NATIONAL GEOGRAPHIC LEARNING'S

Visual Geography of
Travel and Tourism

FIFTH EDITION

NATIONAL GEOGRAPHIC LEARNING'S

Visual Geography of
Travel and Tourism

FIFTH EDITION

Jan van Harssel

Richard Jackson

Lloyd Hudman

NATIONAL GEOGRAPHIC LEARNING | CENGAGE Learning

Australia · Brazil · Japan · Korea · Mexico · Singapore · Spain · United Kingdom · United States

National Geographic Learning's Visual Geography of Travel and Tourism, 5th edition
Jan van Harssel, Lloyd Hudman, Richard Jackson

Vice President, General Manager, Skills and Product Planning: Dawn Gerrain

Senior Product Manager: Jim Gish

Senior Director, Development-Career and Computing: Marah Bellegarde

Senior Product Development Manager: Larry Main

Senior Content Developer: Anne Orgren

Marketing Manager: Scott Chrysler

Senior Production Director: Wendy Troeger

Production Manager: Mark Bernard

Senior Content Project Manager: Glenn Castle

Senior Art Director: Pam Galbreath

Cover image(s): © Richard Nowitz, National Geographic Creative

© 2015, 2003, 1999, 1994, 1990 Cengage Learning

For product information and technology assistance, contact us at
Cengage Learning Customer & Sales Support, 1-800-354-9706
For permission to use material from this text or product, submit all requests online at **cengage.com/permissions.**
Further permissions questions can be emailed to **permissionrequest@cengage.com**

Library of Congress Control Number: 2013957239

ISBN-13: 978-1-133-95126-1

Cengage Learning
200 First Stamford Place, 4th Floor
Stamford, CT 06902
USA

National Geographic Learning
20 Channel Center Street
Boston, MA 02210
USA

Cengage Learning is a leading provider of customized learning solutions with office locations around the globe, including Singapore, the United Kingdom, Australia, Mexico, Brazil, and Japan. Locate your local office at:
www.cengage.com/global

Cengage Learning products are represented in Canada by Nelson Education, Ltd.

To learn more about Cengage Learning, visit **www.cengage.com**

Purchase any of our products at your local college store or at our preferred online store **www.cengagebrain.com**

Notice to the Reader
Publisher does not warrant or guarantee any of the products described herein or perform any independent analysis in connection with any of the product information contained herein. Publisher does not assume, and expressly disclaims, any obligation to obtain and include information other than that provided to it by the manufacturer. The reader is expressly warned to consider and adopt all safety precautions that might be indicated by the activities described herein and to avoid all potential hazards. By following the instructions contained herein, the reader willingly assumes all risks in connection with such instructions. The publisher makes no representations or warranties of any kind, including but not limited to, the warranties of fitness for particular purpose or merchantability, nor are any such representations implied with respect to the material set forth herein, and the publisher takes no responsibility with respect to such material. The publisher shall not be liable for any special, consequential, or exemplary damages resulting, in whole or part, from the readers' use of, or reliance upon, this material.

Printed in the United States of America
1 2 3 4 5 6 7 16 15 14

BRIEF CONTENTS

CONTENTS

p.36

p.43

p.63

p.75

p.103

p.157

p.207

p.243

p.276

p.348

p.382

p.409

p.469

p.481

p.511

p.544

Tourism is one of the leading export industries in the world. In 2012 the world recorded over 1 billion international travelers, a doubling in two decades. For some countries and regions, it is the primary economic activity.

The traditional areas of tourist destinations, such as beaches, theme parks, winter ski areas, and cultural attractions, continue to attract millions of visitors. At the same time, new areas or nontraditional destinations are becoming important. One growth area is destinations practicing sustainable tourism and ecotourism.

The primary factor that attracts tourists is geography. Whether it is the combination of climate and landforms as in sea and ski areas, such as the Alps or the Mediterranean, or cultural-historical geography as in Paris or China, the geographic factors that give character to a place are what attracts tourists.

Visitors are attracted to destinations that express a *sense of place*. If the geography of the earth was uniform, there would be no incentive to travel. Since each place on the face of the earth is different from all others, however, people will always have a desire to see what other places with varied cultural landscapes are like.

This text is designed to provide students, tourism professionals, and other interested readers a working knowledge of the geography of the world as it relates to tourism. The text provides a basic and current geographic overview of the world and each major geographic region to provide insights about geographic characteristics and relationships that compose the setting for tourism in a specific region.

Features

The text also introduces and describes the major attractions in each area. The intention of this introduction is not to provide an encyclopedic or exhaustive listing, but to give an overview of the character of a tourist destination region. By understanding the major attractions of a destination, readers will be able to develop their own mental map of destinations, a mental map sufficient to become familiar with the travel regions of interest to them.

Readers will develop an understanding of the relationship between geography and tourism, including a comprehensive understanding of, and familiarity with, the character of the major regions of the world. Otherwise, after all, the only thing strange in a strange place is the stranger who visits it.

The key terms and words listed at the beginning of each section are terms and words important to understanding that region. While some are explained in the context of the chapter, others are used in a sentence assuming the reader understands the word. If the reader is unfamiliar with the word, all terms and words listed are defined in the glossary.

Maps and descriptions of physical geography combine with vivid photos, as well as cultural and travel information, to convey the unique features of each area and encourage a deeper understanding of attractions and seasonality.

Major geographic characteristics, major tourism characteristics, major climate characteristics, and major tourist destinations are also listed at the beginning of each section, introducing the reader to concise key facts about each region of the world.

All regions or countries have a brief overview of the political, cultural, physical, and tourism characteristics of the region or country. Cultural capsules provide tips about actions that are acceptable and others to avoid. Information is also provided for each country on entry requirements, population, currency, capital, languages, religions, national holidays, and Internet TLDs. While it is difficult to provide geographic depth, readers should be able to obtain their own perception of each tourist destination region in terms of its geographic and tourism characteristics and related attractions.

The text also provides a basic understanding of world travel patterns, including annual arrival numbers and seasonality of travel to a particular region. The regional patterns illustrate how travel and tourism themselves contribute to the geography of each region. The general patterns of world and regional travel change only slowly, barring dramatic events such as wars, terrorism, and environmental disasters. Updated statistics from the World Bank are featured throughout this edition.

Review questions at the end of each chapter help the reader reflect upon and digest the information in the chapter.

What's New About this Edition

Now produced in partnership with the National Geographic Society, the fifth edition features the Society's maps, country flags, and descriptions from *National Geographic's Atlas of the World*, and articles from *National Geographic Magazine* and *National Geographic Traveler*.

Thoroughly revised to present an accurate, current view of our dynamic world, the text includes updated statistical, political, entry documentation, population, and government information for tourist destinations around the globe.

This exciting new edition includes:

- A new, full-color design that brings destinations to life via engaging photographs, detailed maps, and illustrations ideal for today's visual learners

- Up-to-date, colorful National Geographic maps of each continent and all important tourism regions

- "Preserving the Future" boxes in each section that put the focus on sustainability, featuring National Geographic articles about environmental issues and efforts within the region

- "Insider Info" and "Through the Visitor's Eyes" boxes in each section featuring National Geographic articles about the region

- "City Highlights" boxes in each section featuring National Geographic articles focusing on a single city within the region

- Internet TLD information for all destination countries

For the Instructor

Instructor Companion Site: Everything you need for your course in one place! This collection of book-specific lecture and class tools is available online via www.cengage.com/login. Access and download PowerPoint presentations and a revised Instructor's Manual with National Geographic web links and activities, test samples, a midterm test, a final exam, and more.

Acknowledgments

Foremost, I wish to express my appreciation to the original creators and writers of the earlier editions of this book, Lloyd Hudman and Richard Jackson. Both are internationally respected and accomplished professors of Geography at Brigham Young University and their mutual friendship, travel, and teaching experience resulted in the vision that created the original publication of this geography of travel and tourism book. I am proud to celebrate their legacy and dedicate this fifth edition to them.

Editing this volume would not have been possible without the inspiration I receive every day from my students and colleagues in The College of Tourism and Hospitality Management at Niagara University.

I wish to express my appreciation to the staff of Cengage Learning who have provided guidance and assistance in the preparation of the manuscript, especially Senior Content

Developer Anne Orgren and Senior Content Developer Nicole Calisi. Special thanks, also, to all colleagues at National Geographic Learning who helped make this publication possible, including Leila Hishmeh, who helped with the maps, and Anna Kistin who was instrumental in helping select the illustrations. I also appreciate the effort of Production Manager Mark Bernard and Senior Content Project Manager Glenn Castle, who provided invaluable assistance.

The assistance of the outside reviewers was equally valuable, and their critical comments were helpful and thoughtful. Reviewers: Debbie Cooper, Seneca College; Christy Jones, Orange Coast College; Nancy Roop, Heartland Community College (Normal, IL); Dave Schapiro, Lynn University; Nancy Warren, Highline Community College; Donna Yargeau, MacEwan University.

Finally, and most importantly, a special thanks to Associate Acquisitions Editor Katie Hall, for making me "stick" with the project. I thank Katie and her entire team for ensuring that the myriad of details involved in moving this edition of *National Geographic Learning's Visual Geography of Travel and Tourism* from manuscript to published volume were so professionally completed. To these, and all others who have been involved in the production of this volume, I express my gratitude.

Jan van Harssel

Cover, Part Opener and Chapter Opener Photo Locations

The cover photo was taken in San Pedro de Atacama, Chile.

The geographic locations of the photographs at the beginning of each part and chapter are as follows:

Part Openers

Part 1: Northeastland, Svalbard, Norway.

Part 2: Snake River, Wyoming, United States.

Part 3: Muskwa-Kechika Management Area, British Columbia, Canada.

Part 4: Santa Catalina Cuilotepec, Puebla State, Mexico.

Part 5: Negril Beach, Jamaica, West Indies.

Part 6: Machu Picchu, Peru.

Part 7: Bergen, Norway.

Part 8: Red Square, Moscow, Russia.

Part 9: Petra, Jordan.

Part 10: Tsavo East National Park, Kenya.

Part 11: The Great Wall, China.

Part 12: One Tree Island, Queensland, Australia.

Chapter openers

Chapter 1: Earth from space.

Chapter 2: Acadia National Park, Maine.

Chapter 3: American side of the Horseshoe Falls, Niagara Falls, New York.

Chapter 4: Myrtle Beach, South Carolina.

Chapter 5: Natchez, Mississippi.

Chapter 6: Chicago, Illinois skyline with frozen Lake Michigan.

Chapter 7: The Rio Grande as viewed from Big Bend National Park, Texas.

Chapter 8: Nebraska wheat field.

Chapter 9: Bryce Canyon, Utah.

Chapter 10: Heceta Head Lighthouse, Oregon.

Chapter 11: Rocky Mountains, Canada.

Chapter 12: Costa Rica.

Chapter 13: San Juan, Puerto Rico.

Chapter 14: Magens Bay, St. Thomas, Virgin Islands.

Chapter 15: Emerald Pool, Dominica.

Chapter 16: Foul Bay, Barbados.

Chapter 17: Hawksbill turtle in the Bahamas.

Chapter 18: Isla del Sol, Lake Titicaca, Bolivia.

Chapter 19: Mt. Fitz Roy, Patagonia, Argentina.

Chapter 20: Aerial view of rainforest at the Araguaia River, border of the states of Mato Grosso and Goias, Brazil.

Chapter 21: Provence, France.

Chapter 22: The Northern Lights over Landmannarlaugar, Iceland.

Chapter 23: Azure Window, Malta.

Chapter 24: City center, Solny Square tenements (rynek), Wroclaw Poland.

Chapter 25: Tree of desires on Olkhon Island, Lake Baikal, Russia.

Chapter 26: Camel beside Sary-Beles mountains, Kyrgyzstan.

Chapter 27: The Dome of the Rock, Jerusalem, Israel.

Chapter 28: Burj Al Arab hotel, Dubai, United Arab Emirates.

Chapter 29: Pyramids at Giza, Egypt.

Chapter 30: The Mosque of Divinity, Dakar, Senegal.

Chapter 31: Zebra herd on the savannah in the Serengeti, Tanzania.

Chapter 32: Boulders Beach Nature Reserve near Cape Town, South Africa.

Chapter 33: Western lowland gorilla, a species that lives in central Africa (especially the forests of the Republic of Congo).

Chapter 34: Kiyomizu-dera temple pagoda, Kyoto, Japan.

Chapter 35: Details of design of royal Lotus Mahal, Queens' Palace, Hampi, Karnataka, India.

Chapter 36: Sai Thip waterfall, Phu Soi Dao National Park, Thailand.

Chapter 37: Tropical landscape in Vietnam.

Chapter 38: Island of Tahiti as viewed from Moorea.

Chapter 39: Tropical island in Fiji.

Chapter 40: Red rocks in the Northern Territory, Australia.

Jan van Harssel is professor at Niagara University's College of Hospitality and Tourism Management where he has taught classes in tourism and geography for 25 years. He received his B.S. degree from Markendael College in The Netherlands, his M.S. degree from The New School for Social Research in New York City, and his Ed.D. degree from the University of Vermont. His research and teaching interest center on world geography and human geography, community tourism planning and design, and heritage tourism.

Richard Jackson is a professor of geography at Brigham Young University. He taught courses to students in the tourism major for over thirty years. He received his Ph.D. from Clark University. He has led student study-abroad experiences in Europe and Russia.

Lloyd Hudman was a professor at Brigham Young University where he taught for over twenty-five years. He traveled extensively and led university study-abroad programs to London, Madrid, Europe, and the Middle East.

Jan van Harssel, lead author on the 5th edition of this book, is pictured at the National Geographic Society Headquarters in Washington, D.C.

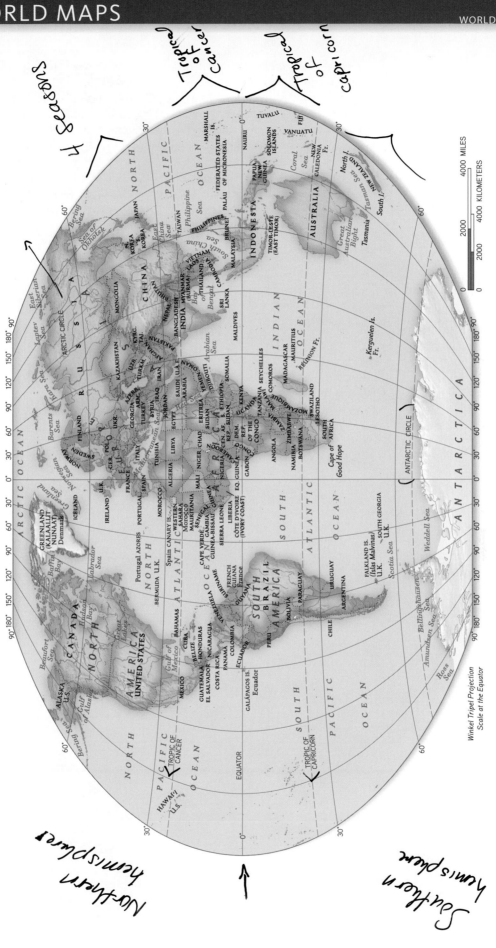

Winkel Tripel Projection
Scale at the Equator

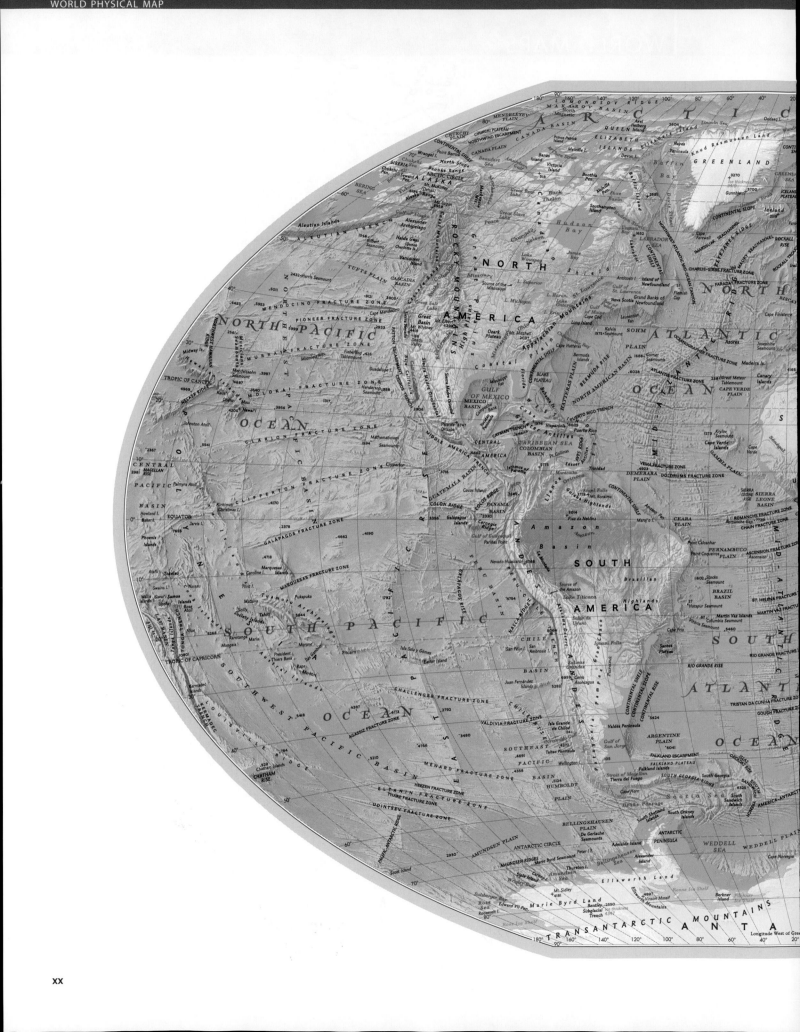

Green-
Vegation (jungle, forest)

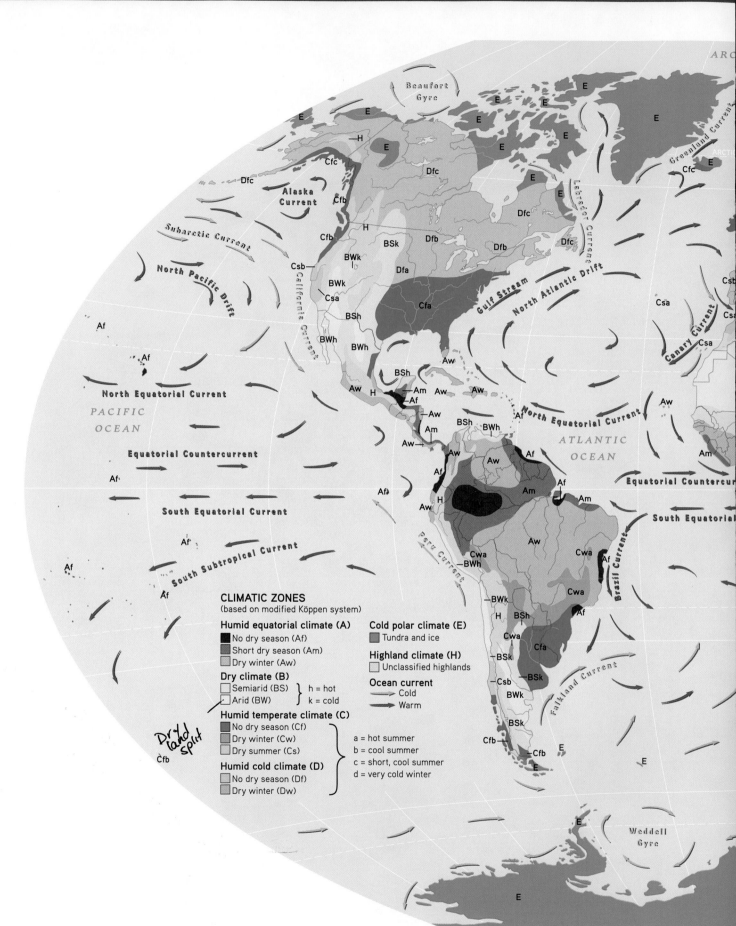

ARC

Beaufort
Gyre

Greenland Current

E

E   E   E

E

E

E   E   Cfc

ARCT

H   E

Cfc   Dfc

Dfc

Alaska
Current

Cfb

E   Dfc

Dfc

Labrador Current

Csb

Csa

Csa

Subarctic Current

H   Dfb   Dfc

North Pacific Drift

Cfb   BSk   Dfb

BWk

Csb   Dfa

BWk   Csa

Csa

Csa

Csa

BSh   Cfa

Gulf Stream   North Atlantic Drift

Af

Af   BWh   BWh

North Equatorial Current

BSh

PACIFIC
OCEAN   Aw   H

Am   Aw   Aw

Aw   Aw

Af   Aw

BSh   BWh

Am   Aw

North Equatorial Current

ATLANTIC
OCEAN

Aw

Af

Am

Equatorial Countercurrent

Af

Af

Af   Aw   Af

Aw   Aw   Af

Am

Am

Equatorial Countercur

South Equatorial Current

Af   H   Am

Aw

South Equatorial

Af   Peru Current   Aw

Cwa   Cwa

Af   Brazil Current

South Subtropical Current   BWh

Af   BWk

Cwa

Af   Falkland Current

Af

CLIMATIC ZONES
(based on modified Köppen system)

Humid equatorial climate (A)
■ No dry season (Af)
■ Short dry season (Am)
□ Dry winter (Aw)

Cold polar climate (E)
■ Tundra and ice

Highland climate (H)
□ Unclassified highlands

H   BSh

Cwa

Cfa

BSk

Dry climate (B)
□ Semiarid (BS) } h = hot
□ Arid (BW) } k = cold

Ocean current
→ Cold
➡ Warm

Csb   BSk

BWk

Dry land split

Humid temperate climate (C)
■ No dry season (Cf)
■ Dry winter (Cw)
□ Dry summer (Cs)

a = hot summer
b = cool summer
c = short, cool summer
d = very cold winter

BSk

Cfb   Cfb

E

Cfb

Humid cold climate (D)
□ No dry season (Df)
■ Dry winter (Dw)

E

E

Weddell
Gyre

E

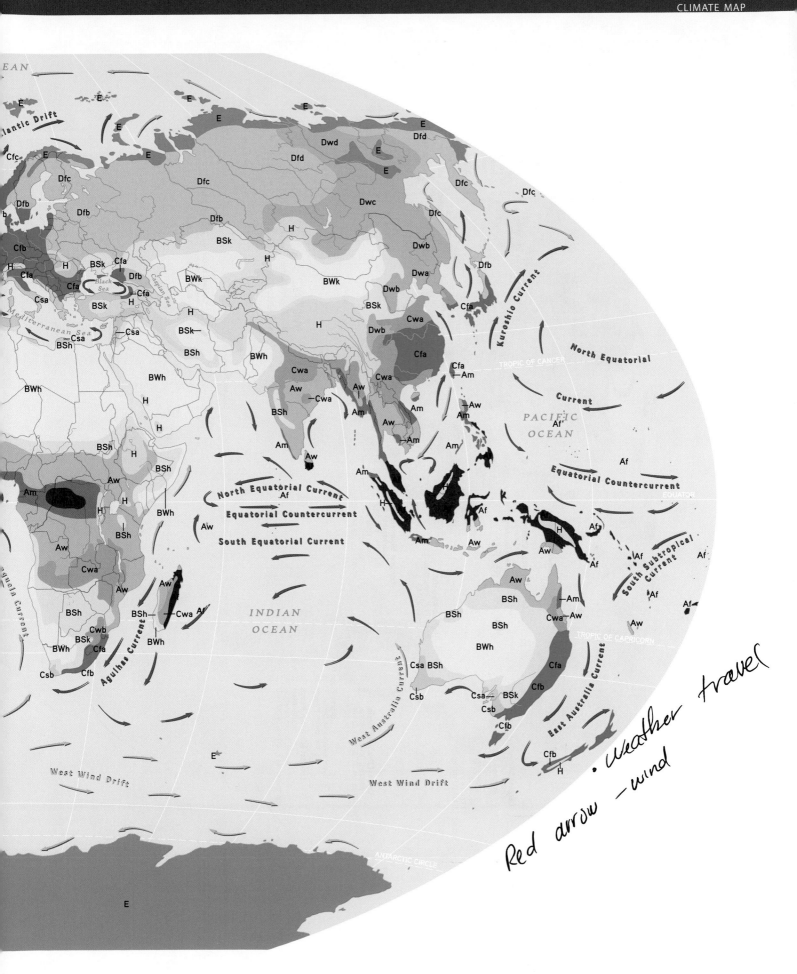

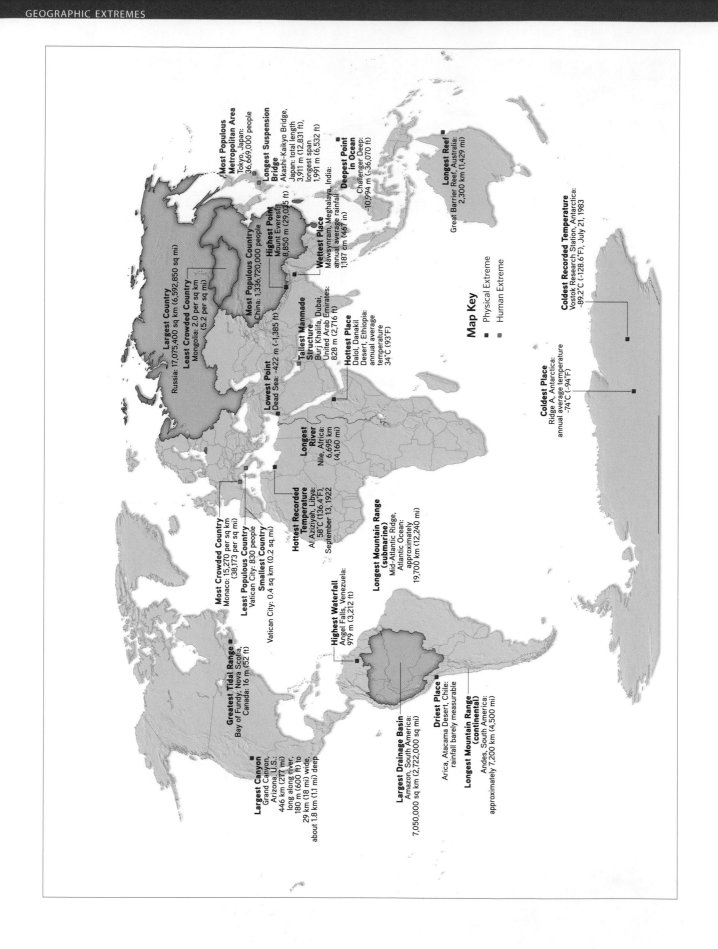

Most Populous Metropolitan Area
Tokyo, Japan: 36,669,000 people

Longest Suspension Bridge
Akashi-Kaikyo Bridge, Japan: total length 3,911 m (12,831 ft), longest span 1,991 m (6,532 ft)

Deepest Point in Ocean
Challenger Deep: -10,994 m (-36,070 ft)

Longest Reef
Great Barrier Reef, Australia: 2,300 km (1,429 mi)

Coldest Recorded Temperature
Vostok Research Station, Antarctica: -89.2°C (-128.6°F), July 21, 1983

Highest Point
Mount Everest: 8,850 m (29,035 ft)

Wettest Place
Mawsynram, Meghalaya, India: annual average rainfall 1,187 cm (467 in)

Largest Country
Russia: 17,075,400 sq km (6,592,850 sq mi)

Least Crowded Country
Mongolia: 2.0 per sq km (5.2 per sq mi)

Most Populous Country
China: 1,336,720,000 people

Tallest Manmade Structure
Burj Khalifa, Dubai, United Arab Emirates: 828 m (2,716 ft)

Hottest Place
Dalol, Danakil Desert, Ethiopia: annual average temperature 34°C (93°F)

Lowest Point
Dead Sea: -422 m (-1,385 ft)

Coldest Place
Ridge A, Antarctica: annual average temperature -74°C (-94°F)

Longest River
Nile, Africa: 6,695 km (4,160 mi)

Hottest Recorded Temperature
Al Aziziyah, Libya: 58°C (136.4°F), September 13, 1922

Most Crowded Country
Monaco: 15,270 per sq km (38,173 per sq mi)

Least Populous Country
Vatican City: 830 people

Smallest Country
Vatican City: 0.4 sq km (0.2 sq mi)

Longest Mountain Range (submarine)
Mid-Atlantic Ridge, Atlantic Ocean: approximately 19,700 km (12,240 mi)

Highest Waterfall
Angel Falls, Venezuela: 979 m (3,212 ft)

Greatest Tidal Range
Bay of Fundy, Nova Scotia, Canada: 16 m (52 ft)

Largest Canyon
Grand Canyon, Arizona, U.S.: 446 km (277 mi) long along river, 180 m (600 ft) to 29 km (18 mi) wide, about 1.8 km (1.1 mi) deep

Largest Drainage Basin
Amazon, South America: 7,050,000 sq km (2,722,000 sq mi)

Driest Place
Arica, Atacama Desert, Chile: rainfall barely measurable

Longest Mountain Range (continental)
Andes, South America: approximately 7,200 km (4,500 mi)

Map Key

■ Physical Extreme
■ Human Extreme

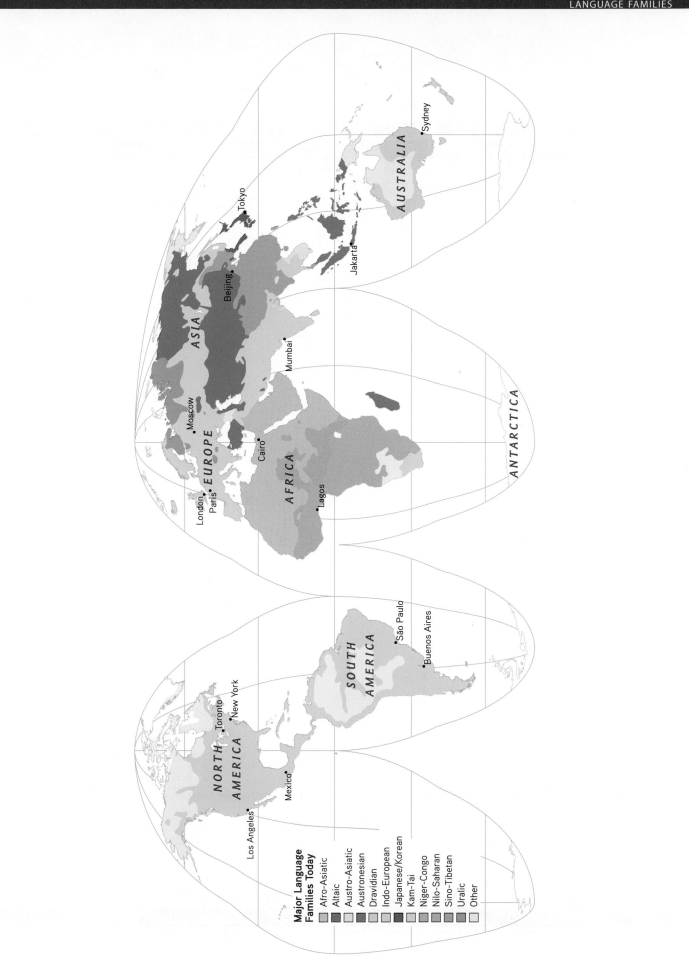

Major Language Families Today

- Afro-Asiatic
- Altaic
- Austro-Asiatic
- Austronesian
- Dravidian
- Indo-European
- Japanese/Korean
- Kam-Tai
- Niger-Congo
- Nilo-Saharan
- Sino-Tibetan
- Uralic
- Other

	1:00 A.M.	2:00 A.M.	3:00 A.M.	4:00 A.M.	5:00 A.M.	6:00 A.M.	7:00 A.M.	8:00 A.M.	9:00 A.M.	10:00 A.M.	11:00 A.M.
-12	-11	-10	-9	-8	-7	-6	-5	-4	-3	-2	-1
	X	W	V	U	T	S	R	Q	P		N

ARCTIC OCEAN

Date Line

V

W

NORTH
PACIFIC
OCEAN

S

U

T

S

R

Q

Q+30
P

NORTH
ATLANTIC
OCEAN

O

Z

N

Z

X W V U T S R Q P O N

M+60

Sunday
Monday
M+120

W+30

M+60
M+60

Date Line

R

Q

S

R+30

Q

P

Q

R

Q

SOUTH
ATLANTIC

P O N

OCEAN

M

INTERNATIONAL DATE LINE
The position of the date line is based on
international acceptance, but it has no legal
status. The island nations of Kiribati and Samoa,
along with Tokelau (a territory of New Zealand)
have advanced their time zones. They are now
the first to start a new day and the first to
celebrate a new year.

M+45

SOUTH PACIFIC OCEAN

	X	W	V	U	T	S	R	Q	P	O	N
-12	-11	-10	-9	-8	-7	-6	-5	-4	-3	-2	-1

The numeral in each tab directly above shows the number of hours to be added to, or subtracted from, Coordinated Universal Time (UTC), formerly Greenwich Mean Time (GMT).

Time Zone

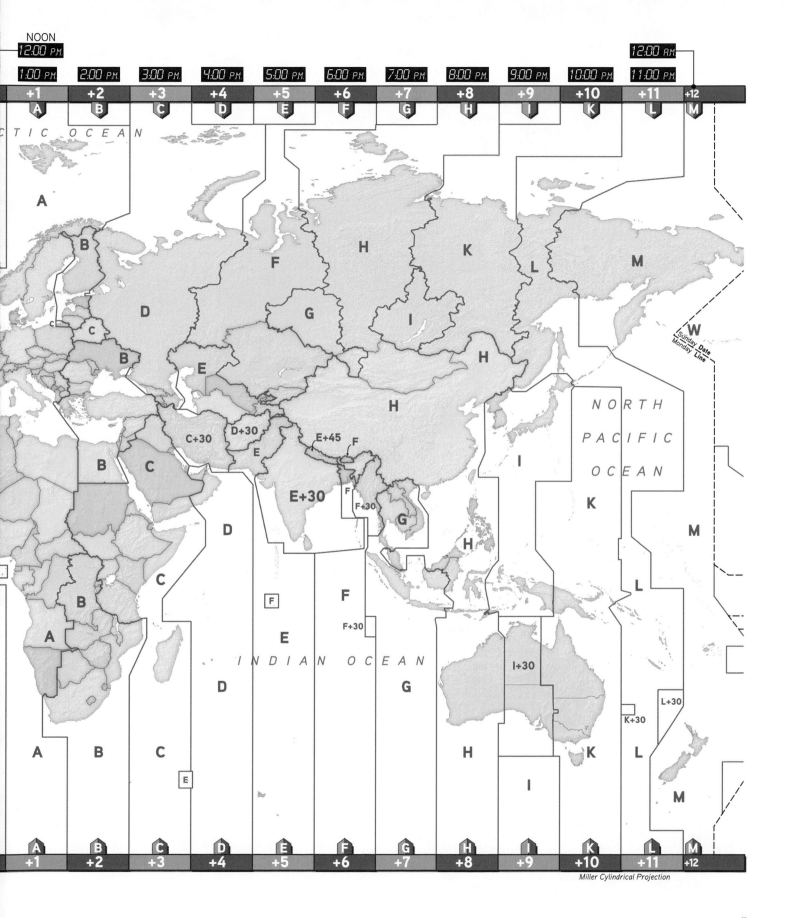

Miller Cylindrical Projection

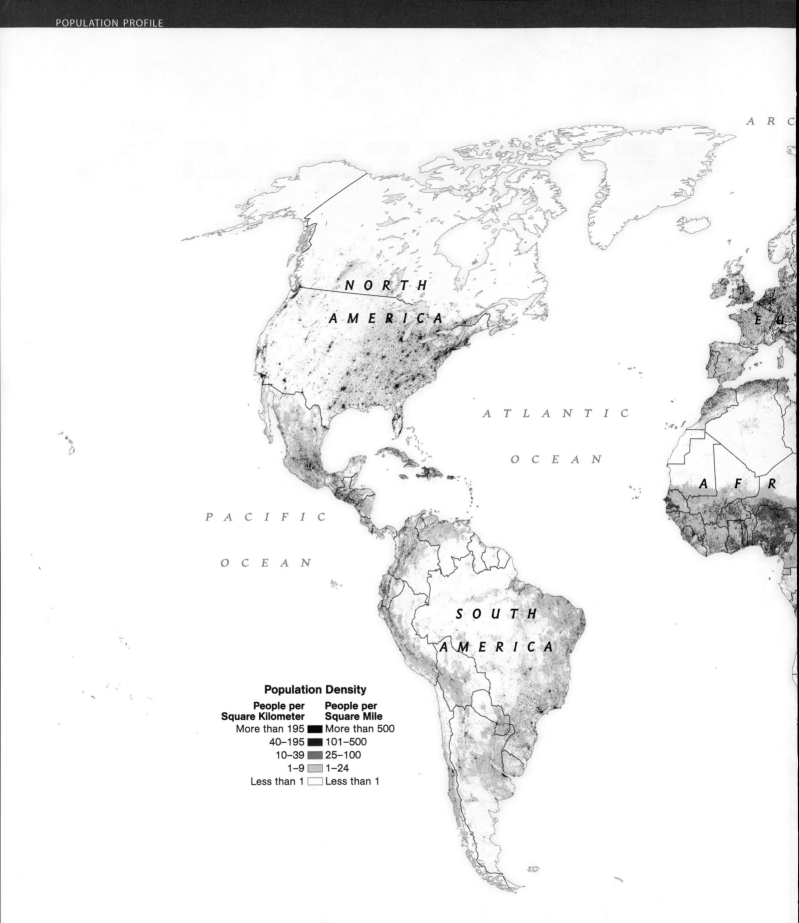

Population Density

People per Square Kilometer		People per Square Mile
More than 195	■	More than 500
40–195	■	101–500
10–39	▦	25–100
1–9	▨	1–24
Less than 1	☐	Less than 1

KEY TERMS AND WORDS

Absolute Location	International Date Line
Accessibility	Intervening Opportunity
Balance of Payments	Landforms
Carrying Capacity	Language
Climate	Latitude
Complementarity	Location
Cultural Geography	Longitude
Destination Countries	Meridians
Economic Development	Parallels
Ecotourism	Perception
Environment	Place
Geographic Location	Pollution
Geography	Preexisting Forms
Geography Information Systems	Prime Meridian
	Relative Location
Global Interdependence	Site
Global Positioning Systems	Situation
Greenwich	Spatial interaction
Hemisphere	Time Zones
Impact	Transferability
Infrastructure	Transportation
Invisible Trade	

chapter 1: GEOGRAPHY AND TOURISM: THE ATTRACTION OF PLACE

Figure 1.1 Coast of Nassau, Bahamas. © Hisham Ibrahim/Getty Images.

For my part I travel not to go anywhere, but to go. I travel for travel's sake. The great affair is to move.

Robert Louis Stevenson

Introduction

People have always traveled. Curiosity, a basic characteristic of humans, has led people of all eras to explore new environments, seek new places, discover the unknown, search for different and strange places, and enjoy other experiences. This suggests that one place is different from another place, or there would be no curiosity about other places. The *National Geographic* and *National Geographic Traveler magazines*, for example, are considered two of the truly fine magazines in the world today. Their primary goal is to illustrate the differences that characterize the world's variety of places and their popularity reflects people's curiosity about other places and cultures.

While people have always traveled, tourism as we know it today is a recent phenomenon. It has only been since World War II that tourism, particularly international tourism, has developed as a major activity in the world. Early travel and early tourism were reserved for the rich or the very brave. One important impetus for tourism was that World War II brought many

people in contact with other people and places. People became more interested in the world. They realized that the events in one part of the world have an important impact on residents in another part of the world.

Growth and change in modes of **transportation** have also encouraged travel. Replacement of transatlantic ships by airplanes introduced the jet age in 1958. Fast, cheap, frequent, and affordable transportation has made world travel a possibility for millions of people.

There are well-developed links between tourism and geography, in that the uniqueness of a place (whether it be an Indian periodic market, a tremendous waterfall, a snowy mountain village, or a resort on a sunny, sandy coast) (Figure 1.1) is the result of the geographic relationships at that place. Successful tourism professionals turn *places* into *destinations.* Through product development, interpretation, and marketing campaigns, places turn into destinations as they earn a reputation, as they get an image, as reasons are created to visit a place, and as they become accessible. **Geography** is the study of the earth as the home of humans. It is concerned with the combination of factors that makes each individual place on the face of the earth somehow unique. Study of geography represents an attempt to gain an understanding of what makes each place unique. Uniqueness results from the combination of the natural (or physical) setting of **climate, landforms,** and resources, and the cultural

Figure 1.2 Rio de Janeiro, Brazil. © Eduardo Garcia/Getty Images.

phenomena created by the residents of that place such as buildings, economy, dress styles, religion, and political or other cultural features (Figure 1.2). The combination of physical and cultural factors that make each place different is the stimulus for human curiosity about other places, which causes the growth and development of tourism.

The process of tourism itself also contributes to the uniqueness of place. Every place on the earth's surface changes over time. Changes in economy, political organizations, culture, population, and the physical **environment** constantly alter the texture and fabric of the complex mosaic that makes up a place. The impact of large numbers of visitors from another place for even a short period of time will affect the visited place, changing its uniqueness, and creating a new and different cultural, political, economic, and physical landscape. Thus, geography and tourism are interrelated in two ways. First, the uniqueness of place creates an attraction. Second, tourism is an agent of change, becoming an element in the uniqueness of place and an important variable in geographic studies.

Elements of Geography

Location

A fundamental aspect of geography that directly affects tourism is the need for measuring and indicating exact locations on the earth. The grid of lines on a map represents the fundamental tool for describing location. The parallel lines extending east and west measure **latitude** north and south of the equator. Latitude is an indicator of how far north or south of the equator a given point is situated. Latitude is measured in degrees of arc from the equator (0 degrees) toward either pole, where the value reaches 90 degrees. All points north of the equator are in the Northern **Hemisphere** and are designated as north latitude. All points south of the equator are in the Southern Hemisphere and are designated as south latitude. These parallel lines (latitudes) are intersected by lines, called **meridians**, extending north and south. Meridians are not parallel, because each of them originates and terminates at the poles; therefore, they converge toward the poles and are most widely separated at the equator. Meridians measure **longitude**. One meridian was chosen as the base point of reference, or the **prime meridian**. The prime meridian was established as the longitude of the Royal Observatory at **Greenwich** near London by the British (Figure 1.3). The British also developed the first accurate system for measuring longitude. Longitude is a measure of a point eastward or westward with respect to the prime meridian of Greenwich. Since the earth is circular, it has 360 degrees of longitude.

Any place can be identified by its latitude and longitude. For example, 40 degrees north latitude, 116 degrees east longitude identifies Beijing, China. The degrees are further subdivided into minutes and seconds for greater accuracy. Therefore, any location may be stated in degrees, minutes, and seconds east or west longitude and north or south latitude. This method makes it possible to identify a location to within a few feet as experienced with GIS (**Geographic Information Systems**) and GPS (**Global Positioning Systems**) technologies.

The world can be divided into hemispheres (halves) in two ways: northern-southern and eastern-western. The Northern-Southern Hemisphere divides the world at the equator, with all **parallels** of north latitude in the Northern Hemisphere and all parallels of south latitude in the Southern Hemisphere. The eastern-western division originates from Greenwich. The Eastern Hemisphere includes all meridians of east longitude from 0 degrees to 180 degrees, while the Western Hemisphere includes all meridians of west longitude.

Time

World time is understood in relation to longitudinal location. East of Greenwich 180 degrees and west of Greenwich 180 degrees are, of course, the same thing. Here, another meridian separates east and west, marking the change in time from one day to another because of the rotation of the earth. The meridian marking the change of date at 180 degrees is called the **International Date Line**. Traveling eastward from one **time zone** to another, clocks are advanced one hour in each time zone, until reaching the line of 180 degrees of longitude, where the day changes to the preceding day. Traveling westward, the opposite occurs; at 180 degrees west longitude, the date changes to the next day.

The surface of the earth is divided into twenty-four time zones. The time of the initial, or zero, zone begins at the prime meridian at Greenwich (London). Each succeeding zone is 15 degrees farther from Greenwich. Also, each zone is designated by a number representing the hours (1 or 2) by which the zone differs from Greenwich. Therefore, if it is 12:00 N. (noon) in London, it is 5 hours (five hours earlier) in New York. When it is 12:00 N. in London, the time in New York is 7:00 A.M. It will be five more hours before the sun is at the midday location in New York. At the same 12:00 N. time in London, it is −3 hours (three hours later) in Moscow. It is 3 P.M. there when it is noon in London.

Because of the International Date Line, if it were Wednesday in Los Angeles, California, it would be Thursday in Sydney, Australia. Travelers flying from Sydney to Los Angeles find they arrive in Los Angeles the same day at an earlier local time than when they departed from Sydney (Sydney time) even after a thirteen-hour flight. Going in the opposite direction, passengers who leave on Friday would arrive on Sunday "losing" Saturday altogether.

Themes of Geography

Absolute Location

Location of places on earth is of special concern to geographers, since location is one of the central elements that contributes to the uniqueness of place. The most obvious aspect is **absolute location** (Where is it?). Absolute location (also referred to as **site**) identifies each location as a precise point on the earth's surface through use of the mathematical grid system that is measured in latitude and longitude. This locational system is used in orientation and measurement of distance. Absolute location does not change over time.

Relative Location

Relative location (also referred to as **situation**) examines the location of places with respect to other places to understand interdependence at local, regional, national, and global scales. The relationship or **spatial interaction** between a place and the rest of the world depends on its relative location, its distance from other places, its **accessibility** or isolation, and its potential for contact. Places that have both a desired characteristic, such as a warm winter climate or access to good ocean beaches (known as **sun-sea-sand**), and important cultural attractions near large population centers are conducive to interaction with other places and development as a tourist center. Countries that have a poor location relative to the wealthy industrialized nations of Europe and North America, such as the interior of Africa, or are isolated by either physical or cultural phenomena, have few tourists even though they may have attractive physical or cultural relationships.

Location has been important in all forms of **economic development** for the various nations of the world. Nations that have excellent connectivity and site characteristics, such as educated citizens and a good resource base, have developed a high standard of living. Countries that have a poor relative location from the rest of the world are apt to have a lower standard of living. Locations that are isolated by mountains, deserts, or cultural phenomena such as **language** have failed to benefit from the technological advances taking place in other areas of the world.

Countries such as Chad, Rwanda, and Burundi, which are located in the interior of Africa and are separated from contact with industrial Europe by physical distance, climate, landform, and culture, lack adequate transportation facilities to assist them in economic development in general or tourism development specifically. Changes in situational and environmental circumstances can cause relative location to change over time, resulting in new or lost tourism development opportunities.

Geographic Location

Geographic location is the combination of absolute location and relative location. Site (absolute location) is a description of the internal characteristics of a **place**, as opposed to situation (relative location), which looks at the external relationships of a place. Site also includes the absolute mathematical location of a place and the qualities or attributes at that place. Site features include the number of people living at that place, their ethnic character, their income, and other attributes of their culture. Site also includes the physical characteristics such as landforms, climates, or resources. The word *place* is general and can refer to the site characteristics of a small area, town, city, county, state, region, or country.

The development of tourism at any specific geographic location depends on its site, its situation (reflecting the ease—usually expressed in time and money—with which a potential tourist can travel to that place), and its relationship to other attractions. More people visit Paris than Oslo because Paris is more accessible and because of the nature and extent of attractions in each city and in surrounding areas. Paris has a central location that facilitates visits to other European attractions such as London, while Oslo has a peripheral location in Europe. Isolated from the main populated and urban areas of Europe, Oslo is less accessible and has fewer attractions for tourists than Paris.

Another important element in the movement of visitors from one place to another is the **perception** by the potential tourist of other places. People have a tendency to react to the world not as it is, but as they think it is. In other words, the perceived and actual character may not be the same. Perception is formed in a cultural context of human behavior with a background steeped in the traditions, values, and goals of a person or group. The perception of an area can either enhance or deter tourism to that place. Travel advertisements may use the public perception of a place if it is positive, or attempt to create programs to change the perception of the place if it is negative. For example, New York City is perceived by many as an unsafe place to visit. This negative view of the city carried over to the state. Realizing this perception, the state adopted the slogan "I Love New York." (This was the origin of all the "I Love…" slogans that are expressed throughout the country.) The idea was to create positive images in the minds of potential tourists, with the hope that they would consider New York as a vacation destination. Tourism to New York increased following the introduction of this program, even flourished after the "rehabilitation" of Times Square, reflecting the success of these and other initiatives to develop a more favorable perception of the city, its people, and its attractions.

Place and Space: The Why of Geography

All places on earth have distinctive tangible and intangible characteristics that give them meaning and character and distinguish them from other places. Geographers generally describe places by their physical or human characteristics. The physical characteristics are derived from the geological, hydrological, atmospheric, and biological processes that produce landforms, water bodies, climate, soils, natural vegetation, and animal life. Human ideas and actions shape the character of places. Places vary in their population composition as well as in their settlement patterns, architecture, kinds of economic and recreational activities, transportation, communication networks, ideologies, languages, and forms of economic, social, and political organization. The nature of the physical environment in each place on the surface of the earth affects the ability of humans to live there and influences travel to each place. Three elements of the physical character of place important for tourism are climate, vegetation, and landforms (Figure 1.3). A second component that makes a place unique is related to the differences among the people who occupy the earth. Each place has unique cultural and human characteristics that make it different from other places. These differences are referred to as the **cultural geography** of a place. The cultural geography that is associated with a place reflects both human changes in the physical environment and the cultural variables (language, religion, race, politics, and economy) that differ from place to place. Much of the difference in places results from variations in culture. Culture is acquired behavior, the way of life held in common by a group of people. It is learned and provides people with similarities in speech, behavior, ideology, livelihood, technology, and language. Culture includes a sense of belonging to a distinct group of people. Cultural landscapes are a combination of the modification of the physical characteristics and the human features existing in a particular place. There are many elements of culture; they all either enhance or deter tourism. Language, food, clothing, political systems, religion, and architectural styles are the elements that affect cultural landscapes.

Movement within Places

Human beings are spread unevenly across the face of the earth. Some live on farms or in the country; others live in towns, villages, and cities. Yet, these people interact with each other; they travel from one place to another; they communicate with each other; and they rely upon products, information, and ideas that come from beyond their immediate environment. Increasing interaction among people at the beginning of the twenty-first century is leading to **global interdependence**.

The most visible evidence of global interdependence and the interaction of places are the means of transportation and communication that now link every part of the world. People now interact with other places almost every day of their lives. This may involve nothing more than a Georgian eating apples grown in the state of Washington that have been shipped to Atlanta by rail or truck. On a larger scale, international trade demonstrates that no country is self-sufficient. Such interaction will continue to change as transportation and communication technologies change. An understanding of the changing technologies will help us to understand the changes taking place in the world in the future.

The uniqueness of place reflects the interaction of the physical and cultural elements at that place in addition to the degree and type of interaction with other places. Geographers are interested in spatial interaction, and tourism is one element in that interaction that affects the character of place. Three terms are important in understanding the interaction between places: **complementarity, intervening opportunity,** and **transferability** (accessibility).

Complementarity

The fact that places are different does not automatically ensure interaction between places. There must be a complementary relationship between two places. Northern Europe is a wealthy (by world standards) area with a damp, cool climate. Its inhabitants like to spend some time in the sunny, warm, sun-sea-sand environment offered by the Mediterranean nations of southern Europe. Thus, a complementary relationship generates interaction in the form of tourism as well as trade in agricultural products; for example, one may grow grapes and other potatoes, and then the two may trade. The two regions are complementary.

Intervening Opportunity

Intervening opportunity refers to the substitution of one place for another, as when growth of a suburban mall leads suburban residents to shop at it instead of going downtown. The mall becomes an intervening opportunity. In tourism, intervening opportunities are common as a nearer or less expensive (in terms of time or money) place is substituted for another. Residents of the western United States might like a Pacific tropical

Figure 1.3 Danxia landform in Zhangye, Gansu of China. © axz700/www.Shutterstock.com.

Travel's ultimate thrill may be that one special discovery—and sharing it with kindred souls.

"So, where are we going for dinner tonight?" I ask. My friend Mariko smiles. "It's a little place. I hope you will like it." We jump into a Toyota taxi with spotless slipcovered seats. Mariko instructs the driver in Japanese, and we zoom off.

I kind of know my way around Tokyo. I can ride the subway without getting lost, and I can tell when I'm in Shinjuku or Asakusa. But not tonight. Two or three turns into a labyrinth of side streets, and I have no idea what neighborhood we are in. Or even if we are still in Tokyo.

"Stop here," Mariko says after a bit. We face a shadowy, empty-looking building illuminated by a dim blue light over the entry door.

Suddenly that door slides open, revealing a warmly lit wood-paneled eatery. A woman in a perfectly wrapped kimono appears, bows, and motions us inside. As we settle ourselves, I notice there are no tables, only a bar. A very, very small bar. I count the seats: One, two, three, four.

That's when I realize what is up. Mariko, a new friend I've made through a mutual acquaintance, is honoring this occasion of our first meeting by presenting me with something special. Something that, as ardent travelers, we both can understand and appreciate, even though we come from very different parts of the world. What Mariko is offering me is the greatest travel gift of all: a secret place.

I've collected secret places since I could crawl—the cabinet under the bathroom sink, the quiet space beneath my bed. Of course my standard for specialness has become a little more sophisticated over the decades; what hasn't changed is the urge to discover marvelous and mysterious nooks around the world that somehow will "belong" to me, finds that I come across spontaneously or after a long and concerted quest.

Most travelers I know share this passion in some form. My friend Laura, for instance, keeps a stack of worn Moleskine books filled with scribbled notes: the address of the tiny café in Budapest where she tasted the ultimate walnut-cream pastry; the telephone number of the unlisted guesthouse in Cartagena, Colombia, where she fell asleep every night to the rolling murmur of the Caribbean sea.

I'm not much of a diarist, so I tend to keep my secret places in my head. To jog my memory, I hold onto pieces of travel ephemera: maps of Ljubljana, menus from restaurants in Shanghai, business cards, *café con leche*-stained paper napkins that I saved from out-of-the-way Buenos Aires *confiterias*.

In a world where everyone can—and does—blog about their favorite obscure noodle stall in Macau, collecting secret places may feel sometimes as obsolete as steamship travel. And yet I continue to make discoveries of places unknown to tourists, guidebook writers, and bloggers, and sometimes even to the people who live in the place I'm exploring. The reason: My definition for a "secret place" has an important qualifier. To get a spot on my list a secret place has to be special—to me.

Ko Samui, in Thailand, is a beach resort that is filled with tourists year-round; the Buddhist temple near the center of town is marked on every map. Yet it became my secret place early one morning when I wandered in and noticed, off to the side of the main altar, a device that looked like a pinball machine. Its main feature was an electrically illuminated statue of Buddha inside the glass case.

I stood in wonder before this pinball Buddha, then noticed a coin slot that read "10 Baht." I had some Thai change in my pocket, so I dropped a 10-baht coin in the slot. Instantly the Buddha's eyes began flashing red, blue, and green as a recorded voice thundered forth in rapid-fire Thai. Then, in a frenzy of flashing, whizzing, and whirring, the machine spit out a piece of paper: my fortune.

To get a spot on my list a secret place has to be special—to me.

What did it say? That remains secret (even to me—most of the text is in Thai). But the next time any friends of mine go to Ko Samui they will certainly be carrying directions to my special pinball Buddha, along with operating instructions. Once you've found that secret place and added it to your collection, there is only one thing you can do to make the experience of it even better: Share it with special friends.

Tokyo is practically ground zero for secret places. There seems to be something about Japanese culture that maintains, even safeguards, a reverence for the hidden, for the spontaneous discovery. At Mariko's secret restaurant, we—along with the lucky patrons in those other two seats—eat one of the best meals I have ever had: course after course of the freshest fish, followed by servings of exquisitely shaped and perfectly steamed vegetables that I'd never heard of. The chef personally presents and explains each dish to Mariko, his regular customer.

Full of heady sake and delight, I ask Mariko if the restaurant has a business card, so I will be able to find it again some day. She laughs.

"It doesn't even have a name."

This secret place, I realize, "belongs" to her. Her traveler's gift is not the place itself, but the sharing of it with me, a like-minded new friend.

—Daisann McLane, *National Geographic Traveler*, March 2010

---

vacation experience. They would be willing to substitute Cancun, Mexico, for Tahiti or Fiji. The British can substitute coastal areas in France for the more distant locations in Spain, Italy, Greece, or the Caribbean. Casino goers on the east coast of the United States may substitute Atlantic City for Las Vegas.

Transferability

Transferability (or accessibility) is the ease (usually expressed in time and money) with which a person can go from one place to another. The greater the accessibility between complementary regions, the greater the interaction. For example, there was only a small degree of interaction by tourists between Europe and the United States before the advent of the jet plane. Travel to Europe across the Atlantic was reduced from six days by ship in 1950 to seven hours by airplane by 1960 and the greater capacity of the larger jet plane greatly reduced the ticket cost.

Those destinations that are perceived as being too expensive in either time or money have little interaction, and tourists seek an alternative destination involving less time and expense. In general, this explains why domestic tourism has greater numbers of tourists than does international tourism. People can travel less expensively and more frequently to destinations within their own country. The next stage has more international tourists within their respective regions, such as Western Europe, North America, East Asia, North Africa, and Eastern Europe, than between regions. Interaction resulting from tourism on an international level occurs most between complementary regions such as between North America and Europe, which have strong cultural complementary characteristics.

Geography and Tourism

Our world is diverse. It is composed of countries with a variety of cultures and customs, rural areas and urban centers each with its own distinct flavor, and so on. The activity we call tourism, with its great economic and social benefits, provides citizens of all countries with an opportunity to explore new places, to meet new people, to learn new things, and, perhaps in the process, to learn more about themselves. Travel is a bridge between people and tourism is a tool for change on a global scale. The tourism activity makes a valuable contribution to the world's economies, employs more people than any other industry, and affects the lives of both hosts and guests in one way or another.

Current International Patterns of Tourism

International tourism has increased steadily since the end of World War II. During the 1960s, the number of world tourist arrivals more than doubled, reaching 183 million international arrivals by 1970, nearly 700 million by 2000, and reaching the 1 billion mark in 2012, according to the UNWTO. By region, Europe was the best performer. Europe accounts for over half of all international arrivals recorded worldwide. Asia and the Pacific reached a total 216 million international tourists. The Americas reached 156 million in total with South America leading the growth (up 10 percent annually since 2010). North America hit the 100 million tourists mark in 2011. Africa maintains international arrivals at 50 million. The Middle East ended 2011 with 55 million arrivals. Worldwide tourists' spending rates parallel the positive trends reported above. Total worldwide spending for domestic and international tourism in 2010 exceeded $9.2 trillion, generating directly or indirectly, 450 million jobs (UNWTO, 2012). In 2000, by contrast, worldwide spending was $4 trillion, and employment stood at 250 million. Earlier,

in 1986, these numbers were $2 billion and 64.3 million jobs (Waters, 1987). Today, the tourism sector is directly responsible for 5 percent of the world's GDP, 6 percent of total exports, and employing 1 of every 12 people in advanced and emerging economies alike (UNWTO, 2012).

During the last two decades the rate of growth in number of arrivals has been greatest in the low-income nations of the world. The increasing growth of tourism to emerging economy countries helps improve their citizens' quality of life. Tourism accounts for a greater percentage of export income for the low-income countries than it does in high-income countries such as the United States.

Destination Countries

Figure 1.4 lists the top ten tourist-drawing countries in order of rank. These twelve countries represent over half of all international tourist visits. European and North American countries dominate the list, indicating the strong attraction that the European region has for tourists. The large number of visitors to European countries can be accounted for by two factors. First, a large number of tourists are from other European nations. Consequently, they travel to other European countries that are close by in search of new experiences. Second, the historical ties of North America with Europe serve to stimulate travel between these two major areas. In general, the Mediterranean countries receive the most tourists, reflecting cost advantages, Mediterranean climates, coastal locations

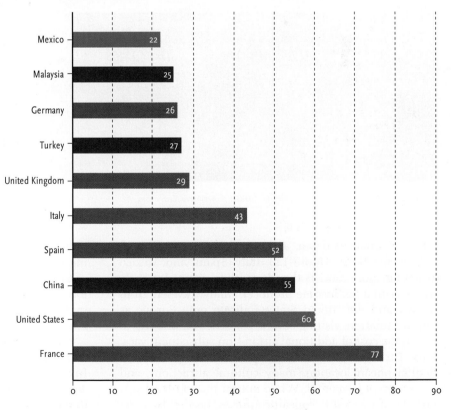

Figure 1.4 Top Ten Tourist Destinations, 2010 (in millions).

Data source: The World Bank: The Data Catalogue. Figure copyright ©2015 Cengage Learning®. All rights reserved.

Figure 1.5 Alcázar fortress in Toledo, Spain. © Ryan McVay/Getty Images.

with sun, sand, and sea, and cultural attractions from early civilizations (Figure 1.5). Italy, Spain, and Mexico attract far more tourists than leave these countries, making tourism a net income producer. Many travelers from Canada and the United States indicate only Europe as their destination, visiting several countries on one trip to reduce the cost of additional airfares on subsequent vacations. Turkey earned a seventh place ranking due to its Mediterranean location, many cultural attractions, and the intrigue of Istanbul. While not on the top ten list, a number of Central European countries, headed by Hungary and the Czech Republic, have become important destinations. In 1986, China moved into the top twelve

destination nations of the world for the first time, indicating growing interest in this country. Since the opening of China in 1978 to international tourism, the increase in tourists to China has been explosive and in 2010 China ranked third in world international tourist arrivals, after France and the United States.

The United States, Mexico, and Canada benefit from large populations with easy access to each other. In addition, the cultural linkage between Anglo-America and Europe serves as an attraction for European travel to the region.

Figure 1.6 shows international tourism arrivals by region. Europe dominates the international arrivals,

What's in your wallet is vital to crossing international borders.

Don't forget to pack your passport and other papers this summer. As of June 1 [2009], the U.S. government will require a passport at sea or land ports of entry. The government isn't alone in tightening restrictions at border crossings. Travel companies are turning away more customers whose paperwork isn't in order. Here's how to make sure you get the green light.

Passport or Passport Card?

- Most travelers will do better with a passport, as a card is valid only for land and sea crossings between the United States and Canada, Mexico, Bermuda, and the Caribbean. The price difference—a card costs $45 for adults, compared with a passport's $100 price tag—isn't worth what you'll give up, in terms of options. An renew your passport at least eight months before it expires, as some countries will reject a passport within six months of the expiration date.
- **Don't Forget the Kids.** If you are traveling alone with a child, bring a letter of permission from the other parent.

The requirements, aimed to prevent child abduction, can vary. For example, children traveling with a single parent in Bolivia may be asked to present a copy of their birth certificates and written authorization from the absent parent or legal guardian, specifically granting permission to travel.

- **Got Your Shots?** Set up a doctor's appointment four to six weeks before your departure, and consult the Centers for Disease Control and Prevention (*www.cdc.gov/travel/contentVaccinations.aspx*) to make sure you're getting all the right inoculations.
- **Need a Visa?** Entry and exit requirements can change quickly. Even though the State Department publishes the latest visa requirements on its site, it's useful to consult with both an experienced travel agent who sells a lot of trips to your destination and the website of the embassy whose country you plan to visit. If you need multiple visas, consider working with a visa expediting service such as Passport Visas Express (*www.passportvisasexpress.com*) or Zierer Visa Service (*www.zvs.com*).
- **Save Some Change for Later.** Many countries—particularly in the Caribbean

and Central America—charge an "exit fee" as high as $30 that must be paid before leaving the country. Some only accept cash. Save a little local currency so you can leave the country. The State Department (*http://travel.state.gov/travel*) lists departure taxes by country in its Consular Information Sheets on its website.

- **Back It All Up.** Keep a paper copy of your airline, hotel, or cruise confirmations, as well as your airline contract of carriage or cruise contract (available on the company's website). Also bring photocopies of your passport, which obviously shouldn't be carried with your passport in case you lose it. If you're renting a car, print your confirmation and carry not only your driver's license but a copy of it as well. (If you're worried about cutting down trees, consider scanning and saving copies of all this in your Hotmail or Gmail "drafts" so that you can access them easily from the road.)

—**Christopher Elliott,** *National Geographic Traveler*, **May/June 2009**

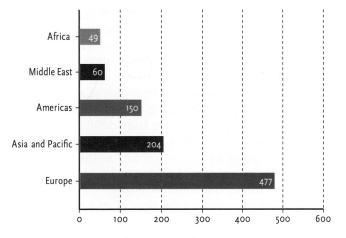

Figure 1.6 International Travel Arrivals by Region 2010.

accounting for 60 percent of tourist arrivals in 2010. The major reason Europe dominates in numbers of international arrivals is the high rate of intraregional travel occurring in Europe. Europe has the highest intraregional travel of all regions of the world. The close proximity of many nations in Europe encourages considerable international travel.

However, there has been a shift in arrivals since the 1980s. Europe's percentage of total world arrivals has declined steadily. Most of the shift has been to East Asia and the Pacific, which increased from 5 percent of the world arrivals in 1980 to over 25 percent in 2011.

The growth of tourism to China had a strong positive effect on tourism to the region. However, sociopolitical problems, the rise of Islamic fundamentalism in the Middle East and North Africa, and the "Arab Spring" events in 2011 have resulted in very little growth for tourism in those regions. In 2011, the area received just 2 percent of all world arrivals. In the Americas there has been little change in the percentage of the world's international tourist arrivals.

The higher rates of growth for the less industrialized regions as well as a smaller intraregional dependency indicates that tourism has many of the characteristics of an income transfer. Tourists and their money flow from the wealthy industrialized nations of the world to the less industrialized nations of the world. This trend is also true even in the European nations. The southern nations of Spain, Portugal, Greece, Italy, and Cyprus are very dependent on travel receipts to sustain their economies.

Tourism-Generating Countries

The economic importance of Western Europe, North America, and China in tourism expenditures is impressive. Figure 1.7 lists in order of rank the ten largest spending

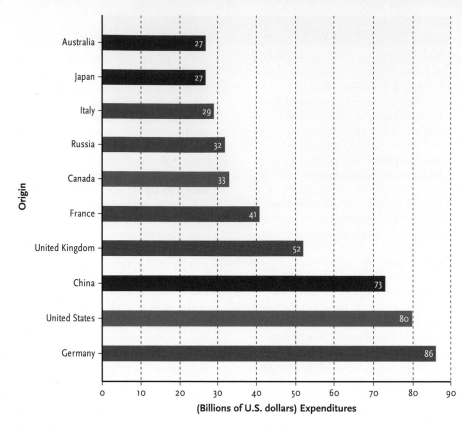

Figure 1.7 Top Ten Spending Countries of the World, 2010.

countries in international tourism. European nations, particularly Western European nations, dominate this list. The four nations outside of Europe, the United States, Canada, Japan, and Australia are all economically advanced nations, and China has the world's fastest growing economy. China multiplied tourism expenditures 4 times since 2000, and achieved the fastest growth rate in a decade. Germany accounts for the most expenditures with 16 percent of the world's total. The United States, second, accounts for 14 percent of the total world expenditures.

The Influence of Tourism

The three major impacts that tourism has on the host nation are economic, social and cultural, and environmental. Most positive comments about the impact of tourism are economic, although other benefits can and do occur from tourism. Most negative comments about the impact of tourism are social-cultural and environmental. Environmental negative impacts will occur unless good planning takes place.

Economic Impact

Tourism is a major factor in providing foreign exchange and tax revenues needed by many nations to raise the standard of living of their citizens. Mexico, Spain, Greece, and the Bahamas are examples of countries that need the

income that the flow of tourist money provides. This transfer of funds is an important factor in tourism and serves to help a country's **balance of payments**. The balance of payments is an accounting of the flow of goods, services, and funds in and out of a country during a given period. If a country pays more money than it receives, it has a deficit in the balance of payments. If it receives more money than it sends, or exports, it has a surplus in its balance of payments.

There are three types of payments and receipts in international accounts:

1. Visible balance of trade, which includes import and export goods

2. **Invisible trade**

3. **Capital transfers**

The visible balance of trade is most familiar, and we hear a great deal about it. The United States exports large quantities of agricultural products, technological innovations, and manufactured items to other countries, and in turn imports such things as raw materials from South America, cars from Japan and Germany, and oil from the Middle East and South America as part of its visible balance of trade.

Tourism is part of the invisible trade in the balance of payments. In some countries, such as Spain, Austria, Greece, Ireland, and Mexico, it is an important source of income (Figure 1.8). Although they have large numbers of tourists, travel expenditures in countries such as the United States and West Germany are not a major part of their balance of payments. In recent years, however, the tourist account is becoming more important in the United States, helping to offset large deficits in the balance of trade account. In many highly industrialized countries, tourism has little impact on the balance of trade payments because the economies of these countries are very diversified and very large.

In an effort to control the flow of money out of the country through tourism, some countries have set limits on the amount of money that can be taken out of the country and countries encourage their citizens to vacation within the borders of their countries. Most limitations on travel and the flow of money in the invisible account occur when the total balance of payments is extremely unfavorable and the country is undergoing serious financial stress. Tourism receipts help stabilize income flow to a country, thereby creating a greater dependency upon tourism receipts than other commodities in the balance of trade payments.

The income that a nation receives from tourism benefits that nation in several ways. The additional money flows into the economy and becomes part of the exchange of goods and services both within and outside of the

Figure 1.8 Parthenon in Athens, Greece. © marcokenya/www.Shutterstock.com.

country, affecting businesses and salaries throughout the country. Income is also generated for the governments in the form of taxes, some of which are paid as part of the general taxes of the country, such as sales tax, or specific tourism taxes that are levied because tourism exists, such as room taxes on hotel rooms or special user taxes on destination facilities, to assist in further development.

In addition to income, tourism creates employment. The tourist industry is a labor-intensive activity. It employs large numbers of people by providing a wide range of jobs from the unskilled to the highly specialized. Employment ranges from semiskilled jobs for maids, porters, gardeners, or custodians, to more skilled positions such as accountants, managers, or entertainers. Further employment is generated in that those hired for tourism jobs then have money to spend; therefore, grocery stores, clothing stores, gas stations, and so on hire additional workers to meet the increased demand. There is more employment generated in tourism in the less industrialized nations than in the industrialized nations, as tourism employs people from population groups that are generally the most severely impacted by unemployment (women and youth). Importantly, employment wages for those in tourism in less industrialized nations are generally higher than the country's wage average; while in the industrialized nations, tourism wages are lower than average wages.

Infrastructure (roads, airports, sewers, tourist facilities, and so on) developed to encourage tourism can also be used by the local residents to improve their quality of life. This is particularly true in less industrialized regions of the world.

There are some negative economic characteristics of tourism. Generally, tourism is seasonal. Thus, income and employment are not always constant. Inflation results from increased demand by tourists, in some cases increasing the cost of living for the local residents. These elements can be further magnified when a country becomes highly dependent upon tourism as the major source of its trade. Planning can partially offset this problem. In Majorca, Spain, for example, the government has imposed a tax on hotels that helps to support unemployed hotel workers during the low-tourist-flow season.

Social and Cultural Impact

One important aspect of tourism is the development of a cultural understanding that could help to reduce international mistrust and suspicion and build a better world. However, in this area there is considerable concern, and much has been written about the negative impact of tourism in the area of social and cultural contact.

Tourism can be important to the host country or area in preserving its history and folk culture. In many countries of the world, many traditional folk costumes and customs are continued or reestablished for the benefit of tourists, and folklore festivals are organized to attract visitors. The establishment of arts and crafts centers among American Indian tribes such as the Cherokee and the Navajo have helped sustain interest in American Indian crafts.

There are many arts and crafts centers throughout the world for the same purpose. Many destinations have cultural centers such as the Polynesian Cultural Center in Hawaii (Figure 1.9), which provides guests with a chance to view some limited historical aspects of a lifestyle as it once was and provides the region an opportunity to maintain its traditions. The growth of these "living museums" can reduce the pressure on local religion and popular beliefs where tourists can profane places of worship and objects of reverence.

Another benefit that can result from tourism is associated with the return to the country or area of their origin by immigrants or their descendants, which serves to bring them closer to their ancestral homeland. Probably the most hoped-for benefit of tourism is the bringing together of people of different views to help them understand each other. It is suggested that tourism can become a tool for effecting understanding among people and cultures by causing people to reconsider their traditional stereotypes of the different cultures.

The level of economic development of a country is an important factor in the degree of cultural stress between groups. Tourism between the more industrialized countries, with their similar societies and well-developed infrastructures, creates little stress, at least until tourism numbers become so great that they create competition for goods and services between residents and travelers. A good example of this is in London, England, where lower airfares have brought record numbers of tourists. Public transportation is crowded throughout the day and so full of tourists that, at times, there is hardly any room for local residents. Shops are full of travelers, forcing British people to change shopping patterns. Subways and streets are filled with visitors, slowing down traffic. Westminster Cathedral has so many tourists that it hardly seems like a church. There is a strong subjective feeling that tourism growth in London cannot continue to increase. Many believe there is a saturation level, at which point residents will declare that enough tourists are enough.

Alienation may be generated in the host area, leading to social unrest between the "haves" and "have nots." A number of factors account for this alienation. One results from the nature of the tourist, who is generally from an industrialized country and used to demanding service and receiving prompt attention, while in many host countries the pace of life may be slower and less

Figure 1.9 Polynesian Cultural Center in Hawaii. © Ritu Manoj Jethani/www.Shutterstock.com.

The noble savage. Primitive and uncorrupted by modern civilization, living a life in harmony with nature and each other. This image has been around for centuries, promulgated by novelists and explorers (including a few from *National Geographic*, truth be told), even as native peoples were conquered and colonized. Despite its inaccuracy, the romantic image endures, perhaps more so now on an always-plugged-in planet.

So the rise of tourism to tribal areas is no surprise. Click on almost any adventure travel site and stereotypical images pop up, from smiling long-necked Padaung women in Myanmar to the "lost world" Pemon Indians of Venezuela. One popular tour company even advertises, "We will search for tribes that have had limited or no contact with Westerners." Although there are estimates that about a hundred "uncontacted" tribes still exist in the world, no one really knows for sure. What we do know is that encounters between outsiders and indigenous peoples have rarely gone well for the latter.

Last year, 30,000 tourists poured into Ethiopia's Omo River Valley to see the Mursi and their seminomadic indigenous cousins before "modern development" overtakes them. The problem is that providing for adventure-seekers—with vehicles, restaurants, accommodations, and other tourism services—prompts the very changes they wish to avoid. Is it possible for the well-intentioned traveler to experience tribal culture without destroying it?

From the Kogi of Colombia to the Huli Wigmen of Papua New Guinea, many of the world's last surviving tribal peoples—already under pressure from profit-hungry industries like timber, mining, and oil—also face tourism's march across Earth. I'm a strong believer that tourism can be a powerful force for good, when planned well. If done badly, however, the consequences are sobering: Despite a government ban on tribal tourism in India's Andaman Islands, during peak season last July dozens of vehicles filled with camera-wielding travelers snaked into a forest reserve set aside for the Jarawa, hunter-gatherers who began to emerge cautiously from the jungle in ones and twos during the late 1990s, and who now number fewer than 400. A video showed corrupt police making girls dance in front of cameras, and candy and biscuits being tossed out of tour bus windows to naked Jarawa children.

Indigenous communities need to be treated as equals in any discussion of tourism, with the power to decide whether and how to balance their priorities with the desires of visitors.

"For many tourists, visiting tribal communities is a way to experience life very different from their own. But tribes are not there for the photo-snapping entertainment of adventure travelers. What they need is to have their land and way of life protected, along with the right to say no to tourism," says Stephen Corry, director for London-based Survival International, a tribal rights advocacy group.

And yet, many tribal groups are actually saying yes to tourism, seeing it as an opportunity for economic and other benefits for their people. Listen to Mamo Santos, a Kogi elder I met in Colombia's Sierra Nevada. Standing serenely beside a grass-roofed house, he surveyed a parade of tourists navigating muddy trails in the jungle. They were bound for Ciudad Perdida—the no-longer-lost stone city cloaked in lianas that was built by his ancestors to escape Spanish conquistadores. "If our little brothers can help protect nature, which is sacred to us, and regain access to our spiritual sites on land that was taken, we welcome them," he told me. "Little brothers," I discovered, is how the Kogi refer to outsiders, including tourists.

"Indigenous societies and tourism rarely get along well, but when they do, it is the result of tribal leaders empowered to make decisions that are best for their own people," says anthropologist Wade Davis, a *National Geographic* explorer-in-residence.

Given the potential for tourism to harm as well as help, indigenous people are reaching out to one another. The National Association of Tribal Historic Preservation Officers in the United States, which represents Native American groups, published a step-by-step *Tribal Tourism Toolkit* (step number three is instructive: "assess the hopes and horrors"). And last year, the newly formed World Indigenous Tourism Alliance collaborated with the Adventure Travel Trade Association to facilitate a dialogue between tour operators and indigenous peoples. One conclusion: Indigenous communities need to be treated as equals in any discussion of tourism, with the power to decide whether and how to balance their priorities with the desires of visitors.

There are positive examples to build on. The Inuit of Nunavik, Canada, have set up carefully monitored tours that allow visitors to experience authentic Inuit culture, including throat singing and foraging for wild foods, while providing jobs and promoting ethnic pride among the youth. In Kenya, where the Maasai have had decades of trial-and-error with tourism, the tribe owns Campi Ya Kanzi, an award-winning eco-lodge in a wilderness reserve on communal land. The Maasai get direct economic benefits, and visitors learn about an age-old way of life while helping to safeguard it. Done this way—by the indigenous people, for the indigenous people—tribal tourism is worth your support. As Mamo Santos said: On our terms, we welcome you.

—Costas Christ, *National Geographic Traveler*, **February/March 2013.**

---

hectic. Therefore, when a tourist demands service, he or she may become impatient with the different culture, creating resentment among the local people.

A second factor creating social conflict, particularly in countries or areas with serious economic problems, is tourist wealth. High-living tourists eat in fine restaurants and live in hotels among splendor in an area of hunger, unemployment, and little opportunity for jobs or education. This has led in some cases to militant revolutionary action. A third factor involved in alienation is the associated change that occurs in the local inhabitants of an area. A fourth factor causing alienation occurs in some less industrialized countries that import foreign workers for the tourism industry. Many multinational corporations bring in workers from other countries who have experience at working in hotels and other tourist-related positions. They are placed in positions of management, giving the local residents a feeling of economic colonialism since the management positions are given to outsiders. The foreign workers generally fill the better-paying jobs and are in many cases supervisors of less-skilled citizens. Because they have the better-paying jobs, they can then compete more favorably for goods and services in the community and country.

Finally, it has been observed that international tourism acts as a catalyst toward the assimilation of traditional customs by Western cultures in developing countries. In other words, tourists' values may be transferred and adopted by the host population. The local population then seeks to imitate the consumption patterns of the tourist. The change in the value system and attitudes of the host population may affect dress, eating habits, and the demand for consumer goods. This phenomenon has been called the demonstration (or imitation effect) and it alters the cultural landscape of the destination and causes a Westernization of the local culture.

Environmental Impact

It seems that some people, in their eagerness to capitalize on opportunities for immediate enjoyment or gratification, do not consider the future consequences of that enjoyment. This characteristic applies particularly in tourist areas where nature itself is the chief attraction. Tourists are attracted to scenic harbors, cascading waterfalls, and large lakes surrounded by high mountains or volcanoes. But in enjoying these attractions, tourists, being human, may threaten the natural beauty because they don't consider the long-term effect of increased tourist use. Increased visits to natural wonders has a tendency to destroy what we find attractive, unless effective plans to balance tourism and the **environment** are developed.

The term *environment* is used rather loosely, indicating both human and physical characteristics. Authors, speakers, and literature often refer to human environment, physical environment, or a combination of both. A term that can be introduced to describe the change that occurs in the character of an area is **preexisting forms**. Preexisting forms characterize an area's human and physical environment before being "discovered" as a major tourist destination area. We use it simply to indicate what an area is like in its cultural and physical setting before tourism invades. The social and cultural impacts of tourism were discussed earlier, and in part deal with the human environment that occurs as a result of tourism.

An excellent example of changing preexisting forms associated with both the human and physical environment is the development of coastal resorts and cities. In Spain, for example, several coastal villages have been changed rather dramatically in the past few years. Promotional images of the area usually highlight the area as it was before tourism. Yet, when visited by the tourist, the scattered villages of Torremolinos, Benidorm, Lloret del Mar, and other small villages are no longer recognizable.

A second factor of large tourist development has been the **pollution** of surrounding areas. Uncontrolled building on coastal stretches of Spain, Italy, and the Adriatic Sea has destroyed completely the natural character of some areas. Hundreds upon hundreds of miles of shoreline have been changed irreparably by the sprawl of hotels, restaurants, bars, and houses. Beaches have been partitioned by unsightly buildings, awash with noise from nightclubs, traffic fumes, and tremendous overpopulation during certain seasons of the year.

It can be expected that some change in preexisting forms will be necessary to accommodate mass tourism. However, location and concentration of development can be controlled carefully by the government in order to take advantage of income and employment opportunities for tourism while reducing its social and cultural impact. Concentration limits the impact on both the social and natural environment.

A common concept used in discussing the environment (whether for tourism or any other use) is the **carrying capacity**. Carrying capacity is that level of tourism development that can occur in the destination or at an attraction that, when exceeded, will create environmental degradation to the area that cannot be relieved with controls or other forms of tourism. Ecotourism is becoming more and more important. **Ecotourism** is environmentally responsible travel to natural areas that helps to preserve the area being visited. It seeks to reduce the impact of tourism on sensitive areas and to protect the indigenous populations of a region by using tourism as a tool for conservation. Tourism has degradation potential for both the indigenous populations and the physical environment.

Elements of environmental degradation that take place as a result of tourism can be divided into a number of subelements.

Pollution

The use of automobiles, taxis, buses, and aircraft has resulted in a number of problems related to polluted air. Air pollution is probably less of a problem for the travel industry than for other industries, yet those locations with a number of conveyances to move people will suffer from some pollution. Two national parks, Yosemite and Shenandoah, among others, have had problems with congestion causing air pollution and damage to vegetation.

Most research and studies on pollution have focused on the discharge of untreated water from resorts or boats into seas, lakes, rivers, and springs.

Noise pollution is a third form of pollution associated with traffic congestion on land and in the air. Also, many recreational vehicles—motorcycles, motorboats, jet skis, snowmobiles, and aircraft—cause excessive noise.

Vegetation

Destruction and degradation of vegetation in an area result from two factors: the large number of visitors that overwhelm an area and physical abuse to the vegetation, either by vandalism or collection. Loss of vegetation leads to soil erosion and further degradation of the environment.

Wildlife

Problems associated with wildlife changes result from the killing of animals or birds and the disruption of normal habits of feeding and breeding (Figure 1.10).

Figure 1.10 Elephant family in Etosha National Park, Namibia. © Jeremy Woodhouse/Getty Images. com.

Natural Landscapes

Construction results in the encroachment of facilities or buildings upon open spaces, both natural and man-made, such as agricultural or pastoral lands. In some cases, the creation of suprastructures and infrastructures removes valuable natural sites from public access and reserves them only for the guests of resorts or hotels.

The Opportunity

The principal environmental benefit of tourism is a rationale for conservation. Tourism often relies on unspoiled natural and cultural environments as basic attractions. Tourism can provide a vital economic justification for maintaining the character and integrity of these environments. In many instances, the highest economic return from these resources is through their conservation as tourism attractions rather than development for commodity production. Classic examples of the relationship are the wildlife refuges in Africa. Without the economic return provided by tourism (also allowing for the protection of resources), these areas might well be converted to agriculture, forestry, mining, or other forms of development, vastly altering their environment.

A second potential benefit of tourism is the environmental improvement that can be associated with tourism development. Tourism, as with other forms of development, can bring with it modern technologies such as sewage-treatment facilities that can protect and even enhance environmental quality. The importance of the environmental effects is rooted in the most fundamental motivation for tourism. In the most rudimentary sense, people engage in tourism to experience different environments. Destinations are attractive to tourists because they posses characteristics that make them distinctive. Contemporary writers often refer to this distinctiveness as "sense of place." Sense of place can be based on features of the natural environment, features of the cultural environment, or—as is often the case—some combination of the two.

Conclusion

The issues described above illustrate that tourism can have multiple economic, cultural, and environmental effects on people and their communities. Tourism can help protect and preserve distinctive communities. Often it is an area's cultural history or heritage that makes it distinctive and there exists a positive

I HAVE A CONFESSION to make. I don't much like cities. In fact, as a kid I hated them. Growing up in the suburbs of New Jersey a few turnpike exits away from Manhattan, I gravitated to the woods, streams, and fields of the Garden State instead of the concrete jungle that was home to my immigrant relatives. Nature made sense to me—it had a rhythm and reason I could understand.

None of this is surprising for a guy who ended up working in the conservation field. But somewhere along the way, I came to appreciate not just the appeal of cities (museums, people, and culture) but also their outsize role in affecting the planet's future. According to the United Nations, half the world's population now lives in cities, and that proportion is expected to increase to more than two-thirds by 2050. If we are to solve our most pressing problems, from climate change to dwindling freshwater resources, we have to get it right in our urban centers. The challenges are immense, but so are the opportunities. Today, cities are sprouting some of the most innovative green projects in the world, redefining a sustainable future for urban dwellers—and attracting travelers, too. Here are just a few.

High-rise shrubbery in Milan: The world's first vertical urban forest is rising above Italy's largest industrial city. Bosco Verticale, scheduled for completion this year, consists of double towers planted with some 700 trees, 5,000 shrubs, and 11,000 smaller plants. The vegetation will create a microclimate that supports birds, butterflies, and other insects, while also absorbing dust—a serious problem in Milan—and CDs, linked to climate change. It will also cut noise pollution and conserve energy. As growing urban populations strain available space, the idea is to expand upward rather than outward. Though questions remain, Bosco Verticale provides a glimpse of a future where skyscrapers might one day double as forests.

Solar trees in Singapore: With environmental awareness on the rise among its youthful population, this clean-cut, high-tech city is emerging as the green capital of Asia. Witness the new Gardens by the Bay (Figure 1.11), an ambitious renewable energy project and ecotourism attraction set on 250 acres of reclaimed land, offering a greener vision of urban renewal. It features 18 solar-powered "supertrees" up to 16 stories tall, made from steel and concrete "trunks" covered in thousands of plants. Two massive, futuristic-looking glass conservatories capture and filter rainwater. Inside is a Noah's ark of some of the world's plants, including, for visitors, interpretations of their modern and traditional uses.

Carbon-sucking spree in Chicago: The famous Millennium Park—surrounded by trendy restaurants and filled with trees and flowers—is actually the largest green roof in the world, stretching some 25 acres over a bustling underground commuter rail station and parking garages. It forms the heart of Chicago's green belt (which covers roughly 17 percent of the metropolis and removes more than 25,000 tons of greenhouse gases from the air annually). The past several years under Mayor Rahm Emanuel and his predecessor Richard M. Daley have seen the city shutter two smog-creating coal-fired power plants that rained pollution onto low-income neighborhoods, call for all new buildings to meet LEED standards, invest in 100 miles of bikeways, and make plans for replacement of 900 miles of leaky city water pipes.

Trash to treasure in Sydney: Australia's first regional food-waste-to-energy power plant, Earth Power can convert over 80,000 tons of food waste each year into renewable energy. An anaerobic process transforms nearly one-third of the city's discarded leftovers (think of the restaurant scraps alone). The results are a biogas that helps power the metropolitan area's electrical grid and the prevention of food rubbish from rotting in landfills and producing methane—a large contributor to global warming.

Electricity-making sidewalks in London: Sidewalk slabs—made from old car tires—that generate electricity from the pressure of a footstep, harnessing the kinetic energy of walking to power streetlights and other electronics? During last year's Olympic Games, temporary slabs made enough energy to light up the walkway between the Tube station and the stadium each night. They are now being installed permanently at the Westfield Stratford City shopping center near the

continues

relationship between tourism and a reawakening or renewal of cultural heritage. The general impact of tourism seems to be positive if the carrying capacity is not exceeded. Tourism has stimulated the rehabilitation of existing historic sites, buildings, and monuments in many parts of the world. Recognition of the need for proper planning to conserve the environment for future generations has, in turn, also resulted in tourism. Clearly, no single subject offers a greater challenge and opportunity for all who work in the global tourism industry and none may be so critical to the image and continued growth of the industry. We all must become more concerned and better prepared if we are to avoid exploitation through too rapid or excessive development and insensitivity to resident needs.

The economic and social impact on a poorer country can be very beneficial, and the greater awareness of life in other lands can lead to a better world. Examination of tourism in individual world regions helps to explain the impact of the ever-growing tourist industry on countries.

Figure 1.11 Gardens by the Bay: Supertrees in Singapore. © Louis W/www.Shutterstock.com.

Olympic Stadium. Airports could be next, capturing the frantic energy of travelers as they rush to catch their flights.

"Things that were unimaginable just a few years ago are now possible," says Jeffrey Sachs, director of Columbia University's Earth Institute. But he also warns that time is running out. "I believe we have maybe two generations to embrace the technologies that allow us the benefits of modern life while sustaining the planet."

That's roughly 50 years. Not a long time, but who would have imagined even a decade ago the apiary that now produces local honey atop New York's Whitney Museum of American Art? I can see a day when city dwellers will take an elevator to the 27th floor to buy organic vegetables from skyscraper farmers using compost to help power the building—and lifting us closer to a sustainable future.

—**Costas Christ,** *National Geographic Traveler,* **May 2013**

REVIEW QUESTIONS

1. Why do people travel?
2. Describe the elements of geography.
3. Compare and contrast *site* and *situation*.
4. What turns places into attractions (destinations)?
5. Why are cultural characteristics of places important to tourism?
6. Define and state the significance of complementarity, intervening opportunity, and transferability.
7. How can tourist activity aid in the preservation of cultural traits?
8. What regions of the world generate the most tourists? Why?
9. Identify the positive and negative economic impacts of tourism.
10. What cultural and social problems may occur as a result of tourism?

part 2: GEOGRAPHY AND TOURISM OF THE UNITED STATES OF AMERICA

© 2015 Cengage Learning

MAJOR GEOGRAPHIC CHARACTERISTICS

- The United States is characterized by urban and ethnically diverse populations.
- The United States has a diversified resource base, including fertile soils that make it the major food-surplus region in the world.
- North America has a high total and per capita consumption of resources and consumer goods.

MAJOR TOURISM CHARACTERISTICS

- Tourism is an important element in the quality of life of residents of the United States.
- U.S. citizens rank near the bottom compared to other industrialized countries in terms of employee vacation time benefits.
- The region is one of the largest origin regions for tourism.
- The region is one of the largest international destination regions of the world.
- The automobile is a major form of travel for domestic tourism.
- The attractions in the region are extremely diversified.

MAJOR ATTRACTIONS

International Visitors

- New York City
- Niagara Falls
- Washington, D.C.
- Las Vegas
- Miami
- San Francisco
- Los Angeles
- New Orleans
- Grand Canyon

Domestic

- Orlando, Florida
- Branson, Missouri
- Yellowstone National Park
- San Diego, California
- Lancaster, Pennsylvania
- Williamsburg, Virginia
- Oahu, Hawaii

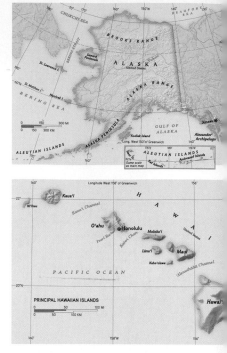

Introduction

50 States

13 colonies

The United States consists of 48 contiguous states and the states, Alaska and Hawaii. Densely populated eastern states cover the Atlantic coastal plain, mostly backed by the low Appalachian Mountains. Central states lie in lowlands drained by the Mississippi river system. The high Rocky Mountains, arid intermontane plateaus, and earthquake-prone coastal ranges occupy the West. Alaska, the largest U.S. state, possesses a vast, rugged terrain, ranging from a mild Pacific coast to a harsh arctic tundra region. Hawaii, a group of volcanic islands, enjoys a tropical climate. Most of the United States experiences a temperate climate. From its founding as a country, immigration has continued building the United States as a multicultural nation. In 2008, the minority population stood at 105 million people—34 percent of all Americans. Whites are about two-thirds of the population, Hispanics 15.4 percent, blacks 13.5 percent, and Asians 5.0 percent. Minority populations tend to concentrate in certain states: California holds the most Hispanics (13.5 million), and they make up 45 percent of New Mexico's population; California also claims the most Asians (5.1 million), but they are a majority in Hawaii at 54 percent; and New York State has the most blacks (3.5 million), although the District of Columbia achieves the highest proportion at 56 percent. The United States declared its independence from Britain in 1776 during the American Revolution. The U.S. Constitution, the world's oldest federal constitution, was written in 1786 and then was ratified by the original 13 states. The new republic expanded westward until the 50th state, Hawaii, was added in 1959. Immigration, innovation, natural resources, free enterprise, and democracy have all combined to make the United States the leading economic power in the world.

From *National Geographic Atlas of the World*, 9th edition. Copyright ©2011 National Geographic Society. Reprinted by arrangement. All rights reserved.

Area	9,826,630 sq km (3,794,083 sq mi)
Population	306,805,000
Government	Federal republic
Capital	Washington, D.C. 4,338,000
Life Expectancy	78 years
Literacy	99%
Religion	Protestant, Roman Catholic, Jewish, Latter-day Saints
Language	English, Spanish, other immigrant and Native American languages
Currency	U.S. dollar (USD)
GDP per Cap	$46,400
Labor Force	0.6% Agriculture, 22.6% Industry, 76.8% Services

From *National Geographic Atlas of the World*, 9th edition. Copyright ©2011 National Geographic Society. Reprinted by arrangement. All rights reserved.

Tourism Characteristics

The United States has a large and varied tourism industry, with a combination of public and private organizations. The United States is the world's third largest market for international tourism, with European destinations such as France and Germany typically ranking ahead in total numbers. The competitiveness of the United States as a destination for international tourists is impressive, considering that unlike France and Germany the United States does not border a large number of wealthy and densely populated countries from which to draw tourists. The United States as a source of tourists to other countries is likewise important, because U.S. tourists spend more money abroad than those of any other country.

Travel and tourism are critical to the American economy (Figure P2.1) and each state has a state tourist agency (destination marketing organization) of some form or another. The principal task of these agencies is to promote travel to and through their respective states, get visitors to stay longer in these states, and encourage citizens of each state to vacation close to home. They accomplish this task by researching existing travel patterns in the state, developing a brand, and sponsoring promotional campaigns for state tourism.

A number of specific organizations serve the private sectors of the tourism industry. The American Society of Travel Agents (ASTA) was created to provide service and information to travel agents and to establish an ethical code of conduct. Regional destination marketing organizations (DMOs) are represented by Destination Marketing Association International (DMAI). The umbrella organization for the entire private industry is a nonprofit organization called the U.S. Travel Association (formerly known as the Travel Industry Association of America). The United States Travel and Tourism Administration (USTTA), which was headed by an Assistant Secretary of Tourism under the umbrella of the United States Department of Commerce, has been replaced by Brand USA, a public–private partnership with the mission of promoting increased international travel to the United States.

The goal of the organization is to make the United States the premier travel destination in the world. A separate agency, the Office of Travel and Tourism Industries, collects and analyzes tourism statistics and data.

In 2010, 62 million international travelers visited the United States (Figure P2.2). This was approximately 6.3 percent of total world international travel, representing 11 percent of global spending on travel and tourism. Canada's 21 million tourists and Mexico's 13.4 million account for over half of all international visitors to the United States (Figure P2.3). The percentage of total international visitors to the United States from Canada and Mexico has declined somewhat during the past decade. This decline reflects the increasing speed and relatively lower costs of overseas travel to the United

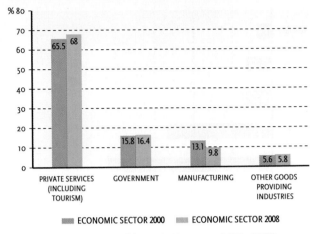

PERCENT OF NONFARM EMPLOYMENT

Figure P2.1 Structure of the U.S. Economy 2000–2008.

Source: Adapted from Statistical Abstracts of the United States, 2010. Copyright © 2015 Cengage Learning®.

Figure P2.2 Times Square, New York, New York. © SeanPavonePhoto/www.Shutterstock.com.

TOP FIVE INTERNATIONAL MARKETS TO THE USA, 2010

Figure P2.3 Tourism to the United States.

Source: Adapted from U.S. Travel Association, 2012. Copyright © 2015 Cengage Learning®.

TOP SEVEN HIGH-GROWTH MARKETS THROUGH 2018 (FORECASTED)

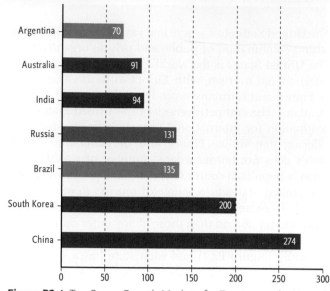

Figure P2.4 Top Seven Growth Markets for Tourism to the United States.

Source: Adapted from U.S. Travel Association, 2012. Copyright © 2015 Cengage Learning®.

States during this time period. Although overseas visitors are increasingly important as a part of U.S. international tourism, Canada and Mexico continue to be very important markets. The next three top international markets are the United Kingdom with 3.8 million arrivals in 2010, Japan with 3.2 million arrivals, and Germany with 1.8 million visitor arrivals. While overseas arrivals represent just 44 percent of all international arrivals, they account for 78 percent of total international travel receipts. Nine of the top 15 countries posted record visitation to the United States: Canada, Brazil, France, South Korea, China, Australia, Italy, Spain, and India. Top leisure travel activities for overseas visitors are: (1) shopping, (2) dining, (3) city sightseeing, (4) visiting historical places, and (5) amusement/theme parks. Direct spending by domestic and international travelers in the United States averages $2 billion a day, $86.6 million an hour, $1.4 million a minute, and $24,000 a second (U.S. Travel Association, 2012).

There is a dramatic shift occurring in the top five high-growth markets (Figure P2.4). The U.S. Travel Association forecasts that arrivals between 2010 and 2018 from China will increase by 274 percent, from South Korea by 200 percent, from Brazil by 135 percent, from Russia by 131 percent, and from India by 94 percent. China has been a fast-growing market for international travelers to the United States since the United States and China signed an agreement that opened the doors for promotion of travel to the entire United States. In 2010 over 800,000 Chinese traveled to the United States (compared with 397,000 in 2005), staying on average 23 nights and spending $7.000 per visit (U.S. Department of Commerce, OTTI, 2012).

In 2012 President Barack Obama signed an Executive Order establishing a new Task Force on Travel and Competitiveness. It called for a set of policies, recommendations, and actions aimed at fostering further growth of the travel industry by reducing barriers, creating opportunities, and improving service levels. The initiative's strategy envisions 100 million international travelers, who will spend

$250 billion annually by 2021 (compared to 62 million international travelers spending $153 billion in 2010).

United States Travelers Abroad

In 2011, 58.5 million citizens of the United States traveled abroad (Figure P2.5). Mexico is the largest destination for U.S. travelers (19.9 million), with slightly more than 34 percent of American tourist travel to that country. Canada is the second largest destination of United States tourists (11.6 million), accounting for nearly 20 percent of all U.S. citizens traveling abroad. Canada's proximity, favorable costs, similar culture in a multicultural context, distinctive and attractive cities, and natural attractions are all factors affecting American visitors.

The two major destinations of overseas trips are Europe (10.8 million or 19 percent) and the Caribbean

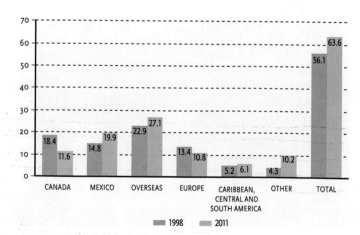

Figure P2.5 Travel from the United States.

Source: Statistical Abstract of the United States, 2012. Copyright © 2015 Cengage Learning®.

Figure P2.6 Orlando skyline. © Songquan Deng/www.Shutterstock.com.

(6 million or 10 percent). The historical ties of Europe to the United States combine with favorable airfares and charters to attract American travelers to Europe. The Caribbean and South America have been the largest growth areas over the past decade due to the increased availability of air routes and increased demand for cruises (U.S. Department of Commerce, OTTI, 2012).

Domestic Tourism

The travel industry is the second largest industry in the United States, but it ranks number one among all U.S. industries in export earnings (U.S. Travel Association, 2011). Direct spending on leisure travel by domestic and international travelers totaled $526 billion in 2010. U.S. residents logged 1.5 billion person-trips for leisure purposes in 2010. The automobile dominates, providing the means of transportation for 79 percent of pleasure trips. Air travel was proportionately greater for people traveling to attend conventions and conduct business, but still clearly second to the automobile. The heavy-use patterns of the automobile are simply an extension of the modern United States in which the auto is important in all private phases of life.

Tourist Destinations and Attractions

The attractions of the United States are diverse and multiple due to the size of the country, its culture, and economic development. The top tourist attractions in the United States reflect that diversity. The single most popular destination in 2011 was Orlando (Figure P2.6) with over 50 million visitors, with the Magic Kingdom at Disney World alone attracting just under 20 million visitors, followed closely by Disneyland in Anaheim, California. However, the diversity of attractions in the United States means that even the Magic Kingdom attracts less than 10 percent of all domestic and international tourists. Popular single-site attractions include Times Square in New York City; Washington, D.C.'s Union Station; the Las Vegas Strip; Niagara Falls;

Faneuil Hall Marketplace in Boston; and the country's many theme parks, events, and national parks. There is a wide geographic distribution and variety in the theme parks in the United States. There are twenty theme parks in the United States that attract 3 million or more visitors each year. National parks are another major attraction, with the Great Smoky Mountains National Park in North Carolina and Tennessee receiving some 10 million visitors yearly (although many of these may reflect combining an automobile trip to Disney World with a visit to this park located between the heavily populated Northeast coastal cities and Florida). Other major attractions include the cities of the country, with New York City, Los Angeles, and other major metropolitan areas attracting tens of millions of visitors annually for their museums, plays, shopping, and other attractions.

The events of September 11th 2001 had a tremendous impact on tourism in the United States. Total domestic trips in the United States declined by some 35 million trips, most accounted for in the last quarter of 2001. As travel began to increase in early 2002, pleasure trips were shorter, closer to home, and by car. The industry began to recover by mid-2002 and four years later it reached the levels of pre-9/11. Growth has been steady although somewhat tempered by a home mortgage lending crises in 2008, leading to a recession followed by several years of double-digit unemployment rates. The tourism industry supports 14 million jobs in the United States; the industry represents nearly 3 percent of the nation's gross domestic product; one out of nine jobs depend on travel and tourism; the industry ranks among the top five in terms of private industry sector employment; and travel is among the top 10 industries in 48 states in terms of employment (U.S. Travel Association, 2011). Nine travel regions in the United States have been identified by the United States Office of Travel and Tourism Industries for the purpose of data gathering and analysis of travel in the country. The regions provide both a convenient geographic grouping for tourism analysis and readily available statistics to allow meaningful comparisons between regions.

chapter 2: NEW ENGLAND

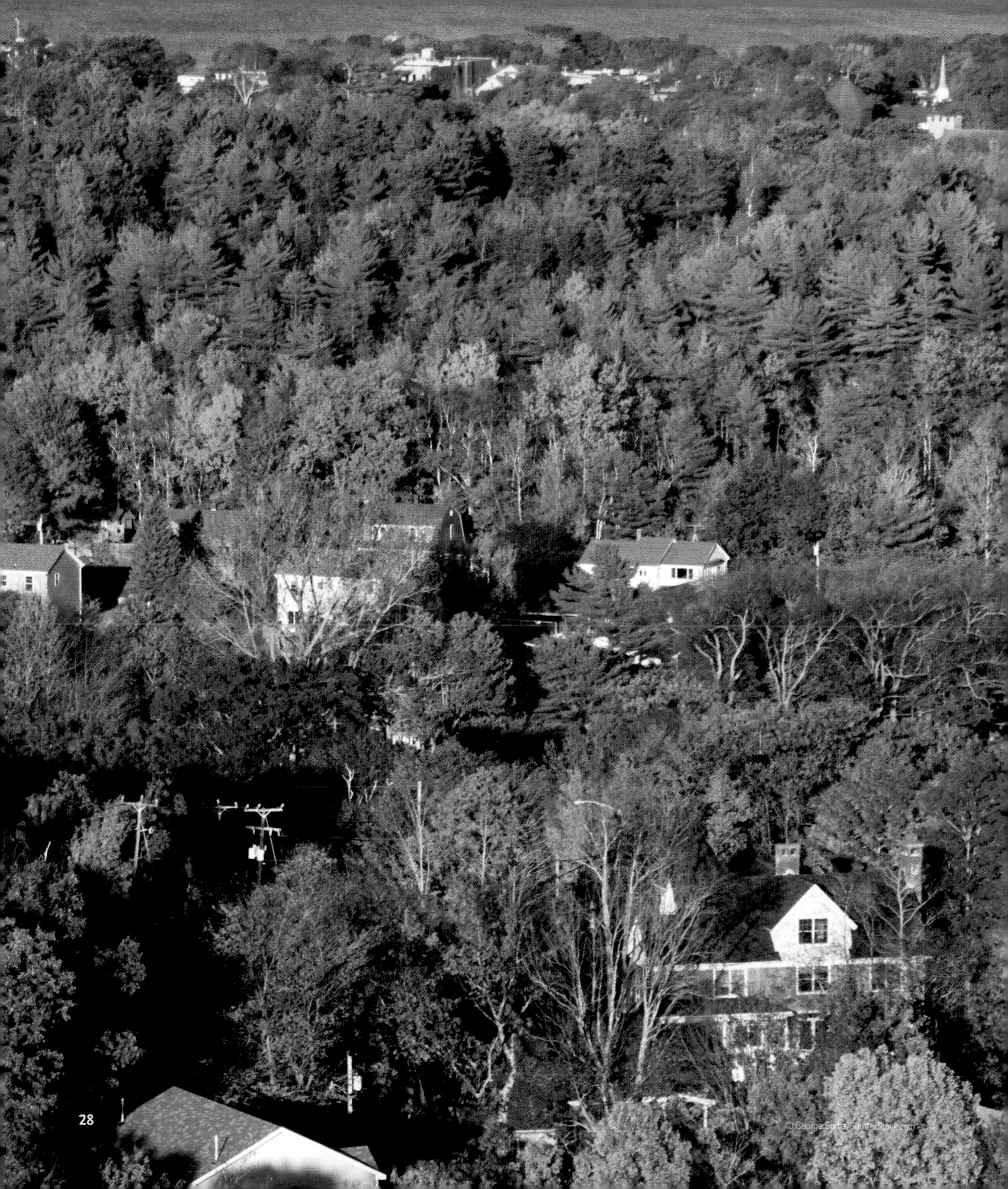

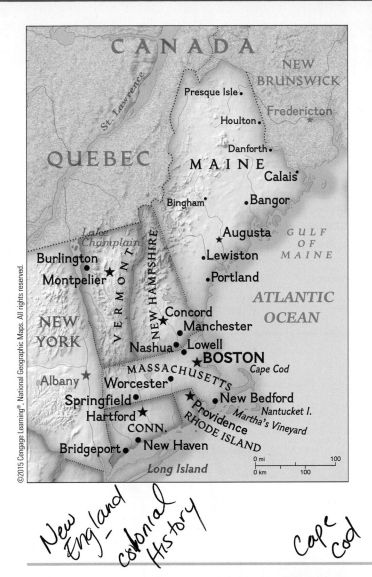

(Handwritten notes: New England – Colonial History; Cape Cod; Beginning of America)

STATE PROFILE

State	Capital	Square Miles	Population (2010)
Connecticut	Hartford	5,544	3,574,097
Maine	Augusta	33,741	1,328,361
Massachusetts	Boston	9,241	6,547,629
New Hampshire	Concord	9,283	1,316,470
Rhode Island	Providence	1,231	1,052,567
Vermont	Montpelier	9,615	625,741

Source: Adapted from U.S. Bureau of the Census, 2011.

With its coasts, mountains, forests, and rich colonial history, New England provides excellent opportunities for outdoor recreation, sightseeing, and entertainment. Winter sports and summer coastal activities are readily available to prospective tourists. Population in the summer resorts along the coast and on the small islands increases dramatically during the summer. The rich colonial history of the area is evident in restored villages (cultural centers) and historical sites. The beauty of the fall season is nationally recognized, attracting people from all over to enjoy the colorful fall foliage of the season. These attributes, coupled with proximity to the populous Great Lakes region and New York, bring many tourists to New England to sightsee, participate in outdoor recreation, and enjoy the entertainment available in the urban centers.

Connecticut

Connecticut's picturesque countryside is dotted with gracefully spired, white-frame churches and small cities. The two largest cities, Hartford and New Haven, are the two major visitor centers. In Hartford, the Mark Twain House and Museum, the Connecticut State Library Museum, and the Wadsworth Athenaeum (the nation's first public art museum) are important attractions aside from the capital itself. At New Haven, the Yale University Art Gallery and the Peabody Museum of Natural History on the grounds of Yale University (founded in 1701) and the nearby Green and Grove Street Cemetery, where Noah Webster and Eli Whitney are buried, are the major attractions. A host of other cities provide glimpses of New England's past. Essex, on the Connecticut River, is a well-preserved Revolutionary War era village. Mystic,

which was the center of early whaling and shipbuilding, has the Museum of America and the Sea (the nation's largest outdoor maritime museum). It has sailing ships, old-time shops, over sixty buildings, museums, an aquarium, and craftsmen demonstrations. Foxwood Resort and Mohegan Sun Casino feature the glamorous glitz of casino gaming.

Constitution State

Area	14,357 sq km (5,543 sq mi)
Population	3,518,000
Capital	Hartford 124,000
GDP per Cap	$50,800
Agriculture	nursery stock; dairy products; poultry, eggs; shellfish
Industry	transportation equipment, metal products, machinery, insurance, tourism

Maine

Maine is the home of Acadia National Park, New England's only national park. The park occupies nearly one-half of Mt. Desert Island and other smaller islands. It is a sea-lashed granite coastal area with forested valleys, lakes, and mountains. Bar Harbor is the entrance to Acadia National Park. Although there is no other national park, the Maine woods, filled with spruce, fir, cedar, birch, and maple are considered Thoreau country. Sugarloaf is one of the finest ski resorts in the Northeast. Along the rocky coast of Maine are lighthouses, sandy beaches, quiet fishing villages, and thousands of offshore islands, bays, and inlets. The two major towns are Bangor and Portland. Bangor is the gateway to excursions in the Maine woods. The Rangeley Lakes, Baxter State Park, and Sebago are easily reached from Bangor. Portland, the childhood home of the poet William Wadsworth Longfellow, which was built in 1785, exhibits the furnishings and personal belongings of the family. Portland, located on beautiful Casco Bay, has stately old homes, historic churches, and charming streets and a renovated waterfront. Freeport is home to the L.L. Bean store, which is the size of small mall attracting 4 million visitors every year.

Pine Tree State

Area	91,646 sq km (35,385 sq mi)
Population	1,318,000
Capital	Augusta 18,000
GDP per Cap	$30,600
Agriculture	seafood; potatoes; dairy products; poultry, eggs; livestock
Industry	health services, tourism, forest products, leather products

From *National Geographic Atlas of the World*, 9th edition. Copyright ©2011 National Geographic Society. Reprinted by arrangement. All rights reserved.

Massachusetts

Massachusetts is the most populous New England state and has many important attractions. Boston is the capital of the state, but it is also a city whose history is an integral part of the entire United States. The two and a half mile Freedom Trail and the Boston Commons (the oldest public park in America) illustrate the history of the city and the nation. It was at the Boston Commons that the British troops assembled for their march on Lexington and Concord. Along the Freedom Trail is the Old North Church, from which the invasion of the British was signaled to Paul Revere, as well as other famous sites. These include Bunker Hill Monument, the ship the U.S.S. Constitution (Old Ironsides); the Boston Tea Party Ship; Old State House; Beacon Hill; Faneuil Hall Market Place (Quincy Market) indoor-outdoor market containing shops and restaurants; and the Old Granary Burying Ground, with the headstones of John Hancock, Paul Revere, Samuel Adams, and others (including one for Mother Goose). The modern part of the city includes an array of important structures, including the Museum of Science, the Museum of Fine Arts (with the new Art of the Wings exhibit), the New England Aquarium, and a striking example of modern architecture, the John F. Kennedy Library. Other popular attractions in the city include 100-year-old Fenway Park and the Sam Adams Brewery. The Boston Harbor Islands National Recreation Area consists of 34 narrow islands scattered in Boston Harbor. Across the river from Boston is Cambridge, which also has numerous historical sites including the location where Washington took command of the Continental Army in July 1775; the Longfellow National Historic Site; Harvard Square

Figure 2.1 The Mayflower at Plymouth, Massachusetts.

© Marcio Jose Bastos Silva /www.Shutterstock.com.

and Harvard University (founded in 1636); and the Massachusetts Institute of Technology. At Lexington Green and Concord Bridge, visitors can reflect on the American Revolution at the Minute Man National

Historical Park and the Minuteman Statue facing the replica of the Old North Bridge.

Near Boston is Plimoth Plantation (Figure 2.1), a re-created historical village where the Pilgrims landed in 1620. Its exhibits illustrate housing, shops, and crafts of these early settlers of the United States. Cape Cod National Seashore is the home of New England's oldest and most popular resorts, including Provincetown and Chatham. Cape Cod has numerous museums, nature trails, beaches, wildlife sanctuaries, picnic grounds, fresh- and saltwater marshes, luxuriant forests, and migrating sand dunes. South of Cape Cod are the islands of Martha's Vineyard and Nantucket. Old Sturbridge Village between Boston and Springfield is a re-creation of an old New England farm community, complete with villagers in period dress demonstrating the crafts and trades of New England between 1790 and 1840. Salem is famous for the 1692 witchcraft trials. At

Springfield is the National Basketball Hall of Fame, located in honor of Dr. James S. Naismith, who founded the sport here in 1891. The Norman Rockwell Museum is in Stockbridge.

Skiing opportunities bring visitors to the Berkshire Mountains located in the western part of the state.

Bay State

Area	27,336 sq km (10,555 sq mi)
Population	6,594,000
Capital	Boston 609,000
GDP per Cap	$48,100
Agriculture	fruits, nuts, and berries, nursery stock; dairy products
Industry	electrical equipment, machinery, metal products, printing, tourism

From *National Geographic Atlas of the World*, 9th edition. Copyright ©2011 National Geographic Society. Reprinted by arrangement. All rights reserved.

New Hampshire

New Hampshire contains less than one-tenth of the region's population. Mount Washington, the most famous mountain in New Hampshire's White Mountains, is a ski area and summer scenic region. The cog railway up Mount Washington (or an eight-mile toll road by car) provide a view into five states and Canada. Franconia Notch is a dramatic eight-mile gorge. A popular attraction, Old Man of the Mountain, made famous by Nathaniel Hawthorne, was a 40-foot-high naturally carved stone face on Mt. Cannon. It collapsed in a rockslide in 2003. The three major cities of New Hampshire are Manchester, Portsmouth, and Hanover. The seacoast town of Portsmouth, the most popular of the three, is famous for its historical houses, including the John Paul Jones House. With its narrow streets, the

older section around Market Square reminds the visitor of the merchant seamen who called Portsmouth home. Hanover is home to Dartmouth College. The state's second largest city, Nashua, owes its rapid growth and prosperity to its proximity to Boston, Massachusetts.

Granite State

Area	24,216 sq km (9,350 sq mi)
Population	1,325,000
Capital	Concord 42,000
GDP per Cap	$38,400
Agriculture	nursery stock; poultry, eggs; fruits and nuts, vegetables
Industry	machinery, electronics, metal products, tourism

From *National Geographic Atlas of the World*, 9th edition. Copyright ©2011 National Geographic Society. Reprinted by arrangement. All rights reserved.

0 percent Sales tax

Rhode Island

Rhode Island's two major cities of Providence, the capital, and Newport are the chief tourist centers. Providence illustrates the architectural heritage of the pre-revolutionary period in many of its buildings. Roger Williams founded Providence while seeking religious freedom. Many of the streets in the city still bear names that Williams gave them such as Benefit, Benevolent, Friendship, and Hope. Slater Mill in nearby Pawtucket was built in 1793

Smallest state

and marked the beginning of the Industrial Revolution in America.

Newport, situated on beautiful Narragansett Bay, is a center of water sports such as yachting and sailing, and the world-famous Newport Music and Jazz Festival. The Touro Synagogue, which was built in 1763, is the oldest synagogue in the United States. On the cliffs overlooking the ocean are many mansions, including the Breakers, a colonnaded four-story mansion overlooking Rhode Island Sound that was built for Cornelius Vanderbilt. Newport is also the home of the International Tennis Hall of Fame and Tennis Museum.

Ocean State

Area	4,002 sq km (1,545 sq mi)
Population	1,053,000
Capital	Providence 172,000
GDP per Cap	$36,300

Agriculture	nursery stock, vegetables; dairy products, eggs
Industry	health services, business services, silver and jewelry

From *National Geographic Atlas of the World*, 9th edition. Copyright ©2011 National Geographic Society. Reprinted by arrangement. All rights reserved.

Vermont

Ver- French
Mount - Green
Mount - mountain

Vermont advertises a green mountain landscape dotted with small towns and covered bridges. It is a popular ski area for the Northeast, with world-class resorts such as Stowe, Sugarbush, Killington, Mount Snow, Jay Peak, Okemo, Stratton Mountain, Smugglers Notch, and Bolton Valley. Vermont's granite rock is the basis for the world's largest granite quarry at Barre, from which comes granite used all across the United States. Like the other New England states, the fall foliage is one of the most important tourist attractions. Picturesque villages include Woodstock, Manchester, and Grafton. Burlington, the state's largest city, is situated on Lake Champlain. South of Burlington is the Shelburne Farms Museum, celebrating outdoor living history. Ben & Jerry's ice cream plant in Waterbury and the Magic Hat beer brewery in South Burlington are two of Vermont's unique tourist attractions.

Green Mountain State

Area	24,901 sq km (9,614 sq mi)
Population	622,000
Capital	Montpelier 8,000
GDP per Cap	$34,900
Agriculture	dairy products; maple products, apples
Industry	health services, tourism, finance, real estate, computer components

From *National Geographic Atlas of the World*, 9th edition. Copyright ©2011 National Geographic Society. Reprinted by arrangement. All rights reserved.

REVIEW QUESTIONS

1. Explain why New England is truly a four-season destination.
2. New England is sometimes called "America's Cultural Heart." Explain.
3. Name five famous universities or colleges in the region.
4. Name five attractions that are associated with the colonial history of New England.
5. What are the attractions in and around Mystic, Connecticut?

chapter 3: MID ATLANTIC

STATE PROFILE

State	Capital	Square Miles	Population (2010)
New Jersey	Trenton	8,215	8,791,894
New York	Albany	53,990	19,378,102
Pennsylvania	Harrisburg	46,059	12,702,379

Source: Adapted from U.S. Bureau of the Census, 2011.

This region is a major population center of the United States, including many of the country's largest cities. It receives many travelers for business reasons and offers a variety of attractions from gambling at Atlantic City, New Jersey, to the historic Liberty Bell in Philadelphia, to the mountainous regions of the Adirondack and Catskill Mountains in New York, and the Poconos in Pennsylvania.

New Jersey

Although New Jersey has the highest population density in the United States, it also offers a number of wooded, coastal, and historical attractions. The most famous attraction today is Atlantic City, with its famed boardwalk offering gambling, nightclubs, shows, and entertainment. The coastal area has a variety of beach resorts. A sample of the many other attractions in New Jersey includes the historic town of Smithville, a recreation of a typical eighteenth-century New Jersey community; the Victorian charm of Cape May at the southern tip of the state; Edison National Historical Site, containing a workshop where Edison worked on the first motion picture camera, tinfoil phonograph, and other electrical items; and Morristown National Historical Park, which provided winter quarters for Washington and his men. Newark Airport is a major gateway for travelers visiting New York City.

Garden State

Area	22,588 sq km (8,721 sq mi)
Population	8,708,000
Capital	Trenton 83,000
GDP per Cap	$45,000
Agriculture	nursery stock, vegetables, grain and hay, fruits and berries
Industry	chemicals, printing and publishing, food processing, machinery

From *National Geographic Atlas of the World*, 9th edition. Copyright ©2011 National Geographic Society. Reprinted by arrangement. All rights reserved.

New York

Both the state of New York and the city of New York are major tourist attractions. The I-Love-New-York theme has been responsible for an increase in visitors to the city and state, but even without it the city is a major destination. It is the most important city in the world because of its combination of financial, manufacturing, and cultural roles.

The major attractions in the city are too numerous to list. Central Park, designed in the 1860s, remains the most important urban park in America, with over 800 acres of recreational attractions and cultural centers. Other major attractions include Fifth Avenue for shopping; Times Square; Lincoln Center for the Performing Arts; Carnegie Hall; Rockefeller Center with Radio City Music Hall; the Empire State Building, the long-time symbol of New York City's skyscraper skyline; the United Nations Headquarters on the East River; South Street Seaport; Wall Street and the American and New York stock exchanges; Ellis Island and the Statue of Liberty National Monuments, the latter a gift from the French people to commemorate the Franco-American alliance of the Revolutionary War. The site of the former World Trade Center Towers destroyed in the terrorist attacks of September 11, 2001 (Ground Zero) is now the site of the Freedom Tower and the National September 11 Memorial.

Not even Rip Van Winkle could sleep through the cultural clarion of today's Hudson Valley. The legendary snoozer in Washington Irving's tale might descend from his Catskill Mountains hollow to find some of the country's best folk musicians at the Clearwater Festival in Croton-on-Hudson. Founded by now 93-year-old Pete Seeger, the festival marks its 35th anniversary in 2013. "The Hudson must surely be one of the world's most extraordinary streams," says Seeger. "Other rivers are longer and start higher, but my wife and I and our daughter look every day from the windows of our two-room house and see the Hudson. Bless it!"

Just a couple hours north of New York City, this is a land of mom-and-pop shops, "u-pick" wildflower fields, and organic farm stands where "chain" is a four-letter word. Between the Culinary Institute of America grads too enchanted to leave Hyde Park and the influx of NYC chefs realizing the land is greener (and apartments bigger) here, area eateries such as Blue Hill at Stone Barns are stoking locavore passions.

Artists of all media find their muses here. Take a drive to the newly expanded Hudson River School Art Trail to see 17 sites in New York that inspired America's great mid-19th-century landscape paintings. "The views that compose the art trail are a national treasure," says Elizabeth B. Jacks, director of the Thomas Cole National Historic Site. Or visit museums such as the outdoor Storm King Art Center sculpture park to see the work of contemporary visionaries.

Artists of all media find their muses here.

Some villages marry art and music famously. In the wonderfully weird and artsy Woodstock, indie performers and music icons rub elbows and grab crusty loaves at Bread Alone Bakery. Budding musicians bring their bongos to the weekly hippie drum circle on the Village Green.

Much like Rip, Hudson Valley wanderers often wake up to find this is where they long to rest their vagabond souls.

—Sascha Zuger, *National Geographic Traveler*, December 2012/January 2013

This list merely mentions some of New York City's most famous sights. The city also includes a host of other things to see and do, including cathedrals, museums, bridges, ethnic neighborhoods, plays both on and off Broadway, outstanding restaurants, zoos, sport stadiums, and the beaches of the Atlantic Ocean. Distinct neighborhoods include Chinatown, Little Italy, Greenwich Village, Soho, and Harlem (uptown). To the east of the city lies Long Island with Montauk and The Hamptons at the eastern end.

The Hudson Valley, which is north of the city, is the home of the United States Military Academy at West Point and the Culinary Institute of America in Hyde Park. The Catskill Mountains are a major resort center with Ice Cave Mountain, the Catskill Game Farm, Woodstock, and the Bethel Woods Center for the Arts. Albany, the capital, is the gateway to the Adirondacks and Saratoga National Historical Park, Saratoga Springs, Lake George, and Fort Ticonderoga. Saratoga National Historical Park is the site of the important Revolutionary battle where France joined the colonies in their battle with England and is regarded as the turning point of the war. Saratoga Springs is a famous resort spa set in a scenic area with a number of operating springs and geysers. It is also a Mecca for horse-racing enthusiasts and home to the National Racing Museum. Lake George, at the foothills of the Adirondacks, serves as a center for winter and summer sports. Fort Ticonderoga is an authentically reconstructed eighteenth-century French fort, containing a large collection of artifacts from the French and Indian and Revolutionary Wars. Travelers to the Adirondack Park (Figure 3.1), the largest wilderness area east of the Mississippi River, can visit Lake Placid and the Adirondack Museum in Blue Mountain Lake.

In the center of the state at Cooperstown is the National Baseball Hall of Fame and Museum. The three major attractions in western New York are Niagara Falls, the Corning Glass Center, and the Finger Lakes region. Niagara Falls, near Buffalo, is one of the broadest and most spectacular falls in the world. *Maid of the Mist* cruises take visitors to the base of the falls. Corning Glass Center is a famous Steuben glassworks center. The Finger Lakes region is an area of lakes, waterfalls, steep gorges, wineries, and scenic vistas. In upstate New York, Rochester is the home of Eastman House, and the Strong Museum; while Syracuse is home of the New York State Fair. Two hours north of Syracuse, at the border with Canada, lies the 1,000 Islands region. Buffalo, the state's second largest city and situated on Lake Erie, has many outstanding architectural landmarks. South of Buffalo is the legendary Chautauqua Institution.

Empire State

Area	141,299 sq km (54,556 sq mi)
Population	19,541,000
Capital	Albany 94,000
GDP per Cap	$49,500
Agriculture	dairy products; cattle, other livestock; vegetables, apples
Industry	printing and publishing, machinery, computer products, finance, tourism

From *National Geographic Atlas of the World*, 9th edition. Copyright ©2011 National Geographic Society. Reprinted by arrangement. All rights reserved.

Figure 3.1 Adirondack Park (Loon Lake). © Doug Lemke/www.Shutterstock.com.

Pennsylvania

Pennsylvania has some of the most important historical and cultural attractions in the United States. Philadelphia, the geographical center of the original thirteen colonies, was the site where the Declaration of Independence was signed and the Constitution of the United States was drafted. It was the first capital of the new nation. The attractions in Philadelphia include Independence National Historic Park with Independence Hall and Carpenters' Hall (two blocks from Independence Hall). Carpenters' Hall was the site of the first Continental Congress called to address the problem of taxation without representation. Christ Church was where George Washington, Ben Franklin, and other Founding Fathers worshipped. It contains the baptismal font used for William Penn's baptism in England. Other historic sites in the city include Congress Hall, America's first capital; Franklin Court; the Betsy Ross House; the Liberty Bell; and nearby Valley Forge State Park. The Philadelphia Museum of Art and the Rodin Museum are among America's largest art museums.

Not far from Philadelphia, in eastern Pennsylvania, are Hershey, Valley Forge, and the Pennsylvania Dutch Country. Hershey, the home of the Hershey® candy bar, has an eighty-one–acre theme and entertainment park in addition to the Hershey Factory. Valley Forge is the most famous site of Washington's Continental Army winter camps. Gettysburg National Military Park is the location of perhaps the most epic battle of the **Civil War**. A dramatic Visitors Center helps travelers understand the three-day events that unfolded here. It houses a spectacular cyclorama of the battlefield. Reading is the factory outlet mall capital of America. In the center of the state is the main campus of Penn State University in State College.

Pennsylvania Dutch Country is a unique area in America. The horse-drawn carriages of the Amish people, brightly colored hex signs on white barns, covered bridges, and rolling farms largely cultivated with horses are reminders of the Amish, Mennonites, Brethren, and other German religious sects who settled the region. A number of visitor centers and displays such as the Amish Farm and House, the Amish Homestead, the Pennsylvania Farm Museum, Kitchen Kettle shops, Intercourse, Ephrata Cloister in Ephrata, and the Plain and Fancy Farm and Dining Room all provide visitors with a view of the unique religious groups that settled in the area. To the west, Pittsburgh, the major city in western Pennsylvania, has undergone a renovation to provide a modern downtown cityscape. Once a gritty steel town, it is now a vibrant urban commercial center whose history is evident in attractions such as the Fort Pitt Blockhouse. Other sites include the Frick Museum, Carnegie Institute, and the Andy Warhol Museum.

Keystone State

Area	119,283 sq km (46,055 sq mi)
Population	12,605,000
Capital	Harrisburg 47,000
GDP per Cap	$35,600
Agriculture	dairy products; poultry, eggs; mushrooms; cattle, hogs; grains
Industry	machinery, printing, publishing, forest products, metal products

From *National Geographic Atlas of the World*, 9th edition. Copyright ©2011 National Geographic Society. Reprinted by arrangement. All rights reserved.

REVIEW QUESTIONS

1. Name the mountain regions in New York and Pennsylvania.

2. You have been asked to plan a three-day visit to New York City for your class. What sites will you visit?

3. The Meadowlands region in New Jersey is home to several sports teams. Name three.

4. Name five major tourist attractions in Pennsylvania.

5. What city is home to Penn State University?

chapter 4: SOUTH ATLANTIC

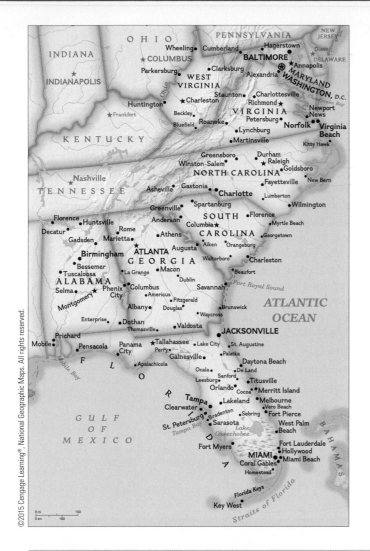

STATE PROFILE

State	Capital	Square Miles	Population (2010)
Delaware	Dover	2,396	897,934
District of Columbia	Washington	68	601,723
Florida	Tallahassee	59,928	18,801,310
Georgia	Atlanta	58,977	9,687,653
Maryland	Annapolis	12,297	5,773,552
North Carolina	Raleigh	52,672	9,535,483
South Carolina	Columbia	31,189	4,625,364
Virginia	Richmond	42,326	8,001,024
West Virginia	Charleston	24,231	1,852,994

Source: Adapted from U.S. Bureau of the Census, 2011.

The South Atlantic region combines history and the nation's capital with the ocean to form a very popular travel region of the United States. The warmer environs extend the travel season in the northern states and the District of Columbia and provide year-round visits to the more southern locations in this region. There is a high degree of travel within the region since during the hot summer many from the southern part of the region move into North Carolina and Virginia for the summer, while in the winter the reverse is true.

Delaware

Delaware, the second smallest state, has a number of summer resorts such as Rehoboth and Bethany beaches along the Atlantic Ocean shorelines. Wilmington, the largest city in the state, is the home of the Du Pont Company. The Winterthur Museum and Gardens, located six miles northwest of Wilmington, is a historical house with over 200 years of early American interior architecture and furnishings in more than 100 rooms. The Hagley Museum displays the history of American industry on a 185-acre complex. Old stone buildings and other buildings have been restored to display the early industries of the United States. The early history of Wilmington can be seen in the Holy Trinity (Old Swedes) Church; Hendrickson House, which is now a museum; Old Town Hall; and Fort Christina Monument, the site of the first Swedish settlement in Delaware. The little town of Lewes, founded in 1631 as a Dutch whaling station, features the striking Zwaanendael Museum. Near Dover is the John Dickinson Mansion, a restored colonial home of the author who wrote the first draft of the Articles of Confederation and who, with Thomas Jefferson, penned the "Declaration of the Causes and Necessity of Taking Up Arms."

First State

Area	6,447 sq km (2,489 sq mi)
Population	885,000
Capital	Dover 36,000
GDP per Cap	$56,400
Agriculture	poultry; soybeans, nursery stock, corn, vegetables; dairy products
Industry	food processing, chemicals, rubber and plastic products, printing

From *National Geographic Atlas of the World*, 9th edition. Copyright ©2011 National Geographic Society. Reprinted by arrangement. All rights reserved.

District of Columbia

The District of Columbia, the nation's capital, can keep a visitor busy for a long period of time. The seat of government provides numerous attractions. The major ones are the Capitol (Figure 4.1) with its marble rotunda, home of the House and Senate chambers, and the Old Supreme Court Chamber; the White House; the Library of Congress, which includes the Gutenberg Bible in its collections; the Bureau of Engraving and Printing, where the government designs, engraves, and prints United States coins, currency, bonds, and postage stamps; the National Archives, which displays a number of historical documents such as the original Declaration of Independence and the Bill of Rights; and a host of other government buildings such as the Department of Justice; Internal Revenue Building; Old Post Office Building; Interstate Commerce Commission; Health, Education, and Welfare Building; Treasury Building; the Federal Reserve Building; and so on. The Washington Cathedral ranks as one of the largest churches in the world.

The John F. Kennedy Center for the Performing Arts, a modern memorial dedicated to the memory of John F. Kennedy, is the national center of performing arts. Other historical sites and memorials are Ford's Theater where John Wilkes Booth shot President Lincoln, the red-brick house where Lincoln died, and the famed Jefferson, Lincoln, and Washington monuments.

The centerpiece of museums in Washington is the Smithsonian Institute, which houses materials ranging from the original Star Spangled Banner that flew over Fort McHenry to the Apollo 11 spacecraft. The Smithsonian is a series of museums, including the National Museum of American History, the National Museum of Natural History, National Museum of History and Technology, the National Museum of the American Indian, Arts and Industries Building, Smithsonian Institution Building, National Air and Space Museum, Freer Gallery of Art, National Portrait Gallery, National Collection of Fine Arts, and the Renwick Gallery. A variety of other attractions, museums, and monuments of interest are found in the city, including Union Station, the Newseum, the National Zoo, the Holocaust Museum, the Vietnam Veterans Memorial, the World War II Memorial, the Dr. Martin Luther King Jr. National Memorial, the National Museum of African History and Culture, and the National Children's Museum.

The Nation's Capital

Area	177 sq km (68 sq mi)
Population	600,000
GDP per Cap	$126,400
Industry	government, service, tourism
Note:	Commonly known as D.C., the District, or Washington, D.C.

Figure 4.1 US Capitol. © Orhan Cam/www.Shutterstock.com.

Florida

Florida is a major winter travel center boasting itself as the playground of America. The state receives more visitors by automobile than any other. South Florida's principal areas are the Florida Keys, Everglades National Park, and Miami. The Florida Keys extend some 135 miles south of the Florida peninsula. They contain marshes, coral reefs, grasslands, and palm trees. The John Pennekamp Coral Reef State Park, near Key Largo, is the first underwater park in the United States. The Ernest Hemingway Home and Museum at Key West was the location at which Hemingway wrote a number of his books. Reef cruises, fishing, boating, swimming, and wading areas are found in the Keys. South Miami Beach has revitalized its art deco architecture and has become a magnet for tourists.

The Everglades National Park is a subtropical wilderness of water, sawgrass, pines, palms, mangroves, alligators, manatees, and other birds and animals. Miami is the home port for many cruise vessels into the Caribbean and has more international travel by ship than any other city in the United States. Two of the city's most noted attractions are the Miami Beach strip of large modern hotels and the kid-friendly Miami Seaquarium, complete with viewing windows, jungle islands, and tidepools. Near Miami is Monkey Jungle, in which visitors in enclosed walkways can watch gorillas, orangutans, chimpanzees, and other primates. It is set in a re-creation of the Amazon rain forest.

Central Florida destinations include Tampa, Orlando, and the Kennedy Space Center. Orlando and the area surrounding it are at the heart of the travel industry in Florida. Walt Disney World Resort includes four major theme parks and several water parks: Magic Kingdom Park (with a new expanded Fantasyland), Epcot, Disney-Hollywood Studios, and Animal Kingdom; Typhoon Lagoon and Blizzard Beach. Downtown Disney and the Disney sports complex are additional attractions providing entertainment, shopping, and food for visitors. Disney's Animal Kingdom presents a unique wildlife experience with a kind of live-action adventure filled with the natural drama of life in the wild. Pleasure Island is a complex of restaurants, shops, and nightclubs built on a six-acre island. A series of theme settings, such as the South Pacific, have been developed for hotels and restaurants. At Disney's Hollywood Studios theme park, visitors can walk through re-creations of palm-lined Hollywood Boulevard and Grumman's Chinese Theater, take a role in a television show (like American Idol Experience), make their own music videos, and get a screen test. Universal Studios Florida is billed as the nation's largest working studio outside of Hollywood and features Islands of Adventure, the Wizarding World of Harry Potter, and Wet 'n Wild Waterpark. Sea World is the world's largest marine park and also features Aquatica, which is SeaWorld's water park.

Accessible from Orlando is Legoland in Winter Haven. Also, Orlando has a wide variety of dinner shows and theme restaurants.

The beaches on both coasts of Florida are world famous. East of Orlando on the Atlantic Coast is Cape Canaveral (Kennedy Space Center), which is open to the public and has a visitor information center. North of Cape Canaveral on the coast, Daytona Beach, home of the Daytona International Speedway, has long been a popular summer resort area. Daytona Beach has become the major destination for students on their annual spring break.

Tampa, on the Gulf of Mexico side of the peninsula, features the Tampa Florida Aquarium and Busch Gardens, where visitors wander through a re-creation of the Serengeti Plain of Tanzania to observe wildlife. Across the bay at St. Petersburg, MGM's Bounty Exhibit has a replica of the three-masted ship Bounty and a Tahitian setting with dioramas, outrigger canoes, and a longboat. The Salvador Dali Museum is in St. Petersburg. Just north of Tampa is Weeki Wachee, where visitors can watch an underwater show in the clear spring waters. Visitors can also take a Wilderness River Cruise, stroll through tropical gardens and rain forest, and see bird shows.

St. Augustine (Figure 4.2) is the oldest permanent settlement on the mainland of the United States. It has been restored to illustrate elements of its original Spanish character. Ponce de León landed near St. Augustine in search of the Fountain of Youth. The most noted attraction is the Castillo de San Marcos National Monument, the old Spanish fort overlooking Matanzas Bay. Other attractions include the Mission of Nobre de Dios, the site of the first permanent Christian mission in the United States, and other reconstructed buildings and houses. St. George Street, where colonial houses have been reconstructed, contains houses and craft shops, including blacksmiths, candle making, leather, pottery, print, and a Spanish bakery.

Just east of Jacksonville stands Fort Carolina National Memorial, a reconstructed sod and timber fort that was first built by the French in 1564. Amelia Island is nearby. The Gulf from Pensacola to Panama City features outstanding beaches, water sports, and resorts. The Naval Aviation Museum and Seville Square, a historic English and Spanish park, are located in Pensacola.

Sunshine State

Area	170,304 sq km (65,755 sq mi)
Population	18,538,000
Capital	Tallahassee 172,000
GDP per Cap	$32,900
Agriculture	citrus, vegetables, field crops, nursery stock; cattle; dairy
Industry	health services, business services, tourism, communications, banking

Figure 4.2 Saint Augustine, the oldest city in the continental United States. © Paul Brennan/www.Shutterstock.com.

History books taught us that Spanish explorer Juan Ponce de León "discovered" Florida 500 years ago in 1513 while seeking the fabled fountain of youth. But before the peninsula was claimed by de León, it was home for more than 12,000 years to Paleo-Indians who built civilizations around its water-filled sinkholes and left behind archaeologically rich middens (giant piles of oyster shells) as proof of their bayside existence.

Today, finding a genuine slice of "Old Florida" can be a scavenger hunt. The breezy Spanish colonial city of St. Augustine is an exception to the rule. A pair of marble lions greets visitors crossing the regal Bridge of Lions into the walled city. Looming over it is Castillo de San Marcos, a seventeenth-century fort surrounded by a moat and occupied at various times by Spanish, British, Confederate, and U.S. soldiers. The fort's warren of chambers echoes with the stories of pirates, three signers of the Declaration of Independence, Spanish-American War deserters, and even Seminole Chief Osceola, who was incarcerated here in 1837 for leading the native resistance against the United States.

Along King Street sit historic Flagler College and the Lightner, an antiquities museum housed in an 1887 Spanish Renaissance Revival masterpiece. It was commissioned by oil tycoon Henry Flagler, who is credited with salvaging the city and planting Florida's tourism seeds. St. George Street, St. Augustine's main drag, may have become overly touristy and crowded with T-shirt emporiums and fudge shops, but the side streets still harbor scrubby garden courtyards and off-the-radar bars, such as the 130-year-old Mill Top Tavern, where you can imagine what Old Florida was like before it became the Sunshine State.

—Adam H. Graham, *National Geographic Traveler*, December 2012/January 2013

Known for peaches

Georgia

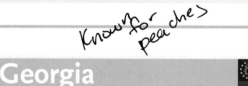

The major attractions in Georgia are in and near the cities of Atlanta and Savannah. Old Savannah, a National Historic Landmark, is over 200 years old. Many of the buildings have been restored. Factor's Walk, a row of business houses, is accessible by a network of iron bridgeways over cobblestone ramps. River Street has shopping and fine restaurants. South of Savannah near the Florida border is the Okefenokee Swamp, an important presence for alligators and other wildlife. Jekyll Island is a popular seaside resort destination. The heart of the South is Atlanta, a thriving city with headquarters of numerous major national corporations, and is considered the transportation, economic, and cultural center of the southeast. The Omni International Center is a sports and convention center that provides all forms of entertainment, shops, and arcades. Atlanta is the home of the High Museum of Art; the Georgia Aquarium; the James E. Carter Presidential Library; and the Dr. Martin Luther King Jr. National Historic Site. Dr. King's grave is at the Ebenezer Baptist Church. Near Atlanta are Stone Mountain Park, a granite dome with sculptures of the Confederate leaders Jefferson Davis, Stonewall Jackson, and Robert E. Lee. As in other large American cities and state capitals there are important museums, gardens, home and civic buildings, and amusement parks and other entertainment for visitors. Atlanta was the site of the 1996 Summer Olympics and several important structures were built to help host the games. Athens, an hour east of Atlanta, is home to the University of Georgia. South of Athens is Augusta, home of the legendary Masters Golf Tournament. In the northwest corner of Georgia is Chickamauga Battlefield, site of one of the bloodiest battles of the Civil War. Dahlonega was one of America's first gold rush towns and has an attractive town square. Nearby, hikers gather at the southern trail head for the two thousand–mile journey on the long Appalachian Trail from Georgia to Maine.

Peach State

Area	153,909 sq km (59,425 sq mi)
Population	9,829,000
Capital	Atlanta 538,000
GDP per Cap	$34,000

Agriculture	poultry, eggs; cotton, peanuts, vegetables, sweet corn, melons
Industry	textiles and clothing, transportation equipment, food processing

Maryland

The major attractions in Maryland are in Baltimore, at Annapolis, and around Washington, D.C. Baltimore is the home of Fort McHenry, where Francis Scott Key wrote the "Star Spangled Banner." Other unique attractions include the B&O Railroad Museum; the Edgar Allan Poe House; the Lexington Market, which has been in continuous operation since 1782; and numerous museums, including the Baltimore Museum of Art. Most famous is the National Aquarium located in the renovated Baltimore Inner Harbor. The Harbor itself is an excellent example of capitalizing on a unique geographic setting both to create a tourist attraction and revitalize a deteriorating inner-city area that includes Oriole Park at Camden Yards. West of Baltimore (and north of D.C.) is Antietam Battlefield. The United States Naval Academy and the Maryland State House, which for a short period of time also served as the capital of the United States, are in Annapolis. Annapolis is one of the most scenic and visitor-friendly cities in the eastern United States. Near Washington, D.C., the Chesapeake and Ohio Canal National Historical Park along the Potomac River provides not only a museum and walking paths but also mule-drawn barge rides in a scenic setting. Assateague Island is famous for its wild ponies.

Old Line State

Area	32,133 sq km (12,407 sq mi)
Population	5,699,000
Capital	Annapolis 37,000
GDP per Cap	$39,200
Agriculture	poultry, eggs; dairy; nursery stock, soybeans, corn; seafood
Industry	real estate, federal government, health and business services

Figure 4.3 Wild horses on Assateague Island. © Helen E. Grose/www.Shutterstock.com.

North Carolina

Attractions are varied in North Carolina, ranging from the mountains through the flatlands to the coastal areas. One of the most beautiful scenic drives in America is the Blue Ridge Parkway. Asheville is the center for trips into the Great Smoky Mountains National Park from the North Carolina side. The Cherokee Indian Reservation has an eighteenth-century Oconaluftee Indian Village, where arts and crafts are demonstrated and the "Trail of Tears," which depicts Cherokee history, is performed.

The Biltmore House and Gardens at Asheville is a large French chateau country house set on an 11,000-acre estate. Nearby is Chimney Rock Park, a towering granite monolith in a beautiful mountain valley. Winston-Salem has Old Salem, a restored planned community, which the Moravians first built in 1766. Over thirty buildings have been restored, of which the Salem Academy and College are the most noted. In and near fast growing Charlotte are the World Golf Hall of Fame, the Mint Museum, Charlotte Nature Museum, the James K. Polk Memorial State Historical Site, and Carowinds, a family entertainment park built around an Old South

theme. Chapel Hill is home to the University of North Carolina. Duke University is in Durham.

The coastal area has outstanding beaches, most notable Cape Hatteras National Seashore; Cape Hatteras Lighthouse, the tallest lighthouse on the East Coast; and the Wright Brothers National Memorial, marking the spot where Orville and Wilbur Wright made their historic first flight at Kitty Hawk. Cape Hatteras is a thin stretch of beach along the Outer Banks barrier islands. Roanoke Island was where Sir Walter Raleigh established a British settlement but the colony vanished after just three years. Cape Fear, to the south, is a quiet beach resort area with activities centering on the lively city of Wilmington.

Tar Heel State

Area	139,389 sq km (53,819 sq mi)
Population	9,381,000
Capital	Raleigh 393,000
GDP per Cap	$35,700
Agriculture	poultry; hogs; tobacco, nursery stock; turkeys; cotton, soybeans
Industry	real estate, health services, chemicals, tourism, tobacco products

From *National Geographic Atlas of the World*, 9th edition. Copyright ©2011 National Geographic Society. Reprinted by arrangement. All rights reserved.

South Carolina

The most dominant attraction in South Carolina is Charleston, one of the oldest cities in the country. Charleston's homes, historic shrines, old churches, lovely gardens, winding cobblestone streets, and intricate iron lace gateways are an outstanding example of historic preservation. A number of museums, such as the Charleston Museum, the Dock Street Theater, the first playhouse in the colonies (1736), and the aircraft carrier Yorktown in the Charleston Harbor all further increase the interest in

the area. George Washington and Robert E. Lee attended services at St. Michael's Episcopal Church. Fort Sumter National Monument marks the site of the beginning of the Civil War. Just north of Charleston are the Magnolia Plantation and Gardens; Cypress Gardens with its giant cypresses, lagoons, azaleas, and subtropical flowers; Boone Hall Plantation (Figure 4.4); and Middleton Place.

Along the coast are a number of resorts such as Hilton Head Island, Myrtle Beach, and Kiawah Island, which provide all forms of sports, especially golf, and amusements. King's Mountain National Military Park, near the North Carolina border, reminds visitors of the southern campaign of the Revolutionary War where the British were defeated by mountain frontiersmen from Carolina, Georgia, and Virginia. A diorama and museum provide information about the battles and the war.

Figure 4.4 Boone Hall Plantation, South Carolina.
© spirit of america/www.Shutterstock.com.

Palmetto State

Area	82,932 sq km (32,020 sq mi)
Population	4,561,000
Capital	Columbia 127,000
GDP per Cap	$28,400
Agriculture	poultry; tobacco, nursery stock; dairy products; cotton
Industry	service industries, tourism, chemicals, textiles, machinery

From *National Geographic Atlas of the World*, 9th edition. Copyright ©2011 National Geographic Society. Reprinted by arrangement. All rights reserved.

Virginia

Virginia's major attractions are concentrated in a triangle between Richmond, Norfolk, and Arlington. Many of Virginia's major attractions relate to the history and founding of the United States. Appomattox Court House National Historical Park, where General Robert E. Lee surrendered to Ulysses S. Grant to end the Civil War; the Virginia State Capitol in Richmond where Aaron Burr stood trial for treason; Colonial Williamsburg, the nation's largest and most authentic privately funded restoration; and Monticello, the beautiful home of Jefferson, are notable examples of historic sites. The Museum of the Confederacy is in Richmond. Others include Jamestown National Historical Site, where Captain John Smith tried to found the first permanent English settlement in America; Cape Henry Memorial, both a popular seaside resort and the place where the first English settlers landed; Yorktown Battlefield, where Cornwallis surrendered his British Army to Washington and Rochambeau; and Mount Vernon, overlooking the Potomac River, where Washington lived and died. Near Washington, D.C., is Arlington National Cemetery with the Tomb of the Unknown Soldier; the gravesites of John and Robert Kennedy; and Arlington House, where Robert E. Lee courted and married Mary Ann Randolf. Washington D.C.'s major airport, Dulles, is located in Virginia.

Old Dominion

Area	110,785 sq km (42,774 sq mi)
Population	7,883,000
Capital	Richmond 202,000
GDP per Cap	$41,800
Agriculture	tobacco; poultry; dairy products; beef cattle; soybeans; hogs
Industry	food processing, communication and electronic equipment

From *National Geographic Atlas of the World*, 9th edition. Copyright ©2011 National Geographic Society. Reprinted by arrangement. All rights reserved.

West Virginia

West Virginia, a mountainous state, has three major attractions: Cass Scenic Railroad near Marlinton, Harpers Ferry National Historical Park, and the West Virginia State Capitol. The Cass Scenic Railroad runs along the Leatherbark Creek and up a steep grade of over 10 percent on logging train rails. Harpers Ferry is situated on a point where the Shenandoah and Potomac rivers meet. John Brown, an abolitionist, launched his famous abortive raid on the federal armory here. Remains of the arsenal, restored buildings, and exhibits recall the experience. The West Virginia State Capitol, at Charleston, is one of the most beautiful state capitals in the United States. It was designed by Cass Gilbert in Italian Renaissance style with a golden dome and a huge Czechoslovakian chandelier. There are a number of resorts throughout West Virginia. The Greenbrier and Berkeley Springs are the most famous. Berkeley Springs is the oldest spa in the nation and was made popular by George Washington. Its official name is Bath, named after a famous spa town in England. The state's many river rapids make it a popular destination for white water rafting enthusiasts. Outdoor enthusiasts also flock to the Monongahela National Forest, a very large wilderness area with over 900,000 acres of dramatic forest and mountain scenery.

Mountain State

Area	62,755 sq km (24,230 sq mi)
Population	1,820,000
Capital	Charleston 50,000
GDP per Cap	$25,500
Agriculture	poultry, eggs; cattle; dairy products; apples
Industry	coal mining, chemicals, metal manufacturing, forest products

From *National Geographic Atlas of the World*, 9th edition. Copyright ©2011 National Geographic Society. Reprinted by arrangement. All rights reserved.

REVIEW QUESTIONS

1. You have been asked to organize a three-day class trip to Washington, D.C. What sights will you include in your itinerary?

2. What large industrial company is headquartered in Delaware?

3. What attractions are major destinations on Florida's Gulf Coast?

4. What major U.S. airline has centralized operations in Atlanta?

5. Name South Carolina's two famous coastal resort destinations.

chapter 5: EAST SOUTH CENTRAL

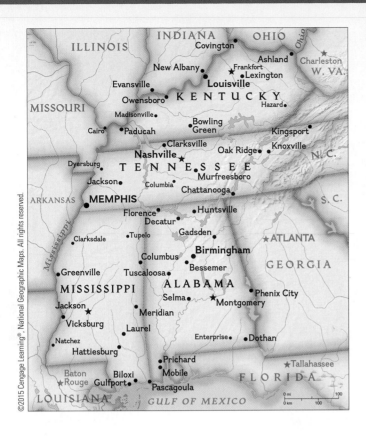

STATE PROFILE

State	Capital	Square Miles	Population (2010)
Alabama	Montgomery	52,237	4,779,736
Kentucky	Frankfort	40,411	4,339,367
Mississippi	Jackson	48,286	2,978,512
Tennessee	Nashville	42,146	6,346,105

Source: Adapted from U.S. Bureau of the Census, 2011.

The East South Central region combines the coastal Gulf States of Mississippi and Alabama with the mountainous environment of Kentucky and Tennessee, offering the visitor a rich variety of historic, environmental, and unique theme park attractions. The East South Central region is the heart of the old South with all the symbols of antebellum homes, icons of the Confederacy and Civil War sites. The area is known for its beautiful gardens and tree-lined avenues. The Gulf Coast States provide sun-sea-sand experiences and in recent years, casino gambling. The northern part of the region provides visitors scenic and outdoor recreation opportunities in the Allegheny and Great Smoky Mountains.

Alabama

Alabama contains the Confederacy's first capital (at Montgomery) and the space center at Huntsville. The Alabama State Capitol, a beautiful colonial-style building, is where Jefferson Davis was sworn in as president of the Confederacy. Across the street is the first Capitol building. Throughout the city are a number of museums, including the Montgomery Museum of Fine Arts, and antebellum homes. The state's numerous Civil War sites can be explored along the Alabama Civil War Trail. The United States Space and Rocket Center at Huntsville has a hands-on type of exhibit where visitors can fire a rocket engine, guide spacecraft by computer, and feel the sensation of weightlessness. The town has a number of museums, including the Twichenham Historic District, a living museum of antebellum architecture.

Near Huntsville is Noccalula Falls at Gadsden, a ninety-five-foot cascade of white water dropping into a great emerald-green pool set in a scenic park. Near Mobile is one of the most beautiful gardens in North America, Bellingrath Gardens and Home. Surrounding a beautiful old brick and wrought-iron mansion are sixty-five acres of gardens, including huge live oaks covered with Spanish moss, giant Indica azaleas, rose bushes, camellias, chrysanthemums, poinsettias, and other flowers. The U.S.S. Alabama and a submarine in the Mobile harbor are open to visitors. Along the coast are a number of beaches such as the Gulf Shores Islands, which offer a complete range of water and fishing sports.

Heart of Dixie

Area	135,765 sq km (52,419 sq mi)
Population	4,709,000
Capital	Montgomery 203,000
GDP per Cap	$29,400
Agriculture	poultry; forest products; cattle; nursery stock, cotton; eggs
Industry	trade, services, government, finance, insurance, real estate

From National Geographic Atlas of the World, 9th edition. Copyright ©2011 National Geographic Society. Reprinted by arrangement. All rights reserved.

Figure 5.1 Mammoth Cave National Park, Kentucky. © Zack Frank/www.Shutterstock.com.

Kentucky

The mention of Kentucky elicits an image of horse racing and well-landscaped beautiful horse ranches. Churchill Downs in Louisville is the site of the world-famous Kentucky Derby, complete with race track and museum. The Man o' War Monument honors one of the great thoroughbred horses in racing history. Lexington is the heart of many of the famous picturesque horse farms.

Fort Boonesborough State Park; Abraham Lincoln Birthplace National Historical Site; the Kentucky State Capitol in Frankfort; and My Old Kentucky Home, where Stephen Foster wrote the song by the same name, are found in the region of Lexington and Louisville. At the Kentucky State Capitol at Frankfort, the Governor's Mansion includes a beautiful replica of Marie Antoinette's reception room at Versailles.

The most famous natural attractions in Kentucky are Cumberland Falls, Mammoth Cave National Park, and the Cumberland Gap. Cumberland Falls near Corbin are second in size in the country only to Niagara Falls. Nearby is Mammoth Cave National Park (Figure 5.1), which has the world's largest, 300 miles, continuous underground passage. The Cumberland Gap National Historical Park, which is shared with Virginia and Tennessee, is the most famous natural pass through the Allegheny Mountains. Early explorers and settlers traveled west through the pass. Kentucky is rich in agritourism resources, including vineyards, orchards, and bourbon distilleries.

Bluegrass State

Area	104,659 sq km (40,409 sq mi)
Population	4,314,000
Capital	Frankfort 27,000
GDP per Cap	$29,700
Agriculture	tobacco; horses, cattle; corn; dairy products
Industry	manufacturing, services, government, finance, insurance

From *National Geographic Atlas of the World*, 9th edition. Copyright ©2011 National Geographic Society. Reprinted by arrangement. All rights reserved.

It's easy to forget about Memphis, a mid-size American city wedged into the southwest corner of Tennessee. Our collective memory of Memphis seems frozen in the mid-twentieth century: Elvis and Graceland, B. B. King and Beale Street, Martin Luther King, Jr., and his "Mountaintop" speech—the last he'd give before his assassination on the balcony of Memphis's Lorraine Motel in 1968.

Certain aspects of Memphis's past stifled the city for decades, snuffing the spirits of residents and scaring away visitors. But there's something newly electric in the air.

The Stax Museum of American Soul Music, located on the grounds of the famous Stax Records, is at the forefront of that revival. The museum, along with its Stax Music Academy and the Soulsville Charter School, celebrates its tenth anniversary in 2013 with concerts, parties, and Stax to the Max, a huge outdoor music festival. It's far from a solo act.

All around Memphis, locals are pursuing grassroots projects more often associated with Brooklyn or the Bay Area.

All around Memphis, locals are pursuing grassroots projects more often associated with Brooklyn or the Bay Area. The nonprofit Project Green Fork has certified dozens of Memphis restaurants as sustainable, linking chefs with farmers and stimulating a vibrant local food community along the way. Running the culinary gamut from down-home Central BBQ to upscale Andrew Michael Italian Kitchen, the eateries are held to admirably high standards in sourcing and sustainability.

And there's no better setting for a grassroots revival. Memphis claims one of the largest urban parks in the country: the 4,500-acre Shelby Farms Park, with 6.5 miles of urban trails and a working farm. The Office of Sustainability supports the city's plans to expand the existing 35 miles of bike lanes to 85 miles and to build a greenway that will link Memphis with cities in Arkansas and Mississippi. "We get to innovate," says city administrator Paul Young. It's a fitting description for Memphis.

—Julie Schwietert Collazo, *National Geographic Traveler*, December 2012/January 2013

Mississippi

Some of the most important attractions in Mississippi are the Mississippi Petrified Forest, Natchez antebellum homes, Natchez Trace Parkway, and Vicksburg National Military Park. The Mississippi Petrified Forest, near Jackson, is a National Natural Landmark composed of a number of ancient giant stone logs in the only petrified forest in the eastern part of the United States. Vicksburg National Military Park commemorates an important Civil War battle. It was the site of a Union siege that lasted forty-seven days. The monuments, markers, and tablets include an exhibit modeled after the Roman Pantheon.

Natchez has one of the best collections of antebellum homes in the south. The Natchez Trace Parkway, a scenic parkway extending from Natchez to Tupelo, follows a trail used by Natchez, Choctaw, and Chickasaw

Indians and early explorers and settlers. Markers along the parkway indicate archaeological, historical, and natural attractions. A resort center on the coast, Biloxi is considered the oldest town in Mississippi. It offers a number of museums and water activities associated with the Gulf.

Magnolia State

Area	125,434 sq km (48,430 sq mi)
Population	2,952,000
Capital	Jackson 174,000
GDP per Cap	$24,400
Agriculture	poultry, eggs; cotton; catfish, soybeans; cattle; rice; dairy
Industry	petroleum products, health services, electronic equipment

From *National Geographic Atlas of the World*, 9th edition. Copyright ©2011 National Geographic Society. Reprinted by arrangement. All rights reserved.

Tennessee

Tennessee bills itself as the capital of country-and-western music. It capitalizes on its music fame and natural beauty to attract visitors. Opryland U.S.A. and the Grand Ole Opry provide country-and-western music lovers all forms of entertainment in Nashville. The Opryland Hotel is among the country's largest hotels. Belle Meade, a well-preserved plantation house; the Parthenon, which is a replica of the Parthenon on the Acropolis in Athens; and the Hermitage, the home of Andrew Jackson, are also located in the Nashville area.

The Hermitage consists of a tailor shop, two homes, and the burial place of President Andrew Jackson. Lookout Mountain at Chattanooga gives the visitor an excellent view of the surrounding Tennessee River Valley and an overlook of the battlefield where a Confederate army surrendered to the Union Forces in November of 1863. Shiloh is home to a National Military Park. Ruby Falls–Lookout Mountain Caverns offer beautiful falls and colorful caves. There are a number of other attractions in the Chattanooga area, including museums and a Confederama, which re-creates the drama of the battle of Chattanooga.

Tennessee also has part of the Great Smoky Mountain Natural Park, one of the most visited and scenic parks in America. The American Museum of Atomic Energy is located at Oak Ridge, where the first atomic bombs were manufactured during World War II. Although there are a number of other historical and scenic attractions, even a brief description of Tennessee would not be complete without recognizing Graceland, the home of Elvis Presley, and his gravesite in Memphis, an old Mississippi River town that is the commercial center of the state and home to the National Civil Rights Museum, the Children's Museum of Memphis, Soulsville Museum, and the Memphis Rock 'n' Soul Museum. Other attractions in the state include the delightful Museum of Appalachia in Norris, and Dollywood in Pigeon Forge.

Volunteer State

Area	109,151 sq km (42,143 sq mi)
Population	6,296,000
Capital	Nashville 596,000
GDP per Cap	$33,800
Agriculture	cattle; cotton; dairy products; hogs; poultry; nursery stock
Industry	service industries, chemicals, transportation equipment

From *National Geographic Atlas of the World*, 9th edition. Copyright ©2011 National Geographic Society. Reprinted by arrangement. All rights reserved.

REVIEW QUESTIONS

1. What is the meaning of the word *antebellum*?

2. Contrast the attractions of this region with those of Florida.

3. Name the attractions in each of Tennessee's two major cities.

4. The country's most visited National Park is located in this region. What is its name?

5. Name Kentucky's three famous natural attractions.

STATE PROFILE

State	Capital	Square Miles	Population (2010)
Illinois	Springfield	57,918	12,830,632
Indiana	Indianapolis	36,420	6,483,802
Michigan	Lansing	96,705	9,883,646
Ohio	Columbus	44,828	11,536,504
Wisconsin	Madison	65,500	5,686,986

Source: Adapted from U.S. Bureau of the Census, 2011.

The East North Central region is the heart of the industrial belt of the United States, often referred to today as the rust belt, since many of its old industries such as steel have declined in importance. The lakes and northern woods attract many to hunt, fish, and participate in water-related activities, hiking, or camping. Tourists to the area are also attracted by the large urban centers, with their rich variety of cities and industrial activities.

Illinois

Chicago (Figure 6.1) is the major tourist center of Illinois. The attractions in Chicago include Lakeshore Drive with beaches, parks, and marinas; the Magnificent Mile; Millennium Park; the Willis Tower (formerly known as the Sears Building), one of the world's tallest buildings; the John Hancock Center; ethnic neighborhoods; Wrigley Field; John G. Shedd Aquarium; the Adler Planetarium; the Art Institute of Chicago, which has the largest collection of French Impressionist paintings in the world; the Field Museum of National History, one of the finest in the world; the Museum of Science and Industry; the Lincoln Park Zoo; and shopping on the Magnificent Mile. Lollapalooza is Chicago's summer music festival with 70 acts and

attracting 300,000 people. In and near Springfield are the Lincoln Home National Historic Site, Lincoln Tomb Historical State Park, Lincoln National Library, and Lincoln's New Salem State Park. The Old State Capitol in Springfield is the site of Lincoln's famous speech "House Divided."

Prairie State

Area	149,998 sq km (57,914 sq mi)
Population	12,910,000
Capital	Springfield 117,000
GDP per Cap	$40,000
Agriculture	corn, soybeans; hogs, cattle; dairy products; nursery stock
Industry	industrial machinery, electronic equipment, food processing

Figure 6.1 Chicago skyline. © Henryk Sadura/www.Shutterstock.com.

Once the largest city in Illinois, Nauvoo has many buildings that have been restored and continues to add others. When the Mormons were driven out of Missouri, they moved to Nauvoo. Reminders of the Mormon history are expressed in the Nauvoo Restoration Visitor Center, which has a number of restored homes and the Joseph Smith Historic Center, which includes the graves of Joseph Smith and his wife Emma. The Old Carthage Jail near Nauvoo is a restored jail, where Joseph Smith and his brother died.

Indiana

Indiana's major attractions are scattered throughout the state. In the north on the shores of Lake Michigan between Gary and Michigan City, the Indiana Dunes National Lakeshore consists of rolling dunes, beaches, trees, shrubs, and bogs, which are centers for plant and animal life. Elkhart is the center of the nation's RV industry and features the National RV Museum and Hall of Fame. In the middle of the state at Indianapolis is one of the most famous speedways in the world, the Indianapolis Motorway, affectionately known as the Brickyard. Other attractions in Indianapolis are the State Capitol, an impressive Corinthian structure of Indiana limestone with a copper dome; Soldiers and Sailors Monument, with a Civil War picture gallery; the World War Memorial Plaza, which is a five-block area dedicated to Indiana residents who lost their lives in the two world wars and the Korean and Vietnam conflicts; the renovated City Market; the Benjamin Harrison Memorial Home; the James Whitcomb Riley House; and the Scottish Rite Cathedral, a Tudor Gothic structure. Northeast of Indianapolis is the Tippecanoe Battlefield State Memorial, commemorating the American-Indian War.

There are a number of attractions in the south, including the Wyandotte Cave, a large five-level cavern over twenty miles long; the George Rogers Clark National Historic Park, commemorating the role of the man "who won the West" in the Revolutionary War; the Lincoln Boyhood National Memorial, gravesite of the president's mother; New Harmony, a utopian village; and the Spring Mill State Park, a restored early nineteenth-century trading fort.

Hoosier State

Area	94,321 sq km (36,418 sq mi)
Population	6,423,000
Capital	Indianapolis 808,000
GDP per Cap	$32,900
Agriculture	corn, soybeans; hogs, poultry, eggs, cattle; dairy products
Industry	transportation equipment, steel, pharmaceuticals and chemicals

From *National Geographic Atlas of the World*, 9th edition. Copyright ©2011 National Geographic Society. Reprinted by arrangement. All rights reserved.

Michigan

The major tourist attractions in Michigan are in two general areas—the Detroit–Grand Rapids area and the northern area along the Great Lakes. In Detroit, the Detroit Zoological Park is one of the largest and most attractive parks in North America. A number of automobile museums and assembly plants are open to visitors. The Detroit Institute of Arts has an outstanding collection of seventeenth- and eighteenth-century Flemish and Dutch paintings. The Charles H. Wright Museum features exhibits on African American history. The Motown Museum celebrates the city's unique musical legacy. Greenfield Village and Henry Ford Museum in Dearborn provide an outdoor historical museum–entertainment park. The Henry Ford Museum is a restored early-American village with shops, tradesmen, and demonstrations. The Civic Center in Detroit is a modern complex of buildings.

Grand Rapids is home to two important museums—the Grand Rapids Art Museum and the Grand Rapids Public Museum. Holland, which is near Grand Rapids, was settled by a group of Dutch people in the 1840s who were seeking religious freedom. Windmill Island provides a picturesque setting like that of Holland, complete with windmills, dikes, and flower gardens. The community stages a popular Tulip Festival in spring (Figure 6.2). To the north, Traverse City celebrates its waterfront location on Grand Traverse Bay and is home to marinas and golf resorts.

In the north, the attractions are mostly natural. They include Isle Royale National Park, Pictured Rocks National Lakeshore, and Sleeping Bear Dunes National

Figure 6.2 Tulip festival at Windmill Village in Holland, Michigan. © csterken/www.Shutterstock.com.

Lakeshore. The three areas provide all types of outdoor experiences, including lakes, forests, dunes, sandstone cliffs, glacial sand, animals, and birds, in beautiful surroundings. Mackinac Island, the "Bermuda of the North," located in the straits between Lakes Michigan and Huron, is very popular. No automobiles are allowed on the island. Bicycles or horse and carriage are the most common forms of transportation used to visit attractions such as the Old Fort, the Indian Dormitory, and the spectacular Grand Hotel.

Great Lakes State

Area	250,494 sq km (96,716 sq mi)
Population	9,970,000
Capital	Lansing 114,000
GDP per Cap	$32,600
Agriculture	dairy products; cattle; vegetables, hogs; corn, nursery stock
Industry	motor vehicles and parts, metal products, machinery, chemicals, tourism

From *National Geographic Atlas of the World,* 9th edition. Copyright ©2011 National Geographic Society. Reprinted by arrangement. All rights reserved.

Ohio

Ohio has many important attractions. Cleveland is the largest city. Located on Lake Erie, its history has been closely tied to trade and industry; but one popular attraction is the Rock and Roll Hall of Fame and Museum, a striking building situated on the shore of Lake Erie.

Other attractions include the Cleveland Museum of Art; the Cleveland Botanical Garden; and Western Reserve Historical Center, with its turn-of-the-century village street and collection of Shaker artifacts. Kings Island is located in the south at Cincinnati, a historic river city that grew into a commercial and business center. It features a replica of the Eiffel Tower overlooking a number of theme parks such as Lion Country Safari, the Happy Land of Hanna-Barbera, Oktoberfest, Coney

Island, and Rivertown. Cedar Point near Sandusky is a popular mile-long beach and amusement resort. The Aviation Hall of Fame at Dayton traces manned flight from the Wright Brothers to space exploration. Also near Dayton is the National Museum of the U.S. Air Force at Wright-Patterson Air Force Base. The Neil Armstrong Air and Space Museum is in Wapakoneta (the birthplace of the first man on the moon). In the center of the state, Columbus has the Columbus Zoo, and the Ohio Historical Center and the Ohio Village, a museum of history, archaeology, and natural science set in a re-created Ohio village.

Roscoe Village, located between Columbus and Cleveland, is a restored Ohio and Erie Canal town. The Schoenbrunn Village State Memorial, which was founded in 1772 by Moravian missionaries, has costumed guides who demonstrate old crafts and recount historical stories. The Football Hall of Fame at Canton houses professional football memorabilia and exhibits.

Sea World has one of the few inland sea world exhibitions in existence. Perry's Victory and International Peace Memorial on the shore of Lake Erie reminds visitors of the victory in the Battle of Lake Erie during the War of 1812. Fishing, particularly in Lake Erie, is important in Ohio's tourism industry.

Buckeye State

Area	116,096 sq km (44,825 sq mi)
Population	11,543,000
Capital	Columbus 755,000
GDP per Cap	$33,600
Agriculture	soybeans; dairy products; corn; hogs, cattle; poultry, eggs
Industry	transportation and electrical equipment, metal products, machinery

From *National Geographic Atlas of the World*, 9th edition. Copyright ©2011 National Geographic Society. Reprinted by arrangement. All rights reserved.

Wisconsin

WISCONSIN
1848

Most of Wisconsin's major attractions are in the south. The north and center of the state have many lakes and forests for hunting, fishing, and other outdoor recreational opportunities. The Apostle Islands National Lakeshore was the center of French and Indian trade. In the south are the Wisconsin Dells, a natural scenic area where the river has carved the river banks into unique formations. The region has the most water parks in the world (many indoors), concentrated at Grand Geneva Resort and Blue Harbor Resort. Other attractions are the Circus World Museum, complete with circus and circus paraphernalia from Ringling Brothers and Barnum and Bailey in Baraboo; Mid-Continent Railway Museum; Villa Louis, a mansion built in 1843 on the banks of the Mississippi River as a trading center; Cave of the Mounds, a colorful cavern of limestone and crystal; and the United States Forest Products Laboratory at

Madison, which gives details on ways to use wood and wood products. Madison is the capital and the home of the University of Wisconsin. Milwaukee, the state's largest city, has a proud beer brewing history and features the Milwaukee Art Museum and many waterfront events in the summer, including Summerfest, an 11-day music festival with 700 acts and nearly 1 million visitors. Lake Geneva, near the Illinois border, is a vacation area popular with visitor from nearby Chicago.

Badger State

Area	169,639 sq km (65,498 sq mi)
Population	5,655,000
Capital	Madison 232,000
GDP per Cap	$35,200
Agriculture	dairy products; cattle; corn; poultry, eggs; soybeans
Industry	industrial machinery, paper products, food processing

From *National Geographic Atlas of the World*, 9th edition. Copyright ©2011 National Geographic Society. Reprinted by arrangement. All rights reserved.

cheese beer football Circus world Museum

REVIEW QUESTIONS

1. What are Illinois' major attractions *outside* Chicago?

2. Name several tourist destinations in Michigan.

3. Ohio is home to two major amusement parks. What are the names?

4. How did Wisconsin Dells succeed in becoming a year-round tourist destination?

5. Name the Great Lakes bordering this region.

STATE PROFILE

State	Capital	Square Miles	Population (2010)
Arkansas	Little Rock	53,183	2,915,918
Louisiana	Baton Rouge	49,654	4,533,372
Oklahoma	Oklahoma City	69,903	3,751,351
Texas	Austin	267,265	25,145,561

Source: Adapted from U.S. Bureau of the Census, 2011.

The West South Central region has a variety of attractions, from coastal to wooded hills and spa resorts, that cut across a number of different cultures.

Arkansas

Arkansas is a beautiful land of mountains and valleys, thick forests and fertile plains. The Ozarks and Ouachita mountain ranges in northern and western Arkansas are known as the Highlands; the southern and eastern parts of Arkansas are called the Lowlands. Its tourist attractions include Bull Shoals Lake Area in the north part of the Ozark Mountains, which offers excellent trout fishing; Dogpatch U.S.A., a family amusement park located south of Harrison; the Ozark Folk Center, which features mountain music and crafts of the mountain people; Petit Jean State Park, which is full of natural wonders such as seventy-foot Cedar Falls, Bear Cave, Growing Rocks, Natural Bridge, and scenic drives. Next to the lake is the Winthrop Rockefeller collection of antique and classic vehicles and Winrock Farms, a prize cattle ranch.

Little Rock is the home of the William Jefferson Clinton Presidential Library. The state capital also has the Arkansas Territorial Capitol Restoration, an outstanding restoration project depicting life in the early nineteenth century.

The capitol itself is a smaller version of the nation's capitol. One of the most noted attractions in Arkansas is the Hot Springs National Park and Hot Springs Resort. Hot Springs contains beautiful wooded hills, valleys, and lakes in addition to its forty-seven warm non-odorous hot springs. A variety of attractions (including Tiny Town, an indoor mechanical village) and Southern Artists Association Fine Arts Center are found in the area. The Crater of Diamonds State Park at Murfreesboro is the only diamond-bearing field in North America. It can be explored by visitors, who can keep any diamonds they find.

Natural State

Area	137,732 sq km (53,179 sq mi)
Population	2,889,000
Capital	Little Rock 190,000
GDP per Cap	$27,800
Agriculture	poultry, eggs; rice, soybeans, cotton, wheat
Industry	food processing, paper products, transportation, metal products

From *National Geographic Atlas of the World*, 9th edition. Copyright ©2011 National Geographic Society. Reprinted by arrangement. All rights reserved.

Louisiana

The visitor attractions of Louisiana are concentrated in New Orleans and Baton Rouge. New Orleans combines a modern city with Southern and French culture to create one of the most interesting cities in North America. The region was badly damaged, including much of downtown, by a devastating flood, caused by Hurricane Katrina in 2008 but cleanup efforts and restoration projects have returned much of the downtown area into an attractive destination once again. The French Quarter is

the most important attraction. It is an exciting, colorful, and historic area in New Orleans. The annual Mardi Gras is the city's most famous festival, held each February. Around New Orleans, the visitor can enjoy the Natchez Steamboat, a replica of an 1887 sternwheeler; the Louisiana Superdome, near the French Quarter; Jackson Square, which was the political, social, and cultural center of the French Quarter; the Aquarium of the Americas; New Orleans City Park, a former plantation with lush lawns around lagoons, an old Spanish fort, and the New Orleans Museum of Art; International Trade Mart, which has an observation deck from which the visitor can see most of New Orleans; Lake Pontchartrain Causeway, the world's longest bridge; Chalmette National Historic Site, where Andrew Jackson won the Battle of New Orleans; and Acadian House Museum, a reminder of the French Canadians who settled in the region.

The Louisiana State Capitol at Baton Rouge is a beautifully designed marble statehouse. Nearby, the Rosedown Plantation and Gardens are a lavishly restored private mansion and gardens in the seventeenth-century French style. Between Baton Rouge and New Orleans is the old River Road paralleling the Mississippi, which passes numerous plantations.

Pelican State

Area	134,264 sq km (51,840 sq mi)
Population	4,492,000
Capital	Baton Rouge 224,000
GDP per Cap	$32,800
Agriculture	forest products; poultry; marine fisheries; sugarcane, rice
Industry	chemicals, petroleum products, food processing, health services

From *National Geographic Atlas of the World*, 9th edition. Copyright ©2011 National Geographic Society. Reprinted by arrangement. All rights reserved.

Oklahoma

The history of Oklahoma is portrayed in a number of attractions such as the Will Roger's Memorial, with memorabilia and manuscripts from and about Will Rogers; the National Cowboy Hall of Fame and Western Heritage Museum in Oklahoma City, illustrating life in the Wild West; Indian City, U.S.A., seven authentically restored Indian villages, complete with dance ceremonies, arts, and crafts; Fort Sill Military Reservation, displaying weapons from field guns to atomic artillery; the J. M. Davis Gun Museum; and the Thomas Gilcrease Institute of American History and Art in Tulsa, which

displays the archaeology and history of the state. Chickasaw National Recreation Area offers mineral springs and nature viewing.

Sooner State

Area	181,036 sq km (69,898 sq mi)
Population	3,687,000
Capital	Oklahoma City 552,000
GDP per Cap	$29,400
Agriculture	cattle; wheat; hogs; poultry; nursery stock
Industry	natural gas production, manufacturing, services, food processing

From *National Geographic Atlas of the World*, 9th edition. Copyright ©2011 National Geographic Society. Reprinted by arrangement. All rights reserved.

Texas

Texas is the largest state in the forty-eight continental states and is second after California in population. In the Fort Worth–Dallas area one can visit the Amon G. Carter Museum of Western Art, containing many works of Charles Russell and Frederic Remington; the Dealey Plaza (now called the John F. Kennedy Plaza) in which John F. Kennedy was shot and killed, which contains the John F. Kennedy Museum; the Biblical Arts Center, with a 20-foot-high mural of the "Miracle of the Pentecost"; Six Flags Over Texas, a large popular theme park; Lion Country Safari for observing game; Will Rogers Memorial Center, containing a number of art museums, a planetarium, and the Museum of Science and History; and the State Fair park, which has a permanent exposition that is open year-round and contains a number of museums on science, art, and history.

Houston is the largest city. It is a center of sites related to the history of Texas, as well as the Astrodome, one of

the first domed stadiums. Astroworld, a theme park; San Jacinto Battleground Park, where Sam Houston won independence for Texas; the NASA/Lyndon B. Johnson Space Center, which is open for visitors; and two historical parks, the Allen's Landing Park and Old Market Square, are other examples of Houston's attractions. The Alamo at San Antonio (Figure 7.1) is the most famous battle site in Texas's fight for independence from Mexico. River Walk is the restored area along the river in San Antonio and hosts boat rides, a number of theaters, restaurants, shops and the Hemisfair Plaza, a cultural and amusement center. The Lyndon B. Johnson National Historic Site in Johnson City near San Antonio is the restored boyhood home of President Johnson. Austin, the state capital, is home to several universities and colleges, and a lively scene that celebrates music and food. *South by Southwest* is the city's world-famous music festival taking place each March.

South on the Gulf Padre Island National Seashore is an eighty-mile-long barrier island of shifting sand and grass that is very popular for fishing and swimming.

Figure 7.1 The Alamo in San Antonio, Texas. © Larry Brownstein/Getty Images.

West on the Rio Grande is Big Bend National Park, a wilderness home for the plants and animals of the desert Southwest. The Chamizal National Memorial at El Paso commemorates the settlement of a boundary dispute with Mexico. The Sierra de Cristo, with a figure of Christ on the Cross on the summit; an Aerial Tramway to Ranger Peak; and the Fort Bliss Replica Museum, expressing the history of the old Southwest; and the Museum of Art are also in El Paso.

Lone Star State

Area	695,621 sq km (268,581 sq mi)
Population	24,782,000
Capital	Austin 758,000
GDP per Cap	$38,000
Agriculture	cattle, sheep; poultry; cotton, sorghum, wheat, rice, hay
Industry	chemicals, machinery, electronics, petroleum and natural gas

From *National Geographic Atlas of the World*, 9th edition. Copyright ©2011 National Geographic Society. Reprinted by arrangement. All rights reserved.

REVIEW QUESTIONS

1. Why is Arkansas called the *natural* state?

2. Name at least five "cultural attractions" associated with New Orleans.

3. Why is Oklahoma home to many Native American events and traditions?

4. Describe the variety of Texas' many tourist regions and attractions.

5. Texas is home to three presidential libraries. Where are they located?

STATE PROFILE

State	Capital	Square Miles	Population (2010)
Iowa	Des Moines	56,275	3,046,355
Kansas	Topeka	82,282	2,853,118
Minnesota	St. Paul	86,943	5,303,925
Missouri	Jefferson City	69,709	5,988,927
Nebraska	Lincoln	77,359	1,826,341
North Dakota	Bismarck	70,704	672,591
South Dakota	Pierre	77,122	814,180

Source: Adapted from U.S. Bureau of the Census, 2011.

The wide open spaces and northern locations of the West North Central region have fewer visitors than other regions of the United States discussed to this point. Many tourists pass through Missouri, Nebraska, and Kansas on the interstate highway and some towns along it capitalize on their locations. Tourism in the northern states is concentrated in the southern portion of each state.

Iowa

Des Moines, the capital of Iowa, features an ornate capitol building and a Living History Farms open-air museum. The Boone and Scenic Valley Railroad provides a ten-mile vintage train ride through the Des Moines River Valley. The Amana Colonies, which were settled in the 1840s by a religious group with members from Germany, France, and Switzerland, are located near Iowa City, site of the state's first capital. The oldest dwelling in Iowa is at Eagle Point Park. New Melleray Abbey is one of four Trappist monasteries in the United States. Both are near Dubuque.

Hawkeye State

Area	145,743 sq km (56,272 sq mi)
Population	3,008,000
Capital	Des Moines 197,000
GDP per Cap	$36,800
Agriculture	hogs; corn, soybeans, oats; cattle; dairy products
Industry	real estate, health services, food processing, industrial machines

From *National Geographic Atlas of the World*, 9th edition. Copyright ©2011 National Geographic Society. Reprinted by arrangement. All rights reserved.

Kansas

Kansas's attractions include Dodge City, where the Wild West is relived along historic Front Street; Fort Leavenworth, which is the oldest army post in continuous existence west of the Mississippi and which has a museum of early history; and the Eisenhower Center near Abilene, including President Dwight Eisenhower's boyhood home and a museum. The eastern portion of Kansas has many lakes and rolling hills, providing regional visitors with fishing and water sports. A number of towns, such as Wichita and Topeka, offer some local attractions for those passing through or visiting friends and relatives in the region.

Sunflower State

Area	213,096 sq km (82,277 sq mi)
Population	2,819,000
Capital	Topeka 123,000
GDP per Cap	$35,000
Agriculture	cattle; wheat, sorghum, soybeans; hogs; corn
Industry	aircraft manufacturing, transportation equipment, construction

From *National Geographic Atlas of the World*, 9th edition. Copyright ©2011 National Geographic Society. Reprinted by arrangement. All rights reserved.

Minnesota

Minnesota has both unique cultural (ethnic settlement patterns) and natural (thousands of lakes) attractions. Around and in the twin cities of St. Paul (the capital) and Minneapolis (the largest city) are the Minnehaha Falls, a very colorful waterfall on the Mississippi river that was made famous by William Wadsworth Longfellow; Betty Crocker Kitchens at General Mills; the Guthrie Theater, a world-famous theater; Valleyfair, a family theme park; the Minneapolis Institute of Arts and the Walker Art Center, with a collection of both famous European artists and American Indian works; and the American Swedish Institute, a museum of Swedish arts, crafts, and pioneer relics. St. Paul hosts a popular Winter Carnival in late January. The Mall of America, in Bloomington, is the largest mall in the United States.

Two important destinations are found in the northern regions of Minnesota: Voyageurs National Park, which is noted for its fishing; and Grand Portage National Monument on Lake Superior, which has a restored stockade and a number of trails used by the early French and Indians.

The woods and lakes are well represented in numerous state parks. The lumber industry is remembered at Lumbertown U.S.A., a restored lumber town, and some early history dating back to the Vikings is found at the Runestone Museum.

Land of 10,000 Lakes

Area	225,171 sq km (86,939 sq mi)
Population	5,266,000
Capital	St. Paul 280,000
GDP per Cap	$41,600
Agriculture	corn, soybeans; dairy products; hogs, cattle, turkeys; wheat
Industry	health services, tourism, real estate, banking and insurance

From *National Geographic Atlas of the World*, 9th edition. Copyright ©2011 National Geographic Society. Reprinted by arrangement. All rights reserved.

Missouri

Missouri combines nature, history, and large urban areas to provide a number of excellent destinations. In the St. Louis area, the 630-foot-high Gateway Arch (Figure 8.1), one of the most creative architectural and engineering feats in North America, commemorates the role of the city as the gateway to the West. At its base is the Museum of Westward Expansion, with fascinating exhibits and memorabilia of the settling of the American West. A tram takes visitors up to an observation platform at the top of the Arch. Other attractions in St. Louis include Six Flags over Mid-America and the Missouri Botanical Gardens, one of the largest in North America. All provide opportunity for a diverse visit.

Kansas City and its surrounding area on the west have the Nelson-Atkins Museum of Art, one of the better art galleries in North America, and the Harry S. Truman Library, Museum, and gravesite. Near Kansas City at Hannibal is the Mark Twain Boyhood Home and Museum. St. Joseph, north of Kansas City, was the departure point for pioneers on their westward journeys.

In the center of the state, in Jefferson City, the Missouri State Capitol has murals that depict the history, legends, and natural beauties of Missouri. To the south are found the Ozark National Scenic Riverways of Adventure in the Ozarks and Silver Dollar City, a re-created pioneer village with performers in authentic

Figure 8.1 St. Louis Arch. © Condor 36/www.Shutterstock.com.

Ozark mountain costume who provide demonstrations of Ozark life. The Lake of the Ozarks has a longer shoreline than the entire state of California. One of the most popular destinations in America today is Branson, Missouri, where country-and-western singers and other performers have built music halls and perform nightly. Located in the Ozark Mountains, Branson's theme parks, attractions, and entertainment venues attract over 8 million visitors every year.

Show-me State

Area	180,533 sq km (69,704 sq mi)
Population	5,988,000
Capital	Jefferson City 41,000
GDP per Cap	$32,800
Agriculture	cattle; soybeans; hogs; corn; poultry, eggs; dairy products
Industry	transportation equipment, food processing, chemicals

Nebraska

Nebraska's attractions illustrate its role in the settling of the West. Omaha is the largest city. Its attractions include the Joslyn Art Museum, the Henry Doorly Zoo, the Union Pacific Museum, and refurbished Old Market area for shopping. The capital, Lincoln, is home to the University of Nebraska and the University of Nebraska State Museum, which has a large collection of fossils and life science exhibits. The Harold Warp Pioneer Village at Minden, which is an outdoor museum of authentic historical buildings, includes a sod hut, school, church, and railroad depot. The Stuhr Museum in Grand Island has similar exhibits. The House of Yesteryear at Hastings exhibits a pioneer grocery store and other historical furnishings and artifacts. Scotts Bluff National Monument

and Chimney Rock National Historic Site, in the scenic North Platte Valley, were important stops along the Oregon and Mormon Trails. The Museum of the Fur Trade at Chadron reflects the color and history of the fur trade and has a replica of the James Bordeaux trading post.

Cornhusker State

Area	200,345 sq km (77,354 sq mi)
Population	1,797,000
Capital	Lincoln 252,000
GDP per Cap	$37,300
Agriculture	cattle; corn; hogs; soybeans, wheat, sorghum
Industry	food processing, machinery, electrical equipment, printing

North Dakota

Most of North Dakota's attractions are in the southern half of the state. Theodore Roosevelt National Memorial Park includes the dramatic badlands of colorful hills, buttes, and tablelands, a petrified forest, and a variety of animals such as deer, antelope, buffalo, and smaller animals. Near Bismarck is Fort Lincoln State Park, where Custer was stationed and left for his famous "Last Stand" at the Little Big Horn. There is also a restored Slant Indian Village on the site. At Fargo, in the east, is the Fort Abercrombie Historic Site, where the state's first U.S. Army post was established, and Bonanzaville U.S.A., a living museum of the bonanza farm of

the nineteenth century. On the Canadian border, in Dunseith, is the International Peace Garden, which is shared with Canada and is dedicated to perpetual peace between America and Canada.

Peace Garden State

Area	183,112 sq km (70,700 sq mi)
Population	647,000
Capital	Bismarck 60,000
GDP per Cap	$37,800
Agriculture	wheat; cattle; sunflowers, barley, soybeans
Industry	government, finance, construction, transportation, oil and gas

South Dakota

Most of South Dakota's attractions are in the west, combining natural attractions and history. The Badlands National Park is a uniquely colorful area of sharp ridges and deep gullies with a variety of wildlife from prairie dogs to mule deer. Wall Drug, at the I-90 exit to the park, is a must see Western-themed attraction, visited by up to 20,000 people daily. Wind Cave National Park is a beautiful cave of limestone labyrinth lined with calcite crystal formations on Elk Mountain. The Homestake Gold Mine in Lead provides visitors the opportunity to watch surface mining. Deadwood was made famous as the place where Wild Bill Hickok was shot. Today it has a museum, a melodramatic Centennial Theater and legalized casino gambling, which has become a major attraction. Nearby is Sturgis, famous for the country's largest Motorcycle Rally held each August. Forty miles west of Rapid City, in the heart of the Black Hills, is Mount Rushmore National Monument with its impressive massive granite faces of former presidents Washington, Jefferson, Lincoln, and Roosevelt carved out of a 6,000-foot mountain. Floodlights are turned on at night and the national anthem is played, providing a moving experience for those in attendance.

At Crazy Horse Monument near Mount Rushmore, sculptor Korczak Ziolkowski began a granite mountain monument to the Sioux chief Crazy Horse in 1948; carving is still ongoing and upon its completion it will be the largest stone carving in the world. South of the Black Hills is Custer State Park with the country's largest herd of free roaming buffalo. In Sioux Falls is an impressive cathedral, while the area of farmland around the area is the center of fine pheasant hunting. West of Sioux Falls, the Corn Palace in Mitchell is decorated with pictures and designs formed by thousands of ears of natural-colored corn and grasses. The red rock gorge at Dell Rapids west of Sioux Falls is a picturesque drive.

Mount Rushmore State

Area	199,731 sq km (77,117 sq mi)
Population	812,000
Capital	Pierre 14,000
GDP per Cap	$37,700
Agriculture	cattle, corn, soybeans, wheat; hogs; hay; dairy products
Industry	finance, services, manufacturing, government, retail trade, utilities, tourism

From *National Geographic Atlas of the World*, 9th edition. Copyright ©2011 National Geographic Society. Reprinted by arrangement. All rights reserved.

REVIEW QUESTIONS

1. What explains the popularity of Branson, Missouri?

2. Name several attractions in the region associated with the westward journey of nineteenth-century migrants.

3. Where is America's largest shopping mall located?

4. Name several attractions in South Dakota's Black Hills region.

5. Name the two rivers of this region. Near what city do they meet?

chapter 9: MOUNTAIN

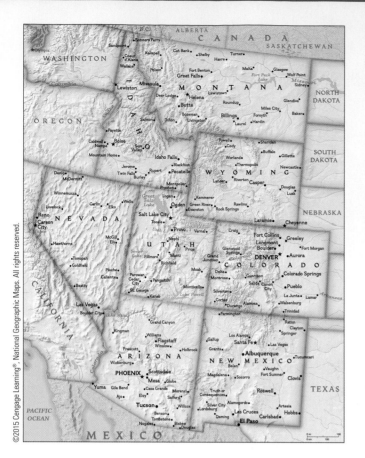

STATE PROFILE

State	Capital	Square Miles	Population (2000)
Arizona	Phoenix	114,007	6,392,017
Colorado	Denver	104,247	5,029,196
Idaho	Boise	83,574	1,567,582
Montana	Helena	147,138	989,415
Nevada	Carson City	110,567	2,700,551
New Mexico	Santa Fe	121,599	2,059,179
Utah	Salt Lake City	84,105	2,763,885
Wyoming	Cheyenne	97,819	563,626

Source: Adapted from U.S. Bureau of the Census, 2011.

The Mountain region is a popular outdoor, cultural, and entertainment travel region. It has a wide variety of physical and cultural phenomena to provide alternative activities and attractions for visitors and residents alike.

Arizona

Arizona is one of the most important tourist states in this region. Its attractions are many and varied, from skiing in the mountains of the north to deserts in the south. In the north, nature has provided a number of outstanding attractions. Grand Canyon, one of the most impressive physical features in the world, was carved by the Colorado River. Most visitors observe the canyon from the south rim, north of Flagstaff. Canyon de Chelly National Monument, also located in northern Arizona, provides a scenic Rim Drive overlooking sheer red sandstone cliffs, sandy canyon floors, Navajo hogans, and beautiful scenic cliff dwellings. A recent, very popular, attraction is the Grand Canyon SkyWalk. It offers visitors a stunning view of the canyon from a glass-bottom horseshoe-shaped "bridge" suspended 3,000 feet above the Colorado River. Northern Arizona also has the Petrified Forest National Park, with its mineralized logs; Monument Valley Navajo Tribal Park, a beautiful red-hued landscape; and Meteor Crater, a huge crater, created by a meteor. Visitors can follow a trail to observe the crater, and there is a museum. Oak Creek Canyon, a scenic canyon that is excellent for fishing, and Sunset

Crater National Monument, a volcanic crater and lava flow, are located near Flagstaff.

Phoenix is the largest city and a popular winter vacation area. The Heard Museum of Anthropology and Primitive Art, which has important holdings of Indian and Spanish arts and artifacts, is in Phoenix. A number of interesting attractions, such as the Phoenix Art Museum, the Phoenix Little Theater, and the Mineral Museum are found in the town. Phoenix also has professional basketball and football teams and Arizona State University. The road from Phoenix to Flagstaff passes the stunning Sedona Red Rock area. Flagstaff is the closest city to the South Rim of the Grand Canyon. The Arizona State Museum at Tucson has many of the world's best Indian archaeological relics. Near Tucson is the Saguaro National Monument, which was established to protect the majestic saguaro cactus; the Arizona-Sonora Desert Museum, with all types of wildlife; and Old Tucson, a combination of an old town and family amusement park. Tumacacori National Monument, a monument to the Franciscan fathers and explorers to the region, and Tombstone, an authentic Wild West town that was famous for its gunfighters, and Boothill, are south of Tucson. Tubac, just north of the Mexican border is a popular arts community and outdoor recreation area.

Grand Canyon State

Area	295,254 sq km (113,998 sq mi)
Population	6,596,000
Capital	Phoenix 1,568,000
GDP per Cap	$32,300

Agriculture	vegetables; cattle; dairy products; cotton, fruits, nursery stock, nuts
Industry	real estate, manufactured goods, retail, tourism, state and local government

Colorado

Colorado is one of the most popular outdoor recreation states in the country with both outstanding skiing and summer outdoor resorts. Denver, the capital and largest city, has the U.S. Mint, and Larimer Square, a restored center of Old Denver that is full of boutiques, restaurants, art galleries, and gift shops. The Denver Art Museum is an impressive structure itself, and the Denver Museum of Natural History is well known for a number of well-presented dioramas of native birds and mammals in their natural settings. The State Capitol Complex, complete with its gold-leaf dome, the Colorado Heritage Center, and a Greek Theater are other Denver attractions.

Just south of Denver at Colorado Springs are the United States Air Force Academy, Pike's Peak, which can be climbed by an eighteen-mile-long road, to the Garden of the Gods. Colorado Springs is home to the Broadmoor Hotel. Southeast of Denver in the plains is Bent's Old Fort National Historic Site, an important trading post built on the north bank of the Arkansas River. North of Denver, the Rocky Mountain National Park is a scenic glaciated park. Picturesque Estes Park serves as the gateway to Rocky Mountain National Park. A number of world-famous ski areas such as Vail, Winter Park, Aspen, Breckenridge, and Snowmass are west of Denver. Boulder is home to the University of Colorado. South of Aspen is Gunnison with the ski town of Crested Butte. Steamboat Springs lies to the north of Denver.

The Great Sand Dunes National Monument near Alamosa is one of the most fascinating natural phenomena in the United States. The Mesa Verde National Park is home to the spectacular cliff dwellings of the Anasazi Indians; the Durango & Silverton Narrow Gauge Train through picturesque rugged mountains; and the Black Canyon of the Gunnison National Monument, a deep chasm and rushing stream, are found in the southwest part of the state. Telluride, north of Durango, is an old silver mining town with excellent skiing. Colorado shares Dinosaur National Monument, which has an impressive visitor center and fascinating dinosaur quarry, with Utah.

Centennial State

Area	269,601 sq km (104,094 sq mi)
Population	5,025,000
Capital	Denver 599,000
GDP per Cap	$41,100
Agriculture	cattle; corn, wheat; dairy products; hay
Industry	real estate, regional government, durable goods, tourism, communications

Idaho

Idaho has a small population, but a great variety of natural attractions. In the north, Lake Coeur d'Alene is considered one of the most beautiful small lakes in the world. Nez Perce National Historical Park surrounds the Snake and Clearwater confluence. It is the site where the Nez Perce defeated the U.S. Army to begin the Nez Perce War. Sandpoint has a year-round tourism industry, centered on Lake Pend Oreille and the Schweitzer Ski Area.

Across the center of the state, the mountain scenery is impressive and rich. Set in the middle of the rugged peaks of Idaho's Rocky Mountains, Hells Canyon–Seven Devils scenic area is the deepest gorge on the continent. The Idaho Primitive Area, including the Salmon River, which is famous for river running, and one of the world's most famous ski resorts, Sun Valley, are in the center of Idaho. The Sawtooth Mountains in this central region are as impressive as the Alps. One of the most unusual monuments is the Craters of the Moon National Monument. It has trails through lava flows and an unusual landscape of cinder cones and craters. Throughout Idaho, outdoor

Potatos

Today Lewis and Clark wouldn't recognize most of their route from St. Louis to the Pacific. But there's one place they'd know in a heartbeat: a 149-mile stretch of the Missouri River in north-central Montana. It still contains the "scenes of visionary enchantment" the explorers found in 1805, where rugged sandstone canyons meet the river, then climb to a seemingly limitless prairie full of life. Bighorn sheep and elk sip from the river while antelope scamper. Eagles scream, coyotes sing, and prairie dogs do that funky dance.

Even bison are back, thanks to the American Prairie Reserve, a group stitching together 3 million acres of public and private land for wildlife.

For locals, this place where erosion slashes the prairie is simply "the Breaks." Some people explore it by canoe, often starting at Fort Benton (make time for the frontier history museums) and paddling for days and days. Others keep their feet dry, but the one thing everybody can find is quiet, the kind of hush that amplifies birdsong, a

flutter of leaf, the melody of wind, your own heartbeat.

It's not easy country. You'll find more cactus and prairie rattlesnakes than people. You'll expose yourself to weather that can peel your skin, freeze your flesh, bake you to the bone. Bring sturdy shoes, lots of water—and an open mind. In the Breaks, you can fill it with something good.

—Scott McMillion, *National Geographic Traveler*, December 2012/January 2013

---

sports such as hunting and fishing are extremely popular. Boise is the largest city and capital, and the Snake River plain is the center of potato production in America.

Gem State

Area	216,446 sq km (83,570 sq mi)
Population	1,546,000
Capital	Boise 205,000
GDP per Cap	$29,900
Agriculture	potatoes; dairy products; cattle; wheat, alfalfa hay, sugar beets
Industry	electronics, computer equipment, tourism, food processing, mining

---

Montana

Montana tourism destinations combine the mountains and the plains. Its largest city is Billings, a regional business center. The scenic areas are best observed in Bob Marshall Wilderness Area and Glacier National Park (Figure 9.1), where the thick forests, scenic lakes, and precipitous peaks and ridges provide both a scenic view and homes for bighorn sheep, grizzly bears, and other wildlife. Attractions in southern Montana include the Beartooth Mountains, and spectacular Big Sky Ski Resort, south of Bozeman. Bozeman is home to the Museum of the Rockies. The Last Chance Gulch at Helena is the picturesque main street in this old mining town. South of Helena, the Lewis and Clark Caverns State Park is one of the largest limestone caves in the United States. Northeast of Helena is Old Fort Benton, a nineteenth-century center for the fur trade. South near the Idaho border, Virginia City is an

Old West mining town complete with wooden boardwalks and a number of well-restored buildings. East of Billings is the Little Bighorn Battlefield National Monument, where the Sioux and Cheyenne destroyed Custer's troops. Missoula, home to the University of Montana, is a very attractive, cultural, and lively city with a unique literary history (host to the Montana Festival of Books).

Treasure State

Area	380,838 sq km (147,042 sq mi)
Population	975,000
Capital	Helena 29,000
GDP per Cap	$28,200
Statehood	November 8, 1889; 41st state
Agriculture	wheat; cattle; barley, hay, sugar beets; dairy products
Industry	forest products, food processing, mining, construction, tourism

Figure 9.1 Glacier National Park. © SNEHIT/www.Shutterstock.com.

Nevada

Nevada calls itself the entertainment capital of the United States. Las Vegas, with its famous hotel and casino strip, Reno, and Lake Tahoe are the entertainment centers, offering all forms of gambling and shows involving famous stars and acts. Las Vegas is the largest city and has become the fantasy vacation destination capital of the world. Fancifully themed mega-resorts have been developed to lure the family and convention markets. All include casinos, hotels, and theme parks.

Virginia City, near Carson, and Hyalite are two old mining towns. The Hoover Dam near Las Vegas is an impressive engineering feat and can now be observed from a unique angle with the completion of a new bridge across the Colorado River just downstream from the dam. The newest national park in the United States is the Great Basin National Park in northeastern Nevada stretching from the base of the Rocky Mountains to the Sierra Nevadas. Lehman Caves in the park is one of the more beautiful small caves in the United States. Reno provides Las Vegas attractions on a smaller scale and also has Harrah's National Automobile Museum, demonstrating the importance and evolution of the auto in America. Burning Man, a weeklong festival, takes place north of Reno in early September.

Silver State

Area	286,351 sq km (110,561 sq mi)
Population	2,643,000
Capital	Carson City 55,000
GDP per Cap	$39,700
Agriculture	cattle; hay; dairy products
Industry	tourism and gaming, mining, printing and publishing, food processing, electrical equipment

From *National Geographic Atlas of the World*, 9th edition. Copyright ©2011 National Geographic Society. Reprinted by arrangement. All rights reserved.

New Mexico

New Mexico combines a variety of outdoor and Southwest culture in a number of destinations. In the north, both nature and culture are displayed in Taos Pueblo, an artist community and one of the most picturesque towns in the world. The Bandelier National Monument, which has a scenic trail along Frijoles Canyon with pink and tan chasms, includes a plateau with ruins of cliff houses up to three stories high with unique cave rooms. Santa Fe is an old Spanish settlement with a picturesque central plaza surrounded by specialty shops. The Palace of the Governors in Santa Fe displays Indian jewelry and pottery. It is the oldest public building in America, erected in 1610 by the Spanish as a capitol. The Museum of New Mexico has an outstanding collection of contemporary American Indian paintings and is set in an impressive historic plaza. The Georgia O'Keeffe Museum in Santa Fe ranks among the most popular art museums in the southwest. Taos, situated north of Santa Fe, is a quintessential New Mexico town with a challenging ski area nearby. Ranchos de Taos has the eighteenth-century San Francisco de Asís Church and Pueblo de Taos, a UNESCO World Heritage Site. A visitor to Albuquerque, the state's largest city, can take a tramway to the top of the Sandia Peak for either skiing in the winter or nature trails in the summer. The city is a combination of Spanish and Mexican historical buildings and shops, with the Indian Pueblo Cultural Center and a celebrated Old Town. The New Mexico Museum of Natural History is located in Albuquerque. The famous Albuquerque International Balloon Festival takes place in early October.

The Acoma Pueblo near Albuquerque is a mesa-topped city high above the countryside. Numerous pueblos can be found throughout the state and most welcome visitors. Further west, El Morro National Monument is famous for its "Inscription Rock," where Spanish conquistadors, early United States Army officers, Indian agents, and others carved their names into the 200-foot-high sandstone bluff.

Two destinations in the south are the White Sands National Monument, with its high dunes of shimmering white sand, the site of the first atomic bomb testing in 1945, and Carlsbad Caverns National Park, one of the most recognized caves in North America. Los Alamos was the site of the Manhattan project leading to the development of the atomic bomb.

Nearby Roswell continues to convince visitors that a spacecraft landed here in 1947.

Land of Enchantment

Area	314,915 sq km (121,590 sq mi)
Population	2,010,000
Capital	Santa Fe 72,000
GDP per Cap	$30,900
Agriculture	cattle; dairy products; hay, chilies, onions
Industry	electronic equipment, government, real estate, oil and gas, tourism

From *National Geographic Atlas of the World*, 9th edition. Copyright ©2011 National Geographic Society. Reprinted by arrangement. All rights reserved.

Utah

Utah combines a varied natural environment with a unique culture to create unusual attractions. It has five national parks, ranging from deep canyons such as Canyonlands National Park to the unique erosional features of Bryce Canyon National Park to the sculpted stone mountains of Zion National Park to the spectacular sandstone formations of Capitol Reef National Park. Erosion has created amazing natural arches in Arches National Park, the most famous being Rainbow Bridge National Monument. Rainbow Bridge National Monument is accessible via Lake Powell, a large man-made lake that is popular for houseboating, swimming, and fishing. The Great Salt Lake is noted around the world for its salty, buoyant waters. Golden Spike National Historic Site near Brigham City commemorates the meeting of the Central Pacific and the Union Pacific railroads, which gave the United States its first coast-to-coast link.

Salt Lake City is the capital, the largest city, and the center of Mormonism. The Temple Square is the most visited attraction in the state with over 4 million visitors annually. Temple Square includes the Temple, the Tabernacle, home of the famous Mormon Tabernacle Choir, and two large visitor centers. The "This is the Place" monument was the site where Brigham Young envisioned the building of this Mormon city. The Genealogical Library is a fascinating destination for many visitors. East of Salt Lake City, the Dinosaur National Monument is located on the border with Colorado. It is home to many different varieties of dinosaurs in addition to crocodiles and turtles. The Rocky Mountains and many lakes provide all forms of outdoor recreational opportunities for visitors to the state. The 2002 Winter Olympics were held in Salt Lake City and vicinity, which brought many more visitors to the region. Nearby ski resorts include Snowbird, Park City, Deer Valley, and Alta. Moab, in the eastern part of the state, is a center for outdoor recreation, especially mountain biking. Sundance hosts a famous Film Festival in January.

Beehive State

Area	219,887 sq km (84,899 sq mi)
Population	2,785,000
Capital	Salt Lake City 182,000
GDP per Cap	$32,000

Agriculture	cattle; dairy products; hay; poultry, eggs; wheat
Industry	government, manufacturing, real estate, construction, banking, tourism

Wyoming

Wyoming's most impressive attractions are in the northwest corner. Yellowstone National Park, with entrances in Montana, Idaho, and Wyoming, is the world's first national park established to preserve its unique natural features. Its hot-water geysers (with Old Faithful the most popular) and vents are world renowned, and the abundant wildlife provides further attractions for the visitor. The Grand Canyon of the Yellowstone offers spectacular views. Grand Teton National Park and Jackson Hole, to the south, are important outdoor centers, providing all forms of outdoor recreation such as hunting, fishing, river rafting, and so on. Skiing is popular at Jackson Hole, and the town is a major resort destination in winter and summer.

East of Jackson Hole at Cody is the Buffalo Bill Historical Center and the Buffalo Bill Museum, which is home to the world's largest collection of artifacts depicting the culture, history, and art of the American West. Also in Cody is the Whitney Gallery of Western Art, which has an impressive collection of Remington's and Russell's works. In the eastern part of the state, Fort Laramie National Historic Site allows visitors to experience what the early fort and trading center was like for travelers going west. The Bighorn Mountains feature the Medicine Wheel archeological site. In the northeastern corner of the state, visitors flock to Devils Tower. The monolith, visible for miles, is the remnant of a volcano's inner core, and has become a magnet for rock climbers.

Equality State

Area	253,336 sq km (97,814 sq mi)
Population	544,000
Capital	Cheyenne 57,000
GDP per Cap	$40,800
Agriculture	cattle; sugar beets; sheep; hay, wheat
Industry	mining, generation of electricity, chemicals, tourism

REVIEW QUESTIONS

1. Name a national park for each of the states mentioned in this chapter.
2. Name five ski resort destination in Colorado.
3. What attractions can be found in or near Colorado Springs?
4. Contrast the attractions of Arizona with those of New Mexico.
5. Name the four states that meet at *Four Corners*.

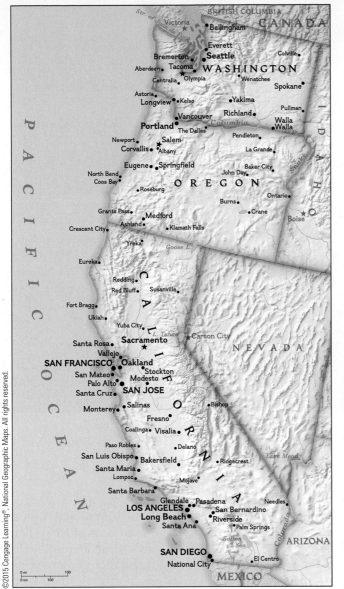

The Pacific region is a popular tourist region that receives large numbers of tourists from all over the world.

STATE PROFILE

State	Capital	Square Miles	Population (2010)
Alaska	Juneau	615,230	710,146
California	Sacramento	158,869	37,253,956
Hawaii	Honolulu	6,500	1,360,301
Oregon	Salem	97,100	3,831,074
Washington	Olympia	70,637	6,724,540

Source: Adapted from U.S. Bureau of the Census, 2011.

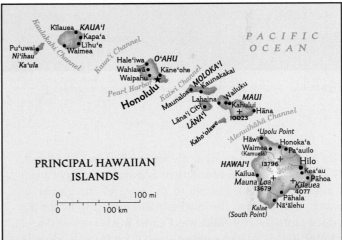

PRINCIPAL HAWAIIAN ISLANDS

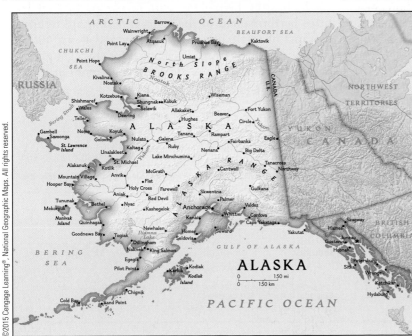

Alaska

Alaska is noted for outdoor adventure. The natural features and scenery are immense, picturesque, and majestic from the Inside Passage in the south to Kotzebue and Nome in the north. The largest state, Alaska is sparsely occupied. Many tourists come via the Inside Passage in the southeast, either by cruise ship or ferries. It is a picturesque trip beneath snow-capped mountains, hurtling waterfalls, massive glaciers, and forests, past unique towns such as Ketchikan, Sitka, and Juneau. Juneau, the state capital, is situated at the foot of majestic mountains in the state's southern panhandle and is only accessible by boat or plane. Attractions include the Alaska State Museum, featuring Alaskan history, flora, and fauna; and the Russian Orthodox Church, which was built in 1894. The Mendenhall

Figure 10.1 Anchorage, Alaska. © Jonathan Nafzger /www.Shutterstock.com.

Glacier near Juneau can easily be reached by car or foot. Glacier Bay National Monument is a short air flight from Juneau. Ships take visitors to the edge of the glacier to watch and listen to the cracking and groaning as the ice crashes into the bay. Sitka was Czarist Russia's New World capital, and is Alaska's oldest town. The Russian church, St. Michael's Cathedral, and the Sitka National Monument, with its many totem poles, are attractions here. Ketchikan, a port on the Inside Passage, is a colorful town. It has a large collection of totem poles at Saxman Park.

With its international airport, Anchorage (Figure 10.1) is the gateway for sightseeing and traveling to south central Alaska, the Kenai Peninsula, and the lower interior. The largest city, Anchorage is a rapidly growing town with an excellent historical museum and is close to the Alyeska resort area and Portage Glacier. Katmai National Monument, some 250 miles south of Anchorage, was created in part by volcanic eruptions and flows. Included in the monument are the Valley of Ten Thousand Smokes and abundant wildlife. Beautiful Kodiak Island is a mecca for fishermen and big-game hunters. North of Anchorage, the Denali National Park and Preserve has spectacular scenery, considerable wildlife, and Mount McKinley, the country's highest peak.

Fairbanks, the second largest city in Alaska, was a gold-rush boomtown. Its attractions include old gold camps, sternwheel riverboat trips, and a pioneer theme park. The Indian villages of Circle and Yukon are nearby. For the visitor who wants a northerly visit, Nome, Kotzebue, and Prudhoe Bay fit the requirement. Nome, which was a gold-rush town, has preserved its frontier atmosphere. Kotzebue, north of the Arctic Circle, has the Living Museum of the Arctic that features performances of the Inupiat (Eskimo) life and a diorama of arctic life. Prudhoe Bay and Point Barrow can be reached from Fairbanks by air. They have become better known with the development of the oil fields and pipeline.

Last Frontier

Area	1,717,854 sq km (663,267 sq mi)
Population	698,000
Capital	Juneau 31,000
GDP per Cap	$43,600
Agriculture	shellfish, seafood; nursery stock, vegetables; dairy products
Industry	petroleum products, state and local government, services, tourism, fishing, trade

From *National Geographic Atlas of the World*, 9th edition. Copyright © 2011 National Geographic Society. Reprinted by arrangement. All rights reserved.

Figure 10.2 Redwood National Park, California. © Michael Nichols/National Geographic Creative.

California

California has more people and receives more visitors than any other state. It can be divided into three broad regions, the north, Los Angeles, and San Diego areas. In the north, the Redwood National Park (Figure 10.2) has trees that are twenty centuries old and the tallest in the world. The drive "Avenue of the Giants" illustrates the character of this park. Lassen Volcanic National Park, also located in the north, is a beautifully proportioned and visible peak set in a natural wonderland. The towns of Eureka and Crescent City are old mining and lumbering towns. Yosemite National Park on the slopes of the Sierra Nevada is one of the most visited parks in the United States. Its lofty granite domes, forests, thundering water-falls, rushing streams, meadows, and giant trees combine to attract large numbers of visitors. The Ahwahnee Lodge, in the heart of the park, is a National Historic Landmark.

California shares Lake Tahoe, a deep blue, cold lake and major summer and winter resort area, with Nevada. Just south of Tahoe, the Sequoia and Kings Canyon national parks have the largest trees and the highest peak in the lower forty-eight states. Sutter's Fort State Historic Park in Sacramento is where John Sutter discovered gold. The fort has been restored. There are many attractions around the San Francisco Bay area. They include Sonoma, where General Maiano Vellejo had his stronghold; Point Reyes National Seashore, where the crashing sea, the cliffs, and fir-forested ridges create beautiful scenery; Great America, a family-fun theme park in Santa Clara; and Marine World in Redwood City. To the north of San Francisco lies the famous Napa Valley wine region.

San Francisco itself has the Golden Gate State Park, a large and beautiful park and home of the Steinhart Aquarium and Morrison Planetarium. The San Francisco Cable Cars take visitors from Union Square to the North Beach or Ghirardelli Square and Fisherman's Wharf. The streets of San Francisco are unique because of their hilly scenic setting and their bustling and interesting activities. Alcatraz National Park, probably the most famous prison in America before its closure, is now part of the National Park Service. The Golden Gate Bridge (Figure 10.3) is the world's second longest single-span suspension bridge and Golden Gate Park is a popular attraction for local residents. The San Francisco Museum of Modern Art is housed in an impressive building, and the Palace of Fine Arts and Exploratorium has some four hundred touch-and-tinker exhibits in a Greco-Roman building. The California Palace of the Legion of Honor has an impor-tant art gallery of prints and paintings. The Asian Art Museum is another special attraction in the city. Other sites include Chinatown and the San Francisco Ferry

Figure 10.3 Golden Gate Bridge San Fransisco, California. © Jeremy Woodhouse/Getty Images. com.

Building (with restaurants, shops, and a farmers' market). Outside Lands is a popular 3-day music festival attracting 200,000 people. Berkeley is situated across the bay from San Francisco. Stanford lies to the south.

The coastal drive between San Francisco and San Diego is very scenic. The Monterey Peninsula has a picturesque rocky coastline and gnarled cypress trees. The cities of Monterey and the artists' colony town of Carmel center on the peninsula, which has white beaches, expansive golf courses, dramatic cypress groves, and large, well-landscaped estates. The Monterey Bay Aquarium is among the finest in the country. Just south of Monterey, the Big Sur Coast has a sandy beach and forested mountains. About halfway between San Francisco and Los Angeles, the Hearst Castle at San Simeon was built in the 1920s as a summer house for publishing tycoon William Randolph Hearst. It was one of the most fantastic and eclectic mansions in America. Within the one hundred–room Hispano-Moorish castle with its twin ivory towers are statuary, tapestries, and other art treasures collected from around the world. Located near Los Angeles, Santa Barbara has an excellent climate, pretty beaches, and a lovely Spanish mission.

The Los Angeles area vies with Central Florida for the title of tourist capital of the United States. The area includes popular beaches such as Zuma Beach, Malibu,

Santa Monica, Venice, Manhattan Beach, Hermosa, Redondo Beach, Huntington Beach, Newport Beach, and Laguna Beach. Theme parks such as Disneyland, Disney's California Adventure, Knott's Berry Farm, and Magic Mountain are large and well planned to occupy the day of a visitor. Movieland Wax Museum, Universal Studios, NBC and Burbank studios, and Mann's Chinese Theater are for those interested in movies, movie making, and the stars. Each of the cities of Pasadena, Beverly Hills, Santa Barbara, Santa Monica, Hollywood, Long Beach, Burbank, and Anaheim has its own personality. History and culture are portrayed at Olvera Street, where Los Angeles was founded by Spaniards in 1781. The Getty Center and Getty Villa, an authentic reconstruction of a Roman villa, the Huntington Library, the Los Angeles County Museum of Art, and Botanical Gardens provide important attractions, as do the Rancho La Brea Tar Pits, with thousands of fossils. The Queen Mary is anchored in the harbor at Long Beach. Just offshore, Catalina Island is a resort center popular for its water sports and beaches. South of Los Angeles, the San Juan Capistrano Mission is famous for the swallows who are supposed to return each year on St. Joseph's Day. San Diego is the third major tourist area of California. It has a world-famous zoo and Sea World. Other attractions include the San Diego Wild

Animal Park, where a visitor can safari through Africa, Asia, Australia, and Central and South America; Old Town, a restored shopping center; and San Diego's Mission. Balboa Park offers museums, art galleries, theaters, and sports facilities. Inland, the Joshua Tree National Monument and Death Valley National Monument characterize the desert environment. Palm Springs, a world-famous winter resort center, has an aerial tramway from Chino Canyon to the top of Mt. San Jacinto. Just north of San Diego is Legoland theme park. West of the city, the Cabrillo National Monument is where Europeans first set foot on the West Coast.

Golden State

Area	423,970 sq km (163,696 sq mi)
Population	36,962,000
Capital	Sacramento 464,000
GDP per Cap	$42,100
Agriculture	vegetables, fruits, nuts; dairy products; cattle; nursery stock
Industry	electronic equipment, aerospace, film production, tourism, food processing

Hawaii

Hawaii, the third major tourist region in the West, relies heavily on tourism and is a leading tourist destination worldwide. It includes twelve islands with their own distinct attractions in spite of general geographic similarities. The island of Oahu, the population and political center of the islands, attracts the most tourists. Honolulu, the largest city, is on this island. Honolulu includes Waikiki (Figure 10.4), probably the most recognized beach in the world, with its high-rise hotels and shopping area concentrated along the beach with its view of Diamond Head. Pearl Harbor serves as a reminder of December 7, 1941, with the impressive USS Arizona Memorial. Outside of Honolulu, major attractions on Oahu are the Iolani Palace, a restored royal palace; National Memorial Cemetery of the Pacific in the Punchbowl, a volcanic crater; and Bishop Museum, an outstanding museum of Hawaiian life and history. On the north side of the island, the Polynesian Cultural Center has a number of re-created native buildings of the Pacific. The dances, arts, and crafts of the various island groups of the Pacific are demonstrated here. At Waimea Bay, famous for its surfing, surfers attract tourists. Waimea Falls is an area of beauty with an expansive valley that is home to tropical growth and exotic birds.

Maui, the Valley Isle, is the second most visited island of the group. High in the clouds, Haleakala National Park, over 10,000 feet in altitude, provides viewing and hiking trails through a volcanic landscape. Many resorts have developed on the coast from Lahaina and Kaanapali to Na Pai and from Kihei to Wailea. Lahaina is a preserved old port town that was once Hawaii's capital. It was also the center of Hawaii's whaling industry, which is represented in the whaling museum that is part of a large shopping center. Hana is somewhat remote from the major tourist resorts, but it is along a picturesque drive and still retains many of the old Hawaiian customs and pace of life. The Seven Pools, near Hana, is reported to be the bathing spots of the Hawaiian kings.

The Big Island (Hawaii) provides views of active volcanoes with the Hawaii Volcanoes National Park. There are a variety of landscapes, from the green lush jungle to the lava flows and streams. Hilo, the largest city on the island, has a number of points of special interest, such as the Rainbow Falls, the Hilo Florist Center, Lyman Memorial Museum (of ancient Hawaiian relics), and the Kalapana Black Sand Beach. Kona, on the leeward side, has become a resort center and is famous because Captain Cook was killed nearby. The city of Refuge south of Kailua is a National Historic Park.

Kauai, the fourth of the major islands, is referred to as the Garden Isle and is known for its lush greenery and deep valleys. Waimea Canyon, a "little Grand Canyon," provides spectacular views of multihued gorges that are nearly 4,000 feet deep. The Fern Grotto is attractive and noted as the setting for many weddings. The coastline is scenic, with beautiful beaches and good natural harbors.

Molokai, the Friendly Isle, is the last of the five major Hawaiian Islands attracting tourists. It is known for the leper colony that was founded there in the eighteenth century. Today it emphasizes sports activities such as hunting, fishing, golf, and swimming. The Kalaupapa Peninsula is a beautiful scenic area. *no flights from us & Canada*

Aloha State

Area	28,311 sq km (10,931 sq mi)
Population	1,295,000
Capital	Honolulu 375,000
GDP per Cap	$38,600
Agriculture	sugarcane, pineapples, nursery stock, tropical fruits; livestock
Industry	tourism, trade, finance, food processing, petroleum refining, stone

Figure 10.4 Waikiki Beach and Diamond Head. © tomas del amo/www.Shutterstock.com.

Oregon

Oregon's major attractions are located in the western half of the state. Portland is the largest city and is famous for its Rose Festival and Fleet Week. Other attractions in and around Portland include the Astoria Column, an observation platform overlooking the Columbia River on the site of Lewis and Clark's visit; the Portland Gardens, home of the world-famous International Rose Test Gardens; the McLoughlin House National Historic Site in historic Oregon City; and Mt. Hood, some 60 miles east, with glaciers, clear streams, blue lakes, and lush meadows. The region south of Portland is known as the Willamette Valley, a rich agricultural region that was the final destination for the thousands who traveled in the 1840 on the Oregon Trail. East of Astoria, the Fort Clatsop National Memorial is a log fort replica of the one built by Lewis and Clark. South is Crater Lake National Park, a deep water-filled caldera and lovely volcanic park. Jacksonville has nearly 80 historic buildings from the nineteenth century. During

the summer, the town is quite active with Wells Fargo stagecoach tours and a number of historic buildings. The Rogue River National Forest has attractive forests of Douglas fir and Ponderosa pine along the Rogue River. One of the most popular and best-known Shakespearean festivals takes place at Ashland in the summer. Sunriver has become a favorite destination for those looking to bike or hike. Near the Rogue River National Forest is the Oregon Caves National Monument.

Beaver State

Area	254,805 sq km (98,381 sq mi)
Population	3,826,000
Capital	Salem 153,000
GDP per Cap	$38,800
Agriculture	nursery stock, hay; cattle; grass seed, wheat; dairy products
Industry	real estate, retail and wholesale trade, electronic equipment

From *National Geographic Atlas of the World*, 9th edition. Copyright ©2011 National Geographic Society. Reprinted by arrangement. All rights reserved.

Figure 10.5 Seattle Cityspace with Space Needle. © Robert Glusic/Getty Images.

Washington

Washington has a number of important attractions that combine history, nature, climate, and culture. The physical environment is represented by Mount Rainier National Park, a scenic glacier-capped mountain, and Olympic National Park, with its beautiful midlatitude forests. Glacier-topped Mt. Olympus dominates the Olympic peninsula, and the rugged coastline provides a scenic drive. History is presented in the Fort Vancouver National Historic Site, a fur-trade center with a reconstructed fort. Whitman Mission National Historic Site, near Walla Walla, is the site where Cayuse Indians killed the Methodist missionary Whitman and his pioneer group. Cheney Cowles Memorial Museum in Spokane deals with Northwest history, and the Pacific Northwest Indian Center, which is also in Spokane, displays Indian history and artifacts. Far to the north is the old seaport of Bellingham with attractive stores and streetscapes. Leavenworth celebrates the region's German culture.

The cosmopolitan metropolis, Seattle (Figure 10.5), is the largest city. The city has become an important cruise ship embarkation port. The skyline is dominated by the Seattle Space Needle, which has a revolving restaurant on top. The Seattle Center, around the Space Needle, has a variety of facilities such as an opera house, a repertory theater, an art museum, and the Pacific Science Center. Nearby, the Seattle Aquarium, Pioneer Square, Pike Place Market, and the Kingdome are important features in Seattle that add to the character of the city. Seattle is also known for its many coffee shops and great seafood restaurants. Fifteen miles north of the city, visitors may visit the Boeing Factory Visitor Center.

Evergreen State

Area	184,665 sq km (71,300 sq mi)
Population	6,664,000
Capital	Olympia 45,000
GDP per Cap	$40,400
Agriculture	seafood; apples; dairy products; wheat; cattle; potatoes, hay
Industry	aerospace, tourism, food processing, forest products

From *National Geographic Atlas of the World*, 9th edition. Copyright ©2011 National Geographic Society. Reprinted by arrangement. All rights reserved.

REVIEW QUESTIONS

1. What would be the highlights of any trip to Alaska?

2. What are three attractions in San Diego, Los Angeles, and San Francisco?

3. What are California's major attractions outside these cities?

4. Name Hawaii's five major islands and list an attraction on each.

5. Name several of the sites that exemplify the impressive natural beauty of the northwestern sta[...]

part 3: GEOGRAPHY AND TOURISM IN CANADA

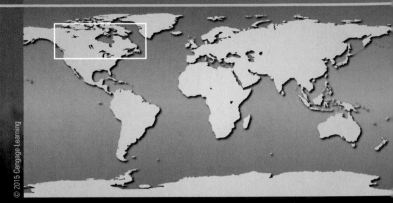

MAJOR GEOGRAPHIC CHARACTERISTICS

- Canada is the world's second largest country, and the largest country in North America.

- Canada is comprised of ten provinces and three territories.

- Despite its large size the country ranks thirty-fifth in world population numbers.

- Population centers are concentrated in and near major cities; the Toronto region is home to nearly 30 percent of the country's population.

- Canada and the United States share many similarities but each has a unique history, political organization, and social fabric.

MAJOR TOURISM CHARACTERISTICS

- Tourism and recreation are important element in the quality of life of residents of Canada.

- The United States is Canada's most important visitor market.

- The attractions in the region are extremely diversified, and center on outdoor activities, urban attractions, and resort based vacations.

MAJOR TOURIST DESTINATIONS

- Toronto
- Niagara Falls
- Montréal
- Edmonton
- Banff
- Québec
- Ottawa-Hull
- Calgary
- Jasper
- Vancouver
- London
- Winnipeg
- Halifax
- Bay of Fundy

81

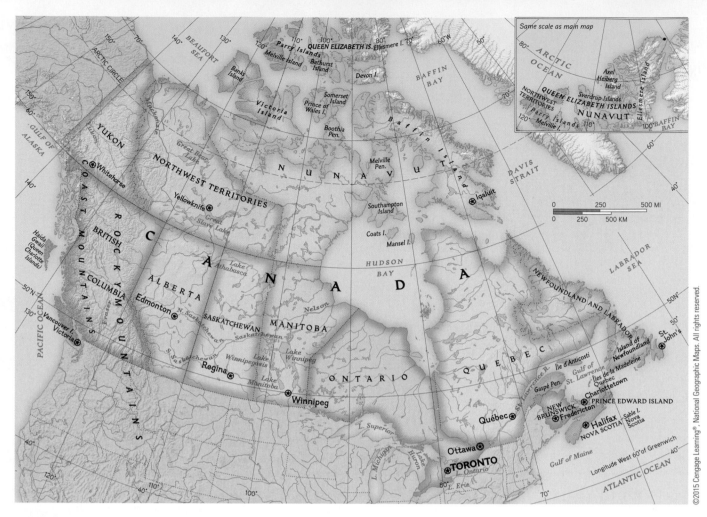

Introduction

Canada is the second largest country in the world (after Russia), but 80 percent of Canadians are concentrated on only 4 percent of the land, most near the U.S.–Canada border. The Arctic region takes up 39 percent of Canada, and the boreal forest covers another third of Canada south of the Arctic—both regions are sparsely populated due to the severe climate. However, climate change affects both areas as temperatures rise and ice melts, and the government allocates increasing resources to preserve and protect its vast northern geography. In addition to the Arctic region, Canada contains four other regions:

- Atlantic Canada offers scenic beaches and delicious seafood and includes the provinces of New Brunswick, Nova Scotia, Prince Edward Island, and Newfoundland and Labrador.

- Central Canada (Ontario and Québec) holds cosmopolitan cities, including Toronto and Montréal. Ontario ranks first in terms of economy and population, home to more than one in three Canadians, and is the second largest province in size. Québec is the largest province in size and is second in population. Québec forms the heartland for French culture, with historic sites and more than 6.8 million French speakers.

- The Prairie region (Manitoba and Saskatchewan), named for the tallgrass prairie, contains countless lakes and First Nations (Indian) and Métis sites.

- The Mountains West region (Alberta and British Columbia) showcases the Rocky Mountains, scenic parks, and the popular cities of Vancouver and Calgary. High immigration from Hong Kong and China has made Chinese the second most popular language, with 570,000 speakers.

Canadians enjoy a high standard of living. A multicultural country, the 2010 census reported more than 200 ethnic groups, with English, French, Chinese, and South Asian being among the largest. Almost 30 percent of Canadians live in southern Ontario, where the multicultural metropolis of Toronto is Canada's commercial hub. Exports range from automobiles and oil to farm and forest products, with most going to the United States.

From *National Geographic Atlas of the World*, 9th edition. Copyright ©2011 National Geographic Society. Reprinted by arrangement. All rights reserved.

Area	9,984,670 sq km (3,855,103 sq mi)
Population	33,707,000
Government	Parliamentary democracy, Federation, and a Commonwealth realm
Capital	Ottawa 1,145,000
Life Expectancy	81 years
Literacy	99%
Religion	Roman Catholic, Protestant
Language	English, French
Currency	Canadian dollar (CAD)
GDP per Cap	$38,400
Labor Force	13% Agriculture, 11% Industry, 76% Services

From *National Geographic Atlas of the World*, 9th edition. Copyright ©2011 National Geographic Society. Reprinted by arrangement. All rights reserved.

TRAVEL**TIPS** 🧳

Entry: A passport or other WHTI-compliant travel document (such as an enhanced driver's license) is required for U.S. citizens traveling to Canada (and return to the United States).

National Holiday: July 1 (Canada Day)

Internet TLD: .ca

Canadians tend to view their country less as a melting pot than as a cultural mosaic. Inuit, Indian Nations (First Nations), French, English, and other immigrant groups have sought to maintain their unique cultural identities.

Cultural hints: Do not compare Canada with the United States. In urban areas, dress appropriately for dinner.

PROVINCE AND TERRITORY PROFILES

Province	Capital	Square Miles	Population (2010)
Alberta	Edmonton	257,287	3,654,474
British Columbia	Victoria	365,948	4,400,075
Manitoba	Winnipeg	250,947	1,208,564
New Brunswick	Fredericton	28,355	751,876
Newfoundland and Labrador	St. John's	155,649	514,456
Northwest Territory	Yellowknife	589,315	41,635
Nova Scotia	Halifax	21,425	921,786
Nunavut	Iqaluit	733,594	31,726
Ontario	Toronto	412,581	12,851,392
Prince Edward Island	Charlottetown	2,185	140,298
Québec	Québec City	594,860	7,903,826
Saskatchewan	Regina	251,866	1,033,398
Yukon	Whitehorse	186,661	32,635

Source: Adapted from Statistics Canada, 2011 census.

Tourism Characteristics

Canada is not as dominant in world travel as the United States, but typically ranks in the top ten in world tourism receipts and expenditures, due in part to its accessibility to its largest market—the United States. In 2011, visitors made 16 million overnight trips to Canada, with Americans counting for 73 percent of all arrivals (Canadian Tourism Commission, 2012).

The infrastructure of the tourism industry in Canada is similar to that of the United States. Many of the hotels and restaurants belong to chains or are members of franchises based in the United States. Numerous United States, Canadian, and international airlines provide direct service to the larger Canadian cities. Competition between government corporations and private industry is a tradition in Canada, evident in both airlines and railways. VIA Rail, Canada's national railroad, runs on both the government-owned Canadian National (CN) tracks and the privately owned Canadian Pacific (CP) tracks. Federal and provincial government tourism departments tend to have larger budgets than their counterparts in the United States. This reflects public acceptance of a higher profile for government in Canada than in the United States and also the fact that because of their smaller size, Canadian businesses have only limited resources for advertising and marketing research.

Agencies of government responsible for tourism development and marketing are found in every provincial and territorial government and at the federal level. These agencies endeavor to cooperate through a system of federal-provincial committees. Some federal financial assistance is provided for mutually agreed-upon projects.

In the private sector, the Canadian Tourism Commission (TIAC) has a role similar to that of the U.S. Travel Association. It represents the viewpoint of the industry to government. In Canada, there are also provincial tourism industry associations, which serve a similar purpose at the provincial level.

One Country, Two Peoples: French Separatism in Canada

Canada is a unique country, and one of the things that makes it especially attractive to tourists is its heritage of both English and French settlement. Canada's total population is more than 33 million, approximately

Figure P3.1 Trail sign in French and English. © SeanPavonePhoto/www.Shutterstock.com.

one-fourth of which claim <u>French </u>as their first language. The French influence is most obvious in the Province of <u>Québec,</u> because the largest percentages and numbers of French Canadians are located in this province. Language is only one of the cultural differences that distinguish the French in Canada, but it is the most easily recognizable to visitors. Eighty-two percent of Québec's over 8 million people speak French, and less than 10 percent claim English as their first language. The only other province with a large percentage of French speakers is <u>New Brunswick</u>, where <u>one-third of the population</u> claims <u>French as their first language.</u> No other province has even 5 percent of its population who are French Canadian, and the result is a French Canadian culture region concentrated along the lower St. Lawrence River Valley in Québec and New Brunswick.

Visitors to this region will find evidence of the French culture everywhere, most obvious being the language, which is evident in the names of towns, newspapers, advertisements, and television and radio. Many names of places and people reflect the Roman Catholic Church, which was a central part of the French culture of early French settlers of the lower St. Lawrence River. Towns beginning with "Sainte" are common in the French culture region of Canada, such as Sainte Foy, Sainte Anne-de-Beaupre, or Sainte Therese-de-Blainville. Individual names in the French region reflect both the

French and Catholic influence in French Canadian culture, such as Jean Paul or Marie. The Catholic Church was the focus of the French Canadian village and is still a prominent part of the French Canadian landscape. The distinctive characteristics of French Canada that appeal to visitors, however, do not reveal the political and cultural tension associated with the presence in Canada of two very different cultures of French and English that dominates the country.

The French were the first to settle Canada, but by 1763 the English had defeated the French in North America, and French settlement was confined primarily to the lower St. Lawrence River Valley. During and after the American Revolutionary War, British royalists settled in the Upper St. Lawrence River Valley, and in 1791 the United Kingdom created two political units in the Canadian Colony, Upper Canada (Ontario) and Lower Canada (Québec and adjacent areas). Known as the Constitutional Act of 1791, this act legitimized the concept of two separate peoples in Canada, the French and English. The ensuing two centuries have seen the emergence of Canada as an independent country, and a series of legislative acts by either the United Kingdom or the Canadian parliament has maintained the importance of Canada as the home of two major cultures. When Canada formally unified as one country in 1867, the government was formed as a federation of distinct cultures, and Canada became one country in which French and English were both official languages (Figure P3.1). Since that time other migrant groups have come to Canada, but the two languages and cultures remain dominant. Later arrivals generally learned English, while the growth of the French-speaking population in Québec and New Brunswick reflected mainly the natural increase of the people already residing there. The result was a gradual decline in the proportion of people speaking French in Canada in the twentieth century.

Recently there has been a remarkable change in the concept of "One Canada, two peoples." French Canadians, worried about the declining percentage of French in Canada, believed that the French were not treated equally with the English in the country. The growth of Montréal's English-speaking peoples led to predictions that the French in Montréal would be a minority in their own city in the twenty-first century and gave impetus to growing French political activism. This culminated in the elections of 1960 in which the National Rally for Independence won control of the Québec provincial government. From 1960 until today there has been a constant, if varying, demand for separatism from Canada among many French in Québec.

Political demands for separatism led to the creation of the separatist Parti Québécois in 1968 and adoption of French-only requirements for the names of stores and businesses in Québec. Concerned that French was being overwhelmed by English, the provincial government passed laws making it difficult for children to attend English-speaking schools, required new immigrants to Québec to learn French, and mandated all government business be conducted in French. In 1980 a referendum was held to determine whether Québec would remain in Canada or not, but the separatists lost by a 60–40 margin.

While the referendum failed to separate Canada into two countries, the result was to concentrate the French even more dramatically. Many large Canadian corporations who were headquartered in Montréal moved to Toronto with the English-speaking employees. Toronto replaced Montréal as the largest city, and Canada adopted the Constitution Act of 1982. This act officially removed the power of the British parliament to be involved in Canadian government, although still recognizing the Queen of England as the official head of the state. All of the provinces ratified the Constitution Act except Québec, which insisted on more recognition of the unique place of French Canada in the country. Constitutional conventions attempting to modify the 1982 Constitution Act failed to do so, as the English majority refused to ratify the proposed changes. The separatists returned to power in Québec in the 1990s with a new political party, the Bloc Québécois. Several referenda were held, but the separatist movement remains defeated in Québec, leaving Québec as an official part of Canada, but recognized as a distinct society.

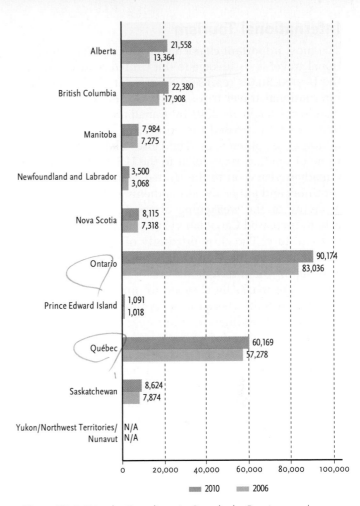

Figure P3.2 Trips by Canadians in Canada, by Province and Territory. Source: Adapted from Statistics Canada, 2012. Copyright © 2015 Cengage Learning®.

Domestic Tourism

Tourism in Canada is largely domestic (Figure P3.2), typically averaging slightly more than 70 percent of all overnight travel by Canadians. Canada's national and provincial governments have been active in promoting both domestic and international tourism within Canada. The federal government travel ministry in Ottawa, the Canadian Tourism Commission, markets the country's distinct Canadian culture and heritage, the national, provincial, and municipal parks, adventure tourism, festivals and events of all kinds, skiing, golf, water sports, dog sledding, snowmobiling, and country resorts.

The two major reasons Canadian residents give for traveling are to visit friends and family (37 percent) and for pleasure (36 percent). Intraprovincial travel for overnight visits is much more common than interprovincial travel, typically comprising some 80 percent of all overnight stays. The two most visited provinces are Ontario and Québec, dominating both intra- and interprovincial travel. The most popular destinations for Canadian residents are Toronto, Montréal, Edmonton, Québec City, Ottawa-Hull, Niagara Falls, Calgary, and Vancouver/ Whistler.

International Tourism

The most important characteristic of Canadian international travel is its linkage to the United States. Trips to the United States represent 93 percent of all Canadian international travel trips. Nearly 30 million overnight trips were taken in 2010 by Canadians to the United States as they crossed the border for shopping, entertainment, or other trips. The close relationship of the value of the Canadian dollar to the U.S. dollar and total Canadian visitation to the United States will no doubt continue, and either the strengthening of the Canadian economy or the weakening of the U.S. economy will lead to increased Canadian visitors to the United States in the future. The close proximity of Canada's population centers to the United States makes it the logical destination for international travel unless other destinations are markedly cheaper. Minimal travel costs to the United States because of its proximity mean that other foreign destinations can rarely compete with the United States, therefore, a decline in Canadian travel to the United States normally translates into substitution of domestic travel within Canada. The traditional ease of border crossing between the two countries was put to the test in recent years as the United States, starting in 2008, required all Canadian travelers entering the country to carry a passport.

More than 70 percent of the international visitors to Canada are from the United States (Figure P3.3). International travel to Canada (overnight trips) reached 17 million in 2011. Nearly 12 million of these were residents of the United States. The close proximity of large population centers in the United States to the Canadian border is a major factor in the dominance of tourists from the United States. The second largest market is the United Kingdom, which accounts for only 4 percent of visitors in 2011. Visitors from the United Kingdom and other European countries (especially France) reflect the cultural linkages existing between Europe and Canada (Statistics Canada, 2012).

There is a marked degree of seasonality in Canadian tourism, with the June to September quarter receiving nearly half of total visitors. International travel by Canadians is also highly seasonal, with most traveling in the summer. Also, the climate of Canada is in itself a major factor in summer travel. Much of the country experiences a northern continental climate with extremes of temperature that in the area of the Great Lakes are accompanied by high humidity in summer and abundant snowfall in winter.

The substantial ties between Canada and the United States and Europe are expressed in the fact that nearly 35 percent of foreign travelers listed visiting friends and relatives in Canada as the primary factor in their visit. Thirty-six percent of the arrivals were for the purpose of holiday or pleasure travel. Nearly 75 percent of foreign arrivals come by automobile, reflecting the proximity of the U.S. markets. Canada also benefits from this

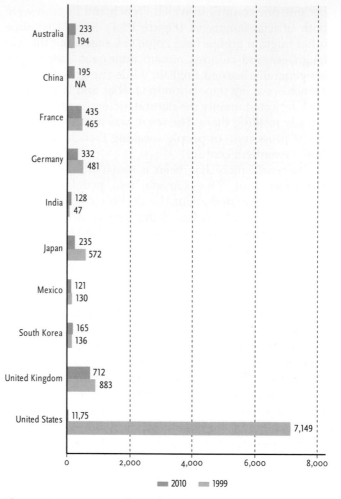

Figure P3.3 International Travel to Canada, 1999–2010.
Source: Adapted from Statistics Canada, 2012. Copyright © 2015 Cengage Learning®.

proximity as almost 30 million additional U.S. visitors come for one-day visits.

Three provinces—Ontario, British Columbia, and Québec—receive the bulk (82 percent) of international expenditures. All are near large United States population centers. The numbers of total non-U.S. international visitors to Canada has remained steady in recent years. Core markets include the United Kingdom with 712,000 arrivals, France (435,000), Germany (332,000), Japan (235,000), Australia (233,000) and China (195,000) (UNWTO, 2012).

Tourism Destinations and Attractions

The province of Ontario is historically and currently the largest attraction for foreign tourists to Canada, particularly the city of Toronto and its environs. The second largest attraction is the province of British Columbia, followed by the provinces of Québec and Alberta. British Columbia's second ranking in overnight international tourists happened rapidly. In part this is the result of the large Asian community in the province, and in part because of growing numbers of U.S. visitors.

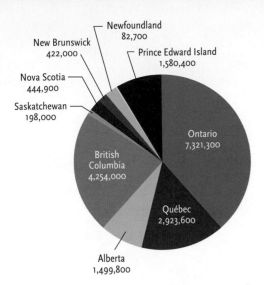

New Brunswick
422,000

Newfoundland
82,700

Nova Scotia
444,900

Prince Edward Island
1,580,400

Saskatchewan
198,000

Ontario
7,321,300

British
Columbia
4,254,000

Québec
2,923,600

Alberta
1,499,800

Figure P3.4 Major Destinations of International Tourists to Canada, 2011. Adapted from *Canadian Tourism Commission, Tourism Snapshot, 2011 Year in Review.,* 2012. Copyright © 2015 Cengage Learning®.

Canada's most outstanding tourism destinations and attractions have historically been its cities and its scenic natural attractions. Canada has an outstanding national park system and vast expanses of virgin forest lands with innumerable rivers and lakes of extraordinary beauty. These attractions are particularly intriguing to visitors from the relatively affluent and crowded countries of Japan, Germany, and other Western European nations. Visitors from the United States have traditionally been attracted by the fishing and hunting opportunities offered by their neighbors to the north, and resort areas such as the Laurentians and the Muskokas are heavily used.

The Canadian government has focused efforts on changing its image to potential tourists in an effort to increase the numbers of visitors. Canada has historically been viewed as a costly vacation with limited historical and cultural scope and as a nation of moose, Mounties, and mountains. In an effort to alter this perception, the government reviewed its tourist product and identified eight major categories that are important for international tourism.

Sporting/Adventure

An outdoor product that is found primarily in sparsely populated areas catering to extended visits and characterized by outdoor activities like hunting, fishing, camping, and canoeing. Similar to the types of products found in Northern Minnesota, Northern Manitoba, and salmon fishing in Scotland.

Wilderness/Expedition

The true wilderness product, characterized by inaccessibility, includes trophy hunting, fishing, safaris, rugged and unforgiving terrain, as in Canada's Arctic. Visitors generally require specialized equipment and qualified guides.

Leisure/Recreation

A leisure-oriented recreational product, easily accessed by local populations and suitable for day trips. These areas are characterized by numerous small-scale recreational and cultural products designed to cater to local populations, such as Southern Ontario.

Beach/Recreation

Recreational product built on beach resources. Similar to leisure/recreation, but with a more significant destination area character that encourages extended visits (such as Prince Edward Island or other beach areas of the world).

Heritage/Culture

Primary features of tourism region are based on either heritage or cultural travel generators and themes such as Québec City or Dawson City.

Urban

Significant urban experience. Cities evaluated as local urban product were not classified as tourist destinations.

Resort

Tourism product characterized by numerous activities and considerable accommodation plant, either contained in a central or major resort product or in groupings of more numerous, smaller products, such as the Laurentians, the Poconos, and Majorca. For analysis of the Canadian product, this category distinguishes between four-season and seasonal resorts.

Scenic

An area characterized by an amalgam of small scenic, heritage, and cultural resources, without a destination travel generator, such as the Gaspé Peninsula and the Lake District.

chapter 11: CANADA

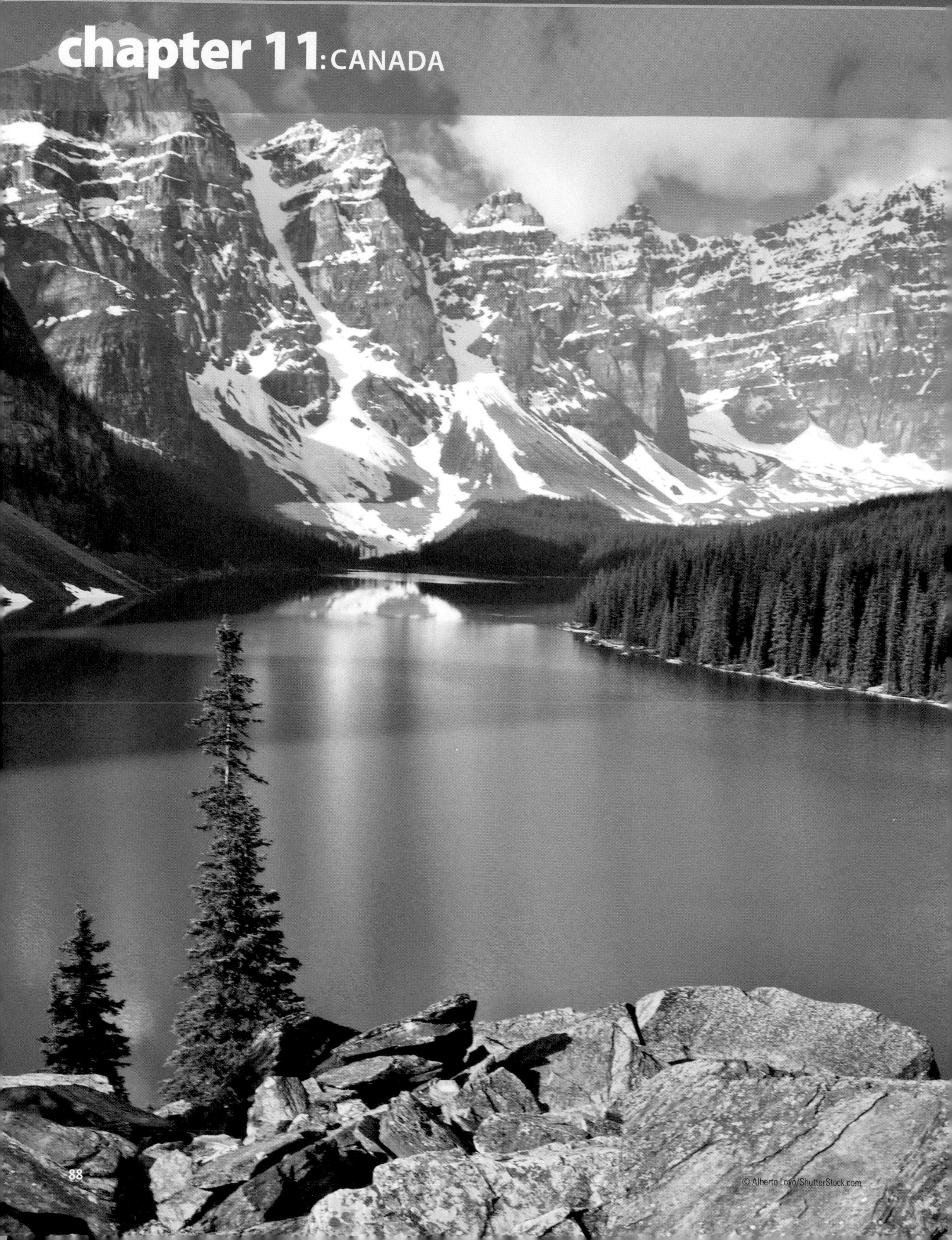

© Alberto Loyo/ShutterStock.com

Figure 11.1 The Northern Lights over the winter landscape of frozen Lake Laberge, Yukon, Canada. © Pi-Lens/Shutterstock.com

Introduction

In 1867, the provinces of New Brunswick, Nova Scotia, Québec, and Ontario formed the Canadian confederation, and they soon acquired what would become the Northwest Territories. Over time, the Northwest Territories were whittled away to create the provinces of Manitoba, Alberta, and Saskatchewan, as well as the territories of the Yukon and Nunavut. Today, Canada is made up of ten provinces and three territories.

The Canadian territories of Nunavut, Yukon, and the Northwest Territories are sparsely populated Arctic regions, making up 40 percent of Canada's land but holding only 0.3 percent of Canadians. Historically, the federal government in Ottawa administered the territories, while provinces possessed their own governments. But in recent years, the federal government has been delegating more authority to the territories, giving each territory a legislature and province-like powers. However, the territories depend on federal funding to provide the necessary public services. Indigenous peoples, including the Inuit and First Nations, are well represented, comprising 85 percent of the people in Nunavut, 51 percent in the Northwest Territories, and 23 percent in the Yukon.

Newfoundland and Labrador

The island of Newfoundland plus Labrador on the mainland create one province. The newest province of Canada, Newfoundland has fishing, scenic, cultural, and historical attractions. Newfoundland as a destination receives the second smallest number of visitors of all the Canadian Provinces, attracting only 1.2 million overnight visitors a year, but about an equal number of same-day visitors yearly. Also, tourism is most seasonal in the Atlantic Provinces in general. Most visitors are from the neighboring provinces and visit during the relatively short summer season.

Since the arrival of the first significant group of British settlers in Newfoundland, the economy has been based upon the sea. In recent years the economy has suffered from overfishing and the closure of military bases. Newfoundland's unemployment is the highest in Canada. It has turned to oil and tourism in an effort to boost its economy, but tourism is limited because of its location. Recently, cruise ships have started calling on

Figure 11.2 St. John's, Newfoundland. © Elena Elisseeva/www.Shutterstock.com.

the region with ships originating from Boston and New York. Newfoundland is noted for its village landscapes with white, tall-spired churches and their adjacent cemeteries. The villages of Newfoundland differ from the New England villages in that they typically lack a village green; but many have covered bridges, which are common through all the maritime regions of Canada. Newfoundland and Labrador have more than 17,000 kilometers of coastline as well as two national parks and more than eighty provincial parks, providing numerous opportunities for sightseeing, camping, or wilderness adventures. A major focus of tourism is the St. John's area (Figure 11.2). St. John's is the capital and largest city. It is one of the oldest settlements in North America and is the eastern terminus of the Trans-Canada highway. It is named after John Cabot, who discovered Newfoundland on June 24, 1497. It was a contested area between the French and English until 1762, when the British defeated the French and recaptured St. John's. The area has a number of national parks and museums that stress history and nature. Water Street in St. John's is the oldest business district on the continent, dating back to 1600. The winding street is accented by the brilliant paint of homes and businesses. Gilbert Hill, where convicted criminals were executed, is another attraction. Fishing for cod and salmon is common in the area. Cabot Tower, located on

Signal Hill, is where the first transatlantic wireless signal was received. Signal Hill National Historic Park is the site of the last battle of the French and English during the Seven Years' War in 1762. It also offers a spectacular view of the city, its harbor, and the adjacent coastline.

The tourist attractions in Newfoundland are associated with the early village and coastal life combined with beautiful coastal and mountain scenery. The Cape Spear Lighthouse is on the most easterly point of North America and is the oldest lighthouse in Newfoundland, serving as a marine beacon from 1836 to 1955. Cape Bonavista Lighthouse was built in 1843 and has been restored to the 1870 period. The Gros Morne National Park area has lakes, coves, fjords, and wildlife ranging from moose to black bear, volcanic sea stacks, caves, sand dunes, and scenic coastal overlooks. Whale watching at Trinity, a village dating back to 1500, is popular because the minke, humpback, and finback whales feed in Newfoundland's eastern fjords. The Hiscock House located in historic Trinity is restored to the 1910 period. At L'Anse-aux-Meadows are a Parks Canada restored Viking settlement and a number of ancient Indian burial grounds, which remind visitors of the early history of the country dating back to A.D. 1000. In combination, Newfoundland's attractions led to the United Nations Educational, Scientific, and Cultural Organization

INSIDER INFO | Cape Breton: Nova Scotia's Treasured Island

During the eighteenth and nineteenth centuries, fishermen and settlers from France and Scotland came to Cape Breton Island, drawn by its rich fisheries, ample timber, and the chance of a better life. Originally settled by the ancient ancestors of the Micmac people, this island off Nova Scotia now lures visitors with its abundant wildlife, natural beauty, and assembly of French, Micmac, and Celtic cultures.

One-fifth of Cape Breton is preserved as a national park, laced by twenty-five hiking paths and looped by the Cabot Trail, a 186-mile driving route frequently ranked among the world's most spectacular.

"I have seen the Canadian and American Rockies, the Andes, the Alps, and the Highlands of Scotland," said inventor Alexander Graham Bell, who spent thirty-seven summers here. "But for simple beauty, Cape Breton outrivals them all."

The mingling of cultures means you can seek a clan tartan at the craft shop at Gaelic College/Colaisde Na Gàidhlig in St. Anns, then explore the French-founded Fortress of Louisbourg on the east coast. In 1745 this garrison withstood a 48-day siege by New Englanders, backed by British naval support, before surrendering. In 2013, the reconstructed fortification celebrates the 300th anniversary of the founding of the French colony of Île Royale (present-day Cape Breton).

—John Rosenthal, *National Geographic Traveler*, December 2012/January 2013

(UNESCO) designating the area as a World Heritage Site. Just 20 miles off the coast of Newfoundland are the French islands of St-Pierre and Miquelon. France's control of these assures access to nearby fishing grounds.

Area	405,212 sq km (156,453 sq mi)
Population	509,000

Capital	St. John's 101,000
GDP per Cap	$41,700
Agriculture	dairy products; poultry, eggs; nursery stock
Industry	oil production, iron ore mining, paper products, tourism

From *National Geographic Atlas of the World*, 9th edition. Copyright ©2011 National Geographic Society. Reprinted by arrangement. All rights reserved.

Nova Scotia

Of the Atlantic Provinces, Nova Scotia is the most popular tourist destination with some 2.7 million overnight visitors a year, and 3.2 million same-day visitors yearly. Acadians established the first permanent European settlement north of Florida at Port Royal in Nova Scotia in 1605. During the next 100 years, Nova Scotia changed hands seven times. In 1713 England and France signed a peace treaty that gave mainland Nova Scotia to England and Cape Breton Island to France. The French built a fortress on Cape Breton Island, which was called Louisbourg. Many Acadians were scattered along the American coast in the British colonies, with a major settlement of Acadians (now called Cajuns in the United States) in the lower Mississippi River area, which was controlled then by France. After the defeat of the French in 1763, some Acadians returned to Nova Scotia and settled principally along the coast, relying on fishing for their livelihood.

Nova Scotia offers the visitor picturesque coastal seaside and fishing villages (Figure 11.3). It is a province of contrasts that is popular with visitors. Nova Scotia celebrates its unique mix of people and culture in its distinct blend of Scottish and Celtic Music. Nova Scotia and Québec are Canada's top two honeymoon destinations. The Cabot Trail on Cape Breton is one of the most spectacular drives in North America and a major destination for visitors to Nova Scotia. It is named after John Cabot and has many lookout points and scenic villages on its route through Cape Breton Highlands National Park and along coastal waters and villages. The rugged mountains of Cape Breton form a sharp, but inviting, contrast with the mainland.

The Alexander Graham Bell Museum exhibits Bell's accomplishments near his family home in Beinn Bhreagh. Bell appreciated the beauty of Cape Breton, stating, "I have travelled around the globe. I have seen the Canadian and American Rockies, the Andes and the Alps, and the Highlands of Scotland; but for simple beauty, Cape Breton outrivals them all." Peggy's Cove is the most visited fishing village in the world. The cove's rugged beauty is part of a beautiful oceanside drive through villages, historic colonial towns, and long white-sand beaches.

Louisbourg National Historic Site is the largest historical reconstruction in North America. Life portrayed within the fortress is a reenactment of military and social existence in 1744. For five decades in the eighteenth century, Cape Breton was called Isle Royale, serving as France's Atlantic bastion. Louisbourg was its capital. It was twice conquered by the English.

Halifax, the world's second largest natural harbor after Sydney, Australia, is considered one of North America's most beautiful cities, complete with a harbor boardwalk system. It was the first English settlement in Canada and has numerous architectural attractions including historic churches, government, and public buildings. Pier 21 celebrates the story of twentieth-century immigration to Canada. The Citadel Fortress at Halifax is Canada's

Figure 11.3 Lunenberg, Nova Scotia. © gary yim/www.Shutterstock.com.

most visited historic site. The Maritime Museum of the Atlantic has a permanent exhibit on the Titanic. Halifax is also home to the Canadian Navy.

Picturesque Lunenburg lies in southern Nova Scotia. Founded in 1753 by German, Swiss, and French Huguenot settlers, Lunenburg has long been known for its shipbuilding, seafaring expertise, and natural beauty. It is home to the Fisheries Museum of the Atlantic.

Nova Scotia is noted for its unique cultural traditions. The Scottish influence is emphasized in annual festivals as people dress in traditional Scottish costumes, bagpipe bands perform, and Scottish games and food are enjoyed on festive days. Distinctive events reflecting the culture of the area include the Celtic Colours International Festival in Cape Breton, the Antigonish Highland Games, the Annual Scotia Gaelic Mod, and the Festival of the Tartans in New Glasgow.

Area	55,284 sq km (21,345 sq mi)
Population	938,000
Capital	Halifax 373,000
GDP per Cap	$33,500
Agriculture	blueberries, apples; livestock; dairy products; lobsters, seafood
Industry	service industries, food processing, paper products, mining, tourism

From *National Geographic Atlas of the World*, 9th edition. Copyright ©2011 National Geographic Society. Reprinted by arrangement. All rights reserved.

New Brunswick

New Brunswick is called the "picture province," and its scenery and natural phenomena are its most important attractions. New Brunswick is a forested region, with the notable exception of the Saint John River Valley, which is farmed intensively. The cities and villages of New Brunswick act as service centers for local areas of farming, fishing, and forestry. St. Andrews is an early and still very popular summer seaside destinations.

Saint John and its suburb Portland have developed serving two rich agricultural areas extending up the Saint John and Kenebecasis rivers. Potatoes are a major agricultural crop. Fredericton, a local service center and lumbering town, became the capital and center of higher education in New Brunswick and is home to the Beaverbrook Art Gallery. Just west of the city is King's Landing Historical Settlement, a living museum re-creating life in the 1880s. New Brunswick's most famous destination is the Bay of Fundy, with a dramatic tidal range that varies as much as fifty feet between low and high tide, the equivalent height of a four-story building. At Moncton, there is the tidal bore on the Petiticodiac River and Magnetic Hill, where drivers can stop their cars, set them in neutral, and seem to coast to the top of the hill. Near Moncton are the Hopewell Rocks (Figure 11.4), which Ripley describes as the world's largest flower pots rocks. The rocks are huge, eerie, sandstone goblets sculpted by the tides over the years. They can be explored at low tide. Sixty miles south of Moncton is the Fundy National Park, and at Saint John is the Reversing Falls. At low tide, the Saint John River rushes into the bay, but at high tide the bay waters rise, seeming to send the river the other way.

Saint John, the oldest incorporated city in the British Empire outside the British Isles, has many historical attractions, including the New Brunswick Museum, which is the oldest public museum in Canada, the Old City Market, and Martello Tower, a fort from the War of 1812. The river road from Saint John north is beautiful and very popular in the fall for its colorful autumn foliage. Near Fredericton, the architecture illustrates the life of the early English settlers. North is the Acadian Historical Village, which illustrates the lifestyle of the Acadians, and the world's longest covered bridge.

Figure 11.4 Hopewell Rocks, Bay of Fundy.

© Natalia Bratslavsky/www.Shutterstock.com.

Area	72,908 sq km (28,150 sq mi)
Population	750,000
Capital	Fredericton 51,000
GDP per Cap	$31,600

Agriculture	lobsters, crabs, other seafood; potatoes; dairy products; poultry
Industry	food and beverage processing, wood, paper products, mining

From *National Geographic Atlas of the World*, 9th edition. Copyright ©2011 National Geographic Society. Reprinted by arrangement. All rights reserved.

Prince Edward Island

Prince Edward Island is mainly a rural area, but tourism is important to the island. Prince Edward Island is the smallest of the Canadian provinces with only 2,185 square miles of total area. In the past, accessibility has been a problem for this island territory with only limited air and ferry connections. Now, the ten-mile-long Confederation Bridge connects Prince Edward Island to the mainland across Northumberland Strait and has increased visitation to the island. The island is a

delightful patchwork of small farming communities, traditional fishing villages, and park lands. Attractions include the small capital city of Charlottetown with its historic Province House National Historic Site where the plan for a unified Canada was first discussed in 1864. While most islanders are descendants of early French, Scottish, English, and Irish settlers, the native Micmac people inhabited Prince Edward Island for a much longer period of time. The Micmac represent about 4 percent of the island's people. The island was discovered by the French explorer Jacques Cartier. The first white settlement was at Port-La-Jove, now Fort Amherst/Port-La-Jove National Historic Site, just across the harbor from Charlottetown. Later, the British occupied the island, deporting the Acadian settlers. Many ended up in southern Louisiana after stays in England and France. In the eighteenth century, it was noted for its shipbuilding around the town of Summerside. In the eighteenth and nineteenth centuries settlers came from Scotland and Ireland, adding to the cultural diversity of the island.

A number of attractions on the island are popular and worth visiting. The Green Gables House at Cavendish served as the backdrop for Lucy Maud Montgomery's novel about the world's favorite orphan, *Anne of Green Gables*. Lobster festivals and sandy beaches are the principal attractions of the area. North Lake is famous for its large bluefin tuna, which average 600 pounds. The scenic drives on the island pass through picturesque fishing villages, along red sand beaches, white sand dunes, and stunted fir and spruce trees.

Area	5,660 sq km (2,185 sq mi)
Population	141,000
Capital	Charlottetown 32,000
GDP per Cap	$30,000
Agriculture	potatoes, barley, blueberries, vegetables; dairy; cattle; seafood
Industry	farm and fish products processing, aircraft parts manufacturing, tourism

From *National Geographic Atlas of the World*, 9th edition. Copyright ©2011 National Geographic Society. Reprinted by arrangement. All rights reserved.

Québec

Québec is the largest province in the area, accounts for 25 percent of the population of Canada, and is the center of French-speaking Canadians. At the time of the establishment of the Canadian nation in 1867, the French-Canada region was largely rural. Montréal and Québec City were the only urban centers. Québec province was largely French in language and custom. The establishment of the federation of Canada guaranteed Québec use of Latin-based French law instead of English common law; and it guaranteed religious liberty. It also established French as one of two national languages. The issue of separatism based on Québec's special constitutional provisions recognizing it as a "distinct society" in Canada remains important in Canadian politics. Québec is the only province for which the United States is not the single most important source for foreign visitors. Only 47 percent of Québec's foreign visitors in 2010 were from the United States, compared with other provinces that receive from 60 to 80 percent of their international visitors from the United States.

The two major tourist destination centers are Québec City (Figure 11.5) and Montréal. Québec City was one of the first French settlements in North America and, in spite of two centuries of English rule, it is still French. The French architecture and beautiful natural setting combine to make it one of the most beautiful cities in North America. Québec City retains the Old World charm and style created by its first French settlers. To visitors, the city provides a sampling of traditional European architecture, excellent restaurants and lively night life. Its rich history is expressed in its older sections. With narrow, cobblestone streets and a citadel, it is a UNESCO site and the only walled city in North America. The citadel is often referred to as the "Gibraltar of America." The narrow streets twist and turn from the Lower Town on the St. Lawrence River upwards to the Upper Town. Its rich history is expressed in the Basilica of Notre Dame des Victoires, which was built in 1688; the hotel Fairmont le Chateau Frontenac; the Ursuline Convent; the Catholic Seminary; Parliament Buildings; the Provincial Museum; and the Bois de Coulange. The wall between Lower and Upper towns has been renovated into a wide promenade overlooking the St. Lawrence River.

Ile d'Orleans, an island in the St. Lawrence River below Québec City, is connected to the mainland by a bridge. This picturesque island retains a great deal of its eighteenth-century French-Canadian architectural influence. "Carnival" is Québec's famous winter festival held each year in February. The Plains of Abraham is the site of the Battle of Québec, which sealed the fate of New France in 1759. Near Québec City is Sainte Anne de Beaupré, a small village dominated by a large cathedral. It is an internationally known religious shrine and attracts millions of pilgrims seeking to be healed. Just twenty-five minutes outside of Québec City is the Mt. Sainte Anne ski resort.

Montréal, founded on an island in the St. Lawrence River, is one of the largest and most cosmopolitan cities in Canada. It is the most culturally diverse city in Québec and the second most popular destination for tourists. The explorer Jacques Cartier discovered an Indian fort and settlement on Montréal Island. A French town grew on the site and became a strategic fur and lumbering trading center. The large French population makes it the second largest French-speaking city in the world. It is a cosmopolitan city with Old World charm expressed in the older sections of the city. Today Montréal is a large and modern city with excellent urban and international transportation.

The principal attractions are the city's rich history, cultural events, museums, and gardens. The Botanical Gardens are considered to be the third largest

Figure 11.5 Québec City and Saint Lawrence River. © GeoStock/Getty Images.

botanical gardens in the world, featuring some 20,000 species of plant life. The Old Quarter (Vieux Montréal) has gas-lamped cobblestone streets, sidewalk cafés, and historic buildings, including Notre Dame Church, opened in 1829; Place Jacques Cartier, a cobblestoned square, which was once the main marketplace; Chateau de Ramezay, a manor built in 1705; and Notre Dame de Bonsecours Chapel, the city's oldest church. Additional attractions are the Biodome, a natural history museum; the futuristic Montreal Museum of Archaeology and History; Chinatown; the Dow Planetarium; Lafontaine Park; and the Olympic park. Another popular attraction is a jet boat tour on the Lachine Rapids, which departs from the old port. The city hosts numerous events, including the Montreal International Jazz Festival and the Montréal World Film Festival.

The Gaspé Peninsula in eastern Québec is a region of picturesque fishing villages, rolling hills, deep gorges, covered bridges, and rocky cliffs. The most impressive attraction is Percé Rock, a 400-million-ton landmark near the town of Percé. The rock juts some 300 feet out of the ocean. Just north of Montréal are the Laurentian Mountains, which have a number of popular resorts offering both winter and summer outdoor sports such as fishing, camping, hiking, and skiing at Mont Tremblant.

Area	1,542,056 sq km (595,391 sq mi)
Population	7,829,00
Capital	Québec 491,00
GDP per Cap	$36,200
Agriculture	dairy; hogs, poultry; vegetables, apples, corn, maple products
Industry	newsprint, other paper products, transport equipment, timber, tourism

From *National Geographic Atlas of the World*, 9th edition. Copyright ©2011 National Geographic Society. Reprinted by arrangement. All rights reserved.

Montreal is like a contortionist. It twists, adapts, folds onto itself in surprising ways. Preternaturally flexible, it is spectacle and entertainment and living thing all at once. Frankly it's kind of crazy that it works at all. But you can't look away.

"It's a question of the spine," says Elena Fomina, a contortion teacher at the city's Ecole Nationale de Cirque–National Circus School. "When I look at the natural flexibility of a back, I can tell whether there is potential. You cannot make a normal person into a great contortionist." Contortionists, apparently, have to be born with elasticity.

Morning sunlight fills the gymnasium where what looks like a surrealist P.E. class is under way. A young woman leaps gracefully onto a narrow bar held at shoulder height by two muscular students. A comic juggler practices throwing himself, repeatedly, against the padded floor. In French with a Slavic lilt, Fomina tells me that before teaching, she toured the world as a member of a swinging-trapeze act.

So you can fly? I ask her. "Yes," she says matter-of-factly.

The National Circus School is housed in a modern steel-and-glass structure in an industrial part of Montreal. Next door sits the international headquarters of the world-famous Cirque du Soleil; beyond that lies a large arena that is home to other homegrown circus troupes. This ensemble, a complex called TOHU and known as "la cité des arts du cirque," is surprisingly vast for a place few would even imagine exists. A giant dream factory that covers nearly 475 acres, it is where every costume and prop for every Cirque du Soleil show is produced, and where future generations of gravity-defying, juggling, human-pretzel performers are learning new tricks.

This city within a city is a place that takes its playing seriously—which is true, too, of the larger metropolis enveloping it. We tourists tend to experience other people's cities as entertainments: three-ring diversions of eating, shopping, and sightseeing. But just as founder Guy Laliberté envisioned Cirque du Soleil as a theatrical show that didn't need a big top, Montreal is a place where the sense of play and originality is free-form and freewheeling. Low rents, a thriving creative class, lively outdoor cafés, and parks in every neighborhood: Enjoying yourself here is a form of collective street theater.

A francophone pocket on a generally English-speaking continent, an island that until recently was iced in every winter, Montreal also knows how to amuse itself with all kinds of festivals for all kinds of folks—jazz, indie, rock, film, art, dance, comedy. Ruby Roy, a knowledgeable local guide who is deeply in love with everything about Montreal except the winters, put it to me this way: "Our festivals are now international attractions, but we did not start them to attract outsiders. They really were for Montrealers—which is why they're all a little different." Note that this enthusiasm for the arts isn't an obsession with box-office takes. "This is a city where documentaries sell out," says Roy.

Like its circus performers, Montreal is imaginative, kinetic— and always part of the show.

And while it's a city where anyone who is asked will tell anyone who will listen that it never takes itself too seriously, there is also something sweetly sincere if not outright boastful about its encouragement of every niche hobby, pastime, and distraction. "Outside Argentina, no one tango dances more than we do," Roy says with civic pride. Take that Ottawa!

Back at the circus school, I ask Fomina if there is a Montreal style of contortion. Her face brightens. "Our style is more rhythmic and dynamic," she says, seeming to speak for all her fellow Montrealers, not only the supple-spined. "It doesn't just show what the body can do; it also shows emotions. It is artistic, expressionistic." The same can be said for this city that created and supported such an unusual industry: Like its circus performers, Montreal is imaginative, kinetic—and always part of the show.

I HAD ARRIVED somewhere between Montreal's summer, when it is an outdoor playland, and winter, when it tends toward tundra. The sky that greeted me was experimenting with different moods: iffy, then sunny, then wet. The locals were unfazed. Even on a gray day as seen from a taxi, the city is pleasant viewing. If, as the late urban theorist Jane Jacobs said, "new ideas require old buildings," the stone edifices of Old Montreal provide much to riff on: the rough-hewn fieldstones of French-built structures, the clean lines of the Brits' cut stones, the red sandstone used by the Scots. Up from the Old Port are buildings in art deco and Chicago styles, and elegant town houses with that Montreal curiosity, exterior rather than interior stairways winding up to the second floor, like urban kudzu. The Olympic Stadium is visible in the distance and the retro-futuristic cubist curiosity Habitat 67 rises across the St. Lawrence River. A pleasure here is that when you are in one neighborhood, you completely forget that an altogether different-looking spot lies just a few blocks away—like the renewable novelty of certain women who change hairstyles to become a completely different person.

Huge chunks of city space are given over to play—such as Parc Jean-Drapeau, which spreads over the islands of Notre-Dame and Sainte-Hélène, and offers inline skating along a race-car circuit and beach volleyball on Plage Jean-Drapeau. There is even a bit of rapids on the river, prompting the intrepid—or delusional—to bring surfboards. In another inspired bit of swords-into-plowshares repurposing, the city's first jail, under Jacques Cartier Bridge, was converted into a public wine cellar.

THE NIGHT I GOT TO TOWN, I went to see a local writer, Adam Gollner, at a café and performance space called Casa del Popolo on Boulevard St-Laurent. Gollner often writes about Montreal, but tonight he was giving a talk about his book *The Fruit Hunters*, on exotic fruits of the world and those who quest for them. Before passing around a giant coco-de-mer fruit from the Seychelles, Gollner talked about the roles of natural selection and human selection in the evolution of fruit. I found myself thinking about how cities, too, are the result of centuries of trial and self-selection. Why does Montreal become a city of the arts while Toronto becomes a hub of commerce? Partially it's circumstantial (it gets cold here; you better have a hobby come winter), eventually it's self-fulfilling (if you want to be in the circus, move to the city that has the top circus school). Later I

continues

asked Gollner why he thought the city was so conducive to the arts.

"The allure of Montreal is that it's the only place in the Western world where you can still be a bohemian," he said. "One of the ways the Québec region has traditionally defined itself is in opposition to things. We have that indie-rock resistance to big American corporate life, a resistance mirrored in the idea that this is a French province that has fought for separatism."

Added to this jumble is an English distaste for appearing to embrace success, along with what Gollner calls "the Nordic instinct to band together to fight the elements." The early settlers were "fat priests guzzling the best wine in the frozen hinterland. That was the Montreal dynamic from the beginning: Though you're in a strange place, you can still live well. You may be broke, radical, and a leftist separatist, but you'll still drink Poire William at the end of a feast and stomp on your hat, saying if we don't protect the French language, we're going to turn into Louisiana."

Barry Lazar, a local journalist and filmmaker who moderated Gollner's presentation, agrees there is some especially playful thing in the Montreal air. In his case that air for a while smelled heavily of smoked meat, when he was producing a documentary on Schwartz's Deli, the venerable "charcuterie Hébraïque" down Boulevard St-Laurent, where meats come in three degrees of fattiness and a frankfurter is considered a side dish. "Now I'm working on a film about a local hip-hop klezmer musician named SoCalled." It's common to have this kind of conversation in Montreal.

I caught a taxi in a misty drizzle and headed down to Au Pied de Cochon, a restaurant known for such rich dishes as foie-gras poutine, stuffed pig's feet, and tripe pizza—all of which should come with their own medical-alert bracelets—to meet up with Mike Boone, a salty veteran city columnist for the Montreal Gazette. Montreal, he tells me, tends to define itself in opposition to Toronto, a place that Boone derides with typical local chauvinism as "Cleveland with Medicare." But it is Montreal's own internal struggles and contradictions, he contends, that make it such a lively and accommodating place to live.

Accommodating, with one big exception.

"Hockey," Boone says. "Spoiled by 24 Stanley Cups, we demand perfection—or, at minimum, artistry. Hockey is the secular religion here, a passion that transcends linguistic, ethnic, demographic, and socioeconomic lines to unite all Montrealers."

THE NEXT DAY I walked down Rue de la Commune along the St. Lawrence River, where bikes for rent encourage you to strike out along miles of paths snaking over to Île Sainte-Hélène and Île Notre-Dame, and through the city itself. From this part of Old Montreal I made my way west toward the commercial center, passing Victoria Square, where a statue of that English queen (looking very trim and youthful) faces a flowery art moderne gate originally made for the Paris Métro, a gift from France. At least one percent of all new public construction budgets in Montreal must be spent on public art, so there is always much to look at—even when locals have fled the cold streets for the commercial catacombs below the city. And no building can be higher than the top line of the city's namesake summit, Mount Royal, which, with its park, is a communal as well as visual focal point of the city. Mount Royal Park was first landscaped by Frederick Law Olmsted, the designer of New York's Central Park, who saw here an opportunity to make the urban mountain a central part of the city's enjoyments.

The sun had come out. This being a city of whim and indulgence, what I wanted was to wander around at leisure, then sit in the sun, drink coffee, and chat. So I arranged to meet with Dennis Trudeau, a long-time television personality, cultural commentator, and all-around suave guy, at a cafe in the student area of St.-Denis. I took a long, looping route there, by way of the Mile End neighborhood, mostly so I could stop at Fairmount Bagels. Perhaps to offset a bitter winter, Montrealers prefer their bagels slightly sweet. Fairmount is known best for its classic small bagels, but it also makes a loony one called a "bozo," which is big, and twisted, and covered in sesame and poppy seeds. It took me most of my walk to finish it.

I found Trudeau waiting at a good seat out on the terrace. Montreal is frequently called the "Paris of North America," but Trudeau said Montreal should stand on its own strengths. "This is a city where you can do pretty much what you like, be it writing or painting or sculpture or inventing something different. It has attracted a lot of people for that reason. It's hard to go anywhere else in Canada after Montreal. Now when I visit other cities I find something missing. Nice, but no garlic, you know?"

Joie de vivre is another term that bugs Trudeau. But, he says, "it is absolutely true here. People like to have parties. In a sense, even Cirque du Soleil is a big party organizer. When I get together with my francophone friends, all we do is laugh. Now, when you get together with your anglophone friends, it might not be so... hilarious. ... " He let the thought trail off.

"Montreal's biggest problem," he resumed, "is that it's on the periphery. This is the last big city in eastern North America before the North Pole. When you're on the edge, and things contract toward the center, you feel it first. We're on the edge, and we're different."

We sipped our warm coffee in the nippy air. "In March, on sunny days, this cafe will be open," Trudeau said, admiringly. "You can have horrible weather here, but as soon as it is 45°F out, this is where Montrealers rush to. To the sunny side of the afternoon street!"

Londoners have their forbearance. New Yorkers, grit. Montrealers, it seems, have a way of finding the sunny side of the afternoon street. I thought again of the circus school, where I'd watched a boy walk lightly forward and backward across a taut wire. "I asked him to visualize it," the boy's teacher told me. Maybe that's what Montreal itself is: a balancing act, a communal decision to keep spirits aloft in spite of weather and other daily challenges. A communal decision to have fun in life. "If he can see it in his head, he can do it," the tightwire teacher had said. "If not, he will fall."

—Adam Sachs, **National Geographic Traveler, March 2009**

Ontario

During the seventeenth and eighteenth centuries, large numbers of immigrants moved into what was then called Upper Canada ("up" river from Quebéc), today's Southern Ontario. Many were former residents of the United States who were loyal to the King of England (Tories). They arrived because of the War of Independence. Other immigrants from the British Isles included Scots and Irish. The population grew rapidly, and Toronto became the largest city of the province. It is the largest metropolitan area in Canada today. The region between Hamilton and Oshawa (including Toronto) has a population of nearly 8 million (or is home to 1 out of every 4 Canadians). The name *Toronto* is from the native language of the Huron people and means "the gathering place." Toronto (Figure 11.6) is a prime example of the multicultural character of Canada's population, with approximately eighty different ethnic communities represented. Ontario remains the destination of the largest number of international tourists to Canada, and Toronto is the major destination city in all of Canada. Part of Toronto's attraction is its cultural diversity, including the largest Italian community outside of Italy. The cultural diversity is a major factor in explaining why Toronto has the highest proportion of non-Canadian tourists (49 percent) among its visitors of any city in Canada.

The population of stately Ontario is concentrated in the southeastern region of the province, located close to a number of U.S. cities that provide an abundance of visitors for short-term visits.

Figure 11.6 Skyline of Toronto, Ontario, Canada. © GeoStock/Getty Images.

Ottawa's selection as the capital of Canada in 1858 ultimately transformed the former mill town into an important capital city of the world. The city is situated on a bluff overlooking the Ottawa River. Tourism's importance in the economy of Ottawa is only exceeded by government's. Ottawa-Hull ranks fourth in number of visitors in Canada.

The heart of Ottawa are the Parliament Buildings on Parliament Hill. They are a massive group of great stone Gothic buildings with copper roofs and spires. This area not only offers the best view of the area, but features one of Canada's outstanding summer attractions, the Changing of the Guard.

Ottawa has many important museums, including the National Gallery, the Bytown Museum, illustrating the history of Ottawa; the Canadian Museum of Civilization; the Canadian Museum of Nature; the Canadian Ski Museum; the Canadian War Museum; the Lag Farm, a re-created farm of 1870; the Museum of Canadian Scouting; the National Aviation Museum; and the National Museum of Science and Technology.

The Rideau Canal in Ottawa, completed in 1832, is a commercial waterway and leisure center. In the wintertime it becomes a five-mile skating rink. Ottawa is the home of a number of festivals, notably the Canadian Tulip Festival in the spring and the Winterlude centered around the ice-bound Rideau Canal. Near Ottawa at Beachburg is the site of white-water rafting on the Ottawa River.

Toronto is one of the most ethnically diverse cities in Canada. It combines elements of the past with some of the most modern skyscraper landscapes of North America. The most outstanding tourist attraction is the world's tallest self-supporting structure, the CN Tower with the new Ripley's Aquarium at its base. In addition, the Metro Zoo, one of the finest in North America; winter sports; national museums and exhibits (including the Art Gallery of Toronto, the Ontario Science Centre, the Royal Ontario Museum, and the Hockey Hall of Fame); and a number of ethnic neighborhoods are important attractions in Toronto. A visitor can take an ethnic tour through the various ethnic neighborhoods: Chinatown; Greek stores and restaurants; Little Italy; and Portuguese fish markets. The St. Lawrence Hall, Mackenzie House, and Casa Loma, a castle built in 1911, are other important attractions.

The Roger's Center hosts major sporting events and is home to the Toronto Blue Jays. The Roger's Center was the world's first stadium with a fully retractable roof. It includes, in addition to a ball field and convention center, entertainment facilities such as movie theaters, health clubs, and restaurants.

Considerable effort has been made by Toronto citizens to develop a pleasing environment in an urban setting. Consequently, Toronto has a multitude of parks and wooded walks. The older buildings, such as the City Hall and Ontario Palace, blend in nicely with the modern buildings. Other important sites include the Air Canada Centre and Paramount Canada's Wonderland. Toronto is the home of one of the world's top film festivals, the Toronto International Film Festival (TIFF). Toronto also has other festivals in the summer, such as the Canadian National Exhibition and Caribana (the Caribbean festival). The Toronto theater is appealing with "Broadway" shows such as *The Lion King* and *Wicked*. Toronto has many theaters. The Four Seasons Centre houses the Canadian Opera Company and the National Ballet of Canada. Roy Thomson Hall houses the Toronto Symphony.

Southwest of Toronto is the center of British culture and popular attractions. Common British names such as Windsor, Stratford, Chatham, London, Woodstock, Brantford, and the River Avon are scattered throughout the region. At Stratford one of the best Shakespearean Festivals in North America is held each summer. The famed Niagara Falls lie at the eastern end of the Niagara Peninsula. Within the town of Niagara Falls sites include the Fallsview Casino; the Butterfly Conservatory; the Skylon Tower; Marineland; and the Scotia Bank Convention Centre. Twenty miles to the north, Niagara-on-the-Lake is one of the best preserved nineteenth-century towns in North America. It was originally named Newark and was the first capital of Upper Canada from 1791 to 1796. The Shaw Festival features plays by Bernard Shaw, from May to October. Between Niagara Falls and Niagara-on-the-Lake dozens of wineries have become popular tourist destinations.

The area between Toronto and Ottawa has many attractions including the long, narrow farms along the banks of the St. Lawrence; numerous provincial parks; white sand bluffs at Picton standing over 30 yards high; Upper Canada Village, an authentic re-creation of an 1867 pioneer village; and Old Fort Henry at Kingston, a dramatic nineteenth-century fort where military displays include the thunder of cannon fire.

Fort William in Thunder Bay is a re-creation of the pioneer heritage and life of the late eighteenth century. The Agawa Canyon provides a scenic trip departing from Sault Ste. Marie along mountain ledges, through dark forests, over rivers and gorges, across a trestle bridge, and into fjord-like ravines. There is an underground tour of the old nickel mine in Sudbury. Historical sites of Sainte-Marie among the Hurons and the Huron Indian Village present a reconstructed sixteenth-century French mission and native community complete with longhouses and timber palisades. Across the road from this site is the Martyrs Shrine where martyred Jesuit missionaries are remembered. Northern Ontario is a rocky area dotted with over 250,000 lakes and has abundant forests and minerals. Outdoor enthusiasts will revel in the provinces recreational resources. Ontario has over 250 provincial parks. In Quetico Provincial Park, near Thunder Bay, visitors can see Kakabeka Falls and Quimet Canyon. Temagami is a canoeist's paradise with 8,000 square kilometers of interconnecting water routes; hikers will be lured by Ontario's mighty Algonquin Provincial Park, just three hours north of Toronto.

Area	1,076,395 sq km (415,598 sq mi)
Population	13,069,000
Capital	Toronto 2,503,000
GDP per Cap	$42,900
Agriculture	dairy products; cattle, hogs; feed crops, nursery stock, fruits
Industry	automobile manufacturing, telecommunications equipment, tourism

From *National Geographic Atlas of the World*, 9th edition. Copyright ©2011 National Geographic Society. Reprinted by arrangement. All rights reserved.

Manitoba

Manitoba does not have a tourism industry comparable to that of Ontario and Québec. It was not settled until late in the 1800s. The major groups were Mennonite settlers from Czarist Ukraine, French Canadians from New England, English, Scots, and Irish. Winnipeg's favorable location on newly constructed rail lines brought additional immigrants to settle and work the land. More recent immigrants of Asian and Caribbean ancestry have added to the ethnic diversity of the region. Although it is a prairie province, its terrain is varied—from the tundra and boreal forest of the north to the rolling, wooded parkland of the central region and the grain-rich plains of the south. Golden fields of wheat blend into a never ending horizon. Manitoba is dotted with thousands of lakes, the largest of which, Lake Winnipeg, ranks fourteenth in size in the world. Buffalo can be seen

on the prairies and outdoor recreational opportunities abound throughout the province.

Winnipeg, the capital of Manitoba, contains more than half of the population of the province. It is Manitoba's largest tourist destination, with its government buildings and Royal Canadian Mint. The Museum of Man and Nature in Winnipeg includes an exhibit of a full-scale replica of the Nonesuch, the first ship to bring furs from the New World to Europe. The Winnipeg Art Gallery has one of the world's finest collections of Inuit art. The Folklorama in Winnipeg is a major festival at which some forty pavilions illustrate Winnipeg's various ethnic groups with food, dance, and entertainment. The French quarter is the largest Francophone community west of Québec.

Outside of Winnipeg are other areas of interest, including Lower Fort Gary National Historical Park (the restored Hudson Bay Company supply center that dates back to the 1830s). Far to the north is Churchill, Manitoba's northernmost settlement, on the shores of Hudson

Bay. Churchill is a tourist center for observing the polar bear migration, the beluga whale, and the northern lights. Also in Churchill, the Eskimo Museum takes visitors back to 1400 B.C. with a collection of local ancient artifacts. Outdoor recreational opportunities abound. They range from an overnight camping experience at Anishinable Camp in Riding Mountain National Park to a visit to the sandy shores of Hecla Provincial Park on Lake Winnipeg. There are more than 200 lakes in Manitoba's Whiteshell Provincial Park.

Area	647,797 sq km (250,116 sq mi)
Population	1,222,000
Capital	Winnipeg 633,000
GDP per Cap	$35,600
Agriculture	canola, wheat, potatoes, oats, flaxseed; hogs, beef cattle; dairy
Industry	food processing, transportation equipment, nickel mining, tourism

From *National Geographic Atlas of the World*, 9th edition. Copyright ©2011 National Geographic Society. Reprinted by arrangement. All rights reserved.

Saskatchewan

The development of the railroads in the late 1800s brought more and more settlers, largely second-generation immigrants, to the region in search of farming opportunities. The migrants created the rolling wheat fields of Saskatchewan, the bread basket of Canada.

The two leading tourist destinations are Regina and Saskatoon. At Regina, the capital of Saskatchewan (named after Queen Victoria), the Royal Canadian Mounted Police have a training center and museum. The museum displays old equipment, weapons, uniforms, and photos documenting history of the Royal Canadian Mounted Police. The farming industry is represented in the Western Development Museum, with its pioneer machinery, vintage cars, and indoor prairie village. One of the newest attractions in Regina is the Science Center with exhibits on the human body, the living planet, astronomy, and geology. Downtown, visitor attention is drawn to Wascana Centre, a 2,300-acre park attracting runners, cyclists, and picnickers. It is one of the largest urban parks in North America and home to the campus of the University of Regina.

The Mendel Art gallery in Saskatoon has works by Chagall, Picasso, and Lawrence Harris. Sask Place, located near the Saskatoon Airport, is one of Canada's busiest indoor arenas and hosts numerous world-class events. The only national park in Saskatchewan is the 1 million acres Prince Albert National Park, which is known for its lakes and fishing. There are a number of historical parks and Saskatchewan's famous Big Muddy Badlands.

Area	651,036 sq km (251,366 sq mi)
Population	1,030,000
Capital	Regina 179,000
GDP per Cap	$42,700
Agriculture	wheat, canola, barley; cattle
Industry	service industries, petroleum and natural gas production, mining of potash and uranium

From *National Geographic Atlas of the World*, 9th edition. Copyright ©2011 National Geographic Society. Reprinted by arrangement. All rights reserved.

Alberta

Alberta is the richest province in Canada and has a variety of spectacular scenery, from the flatlands of the east to the Rocky Mountains in the west. It is a showcase of the splendors of the Rockies. The two most famous attractions in Alberta are Banff and Jasper National Parks. Both are well known for their outstanding scenery, with hot springs and ice fields. The most famous of the latter is the Columbia ice field, which is the largest permanent body of ice between the Arctic and Antarctic. Spectacular Fairmont Chateau Lake Louise offers breathtaking views of Lake Louise. Between Lake Louise (Figure 11.7) and Jasper is one of the most scenic drives in Canada (the Icefields Parkway). Snow-capped peaks, wildlife, Peyto Lake, and the Athabasca Glacier are a few of the attractions along the trail. Two other attractive national parks in Alberta are Waterton Lakes and Wood Buffalo.

The two main destination cities of Alberta are Edmonton and Calgary. Edmonton ranks third in visitors for all Canadian cities. The big events in Edmonton are the annual 10-day Klondike Days, and the Edmonton International Fringe Theatre Festival in August. The West Edmonton Mall is one of the world's largest shopping malls. The Water Park, located inside the mall, is the length of five football fields and offers water skiing and body surfing on artificial waves. A roller coaster inside the Mall is twelve stories high. The Edmonton Space Sciences Center is Canada's largest planetarium, featuring an IMAX theater, observatory, and science exhibits. Syncrude Gallery displays artifacts associated with the area's rich Aboriginal culture. Historic Fort Edmonton Park includes villages depicting Edmonton in 1885, 1905, and 1920 plus a replica of a fur-trading post.

Calgary, the gateway to the Rocky Mountains, ranks fifth in visitors for Canadian cities. Two popular sites in Calgary are Heritage Park and the Calgary Tower. Heritage Park is a 66-acre park depicting a prairie railroad town

Figure 11.7 Lake Louise in the Canadian Rockies. © karamysh/www.Shutterstock.com.

Wood Buffalo largest national park.

with over 100 exhibits, including operative steam trains and a paddlewheel boat. Calgary Tower provides a view of the city and surrounding area from either an observation terrace or the revolving restaurant. The Calgary Zoo, the second largest in Canada with over 1,400 animals and birds, also features a Prehistoric Park with many life-size replicas of ancient dinosaurs. The most famous attraction for visitors is the Calgary Stampede, the greatest outdoor show on earth, every July. Just west of Calgary is Canada Olympic Park, which was the site of the luge and bobsled events during the Olympic Winter Games of 1988.

An hour and a half's drive northeast of Calgary is a dinosaur land in the Red Deer River Valley. The Dinosaur Trail includes the Royal Tyrell Museum of Paleontology at Drumheller. The Drumheller Dinosaur and Fossil Museum features exhibits that explain the occupancy of the inland sea, petrified forests, coal formation, processes of fossilization, and many varieties of dinosaur remains found in the area. It is the world's largest display of dinosaur specimens.

Area	661,848 sq km (255,541 sq mi)
Population	3,688,000
Capital	Edmonton 730,000
GDP per Cap	$66,300
Agriculture	cattle; wheat, canola, barley; timber
Industry	petroleum and natural gas production, chemical manufacturing, tourism.

From *National Geographic Atlas of the World*, 9th edition. Copyright ©2011 National Geographic Society. Reprinted by arrangement. All rights reserved.

British Columbia

top 3 for Tourism

The combination of the Pacific Ocean, beautiful wooded mountains, and a west coast marine climate makes British Columbia an outstanding destination for tourists. Culturally, its residents were mostly English with small groups of Russian, German, Japanese, and Chinese. The more recent heavy migration from Asia, particularly of Chinese, has created a new ethnic mix. British Columbia has nearly 17,000 miles of beautiful fjord-like coastlines, inland lakes, emerald forests of Douglas fir, and great rivers that breed more salmon than any place in the world. Coastal communities are connected with a ferry system that links Vancouver with Alaska (the Inside Passage). Both Vancouver Island and the entire region have wild and beautiful natural settings that do not fail to impress visitors. Settings for a variety of water sports are available, from well-kept, long, sandy beaches to fishing for salmon in the bays and fast-running rivers. Beautiful gardens and parks abound throughout the region. A short distance from the city of Vancouver is Vancouver Island and the

Ever in the mainland's shadow, **Vancouver Island** is now taking center stage in the slow food rediscovery of its seafood and farmland bounty. Pack those roomy pants and base yourself at Spinnakers, a Victoria brew pub with three guesthouses directly across the street. Expect to be tempted by the pub's hoppy Nut Brown Ale and hearty fare, but tear yourself away for an epicurious exploration of verdant Cowichan Valley. This Provence-like landscape of rolling hills and tree-shaded roads is studded with signs pointing to foodie pit stops: Cowichan Bay Farm for duck confit,

Organic Fair Farm's homemade chocolate bars, Venturi-Schulze Vineyards for balsamic vinegars and sparkling wines.

While wineries are de rigueur here, Cobble Hill's Merridale Estate Cidery is a must. Local apples are pressed into service to create eight varieties, including eye-popping Scrumpy and oak-aged Cidre Normandie. Sip some with brick-fired pizza on the orchard-view deck.

"The quality of food and drink here is outstanding," says Alison Philip of Damali Lavender Farm, a magnet for culinary travelers, many of whom find their way to

Amusé Bistro. Rhode Island–born Bradford Boisvert is the chef at this tiny, French-influenced Shawnigan Lake restaurant, which turns out meals that rival the fare at top city eateries. Dedicated to regional ingredients (leaves for the nettle bisque grow out back), he uses forest-foraged morels, Pender Island scallops, and Cowichan Valley lamb. "I love the challenge of not knowing what's going to be available on a daily basis. It makes every menu I create an adventure," says Boisvert.

—John Lee, *National Geographic Traveler*, **April 2009**

---

provincial capital Victoria which is a major destination for visitors. Vancouver Island also includes the world-famous Butchart Sunken Garden and the Pacific Rim National Park. Thunderbird Park contains a collection of nineteenth-century totem poles. Victoria claims to be more British than England, complete with big red double-decker buses. The center of historic buildings is the inner harbor with the Royal British Columbia Museum and Victorian-era Parliament Buildings, beautifully outlined at night with thousands of sparkling lights. The western coastline of Vancouver Island permits the watching of hundreds of migrating great gray whales and orca whales.

Vancouver is a new city with modern architecture and the second largest Chinatown in North America. The University of British Columbia's Museum of Anthropology contains exceptional Northwest Indian art, including totem poles, ceremonial objects and other artifacts. The historic Gastown area was the original settlement and has buildings dating back to the 1800s. The thousand-acre Stanley Park (with the Vancouver Aquarium) borders the sea and provides a dazzling view of the city, port, and north-shore mountains. Just two hours north of Vancouver is the famous ski resort Whistler/Blackcomb

which has emerged as one of North America's prime ski resorts and was host to the 2010 Winter Olympics.

The interior of the province through the Caribou-Chilcotin range offers exciting views of deep canyons, impressive mountains, and the Indian villages of Ksan, Kispiox, Kitwanga, and Kitwancool with their totem poles.

The various areas of British Columbia also have tourist attractions related to the history and culture of the province. The Fort St. James National Historical Park illustrates the fur trade era of the 1880s in the Northwestern region. The Bakerville Historic Town takes visitors back to the gold rush dates of the 1860s and 1870s.

Area	944,735 sq km (364,764 sq mi)
Population	4,455,000
Capital	Victoria 78,000
GDP per Cap	$39,500
Agriculture	nursery stock and ornamental flowers; dairy products; salmon
Industry	wood and paper products, food processing, refined-fuel products, tourism

---

Northwest Territories

The Northwest Territories span four time zones with a population of only 42,000 people. The environment is important to the region for ecotourism and preservation. Four rivers are part of the Canadian Heritage River System, and four national parks (of which two are

UNESCO World Heritage Sites) serve as examples of the region's commitment to preservation.

Tourism is important to this sparsely populated north land, home to the Inuit and Dene Indians. Total numbers of tourists are low, however, due to the isolation of the region. The land of the midnight sun, with its short summer and beautiful, picturesque flowers, has tremendous fishing opportunities. The primitive nature of the area is a unique attraction in itself. Opportunities abound to watch all types of creatures in their natural habitats (Figure 11.9).

Sometimes you can see both the forest and the trees. The Great Bear Rainforest (Figure 11.8), the planet's largest intact coastal temperate rain forest, is an untamed strip of land stretching 250 miles along British Columbia's coast that harbors extensive tracts of giant hemlock, Sitka spruce, and red cedar. The mighty trees rise high above a moist and ferny forest floor patrolled by coastal wolves, minks, Canada's largest grizzly bears, and rare white Kermode spirit bears.

This tranquility has recently been rocked by a proposal to send tar sands crude oil from Alberta to a terminal at Kitimat in the Great Bear Rainforest. The project would entail two pipelines crossing some of the world's largest salmon-producing watersheds and a steady procession of supertankers plying the narrow channels. The local First Nations and environmental groups are vehemently opposed, fearing the catastrophic effects of an *Exxon*

Figure 11.8 The Great Bear Rainforest. © Paul Nicklen/National Geographic Creative

Valdez–type spill. "This is a wilderness sanctuary, a very spiritual place," says Ian McAllister, founding director of Pacific Wild. "The pipelines would fundamentally alter the coast forever." A decision on the pipelines could come by the end of 2013.

—**Robert Earle Howells,** *National Geographic Traveler*, December 2012/January 2013

Figure 11.9 Buffalo grazing in Northwest Territories. © Danny Xu/www.Shutterstock.com.

Visitors can observe great gatherings of sea mammals (beluga and bowhead whales, narwhals and tusked walruses, ringed and bearded seals) and land mammals (moose, mountain sheep, bearded muskoxen, grizzly bears, and polar bears).

From May through July the sun never sets. Golfers can tee off at midnight, which they do at the Western Midnight Sun Golf Tournament at Yellowknife. It is an outdoor wonderland for active people. A visitor can hike the boreal forest in search of nesting birds and hardy wildflowers or rigorously climb amid the rock spires of Baffin Island's Auyuittuq National Park. Visitors may canoe or raft through the legendary Nahanni River and view the magnificent Virginia Falls (which are twice as high as Niagara Falls). Other attractions include fishing for fat Arctic char, kayaking the ice-floe edge where seals play, driving a dog team, hunting for polar bear using dog teams, or camping in igloos or tents on ice floes. Cultural attractions include meeting various native people and going to museums such as the Prince of Wales Northern Heritage Center, which traces the history of the Northwest Territories. Native artifacts, crafts, and paintings are also displayed in the Center. In the past decade, ecotourism to the Northern Rivers, exploration of the Arctic, Inuit village stays, whale watching, seal flow observations, and sea kayaking have become more popular.

Area	1,346,106 sq km (519,734 sq mi)
Population	43,000
Capital	Yellowknife 19,000
GDP per Cap	$95,000
Agriculture	NA
Industry	diamond mining, gold mining, oil and natural gas production

From *National Geographic Atlas of the World*, 9th edition. Copyright ©2011 National Geographic Society. Reprinted by arrangement. All rights reserved.

Yukon Territory

Many visitors combine travel to Alaska with visits to the Yukon, making tourism an important part of the economy. Many cruise ships and Alaskan ferries stop at Skagway, where passengers can take the train or motorcoach to Whitehorse over the historic White Pass on the Klondike Highway. Many visit Dawson from Alaska itself; thus, Dawson and Whitehorse are two heavily visited cities. Booming centers in gold rush days, both are now important tourist centers. Dawson City has a gambling casino, and there are many reminders of the glory days of the gold rush. Diamond Tooth Gertie's and the Palace Grand Theater/Gaslight Follies provide gold rush–era entertainment.

Whitehorse is another city re-creating the gold rush days, with the Frantic Follies Vaudeville Revue and the MacBride Museum. It also includes the important Yukon Gardens, Canada's only northern botanical gardens. Here, flora and vegetation of the territory and the Old Log Church Museum are found. Hikers who wish to re-create the gold rush era can follow the "Trail of '98," the Chilkoot Trail from Skagway, Alaska, to Bennet Lake. Mount Logan (19,524 ft), Canada's highest mountain is located in Kluane National Park.

Area	482,443 sq km (186,272 sq mi)
Population	34,000
Capital	Whitehorse 20,000
GDP per Cap	$49,100
Agriculture	greenhouse vegetables; hunting, fur trade; fishing
Industry	mining of metal ores, lumber, tourism

From *National Geographic Atlas of the World*, 9th edition. Copyright ©2011 National Geographic Society. Reprinted by arrangement. All rights reserved.

Nunavut Territory

In the Far North of Canada flanking Hudson's Bay and including the Arctic islands of Canada is the newest political unit in North America—the territory of Nunavut. It was established in 1993 in recognition of the degree of autonomy for the indigenous people of the region. Occupying one-fifth of the total territory of Canada, this new territory is inhabited by only 32,000 people. Nunavut has three official languages: Inuktitut, English, and French. In the native language the name of the territory means "our land." Major settlements like the capital, Iqaluit, have only a few thousand inhabitants. Most of the people of the territory are Inuit, descendants of Canada's First Nations, the Native Americans occupying North America when the first European explorers and colonists arrived. The majority of the residents of Nunavut still rely on traditional economic activities such as hunting and fishing for their livelihood. Because much of the territory lies north of the Arctic Circle, summers are short but with little or no darkness, while winters are long and dark.

Tourism attractions in Nunavut are primarily classified as adventure or wilderness tourism. There are no roads connecting the territory with the rest of Canada, and tourists must fly into the capital Iqaluit and transfer to boats or small planes to visit even more remote areas.

Figure 11.10 Inuit inukshuk in a fjord of Baffin Island, Nunavut, Canada. © City Escapes Nature Photography/www.Shutterstock.com.

Attractions include the Nunatta Sunakkutaangit Museum in Iqaluit, which contains historical Inuit artifacts, tools, and clothing; hiking, camping, hunting (with cameras or weapons), and fishing; and a variety of national parks and wilderness attractions. Significant national parks are found on Baffin Island (Auyuittuq, Sirmilk) and Ellesmere Islands to the north, which have beautiful mountain scenery, glaciers, fjords, and rushing streams that provide fishing and camping for the few visitors (Figure 11.10).

Area	2,093,190 sq km (808,185 sq mi)
Population	32,000
Capital	Iqaluit 6,000
GDP per Cap	$36,700
Agriculture	NA
Industry	government and education services; mining of zinc, gold, and lead; fishing, trapping

From *National Geographic Atlas of the World*, 9th edition. Copyright ©2011 National Geographic Society. Reprinted by arrangement. All rights reserved.

REVIEW QUESTIONS

1. Differentiate between a *province* and a *territory*.

2. What is Canada's major tourism market? Why?

3. Which region outside of North America is the most important source of international tourists to Canada? Why?

4. Identify the key attractions of Canada's Maritime Provinces.

5. Describe and discuss the general divisions of tourism attractions in Canada.

part 4: GEOGRAPHY AND TOURISM IN MEXICO AND CENTRAL AMERICA

een/National Geographic Creative

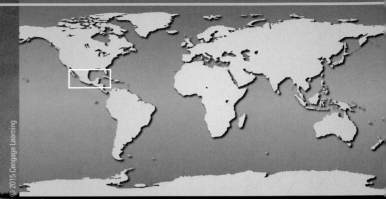

MAJOR GEOGRAPHIC CHARACTERISTICS

- Diverse physical and cultural environment
- Accessible to major markets in North America
- Important colonial influence on the region
- Continued dependency upon plantation agriculture
- Distinct climate zones that reflect topography
- Marked contrasts between rich and poor

MAJOR TOURISM CHARACTERISTICS

- The region includes major archaeological sites of early American civilizations.
- This is emerging as a major cruise region of the world.
- Lengths of visits vary from one week (resort based tourism) to one day (cruise visit).

MAJOR TOURIST DESTINATIONS

- Capital cities of each country
- Colonial towns
- Archaeological sites in Mexico, Guatemala, Honduras
- Beach resort towns of Cancún, Mazatlán, Acapulco, Ixtapa, Puerto Vallarta
- Border towns on the United States–Mexico border

KEY TERMS AND WORDS

Arawaks	Ibero-European
Barrios	Maquiladoras
Border Towns	Mayan World Circuit
Calderas	Mestizos
Cathedrals	Middle America
Central America	NAFTA
Cinder Cones	Pyramids
Colonial Territories	Rain Forest
Cruise Ships	Sinkhole
Hurricanes	

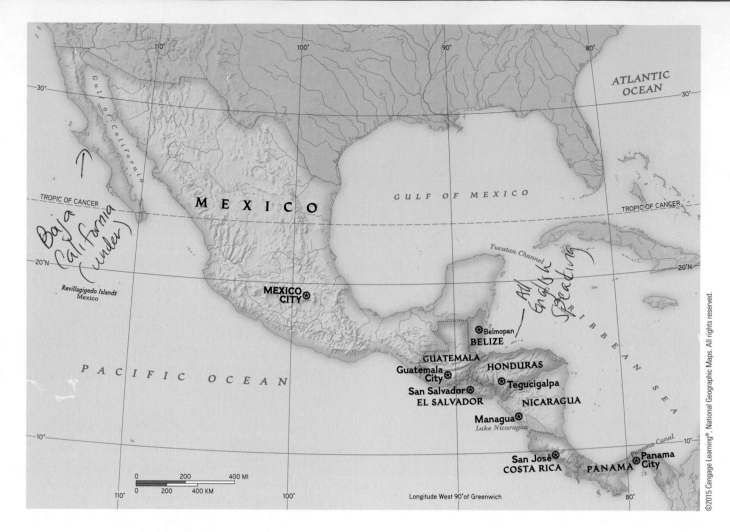

Introduction

Mexico and Central America are some of the world's most important tourism destinations. The proximity of the region to the two major industrial countries of North America—the United States and Canada—as well as historic colonial ties with Europe, are major factors in the region's ability to attract a high number of visitors. The continued growth in the region is due to its mild climate, clear blue waters, and cultural attractions. Mexico and Central America are in some ways similar to the Caribbean but their respective tourist industries differ markedly in size and income generated. Factors such as location, political stability, and concern for personal safety help explain these differences.

The region consists of the countries from Mexico to Panama, typically being referred to as Mexico and Central America. In many regional geographical references, however, Mexico is included as part of North America; but in others it is included in a region called **Middle America** with the countries from Guatemala to Panama. In this text we will refer to all of the continental countries from the United States border to South America as Mexico and Central America to make it clear Mexico is included.

Mexico and Central America were among the first areas where the Spanish imposed their colonial rule and began the process of developing an exploitative economy. There are major differences in the countries of the region, particularly between Mexico and the other seven countries.

Mexico is the third largest independent state in Latin America and has the second largest population. It receives more tourists than any other country or island in the region and is one of the major generators of tourism receipts. Geographically, Mexico is complex, ranging from the arid and semiarid north to the moderate highland climates of central Mexico (where the majority of the population live) to the tropical southern and eastern lowlands. More than one-half of the population is concentrated in the valleys and basins of central Mexico, particularly around Mexico City proper.

The poorest Mexicans are those who are classified as Indian, not necessarily according to their ethnic background, but according to their culture. Indians speak a native language (even though they may also speak Spanish), emphasize Indian rather than European customs, and are primarily involved in agriculture.

Approximately 10 percent of Mexicans remain illiterate, and nearly one-third live in poverty. In rural areas, Indians practice their traditional agriculture on even the steepest slopes in the highland valleys. Production of corn, beans, squash, and other traditional crops remains important for this sector of the agricultural economy.

In the cities, major industries include textiles, steel, automobiles, electrical products, and food processing. The dominant manufacturing center is the Valley of Mexico, where more than 75 percent of the country's industry is concentrated. In the past few years border towns have become the focal point for industries and rapid population growth. Through trade agreements with the United States a large number of assembly plants have located along the border. Imports from these plants (known as maquiladoras) have lower tariffs on their exports to the United States.

Mexico joined the United States and Canada in an economic union called the North American Free Trade Association (**NAFTA**) in the early 1990s. NAFTA has resulted in increased economic growth in Mexico and greater movement of Mexicans to the United States and vice versa.

The concentration of industrial activity in the Valley of Mexico and along the United States border has created urban problems on a scale rivaled in only one or two other cities of the world. Mexico City is one of the world's largest cities, with over 21 million people in the metropolitan area. Urban problems range from lack of housing and jobs to massive air pollution and vast slum areas (**barrios**) inhabited by migrants from rural areas. Mexico has significant oil reserves, but its tourism industry has developed to such a level that tourism ranks second to oil as a major earner of income for the country.

The seven countries of Central America consist of the nations of Guatemala, Belize, El Salvador, Honduras, Nicaragua, Costa Rica, and Panama. This region is the least traveled part of Mexico, Central America, and the Caribbean. In part this results from political instability and conflict such as that in El Salvador, Nicaragua, and Guatemala in the 1980s and 1990s. Even the stable countries of the region were often perceived as unsafe by potential tourists because of past violence in the others. Although the region was more peaceful after 2000, **hurricanes** frequently pose a threat to the tourism infrastructure of the countries in the region.

The seven countries of Central America have many similarities. Their physical geography is dominated by complex mountain systems. The mountains include spectacular volcanic mountains with **cinder cones**, **calderas**, and other volcanic features (Figure P4.1), and sedimentary mountains composed primarily of limestone. The climate is generally tropical or subtropical and is characterized by heavy rains during the hot summers and by decreased rainfall in the winter. But there is no truly dry season anywhere in the region. These seven countries typify the less industrialized regions of Latin America, relying on a few exports, with high

Figure P4.1 Active volcano Arenal in Costa Rica.
© Henner Damke/www.Shutterstock.com.

illiteracy rates and great disparities between rich and poor. The economies of all these countries rely heavily on tropical agricultural exports, especially bananas and coffee, but they also have been based largely on foreign capital. In general, these countries lack good communication systems, capital for investments to develop more rapidly, and political stability.

Climate Characteristics

The diversity of the climate in Central America and Mexico results from latitudinal location, altitude influence, and land-water relationships. Northern Mexico's climate is controlled by its mid-latitude location, which combines with the high plateau to create an arid environment on the plateau and the western coastal areas of Mexico. The southern two-thirds of Mexico is influenced by tropical location and altitude. Altitude affects climate in the same ways latitude does. An increase in elevation is associated with cooler temperatures. Increased elevation creates altitudinal zones of climate in the mountainous areas of the region. There are three major climate zones recognized in this region. The *tierra caliente*, or hot land, is the lowest zone, extending up to approximately 3,000 feet (900 meters). This has all the characteristics of a tropical rain forest climate, and population densities are low. The economy is based on plantation agriculture, bananas, sugar cane, rice, cocoa, and nutmeg for export. The second zone is the *tierra templada*, or temperate land. This zone has a cooler climate with conditions similar to the humid subtropical climates. The Europeans settled here. A major activity is coffee production. The

Figure P4.2 Maya Pyramid of the Magician, Adivino. Uxmal, Merida, Yucatan, Mexico. © f9photos/www.Shutterstock.com.

third zone, the *tierra fria*, or cold climate, is above about 6,000 feet. It is the home of much of the Indian population of Central America, who practice a subsistence agriculture with corn, squash, and small grains as dominant crops. The largest concentration of *tierra fria* in the region is in Mexico and Guatemala, which are among the most densely populated areas of Middle America.

The eastern shores of Central America and Mexico are influenced by the warm currents of the Caribbean Sea and the Gulf of Mexico, creating either a humid subtropical climate along the east coast of Mexico or a true tropical climate southward into South America. Many of the popular tourist locations such as the Yucatán are in an area of tropical savanna, or tropical monsoon-type climate with tropical hurricanes from July through October. The hurricanes in both these locations and the Caribbean make tourism to both regions highly seasonal. During the hurricane season, tourism is dramatically reduced. Hurricanes can result in significant damage to the tourist infrastructure, affecting visitation for years afterward. Warm ocean currents also affect the western coasts of much of Central America and southern Mexico. However, northern Mexico's west coast is affected by the cold water of the California current,

which brings cool, pleasant, year-round temperatures along the coast.

Cultural Characteristics

The cultures of the region, like the physical characteristics, are diverse. Mexico and the other countries of Central America include a variety of ethnic, social, political, and economic patterns unmatched in the world in an area of comparable size. There are two major languages—Spanish and English—plus numerous Indian tongues. Within these languages, there are a number of complex, local dialects.

The region was an Indian world before the arrival of the Europeans and Africans. The Southern Central Plateau of Mexico, the Yucatán, and the highlands and coastal lowlands of Central America were inhabited by technologically advanced Indians with high population densities, large cities, and an intensive agricultural base. The remnants of these early civilizations, the Mayas of Guatemala and Yucatán and the Aztecs of Central Mexico, have become centers of attraction for a modern tourism industry (Figure P4.2). In the Caribbean and the arid portions of Mexico, the Indian population was smaller and less technologically advanced. The Caribs and **Arawaks**, both originally from South America, settled in the Caribbean. They practiced primitive agricultural techniques, hunted, and fished. The Carib, the more warlike and primitive of the two, reportedly practiced cannibalism and relied more on food gathering, hunting, and fishing than agriculture.

The conquest and settlement of Middle America and the Caribbean by the Europeans after the voyage of Columbus changed the map. The Spanish, English, French, Dutch, Danes, Portuguese, and eventually Americans contributed to the present ethnic makeup of the region. Spain was by far the most dominant force in Mexico and Central America, imposing its language, religion, and customs upon the new colonial empire. Colonial activity by English, French, Dutch, and Danes added to the European impact in the Caribbean. Wars and battles changed some of the **colonial territories**. Jamaica, for example, was seized from the Spanish by the British. The French gained possession of Haiti, and the French, Dutch, and Danes obtained the various islands of the Lesser Antilles. Plantation crops were introduced, requiring additional African slaves, and Africans soon outnumbered their European masters by a wide margin. Indians from India were later imported to some Caribbean islands, further complicating the cultural ways. All of the groups interacted with one another to a greater or lesser extent, creating cultural groups distinct from European, African, Indian, or Asian. The present cultural landscape can be divided into Euro-African, Euro-Asian, Euro-Indian, and Mestizo groups.

Descendants of African, European-African, or Indian-African intermarriages are concentrated in the coastal lowlands of Central America (where plantation agriculture was practiced), Cuba, Puerto Rico, the Dominican Republic, Haiti, the Netherlands Antilles, British West Indies, Martinique, Guadeloupe, St. Lucia, and Grenada. The appearance of each of these groups varies, reflecting intermarriage with specific groups (such as the French in Haiti, the Spanish in Puerto Rico or Cuba) or specific North European groups (as in British West Indies or the Netherlands Antilles). In each country, there is generally a group that classifies itself as of "pure" European ancestry, but they often reflect only the group with the greatest social or economic prestige rather than a distinct ethnic origin.

The mainland areas of Mexico and Central America are generally inhabited by descendants of Indians and Europeans. Indian influence is most dominant in the southern basins of Mexico, the Yucatán Peninsula, southern Mexico's highlands and Guatemala, and western Honduras and western Nicaragua. Descendants of intermarriage between Europeans and Indian (mestizos) dominate in Central Mexico, El Salvador, Honduras, Nicaragua, and Panama. Europeans are concentrated in Costa Rica and northern Mexico, although each area

has representatives of all three groups. Asians (Indians from India primarily) are found in Antigua, Jamaica, and Trinidad and Tobago, which have the largest concentration of East Asians.

Thus, the cultural groups in Middle America include the remnants of the original Indian inhabitants, the descendants of mixed marriages between Indians and Europeans (mestizos), the black population descended from slaves in the Caribbean or European-African intermixing, and descendants of mixtures of European-Mestizo-African combinations.

Tourism Characteristics

Tourism to the region is dominated by Mexico (Figure P4.3), largely because of its proximity to Canada and the United States. Distances, intervening opportunities represented by Mexico (and the Caribbean), and political conditions in the region south of Mexico have led to a smaller travel industry in that region. Mexico and the Caribbean compete with Hawaii for the same market. The average length of stay in Mexico is nine days per visitor.

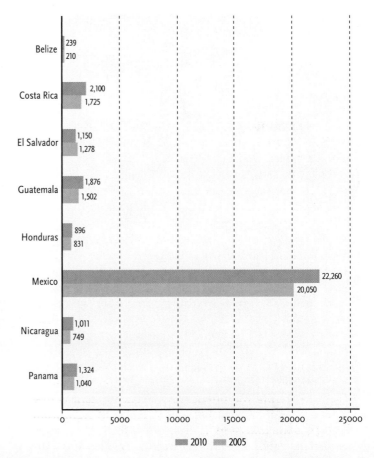

Figure P4.3 International Tourism to Middle America (000) 2005–2010.

Source: *The World Bank: The Data Catalogue.* Figure copyright ©2015 Cengage Learning®. All rights reserved.

chapter 12: MEXICO AND CENTRAL AMERICA

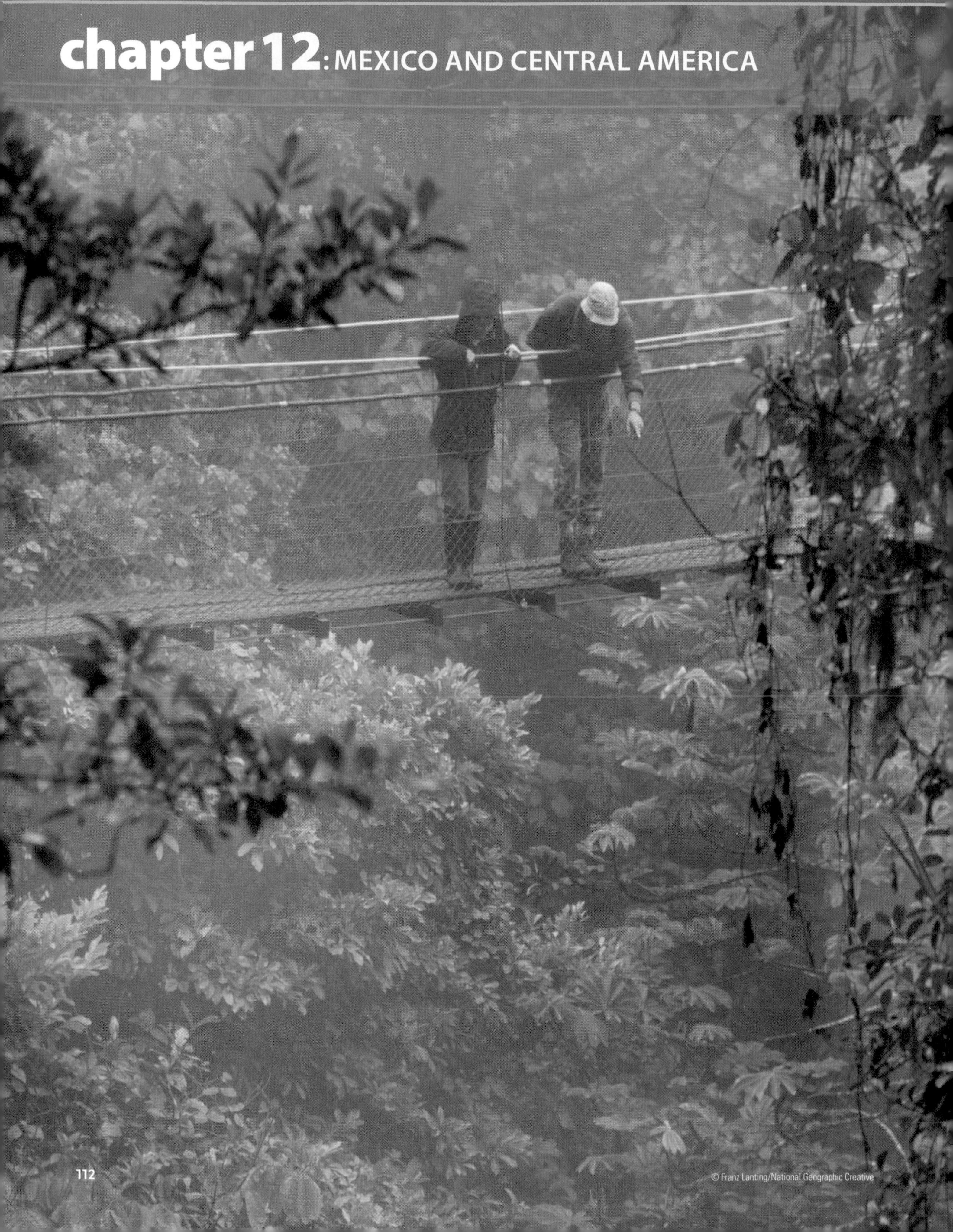

Mexico

Introduction

A large part of Mexico is high plateau flanked by mountain ranges to the east and west. In the southeast lies the Yucatán Peninsula, an extensive limestone plain that is only slightly above sea level. The climate depends on latitude and altitude: lowlands are hot and humid; the high plateau is cooler in summer and cold in winter; the north is arid; and the southern coastal regions get the most rainfall. Situated atop three tectonic plates, Mexico experiences frequent earthquakes and volcanic activity. Mexico is the world's most populous Spanish-speaking country, and the population is heterogeneous and multicultural. Mexicans are highly urbanized and most reside within the densely populated central plateau region, or "waist," of the country, including the cities of Veracruz, Mexico City, and Guadalajara. The majority of Mexicans are of mixed Spanish and Indian descent, but there are also fifty-six indigenous groups recognized by the government, totaling some 12 million people. Indigenous Indian languages are still spoken; the most popular are Nahuatl (language of the Aztec Empire), with 1.5 million speakers, and Mayan, with 1.2 million speakers. Many of the indigenous languages are in decline, and UNESCO lists 143 as endangered. Mexico declared independence from Spain in 1810 and went through a series of autocratic governments before the 1910–17 Mexican Revolution. The 1917 constitution made Mexico a federal democracy (like the United States). Mexico has evolved into a highly industrialized economy and is a major oil producer. It has free trade agreements with more than forty countries, including the United States. Mexico is highly dependent on U.S. trade, sending 80 percent of its exports to the United States. Also, millions of American tourists visit Mexico each year. An estimated 12.7 million Mexican immigrants live in the United States (half illegally), sending billions of dollars in remittances to their families in Mexico.

From *National Geographic Atlas of the World*, 9th edition. Copyright ©2011 National Geographic Society. Reprinted by arrangement. All rights reserved.

Area	1,964,375 sq km (758,449 sq mi)
Population	109,610,000
Government	Federal Republic
Capital	Mexico City 19,028,000
Life Expectancy	75 years
Literacy	91%
Religion	Roman Catholic, Protestant
Language	Spanish, Mayan, Nahuatl, other indigenous languages
Currency	Mexican peso (MXN)
GDP per Cap	$13,500
Labor Force	13.7% Agriculture, 23.4% Industry, 62.9% Service

From *National Geographic Atlas of the World*, 9th edition. Copyright ©2011 National Geographic Society. Reprinted by arrangement. All rights reserved.

TRAVEL TIPS

Entry: A passport or other WHTI-compliant travel document (such as an enhanced driver's license) is required for U.S. citizens traveling to Mexico. A tourist card is also required and can be obtained at travel agencies, airports, border crossing facilities, and Mexican government tourism offices.

Peak Tourist Seasons: March and December

National Holiday: September 16 (Independence Day)

Health: Some areas require malaria suppressants.

Shopping: Typical items are silver, copperware, blown glass, onyx, pottery, handwoven fabrics such as rugs and serapes, embroidery, and Indian arts. Reproductions of artifacts of ancient civilizations are available near archaeological sites.

Internet TLD: .mx

CULTURAL CAPSULE

Sixty percent of the people of Mexico are mestizo (mixed Spanish and Indian). Thirty percent are pure Indian, descendants of the Mayans and Aztecs. Nine percent are European. While Spanish is the official language, there are nearly one hundred Indian languages spoken in parts of Mexico.

Cultural hints: Greet by a soft handshake or a nod of the head. Let women make the first move toward the handshake. Mexicans stand close when talking to each other. Mexicans like to touch others as a sign of friendliness. Be patient when encountering delays. Dress conservatively (no shorts or tank tops) when visiting religious sites. On the street eat food at the stand, rather than eating and walking. Food basics are corn, beans, and chili. Typical foods are corn tortillas, frijoles refritos (refried beans), tortas (hollow roll stuffed with meat or cheese), quesadillas (tortilla baked with cheese), moles (spicy sauce on many food items), and tacos (folded tortilla filled with meat, cheese, and onions). Regional variations exist.

Tourism Characteristics

The Mexican government is very active in tourism development. Next to oil, tourism is the largest earner of foreign exchange for the country. The country is ranked as the tenth major destination for international tourist arrivals (UNWTO) with 22 million arrivals in 2010. Although an increasing number of manufacturing assembly plants (**maquiladoras**) in **border towns** along the United States–Mexico border have created a booming economy, tourism is important even in these towns despite recent outbreaks of drug trafficking–related violence.

The government has been involved in large-scale development and planning projects, with economic assistance through Fondo Nacional De Fomento al Turismo (FONATUR), and has also actively pursued attracting more tourists through innovating highly visible policies. One such policy is Mexico's Tourist Patrol service, which provides free emergency assistance to motoring tourists in case of highway problems. It is operated by the Mexican government's Ministry of Tourism, which hires English-speaking drivers who patrol the heavily traveled tourist routes in green patrol cars with emergency supplies of gas and first-aid equipment. These cars pass check points twice a day every day of the year.

FONATUR developed fifteen mega-tourism projects throughout Mexico. Upgrading some of the existing resorts was included. Acapulco underwent a massive upgrading and renovation capped by the construction of a motorway from Mexico City. Two of the new projects are Huatulco and Baja California. The government has been working cooperatively with Belize, Guatemala, El Salvador, and Honduras to develop and market jointly a **Mayan World Circuit** (el Circuito Mundo Maya) tourist itinerary including some of the most impressive archeological sites in the world.

Although Mexico has had a high rate of inflation, the continued devaluation of the peso and partial deregulation of Mexico's airlines have effectively reduced airfares, creating one of the greatest travel bargains in the world. Also, the all-inclusive packages that have become popular from the United States and Europe have generated increasing numbers of visitors to Mexico. By 2010 tourism had reached more than 22 million visitors. The United States is the dominant source of tourists who enter Mexico for longer than one day. Over 80 percent of the tourists to Mexico are from the United States. When Canada is included, the number is close to 90 percent. Mexico has a strong tourist trade year-round, although the winter has the largest number of visitors. Coastal areas and the Yucatán have their peak tourist season in the winter months, since the weather is better here at this time of the year and worse in the United States and Canada. Tourism in the inland areas, such as Mexico City and Merida, peaks in the summer during the normal school vacation months of the industrial countries.

Tourist Destinations and Attractions

While tourism is strong throughout Mexico, the dominance of United States trade can be seen in the northwest zone of Guadalajara and the coastal regions of Mazatlán and Puerto Vallarta, which receive over 30 percent of the visitors to Mexico. The central zone of Guanajuato, Mexico City, and San Miguel Allende receives 23 percent of all visitors to Mexico. The four leading destinations are Cancún, Acapulco, Mexico City, and Guadalajara.

The major tourist regions of Mexico are as follows:

Border Towns

The border towns of Tijuana, Ciudad Juárez, Nuevo Laredo, Reynosa, and Matamoros attract millions of day trippers, mainly for shopping. Tourist numbers have been impacted by publicity about drug cartel–related violence but these conditions are not a reflection of the rest of Mexico.

Baja California

largest # visitor

Ecotourism and the newly developing coastal resorts are important to Baja. Coastal towns include Ensenada on lovely Bahía de Todos los Santos, Bahía de los Angeles on the Sea of Cortez, and La Paz, capital of Baja California Sur. Guerrero Negro is one of the better places in the world for whale watching, as the California gray whales head for Scammon's Lagoon from November through February to breed and train their young. The high desert of the Baja in the winter provides a kaleidoscope of desert colors for those interested in ecotourism. The new development taking place in the southern tip of Baja when complete will rival the other west coast resorts and towns of Puerto Vallarta and Mazatlán. The Los Cabos area in this region is one of the fastest-growing destinations in Mexico.

Northwest Region

The northwest region includes Guadalajara and the coastal towns of Mazatlán, Guaymas, Puerto Vallarta, and Manzanillo. Guadalajara is the second largest city in Mexico. It has an impressive town square focused on the Cathedral and Palace de Gobierno (Palace of the Governor). The church of Santa Mónica, which is intricately carved in the Churrigueresque style, was completed about 1720. The churches of San Francisco and Aranzazu both face the shady Jardín de San Francisco. The church of San Francisco has a most impressive exterior. The Hospicio Cabañas represents the best work of muralist Orozco, whose paintings decorate the chapel. To provide ease of viewing the ceiling, benches are available to lie on. The State Museum, which is located near the central plaza, contains art galleries and exhibits covering history, zoology, and archaeology. Across the street from the park and the flower market, the State Library exhibits contemporary art, including the great three-dimensional mural by Gabriel Flores on the ceiling of the auditorium dome.

A number of small villages surround Guadalajara. These include Tiaquepaque, noted for its pottery; Ajijic, with its lovely embroidery and hand-loomed cotton and wool fabrics; and Zapopán, which is famous for its Huichoes Indian handicrafts. This region, which includes Lake Chapala, draws many North American retirees visiting to escape the cold, damp North American winter. The coastal resorts centered in Guaymas, Mazatlán, and Puerto Vallarta are within easy access of the western United States and provide year-round resorts focused on the Pacific. All of the resorts offer a variety of water sports, such as surfing, deep-sea diving, waterskiing, and some of the best fishing in the world. Puerto Vallarta is the most

This is the town Laguna Beach always wanted to be: a seaside artist retreat steeped in an historic Old California setting. (California's history is rooted in these small Baja California villages.) Everywhere you turn, there's a patch of antiquity waiting to be sketched: the mission church facing a centuries-old plaza, ruins of an old sugarcane mill, weather-beaten adobe walls painted in vibrant colors. "Todos Santos has a quality of light equal to Taos or the High Andes in Peru," says Jill Logan, an artist who owns one of the 15 art galleries here (more per capita than any town in Mexico). Inspired by their surroundings, this community of 4,000—including hundreds of expats—works hard to preserve them. Zoning regulations are in place to protect Todos Santos from the kind of development consuming Cabo San Lucas 43 miles to the south, while sustaining its historic appeal. A former sugar baron's mansion became the Todos Santos Inn, a chic bed-and-breakfast, while a gutted sugar warehouse was transformed into Los Adobes, serving haute Mexican food. Since this is Baja, you can always pick up traditional fish tacos at a street stand on your way out of town. The road south leads to the kind of sweeping, development-free beaches that disappeared from California decades ago: Pelicans wheel overhead, whales spout on the horizon, a sprinkling of surfers bob in the swell. **The High:** Check out the historic Casa de Cultura near the main plaza for artist workshops and cultural events. **The Low:** Even when the surf looks calm, riptides plague most beaches here.

—**Charles Kulander,** *National Geographic Traveler,* January/February 2010

unspoiled of these west coast resorts. Puerto Vallarta was made famous as the site for the movie *The Night of the Iguana,* starring Elizabeth Taylor and Richard Burton. It is a highly picturesque town with flaming bougainvillea and blue jacaranda bushes hugging stucco walls. Mazatlan is a lively resort destination with miles of sandy beaches. It is a shipping port with ferry service to Baja California. An important ecotourism attraction is Copper Canyon. The canyons are located in the Tarahumara Range of the Sierra Madre. This formidable landscape possesses the world's largest proliferation of major canyons confined to a relatively small area. It is deeper and larger than the Grand Canyon in the United States. It is located between Chihuahua and Los Mochis on the coast.

Central Highlands

The central highlands area is centered around Mexico City (Figure 12.1) and the old city of Puebla. Mexico City, Mexico's capital, is the oldest city in North America.

Figure 12.1 Cityscape of Mexico City. © Jess Kraft/www.Shutterstock.com.

Mexico City is made up of dozens of villages that have merged over the past hundred years of overpopulations and an urban web of construction projects. This development has created a complex, fascinating urban sprawl, with a mix of modern and traditional neighborhoods. Colonia El Toro, my neighborhood in Mexico City, is a place where these traditional and modern Mexicos converge, and everything happens. Especially noise.

Just this morning the knife grinder pedaled past my house on his bicycle, blowing his whistle; the garbage truck announced itself with the ringing of a brass bell; the gas truck was accompanied by a man announcing, "El gas!"; and the ironmonger walked past, hands cupped around his mouth, broadcasting his willingness to buy metal scraps or old newspapers. His voice was soon overtaken by a pickup truck with a megaphone playing an unintelligible recording about the price of the oranges it was selling.

At noon, the neighborhood crier proclaimed the latest local crimes: Senor Diaz the mechanic had killed his wife; an ATM machine had been vandalized; two chickens were found dead inside a green Volkswagen.

Next it was a man armed with yet another megaphone calling out the arrival of the circus at the end of the week. "We bring real Indian tigers. We bring an elephant. We bring a boy with three eyes."

He was followed by Senor Primitivo, an elderly man shepherding three cows. One cow limped. Senor Primitivo explained that the cow was hit by a man driving a BMW and talking on his cellphone. He shook his head while making the hand gestures of driving and talking on the phone.

As evening arrived, a man pushed a steaming cart down my street, and the air filled with the scent of sweet potatoes and bananas. Then the tamale vendor walked past, crying, "Tamales from Oaxaca. Tasty, delicious tamales for sale."

Now, at midnight, I heart soft, comforting whistle of the watchman as he makes his rounds under a sky that no longer twinkles with stars, thanks to pollution and electric lights. But it still has the moon. The Mexican moon.

—Jennifer Clement, *National Geographic Traveler*, October 2009

Pre-dating European settlement, Mexico City is located on the site of the Aztec capital, Tenochtitlán, in the Valley of Mexico. It is surrounded by volcanic mountains. It has fourteenth-century Aztec ruins, sixteenth-century colonial buildings, and modern skyscrapers. It is the second largest city in the world. With the tremendous industrial development and heavy migration of people, air pollution and poverty are major problems. Many of its residents live in rather poor conditions, many as squatters on the edge of the city. Nezahualcoyotl, on the east side, is an immense squatter settlement with over 2 million poor residents. While great effort is made by the government, the size of the population migration to the city overwhelms their efforts.

The city boasts a number of outstanding museums. There are native cultural events, such as concerts with marimbas, mariachis, singers, and dancers, which can be seen in Mexico City and in other Mexican cities and towns. Chapultepec Park is a cultural and recreational center. It is home to one of the most impressive museums in the world. With its 168-ton figure of Tlaloc, the rain god, within the National Museum of Anthropology is an impressive architectural building in its own right. Its collections and displays are equally as impressive as the building. Three more of the country's finest museums—the Museum of Modern Art, Chapultepec Castle, and the Museum of Natural History—three lakes with boating facilities, a variety of playground equipment, an amusement park, complete with a large roller-coaster ride, and a number of flower gardens, fountains, and sculptures are also located in the park.

The seat of government and religion for the country is the Zocalo. Two municipal palaces—the Supreme Court building, the National Palace where the Palace of Montezuma once stood, and the magnificent Metropolitan Cathedral—are on the Zocalo. Leading away from the Zocalo, the Avenida Madero, renamed to honor the leader of the Revolution of 1910, has a number of excellent reminders of the history of Mexico. The Church of La Profesa was built by the Jesuits in the sixteenth century; the Palace of Iturbide, constructed in 1779, has a private dwelling built by the Count of San Mateo; the Church and Monastery of San Francisco was a dominant force in the spiritual and social life of the people from 1524 until 1850; the House of Tiles was built in 1708 as the town house of the Counts of Orizaba; and the Numismatic Museum has a collection dating back before the European Conquest.

There are many notable attractions within a one hundred-mile radius in Mexico. They include the floating gardens of Xochimilco, including a colorful market and park; Cuernavaca, a Spanish colonial city; Xochicalco, an archaeological site near the Pyramid of Teopanzalso; Taxco, a hillside silver-mining town with cobblestone streets, flower-decked shops, and colorful houses; Tula, the capital of the ancient Toltec civilization; the spectacular Pyramids of Teotihuacan, the once holy site of the Toltec civilization; and Puebla, an ancient colonial city that was founded in 1521.

Central Coastal Resort Towns

The central coastal resort towns include Acapulco, Zihuatanejo, Ixtapa, and Huatulco. Acapulco, the oldest of the towns, has historically been the fashionable resort of Mexico, with its famous cliff divers (Figure 12.2)

Figure 12.2 Cilff Diving in Acapulco. © Vilant/www.Shutterstock.com.

founded the city in 1519. Activity centers on the waterfront with fish and food markets, arcades, and curio shops. Veracruz is also excellent for fishing.

The Yucatán

The Yucatán combines outstanding archaeological sites and Caribbean resorts. Palenque features temples in a picturesque setting. Chichen Itza, Uxmal, Tulum, and Ruta Maya are religious centers of the Mayan culture that are adorned with **pyramids**, temples, arches, vaults, and beautifully carved friezes. Cozumel is one of the top scuba-diving areas of the world, while Cancún is a planned destination resort and Mexico's most popular coastal resort. Cancún was developed by FONATUR using a computer-generated development plan. Although it is an excellent location, the sand had to be brought in to create the white sandy beaches. The crystal-clear Caribbean waters and the abundance of fresh seafood, fruit, and vegetables make Cancún, Cozumel, and Riviera Maya ideal Caribbean playgrounds that are easily accessible to the United States and Canada. Puerto Maya has the region's newest cruise port facility. Merida, the capital of Yucatán, combines old colonial buildings and modern homes with thatched Indian huts, presenting a unique setting. The region has a number of wildlife reserves, and the karst topography offers a unique physical environment for the visitor. The major attractions in Merida are the fortress-type cathedral; the Montejo mansion, which was built by the Spanish conqueror and founder Francisco de Montejo; and the Museum of Archaeology, which displays Mayan artifacts.

and a large well-developed tourist infrastructure along its coastal areas. Acapulco is set at the base of mountains on a partly enclosed bay. The three resort towns are in a more tropical environment than the northwest coastal areas, thus the waters are much warmer. The town of Zihuatanejo is the support center for the beach resort development of Ixtapa with its sixteen-mile-long white sand beach, which is an excellent example of state planning and development of tourism. It was the first of FONATUR's developments that used modern technology to build a quality tourism environment in an outstanding setting while preserving the Mexican culture.

East Coastal Towns

The main east coastal towns are Tampico and Veracruz. These are old colonial towns on the Gulf of Mexico. They exhibit the planning that the Spanish used in establishing their cities in the New World. Both are in the hot tropical coastal zone. Tampico is particularly good for fishing and hunting. Veracruz is the main port on the east coast of Mexico. Cortez landed in the harbor and

The Southwest

Tourism in the Southwest centers around Oaxaca. Oaxaca represents the Indian culture of Mexico and still has a local periodic market. It is a colorful city where the Indian population still wears clothing that identifies them as being from a specific village. Oaxaca is known for its crafts of pottery, gold and silver jewelry, skirts, blouses, men's shirts, tablecloths, and knives. Near Oaxaca, Monte Alban is an impressive archaeological site high on a mountain. Monte Alban is composed of a huge central plaza and several tombs. Another impressive architectural wonder, the ancient town of Mitia, is also near Oaxaca. Mitia was a Zapotec-Mixtec ceremonial center. Particularly impressive is the intricately carved stone fretwork on the façades of the temples. A number of small Indian villages around Oaxaca are interesting to tourists. These include Azompa, which is known for its pottery; Santo Tomás, which specializes in weaving of sashes using the backstrap loom; Ocotlán, which offers baskets and embroidered and pleated blouses; and Teotitlán del Valle, which produces sarapes found in the markets in the region.

Belize

Introduction

An Anglo-Caribbean culture sets off Belize from its Spanish-speaking Central American neighbors. Known as British Honduras before gaining independence in 1981, Belize enjoys a tradition of democratic government, helping it avoid the political turmoil of nearby countries. Although English is the official language, English Creole (known as Kriol) and Spanish are also common. The Caribbean coast offers visitors the longest barrier reef in the Americas, with coral gardens and colorful fish. The country's interior holds **rain forests**, waterfalls, mountains, and ancient Maya temples.

From *National Geographic Atlas of the World*, 9th edition. Copyright ©2011 National Geographic Society. Reprinted by arrangement. All rights reserved.

Area	22,966 sq km (8,867 sq mi)
Population	329,000
Government	parliamentary democracy and a Commonwealth realm
Capital	Belmopan 16,000
Life Expectancy	73 years
Literacy	77%
Religion	Roman Catholic, Protestant
Language	Spanish, Creole, Mayan dialects, English, Garifuna (Carib), German
Currency	Belizean dollar (BZD)
GDP per Cap	$8,100
Labor Force	10.2% Agriculture, 18.1% Industry, 71.7% Services

From *National Geographic Atlas of the World*, 9th edition. Copyright ©2011 National Geographic Society. Reprinted by arrangement. All rights reserved.

TRAVEL**TIPS** 🧳

Entry: A passport is required for U.S. citizens traveling to Belize. No visa is required for visits of less than thirty days.

Peak Tourist Season: December through March

National Holiday: September 21 (Independence Day).

Health: Check for malaria, yellow fever, and cholera before visit.

Shopping: Good buys are wooden handicrafts. Care must be taken buying Mayan arts and tortoise shell crafts. They may be restricted or not allowed in the United States.

Internet TLD: .bz

CULTURAL CAPSULE Belize is one of the most sparsely populated countries in Central America. Most Belizeans are of multiracial mixture. More than 45 percent are of African ancestry. A little more than 25 percent are mestizo. Another one-fifth is Carib, Mayan, and other Amerindian ethnic groups. The remainder includes Europeans, East Indians, Chinese, and Lebanese. Over the past few years the population has increased significantly from an inflow of Central American refugees, mostly from El Salvador and Guatemala. English is the official language and is spoken by almost all of the population except recently arrived refugees. Spanish is the native tongue for about half of the people and is spoken as a second language by another 20 percent. The various Indian groups still speak their original language. An English-Creole dialect similar to that of the English-speaking people of the Caribbean islands is also used. About half of the people are Roman Catholic, while the Anglican Church and Protestant Christian groups make up most of the rest.

Cultural hints: Greet with a handshake. Keep hands above table when eating. The best restaurants are in the hotels. Foods include seafood, beef and chicken, and rice and beans.

Tourism Characteristics

Belize has established a reputation as an excellent ecotourism destination (Figure 12.3). Tourist arrivals reached 240,000 in 2011. The United States is the major market. The government does not want to expand too rapidly, but continued managed growth would be beneficial to the country. The joint marketing of the Mayan World Circuit, its ecotourism potential, its long barrier reef, its pristine beaches, and the fact that it is English-speaking should certainly encourage future growth.

Figure 12.3 Loggerhead turtle swimming in Belize. © Sharon K. Andrews/www.Shutterstock.com.

Tourist Destinations and Attractions

The capital has been moved from Belize City to Belmopan, a safer upland area than the coastal location of Belize City, which is vulnerable to hurricanes. Belize City still remains the major tourist destination. It has the oldest Anglican cathedral in Central America—St. John's Cathedral—built in 1857. The Government House, the residence of the British governor, was built in 1814. The remnants of former slave quarters are still evident along Regent Street. The Supreme Court building, overlooking Central Park, continues elements of the British colonial style. Belize is, in many ways, similar to many of Britain's former West Indies island colonies.

The coastal area has excellent beaches. A mosaic of islands off the barrier reef, the largest in the Western Hemisphere, provides outstanding scuba diving and game fishing. Jacques Cousteau explored the waters of Belize in the 1970s. His exploration of a five-hundred-foot-deep karst **sinkhole** now known as the "Blue Hole" transformed this area into a remarkable recreational paradise for divers. Belize has a wealth of Mayan ruins. Major sites are at Altún Ha, a small rich ruin, 30 miles northwest of Belize City and Xunantunich, 80 miles southwest of Belize City. At Lamanai stand 700 ceremonial structures in which 75,000 Mayans once lived. **Cruise ships** call on Belize City and Punta Gorda.

The country is developing its ecotourism resources. The Mountain Pine Ridge is famed for its orchids and wildlife. There are some 450 varieties of birds. The Cayo district contains a jaguar reserve, a baboon sanctuary, numerous wildlife and marine reserves, national parks, and an active Audubon Society.

Guatemala

Introduction

Guatemala, meaning "land of the trees," is a heavily forested and mountainous nation—and the most populous in Central America. The Pacific coast lowlands in the south rise to the volcanic Sierra Madre and other highlands, then the land descends to the forested northern lowlands, including the narrow Caribbean coast. The highlands, where most Guatemalans live, are temperate in climate, especially when compared with the tropical lowlands.

A thousand years ago the Maya civilization flourished, and its ruins dot the landscape. Today more than half of Guatemalans are descendants of the indigenous Maya peoples; most live in the western highlands and are poor subsistence farmers. By contrast the rest of the population are known as Ladinos (mostly mixed Mayan-Spanish ancestry). The more urbanized Ladino population dominates commerce, government, and the military. By 1960, Guatemalan society had grown increasingly polarized between the military rulers, Ladino upper class, and indigenous lower class, and a revolt started civil war. Warfare between mostly indigenous guerrillas and government forces cost 200,000 lives and displaced half a million people. In September 1996 the government and the guerrillas agreed on terms to end the 36-year-long civil war. The democratic government faces problems of crime, illiteracy, and poverty; but it is making progress in moving the economy away from agriculture and toward manufacturing (notably textiles) and tourism.

From *National Geographic Atlas of the World*, 9th edition. Copyright ©2011 National Geographic Society. Reprinted by arrangement. All rights reserved.

Area	108,889 sq km (42,042 sq mi)
Population	14,027,000
Government	constitutional democratic republic
Capital	Guatemala City 1,024,000
Life Expectancy	70 years
Literacy	69%
Religion	Roman Catholic, Protestant, indigenous Mayan beliefs
Language	Spanish, 23 officially recognized Amerindian languages
Currency	quetzal (GTQ); U.S. dollar (USD); others allowed
GDP per Cap	$5,200
Labor Force	50% Agriculture, 15% Industry, 35% Services

From *National Geographic Atlas of the World*, 9th edition. Copyright ©2011 National Geographic Society. Reprinted by arrangement. All rights reserved.

TRAVEL**TIPS** 💼

Entry: A passport is required for U.S. citizens traveling to Guatemala.

Peak Tourist Season: January through April

National Holiday: September 15 (Independence day).

Health: Food should be cooked (no raw meat or fish) and hot. Drink boiled or bottled water. At times visitors need protection for malaria, cholera, and yellow fever. Consult with health officials or your physician before travel.

Shopping: Popular items are Indian handicrafts including antique embroidery, handwoven fabrics, silver jewelry, handwoven bags, basketwork, and huipiles (Indian blouses).

Internet TLD: .gt

Over half of the population are descendants of Mayan Indians, most living in the mountain area. Ladinos—Westernized Mayans and mestizos (Spanish-Indian)—live in a crescent-shaped area running from the northern border on the Pacific, along the coastal plains, and up through Guatemala City to the Caribbean. The dominant religion is Roman Catholicism, which many Indians have superimposed onto their traditional forms of worship. While Spanish is the official language, there are some thirty Indian dialects. Some Indians do not understand Spanish.

Cultural hints: Good eye contact during greetings and talking. Ask permission to take photographs of people. It is polite to finish all the food on your plate. For the bill, raise your hand and then make a writing motion on your hand. Common foods are tortillas, black beans, rice, tamales, meats (beef, pork, and chicken), and fried platanos (bananas). Papaya and breadfruit are also common.

Tourism Characteristics

Guatemala's tourist industry suffered because of the political instability of the region, but in 1996 a peace treaty ended the civil war. It is easily accessible from the southeastern United States, and as the government became more stable, tourism increased rapidly. Nearly 2 million tourists visited the country in 2010; many attracted by the ancient Maya Empire sites. The United States is the second biggest market for Guatemala, after its neighbor El Salvador. Like other Central American countries the peak tourist season is winter and spring, with the low season in September and October due to the hurricane and rainy seasons in the summer and fall.

Tourist Destinations and Attractions

There are currently five principal destinations of interest to tourists. Guatemala City, the capital, has museums and buildings that remind the visitor of Mayan Indian history and the city's role as a colonial capital. Lake Atitlán, a volcano-surrounded lake, is considered by many to be one of the most beautiful lakes in the world. The lake is ringed by a number of villages, each with its Indian tribe with distinctive colorful costume and periodic markets for the Indians. Chichicastenango and other mountain market towns are another attraction. Chichicastenango has become one of the outstanding Mayan market towns in all of Latin America. In addition to the market, a number of religious ceremonies are performed on the steps and inside the church of Santo Tomás. It is a picturesque

mountain village of cobbled streets, red-tiled roofs, and whitewashed houses. The colonial city of Antigua was the capital until it was devastated by earthquakes. It has fascinating colonial buildings and ruins, and is a World Heritage Site. The Tikal Mayan ruins are one of the most extraordinary archaeological sites in Latin American or, indeed, the entire world. The mutual marketing of Tikal as part of the Mayan World Circuit would be an additional growth factor for the country. Tikal sits in 222 square miles of dense rain forest. The city sprawls for some 50 square miles. Five imposing temples and thousands of stately structures emit an aura of power. Until recently, most visits were by air for a day trip, but the area now has several hotels. Tikal's Temple IV is the tallest pre-Columbian structure in the Americas at 212 feet. The city of Peten is a good starting point to access Tikal. One of the advantages of tourism in Guatemala is that all these destinations, with the exception of Tikal, are relatively close to each other and are located in the high elevations with pleasant climates.

Honduras

Introduction

The second largest country in Central America, Honduras possesses a landscape that is about 80 percent mountainous. Lowland areas exist along the long Caribbean and short Pacific coasts. The inland mountains are cooler and drier compared with the hot and humid coastal regions. Much of Honduras is forested, but illegal logging claimed more than 37 percent of the forests between 1990 and 2005. The largely mestizo population speaks Spanish. English is common in major cities, along the northern coastal region, and on the Bay Islands. Amerindians, about 7 percent of the population, inhabit northern and western Honduras; the largest groups are the Lenca and Miskito. The Garifuna, an Afro-Caribbean people, populate northern coastal areas. Honduras is one of the poorest countries in the Americas, and most citizens are subsistence farmers. Major exports include bananas and coffee, and there is a growing textile industry.

From *National Geographic Atlas of the World*, 9th edition. Copyright ©2011 National Geographic Society. Reprinted by arrangement. All rights reserved.

Language	Spanish, Amerindian dialects
Currency	lempira (HNL)
GDP per Cap	$4,200
Labor Force	39.2% Agriculture, 20.9% Industry, 39.8% Services

From *National Geographic Atlas of the World*, 9th edition. Copyright ©2011 National Geographic Society. Reprinted by arrangement. All rights reserved.

TRAVEL **TIPS** 💼

Entry: A passport is required for U.S. citizens traveling to Honduras.

Peak Tourist Season: Coastal, January through April

National Holiday: September 15 (Independence Day).

Health: Water must be boiled and filtered. Fruits and vegetables must be cleaned carefully and meats cooked well. Protection for malaria, typhoid fever, and cholera is advised. Check with health officials or physician before travel.

Area	112,090 sq km (43,278 sq mi)
Population	7,466,000
Government	democratic constitutional republic
Capital	Tegucigalpa 946,000
Life Expectancy	72 years
Literacy	80%
Religion	Roman Catholic, Protestant

Figure 12.4 Copán ruins, Honduras. © Kim Briers/Shutterstock.com

Shopping: Wooden carvings, Panama hats, woven straw items, and pottery are popular items.

Internet TLD: .hn

 The population of Honduras is 90 percent mestizo with small minorities of European, African, Oriental, and American Indian ancestry. Most Hondurans are Roman Catholic. Spanish is the predominant language, although some English is spoken along the northern coast and on the Caribbean Bay islands. Native Indian dialects and Garifuna are also spoken. Honduras is one of the poorest countries in the Western Hemisphere. Its economy is rural, exporting bananas, coffee, sugar, cotton, timber, and some metals.

Cultural hints: Hondurans have close personal space, standing near to converse. Touching the finger below the eye warns caution. Foods include beans, corn, tortillas, rice, and fruit. Typical dishes are tapado (a stew of beef, vegetables, and coconut milk), mondongo (tripe and beef), and nacatamales (pork).

Tourism Characteristics

Like the other Central American nations, Honduras feels tourism is important but has not yet developed a substantial tourist infrastructure. Its development was hindered by its position between Guatemala and Nicaragua. Since the end of the civil war in Nicaragua and El Salvador, its tourism industry has grown reaching 900,000 arrivals in 2011. The United States is the largest market, accounting for nearly one-third of total visitors. Honduras will benefit from political stability and increased tourism to Guatemala as its major Mayan site is close to the border between the two countries.

Tourist Destinations and Attractions

The most famous attraction in Honduras is Copán (Figure 12.4), an ancient religious and cultural center for the Mayan Indians. It is considered to be an outstanding example of ancient Mayan civilization and is included in the Mayan World Circuit promotion and marketing with other Central American countries. Structures such as stone temples, courts, and an amphitheater have been restored. Comayaguela, a remarkably well-preserved sixteenth-century town, is a major attraction. The capital, Tegucigalpa, is a picturesque city with winding cobblestone streets. Honduras has sandy beaches on both the Pacific and Caribbean coastal areas. This combined with the Bay Islands in the Caribbean with their pristine beaches and coves provide a potential base for the development of a tourism industry, but it has yet to be realized.

2

El Salvador

Introduction

The smallest and most densely populated country in Central America, El Salvador adjoins the Pacific with a narrow coastal plain, backed by a volcanic mountain chain, and a fertile plateau. The country experiences volcanic and seismic activity, and the Santa Ana volcano is notably active. The climate is tropical with pronounced wet and dry seasons. The rainy season is May to October. About 90 percent of Salvadorans are mestizo, 9 percent claim Spanish descent, and only 1 percent of the people are indigenous. The rich volcanic soils attracted coffee plantations—where rich landowners subjugated the peasant population. Economic inequality led to the 1980–1992 civil war; many Salvadorans, rich and poor, fled to the United States. At present, El Salvador's democratic government shows success in improving education and adding manufacturing jobs—but faces the challenges of poverty, crime, and natural disasters.

From *National Geographic Atlas of the World*, 9th edition. Copyright ©2011 National Geographic Society. Reprinted by arrangement. All rights reserved.

Area	21,041 sq km (8,124 sq mi)
Population	7,339,000
Government	republic
Capital	San Salvador 1,433,000
Life Expectancy	71 years
Literacy	80%
Religion	Roman Catholic, Protestant
Language	Spanish, Nahuatl
Currency	U.S. dollar (USD)
GDP per Cap	$7,100
Labor Force	19% Agriculture, 23% Industry, 58% Services

From *National Geographic Atlas of the World*, 9th edition. Copyright ©2011 National Geographic Society. Reprinted by arrangement. All rights reserved.

TRAVEL **TIPS** 🧳

Entry: A passport and a visa are required.

Peak Tourist Season: November and December

National Holiday: September 15 (Independence Day).

Health: Precautions for malaria, yellow fever, and cholera advised. Check with local health officials before trip.

Shopping: Gold, ceramics, wood carvings, dolls, leather goods, and textiles are popular.

Internet TLD: .sv

CULTURAL CAPSULE The people of El Salvador are very homogeneous (90 percent mixed Indian and Spanish). There are a few Indians who have retained their old customs and traditions, while the vast majority have adopted the Spanish language and culture.

Cultural hints: It is impolite to point with finger or feet. Men stand when women leave the table. Food includes black beans, refried beans, tortillas, rice eggs, meat, and fruit. Food is less spicy than in other Latin American countries.

Tourism Characteristics

In the past El Salvador, like Guatemala, had a reasonably strong tourist trade even though it was the smallest country in Central America. It is the most densely populated and most industrialized of the Central American countries.

Because of past political problems, tourism to El Salvador was stagnant for a long time. Since 1995 El Salvador has had the fastest growth rate of tourist arrivals in Central America, increasing to over 1 million visitors in 2010. Unlike most of the Central American countries the United States is not the dominant market for El Salvador, rather neighboring Guatemala is the largest, providing nearly half of total visitors. Among Central American countries, El Salvador does receive the largest percentage of European visitors. They have good accommodations and many tourist facilities that are currently underused.

Tourism Destinations and Attractions

El Salvador has some very scenic mountains, 25 volcanoes, and 14 lakes. Surrounding the lakes are unique Indian villages where the inhabitants still wear traditional dress and use traditional markets. El Salvador also has excellent beaches along its Pacific coastline. There are a number of pre-Columbian ruins near Taxumal and San Andreas. The capital, San Salvador, is a modern city. The culture and art of the country are expressed in the museums and palaces of San Salvador. One of El Salvador's most impressive sites is Joya de Cerem, a village buried by a volcano 1,400 years ago. Due to the swift eruption, the village was left largely intact and quite well preserved. San Miguel is home to fabulous beaches, including Playa Las Flores, Playa El Esteron, Intipuca Beach, and El Cuco.

Nicaragua

Introduction

Nicaragua lies at the heart of Central America. The Pacific coastal region is fertile lowland plain, with active volcanoes and lakes; this is Nicaragua's most populous and developed region. The northern highlands region (north of Lake Managua to the Honduran border) is mountainous and cooler and contains cloud forests. The Caribbean coastal region, taking up about 60 percent of the country, features a lowland plain covered by tropical rain forests. Volcanoes and earthquakes along the Pacific coast are a constant threat, and hurricanes often hit the low-lying Caribbean coast. Since independence from Spain in 1821, Nicaragua has endured dictatorships, military interventions, and civil war. Elections in 1990 brought democracy and economic growth, but poverty and corruption continue to be major problems. Nicaragua is one of the poorest countries in the Western Hemisphere, and it depends on international economic aid.

From *National Geographic Atlas of the World*, 9th edition. Copyright ©2011 National Geographic Society. Reprinted by arrangement. All rights reserved.

Area	130,370 sq km (50,336 sq mi)
Population	5,669,000
Government	republic
Capital	Managua 920,000
Life Expectancy	71 years
Literacy	68%
Religion	Roman Catholic, Evangelical
Language	Spanish
Currency	gold cordoba (NIO)
GDP per Cap	$2,800
Labor Force	29% Agriculture, 19% Industry, 52% Services

From *National Geographic Atlas of the World*, 9th edition. Copyright ©2011 National Geographic Society. Reprinted by arrangement. All rights reserved.

TRAVEL **TIPS** 💼

Entry: A passport is required for U.S. citizens traveling to Nicaragua.

Peak Tourist Season: December and January

National Holiday: September 15 (Independence Day).

Health: Precaution advised for malaria, yellow fever, and cholera. Check with local health officials before travel. Food and water in better restaurants is generally safe.

Shopping: Brass, leather goods, wood carvings, masks, jewelry, and handwoven fabrics are common items purchased.

Internet TLD: .ni

CULTURAL CAPSULE Most Nicaraguans are mestizo. The Indians of the Caribbean coast remain ethnically distinct and retain tribal customs and dialects. A large African minority (of Jamaican origin) is concentrated on the Caribbean coast. Nicaraguan culture follows the lines of its **Ibero-European** ancestry with the Spanish influence prevailing. Roman Catholicism is the major religion, but Evangelical Protestant sects have increased recently. Spanish is the official language with English spoken on the Caribbean coast.

Cultural hints: Smiles are important. Nicaraguans have close personal space, standing closely in conversations. Food staples are beans and rice. Typical dishes are tortillas, enchiladas, nacatamales (meat and vegetables), mondongo (tripe and beef knuckles), and baho.

Tourism Characteristics

Nicaragua's visitors include more politically motivated rather than pleasure travelers than other Central American countries. Its similarity to other Central American countries and its political problems have been factors in its small tourist industry. Nicaragua has a growing industry, expanding to 950,000 in 2011. The United States represents the largest share of visitors but other Central American countries are important markets for Nicaragua. The Nicaraguan government encourages tourism and tourism-related projects as part of its attempt to restore the country's economy.

Tourism Destinations and Attractions

Nicaragua's attractions include its Indian heritage; ancient Spanish cities such as Grenada, the oldest Spanish city in Nicaragua; Leon, near the scores of excellent sandy beaches that dot the coastline from the Gulf of Fonsceca to the Costa Rican border; beautiful lakes and volcanoes; and the old English colonial town of Bluefield, with its houses built on stilts and surrounded by coconut palms. In addition, Nicaragua has coastal resorts on both the Pacific (Masachapa and Pochomil) and the Caribbean, which are undergoing development for tourists. Fifty miles offshore from Bluefield are two small, beautiful, peaceful, unspoiled islands, with white sand beaches bordered by coconut trees and clear turquoise water—the Corn Islands. Development is now taking place to provide access for international visitors to the wonderful snorkeling, horseback riding, and hiking on the islands.

Following on the heels of it ecoappealing neighbor to the south, Nicaragua is emerging as "the next Costa Rica." A civil war in its not too distant past (Nicaragua become a democracy in 1995), the country's gracious locals, six active volcanoes, adventure activities, rich ecosystems, bountiful crafts, and Spanish colonial influence add up to a great, affordable getaway.

A half-hour drive from Managua airport, Masaya is home to the country's most active volcano. You can drive right up to its lip, as long as you park with your front wheels facing out in a case a quick, eruptions-provoked exist is necessary. If you visit in the afternoon, you may hear the singing of thousands of parakeets

nesting in the crater walls, apparently unfazed by the heat and gas.

Masaya has long been an exciting center of Nicaraguan art and culture. Mercado Artesanias, a fortresslike structure, is filled with some of Central American's most colorful souvenirs, from woven hammocks to woodcrafts. The colonial city of Granada, famous from its adobe architecture awash in tropical tones, is another 30-minute drive south. From the parquet central, take a city tour in one of the horse-drawn carriages (taxi for locals and travelers). For an above-it-all view, climb the Iglesia de la Merced bell tower (fee: $1). Come dinnertime, try the fire-grilled meat or fish at El Zaguan, right behind the Granada cathedral.

A two-hour drive south of Granada brings you to Morgan's Rock Hacienda & Ecolodge, where howler monkeys make you feel most welcome. After crossing a canopy-level suspension bridge, you'll see the lodge's wooden bungalows, each with an open-air shower; just below break the waves of the ocean. Surfing, hiking, horseback riding, and kayaking are on-site options; making breakfast at the property's working farm and ziplining at the nearby surf town of San Juan del Sur are off-campus delights.

—Caren Osten Gerszberg, *National Geographic Traveler*, March 2009

Costa Rica

Introduction

Located in Central America, Costa Rica has coastlines on the Caribbean Sea and Pacific Ocean. The tropical coastal plains rise to mountains and a temperate central plateau, where most of the major cities are found, including San José, the capital. Costa Rica is famous for its volcanoes; there are more than 110 of them, mostly in the northern part of the country. Arenal Volcano, one of the most active volcanoes in the world, is a tourist destination, with nearly daily eruptions featuring glowing rocks and ash. The only country in Central America with no standing army, Costa Rica enjoys continuing stability after a century of almost uninterrupted democratic government. Most Costa Ricans are well educated and of European descent. Tourism and manufacturing have replaced coffee and bananas as economic mainstays. The nation preserves more than 25 percent of its land with a variety of national parks, reserves, and wildlife refuges.

From *National Geographic Atlas of the World*, 9th edition. Copyright ©2011 National Geographic Society. Reprinted by arrangement. All rights reserved.

Area	51,100 sq km (19,730 sq mi)
Population	4,509,000
Government	democratic republic
Capital	San José 1,284,000
Life Expectancy	79 years
Literacy	95%
Religion	Roman Catholic, Evangelical
Language	Spanish, English
Currency	Costa Rican colon (CRC)

GDP per Cap	$10,900
Labor Force	14% Agriculture, 22% Industry, 64% Services

From *National Geographic Atlas of the World*, 9th edition. Copyright ©2011 National Geographic Society. Reprinted by arrangement. All rights reserved.

TRAVEL **TIPS** 🧳

Entry: A passport is required for U.S. citizens traveling to Costa Rica

Peak Tourist Season: Year-round

National Holiday: September 15 (Independence Day).

Major cities: San Jose.

Health: Some areas have cholera. Check with local health officials.

Shopping: Items include carved wood (mahogany), native dolls and costumes, leather, and embroidery.

Internet TLD: .cr

Figure 12.5 In Costa Rica, **a.** coppery-headed emerald hummingbird © Rosalie Kreulen/www.Shutterstock.com **b.** Red-eyed tree frog © Nacho Such/www.Shutterstock.com **c.**Squirrel monkey © Dirk Ercken/www.Shutterstock.com. **d.** Chestnut-mandibled toucans. © BMJ/www.Shutterstock.com

CULTURAL CAPSULE Costa Ricans are largely European (Spanish ancestry), with a few Africans, descendants of Jamaican immigrant workers. There are about 1 percent native American Indians and another 1 percent ethnic Chinese. Spanish is the official language, with English widely understood. Creole English is spoken by the Black population, and Bribri is spoken by Indians. About 95 percent of the population is Roman Catholic. Costa Rica has the most politically stable government in Central America.

Cultural hints: People waiting for public transportation line up in an orderly manner. Eye contact is important. It is impolite to talk with food in your mouth. Chewing gum while speaking is impolite.

Tourism Characteristics

Costa Rica is more economically advanced than the other Central American countries, and it is one of the most stable countries of Central America. In 1985, recognizing tourism potential, the government began a tourism-development program that resulted in the development of a number of new hotels and an increase in marketing to the North American market. Although most of its tourists are from other Latin American countries, the United States is a significant and growing

market, as it accounts for nearly half of all the visitors to Costa Rica. The number of visitors doubled in just one decade between 2000 and 2010 from 1 million to nearly 2 million.

Costa Rica has become the most dynamic ecotourism destination in Central America, largely based on its biodiversity. In an area the size of West Virginia, it has a rain forest, high mountain cloud forests, coral beaches, and 66 national parks, beaches, and protected areas set aside to preserve their natural ecology. The parks contain more than 850 species of birds, 1,500 varieties of orchids, and a number of other fauna and flora (Figure 12.5 a through d). Costa Rica now protects some 25 percent of the country's territory. The country practically invented the concept of exploring the forest canopy first by introducing aerial walkways (Figure 12.6), and now ziplines span trees and canyons.

Tourism Destinations and Attractions

The country's most noted attractions are its volcanic scenery, national parks, and oceans. The capital, San José, has some excellent museums and is a good representative of Costa Rican culture. The national parks

Figure 12.6 Hanging Bridge, Monteverde Cloud Forest, Costa Rica. © J. L. Levy/www.Shutterstock.com.

exhibit a variety of flora and fauna with a remarkable collection of birds, flowers, mammals, and fish.

The Central Highlands contain the majority of the population, virtually all of the colonial town's **cathedrals**, and the majority of the country's most dramatic natural beauties, such as the great steaming volcanoes, the luxuriant misty cloud forests, the rocky gorges, waterfalls, and rushing streams.

A short day's trip from San José is Puerto Limón. Puerto Limón is the only deep-water port on Costa Rica's Caribbean coast. The coast south of the port is lined with superb beaches. One of the best and most popular in Central America is Cahuita National Park, with its white and black sand beaches, coral reefs, and transparent waters. Great diving, swimming, sunning, and beachcombing are available.

The stability of the government, the moderate climate, and the variety of attractions from beaches to rich national parks provide a resource for expanding its tourism industry

Panama

Introduction

Panama occupies the narrow land bridge connecting North and South America. In the west, a mountain range runs through the country's center; in the east, the region adjacent to the Colombian border is covered by dense tropical rain forest. The Panama Canal connects the Atlantic and Pacific Oceans and was built by the United States after Panama's independence in 1903 from Colombia. The canal, completed in 1914, was governed as a U.S. territory until 1979,

PANAMA

when joint U.S.–Panamanian control was established. The U.S.–Panamanian relationship remained close over the years, with thousands of Americans working in the canal zone. In 1989, U.S. troops overthrew General Manuel Noriega, after the Noriega regime annulled an election. Panama assumed full control of the Panama Canal in 1999. The economy is stable, with a well-developed service sector that is based on the canal, trade in the Colon Free Zone, and international banking.

From *National Geographic Atlas of the World*, 9th edition. Copyright ©2011 National Geographic Society. Reprinted by arrangement. All rights reserved.

Area	75,420 sq km (29,120 sq mi)
Population	3,454,000
Government	constitutional democracy
Capital	Panama City 1,281,000
Life Expectancy	75 years
Literacy	92%
Religion	Roman Catholic, Protestant
Language	Spanish, English
Currency	balboa (PAB); U.S. dollar (USD)
GDP per Cap	$11,900
Labor Force	15% Agriculture, 18% Industry, 67% Services

From *National Geographic Atlas of the World*, 9th edition. Copyright ©2011 National Geographic Society. Reprinted by arrangement. All rights reserved.

TRAVEL**TIPS**

Entry: A passport and a visa are required for U.S. citizens traveling to Panama.

Peak Tourist Season: January through April

National Holiday: November 3 (Independence Day).

Health: Concern for malaria, yellow fever, and cholera. Check with local health officials before travel.

Shopping: Panama is a duty-free country for goods from around the world. Local handicrafts such as embroidery beaded collars, leather, straw, and wooden goods are typical of the country.

Internet TLD: .pa

CULTURAL CAPSULE The people of Panama are predominantly Caribbean Spanish. Ethnically, the majority are mestizo, or mixed Spanish, Indian, and West Indian. A number of minorities exist such as elements of the West Indians and indigenous Indian groups. Spanish is the official language; however, English is a common second language.

Cultural hints: Women should dress conservatively. Eye contact is important. Typical foods are kidney beans, rice, plantains, corn, fish, beef, chicken, pork, and tropical fruits.

Tourist Characteristics

Panama was a relatively stable country until 1988, but tourists traditionally stayed only for a short time. Most of its visitors were in transit, either from cruise ships traveling through the Panama Canal or international flights between South America and North America. The number of visitors has risen to over 1 million in 2010. This is partly due to the United States government, who appropriated $30 million to improve tourist facilities and related employment in Panama. Panama's currency, the balboa, has been tied to the United States dollar, which is attractive to tourists and helps account for the increase of visitors from the United States. The United States is Panama's largest market, accounting for one-fifth of its visitors. Panama's neighbors, Colombia and Costa Rica, account for most other visitors.

Panama's strategic location has allowed the development of a tourist industry. Although the United States' and Panama's neighbors are the most important contributors to its tourist industry, Panama attracts tourists from a much greater diversity of nations than do other Central American countries because of ships passing through the Panama Canal.

Tourism Destinations and Attractions

The tourist industry centers on the capital, Panama City, and its duty-free shopping, nightlife, and treasures from its history of colonialism and piracy. The Altar of Gold in the Church of San José is an important attraction. Panama City is a modern, thriving metropolis and has established itself as a destination for fashion, fine dining, arts, and education. Panama is trying to emphasize other attractions such as its beaches and offshore islands, which offer fishing, water sports, and other resort amenities, in an effort to increase the length of stay of tourists.

Naturally, Panama's single, most important attraction is the Canal and locks (Figure 12.7). For observing the Canal, Cristóbal and Colón on the Atlantic and Balboa on the Pacific are major points of interest. A short flight from Panama City, San Blas Island is the home of the Cuna Indians who have maintained their unique language and customs for thousands of years. The country is earning a reputation as an ecotourism destination due to its diversity of wildlife (over 900 bird species). Portobelo has well-preserved Spanish Forts and Coiba National Marine Park is frequently referred to as the Galapagos of Central America,

PRESERVING THE FUTURE | Panama: Eco-Wonderland

As a bridge between continents, Panama, 51 miles sea-to-sea at its midpoint, only looks slight. The Panama Canal, which capitalized on the Central American country's slim waistline to become a literal nexus of global trade, will expand with two new sets of locks, one on the Pacific side of the canal and one on the Atlantic, designed for massive, 13,000-container cargo ships, due to be completed in 2014. World traders occupy gleaming new hotels that modernize the colonial capital.

But Panama's indigenous gifts trump industry in 2012 with the debut of the "Biomuseo," the Museum of Biodiversity. American architect Frank Gehry designed the fractured, oceanfront building. Inside, exhibits tell the story of continents colliding and mountains rising, leaving Panama with twelve distinct ecosystems and wildlands comparable to its more touristed neighbor, Costa Rica.

Abundant nature surrounds you anywhere you go. The canal-bordering tropical lowlands of Soberanía National Park ring with the cries of howler monkeys and the chatter of toucans. The cool, flower-filled highland town of Boquete sits in the shadow of the country's tallest volcano. At the offshore Coiba National Park, where a maximum of only forty overnight visitors are allowed, divers share the pristine waters with scientific researchers and whale sharks.

—Elaine Glusac, *National Geographic Traveler*, **November/December 2011**

Figure 12.7 Panama Canal. © andrej pol/www.Shutterstock.com.

REVIEW QUESTIONS

1. Discuss the climatic zones associated with altitude and their importance in terms of crops and population characteristics in Middle America.

2. What factors account for Mexico dominating travel to Central America?

3. Describe the seven major tourist regions of Mexico. Which is the most important? Why?

4. Describe the life of Central American Indians (Aztecs and Mayans) and their contributions to tourism in the area.

5. Which of the Middle American countries below Mexico has the greatest potential for tourism? Why?

part 5: GEOGRAPHY AND TOURISM IN THE CARIBBEAN

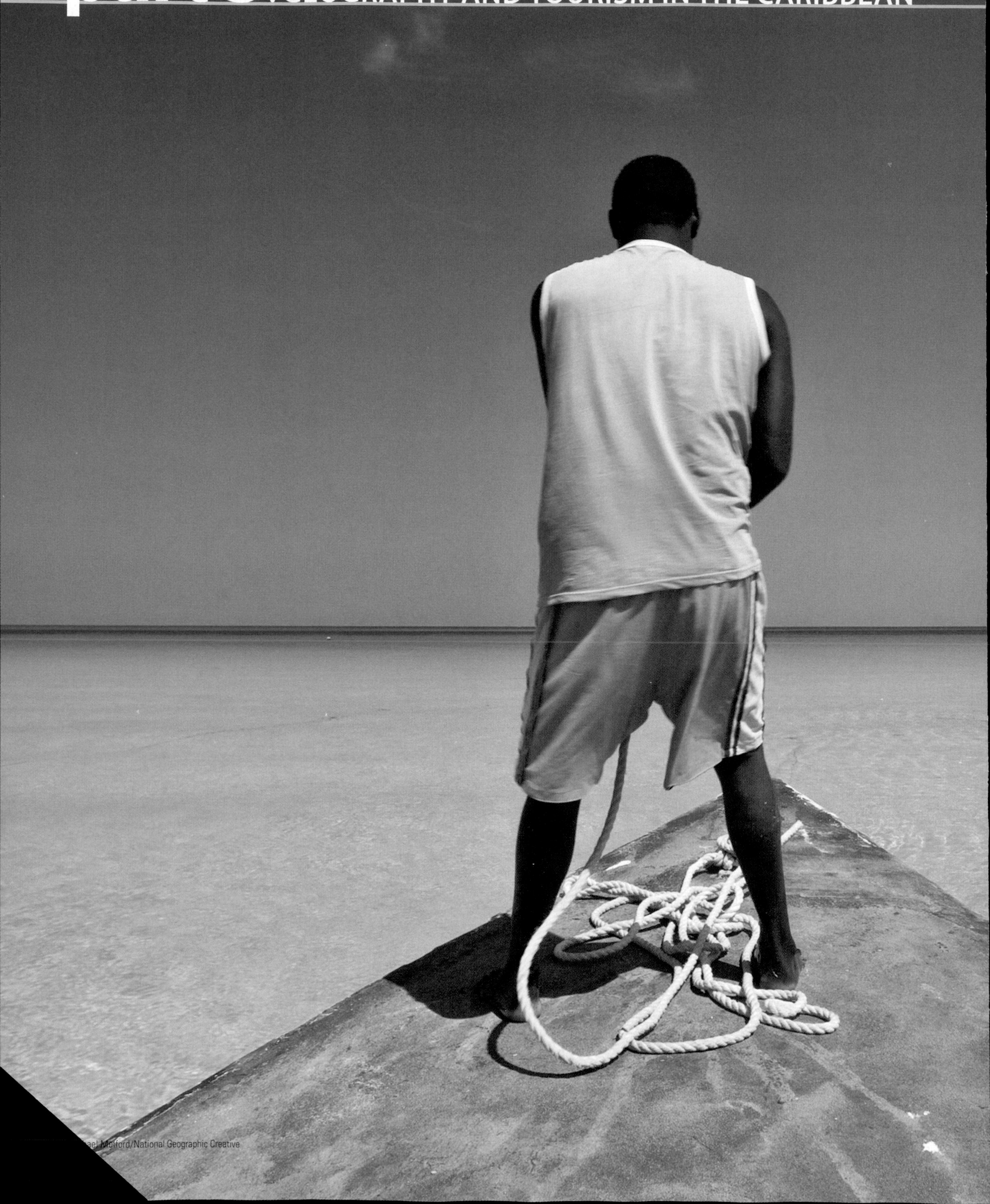

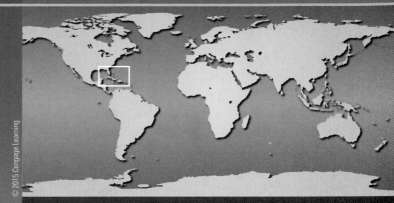

MAJOR GEOGRAPHIC CHARACTERISTICS

- Highly diverse cultural environment
- Accessible to major markets in North America and Europe
- Important colonial influence on the region

MAJOR TOURISM CHARACTERISTICS

- The major attraction of the region is sun-sea-sand.
- Tourism is highly seasonal.
- This is the major cruise region of the world.
- Lengths of visits vary from one week (resort-based tourism) to one day (cruise visit).

MAJOR TOURIST DESTINATIONS

- Resorts of the Caribbean islands
- Bahamas
- Jamaica
- Puerto Rico
- United States Virgin Islands
- Dominican Republic
- St. Maarten
- Aruba
- Barbados

KEY TERMS AND WORDS

ABC Islands	Creole
African	Cruise Ships
Arawaks	Cultural Links
Archipelago	Ecotourism
Calypso	Hurricanes
Carib	Leeward
Caribbean	Windward
Caribbean Tourism Organization	

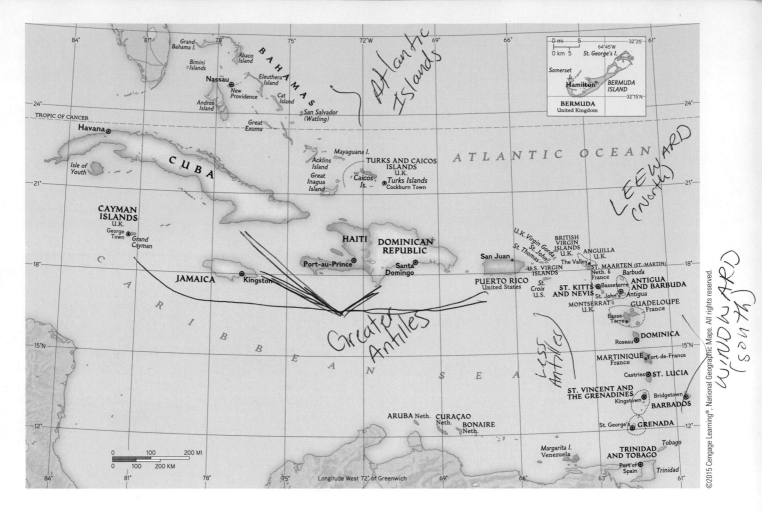

Introduction

The Caribbean, one of the world's most popular tourist destinations, is an arc of islands extending about 1,700 miles from offshore Florida to the coast of South America. The Caribbean was discovered and claimed by Columbus for Spain during his four voyages in search of a route to the riches of the Far East. The most densely populated region of the Americas, the Caribbean, is also one in which there are great differences between the rich and poor. Although it is a region with a low per capita income for many of its people, abject poverty is the exception apart from Haiti. Haiti has little industry or tourism, relies on agriculture that has resulted in erosion and small farms as the population has increased dramatically, and has an unstable government. Some countries are exceptions to the lower standard of living found in some of the Caribbean countries, particularly Puerto Rico (which is a commonwealth of the United States); the British Virgin Islands, a British dependency; and some small islands, such as the United States Virgin Islands, an unincorporated territory of the United States. All three receive high revenues from tourism and economic assistance from Britain or the United States.

The Caribbean region is a tropical, lowland environment with most of its 35+ million people living at elevations below 1,000 feet. With a diversity of environmental characteristics, it can be divided into three major regions: the Greater Antilles, the Lesser Antilles, and the Continental Islands.

Climate Characteristics

Although they are located in a tropical environment, the Caribbean islands are considered temperate. The islands are swept by the easterly trade winds (Figure P5.1), which moderate the hot tropical climate. The major attraction of the Caribbean as a tourist area is its beautiful year-round warm temperature. It can be expected that temperatures in the Caribbean will range from daytime highs of up to about 85 degrees Fahrenheit to lows of 70 degrees Fahrenheit. This is not a particularly high temperature, but the feeling of warmth reflects the effect of heat plus relative humidity. Therefore, fluctuations in rainfall are as important as the temperatures in attracting tourists.

There is a tremendous increase in rainfall from early summer into late November. This increases the

Figure P5.1 Aruba palm blowing in the trade winds.
© serifa/www.Shutterstock.com

humidity and adds an additional five to ten degrees to the apparent temperature. Therefore, the atmosphere in the Caribbean from late April until the first part of December seems more muggy and uncomfortable than during the winter and early spring months. The humidity is modified somewhat by the offshore breezes that constantly blow throughout much of the Caribbean, especially at locations near the water. In addition, in some islands (like Haiti with its higher mountains), wind movement up the hills combines with the cooler temperatures at higher elevations to create a much more comfortable environment. The hurricane season is from August through October, which adds to the discomfort during the summer and early fall.

Discomfort caused by high temperatures and increased humidity takes its toll on the tourist industry. The rainy season seriously interferes with enjoyment of the beaches. The best time to travel in the Caribbean is from December through April. The industry tries to stimulate demand in the slow season by offering bargain rates during the months from May through the early part of December.

The Caribbean Tourism Association has called the April through December 15th period "the season of sweet savings." During that period, nearly half of the Caribbean Tourism Association members reduce their rates from 10 to 30 percent on shopping, travel, and lodging. But, of course, the bargain-hunting tourist is gambling on the weather. The Caribbean has frequent hurricanes, which pose problems on given years for the tourism industry. Most hurricanes develop between August and October.

Tourism Characteristics

One of the most popular tourist destinations in the world today, the Caribbean is the most densely populated region of the Americas. It is a region of extreme wealth and extreme poverty. The economy of the region has long been associated with one major crop or resource. Sugar has been the chief source of income and at one time brought in much wealth. After an initial era of prosperity, however, the sugar economy collapsed due to the cultivation of sugar beets in northern climates. Since that time, many of the Caribbean people have struggled to obtain a livelihood. Tourism has offered some relief and will continue to grow in importance to the economy of the region. Millions have migrated, especially to the United States, with the Caribbean being the third largest source of immigrants to the United States in the last two decades.

For most of the people in this area, life is deficient due to the lack of arable land and the uncertainties of an agriculture-based economy. Years of drought, cold weather, and hurricanes have spelled hardships for many families.

With a limited economic base, the Caribbean nations have seen tourism as a way to improve their standard of living. Tourism is not only a capital investment but a labor-intensive industry that employs many individuals, both skilled and unskilled. Despite the serious problems and drawbacks that are part of tourism in this area, it has become a leading moneymaker for many Caribbean nations; and its future looks hopeful, promising steady growth.

Tourism has become the region's leading industry despite damage from hurricanes, civil unrest, tour operators' challenges, and volcano eruptions. Direct scheduled air service from the American market reaches a number of islands. The Caribbean is the largest cruise destination in the world (Figure P5.2). However, while the cruise industry continues to grow, the longer-stay tourist market has declined with competition from resorts in Florida and Mexico.

In the past, the flow of wealthy visitors to this region sometimes led to hostility among some local residents. They resented the free-spending and raucous tourists whose demands that the native hosts adapt to their tastes and attitudes debased the island culture. Tourism, then, is a mixed blessing in the Caribbean, but it endures because it provides much-needed income to the residents.

Travel Patterns

The Caribbean region is dominated by tourists from North America. Over half of its visitors are from the United States and Canada.

Although the United States is the most important source of visitors to the area, its share has been falling. During the same period the European and South

Figure P5.2 Cruise ship entering port of Nassau, Bahamas. © Ruth Peterkin/www.Shutterstock.com

American markets increased. In addition, the Europeans stay longer, thus having an even bigger impact than may be expressed in numbers of visitors.

The nearness of the United States with its large population along the eastern seaboard and the lack of warm winter weather in Canada are two reasons for this influx of visitors from North America. The two major forms of transportation to the Caribbean are ship and airplane. There are well over two hundred cruise departures a year from ports along the North American coasts, such as Miami, New York, Port Everglades, and San Juan, and within the Caribbean islands themselves. Cruise ships visit between four and six islands, depending upon the length of the cruise. While many of the Caribbean islands are not part of the major cruise itineraries, several airlines offer all-inclusive programs for North American customers that have both enhanced the opportunities of the small islands and brought many tourists from the western United States as well. In addition, there are flights and connections from European cities such as London, Paris, and Amsterdam to their former Caribbean colonial islands. The European share of tourists has increased to over 30 percent, aided by the greater number of air charter packages available in Europe.

Tourism to the Caribbean is strongest from January through April and declines slightly during the rainy summer season. Hurricane season is well illustrated with the smallest amount of visitors in September and October. Visitors from the United States and Europe prefer the summer, while Canadians prefer the winter with a slightly higher percentage in the winter than the summer. The two largest receivers of Americans are the Bahamas and Puerto Rico. Together they receive almost half of the total visitors from the United States. The Europeans' major destinations are the Dominican Republic, Cuba, Guadeloupe, and Martinique. This is a reflection on the two major markets in Europe, the United Kingdom and France, which are followed closely by Germany. It also illustrates the increasing opening of Cuba to the West and Europe's interest in it.

The three largest cruise destinations in the Caribbean are the Bahamas, the U.S. Virgin Islands, and Puerto Rico. They account for over 50 percent of the arrivals by cruise ships in the Caribbean.

Cultural links with European nations have added to the attractiveness of these islands for Europeans. The three major European groups of tourists to the Caribbean are English, French, and German. England and France have developed strong patterns of tourism from their long colonial ties, and Germany has a prosperous population looking for exotic places to spend money in the sun. This European linkage is observed in Guadeloupe, with 87 percent of its visitors from France, and Martinique, with 85 percent of its visitors French, and in the high number of Europeans who visit the British Virgin Islands, Barbados, Antigua, Barbuda, Curacao, and Bermuda.

While not geographically part of the Caribbean, Bermuda, the Bahamas, and Turks and Caicos are included because most international organizations include them in the Caribbean for statistical purposes even though they are technically Atlantic islands. The greatest growth in the last two decades was in the cruise industry. The most visited islands are the Bahamas,

It's 1977 and I'm sitting by a smoldering fire of coconut husks on Pinney's Beach in Nevis. A guy in dreadlocks named Bushes torches a spliff and invites me to "reason" with him. Our conversation roams from the mundane to the metaphysical until the pink glow of daybreak, when he turns prophetic: "Dem crazy bald heads pollute di Earth 'til what future we gonna have?"

Pretty potent stuff for an idealistic marine biology intern with the Island Resources Foundation. This conservation group was among the first to conduct an environmental survey of the islands and publicize the growing damage to the region's fragile marine habitats.

Some three decades later, government inaction and the tourism industry's unchecked sun-and-fun mentality make 1977 look like the good old days. Seventy-five percent of the Caribbean's reefs are threatened, more than any other marine region on the planet except for Asia's Coral Triangle, according to the World Resources Institute. And nearly three-quarters of beaches are eroding away, the result of relentless development of coastal areas, including clear-cutting mangrove forests and dredging up sea grass beds. Coral reefs have also been ripped out to create larger cruise ship ports to accommodate the new breed of giant ocean liners that carry up to 8,700 passengers and crew. It's not just the beaches and reefs disappearing but fish, too, their spawning sites collapsing from pollution, habitat destruction, and overfishing. It's enough to make a tropical island lover swig a bottle of rum in despair.

But it may not be time to drown in drink just yet. With tourism in the Caribbean generating roughly $20 billion in annual revenues and supporting two million jobs—employing one out of eight people (the Caribbean is the world's most tourism-dependent region)—local government leaders are finally making the connection between a healthy environment and those postcard-pretty island images. In what could be the most ambitious marine conservation effort ever undertaken, ten governments have formed the Caribbean Challenge Initiative.

The goal is to conserve at least 20 percent of each island's marine and coastal habitat—an unprecedented target that would nearly triple the Caribbean's marine protected areas to some 20 million acres.

In what could be the most ambitious marine conservation effort ever undertaken, ten governments have formed the Caribbean Challenge Initiative.

"The tourism economy of our region relies to a great extent on protecting our natural heritage. The success of the Caribbean Challenge Initiative speaks to the very survival of the Caribbean as a travel destination and the prosperity of our people," says Prime Minister Tillman Thomas of Grenada, where three new marine national parks were recently created.

Other island governments are also putting their words into action: Since the initiative was unveiled in 2008, the Bahamas has set aside 1.2 million acres of unspoiled coast—one of the region's last true wildernesses—as the Andros Westside National Park. St. Kitts and Nevis has completed an integrated marine conservation zoning plan, and Jamaica has declared ten fish sanctuaries.

In a major conservation move, the Dominican Republic—one of the Caribbean's most biodiverse countries—created 32 new protected areas, safeguarding 2.7 million acres of marine habitat, including coral reefs and meadows of sea grass that are home to endangered species such as manatees and sea turtles.

"If these island nations can pull off protecting a full 20 percent of their marine ecosystems, the Caribbean will show the world that even small nations can deliver huge conservation results and provide a model that other islands can learn from," says John Myers, deputy director for the Caribbean Program at the Nature Conservancy, which is providing technical assistance.

The task will not be easy. Despite some impressive strides, much more still needs to be done. Next spring, the prime ministers of Grenada and British Virgin Islands will join sustainability advocate and Virgin CEO Richard Branson in cohosting other Caribbean government leaders, business representatives, and marine conservationists at Branson's private retreat in the British Virgin Islands. Together they will wrestle with some of the most intractable challenges. On the agenda: Raise money to finance the project (at least $50 million is needed), get the support of the tourism sector—including businesses that have long benefited from lax environmental regulations (think cruise ships and megaresorts)—and encourage other Caribbean governments to sign on. (Where are you, Guadeloupe and Martinique? And what about you, Barbados?)

The good news is that it's not too late for the Caribbean. As local governments and concerned groups grapple with setting policy, what can reef-snorkeling, sun-basking travelers do? We can reward the islands that are trying to do the right thing by snorkeling, basking, and spending money on their shores: Antigua and Barbuda, the Bahamas, the Caymans, Dominican Republic, Grenada, Jamaica, Puerto Rico, St. Lucia, St. Kitts and Nevis, and St. Vincent and the Grenadines. Bushes, from Nevis, would call that "good reasoning."

—Costas Christ, *National Geographic Traveler*, November 2012

---

the Dominican Republic, Jamaica, and Cuba. Cuba had the greatest growth. The Cuban government encouraged tourism in an effort to help the economy of Cuba because support from the Soviet Union ended after its breakup in the early 1990s.

The major beneficiaries of the increased growth of the cruise visitors to the Caribbean are the Bahamas, the U.S. Virgin Islands, and Puerto Rico. The Caribbean is the most popular cruise destination in the world, with cruise visitors accounting for 45 percent of all arrivals. The next largest region for cruises is the Mediterranean, with only 14 percent of the world cruise passengers. Total revenue to the Caribbean from noncruise tourists is approximately three times greater than revenue from cruise passenger arrivals however.

The average length of stay varies from 2.7 days in Puerto Rico to 12.9 in Martinique. The longer average stay for tourists visiting Barbados, Cuba, the Dominican Republic, Jamaica, Martinique, and St. Vincent and the Grenadines results from the large number of European travelers to this area. The varied cultural backgrounds of the inhabitants of this area have produced a unique pattern of life that is expressed in the language, music, dance, art, architecture, and foods of the region. Basic languages include French, English, Spanish, and combinations of words from two or more languages to create a distinctive language known as **Creole**. English is the official language spoken in former British possessions, French in the former French possessions, French Creole in Haiti, and Spanish in Cuba and the Dominican Republic. Both Spanish and English are official languages accepted in Puerto Rico, but most business is conducted in English. In the Netherlands Antilles, Dutch is the official language, but English is spoken in all islands. In the southern islands, most of the people speak Papiamento, a Creole language that mixes Dutch, Spanish, Portuguese, English, and African words. To the African-modified forms of English and French heard in the Caribbean, there can be added several imported languages, with Hindi especially strong in Trinidad.

Catholicism dominates religion on most of the islands, with the exception of the former British islands where Protestant denominations, particularly the Anglican Church, dominate. On most islands, religious tolerance is the norm.

The Caribbean area also has an important legacy from Africa. In places, it strongly resembles western equatorial Africa in the construction of village dwellings, the operation of open markets, the role of women in rural life, the preparation of certain foods, the methods of cultivation, and artistic expression. The mixture of Blacks with Whites varies from 90 percent Black in Haiti to 15 percent Black in the Dominican Republic. This composition is further enhanced by the presence of Asians from India and China and other small populations from other countries.

During the nineteenth century, the emancipation of slaves and the later importation of laborers brought some far-reaching changes. For example, 100,000 indentured Chinese laborers were brought in to work in the sugar fields. In Jamaica, Trinidad, Guadeloupe, and Martinique, a quarter of a million East Indians arrived for the same purpose. This helps to explain the ethnic and cultural variety of Caribbean America.

A combination of the African, European, and Asian led to a unique and lively style of music and dance. The Caribbean has long been known for its **calypso** music and steel bands, with calypso flourishing especially in Trinidad. African rhythms and European dances are combined for a wealth of festive sound to delight tourists. Carnivals held throughout the Caribbean, such as the pre-Lenten carnival in Trinidad and the annual June merengue festival in the Dominican Republic, are popular tourist attractions. People come from all parts of the world to enjoy the rhythms and activities associated with them. Dance is as varied throughout the Caribbean as the language.

Art is also an expression of the Caribbean's rich history. The art of the original people of the Caribbean, the Arawak and the **Carib**, in addition to the primitive art of Africa and the variety of European traditions, offers travelers a rich opportunity to enjoy a variety of styles no matter which nation they visit.

The varied architecture of the Caribbean (Figure P5.3) instantly captures the visitor's eye, providing the

Figure P5.3 Caribbean architecture. © Kamira/www.Shutterstock.com

backdrop for music, dance, and art. Most buildings feature the distinctive patterns of the colonizing nations modified by climate and the changes wrought by history. The former Spanish West Indies, which are now the United States Virgin Islands, are marked by Danish influence, particularly the town of Christiansted on St. Croix. Those islands formerly under Dutch rule in the Caribbean echo the architecture of Holland, with Willemstad, Curacao, as the best example. Spanish architecture can be seen in Puerto Rico and the Dominican Republic. Victorian English details have been transplanted to the islands that were under British control, particularly in Frederiksted, St. Croix.

As might be expected, a wide variety of food is available, with various specialties from each culture throughout the islands. This variety results from the adaptation of European foods to the region, the incorporation of cuisines from the various settlers, the creation of specialties of the islands, and the availability of seafood. The variety of foods and cuisines has helped the Caribbean to attract tourists.

The cultural heritage of diversity in language, food, music, and dance has led to a special effort by many Caribbean countries to preserve the traditions of the past in museums, theaters, and organizations of performing artists. These, along with the traditional carnivals and festivals, have saved the tremendous cultural variety of the people. While entertaining to the tourists who visit the Caribbean, it is important to remember that it is part of the life of the people of the region.

chapter 13 : GREATER ANTILLES

© Songquan Deng/ShutterStock.com

139

The Greater Antilles are Cuba, the Caymans, Dominican Republic, Haiti, Jamaica, and Puerto Rico.

Cuba

Introduction

The Republic of Cuba encompasses more than 4,000 islands and cays. The main island, slightly smaller than Pennsylvania, is the largest in the Caribbean. The northern coastline is steep and rocky, but mangrove swamps are prevalent along the south and southwest coasts. Fertile plains cover most of Cuba, but the Sierra Maestra rises in the southeast as the highest mountain range, reaching 1,974 meters (6,476 feet). The climate is subtropical, warm, and humid. Cuban society is multiracial and based largely on Spanish and African origins. About half are considered mulatto or mestizo, 37 percent white, and 11 percent black. There is a small Chinese minority. Sustained declines in fertility and mortality contribute to an aging Cuban population. The United States took Cuba from Spain in 1898, giving the island independence in 1902. U.S. trade and investment in Cuba continued until the 1959 revolution, when Fidel Castro nationalized U.S.-owned properties. In response, the United States imposed an embargo in 1960 and broke off diplomatic relations with the communist state in 1961. Despite the long embargo, Cuba's economy is improving due to Canadian, European, and Latin American investments—especially in tourism. Some 2.4 million tourists arrived in 2009, with many coming for the exotic blend of sun, sea, sand, and socialism. In southeastern Cuba, the United States maintains a presence at Guantanamo Bay; the 1934 treaty between Cuba and the United States grants a perpetual lease for the naval base.

Area	110,860 sq km (42,803 sq mi)
Population	11,225,000
Government	communist state
Capital	Havana 2,174,000
Life Expectancy	78 years
Literacy	100%
Religion	Roman Catholic
Language	Spanish
Currency	Cuban peso (CUP); Convertible peso (CUC)
GDP per Cap	$9,700
Labor Force	20% Agriculture, 19.4% Industry, 60.6% Services

TRAVEL **TIPS**

Entry: U.S. citizens need a Treasury Department license. U.S. citizens cannot transact financial trade in any form to support tourism to Cuba.

Tourist Season: December to April

National Holiday: January 1 (Triumph of the Revolution).

Health: No requirements.

Internet TLD: .cu

CULTURAL CAPSULE Cuba is a multiracial society with a population mostly of Spanish and African ancestry. The organized religion is Roman Catholic.

Tourism Characteristics

Tourism to Cuba from the United States is restricted, which handicaps Cuban industry considerably. Travel to Cuba has increased each year. The number of tourists is increasing, reaching 2.5 million in 2011. They arrive on European, Russian, and Cuban airlines. Cuba also has connections to Canada, Mexico, Venezuela, and other Latin American countries.

Major new Cuban development has been taking place outside of Havana with the help of European investors from Germany, Italy, Spain, and Austria. In 1992 Cuba became a member of the **Caribbean Tourism Organization**, which helps in marketing Cuba as part of the Caribbean outside of the United States.

Tourist Destinations and Attractions

Havana, the capital, has become somewhat run-down, but the old town near the docks is still the focal area for visitors. The city was founded in 1515, and many of the ancient palaces, plazas, colonnades, churches, and monasteries are still part of the landscape (Figure 13.1). Around the old town, there are narrow and picturesque streets. The presidential palace now holds the museum of the Revolution. Near Havana is Guanabacoa, a well-preserved, small colonial town with a historical museum containing a voodoo collection located in the former slave quarters.

Figure 13.1 The Cathedral of Havana and the famous nearby square. © Kamira/www.Shutterstock.com

Figure 13.2 Beach on the coast of Cuba. © Sexto Sol/Getty Images

Cuba has some excellent beaches (Figure 13.2) and deep bays that are good for snorkeling and other water sports. Santiago de Cuba on the east side of the island is home to a number of museums, the most noted of which is the Colonial Museum located in the Diego Velasquez house.

Cayman Islands

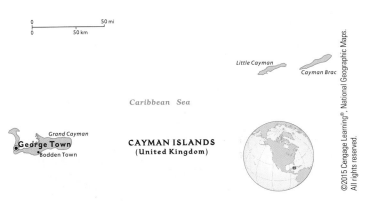

Introduction

The three small Cayman Islands are south of Cuba in the Caribbean Sea. Grand Cayman holds 94 percent of the people and gets most of the tourists with Seven Mile Beach. Cayman Brac boasts great bird-watching and Little Cayman offers spectacular diving sites.

From *National Geographic Atlas of the World*, 9th edition. Copyright ©2011 National Geographic Society. Reprinted by arrangement. All rights reserved.

Area	264 sq km (102 sq mi)
Population	55,000
Capital	George Town 28,000
Religion	Church of God, United Church, Roman Catholic, other Christian
Language	English, Spanish

From *National Geographic Atlas of the World*, 9th edition. Copyright ©2011 National Geographic Society. Reprinted by arrangement. All rights reserved.

TRAVEL**TIPS** 🧳

Entry: A passport is required for U.S. citizens traveling to the Cayman Islands.

Peak Tourist Season: March and December.

National Holiday: First Monday in July (Constitution Day).

Major cities: George Town

Shopping: Grand Cayman has duty-free goods and no sales tax, which is beneficial to visitors. Jewelry from black coral (an environmental concern), wood carvings, lacework, and local crafts are popular items.

Internet TLD: .ky

CULTURAL CAPSULE

The Cayman Islands are inhabited by an English-speaking population. The food specialties are turtle soup, turtle steak, oyster, conch pie, snapper, and barracuda.

Tourism Characteristics

The Caymans were first sighted by Columbus on his last voyage in 1503 and he named them Las Tortugas, the island of turtles. More than 75 percent of the 280,000 annual visitors in the Caymans are from the United States. However, visitors from Europe increased by 50 percent from 2000 to 2010. The only two island industries are tourism and international banking. They offer a wide range of accommodations and eating establishments.

Tourist Destinations and Attractions

George Town, the island group's capital, is a vibrant city with some of the Caribbean's best shopping, a renowned National Gallery, and the Cayman National museum. The Cayman Islands beaches are among the best in the Caribbean. The Seven Mile Beach, with its dazzling white sand and tall Australian pines, is becoming famous as a destination wedding and honeymoon destination. The reef and the many shipwrecks attract all kinds of underwater tropical fish and both snorkelers and scuba divers (Figure 13.3). In addition to great beaches, the coastline provides other water-related experiences such as blowholes and unusual rock formations. The Cayman Turtle Farm on Grand Cayman is the only commercial turtle

Figure 13.3 Divers swimming near the Tibbetts, a Russian frigate that was sunk in the waters off Cayman Brac. © Durden Images/www.Shutterstock.com

farm in the world and an interactive maritime park with sea turtles, sharks, and a snorkeling lagoon. Stingray City is another family attraction. Cayman Brac and Little Cayman provide visitors with a more relaxing lifestyle, as both have small populations of warm and friendly people. Both small island escapes offer excellent walking and hiking trails.

Dominican Republic

Introduction

The Dominican Republic occupies the eastern two-thirds of the island of Hispaniola, which it shares with Haiti. The second largest country in the West Indies (after Cuba), the Dominican Republic is a mountainous land that includes the Cordillera Central (Central Range) and Pico Duarte—the highest point in the Caribbean at 3,175 meters (10,416 feet). But there are also fertile valleys and a wide Caribbean coastal plain, where sugar plantations have existed for centuries. The country has a tropical climate, with a varying rainy season. The northern coast receives rain November through January, but the rest of the country experiences the rainy season from May through November. Tropical storms and hurricanes usually strike the southern coast.

Most Dominicans represent a blend of Spanish, Indian, and African ancestries. There is a strong African folk culture, especially in music. Haitians form a large minority, estimated at nearly one million.

The Spanish colonized the island in 1493. Santo Domingo, founded in 1496, is the oldest European settlement in the Western Hemisphere. The colonial center of Santo Domingo became a UNESCO World Heritage site in 1990. Gaining independence in 1844, the Dominican

Republic endured decades of political instability and repressive governments. Today it is a democracy, economically dependent on agriculture and tourism.

Area	48,670 sq km (18,792 sq mi)
Population	10,090,000
Government	democratic republic
Capital	Santo Domingo 2,154,000
Life Expectancy	72 years
Literacy	87%
Religion	Roman Catholic
Language	Spanish
Currency	Dominican peso (DOP)
GDP per Cap	$8,300
Labor Force	14.6% Agriculture, 22.3% Industry, 63.1% Services

TRAVEL**TIPS** 🧳

Entry: A passport and a 30-day tourist card are required for U.S. citizens traveling to the Dominican Republic.

Peak Tourist Season: December through April.

National Holiday: February 27 (Independence Day).

Health: Cholera. Check with local health officials before visit.

Shopping: Amber jewelry is the most noted item. Devil masks, cigars, and ceramic lime figurines that symbolize the Dominican culture are valued by visitors.

Internet TLD: .do

CULTURAL CAPSULE The Dominican Republic was originally occupied by a branch of the Arawak people from South America. After the discovery by Columbus, the native population was reduced. The Spanish began bringing African slaves to the island in 1503. During the 1600s, the French settlers occupied the western end of the island, which is now Haiti. The population today is mixed with a sizable European minority. Baseball is the national pastime and provides many major league players to the professional leagues in the United States.

Cultural hints: The handshake is a common greeting. The basic cooking is Spanish with a number of foreign ethnic restaurants such as Italian, Chinese, and French. Typical foods are sancocho (thick, heavy soup-cum-stew of pork, yams, sausages, onions, tomatoes), arroz con pollo (chicken and rice), pastelitos (small pastries filled with chicken or other meat), empanadas (meat patties), and fritos (assorted fritters).

Tourism Characteristics

The Dominican Republic is increasing its tourist trade and has many attractions that can be used to generate tourism. Tourism is by far the largest earner of income in their international trade. Tourism arrivals doubled in just one decade, reaching 4 million in 2011. The Dominican Republic has become one of the major destination countries of the Caribbean. The fastest growth in arrivals is from Europe. There are large numbers of charters from the European countries of the United Kingdom, Germany, Spain, Switzerland, and France as well as an increase from Canada.

Tourist Destinations and Attractions

The capital and major seaport, Santo Domingo, is the center of the tourism industry to the Dominican Republic. It was founded by Bartholomew, the brother of Christopher Columbus. The city was the base for the Spanish exploration and conquest of the American continent. Today there are many colonial buildings that have been restored as major tourist attractions. The Cathedral of Santa Maria La Menor (Figure 13.4) is the oldest cathedral in the New World, and the remains of Christopher Columbus were buried there. In 1992, the remains were moved to a new monument at Playa Dorado where an eleven-story lighthouse in the shape of a cross was completed for the five-hundredth anniversary of Columbus's discovery of the

Figure 13.4 Cathedral of St. Mary of the Incarnation (Cathedral of Santa Maria la Menor) in Santo Domingo, the oldest cathedral in the Americas. © Zoran Karapancev/www.Shutterstock.com

New World. Other impressive buildings are the Torre del Homenaje, which was built in 1503–1507 and is the oldest fortress in America; the Museo De las Casas Reales, a reconstructed early sixteenth-century building; the Alcazar de Colon, which was built by Diego Colon (Columbus's son) and was the seat of the Spanish Crown in the New World; and the ruins of the Monasterio de San Francisco, the first monastery in America. The region along the coast from Santo Domingo contains a number of popular resorts, towns, and beaches. Boca Chica, eighteen miles east of Santo Domingo, is the most popular resort. It has a reef-protected shallow lagoon and good beaches. Juan Dolio is also a popular beach. La Romana has an artist enclave and offers golf, polo, horseback riding, and a marina.

With its rugged landscape, the interior provides the scenery for hill resorts. The town of Jarabacao and the Constanza region have many beautiful pine forests, rivers, waterfalls, and impressive peaks, of which the Pico Duarte is the highest in the Caribbean.

The majority of international visitors interested in sun-sea-sand enter the country at Puerto Plata, which was founded by Columbus. It is here at Playa Dorado that the Columbus memorial referred to was built. It is also a major stop for many cruise companies. In both directions from Puerto Plata along the Atlantic coast, there are excellent beach resorts, providing diving and water sports. San Filipe Fort was used by the Spanish in the sixteenth century to fight off pirates.

Haiti

Introduction

Haiti, the first Caribbean state to achieve independence, occupies the western third of the island of Hispaniola. Mountainous (Fig 13.5) with a tropical climate, it is the poorest country in the Americas due to decades of violence and instability. The country is prone to devastating tropical storms, hurricanes, floods, and earthquakes. There is a huge income gap between the Creole-speaking black majority and the French-speaking mulattos (mixed African and European descent). Mulattos, only 5 percent of the population, control most of the wealth. To escape poverty and natural disasters, Haitians have migrated mostly to the United States, but also to Canada, the Dominican Republic, and other Caribbean neighbors. Most of the 535,000 Haitians in the United States live in Florida and New York. Remittances from millions of Haitians living abroad are vital to the country's economy.

Haiti became the first black republic in 1804 after a successful slave revolt against the French. As Haiti celebrated 200 years of independence, a rebellion toppled the government in February 2004. An interim government, bolstered by international peacekeeping forces, ruled until a new president was elected in 2006. Since 2004, the UN Stabilization Mission in Haiti (MINUSTAH) has helped create a stable political environment with more than 7,000 troops and 3,000 police. On January 12, 2010, a magnitude 7 earthquake hit Haiti's capital, Port-au-Prince, destroying the city and killing some 230,000 people.

From *National Geographic Atlas of the World*, 9th edition. Copyright ©2011 National Geographic Society. Reprinted by arrangement. All rights reserved.

Area	27,750 sq km (10,714 sq mi)
Population	9,242,000
Government	republic

HAITI

Capital	Port-au-Prince 1,998,000
Life Expectancy	58 years
Literacy	53%
Religion	Roman Catholic, Protestant, Voodoo
Language	French, Creole
Currency	gourde (HTG)
GDP per Cap	$1,300
Labor Force	66% Agriculture, 9% Industry, 25% Services

From *National Geographic Atlas of the World*, 9th edition. Copyright ©2011 National Geographic Society. Reprinted by arrangement. All rights reserved.

TRAVEL**TIPS**

Entry: A passport is required for U.S. citizens traveling to Haiti.

Peak Tourist Season: December

National Holiday: January 1 (Independence Day).

Health: Concern for malaria and yellow fever. Check with local health officials before travel.

Shopping: Best buys are wooden statuettes, inlaid boxes and trays, embroidered clothes, copper jewelry, heavy bedspreads and draperies, and paintings by local artists.

Internet TLD: .ht

Figure 13.5 Coast of Haiti. © FloridaStock/www.Shutterstock.com

CULTURAL CAPSULE Haiti is one of the world's most densely populated countries. Its population is almost 95 percent of African ancestry. The remainder are mixed African Caucasian (mulattoes). Language is French based, with Creole the most common. Roman Catholic is the dominant religion, but voodoo practices are widespread.

Cultural hints: Greet with a friendly handshake. Many residents offer to be guides. Food is based on French cuisine creating Creole specialties, combining French, tropical, and African ingredients. Typical dishes are guinea hen, tassot de dinde (dried turkey), grillot (fried island pork), diri et djondjon (rice and black mushrooms), riz et poils (rice and kidney beans), lobster, pork chops, and various sauces.

Tourism Characteristics

Tourism to Haiti suffered due to political problems since the ending of the Duvalier dictatorship in 1986. It is the least developed country in the Western Hemisphere and the country's troubles deepened when a devastating earthquake (7.0 scale) hit the island in 2010. Until recovery efforts are successful, the tourist industry will continue to suffer. Haiti desires to have tourists and the people have been very friendly toward visitors. In the past, nearly 85 percent of the visitors were from the United States and Canada. It has had excellent connectivity with

a number of carriers providing air service and Port-au-Prince was a major port stop for cruise lines from the United States. However, political unrest and a slowly recovering tourism industry infrastructure have left the tourist industry in disarray, and Haiti in now one of the least visited destinations in the Caribbean.

Tourist Destinations and Attractions

Haiti offers intrepid tourists at least four important attractions: its culture, including African voodoo and associated African music; shopping, especially in the Iron Market; the unique scenery; and outstanding beach resorts.

Port-au-Prince, the capital and port city, is located on a beautiful deep bay with high mountains in the background. The houses are colorful and unique in architectural style. A short distance up the mountains at Pétionville, the cooler mountain environs were the primary location of the Europeans. The Iron Market in the center of town is crowded with people (both inside and outside) buying and selling their wares.

A number of museums display Haitian art, relics, costumes, paintings, and historical items of the better coral reefs in the world. A second major area of interest centers on Cap Haitian, which is the second largest city in Haiti. The coastal area around Cap Haitian has a number of excellent beaches and locations providing good access to the coral reefs.

One of the most important attractions in the area near Milot is the Citadelle, a large ruined fortress built for King Henri Christophe in the 1800s. The Haitians regard it as the eighth wonder of the world. It is on top of a mountain accessible by either a two-hour walk or a horseback ride. The ruins of the Sans Souci Palace, which was built in the early nineteenth century as a rival to Versailles, are also located at Milot.

Jacmel, a port city on the south coast, is an area of many beaches, some with black sand and others with white. The area provides some scenic steep and rocky mountains, including Pic de Macaya (7,700 feet), with waterfalls and bays.

Jamaica

Introduction

Jamaica is the third largest Caribbean island, after Cuba and Hispaniola. Its sugary sands and beach resorts share the densely populated coastal plains with major cities, such as Kingston and Montego Bay. Inland there are hills, plateaus, and the forested Blue Mountains, named for the blue haze surrounding the high peaks. The climate is tropical but cooler inland.

Columbus landed here in 1494, and the Spanish soon brought in slaves as the native Arawak Indians died out—today 90 percent of the population is of African descent. The British seized the island in 1655, granting independence in 1962. The African culture has produced Rastafarianism, reggae, and Jamaican jerk seasonings. Tourism is a steady earner, but unpredictably priced products, such as bauxite and sugar, cause uneven growth. Crime is a problem due to the drug trade and unemployment, and many Jamaicans immigrate to the U.S. Remittances from overseas Jamaicans contribute billions to the economy.

From *National Geographic Atlas of the World*, 9th edition. Copyright ©2011 National Geographic Society. Reprinted by arrangement. All rights reserved.

Area	10,991 sq km (4,244 sq mi)
Population	2,702,000
Government	constitutional parliamentary democracy
Capital	Kingston 580,000
Life Expectancy	72 years
Literacy	88%
Religion	Protestant (Seventh-Day Adventist, Pentecostal, Church of God, Baptist)
Language	English, English patois
Currency	Jamaican dollar (JMD)
GDP per Cap	$8,200
Labor Force	17% Agriculture, 19% Industry, 64% Services

From *National Geographic Atlas of the World*, 9th edition. Copyright ©2011 National Geographic Society. Reprinted by arrangement. All rights reserved.

TRAVEL **TIPS**

Entry: A passport is required for U.S. citizens traveling to Jamaica.

Peak Tourist Season: January through March

National Holiday: August 6 (Independence Day).

Health: Concern for yellow fever and cholera.

Shopping: Local items are Jamaican cigars, rum, calypso music boxes, shells, carvings, pottery, clothing, fabrics, and straw work.

Internet TLD: .jm

CULTURAL CAPSULE The population of Jamaica is primarily of African origin. Minorities are Afro-Europeans (15 percent), Afro-East Indians and East Indians (3 percent), Caucasians of European descent (3 percent), and some Chinese and other groups. The Anglican Church is the largest of the established churches, followed by many Baptist sects, the Roman Catholic, and the Methodist. Jamaica has several Muslim and Hindu groups, along with a small Jewish community. Rastafarians, who see former Ethiopian Emperor Haile Selassie as the embodiment of God (Jah), are also found here.

Cultural hints: Greetings are a nod, bow, or handshake. Abundant hand gestures are common when talking. Meals are relaxed and sociable. Foods are spicy. Typical dishes are ackee and saltfish, rice and beans, jerked (grilled) pork and chicken, and pepper pot soup.

Tourism Characteristics

Tourism started in Jamaica in 1905 at Port Antonio. Many of the early tourists were English visiting the beautiful tropical resort. The continued growth in tourism has been important as Jamaica's other industries have

Figure 13.6 Doctor's Cave Beach Club, Montego Bay (also known as Doctor's Cave Bathing Club) has been one of the most famous beaches in Jamaica for nearly a century. © col/www.Shutterstock.com

declined. North America dominates tourism trade to Jamaica, accounting for 75 percent of all arrivals (2 million in 2011). Tourism from the United Kingdom is growing and becoming more important. This is reflected in the increased number of flights from London. Jamaica's principal ports of Ocho Rios and Montego Bay are popular cruise ship stops. Today tourism is the largest earner of foreign exchange and the island's major employer.

Tourist Destinations and Attractions

An important attraction in Jamaican trade has been the development of the all-inclusive resorts, where one price includes the entire cost of the holiday from food and accommodations to water sports and drinks.

The Montego Bay-Negril-Mandeville region is Jamaica's principal tourist center and has an international airport. Around Montego Bay, there are beautiful coastlines of white sand beaches and deep blue water (Figure 13.6), which provide for all types of water activities year-round. The majority of its hotel and motel rooms are in this area and shopping on Gloucester Avenue is a popular activity. The second major resort area is Ocho Rios, which is on a sheltered bay. It claims some of the best

beaches on the islands (Runaway Bay and Discovery Bay) and is a popular stop for cruise ships. Near Ocho Rios are the beautiful Fern Gully and two falls, Roaring River Falls and Dunn's River Falls, where visitors can be seen climbing through the waterfalls enjoying the cool, fresh water. Falmouth, wedged between Montego bay and Ocho Rios, recently opened the Caribbean's newest cruise port.

The third area is around Port Antonio, cradled between the Blue Mountains and the shores of the Caribbean Sea. It was the home of actor Errol Flynn. He was reported to have said that Port Antonio was among the most beautiful places known. West of the town near Buff Bay is Crystal Springs, a nature reserve home to 23,000 orchids and hundreds of tropical birds. It is the island's oldest tourist area, and its beaches are less crowded than the two more popular resorts at Montego Bay and Ocho Rios. It also has good fishing. However, one of the major attractions is in the mountains, where visitors ride two-person bamboo rafts down the rapids of the Rio Grande to a point on the coast near Port Antonio. Southeast of town is Nonsuch Caves at Athenry Gardens, with lovely stalagmites, stalactites, and fossilized sponges. Blue Mountain Peak, at 7402 feet, is a challenge even for experienced

Until the '50s, this rickety banana port was Jamaica's epicenter for tourism. Big modern resorts have since been built elsewhere, leaving Porty's provincial character unscathed. "Here on a personal level you can still experience the heart and soul of Jamaica," says Shireen Aga, co-owner of the ten-room Hotel Mocking Bird Hill, a pioneer in sustainable tourism. "Whether walking around our twin harbors or eating lobster at Cynthia's hut on Winnifred Beach, visitors can interact with locals a million different ways." There's nothing generic about Porty, from "da' jelly" (chilled coconut water) sold at Musgrave market to its quirky hotels, ranging from the delightfully decrepit DeMontevin Lodge to celebrity-fave Geejam with its veranda whirlpools and in-house recording studio.

Five splendid beaches etch the coastline, Monkey Island entices offshore, and spring-fed Blue Lagoon—a 180-foot-deep indigo hole—opens to the sea. The misty mountain backdrop is Maroon country, the communally owned, self-governing homeland of former runaway slaves granted their freedom after a peace treaty was signed with the British in 1740. Navigate eight miles through its heart on the Rio Grande River, gliding on a bamboo raft, your guide poling through the riffles. "Up here with the Maroons, you can hike to the ruins of an 18th-century plantation, or learn how to make bammy, unleavened bread made from cassava flour," says Aga. In Charles Town, Maroon leader Colonel Frank Lumsden will show you around the museum, meant to keep Maroon culture

intact. If Maroons are the safe-keepers of Jamaica's origins, the Blue Mountains are its spiritual home. Explore them on trails dappled with exotic birds, more than 200 species. And if you need an attitude adjustment, sample Jamaica's most famous (and legal) backcountry crop. Yep, Blue Mountain coffee, arguably the world's most delicious bean. **The High**: Ask around in Porty or Charles Town to see if the Charles Town Drummers, a Maroon heritage drumming group, are performing. **The Low:** Deep potholes, steep hills, steering wheel on the right: Driving here is not for the fainthearted

—**Charles Kulander, *National Geographic Traveler*,** January/February 2010

---

hikers. The island is rich with formal gardens, including Hope Botanical Gardens, Shaw Park Gardens, Coyaba River garden, and Cranbrook Flower Forest.

Kingston, the capital and largest city, is located on the southern coast. It receives few tourists, but does have some museums with historical relics of the Arawak

culture and also the popular Bob Marley Museum. A number of old homes and villages throughout the island are open to visitors. These include Spanish Town, the former capital, with historical reminders of the English and the Spanish. Rose Hall and Greenwood, two great houses, are near Montego Bay.

Puerto Rico

Introduction

Puerto Rico, in the northern Caribbean, became a U.S. possession in 1898, and Puerto Ricans have been U.S. citizens since 1917. The Spanish name means "rich port," which still applies to the island's prosperous urban centers, resort beaches, and lush rain forests.

From *National Geographic Atlas of the World*, 9th edition. Copyright ©2011 National Geographic Society. Reprinted by arrangement. All rights reserved.

Location	Caribbean Sea
Area	13,790 sq km (5,324 sq mi)
Population	3,971,000
Capital	San Juan 2,690,000
Religion	Roman Catholic, Protestant
Language	Spanish, English

From *National Geographic Atlas of the World*, 9th edition. Copyright ©2011 National Geographic Society. Reprinted by arrangement. All rights reserved.

TRAVEL**TIPS**

Entry: No visa or passport required for U.S. citizens.

Peak Tourist Season: December to May

National Holiday: July 4 (U.S. Independence Day).

Shopping: Local items of hand-carved wooden religious figures, tortoiseshell, embroidery, jewelry, ceramics, woven hammocks, and fine

Figure 13.7 Fort El Morro, Puerto Rico. © Sexto Sol/Getty Images

cigars. Also a musical instrument similar to a 12-string guitar called a cuatros and hand-screened fabrics are popular items.

Internet TLD: .pr

CULTURAL CAPSULE The population of Puerto Rico is over 95 percent Hispanic. The official languages are Spanish and English with Spanish the most heavily used. Eighty-five percent of the population are Roman Catholics, and Catholic traditions and customs prevail.

Cultural hints: Use handshake when greeting. Summon waiters with a "psst" sound. Puerto Rican food dishes are Spanish in character. Common foods are rice and beans, arroz con pollo (chicken and rice), paella (includes shrimp, mussels, lobster, and other seafood), suckling pig roasted on a spit, fish, and chicken barbecue.

Tourism Characteristics

Puerto Rico has a strong tourist industry because of its political ties, and accessibility, to the United States. It receives more visitors than any other island in the Caribbean. Most of its 3.5 million annual visitors are from the United States. Europe accounts for only 5 percent of the market. A large number of former Puerto Ricans residing in the United States return to visit friends and relatives. The excellent airline connections (it is the major hub for American Airlines in the Caribbean), the common use of English, and the climate are also important factors to the large number of visitors. It also has become a major cruise center, ranking third in cruise passenger arrivals in the region.

Tourist Destinations and Attractions

San Juan, the oldest city under the U.S. flag, is both the capital and the principal tourist center in Puerto Rico. Its main attraction is its Spanish culture. San Juan is one of the oldest cities in the Western Hemisphere, with narrow, shaded streets, Spanish-style architecture, and beautiful patios and gardens. Many of the old houses have been restored and now serve as museums. Others have been whitewashed and decorated with an intricate lacing of black wrought iron to provide tourists with a view of the area when it was the commercial, governmental, and major residential area in its early history. All of these cluster around the large fortress to offer the traveler days of great scenic enjoyment. Two of the most dominant features of San Juan are the two forts of El Morro and San Cristóbal. El Morro (Figure 13.7), completed in 1785, is an impressive fortress guarding the entrance to the harbor. Fort San Cristóbal was begun in the seventeenth century to protect San Juan from land attacks. It is larger than El Morro and provides magnificent views from its ramparts and gun emplacements. La Fortaleza, the Governor's Palace, was built between 1533 and 1540 as a fortress and later expanded. The Institute of Culture restores and renovates all buildings. There are a number of excellent museums of art and history, including the Institute of Puerto Rico Culture and the Las Americas Museum.

Puerto Rico has a number of excellent resorts with Isla Verde the closest to San Juan. Luquilla Beach and the Dorado area have outstanding facilities and excellent beaches. All types of sports, including horseback riding, swimming, fishing, and snorkeling, are found in abundance on and around the island. Combined with the water sports Puerto Rico has been a golfing mecca with 25 world-famous courses.

El Yunque National Forest is a tropical rain forest complete with a large species of birds and varieties of trees. It is one of the most luxuriant rain forests in the world, with giant ferns, exotic trees, wild orchids, green vines, brilliantly colored parrots, and scenic waterfalls.

Ponce, the second largest city, has a fine art museum, and its ancient firehouse (Parque de Bombas) is the most photographed site in Puerto Rico. Near Ponce is Phosphorescent Bay, where the slightest movement sets the water sparkling. San Germán, the second oldest town (1573) on the island, still has preserved its Spanish colonial atmosphere.

REVIEW QUESTIONS

1. Explain the Dominican Republic's special role in preserving Columbus's legacy.

2. Take a good look at the size of the island of Cuba. How could the tourism industry in Florida be impacted if the United States normalized relationships with Cuba?

3. Why is the Dominican Republic an important destination for European travelers?

4. What are major attractions in Jamaica for cruise ship passengers?

5. How does Puerto Rico benefit from its special relationship with the United States?

chapter 14: LESSER ANTILLES

The Lesser Antilles are the United States Virgin Islands, British Virgin Islands, Anguilla, Antigua, Barbuda, St. Kitts-Nevis, French Antilles, Martinique, Guadeloupe, Netherlands (or Dutch) Antilles, Windward Islands, Dominica, St. Lucia, St. Vincent and the Grenadines, and Grenada.

United States Virgin Islands

Introduction

The U.S. Virgin Islands, in the northern Caribbean, consist of three main islands: St. Thomas, St. John, and St. Croix. St. Thomas is a lively tourist destination, most of St. John is a national park, and St. Croix has industry.

From *National Geographic Atlas of the World*, 9th edition. Copyright ©2011 National Geographic Society. Reprinted by arrangement. All rights reserved.

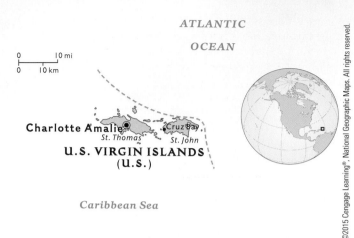

Area	386 sq km (149 sq mi)
Population	109,000
Capital	Charlotte Amalie 53,000
Religion	Baptist, Roman Catholic, Episcopalian
Language	English, Spanish or Spanish Creole, French or French Creole

From *National Geographic Atlas of the World*, 9th edition. Copyright ©2011 National Geographic Society. Reprinted by arrangement. All rights reserved.

TRAVEL **TIPS** 💼

Entry: No passport is required, but it is advisable to carry proper U.S. citizenship documentation.

Peak Tourist Season: January through March

National Holiday: July 4 (Independence Day).

Shopping: Popular items are liquor, linens, imported china, crystal, jewelry, hand-painted batik, and hook bracelets.

Internet TLD: .vi

CULTURAL CAPSULE The majority of the population is a mixture of West Indian (74 percent born in the Virgin Islands and elsewhere in the West Indies). Minorities are Puerto Ricans and United States mainland people who have moved to the Virgin Islands. English is the official language, but Spanish and Creole are widely spoken. In 1992, the islands celebrated the seventy-fifth anniversary of their transfer from Denmark to the United States for $25 million.

Cultural hints: Greeting is a handshake and smile. Typical dishes are fish soups, fungi (spiced cornmeal paste), turtle, kalaloo (spinach-type soup), gundy (herring balls), and soursop (a local fruit and cream).

Tourism Characteristics

Tourism is very important to the Virgin Islands as almost all of their income comes from tourism. They have a strong tourist industry with excellent airline and cruise connections to the United States. The number of cruise visitors to the Virgin Islands is exceeded only by the Bahamas, averaging 2.5 million in 2010. There is a well-developed infrastructure to provide all services required by visitors. Visitors from the United States represent the vast majority of all tourists.

Tourist Destinations and Attractions

The duty-free shops (rum, jewelry, and cigarettes are popular items) in Charlotte Amalie on St. Thomas can be crowded, especially when more than two cruise ships are in port at one time, which is common. The town was built by Danes, and visitors can see old Danish houses, picturesque churches, and one of the oldest synagogues in the Western Hemisphere. The well-known beaches of Magens Bay and Sapphire are active and noisy at times. However, the real St. Thomas is secluded beaches, endless vistas, and restaurants ensconced in Danish manor homes. It's a world of water sports, tennis, and the cliffside golf resort at Mahogany Run.

St. John, five miles east of St. Thomas, is, in part, a United States National Park. It has a number of hiking trails. The pace is much slower than at St. Thomas. St. John has a unique water snorkeling trail that is maintained by the National Park Service. St. Croix (pronounced St CROY), which is thirty-five miles south of St. John, has a number of restored sugar mills and museums that remind the visitor of the Danish rule. The two major towns are Christiansted, which is the old Danish capital, and Frederiksted. The focal point in Christiansted is the old town square and waterfront area, with its shops and restaurants. The red-roofed pastel houses found throughout Christiansted are reminders of the Danes. Seventeen miles from Christiansted, Frederiksted is best noted for its charming gingerbread architecture. Buck Island Reef Monument has a marked snorkeling trail.

British Virgin Islands

Introduction

Tortola, the largest island, is home to more than three-quarters of the population. This U.K. territory, east of Puerto Rico in the Caribbean, comprises some 40 islands and cays; only 16 are inhabited. Tourism drives the economy.

From *National Geographic Atlas of the World*, 9th edition. Copyright ©2011 National Geographic Society. Reprinted by arrangement. All rights reserved.

Area	151 sq km (58 sq mi)
Population	24,000
Capital	Road Town 9,000
Religion	Protestant
Language	English

From *National Geographic Atlas of the World*, 9th edition. Copyright ©2011 National Geographic Society. Reprinted by arrangement. All rights reserved.

TRAVEL**TIPS** 🧳

Entry: A passport is required for U.S. citizens traveling to the British Virgin Islands.

Peak Tourist Season: December through March

National Holiday: July 1 (Territory Day).

Shopping: The best items are art, jewelry, and clothing.

 CULTURAL CAPSULE The population is dominantly Black (90 percent) with minorities of Asian and White. Language is English, and there is a mixture of religious groups, mostly Protestant (86 percent).

Cultural hints: Typical dishes are seafood and local West Indian dishes.

Tourism Characteristics

Most visitors come from North America, with the United States accounting for over half of all visitors. The British Virgin Islands have good connections with other Caribbean islands. They have a small number of cruise visitors compared to the United States Virgin Islands.

Tourist Destinations and Attractions

Of the approximately 60 islands in the British Virgin Islands, the population and tourism are concentrated on Tortola and Virgin Gorda along with the groups of Anegada and Jost Van Dyke. Tortola has a rain forest with superb walking tours. The capital, Road Town, has a cruise ship dock and is the main location for charter boats. The Baths on Virgin Gorda is a coastal area where boulders as big as houses have fallen together to form grottoes, caverns, and pools (Figure 14.1). The British Virgin Islands have excellent snorkeling, and diving sites. A popular dive site is the wreck of the Rhone. Guana Island has a wildlife sanctuary for species like the masked booby. The region is a paradise for yachting with many opportunities for protected anchoring sites.

Figure 14.1 The Baths on Virgin Gorda, British Virgin Islands. © Achim Baque/www.Shutterstock.com.

Anguilla, Antigua, Barbuda, and St. Kitts-Nevis

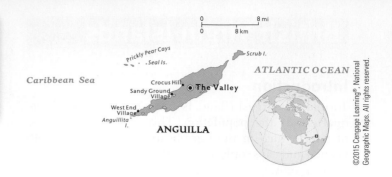

Anguilla

Small, only about 26 kilometers (16 miles) long, this Caribbean island lures tourists, mostly from the United States, with thirty-three powder-soft, white-sand beaches on pristine, turquoise seas. Tourism and banking are the most important industries.

From *National Geographic Atlas of the World*, 9th edition. Copyright ©2011 National Geographic Society. Reprinted by arrangement. All rights reserved.

BRITISH OVERSEAS TERRITORY

Location	**Caribbean Sea**
Area	96 sq km (37 sq mi)
Population	16,000
Capital	The Valley 1,500
Religion	Anglican, Methodist, other Protestant, Roman Catholic
Language	English

From *National Geographic Atlas of the World*, 9th edition. Copyright ©2011 National Geographic Society. Reprinted by arrangement. All rights reserved.

Religion	Anglican, Seventh-day Adventist, Pentecostal, Moravian, Roman Catholic
Language	English, local dialects
Currency	East Caribbean dollar (XCD)
GDP per Cap	$18,100
Labor Force	7% Agriculture, 11% Industry, 82% Services
Industry	tourism, construction, clothing, alcohol, appliances

From *National Geographic Atlas of the World*, 9th edition. Copyright ©2011 National Geographic Society. Reprinted by arrangement. All rights reserved.

Antigua and Barbuda

English settlers arrived in 1632, and the islands remained a British dependency until 1981. The country consists of three low-lying islands in the eastern Caribbean: Antigua, Barbuda, and Redonda. Most of the population lives on Antigua, only 1,500 inhabit Barbuda, and uninhabited Redonda is a nature preserve. Most Antiguans are of African origin, descendants of slaves brought here centuries ago to work in the sugarcane fields. Tourism has replaced agriculture as the main employer, with Antigua boasting 365 beaches—one for each day of the year.

From *National Geographic Atlas of the World*, 9th edition. Copyright ©2011 National Geographic Society. Reprinted by arrangement. All rights reserved.

Location	Caribbean Sea
Area	442 sq km (171 sq mi)
Population	88,000
Government	constitutional monarchy with a parliamentary system of government and a Commonwealth realm
Capital	Saint John's 26,000
Life Expectancy	73 years

St. Kitts-Nevis

The northeastern Caribbean island country of St. Kitts and Nevis was once known as the Gibraltar of the West Indies due to the massive seventeenth-century fortress atop Brimstone Hill on St. Kitts. The twin islands are both volcanic with black sand beaches and a warm, wet climate. Independent of Britain since 1983, it closed down the sugar industry in 2005, and is diversifying its economy. Tourism, banking, and light manufacturing now bring in revenue. Nevis, smaller in size than St. Kitts, has fewer people, but it attracts nature lovers to coral reefs and historic sites.

From *National Geographic Atlas of the World*, 9th edition. Copyright ©2011 National Geographic Society. Reprinted by arrangement. All rights reserved.

Location	Caribbean Sea
Area	269 sq km (104 sq mi)
Population	50,000
Government	parliamentary democracy and a Commonwealth realm
Capital	Basseterre 13,000
Life Expectancy	70 years
Religion	Anglican, other Protestant, Roman Catholic
Language	English
Currency	East Caribbean dollar (XCD)
GDP per Cap	$15,200
Industry	tourism, cotton, salt, copra, clothing, footwear, beverages

From *National Geographic Atlas of the World*, 9th edition. Copyright ©2011 National Geographic Society. Reprinted by arrangement. All rights reserved.

ST. KITTS AND NEVIS

TRAVEL**TIPS** 🧳

Entry: A passport is required for U.S. citizens.

Peak Tourist Season: December through March

Health: Concern for yellow fever.

Shopping: Local items of interest are straw hats, baskets, batik, pottery, and hand-printed cotton clothing.

Figure 14.2 The island of St. Kitts with Nevis in the background. © John Wollwerth/www.Shutterstock.com.

CULTURAL CAPSULE

The peoples of the Leeward Islands are dominantly African with a small minority of British and Portuguese in Antigua and Barbuda. All speak English and are Protestant, mainly Anglican. Seafood is used in the main dishes. Lobster and some West Indian curry are common specialties.

Tourism Characteristics

Anguilla, Antigua and Barbuda, and St. Kitts-Nevis are all part of the Leeward Islands. They have a common English-speaking background and are all well endowed with beaches and water sports. Anguilla has quite unspoiled and nearly deserted dazzling white beaches, clear turquoise water, and colorful undersea gardens. Recently it is becoming the playground for the royalty and wealthy of Britain.

The United States is the largest single generator of visitors, accounting for over half of visitors. The peak season accounts for approximately 45 percent of all visitors from December to March. Concern is being expressed because of the fragile ecosystems of the sandy beaches. The lack of adequate development controls allows many new accommodation projects to be built on the beachfront.

Travel Destinations and Attractions

Attractions in Anguilla include beaches at Rendezvous Bay, Cove Bay, and Mead's Bay. Activities on the island include horseback riding, bird watching, and visits to over a dozen art galleries. Carnival in August features a parade popular with residents and visitors alike. Antigua also has white sandy beaches and the Restored Nelson's Dockyard, dating to 1725, at English Harbor where Admiral Lord Nelson dropped anchor. It is part of a National Park that also houses Naval Officer's House, a museum that interprets the history of the area. Antigua is more lively than Anguilla in that it has gambling casinos and luxurious resorts. Untouched by progress, Barbuda is a small island forty miles to the north. It is a coral island with sandy beaches but little tourism development.

The two-island nation of St. Kitts-Nevis is located west of Antigua. It is a member of the West Indies Associated States and the British Commonwealth. St. Kitts (Figure 14.2) is a mountainous island with both black and white sand beaches. Nevis offers golden sand beaches and snorkeling on the coral reef. Both St. Kitts and Nevis are trying to expand their tourism and have encouraged cruise ships to add the island to their ports of call with little success.

French Antilles

The French Caribbean Islands consist of Martinique and Guadeloupe and its offshore islands of Marie Galante, Les Saintes, La Desirade, Saint Barthelemy, and St. Martin. These islands are represented by officials in the French Parliament. The tourism industry to the French Caribbean is dominated by visitors from France because of cultural ties.

Martinique

Martinique, in the eastern Caribbean, has an active volcano in the north, with luxury resort beaches in the south. Martiniquais are French citizens, because the island is an overseas department of France. Most people are of mixed ancestry, descendants of French settlers and African slaves.

Location	Caribbean Sea
Area	1,100 sq km (425 sq mi)
Population	406,000
Capital	Fort-de-France 93,000
Religion	Roman Catholic, Protestant, Hindu, Muslim
Language	French, Creole

Tourist Destinations and Attractions

Martinique has been a French island since 1635. Fort-de-France is a major port of call for cruise vessels in the Caribbean. It is similar in character to New Orleans and boasts of being the birthplace of Napoleon's wife, the Empress Josephine. The Martinique Museum contains material found from the Arawak and Carib period. It has a colorful market (Figure 14.3) and a popular artisan center that visitors from the cruise ships enjoy. Pointe du Bout is the island's main resort area. Of all visitors to the island in 2010, 95 percent arrived from France.

Guadeloupe

In the eastern Caribbean, Guadeloupe includes the main islands of Basse-Terre and Grande-Terre, which together form a butterfly shape. Tourism is a focus of the economy; most visitors come from France.

Location	Caribbean Sea
Area	1,705 sq km (658 sq mi)
Population	409,000
Capital	Basse-Terre 12,000
Religion	Roman Catholic, Protestant, Hindu, Muslim
Language	French, Creole

Figure 14.3 Stall of spices in Martinique. © Pack-Shot/www.Shutterstock.com.

Tourist Destinations and Attractions

Pointe-à-Pitre is the major port and commercial center. It has a picturesque harbor with a colorful central marketplace. Visitors can see several museums, a zoo, and an orchid garden. On Grande-Terre, away from Pointe-à-Pitre, the most important attractions are the ruins of the eighteenth-century fortress, Fort Fleur d'Epee; Gosier, the resort center; and Sainte-Anne, a popular beach resort.

The west side of the island is a nature lover's paradise with a very diverse wildlife. Basse-Terre is a port town of narrow streets and well-planned squares with palm and tamarind trees offering a picturesque setting between the sea and the La Soufriere volcano. It has a seventeenth-century cathedral and the ruins of Fort St. Charles.

The outer islands of Guadeloupe are some of the prettiest in the West Indies. They have a number of excellent beaches and unique fishing villages such as those of the Breton fisherman. Of all visitors in 2010, 95 percent arrived from France.

Netherlands Antilles

The Caribbean island of Curacao displays European flavor and an African heritage. The Dutch came in 1634, making the island a slave depot, which produced a rich African Caribbean culture. Willemstad, the capital city, features historic Dutch buildings and is a UNESCO World Heritage site. Dutch architecture and ideal tropical weather welcome tourists to Aruba. Its southwest Caribbean location that is south of the hurricane belt ensures maximum sunshine. Tourism and oil refining provide high living standards. "Diver's paradise" is Bonaire's motto, and visitors come to explore extensive coral reefs, colorful fish, and seahorses. Tourist attractions also include windsurfing, kite surfing, national parks, and thousands of flamingos. In 1986, Aruba was granted separate status. It became fully independent in 1996.

SELF-GOVERNING NETHERLANDS TERRITORY

Location	Caribbean Sea
Area	444 sq km (171 sq mi)
Population	141,000
Capital	Willemstad 120,000
Religion	Roman Catholic, Pentecostal
Language	Papiamento, English, Dutch, Spanish

From *National Geographic Atlas of the World*, 9th edition. Copyright ©2011 National Geographic Society. Reprinted by arrangement. All rights reserved.

TRAVEL**TIPS** 🧳

Entry: A passport is required for United States citizens traveling to the Netherlands Antilles.

Peak Tourist Season: December through March

National Holiday: April 30 (King's Day).

Shopping: Most items are imported and are an excellent buy.

Internet TLD: .an

CULTURAL CAPSULE The population on Aruba is mixed European/Caribbean Indian, while the population on Bonaire and Curacao is mainly African with minorities of Carib-Indian, European, Latin, and Oriental. Some forty nationalities are represented in the Netherlands Antilles and Aruba, but the mixture varies from island to island. Dutch is the official language, but Papiamento, a Spanish-Portuguese-Dutch-English-Creole dialect predominates. English is widely spoken.

Tourism Characteristics

Aruba, Curacao, and St. Maarten have the most tourists and the best-developed tourist industry. The other three are more relaxed and offer a slower pace. Constant sunshine combined with unique scenic surprises give the islands considerable tourist potential. However, growth will be somewhat limited because of the location of the islands off the coast of Venezuela. Tourism competes with oil refining as the major generator of foreign income. There are several oil refineries scattered through the islands, taking advantage of the oil production in Venezuela.

Aruba, now an independent country, was originally named "Oro Uba" by the Spanish conquistadors. To help solve the high unemployment problem, which is compounded by crop failures, the government of Aruba has developed an aggressive tourism promotion program. It focuses on the North American market. The island hosted nearly one million visitors in 2010.

Tourist Destinations and Attractions

Aruba has two locations considered to be both picturesque and good for surfers at Andicouri and Dos Playas. Druif, Eagle, and Palm are broad, white beaches fronted by a pedestrian walkway. The northwest coast is popular for wind surfing, parasailing, and kite surfing. The countryside is picturesque, with cactus fences, Aruban cottages, bougainvillea, oleanders, flamboyant hibiscus, and other tropical plants. A hike up 541-foot Mount Hooiberg is a popular activity. Oranjestad, the capital of Aruba, is a free-port town, with some Dutch character expressed in a few of the homes, the Olde Molen, and Fort Zoutmeer.

On Curacao, Willemstad, which has an outstanding harbor, provides many examples of Dutch architecture in pastel colors, rococo gables, arcades, and bulging columns on homes, shops, and government buildings. The Dutch colony house of Willemstad is a prime example of this unique Dutch architecture. Other buildings of interest are the Mikve Israel Emanuel synagogue, probably the oldest in the Western Hemisphere; an eighteenth-century Protestant church; the Governor's Palace; and the Maritime Museum, the Sea Aquarium, and the Curacao Postal Museum. The Floating Market is a unique market comprised of Venezuelan, Colombian, and other schooners in the small canal leading to the Waaigat. The western end of the island has beautiful beaches and Christoffel Park with wind-swept divi-divi trees and a road up Mount Christoffel and the reward of amazing vistas in every direction.

Bonaire (Flamingo Island), one of the most beautiful islands in the Caribbean, is only beginning to awaken to its potential as a tourist center. The coral reefs surrounding Bonaire rank just behind the Caymans and Cozumel for diving and snorkeling. The beaches and water sports are the main attractions. The capital, Kralendijk, has little to offer the tourist other than a folklore museum.

St. Maarten's slogan "Two for the price of one" stresses the two cultures of the island, French (Saint Martin) and Dutch (Sint Maarten), complete with architecture and cuisine, set amid white beaches (Figure 14.4) and tropical blossoms. The international airport (with a challenging runway), and most of the tourist development is on the Dutch side of the island. St. Maarten, a historical townhouse in Philipsburg and the capital of the Dutch side, is a popular shopping area for visitors from cruise ships. In 2010, 440,185 travelers visited St. Maarten.

The island of Saba is unique in that it has no beaches, but rises 2,900 feet from the ocean to its large volcanic mountain top. The principal population center and capital, The Bottom, is inside the crater of the volcano. In spite of the lack of beaches, Saba is a major attraction with its scuba diving, cool climate, and beautiful environment of flowers and trees.

St. Eustatius (Statia) is quiet and mostly visited on day trips from St. Maarten. It has a few historical sites, including a Jewish synagogue, a Reformed Church, and Fort Oranje, which is the seat of the government.

Figure 14.4 Tropical beach on St. Maarten. © Travel Bug/www.Shutterstock.com.

REVIEW QUESTIONS

1. What is unique about the National Park in St. Croix?

2. What explains the popularity of Martinique and Guadeloupe with French tourists?

3. What two countries "share" St. Maarten?

4. What is a divi-divi tree?

5. The Dutch ABC islands (Aruba, Bonaire, and Curacao) are also called the Continental Islands. Why?

chapter 15: OTHER WINDWARD ISLANDS

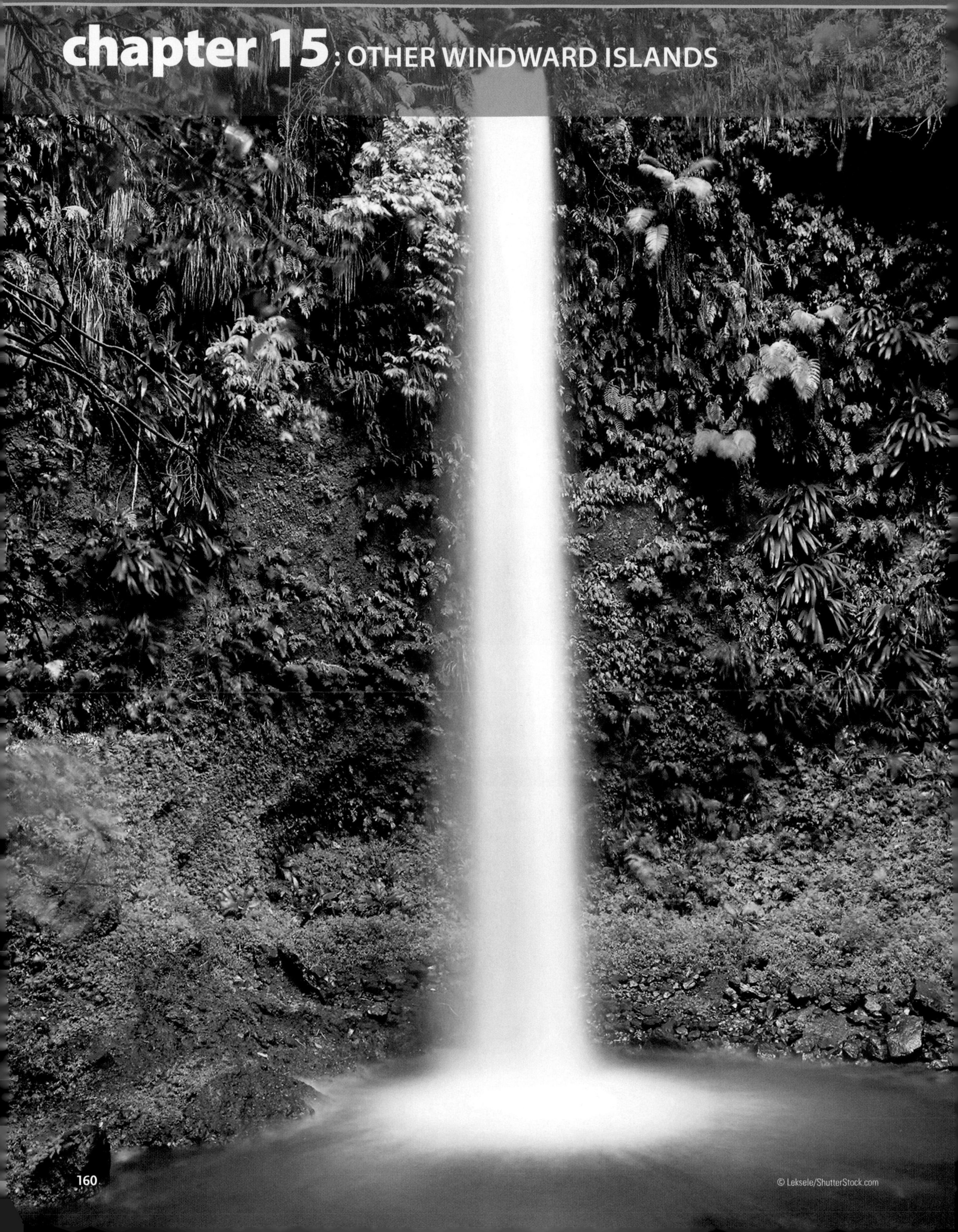

The rest of the Windward Islands are small and have had English connections. All have their major tourist season between January and March, with February being the peak tourist season. From April to December, the climate is hotter than in the Leeward Islands. However, the climate is somewhat moderated by the trade winds. The weather between June and October is particularly unpredictable. The terrain is generally mountainous, with a considerable portion volcanic. The Windward Islands are small, ranging from slightly larger than Washington, D.C., to considerably smaller than Rhode Island. The people are mostly of African ancestry, and the Roman Catholic religion dominates, although there are some Anglican, Methodist, and Seventh-Day Adventist groups. English is the official language, with some French spoken throughout the islands. All the islands use the East Caribbean dollar. They are all dependent upon tourism and continue seeking methods to increase visitor numbers.

Dominica

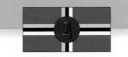

Introduction

Mountainous, densely forested, and with exotic birds, much of the Caribbean island of Dominica is protected as national wilderness. Volcanic activity provides boiling pools, geysers, and black sand beaches. Most Dominicans are descendants of African slaves brought in by colonial planters. Independent from Britain since 1978, Dominica remains poor and dependent on banana exports. The government tries to broaden the economic base with tourism and light industry. Home to 3,000 Carib Indians, Dominica is the last bastion of this once populous Caribbean tribe.

No airport

From *National Geographic Atlas of the World*, 9th edition. Copyright ©2011 National Geographic Society. Reprinted by arrangement. All rights reserved.

Area	751 sq km (290 sq mi)
Population	72,000
Government	parliamentary democracy
Capital	Roseau 14,000
Life Expectancy	75 years
Literacy	94%
Religion	Roman Catholic, Seventh-day Adventist, Pentecostal
Language	English, French patois
Currency	East Caribbean dollar (XCD)
GDP per Cap	$10,200
labor force	40% Agriculture, 32% Industry, 28% Services

From *National Geographic Atlas of the World*, 9th edition. Copyright ©2011 National Geographic Society. Reprinted by arrangement. All rights reserved.

Tourist Destinations and Attractions

Dominica, the largest of the Windward Islands, has one of the least developed tourist industries in the region. It is mountainous and rugged, with a tropical jungle and few settlements to support tourism. Dominica is popular with day trippers from Guadeloupe and Martinique. As the largest and most mountainous Windward Island, it has a number of hiking trails, dramatic scenery, lush forests, stunning waterfalls (Figure 15.1), orchids, and other wild plants. The island has a great deal to offer for travelers in search of adventure. The Rainforest Aerial Tram offers a 70-minute journey through the treetop canopy. The remnants of the original inhabitants live on the Carib Reserve. Other attractions are the market in Roseau, the capital, and the ruins of the eighteenth-century Fort Shirley near Portsmouth.

Figure 15.1 Emerald pool in Dominica. © Sorin Colac/www.Shutterstock.com.

St. Lucia

Introduction

Saint Lucia, an island in the eastern Caribbean Sea, gained independence from Britain in 1979. Tropical forests cloak a mountainous interior flanked by twin volcanic peaks, known as pitons. Oil transshipment via a U.S.–built terminal and exports of manufactured goods supplement agriculture and tourism. In recent years, revenue from tourism has replaced that from bananas. Tourists come for the beaches, rain forest canopy zip lining, and ATV adventures.

From *National Geographic Atlas of the World*, 9th edition. Copyright ©2011 National Geographic Society. Reprinted by arrangement. All rights reserved.

Area	616 sq km (238 sq mi)
Population	172,000
Government	parliamentary democracy and a Commonwealth realm
Capital	Castries 14,000
Life Expectancy	73 years

Literacy	90%
Religion	Roman Catholic, Seventh-day Adventist, Pentecostal
Language	English, French patois
Currency	East Caribbean dollar (XCD)
GDP per Cap	$10,900
Labor Force	21.7% Agriculture, 24.7% Industry, 53.6% Services

From *National Geographic Atlas of the World*, 9th edition. Copyright ©2011 National Geographic Society. Reprinted by arrangement. All rights reserved.

Tourist Destinations and Attractions

St. Lucia combines outstanding water sports utilizing great beaches and warm sea and sunshine with some of the best mountain scenery in the Caribbean islands. The twin peaks of Piton are beautiful and scaled by experienced climbers. A volcano provides a visitor with views of pools of boiling water, sulfur baths, and steam venting from the volcano. Castries, the capital, was rebuilt after a fire in 1948. It is on a natural harbor with beautiful mountains in the background. It has an excellent market and an old fortress. Excellent beach resorts can be found at Rodney Bay and Soufriere.

St. Vincent and the Grenadines

Introduction

This eastern Caribbean country consists of volcanic St. Vincent Island and the Grenadines, thirty-two smaller islands and cays. St. Vincent is hilly with rich volcanic soils, and its volcano, Soufrière, last erupted in 1979—the year of independence from Britain. Most Vincentians are descendants of African slaves. Hydroelectric plants help power St. Vincent's diversifying economy, dependent in part on exports of bananas. Tourism is of growing importance, especially in the Grenadines. The country experiences high unemployment and emigration. *leaving the island*

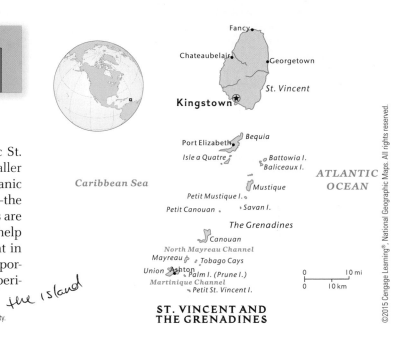

ST. VINCENT AND
THE GRENADINES

Area	389 sq km (150 sq mi)
Population	110,000
Government	parliamentary democracy and a Commonwealth realm
Capital	Kingstown 26,000
Life Expectancy	72 years
Literacy	96%
Religion	Anglican, Methodist, Roman Catholic
Language	English, French patois
Currency	East Caribbean dollar (XCD)
GDP per Cap	$18,100
Labor Force	26% Agriculture, 17% Industry, 57% Services

Tourist Destinations and Attractions

St. Vincent, known as the "Breadfruit Island," is a picturesque island with fishing villages, coconut groves, and fields of arrowroot. Kingstown, the capital, is on a sheltered bay and has the famous Botanical Gardens with the first breadfruit tree, which was planted by Captain Bligh of the Bounty. Fort Charlotte, an early British outpost, sits atop a bluff in Kingstown.

St. Vincent has some excellent beaches, most of which have the black sand that is common around volcanic islands. The mountains provide scenic drives with lush valleys and sea views.

The Grenadines (some are administered by Grenada and some by St. Vincent) are composed of over one hundred islands and are particularly good for yachting, fishing, and snorkeling. Carriacou and Petit Martinique are the part of the Grenadines that are administered by Grenada. They are attractive sandy islands with good underwater reefs. Bequia and Mustique are the largest of the St. Vincent dependencies and receive the most tourists.

Peak Tourist Season: December through March

Internet TLD: .vc

It's one of the last truly Caribbean islands, not yet overwhelmed by resorts and cruise ship crowds. The charm of this lush island lies beyond the white-sand beach of Grand Anse and its string of hotels.

Grenada's capital, St. George's, is one of the prettiest towns in the Caribbean, its jumble of orange roofs tumbling down to the harbor. There, the gray stones of Fort George evoke a history that runs from 1705 through the dark days of 1983, when a military coup by a Communist hard-liner prompted President Ronald Reagan's invasion of the island.

That was an unhappy exception to a happy rule: Grenadian traditions are an amiable mix of African, Indian, and European—much of it coming together every April on the country's little Carriacou island.

Grenadian traditions are an amiable mix of African, Indian, and European—much of it coming together every April on the country's little Carriacou island.

The Maroon Festival features drums, string bands, dances, and the "Shakespeare Mas," in which costumed contestants hurl island-accented recitations from Julius Caesar at each other. Really.

The weekly "Fish Friday" festival in Gouyave, Grenada's seafood town, offers a marine taste of true Caribbean. Vendors fill the air with scents of fish cakes, shrimp, conch, and beer. Street music makes it a party, with visitors welcome. For most Grenadians, tourists are guests, not sales targets.

Nutmeg, cloves, ginger, cinnamon, and mace made Grenada the "Spice Island," and culinary opportunity persists today. The Belmont Estate serves up such local fare as callaloo soup and bergamot ice cream. The dark slabs from the Grenada Chocolate Company are so determinedly organic that chocolate bars exported to Europe have been shipped by wind power on a square-rigged brigantine.

With mangrove-fringed coastlines and coral reefs just offshore, there's plenty of nature. At Mount Hartman, with the right guide at the right time, you might see the national bird: the shy Grenada dove. Fewer than 150 remain on Earth. Indeed, Grenada is becoming a rare bird itself.

—Jonathan B. Tourtellot, *National Geographic Traveler*, December 2012/January 2013

Grenada

Introduction

Grenada, located in the southeastern Caribbean, consists of the islands of Grenada, Carriacou, and Petite Martinique. Most Grenadians are of African descent. Nutmeg replaced sugar as the main crop after the British took the island from France in 1783. Small farms replaced sugar plantations, slavery was abolished, and today the sweet smells of nutmeg and other spices waft on balmy breezes. Since independence in 1974, Grenada has seen growth in tourism, medical schools, and banking.

Area	344 sq km (133 sq mi)
Population	106,000
Government	parliamentary democracy and a Commonwealth realm
Capital	St. George's 32,000
Life Expectancy	74 years

Literacy	96%
Religion	Roman Catholic, Anglican, other Protestant
Language	English, French patois
Currency	East Caribbean dollar (XCD)
GDP per Cap	$10,800
Labor Force	24% Agriculture, 14% Industry, 62% Services

Tourist Destinations and Attractions

St. George's, the capital, is one of the most picturesque towns of the Caribbean with terraces of pale, color-washed houses with red roofs. It blends the character of the French in typical eighteenth-century provincial houses with English Georgian architecture.

Grenada has some outstanding beaches. Grand Anse, a two-mile stretch of white sand beach, is considered one of the best in the world. The island has a rich agricultural tradition and produces cinnamon, cocoa, and nutmeg, earning it the "spice island" nickname.

REVIEW QUESTIONS

1. Describe St. Lucia's unique landscape and natural beauty.

2. What adventure activities await a visitor to St. Lucia?

3. What is the meaning of the words **Leeward** and **Windward**?

4. Comment on Dominica's unique status as an "ecotourism" destination.

5. How has Grenada diversified its economy?

Barbados

Introduction

Sugar production was the basis for the economy when this eastern Caribbean island achieved independence from Britain in 1966. Today the island runs on tourism, with banking and financial services growing in importance. The country promotes vacations for all tastes and budgets. The island's west coast features a modern cruise ship terminal and luxury beach resorts, while the south coast accents less pricey lodgings but great beaches. The windy, Atlantic-battered east coast is a top surfing spot, and central Barbados shows off rolling hills and historic plantation homes.

From *National Geographic Atlas of the World*, 9th edition. Copyright ©2011 National Geographic Society. Reprinted by arrangement. All rights reserved.

Area	430 sq km (166 sq mi)
Population	281,000
Government	parliamentary democracy and a Commonwealth realm
Capital	Bridgetown 116,000
Life Expectancy	77 years
Literacy	100%
Religion	Anglican, Pentecostal, Methodist, Roman Catholic
Language	English
Currency	Barbadian dollar (BBD)
GDP per cap	$18,500
Labor Force	10% Agriculture, 15% Industry, 75% Services

From *National Geographic Atlas of the World*, 9th edition. Copyright ©2011 National Geographic Society. Reprinted by arrangement. All rights reserved.

TRAVEL**TIPS** 💼

Entry: A passport is required for United States citizens traveling to Barbados.

Peak Tourist Season: December and March

National Holiday: November 30 (Independence Day).

Shopping: Local goods including straw mats, custom-made clothing, coral jewelry, wood carvings, basket work, pottery, woven goods, and Barbados rum. Duty-free goods (particularly British woolens) are abundant.

Internet TLD: .bb

CULTURAL CAPSULE The original peoples of Barbados were Arawak and Carib Indians. The British settled in the 1600s and brought African slaves to the island. Today Africans dominate, with 80 percent of the population. The official language is English. Bajan, descendants of African slaves, also use a dialect that can be understood by English speakers. Seventy percent of the people are Anglican and a mixture of other religions.

Cultural hints: A handshake and smile is a common greeting. Taxis and buses are called by waiving. Typical dishes are seafood (flying fish, lobster, shrimp, dorado, red snapper, turtle, tuna, and kingfish), cou cou (okra and corn meal), white sea urchin eggs, tropical fruits, pepperpot (a spicy stew), and jug-jug (Guinea corn and green peas).

Tourism Characteristics

Barbados has one of the best-developed tourist industries and receives the largest number of tourists in the eastern Caribbean. Arrivals topped a half million in 2010. The connectivity with the United Kingdom is strong, with a number of international flights between Barbados and London. Barbados is highly dependent upon tourism.

Tourist Destinations and Attractions

Barbados is probably the most typical English island. Standing near Trafalgar Square or on Bond Street in Bridgetown, you get the feeling that you are in London—but in a London with no fog, only sunshine. Bridgetown (Figure 16.1), the capital and center of tourism, has a number of excellent tourist attractions. The old part of town with wooden houses contrasts with the modern part of town. Other attractions are Broad Street, Independence Square, Nelson's statue, the Cathedral, and the Straw Market. Sunbury Plantation House contains a collection of seventeenth-century artifacts and antiques. Other museums include the Barbados Concorde Experience, and the Barbados Museum in Bridgetown. The island's premier festival, Crop Over, lasts for five weeks and includes markets, concerts, and parades. In Speightstown visitors find the Arlington House, a beautifully restored, interactive exhibit on the town's former glory as a major port. Gun Hill Signal Station was used to send smoke signals and people flock here to see the statue of a lion carved from one piece of rock. There are some excellent beaches on the south and west coasts, where most of the tourism of the island is located. In St. Peter is the Barbados Wildlife Reserve. The island is also a major cruise destination and the turnaround point for many eastern Caribbean cruise ship itineraries originating from Puerto Rico or the U.S. Virgin Islands.

Figure 16.1 Promenade in Bridgetown, Barbados. © Pixachi/www.Shutterstock.com.

Trinidad and Tobago

Introduction

Trinidad and Tobago, the most southern island country in the Caribbean, is just off the coast of Venezuela. Trinidad features plains and hills, with the highest elevations being in the Northern Range. Smaller Tobago is mostly hilly, but the southwest is largely flat. The islands are south of the hurricane belt, so they seldom suffer damage. They enjoy a warm, sunny climate, and the rainy season is from June to December. Trinidad and Tobago's people are mostly of African or East Indian descent. Britain granted independence to the islands in 1962, and it is the second largest English-speaking country in the Caribbean after Jamaica. Unlike other Caribbean nations, it is a major oil and natural gas producer; in addition, Trinidad contains Pitch Lake, a

huge asphalt deposit. High priorities for the economy are increasing gas production, aggressive promotion of foreign investment, and industrial and agricultural diversification.

From *National Geographic Atlas of the World*, 9th edition. Copyright ©2011 National Geographic Society. Reprinted by arrangement. All rights reserved.

Limin', or hanging out, is an acquired skill best learned on the island that has elevated it to a true art form: Tobago. The fine beach at Pigeon Point Heritage Park is the perfect place to begin some introductory limin'. (Start with rum punch, add sunset and dominoes.) Once you get the hang of it, head for Tobago's fabled northwest coast, passing hillside hamlets with fairytale names—Harmony Hall, Providence, Whim—to reach the quiet beaches of Castara, Charlotteville, and Parlatuvier, traditional places where you can still lend a hand by helping villagers tug their seine nets onto the sand in return for a share of the catch. Relaxation comes later, kicking it back at the tiny rum shops or beachfront dining shacks such as Boat House in Castara, where the local steel pan band

plays Wednesday nights. Village guesthouses and small hotels are integrated into community life, like the eco-sensitive Castara Retreats, a six-cabin aerie overlooking village and sea, and backed by the island's most precious resource: the Tobago Rain Forest Reserve. "It's the oldest legally protected rain forest in the Western Hemisphere, established in 1776 to protect the sugar plantation watershed," says guide and local ornithologist David Rooks.

The island's primordial bounty allows for prolific birdwatching, diving with manta rays, plunging into refreshing waterfalls, and snorkeling over the largest brain coral colony in the world.

The island's primordial bounty allows for prolific birdwatching, diving with manta rays, plunging into refreshing waterfalls, and snorkeling over the largest brain coral colony in the world. Come Sunday, attend "Sunday school" at Buccoo Beach, the island's largest nondenominational beach party: steel pan band, crab-and-dumpling stalls, and dancing into the wee hours. By now, you'll be limin' like a true Tobagonian. **The High:** J'ouvert, the muddy (old clothes, please), rum-fueled, music-blasting start to the two-day Carnival celebrations (Feb. 15–16) kicks off at 4 a.m. **The Low:** Expecting to find peace and relaxation during same Carnival.

—Charles Kulander, National Geographic Traveler, *January/February 2010*

Area	5,128 sq km (1,980 sq mi)
Population	1,333,000
Government	parliamentary democracy
Capital	Port of Spain 54,000
Life Expectancy	69 years
Literacy	99%
Religion	Roman Catholic, Hindu, Anglican, Baptist, Pentecostal, Muslim, Seventh-Day Adventist, other Christian
Language	English, Caribbean Hindustani, French, Spanish
Currency	Trinidad and Tobago dollar (TTD)
GDP per Cap	$23,100
Labor Force	3.8% Agriculture, 33.2% Industry, 62.9% Services

From *National Geographic Atlas of the World*, 9th edition. Copyright ©2011 National Geographic Society. Reprinted by arrangement. All rights reserved.

TRAVEL **TIPS** 🧳

Entry: A passport is required for U.S. citizens traveling to Trinidad and Tobago.

Peak Tourist Season: February

National Holiday: August 31 (Independence Day).

Health: Concern for yellow fever. Check with local health officials. Do not drink water from an unknown source.

Shopping: Good buys are Asian and East Indian silks and cottons. Local crafts from straw and cane are also popular.

Internet TLD: .tt

 CULTURAL CAPSULE The peoples of Trinidad and Tobago are mainly African or East Indian. Almost all speak English, ranging from standard British English to local dialects. Some speak Hindi, French patois, and several other dialects. The two major folk traditions are Creole (a mixture of African influenced by Spanish, French, and English culture) and East Indian.

Cultural hints: Foods are mixture of English, American French, Indian, or Chinese. Some popular Creole dishes are callaloo soup, stewed ta-too (armadillo), crab backs, fried iguanas or tum tum (mashed green plantains), and cascadura (fresh-water fish).

Tourism Characteristics

While Trinidad and Tobago have a well-established tourism industry, tourism is not as important to them as it is to other Caribbean islands because they have a stronger industrial base, including oil production and refining. Tobago, in contrast to Trinidad, is much more of a quiet vacation island with cozy resorts and great beaches.

Tourist Destinations and Attractions

Reflecting the Hindu culture that was imported with Indian laborers in the last century, Trinidad and Tobago surprise the eye with Hindu temples and Indian saris. The architectural mixture of English and Indian creates a unique landscape. Trinidad is the birthplace of the calypso, and the steel drum was first developed there. Carnival in February is one of the great festivals of the year and accounts for the large number of tourists visiting the island in that month.

Port of Spain, the capital, has a mixture of old wooden houses dotting the modern landscape. Important buildings of interest are the Red House, the Anglican Cathedral, Church of Holy Trinity, the Roman Catholic Cathedral, and a Hindu temple. A principal tourist site outside Port of Spain is Pitch Lake, which is about 110 acres of black tar. The beaches are not as good as on the other islands.

Tobago claims to be the island of Robinson Crusoe. The tradition and the beautiful setting of the island make it an interesting notion. It has a number of excellent beaches and fine snorkeling and swimming. Throughout the island, exotic tropical birds such as brown pelicans can be observed.

REVIEW QUESTIONS

1. Tourism in Trinidad and Tobago is not as important as it is in the other Caribbean islands. Why?

2. Barbados is "the most British" of all the Caribbean islands. Explain.

3. Barbados is often a "turnaround" island for the cruise ships. Explain.

4. Name several of Barbados' unique features and attractions.

5. What was the origin of the steel drums used in Calypso music?

© Matt9122/ShutterStock.com

Although the island groups discussed here, particularly the Turks and Caicos Islands, the Bahamas, and Bermuda are physically part of the Atlantic, they are often included in programs and itineraries with the Caribbean.

Turks and Caicos Islands

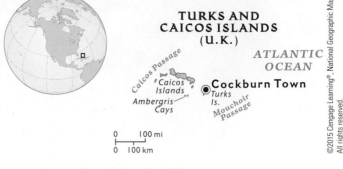

Introduction

Some forty islands and cays make up the Turks and Caicos Islands; only six of them are inhabited. These Caribbean islands are mostly barren and dry, making the surrounding waters clear, which brings in tourists for snorkeling and scuba diving.

From *National Geographic Atlas of the World*, 9th edition. Copyright ©2011 National Geographic Society. Reprinted by arrangement. All rights reserved.

TRAVEL**TIPS** 🧳

Entry: A passport is required for United States citizens traveling to the Turks and Caicos Islands.

Peak Tourist Season: February and March

National Holiday: August 30 (Constitution Day).

Shopping: Baskets woven from local grasses and small metal products are the only native crafts available.

Internet TLD: .tc

The people of Turks and Caicos Islands are mainly African who speak English. Religion is dominated by a Protestant mixture of Baptist, Methodists, Anglican, and Seventh-Day Adventists. Eating is mostly in hotels, and specialties are mostly seafood.

Tourism Characteristics

Tourism and fishing for conch and crayfish are the major sources of income for the islands. However, they do not receive large numbers of visitors. Almost 80 percent of their visitors are from North America, with the United States accounting for 70 percent of all visitors. They are reasonably accessible, with airline connections to Florida and the Bahamas and charter services to Europe.

Tourist Destinations and Attractions

Grand Turk is principally a resort island. Early in the year (from January through March) visitors flock to Salt Cay to spot the migrating humpback whales. A second international airport has been developed at Provo (East Caicos), and it has become a hub of tourism. It already has attracted numerous resort developers. In addition to the usual water sports, the area has some outstanding bonefishing waters.

The Bahamas

Introduction

An **archipelago** of some 700 coral islands and 2,400 cays, the Bahamas are famous for being the landfall of Christopher Columbus in 1492, a pirate haven in the 1600s, and a tourism paradise starting in 1898. The Bahamas became independent in 1973 after 325 years of British rule. Tourism drives the economy, which is focused on tiny New Providence island, home to 70 percent of Bahamians—add Grand Bahama and Abaco islands to get 90 percent of the people living on just three islands. Most Bahamians are of West African descent, with 12 percent being of European ancestry.

From *National Geographic Atlas of the World*, 9th edition. Copyright ©2011 National Geographic Society. Reprinted by arrangement. All rights reserved.

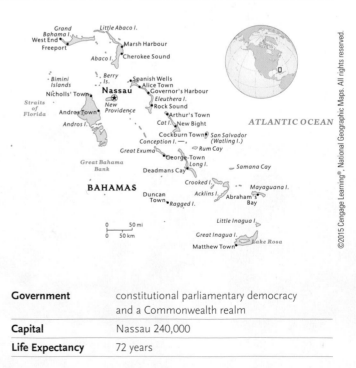

Area	13,939 sq km (5,382 sq mi)
Population	341,000
Government	constitutional parliamentary democracy and a Commonwealth realm
Capital	Nassau 240,000
Life Expectancy	72 years

Religion	Baptist, Anglican, Roman Catholic, Pentecostal, Church of God, other Christian
Language	English, Creole
Currency	Bahamian dollar (BSD)
GDP per Cap	$29,800
Labor Force	2% Agriculture, 18% Industry, 80% Services

From *National Geographic Atlas of the World*, 9th edition. Copyright ©2011 National Geographic Society. Reprinted by arrangement. All rights reserved.

TRAVEL **TIPS** 🧳

Entry: A passport is required for U.S. citizens traveling to the Bahamas.

Peak Tourist Season: March

National Holiday: July 10 (Independence Day).

Shopping: Local items include basketwork, and conch shell and tortoise shell souvenirs.

Internet TLD: .bs

 CULTURAL CAPSULE The people of the Bahamas are of African ancestry who speak English and some Creole. The most distinctive food dishes are from the sea such as the conch (a shelled mollusk), boiled crawfish, green turtle pie (turtle meat baked in a shell with vegetables), and desserts of coconut and guava duff.

Tourism Characteristics

The Bahamas have one of the strongest tourist industries in the region. It is close to Florida (only 60 miles from Miami) and has many cruise ships that either focus on the Bahamas or make stops as a major part of their program. The Bahamas receive by far the greatest number of cruise passenger arrivals in the Caribbean region. Eighty-seven percent of the visitors are from North America, with the United States accounting for 82 percent of the total. Tourism and banking are the major sources of income for the Bahamas. Tourism now accounts for nearly 60 percent of the jobs on the islands.

Tourist Destinations and Attractions

The Bahamas, flamboyant next-door neighbors to the United States and a former British colony, boast a glorious year-round climate with brilliant sky and sea, lush vegetation, bright-feathered birds, vivid fish, and multicolored coral. The pomp and ceremony remaining from years as an English colony combine with the other attractions to draw many visitors to the islands.

The two major islands are New Providence and the Grand Bahamas. Nassau, the capital, and Paradise Island (Figure 17.1) are the most visited destinations thanks to

Figure 17.1 Paradise Island in Nassau, Bahamas. © Worachat Sodsri/www.Shutterstock.com.

its international airport and busy cruise dock. It provides the visitor with all types of water sports, including fishing, skin diving, skiing, and boating. It has some attractive local architecture of white and pink houses, and houses built of limestone with wide wooden verandas. A fine aquarium near the unique Ardasta Gardens is the home of the famous trained flamingoes. On the harbor front is the Straw Market, which is constantly crowded with cruise passengers.

The Grand Bahamas is the nearest to the United States, and its casinos make it an attractive place to visit for a short stay for gaming. It has some of the best beaches in the Bahamas, as they face south and are protected from the northerly winds. Freeport is the major city and international airport. It has a number of attractions. Like Nassau, Freeport has an International Bazaar for duty-free shopping, a Museum of Underwater Exploration (headquarters of the Underwater Explorers Society), and a central location for access to a number of fine beaches. In Lucayan National Park visitors can view flamingos, parrots, and other exotic birds. Andros is the largest island in the Bahamas, and boasts to have the second-largest coral reef in the Western Hemisphere.

Swimming with pigs

Bermuda

Introduction

The Gulf Stream current warms the 138 coral islands and islets of Bermuda, located in the Atlantic Ocean. Tourism is the major employer, and some 500,000 visitors come each year to delight in the pink-sand beaches (Figure 17.2) and balmy climate.

From *National Geographic Atlas of the World*, 9th edition. Copyright ©2011 National Geographic Society. Reprinted by arrangement. All rights reserved.

Area	54 sq km (21 sq mi)
Population	64,000
Capital	Hamilton 11,000
Religion	Anglican, Roman Catholic, African Methodist Episcopal, other Protestant
Language	English, Portuguese

From *National Geographic Atlas of the World*, 9th edition. Copyright ©2011 National Geographic Society. Reprinted by arrangement. All rights reserved.

TRAVEL**TIPS** 💼

Entry: Passport is required for U.S. citizens.

Peak Tourist Season: May through August

National Holiday: May 24 (Bermuda Day).

Shopping: In addition to British goods, local items include wood carvings, shell jewelry, copper enamel, basketwork, ceramic tiles, pottery, antiques, and angelfish and seahorse souvenirs.

Internet TLD: .bm

 CULTURAL CAPSULE Nearly two-thirds of the Bermudians are of African descent. There are both Americans and Britons living in Bermuda. The language is English with a distinctive Bermudian accent. The Church of England predominates, though many other sects are represented. Most of Bermuda's food is imported, but there are local tropical fruits and vegetables. The specialty dish is cassava pie (pork and chicken in a pie crust made from the grated root of the cassava plant). Bermuda is quite expensive and formal. Formal attire for restaurants is a must.

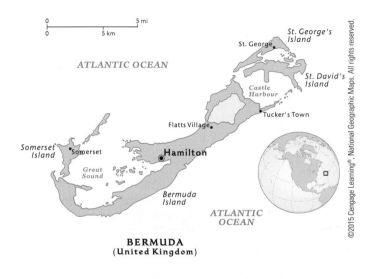

ATLANTIC OCEAN

St. George's Island
St. George
St. David's Island
Castle Harbour
Tucker's Town
Flatts Village
Somerset Island
Somerset
Hamilton
Great Sound
Bermuda Island
ATLANTIC OCEAN

BERMUDA
(United Kingdom)

Tourism Characteristics

Bermuda receives most of its income from tourism. It has developed excellent services and good airline connectivity. It also receives a number of cruise ships. Two new cruise ports recently opened, one in St. George's and the other at the Dockyards in Somerset. The number of cruise passengers has increased in recent years with the introduction of more scheduled departures from cities like Boston and New York. Because it limits the number of automobiles, mopeds and motorbikes are quite popular. Tourists cannot rent cars.

Tourist Destinations and Attractions

The two major towns, St. George and Hamilton, are picturesque harbor towns in an English setting with a very quiet lifestyle. They are the center of tourism for

Figure 17.2 The pink sand of Horseshoe Bay Beach, Bermuda. © V. J. Matthew/www.Shutterstock.com.

Bermuda. Hamilton, the capital and major commercial center, houses the world's second oldest parliament and has a historical museum and Bermuda Aquarium. There are excellent coastal sites nearby with deep tidal pools and a variety of wildlife. St. George, the capital from 1612 to 1815, is an interesting old-world town. The Royal Naval Dockyards feature the Maritime Museum and the Bermuda Arts Centre are in Somerset. St. Peter's Church is the oldest Anglican church in the Western Hemisphere. It also has a number of museums of interest. Other island highlights include the Botanical Garden, the Underwater Exploration Institute, and Crystal Caves.

REVIEW QUESTIONS

1. The Bahamas have one of the strongest tourism industries in the region. What are contributing factors?

2. Name several of the famous destination resort hotels in the Bahamas.

3. Why should a traveler be cautious about vacationing in Bermuda during the winter months?

4. What impact does seasonality have on tourism to the Caribbean?

5. For the entire Caribbean region, name three island destinations that have developed a tourism economy based on visits by cruise ships. Name three island destinations that have developed a tourism economy based on resorts.

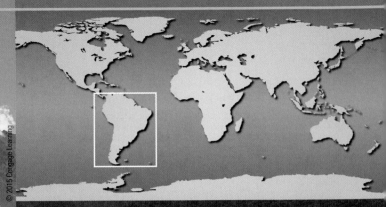

MAJOR GEOGRAPHIC CHARACTERISTICS

- South America is dominated by two mountain regions and three river basins.
- The level of economic development in the continent varies widely both within and between individual countries.
- Most countries rely on only one or two exports.
- Settlement and population patterns reflect the effect of topography and colonialism.
- The continent has historically been governed by a power base of large landholders, the army, and the Catholic Church.

MAJOR TOURISM CHARACTERISTICS

- The region is relatively isolated from major tourist-generating countries.
- South America is one of the least-visited tourist regions of the world.
- The region is rich in relics related to the Inca culture.
- The cultural diversity and archaeological sites are the major attractions for visitors from outside of the continent.
- The length of stay is one of the shortest for any major region of the world.
- Prominent events, like the Brazil Summer Olympics and FIFA Worldcup help South America earn an important emerging role among the world's leading travel destinations.

MAJOR TOURIST DESTINATIONS

- Capitals
- Colonial towns
- Cartagena, Colombia
- Cuzco and Machu Picchu, Perú
- Galapagos Islands, Ecuador
- Iguassu Falls, Brazil
- Carnival (Río de Janeiro, Brazil)
- Amazon River (Manaus, Brazil and Iquitos, Perú)
- Angel Falls, Venezuela

KEY TERMS AND WORDS

Altitudinal Zonation   Colonial   Jungle   Tierra Caliente

Amazon   Gauchos   National Museum   Tierra Fría

Andes   Indian   Pampas   Tierra Templada

Archaeological   Indian Markets   Patagonia

Castellano   Intervening Opportunities   Plateau

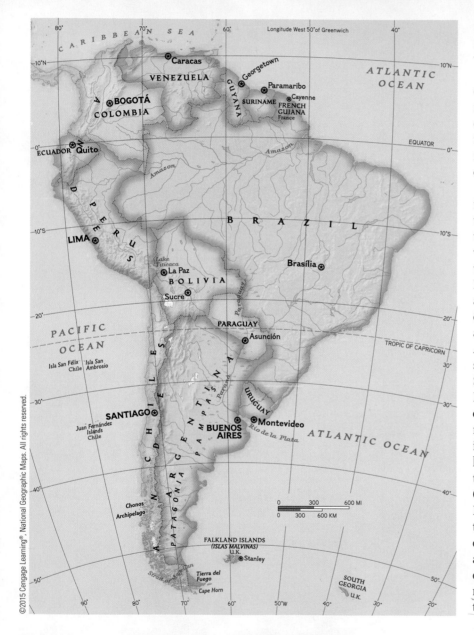

many South American countries are more often visiting for business than visitors to other regions in the world.

The region has only a small number of visitors in spite of the fact that it has magnificent scenery, outstanding beaches, excellent skiing, picturesque towns, cities of great cultural diversity, venues for major sporting events, and **archaeological** sites as impressive as any in the world.

There are several factors that account for South America's inability to attract tourists in larger numbers. First, the tourism industry is still largely underdeveloped. Second, it is far from the main tourist-generating countries of the world, North America and Europe. Third, there are a number of countries that are both closer to Canada and the United States and less expensive to visit than South America. These other countries offer some of the same general attractions as South America and are located between North and South America (**intervening opportunities**). Fourth, potential tourists may perceive the service in South America as poor and many areas as unsafe. This has become more of a concern today with the problems of drugs and drug wars in Colombia and elsewhere in the continent. Individuals traveling alone are cautioned to be careful as they may be suspected of being involved in drug movement in addition to being caught in the middle of drug raids. With political problems in a number of countries travelers are reluctant to travel in and to South America.

Although most travelers to the countries of South America come from the other countries of South America, many come from outside the region. The United States is the single most important tourist source country outside of South America. There are also some important European linkages that account for foreign tourists such as linkages between Germany and Bolivia, Portugal and Brazil, the Dutch and Suriname, and Italy and Argentina.

Introduction

Although South America has a great variety of tourist attractions, it still attracts less than 5 percent of world tourists. Tourists to South America also stay for a short amount of time, averaging only 4.2 days. Visitors to

Figure P6.2 The Amazon of Peru. © Anton_Ivanov/www.Shutterstock.com.

Climate Patterns

Climate patterns in South America are diverse and complex. The dominant climate feature is the tropical nature of the continent. A belt of tropical rain forest extends across the Amazon Basin (Figure P6.2). Savanna climates are found north and south of this tropical rain forest, while subtropical climates are located in the southern portions of Brazil and in Argentina. They are characterized by high temperatures throughout the year, with only the subtropical area of southern Brazil and northern Argentina having very rare periods of frost. None of the subtropical, tropical rain forest, or savanna climates experiences the extreme winter temperatures found in North America.

The other climatic types of South America consist of a small area of Mediterranean climate in central Chile, a small area of marine west coast climate in southern Chile, and dry steppe and desert climates in Argentina, Paraguay, Northern Chile, and Perú. These dry climates, especially in Argentina, are important for livestock ranching, which was introduced by Europeans.

Climates in the Andes are modified by elevation, which geographers identify as distinct **altitudinal zonation**. The *tierra caliente* (hot land) is the lowest zone, extending to about three thousand feet elevation; the *tierra templada* (temperate lands) occupy a zone from about three to six thousand feet elevation; while the *tierra fría* (cold lands) are above six or seven thousand feet. Each zone is characterized by distinctive crops and human activity.

Tourism Regions

South America can be divided into three distinct physical and cultural regions that influence tourism: the **Andes** countries, including Venezuela, Colombia, Ecuador, Perú, Bolivia, and Chile; the middle-latitude

countries of Argentina, Uruguay, and Paraguay; and Brazil, which by both its size and cultural distinctiveness is a region by itself.

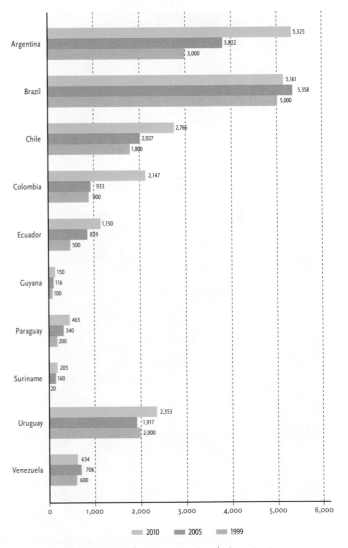

Figure P6.1 International Tourism to South America in Thousands, 1999–2010. Data source: *The World Bank: The Data Catalogue.* Figure copyright © 2015 Cengage Learning®. All rights reserved. Copyright © 2015 Cengage Learning®.

chapter 18: THE ANDES COUNTRIES

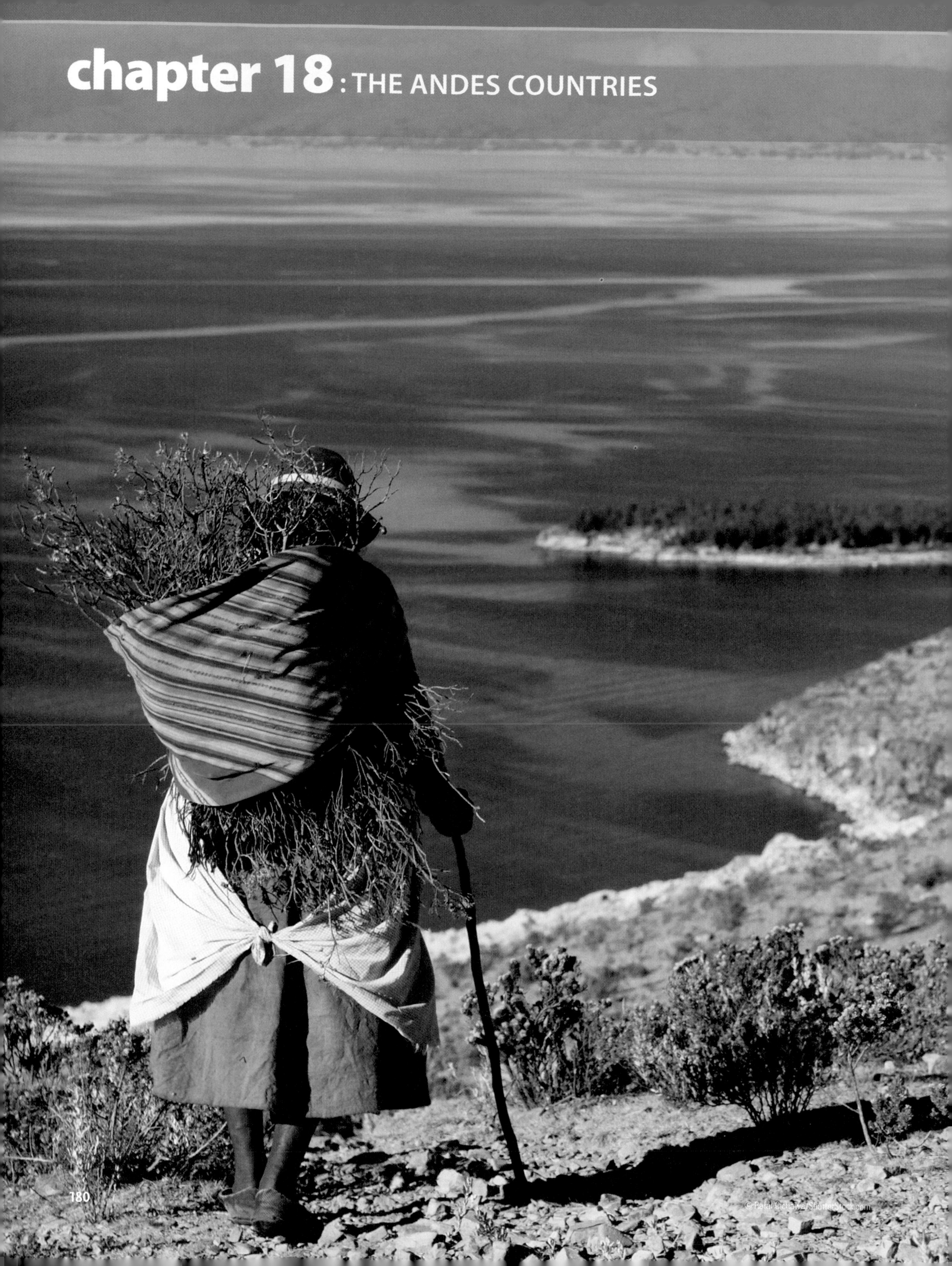

The Andes countries are one of the most important tourist regions in South America because of their unique historical and cultural attractions. The people of the Andes differ in each climatic zone. The **Indian** and mestizo (mixed Indian and European ancestry) peoples are concentrated in the *tierra fría* (high altitudes), the European population is more highly concentrated in the moderate valleys and basins of the *tierra templada* zone, and a combination of Indians, mestizos, and descendants of African workers who were imported to exploit mineral and agricultural potential live in the *tierra caliente* of the lowlands. Ecuador, Perú, and Bolivia are less industrialized countries and share the major economic problems of other countries in Latin America. They have predominantly Indian populations, concentrated mostly in the highlands and engaged in farming. Social and economic problems, especially land ownership, have led to revolutions in all three countries. The richest country of the Andes is Venezuela. Its wealth primarily comes from oil deposits in the Lake Maracaibo region.

Venezuela

Introduction

Venezuela, in northern South America, was named for Italy's Venice by fifteenth-century European explorers. The Lake Maracaibo basin splits the Andes into two mountain ranges. Mild temperatures exist on the mountains, where most people live, while the Maracaibo basin swelters in tropical heat. South of the mountains is the Orinoco River basin, a vast plain of savanna grasses known as the Llanos (YAH-nohs). South of the Orinoco are the remote Guiana Highlands—with the world's highest waterfall, Angel Falls (Figure 18.1). Most Venezuelans reside in urban areas along the coastal mountains. Estimates indicate that two-thirds of the population are mestizo, and about 21 percent are white. Blacks account for 10 percent, and indigenous groups make up just 2 percent of Venezuelan society. Venezuela is one of the oldest democracies in South America (elections since 1958). A founding member of the Organization of Petroleum Exporting Countries (OPEC), the nation has the largest proven oil and natural gas reserves in South America. The petroleum industry accounts for half the government's revenue; however, many Venezuelans still live in poverty, which contributes to political instability. According to the World Bank, the Venezuelan government pushed down the poverty rate. The country has also made progress improving slums and controlling diseases, like malaria. Recent political realities have centered on President Hugo Chavez. Elected by a 54 percent majority for a fourth 6-year term in 2012, he had been influential in setting an agenda that is transforming the country, but vilifying much of the world. President Chavez died in 2013.

From *National Geographic Atlas of the World*, 9th edition. Copyright ©2011 National Geographic Society. Reprinted by arrangement. All rights reserved.

Area	912,050 sq km (352,144 sq mi)
Population	28,368,000
Government	Federal Republic
CAPITAL	Caracas 2,985,000
Life Expectancy	73 years
Literacy	93%
Religion	Roman Catholic

Language	Spanish, numerous indigenous dialects
Currency	bolivar (VEB)
GDP per Cap	$13,100
Labor Force	13% Agriculture, 23% Industry, 64% Services

From *National Geographic Atlas of the World*, 9th edition. Copyright ©2011 National Geographic Society. Reprinted by arrangement. All rights reserved.

TRAVEL **TIPS**

Entry: A passport and a visa are required for U.S. citizens.

Peak Tourist Season: February and March

National Holiday: July 5 (Independence Day).

Health: Concern for malaria, yellow fever, and cholera. Check with local health officials before travel.

Shopping: Best buys include Indian wall hangings, hammocks, hand-woven blankets, heavy wooden furniture, leather work, gold trinkets, wood carvings, and masks.

Internet TLD: .ve

CULTURAL CAPSULE Over 80 percent of the people of Venezuela live in urban areas. Although the people are mostly Roman Catholic, the church is somewhat less important than in other Latin American countries. Spanish is the official language, but English is required as a second language. It is not uncommon to hear Portuguese as well as a number of native languages. Simón Bolívar, the South American liberator, was a

Figure 18.1 Angel Falls, the world's highest waterfall. © Vadim Petrakov/www.Shutterstock.com.

Venezuelan. Consequently, most cities have a Plaza Bolívar near the city center. It is rude to behave disrespectfully in the plaza.

Cultural hints: Greet and depart with a handshake. People stand close, and it is not polite to back away. Keep feet on floor when seated.

Tourism Characteristics

Venezuela has the highest percentage of visitors traveling for business in South America. Both the purpose of visit and the origin of visitors to Venezuela illustrate the importance of the country's large petroleum and natural gas deposits. Venezuela is one of the world's fifth largest exporters of oil. Europe and the United States annually account for more than two-thirds of total visitors. As with visitors from the United States, most visitors from Europe are from countries associated with the oil industry. The business linkage is reinforced by the good airline connectivity to the United States and Europe.

The government has for a number of years encouraged the development of hotels and resorts in an effort to increase the number of visitors to reduce the export dependency on oil and give Venezuela a more diverse economy. The number of visitors has remained stable, at around 750,000, in recent years due to strained relationships between the Chavez administration and much of the

Western world. Some cruise ships stop in Venezuela at the port of La Guaira.

Tourist Destinations and Attractions

The country's main attractions are its superb beaches surrounded by backgrounds of beautiful mountains and forests. Two popular beach resorts include Macuto and Margarita Island. Caracas (Figure 18.2), an important tourist center, is a modern city with botanical gardens, museums, parks, and a cable-car trip to the top of Mount Avila that offers a breathtaking view. Because of rapid growth, colonial buildings have been replaced by modern buildings, many of which are quite impressive. These include the University City, the twin towers of the Parque Central, the Centro Simón Bolívar, and the Círculo Militar. Two important national monuments are the Pantheon Nacional, where the remains of Simón Bolívar lie, and the Capitolio Nacional. There are a number of other museums in Caracas, such as Casa Natal del Libertador, a reconstructed house where Bolívar was born. The Santa Teresa Basilica contains the grave of Simón Bolívar. In addition to the beaches around Caracas (especially Macuto), the Los Roques Islands (requiring

Figure 18.2 Caracas, Venezuela. © avarand/www.Shutterstock.com.

an overnight trip) provide beautiful islands with long stretches of white beaches and an excellent coral reef. Popular Margarita Island is near the Dutch ABC islands. Venezuela is an important destination for ecotourism. Environmental protection has been effectively implemented, and now national parks or monuments represent nearly 22 percent of the country's territory.

Bolívar, another delightful city, is noted for its handicrafts in gold. It is an active town with river craft bringing all forms of items to the city for trade. Bolívar is popular for shoppers. It also serves as an excellent starting place for

tourist excursions into the Indian villages. Bolívar, along with Canaima National Park, is a good place to see the magnificent Angel Falls, which along with Devil Mountain is a scenic wonder. Angel Falls is the highest falls in the world with a drop of 2,937 feet. The falls were first spotted by American pilot Jimmy Angel in 1935. In Canaima tourists sleep in thatched cabanas on the edge of a pink lagoon that is surrounded by an orchid-filled jungle. The muffled roar of the La Hacha waterfalls serves as background to the panorama—the Río Currao tumbling over several falls and the pink lagoon with its soft beige beach.

Colombia

Introduction

The only South American country with coastlines on both the Pacific Ocean and Caribbean Sea, Colombia is the third most populous nation in Latin America, after Brazil and Mexico. Three north-south Andean mountain ranges separate the western coastal lowlands from the almost empty eastern jungles. The Andes divide Colombia's people into separate clusters. Some live in the Caribbean lowlands in cities like Barranquilla and Cartagena, while others inhabit isolated mountain valleys—in alpine cities like Bogotá, Cali, and Medellín. Bogotá, the capital and largest city, is in a remote mountain

Four off-the-beat excursions in Cartagena

With Colombia's drug-related violence mostly a thing of the past, the old Caribbean port town of Cartagena—arguably the finest colonial city in the Western Hemisphere—contributes to a boarder Colombian reawakening, attracting a crowd of global style-seekers. The city of gold and pirates has long been on the itinerary of cruise ships transiting the Panama Canal during October-to-April cruising season.

Around the Old City (3 hours)

Walk through Cartagena's walled district, especially El Centro, to find the most historic plazas, churches, and museums. This maze of a neighborhood brims with sixteenth- and seventeenth-century man-sion, festooned with flower-filled balconies. But more sober reminders of the city's past remain, like **Plaza de los Coches**, site of the largest slave market in the New World.

The Museum Beat (90 minutes)

Cartagena's best museums all lie within a short walk of each other in the walled city and are small enough to be seen in a brief visit. The **Museo de Arte Moderno** has ongoing exhibition of contemporary Colombian artist. The **Gold Museum** in the Plaza de Bolivar stores a trove of pre-Columbian gold in its baroque mansion.

Márquez's Neighborhood (3 hours)

Cartagena proudly claims Nobel Prize–winning novelist Gabriel García Márquez as its most famous resident. The writer of so-called magic realism set *Love in the Time of Cholera* in Cartagena, and his home stand at the corner of Calle Zerrezuela and Calle del Curato in the San Diego district. Marquez occasionally stops by for a small cocktail across the street at the **Sofitel Santa Clara** hotel, a former monastery.

Rhythm of the Night (4 hours)

Local and Cuban rhythms infuse Cartagena's nightlife. Get on Board a *rumba chiva* (about $13), which leave around 8 p.m. from local hotels and cruises the city fueled with music and seemingly unlimited quantities of rum.

—Everett Potter, *National Geographic Traveler,* January–February 2011

---

basin at 2,700 meters (8,500 feet). Colombia lies within the tropics, but climate varies greatly according to elevation, from tropical lowlands to freezing Andean peaks. With one of the most ethnically diverse populations in the Western Hemisphere, Colombia counts 85 different ethnic groups. The country is a melting pot of European, indigenous, and Afro-Caribbean cultures. About 20 percent claim European descent. Native Indians, less than 2 percent of the population, are found mostly in the tropical jungles of Colombia's Amazon region. Colombia is a highly urban country, with more than 70 percent of Colombians living in just ten cities. Colombia maintains a stable democracy, with the longest democratic legacy in Latin America, and a strong, growing economy. Colombia's government has achieved some successes in battling guerrilla groups and their illegal drug trade, using a combination of military operations and economic programs. "Plan Colombia" eradicates coca crops and provides incentives for farmers to grow legal crops. The diversified economy produces many agricultural products, such as coffee and bananas; mining products, including coal, emeralds, and oil; and manufacturing products, ranging from metals to textiles.

Area	1,138,914 sq km (439,737 sq mi)
Population	45,065,000
Government	Republic
Capital	Bogotá 7,772,000
Life Expec	72 years

Literacy	90%
Religion	Roman Catholic
Language	Spanish
Currency	Colombian peso (COP)
GDP per Cap	$9,200
Labor Force	22.4% Agriculture 18.8% Industry 58.8% Services

TRAVEL**TIPS**

Entry: A passport is required for U.S. citizens. No visa is required for stays up to 60 days.

Peak Tourist Season: No peaks; however, North Americans prefer February and March.

National Holiday: July 20 (Independence Day)

Shopping: Preferred items include emeralds, brightly colored woolen ponchos, silver work, leather goods, and pottery.

Internet TLD: .co

CULTURAL CAPSULE

Colombia is the second most populous country in Latin America. There has been a large migration from rural to urban areas. The urban population of the country is now over 70 percent. There is a diversity of ethnic origins resulting from the intermixture of indigenous Indians and Spanish (58 percent mestizo) and African (15 percent mulatto) colonists. Today, only about 1 percent of the people can be identified as fully Indian on the basis of language and customs. The official language is Spanish; however, English is widely understood in the cities and required as a second language in school. There are some forty different Indian languages throughout the country. The state religion is Roman Catholic (95 percent of the population).

Cultural hints: Be careful to spell the country's name correctly. It is Colombia, not Columbia. Use a warm, friendly handshake as a greeting and upon departure. Yawning in public is impolite. Typical foods are fruit, eggs, soup, rice, meat, potatoes, salad, and beans. A common dish is arroz con pollo (chicken with rice).

Tourism Characteristics

The tourism industry in Colombia has been handicapped by drug trafficking and related tourist fears of kidnapping. Because of this concern for safety, the tourism industry is largely made up of domestic and international business travel. At present the government is more concerned with solving the drug-trafficking problem than establishing a better infrastructure for tourism. The location and quality of beaches gives Colombia a rich resource for tourism development. There have been some mega-resort developments along the coast and on small islands.

Colombia attracts just over a million visitors a year, and the United States accounts for one-fifth of these visitors. The major origin countries for visitors to Colombia are regional in character. Other than the Americas, the only other major origin country is Spain.

Tourist Destinations and Attractions

The Andean ranges, interspersed with green valleys and dense jungles, offer a spectacular tourist environment. In addition, as with other Latin American countries, there are some interesting archaeological attractions.

Bogotá, the capital, is in a remote mountain basin on a high **plateau** with a mixture of colonial and modern buildings. The Palace of San Carlos where Simón Bolívar once lived, the Cathedral, La Toma de Agua, the Muséo de Oro with more than 15,000 pieces of pre-Columbian gold, the **National Museum**, the Planetarium, and the Museum of Natural History are some interesting places to visit. A funicular railway takes visitors to the top of Monserrate for a good view of Bogotá. Around the Plaza Bolívar, the old quarter of the city has barred windows, carved doorways, brown-tiled roofs, and sheltering eaves. Visitors to Bogotá will experience a contrast between traditions of times past and the frantic pace of the new.

North of Bogotá, tourists can visit the salt mine of Zipaquirá, which has an underground "Salt Cathedral" that was carved by the Chibcha Indians. It holds about ten thousand people. Cartagena (Figure 18.3) is one of the major attractions of South America. Founded by Pedro de Heredia in 1533, the "Heroic City" was built as a Spanish base for the conquest of the continent—an impregnable port with a heavily armed garrison to protect the gold routes and slave trade. Surrounded by the Caribbean Sea, the Bay of Cartegena, and lakes and lagoons, the old walled city has many forts and other reminders of the early Spanish era, such as parade grounds, colonial baroque architecture with typical balconies, cloisters, patios, stone entrances, and wood doors. It is a popular stop for cruise ships traveling in and out of the Panama Canal. Santa Marta is a nearby resort destination and was the place where Simón Bolívar died. Barranquilla is another coastal city and host every year to the world's second largest carnival celebrations. Farmers raise world renowned coffee on the Andean slopes and the country provides much of the world's emeralds.

Figure 18.3 Cartagena, Colombia. © Alberto Loyo/www.Shutterstock.com.

Ecuador

Introduction

Ecuador's name comes from the Equator (Figure 18.4), which divides it unequally. It is one of South America's smaller countries—but with four distinct regions. The Costa (coastal plain) grows enough bananas to make the country a top exporter. The Sierra (highlands) is a north-south belt of mountainous terrain dominated by the Andes. The Oriente (east), also known as the Amazon region, features lowland rain forests east of the Andes. The fourth region consists of the Galápagos Islands, a national park of 13 main islands 1,000 kilometers (620 miles) west of the Ecuadorian coast. Most Ecuadorians (65 percent) are considered mestizo, indigenous people make up about 25 percent, and the other 10 percent are Spanish descendants and other ethnic groups. The population is almost evenly divided between the Costa and Sierra region. Only 3 percent live in the Oriente region, but oil development has damaged the pristine environment. Growing migration to the Galápagos threatens the park with pollution and overfishing. Those of Spanish descent often are engaged in large land ownership in Quito and the surrounding Andean highlands; this is also where most of the indigenous people live—many are subsistence farmers. As a result, land-tenure reform is an explosive issue. The city of Guayaquil dominates the coastal plain, largely populated by mestizos. Guayaquil—the country's largest city, major port, and leading commercial center—is a rival to Quito. Regional rivalries and ethnic issues contribute to political instability for Ecuador's democracy.

From *National Geographic Atlas of the World*, 9th edition. Copyright ©2011 National Geographic Society. Reprinted by arrangement. All rights reserved.

Figure 18.4 Monument Mitad del Mundo near Quito in Ecuador. © Pablo Hidalgo/www.Shutterstock.com.

Area	283,561 sq km (109,484 sq mi)
Population	13,625,000
Government	Republic
Capital	Quito 1,701,000
Life Expectancy	75 years
Literacy	91%
Religion	Roman Catholic
Language	Spanish, Quechua, other Amerindian languages
Currency	U.S. dollar (USD)
GDP per Cap	$7,400
Labor Force	8.3% Agriculture, 21.2% Industry, 70.4% Services

From *National Geographic Atlas of the World*, 9th edition. Copyright ©2011 National Geographic Society. Reprinted by arrangement. All rights reserved.

TRAVEL **TIPS** 💼

Entry: A passport is required.

Peak Tourist Seasons: January, July, and December

National Holiday: August 10 (Independence Day).

Shopping: Purchases of hats, handwoven rugs and ponchos (Figure 18.5), wood carvings from native wood, pottery, basketwork, tsantas (goatskin replicas of Jivaro headhunter shrunken heads), gold, and silver are common.

Internet TLD: .ec

CULTURAL CAPSULE The population of Ecuador is ethnically mixed, combining mestizo, African, Spanish, and other European strains. The dominant pre-European group was the Inca. In the fifteenth century, the Inca Empire spread from Perú into what is now Ecuador. Spaniards later took advantage of Inca weakness and tribal resentment to subdue Quito. The people in the Amazon region are mostly Indians and are culturally distinct from others. Ecuadorians maintain their own traditions even in the cities. Spanish is the official language, with Quechua (the Indian language) spoken in the highlands. English is understood by business and tourism officials.

Cultural hints: A firm handshake is the common greeting. Touching and closeness are common. Common foods are corn, potatoes, rice, beans, fish, soup, and fruit. Typical dishes are arroz con pollo (fried chicken with rice), locro (soup of potatoes, cheese, meat, and avocados), llapingachos (cheese and potato cakes), ceviche (raw seafood marinated in lime and served with onions, tomatoes, and other spices), fritada (fried pork), and empanadas (pastries filled with meat or cheese).

Tourism Characteristics

The tourism industry in Ecuador is small but growing rapidly with annual arrivals exceeding 1 million. The tourism industry's development is made possible by revenue from oil production now topping Ecuador's export list. Ecuador's neighbors account for one-third of the total visitors with most arriving by land. The primary purpose of trips to Ecuador is for holiday. The North Americans and Europeans arrive by air and stay longer than do visitors from the region. The United States accounts for one-fifth of all visitors. Because

Figure 18.5 Textiles in Ecuador. © Eleonora Kolomiyets/www.Shutterstock.com.

of its equatorial location, Ecuador does not have one dominant season, although the peak season is in July and August, which may be a result of the visitors from the United States and Europe taking advantage of their traditional summer vacation to travel. January and December are secondary peaks of tourism as tourists take advantage of Christmas and New Year's vacations.

Tourist Destinations and Attractions

The country's high mountains and volcanic ranges are important attractions, offering spectacular beauty with Indian culture. Quito, the capital and third largest city in Ecuador, is set in a hollow at the foot of a volcano. It is very picturesque. The old colonial area has been preserved with its buildings painted white and blue. Quito has many churches such as San Francisco, Monastery of Santo Domingo, and La Companía. Quito also has a number of excellent art museums such as the Casa del La Cúltura Ecuatoriana, the Museum of Colonial Art, the Muséo de Santo Domingo, the Muséo de San Agustín, the Archaeological Museum, and the Muséo Colonial y de Arte Religioso. From Panecillo Hill there is a glorious panoramic view of Quito. The enormous statue of the Virgin of Quito is located on the hill's summit. Not far from Quito is Mt. Cotopaxi, a National Park.

One of the most interesting market towns in South America is at Otavalo (Figure 18.5). In addition to its colorful **Indian markets**, Otavalo offers a number of other interesting features such as cockfights, bull-fights, and a unique ball game. There are actually three markets taking place: a woolen fabrics and shawls market, an animal auction, and a produce market. It is a very busy place on Saturdays.

Santo Domingo, a scenic 80 miles from Quito, is the center for trips into the Colorado Indian villages. Guayaquil is the most important port in Ecuador and a major commercial city. It is a popular cruise port and is

Surrounded by bunches of bright sunflowers and chamomile, Rosa Lagla gently performs soul-cleansing *limpia* treatments in a market just a few blocks from Plaza de San Francisco, hub of Quito's restored Old Town. Rubbing handfuls of stinging nettles, sweet herbs, and rose petals into the skin drives out bad energy, she says, working the plants to a pulp. With botanicals brimming from plastic bags, Lagla brings the Andean healing practice to guests of the newly restored Casa Gangotena on the plaza. Healer and hotel span two worlds, the traditional and the modern, both reinvigorating this city of 1.6 million.

For too long, travelers have neglected Ecuador's capital city en route to the nation's marquee attraction, the Galápagos Islands. Though its Spanish colonial center has been enshrined as a UNESCO World Heritage site since 1978, the area has more recently undergone a renaissance warranting longer stays. In the past decade, city officials have invested nearly $500 million to make improvements to its historic quarter.

In the past decade, city officials have invested nearly $500 million to make improvements to its historic quarter.

At Quito's heart, cobblestoned streets and pastel-colored mansions hem the revitalized San Francisco Church. Many restorers of the landmark learned to apply gold leaf, inlay wood, and chisel statuary in a nearby workshop with a mission to teach skills to impoverished teenagers with an aptitude for art. People are primary in Quito's new museums. Emphasizing storytelling, Casa del Alabado arranges its pre-Columbian art and artifacts thematically to dramatize the mystery of the ancients. Quito's historic center is now beginning to cultivate a vibrant nightlife. On Calle La Ronda, music sings out from restaurants and bars. But Lagla lifts spirits the old way. Sweeping up sage post-ritual, she says, "*Se fue, el espanto. La energia vuelve*—It's gone, the fright. Energy returns." She could be speaking of Quito, too.

—Elaine Glusac, *National Geographic Traveler*, December 2012/January 2013

---

also the departure point for visits to the Galápagos Islands. The city has many monuments and churches including Santo Domingo and the Church of San Francisco. Built in 1548, the Church of San Francisco is the oldest church in Ecuador. Across the street from the Church of San Francisco is Parque Bolívar, the home of many land iguanas, with trees filled with the prehistoric-looking reptiles. A city with much promise is Cuenca. It is expected to be the "next destination" to be discovered, and will soon rival Quito and Guayaquil as the country's top visitor attraction. It has many historic buildings that are well preserved.

A fascinating attraction bringing tourism revenue to Ecuador are the Galápagos Islands with their unique plant and animal life. Located six hundred miles off the west coast, they consist of six main islands and twelve smaller islands. The islands are the peaks of volcanoes. Darwin described the Galápagos Islands as "a separate center of creation," and they served as an inspiration for his origin of species theory. A number of plants and animals found here are unique to these islands. The most fabled species are the giant tortoise, marine iguana, land iguana, hammerhead sharks, Galápagos albatross, and a number of exotic birds (Figure 18.6). The land iguanas are so abundant that visitors almost step on them. Santa Cruz is home to the Charles Darwin Research Center, where visitors can visit the breeding pens of the giant tortoises and land iguanas. The main attraction is the Galápagos National Park, but other attractions include Tortuga bay, Sierra Negra Volcano, the Wall of Tears, and Los Tuneles. The government limits visitation to the islands so reservations should be planned years in advance. Back on the mainland there are twenty-six national parks and forty-four protected areas. Beach resort destinations include Bahia de Caraquez, Manta,

Figure 18.6 Blue-footed booby at the Galapagos island of North Seymourc. © BlueOrange Studio/www.Shutterstock.com.

San Jacinto, and San Clemente. Banos, in the heart of the country, is the gateway city to the **Amazon**. It is situated on the side of Tungurahua, the largest (and active) volcano in Ecuador.

Peru

Introduction

Perú lies on the Pacific coast of South America just south of the Equator. The entire coast is desert that gets little rain. The Andes rise steeply from the coastal plain and contain high plateaus, fertile mountain valleys, and deep canyons. East of the mountains, lies the vast rain forest of the Amazon Basin. The climate is arid but mild along the coast, temperate to cold in the Andes, and hot and humid in the eastern lowlands. The majority of Peruvians are either Spanish-speaking mestizos or Quechua-speaking indigenous groups. Most mestizos live in urban areas along the coast. Lima holds more than 30 percent of Perú's people, and most are of European descent or mestizo. The Andean highlands occupy about a third of the country and serve as the home of the Quechua-speaking Indians. Quechua (a language family with many dialects) is an ancient language, and the Inca Empire spread it into new areas, such as Bolivia. To the indigenous Quechua Indians, Perú means "land of abundance." Sites such as Machu Picchu (Figure 18.7) and Cusco recall the wealth of the Inca civilization, which was destroyed in the early sixteenth century by Spaniards, who built an empire on Perú's gold and silver. Today Perú ranks among the world's top producers of gold, silver, copper, and zinc. Government redistribution of mining tax income is benefiting some of the poorer highland areas. Poverty is falling as the democratic government advances economic development throughout the country.

From *National Geographic Atlas of the World*, 9th edition. Copyright ©2011 National Geographic Society. Reprinted by arrangement. All rights reserved.

Figure 18.7 Machu Picchu. © David Madison/Getty Images.

Area	1,285,216 sq km (496,224 sq mi)
Population	29,165,000
Government	Constitutional Republic
Capital	Lima 8,012,000
Life Expectancy	72 years
Literacy	93%
Religion	Roman Catholic, Evangelical
Language	Spanish, Quechua, Aymara, minor Amazonian languages
Currency	Nuevo Sol (PEN)
GDP per Cap	$8,600
Labor Force	0.7% Agriculture, 23.8% Industry, 75.5% Services

From *National Geographic Atlas of the World*, 9th edition. Copyright ©2011 National Geographic Society. Reprinted by arrangement. All rights reserved.

Figure 18.8 Colca Canyon, the world's deepest canyon. © Christian Kohler/www.Shutterstock.com.

Entry: A passport is required.

National Holiday: July 28 (Independence Day).

Shopping: Common purchases include alpaca goods, gold, silver, and handwoven fabrics.

Internet TLD: .pe

The people of Perú are ethnically diverse, consisting of Indians (45 percent), mestizos (37 percent), and Hispanic Europeans (15 percent). Other minorities include Blacks, Japanese, and Chinese. Spanish and Quechua (Indian) languages are both officially recognized. Another Indian language, Aymara, is spoken widely. English is understood in businesses and tourist attractions. Most people are Roman Catholic, and the Indians mix their traditional Indian beliefs with their Christian beliefs. There are also Protestant and evangelical churches in the country.

Cultural hints: Shake hands upon greeting and departing. Ask permission to photograph Indians. Typical food includes rice, beans, corn, fish, potatoes, and tropical fruits.

Tourism Characteristics

Perú views tourism as an important element in its economic development, and encourages growth in visitor numbers. Tourism almost doubled between 2000 and 2010,

and by 2010 Perú was receiving over 2 million tourists a year. Although several factors help to explain this rapid growth, including the government support for tourism, the most important factors have been the decline in guerrilla-related conflicts in Perú and a more stable government.

Perú is actively promoting itself as an international tourist destination. However, the country lacks funding for essential infrastructure and private sector investment in hotels. Domestic air services have reached the saturation point at certain times of the year and hotel capacity will need to be expanded.

The United States accounts for nearly 15 percent of visitors to Perú. Although data are not currently available for explaining the purpose for visiting, it can be assumed that a high percentage of visitors are from the United States because of the quality and type of attractions. Because of this, the country has also started to attract more tourists from neighboring countries. July and August constitute the peak season for visitors, reflecting the vacation period in the major markets of Europe and the United States.

Tourist Destinations and Attractions

The most famous attraction in Perú is Machu Picchu, the legendary "Lost City of the Incas," with over

1,500 people visiting the site daily. It sits in the high Andes on a saddle of a mountain with terraced slopes. At least a day is required to see the ruins, consisting of staircases, terraces, temples, palaces, towers, fountains, sundials, and the Muséo de Sítio below the ruins. A hike up an adjacent mountainside provides a tremendous view of the site. The two most popular tours consist of a visit to Machu Picchu by a train that departs from Cuzco early in the morning and returns the same day, and a four day and three night hike along the famous Inca Trail. Cuzco, the old Inca capital, recalls the wealth of this early civilization. In addition to Cuzco and Machu Picchu, the Urubamba Valley has a number of ruins, two well-known folk markets, the town of Puno, and Lake Titicaca, which combines scenery with the floating islands and archaeological ruins at Tiahuanaco to attract tourists to the southeast of Perú.

Lima, the capital of Perú founded in 1535, was the major city of Spanish South America. Perú has tried to maintain the colonial days in the heart of the city. The Plaza de Armas was the site of Spanish conquistador Pizzaro's palace, and the Museum of the Inquisition at Plaza Bolívar is where inquisition trials took place. The city has important museums, such as the Gold Museum, the National Museum of Art, the Museum of Anthropology and Archaeology, the Museum of Peruvian Culture, and the Bullfight Museum. These and others display the rich Incan and Spanish history of the region. Nearby, Callao is the country's cruise port. At Nazca, some 280 miles south of Lima, flights can be taken over the Nazca lines, which are tracings of symbols, animals, and other features (a dog, monkey, birds, a spider, and a tree) extending for miles across the desert. The valley is full of ruins, temples, and cemeteries.

Between Lima and Nazca, there are a number of coastal towns and a national park with sea lions and condors. The Colca Canyon (Figure 18.8) is the world's deepest canyon and has a string of Spanish colonial churches in villages, with a culture and costume distinct from other areas. It is being developed into a tourism destination. The Amazon, centering on Iquitos, has become a popular trip for a **jungle** adventure. River trips are taken from Iquitos into the jungle to observe jungle activity. Belén, a floating village, has a floating market of canoes canopied with palm thatch. Visitors may observe the buying and selling of tropical fruits, fish, and vegetables. The jungle camps provide access to jungle flora and fauna (Figure 18.9) in unique settings.

Figure 18.9 Poison arrow frog on a branch. © Dirk Ercken/www.Shutterstock.com.

Bolivia

Introduction

La Paz, the world's highest capital city, approved a new constitution in 2009, with lofty ideals for indigenous peoples and a new country name: Plurinational State of Bolivia. *Plurinational* is a term designed to give Bolivia's indigenous groups, at 55 percent of the population, more power in a government historically dominated by whites and mestizos. While Bolivia is rich in energy resources, most Bolivians live in poverty, especially on the Altiplano (high plateau). In 2006, Bolivia took control of foreign energy firms and moved to redistribute land to the poor. Many in the affluent eastern lowlands resist the reforms.

Area	1,098,581 sq km (424,164 sq mi)
Population	9,863,000
Government	Republic; Constitutionally defined as a "Social Unitarian State"
Capital	La Paz (administrative) 1,590,000; Sucre (legal) 243,000
Life Expectancy	65 years
Literacy	87%
Religion	Roman Catholic, Protestant
Language	Spanish, Quechua, Aymara
Currency	Boliviano (BOB)
GDP per Cap	$4,600
Labor Force	40% Agriculture, 17% Industry, 43% Services

TRAVEL**TIPS** 🧳

Entry: A passport and a visa are required.

Peak Tourist Season: May through November

National Holiday: August 6 (Independence Day).

Shopping: Local items include vicuna ponchos, alpaca sweaters, fabrics, gold and silver jewelry, wood carvings, and pottery.

Internet TLD: .bo

CULTURAL CAPSULE The population is approximately 60 percent indigenous Aymara and Quechua Indian, 30 percent mestizo, and 15 percent European (mostly Spanish). Spanish, Quechua, and Aymara are all official languages. Ninety-five percent of the people are Roman Catholic with a number of Protestant minority groups and some indigenous tribal religions that mix Indian beliefs with Catholic.

Cultural hints: A warm handshake is a common greeting. Close personal space is tolerated. Eat everything on plate. Common foods are potatoes, rice, soups, and fruits. A typical dish is saltenas (meat or chicken pie with potatoes, olives, and raisins).

Tourism Characteristics

Bolivia, named after Simón Bolívar, is a poor and landlocked country. Tourism to Bolivia has not been important, and its government has done little to encourage it. Only 800,000 tourists a year visited Bolivia in 2010. There are, however, a number of excellent resources to attract tourists, including the Beni Biosphere Reserve, Madidi National Park, and Salar de Uyuni, the world's largest salt flat (Figure 18.10).

The major markets for Bolivia are regional in character, with the four neighboring countries accounting for over half of the total visitors to Bolivia. The overseas market is small and very diverse with few tourists coming from many countries to visit Bolivia. Holidays

Figure 18.10 Salar de Uyuni, the world's largest salt flat.

Figure 18.11 La Paz, Bolivia. © Adalberto Rios Szalay/Sexto Sol/Getty Images.

are the major purpose for visiting, and January and February are the peak season.

Tourist Destinations and Attractions

La Paz (Figure 18.11), the highest capital in the world at twelve thousand feet, is in a natural basin or canyon, with Mount Illimani towering over the city. There are some colonial buildings left, particularly in the Calle Jaen. Around the Plaza Murillo in the center of town, tourists can visit the huge cathedral, the Presidential Palace, the National Congress, the Muséo Nacional del Arte, and a central market (Mercado Camacho) where Indian vendors sell their goods. The market is characterized by Indians sitting on the ground or in stalls, selling everything from cheese empanadas, to steel wool, canned goods, powdered soup, brazil nuts, sausages, and so forth. Mercado de Hechiceria is a daily witchcraft market sure to fascinate visitors. The monastery of San Francisco, which was built in the colonial period; Santo Domingo; La Merced; and San Sebastian, the first church to be built in La Paz, are attractive churches in La Paz.

Near La Paz, the ruins of Tiahuanaco near the southern end of Lake Titicaca are impressive and are being reconstructed. Lake Titicaca (Figure 18.12) provides a number of good attractions for visitors, including a ride on boats built from the local reed plant. Copacabán, an attractive little town on the lake, is noted for its restored church and miracle-working Dark Virgin of the Lake. The most popular excursion is to ride on the lake to visit the Island of the Sun, a worship site of the Incas.

Figure 18.12 Isla del Sol on Lake Titicaca. © Rafal Cichawa/www.Shutterstock.com.

Chile

Introduction

Long and narrow, Chile is more than 4,300 kilometers (2,700 miles) from north to south but never more than 180 kilometers (110 miles) wide. This South American country is well defined by its geography: to the west, the Pacific Ocean; to the east, the Andes mountains; to the north, the Atacama Desert, driest in the world; and to the south, the Chilean **Patagonia**, covered with glaciers and ice fields. Midway along the length of the country is Santiago (Figure 18.13), the nation's capital. Santiago forms the center of an urban complex, which is situated in a sheltered, temperate valley between the coastal mountains and the Andes. Some 40 percent of Chileans live in greater Santiago. Most Chileans claim European ancestry, with Spanish being dominant, but there are also Irish, English, and German descendants. Only about 800,000 Native Americans live in Chile, mostly in the south-central part of the country. The Mapuche tribe is the largest. Chile is one of South America's most stable democracies and prosperous economies. It is the world's largest producer of copper, but other exports, such as fish, fruit, and wine, enjoy strong growth. The government promotes conservation and renewable energy technologies to reduce greenhouse gas emissions.

Figure 18.13 Santiago, Chile. © Pablo Rogat/www.Shutterstock.com.

CITY HIGHLIGHTS | Valparaíso: Chile's Soulful Port Apart

Generations of creative pilgrims have been hooked by Valparaíso's weathered beauty and bohemian vibe. Travelers have followed suit, coming for the romantic allure of its forty-two *cerros* (hills) that ascend sharply from the water. Stacked high with faded mansions, nineteenth-century funiculars, and battered cobblestones, Valparaíso stands in contrast to the glitzy Viña del Mar resort town to the north. As Chile's vital harbor, it retains the signature grittiness and edge that often endow ports. But Valparaíso is also welcoming a boom of eateries serving inventive Chilean fare, quirky bars offering hoppy microbrews, and antiques-packed B&Bs.

Pablo Neruda, whose former home, La Sebastiana, still lords over Cerro Bellavista, wrote Valparaíso-inspired verse: "I love, Valparaíso, everything you enfold, and everything you irradiate, sea bride ... I love the violent light with which you turn to the sailor on the sea night." A meander through its tangle of steep alleyways and stairways reveals eye-catching street art and ocean views from pedestrian passages that hug the slopes. Then a cool breeze comes off the Pacific, night falls, and silhouettes of hills appear against darker skies, infusing Valparaíso with poetry that seeps through its every pore.

— **Anja Mutić,** *National Geographic Traveler*, December 2012/January 2013

Area	756,102 sq km (291,933 sq mi)
Population	16,970,000
Government	republic
Capital	Santiago 5,720,000
Life Expectancy	78 years
Religion	Roman Catholic, Evangelical
Language	Spanish, Mapudungun, German, English
Currency	Chilean peso (CLP)
GDP per Cap	$14,700
Labor Force	13.1% Agriculture, 23% Industry, 63.9% Services

From *National Geographic Atlas of the World,* 9th edition. Copyright ©2011 National Geographic Society. Reprinted by arrangement. All rights reserved.

TRAVEL**TIPS** 🧳

Entry: A passport and a visa are required.

Peak Tourist Season: December through February

National Holiday: September 18 (Independence Day).

Shopping: Local items include copperware fabrics, Chilean wine, woolen rugs, wooden carvings from Easter Island, leather goods, black pottery, and lapis lazuli jewelry.

Internet TLD: .cl

CULTURAL CAPSULE Chile is an urbanized nation with 85 percent of its population living in urban centers. The largest group of people are Spanish or Mestizo (over 95 percent). Only 3 percent are Indians, and the rest are Irish, English, German, Italian, Yugoslav, French, and Arab. More than 80 percent of the population is Roman Catholic with minority groups of Protestant, Christian, Jewish, and some Indians. Spanish is the official language, but unlike the rest of South America's Spanish dialect, Chile uses **Castellano**. English is taught in schools and understood by many in the large cities. Chile has a booming economy, and its people enjoy one of the highest standards of living found in South American countries.

Cultural hints: Men rise when women enter the room. Good posture while seated is important. Common foods are fish, seafood, chicken, beef, beans, eggs, and corn. Typical dishes are empanadas de horno (meat turnovers with beef, hard-boiled eggs, onions, olives, and raisins), humitas (grated corn, fried onions, sweet basil, salt, and pepper), pastel de choclo (beef, chicken, onions, corn, eggs, and spices), and cazuela de ave (chicken soup).

Tourism Characteristics

Chile's tourist industry is in transition. It received nearly 3 million visitors in 2010, more than double the amount of just ten years earlier, with one-third coming from its neighbor Argentina. The government had invested significantly in developing the tourist industry, and is still encouraging new hotel development and personnel training in tourism. Tourist arrivals from the United States have increased rapidly in recent years.

Visitor's to Chile come primarily for holiday. Holiday activities account for nearly two-thirds of all visits by tourists, with business and visits to family friends a distant second and third. Chile's tourist industry is very seasonal. The summer months of January and February are the strongest, drawing 29 percent of total visitors.

Tourist Destinations and Attractions

The country has a variety of attractions to offer. Located in the lush central valley, Santiago, the capital and main tourist city, has a Mediterranean-type climate. Nearly 70 percent of the population is concentrated in this central heartland. Santiago was founded in 1541 and is a well-planned city. The beautiful snow-covered Andes provide a picturesque panorama. The center of the city contains the Cathedral and the Archbishop's palace, the Palacio de La Real Audiencia with the Muséo Histórico Nacional inside, the Congressional Palace, and Casa Colada, which was the home of the governor in colonial times and is now a museum of the history of Santiago. There is an excellent view of the city from the first Spanish fort built in Chile at the top of Santa Lucia.

Valparaíso, the second largest city and major port, is also a favorite tourist spot. It is built on a bay with a crescent of hills around it. The snow-capped peaks can be seen in the distance. Few buildings remain from the colonial times because of a number of earthquakes. The city does have a variety of landscapes, from the narrow, clean, winding streets around the center to the hills with tattered houses and shacks and littered back streets. There are a number of excellent seaside resorts around Valparaíso, including the Viña del Mar, which is the most famous and is the summer palace of the president. Visitors can go by ship from Valparaíso to legendary Easter Island, which has huge stone monoliths (moai) (Figure 18.14) and has only recently been developed as a tourist attraction.

However, since it is nearly 2,400 miles west, most visits are by air as it is the world's most remote inhabited island. The island is home to 5,500 residents and 50,000 tourists visit every year. Juan Fernandez, the setting for the classic story of Robinson Crusoe, is another island to visit.

Located between the Lastarria Range and Reloncavi Sound, the lake region is one of the most picturesque areas in Chile. Chile has also developed a number of mountain resorts in an effort to utilize the many ski slopes in the country, with Portillo claiming to be South America's best ski resort destination. Torres del Paire National Park (Figure 18.15) is a fascinating destination located in Chile's Patagonia region.

Figure 18.14 Moai at Easter Island. © Leonard Zhukovsky/www.Shutterstock.com.

Figure 18.15 Torres del Paine National Park, Patagonia, Chile. © David Thyberg/www.Shutterstock.com.

REVIEW QUESTIONS

1. What caused tourism to Venezuela to stagnate in recent years?

2. What are the major attractions on the Galapagos Islands? How do most travelers arrive at this destination?

3. Portillo in Chile has been mentioned as a potential site for a future Winter Olympics. What would be pros and cons of selecting this location to stage this event?

4. Colombia's coastal city of Cartagena earned a UNECSO World Heritage Site designation. What is the city's historic significance and cultural legacy?

5. On a trip to Perú, what attractions would you want to visit?

chapter 19 : MIDDLE-LATITUDE SOUTH AMERICA

© Curioso/ShutterStock.com

Argentina, Paraguay, and Uruguay are located in the middle latitudes. They have a climate that does not share tropical conditions with the bulk of Latin America.

Historically, this region did not have the advanced Indian civilizations of Mexico and the highlands of the Andes, so its development is based on European immigration.

Argentina

Introduction

The Pampas is the center of Argentina, and the country's most famous region; this land of fertile plains holds half the nation's population and includes Buenos Aires, the sprawling capital city. But Argentina, South America's second largest country, spreads beyond the Pampas. In the northeast, between the Paraná and Uruguay rivers, lies the "Argentine Mesopotamia," a land of rain forests, which includes Iguazú Falls, one of the world's largest waterfalls. South of the Pampas, dry and windswept Patagonia stretches from the Andes to the sea and to the southernmost tip of South America. The country's climate is subtropical in the north, subantarctic in southern Patagonia, and mild and humid in the Pampas. Argentina is a nation of immigrants: Ninety-five percent of its population is of European ancestry, mostly Spanish or Italian, with significant French, German, and Polish minorities—the pure indigenous population is estimated at less than 1 percent. Also, there are some 3.5 million Arab Argentines and about 200,000 Jews. Over the years, immigration has produced a modern society, with an urbanized middle class, a diversified economy, and an enduring democracy. But the legacy of military rule from 1976 to 1983 is still an open wound for Argentine society—a time when thousands were tortured and killed. One of the last acts of the military regime was the 1982 invasion of the British-controlled Falkland Islands (called Islas Malvinas by Argentina). Britain retook the islands in a costly war, leading to the collapse of military rule and the restoration of democracy. However, Argentina's democratic government still claims sovereignty over the islands, adding to international tension.

From *National Geographic Atlas of the World*, 9th edition. Copyright ©2011 National Geographic Society. Reprinted by arrangement. All rights reserved.

Area	2,780,400 sq km (1,073,518 sq mi)
Population	40,276,000
Government	Republic
Capital	Buenos Aires 12,795,000
Life Expectancy	75 years
Literacy	97%
Religion	Roman Catholic
Language	Spanish, Italian, English, German, French
Currency	Argentine peso (ARS)

0 — 350 mi
0 — 350 km

ARGENTINA

GDP per Cap	$13,800
Labor Force	5% Agriculture, 23% Industry, 72% Services

From *National Geographic Atlas of the World*, 9th edition. Copyright ©2011 National Geographic Society. Reprinted by arrangement. All rights reserved.

TRAVEL**TIPS**

Entry: No visa required. Passport required.

Peak Tourist Season: December through March

National Holiday: May 25 (Revolution Day).

Shopping: Local items include leather goods, furs, silver work, and gaucho souvenirs.

Internet TLD: .ar

CULTURAL CAPSULE

Argentina's population has been influenced by the waves of European immigrants who came in the nineteenth and twentieth centuries. Italian and Spanish are the dominant groups (85 percent). Mestizos and Indians make up the remaining 15 percent. There is a sizable number of Syrian, Lebanese, and other Middle Eastern immigrants; most are city dwellers. More than 90 percent of Argentines are Roman Catholic. Although Spanish is the official language, many people speak some English, German, French, or Italian. Argentina is famous for its horse ranches and **gauchos** (cowboys) in the **Pampas** region. Beef is the single most important food. It is so much a part of the culture that steak is even eaten for breakfast. Also, Argentina was the place of origin and is still home to the tango. It was started in Buenos Aires by a Frenchman, Carlos Gardel. The highest peak in the Western Hemisphere, Aconcagua, dominates the Andes at 22,834 feet.

Cultural hints: Argentine culture includes close personal space, so people stand close when talking. Hands on hips indicates anger or a challenge. When finished eating, cross the knife and fork in the middle of your plate. Beef is the most important staple. Common foods include beef, corn, potatoes, and hot tea. Popular meals feature barbecue, meat pies, and locro (a stew of meat, corn, and potatoes).

Tourism Characteristics

The National Tourist Office is actively engaged in promoting tourism. It has sought assistance from the Organization of American States for technical advice on the preservation of its colonial cities and towns. Gross receipts from international tourism are now the largest single item in export earnings. As a result, tourism now represents more than 20 percent of total foreign exchange receipts from commodity exports, double what it was 10 years ago. Improved economic conditions have brought about an increase in domestic tourism and more travel by Argentines to other countries, mostly Chile and Uruguay.

Argentina has a well-developed tourism infrastructure, with excellent accommodations to support an important tourist industry. The 5 million visitors in 2010 represent only a slight increase over 2000. Most arrivals are from neighboring countries. The two leading European countries of origin, Italy and Spain, have long-established immigration and language ties with Argentina. The United States has also become an important visitor source.

Tourist Destinations and Attractions

The country has a wide variety of landscapes, from tropical rain forests to the glaciers of Antarctica. Argentina's most famous tourist attraction is the capital city of Buenos Aires (Figure 19.1), the location of the world's widest thoroughfare and the world's largest opera house (Teátro Colón). Although the city has very few of its old buildings left, it has maintained its original design with narrow one-way streets. The historic Cabildo (the town hall), the pink Casa Rosada (Presidential Palace), and the cathedral are located in the Plaza de Mayo, the heart of the city. The city also has numerous museums, libraries, and art exhibitions. The historical landmarks, cathedrals, palaces, and museums are all tourist inducements that complement the country's excellent cuisine.

The famous Iguazú Falls of the Parana River can be reached from Argentina, but most visitors come to the Brazil side of the falls.

Outside of Buenos Aires, there are many other tourist attractions. Tigre is a popular weekend and holiday spot, situated in a delta of the Parana River 18 miles from Buenos Aires. The long coastal areas offer a number of excellent seaside resorts with casinos and wide, sandy beaches. The Mar del Plata, about 250 miles south of Buenos Aires, is a famous resort and playground with private clubs and summer estates of the wealthy.

Figure 19.1 Buenos Aires. © sunsinger/www.Shutterstock.com.

Figure 19.2 Perito Moreno Glacier, Argentino Lake, Patagonia, Argentina. © Pichugin Dmitry/www.Shutterstock.com.

In the northwest region, Córdoba, the capital city of Córdoba Province, is the second largest city of Argentina. It has a mixture of old churches and modern buildings. Some points of interest are the old colonial building (the Viceroy's House), the Church of La Merced, and the Church of La Companía. Mendoza, near the Chilean border, has a thriving wine industry.

The foothills of the Andes are in southern Argentina in Patagonia. Patagonia stretches from Central Argentina to the Strait of Magellan. This region contains two completely different geographical areas. First is the towering Andes and a vast terrain covered with sheets of ice and glaciers that spill into huge lakes. Glaciers National Park contains 300 glaciers, including Perito Moreno (Figure 19.2), the park's centerpiece. The second area, the Peninsula of Valdés in the east of Patagonia, offers a perfect vantage point for the observation of whales, penguins, huge sea elephants, and all kinds of marine life. The area includes the mountain scenery Bariloche and the southern lake district, which attract tourists for a multitude of sporting activities such as hunting, fishing, skiing, and golfing. It is often referred to as the Switzerland of South America. Even farther south, Tierra del Fuego has a large number of species of birds (Figure 19.3), snow-capped peaks, waterfalls, deep red forests, lakes, and glaciers for the hardy traveler, and is home to the world's southernmost city, Ushuaia. From here, cruise ships depart to explore the Antarctic region to the south.

Figure 19.3 Gentoo Penguins on the beach on Isla Martillo near Ushuaia, Tierra del Fuego, Argentinian Patagonia.
© jorisvo/www.Shutterstock.com.

Paraguay

Introduction

Paraguay is a landlocked country in central South America. The Paraguay River divides the country into a hilly, forested east and a flat plain (known as the Chaco) in the west. The Chaco is marshy near the river but turns to semi-desert grasslands and scrub forest farther west; it takes up 60 percent of the country but is home to only 2 percent of the people. The climate is subtropical.

Paraguayans are mostly a mixture of Spanish and Guaraní Indian, and they are the most racially homogeneous people in South America. The majority of the population understands Spanish but prefers to speak Guaraní. Paraguay enjoys plenty of electric power thanks to hydroelectric dams like Itaipú, the world's largest, built and operated jointly with Brazil. Democracy replaced dictatorship by 1993, but the government faces problems in dealing with poverty, deforestation, and smuggling.

From *National Geographic Atlas of the World*, 9th edition. Copyright ©2011 National Geographic Society. Reprinted by arrangement. All rights reserved.

Area	406,752 sq km (157,048 sq mi)
Population	6,349,000
Government	Constitutional Republic
Capital	Asunción 1,870,000
Life Expectancy	71 years
Literacy	94%
Religion	Roman Catholic, Protestant
Language	Spanish, Guaraní
Currency	Guarani (PYG)
GDP per Cap	$4,100
Labor Force	26.5% Agriculture, 18.5% Industry, 55.0% Services

From *National Geographic Atlas of the World*, 9th edition. Copyright ©2011 National Geographic Society. Reprinted by arrangement. All rights reserved.

Tourism Characteristics

The country is now stressing the development of tourism by organizing tourist events, national festivals, and other special promotions. In 2010, Paraguay attracted 450,000 tourists. Argentina and Brazil account for more than 80 percent of the tourists to Paraguay, again indicating the considerable intraregional travel within South America.

TRAVEL **TIPS** 💼

Entry: A passport and a visa are required.

Peak Tourist Season: December through March

National Holiday: May 14 (Independence Day).

Shopping: Local items include alpaca goods, gold, silver, and hand-woven wool fabrics.

Internet TLD: .py

CULTURAL CAPSULE

Paraguay's population is the most homogeneous in South America. It is about 95 percent Spanish, Guarani Indian, and mestizo. There are small minority groups of Italians, Germans, Koreans, and Japanese. The two official languages are Spanish and Guarani. Nearly 90 percent of the population belongs to the Catholic Church.

Cultural hints: Women should dress conservatively and modestly. Paraguayans have a close personal space during conversations. Common foods are chicken, pork, beef, corn, rice, and vegetables.

Tourist Destinations and Attractions

There are a variety of attractions, from the vast Chaco, which for years was inhabited only by scattered Indian tribes and Mennonite settlements, to Asunción, the capital, to the Paraguay (Parana), Alto Parna, and Pilcomayo rivers that form Paraguay's boundaries. Asunción is usually the traveler's first choice of a city to visit. It is the largest city, containing many palaces, churches, and museums. The large modern church of La Encarnación is the focal building in the city. Asunción has a number of excellent parks such as Parque Caballero with waterfalls and plantations and the Botanical Gardens.

The small, ancient town of nearby Itaugua with its reddish tile roofs is another frequently visited attraction. Famous for spider-web lace, it has all types of other handicrafts, from hammocks to dresses. Ypacarai and Ypoa are Paraguay's major lakes. Both are resort centers with beautiful tropical trees and flowers. Other important attractions are the Indian culture, the open-air markets, and the excursions into the primitive Chaco jungles. Iguazú Falls is on the border of Brazil, Argentina, and Paraguay. However, Paraguay benefits far less from it as a tourist destination than the other two countries.

Uruguay

Introduction

Uruguay, a land of low prairies, is located on the Atlantic coast of southern South America, and is the continent's second smallest country (after Suriname). The coastal area features many lagoons, sand dunes, and scenic beaches. The climate is subtropical and pleasant. Uruguay has one of the highest urbanization and literacy rates in South America, and it claims the lowest poverty and population growth rates. About 92 percent of Uruguayans, most of Spanish or Italian descent, live in cities, with Montevideo home to nearly one-half of Uruguayans. Education is compulsory and free. Uruguay's economy remains dependent on agriculture, mostly cattle and sheep ranching, and services. Economic diversification, including development of hydroelectric power, has spread optimism; tourists flock to Atlantic beach resorts, such as Punta del Este.

From *National Geographic Atlas of the World*, 9th edition. Copyright ©2011 National Geographic Society. Reprinted by arrangement. All rights reserved.

Area	176,215 sq km (68,037 sq mi)
Population	3,364,000
Government	Constitutional Republic
Capital	Montevideo 1,513,000
Life Expectancy	76 years
Literacy	98%
Religion	Roman Catholic, other Christian, nondenominational
Language	Spanish
Currency	Uruguayan peso (UYU)
GDP per Cap	$12,700
Labor Force	9% Agriculture, 15% Industry, 76% Services

From *National Geographic Atlas of the World*, 9th edition. Copyright ©2011 National Geographic Society. Reprinted by arrangement. All rights reserved.

TRAVEL **TIPS** 🧳

Entry: Visa not required for stays up to three months. A passport is required.

Peak Tourist Season: December through March

National Holiday: August 25 (Independence Day).

Shopping: Local items include furs, leather goods, woolen goods, ostrich bags, jewelry and precious stones, and gaucho souvenirs of dolls and bombillas.

Internet TLD: .uy

CULTURAL CAPSULE: The population is mostly Spanish and Italian (over 80 percent). Mestizos only account for 8 percent and Blacks for 4 percent of the population. Most are Roman Catholics (65 percent), with the rest belonging to various Christian and Protestant faiths. There is a small minority of Jewish faithful.

Cultural hints: Uruguayans have close personal space. Keep feet on the floor. Common foods are meats, fish, vegetables, and fruits. Typical dishes are roasts, stews, and meat pies.

Tourism Characteristics

With the assistance of the Organization of American States, Uruguay has been developing programs to improve its tourism industry. Argentina and Brazil account for the majority of the more than 2 million visitors to Uruguay. The country has not been successful in attracting visitors from the United States or Europe because there are few direct flights and Uruguay is often not included in the Latin American circuit by tour operators. Seasonality of visitors to Uruguay is very marked, with the peak number arriving in January and declining rapidly through March, reaching lows in early summer. Visitor arrivals increase in December, resulting in a December to March major tourist season.

Tourist Destinations and Attractions

The principal attraction is Montevideo, the capital, which is situated on a bay with beautiful beaches. The major attraction in Montevideo is the Palacio Salvo. The Municipal Palace contains two fine museums: the Museum of Art History and the Museum of Pre-Columbian and Colonial Art. The Palacio Legislativo has pink granite pillars, mosaic floors, and historic wall murals. The Teátro Solís (Theater of the Sun) and the Museum of Natural History are significant attractions. On top of the Cerro (Hill), there is an old fort, which is now a military museum, and the oldest lighthouse in the country. Extending north toward Brazil, there are a number of beaches and resorts, all popular with Argentine and Brazilian tourists. The most popular is Punta del Este (Figure 19.4), which has excellent beaches backed by sand dunes covered with pines.

Figure 19.4 "The Hand," a famous sculpture in Punta del Este, Uruguay. © Kobby Dagan/www.Shutterstock.com.

REVIEW QUESTIONS

1. Paraguay is one of South America's two landlocked countries. What is the name of the other country?

2. Argentina is emerging as a magnet for tourism. What are the country's major attractions?

3. The "Riviera of South America" is located in Uruguay. What are its unique features?

4. What region in Argentina is often compared to Switzerland?

5. What is the name of the vast region in Argentina situated east of the Andes mountain range?

chapter 20: BRAZIL AND THE GUYANAS

Brazil

Introduction

South America's largest country and the world's fifth largest nation, Brazil holds Earth's most extensive rain forest and greatest river system—the Amazon. The Amazon River's drainage basin covers some 60 percent of the country. Most of Brazil has a tropical climate, but most Brazilians live near the coast, where highlands and sea winds moderate temperatures. Brazil, a federal republic, has twenty-six states and a federal capital district, which are often grouped into five regions: The North region covers 39 percent of Brazil, from the state of Amazonas east to Tocantins and Pará, but holds only 6 percent of the population. Many migrated to this region from the densely populated Northeast, causing rapid deforestation, but the government now pushes sustainable development. With 18 percent of Brazil's land and 28 percent of its people, the semiarid Northeast region cradles Afro-Brazilian culture. The Northeast ranges from Maranhão south to Bahia, including smaller coastal states. Portuguese colonization originated here, as did much of Brazil's music, folklore, and cuisine. The West Central region (Goiás, Matto Grosso, and Matto Grosso do Sul states) holds 25 percent of the land and 7 percent of Brazilians. This grassland region was a development target when Brasília, the capital, was founded in 1960. The Southeast is Brazil's most densely populated region and economic hub; it has 11 percent of the land and 44 percent of the people—many housed in São Paulo and Rio de Janeiro, Brazil's largest cities. The mountains of Minas Gerais state hold vast mineral wealth, feeding industrialization. The South, with 7 percent of the land and 15 percent of the population, lies south of São Paulo state; it is small but highly developed—attractions include Florianópolis and Iguaçu Falls.

From *National Geographic Atlas of the World*, 9th edition. Copyright ©2011 National Geographic Society. Reprinted by arrangement. All rights reserved.

Area	8,514,877 sq km (3,287,612 sq mi)
Population	191,481,000
Government	Federal Republic
Capital	Brasília 3,599,000
Life Expectancy	73 years
Literacy	89%
Religion	Roman Catholic, Protestant
Language	Portuguese
Currency	real (BRL)
GDP per Cap	$10,200
Labor Force	20% Agriculture, 14% Industry, 66% Services

From *National Geographic Atlas of the World*, 9th edition. Copyright ©2011 National Geographic Society. Reprinted by arrangement. All rights reserved.

TRAVEL **TIPS**

Entry: A passport and a visa are required.

Peak Tourist Season: February

National Holiday: September 7 (Independence Day).

Shopping: Local items include jewelry, gemstones, hardwood items, clay figurines, pottery, soapstone carvings, bone carvings, leather work, snake skin, tiles, basketwork, cotton fabrics, antique silver, and Indian miniature souvenirs.

Internet TLD: .br

CULTURAL CAPSULE Brazil is the largest and most populous country in Latin America. Most of the people live in the south-central area, which includes the industrial cities of São Paulo, Río de Janeiro, and Belo Horizonte. Four major groups comprise the Brazilian population: indigenous Indians of Tup and Guarani language stock; the Portuguese, who colonized in the sixteenth century; Africans brought to Brazil as slaves; and various European (German and Italian) and Asian immigrant groups. Soccer is the national sport and is played and watched passionately.

Cultural hints: A warm, friendly handshake is the common greeting and departing gesture. Good friends embrace (Abrazo). To get someone's attention people say "pssst." Do not drink directly from a can or bottle. Common foods are bread, cheese, beans, rice, meat, and fruit. Typical dishes are imbu (potatoes and bread), feijoada (black beans with beef, pork, sausage, tongue), and meat with egg and French fries.

Tourism Characteristics

Brazil continues to improve its tourist industry and is now the most popular destination country in South America. In 2010 there were over 5 million visitors. Like the other South American countries, Brazil has a strong intraregional tourist bias, but overseas markets are increasing in importance. Visitors from Europe have increased (with Italy and Germany having the largest percentage). The increasing number of tourists from Europe results from the increasing number of low-cost flights and strong marketing by the Brazilian government in an effort to penetrate the European market. Both the high percentage of trips for holidays and a peak season in January and February illustrate the typical vacation period for South American countries and the attraction of Carnival for

Figure 20.1 a. Toucan. © holbox/www.Shutterstock.com. **b.** Red tree frog. © Dirk Ercken/www.Shutterstock.com. **c.** Jaguar. © guentermanaus/www.Shutterstock.com. **d.** Amazon river dolphin. © guentermanaus/www.Shutterstock.com.

many tourists from North America and Europe. A very strong economy during the first decade of the twenty-first century spurred the development of many tourism indus-try–related infrastructure projects throughout the country resulting is a boost in domestic travel. Mega events such as the FIFA World Cup and Summer Olympics will help increase international tourist arrivals in 2014 and 2016.

Tourist Destinations and Attractions

The three principal tourist areas are Amazonia, the northeast, and the triangle formed by Río de Janeiro, Brasília, and São Paulo. In Amazonia, the Amazon River's exotic wildlife and vast rain forests offer an expe-rience unequaled anywhere (Figure 20.1). Amazon tour-ist activity centers in the area of Manaus. The river trip from Belén to Manaus is becoming increasingly popular. Dominating Manaus is its famous theater (opera house).

Attractive local culture, beautiful church architecture, and pretty towns and cities such as Recife, the "Venice of America," can be found in the northeast. Salvador, the capital of Bahía State, has many churches, fortifications, and other old buildings. The older parts of the city are now a national monument, and considerable restoration

Figure 20.2 Christ the Redeemer statue in Rio de Janeiro, Brazil. © LaiQuocAnh/www.Shutterstock.com.

work has been completed. As in many Brazilian towns, Carnival in Salvador is exciting and entertaining. There are a number of outstanding beaches in the region. With its thirty-four islands, the Bahía de Todos os Santos provides all types of water experiences.

Río, with its famed Copacabana, Leblon, Barra de Tijuca, and Ipanema Beaches, architecture, monuments, and festivals, forms one corner of the tourist triangle, and the capital city of Brasília forms another.

The triangle is completed by São Paulo, a modern city with gourmet food, waterfalls, and beautiful beaches, all important to the development of the strong tourist industry in this area. Rio's coastal landscape is one of the most beautiful on the continent. The city is known for the samba and Bossa Nova. Landmarks include the giant statue of Christ the Redeemer (Cristo Redentor) (Figure 20.2) atop Corcovado mountain, and Sugarloaf mountain with its cable car.

Figure 20.3 São Paulo, Brazil. © Celso Diniz/www.Shutterstock.com.

PRESERVING THE FUTURE | Waterworld Brazil

Welcome to an island playground fiercely protected for its fragile ecosystem and respectfully savored by surfers and divers

Even Brazilians are surprised to find we have an island paradise on a par—and then some—with Hawaii and Tahiti. Yes, Fernando de Noronha, a twenty-one-island archipelago about one hundred miles off the mainland, has bluer-than-blue waters, star rock formations, and indigenous birds and blooms, but it is blessedly less trampled and more exotic than better-known paradise spots. It sits four degrees south of the Equator, giving it geographic bragging rights.

Talk about transformation. In the 1800s, Noronha functioned as a penal colony. The islands were discovered by environmentalists and biologists in the

Named a World Heritage site in 2001 for its diversity of sea animals, including a wealth of dolphins, the archipelago is possibly the only destination in Brazil that imposes a visitor limit in order to maintain the place's untouched essence.

late twentieth century and reborn as a sustainable development locale. My friend Claudio Bellini is one of the oceanologist responsible for project TAMAR, which studies and preserves the green turtles that come to lay their eggs on the sand here. Named a World Heritage site in 2001 for its diversity of sea animals, including a wealth

of dolphins, the archipelago is possibly the only destination in Brazil that imposes a visitor limit in order to maintain the place's untouched essence.

For me, Noronha's perfect waves are a great lure, for surfing atop and diving below. The water is so warm that I can head down as deep at 120 feet without a wet suit.

Afternoons are for hiking up a mountain, then staying put for the water views and the sunset. Sometimes magic happens, with bird and dolphins gathering at the same time, all beings seemingly knowing there is a no better place on Earth.

— **Oskar Metsavaht,** *National Geographic Traveler,* **October 2009**

Brasília, the capital, is a relatively new city designed to attract some of the population inland from the coast. The public buildings were designed by architect Oscar Niemeyer. The center is the Plaza of the Three Powers, with marble buildings, reflecting pools, and metal sculpture. Brasília is famous for its large number of modern sculptures.

São Paulo (Figure 20.3), the largest city in Brazil and South America, has a modern dynamic skyline.

The Butanta Institute, a snake farm, and the old Municipal Market are on the outskirts of town. São Paulo has fine beaches and resorts and small colonial villages.

Iguazú Falls, in the south, is visited heavily from Brazil since the Brazilian side offers the best panoramic view (Figure 20.4).

Figure 20.4 Iguazú Falls, Brazil. © iladm/www.Shutterstock.com.

Guyana

Introduction

Tropical rain forests shroud more than 80 percent of this English-speaking former British colony on the north coast of South America. More than 90 percent of the population resides on the narrow coastal plain. Guyana gained independence in 1966. During 150 years of British rule, laborers were brought here from Africa and India. Today, the Guyanese population is 43 percent East Indian, 30 percent African, 17 percent mixed, and 9 percent Amerindian. Sugar, bauxite, and gold are leading exports; however, Guyana's high debt burden hampers the democratic government.

From *National Geographic Atlas of the World*, 9th edition. Copyright ©2011 National Geographic Society. Reprinted by arrangement. All rights reserved.

Figure 20.5 Kaieteur Falls. © ecoventurestravel/www.Shutterstock.com.

Area	214,969 sq km (83,000 sq mi)
Population	773,000
Government	Republic
Capital	Georgetown 133,000
Life Expectancy	66 years
Religion	Christian, Hindu, Muslim
Language	English, Amerindian dialects, Creole, Caribbean Hindustani, Urdu
Currency	Guyanese dollar (GYD)
GDP per Cap	$3,800

From *National Geographic Atlas of the World*, 9th edition. Copyright ©2011 National Geographic Society. Reprinted by arrangement. All rights reserved.

TRAVEL**TIPS**

Entry: A Passport is required.

Peak Tourist Season: July and August

National Holiday: February 23 (Republic Day).

Shopping: Local items include Indian handicrafts, such as beaded aprons, basketwork, blowpipes, pottery, and clothing.

Internet TLD: .gy

CULTURAL CAPSULE The population comprises five main ethnic groups: East Indian, African, Amerindian, Chinese, and Portugese. The population is concentrated along the coast. Religion is an expression of the population, consisting of a number of Christian faiths, large numbers of Hindus, and a sizable minority of Muslims.

Tourism Characteristics

Guyana has a limited tourism industry averaging less than 150,000 visitors a year. The United States and Canada account for over 70 percent of all visitors to Guyana. Other than Anglo-America and the Caribbean, the United Kingdom is the only other country with a large number of visitors to Guyana, a reflection of the political and cultural linkages of colonialism. The peak tourist season in July and August is reflective of the vacation periods in the United States, Canada, and the United Kingdom. The major attraction is the capital, Georgetown, which contains attractive Georgian-style houses of wood supported on stilts. Some of the better sights are the City Hall, St. George's Cathedral, the Law Courts, the president's residence, and the Parliament Building. The botanical gardens have a large number of birds as well as a collection of palms, orchids, and ponds. The Kaieteur Falls (Figure 20.5) on the Potaro River is in a class with Niagara and Victoria Falls. The falls are nearly five times the height of Niagara Falls. Located in a jungle, they can be reached only by small aircraft. Recent explorations of off-shore oil reserves hold the promise of transforming the country's economy.

Suriname

Introduction

Along the north coast of South America, Suriname is a small but ethnically diverse country. Most people are descendants of Indian or Indonesian servants and African slaves brought over by the Dutch to work in agriculture. Suriname, formerly known as Dutch Guiana, gained independence in 1975. Most Surinamers live along the narrow coastal plain, and access to the interior rain forest is limited. Bauxite, gold, and oil dominate trade and investment. Environmental issues focus on deforestation and waterway pollution from mining operations. Suriname disputes land and maritime boundaries with Guyana and French Guiana.

From *National Geographic Atlas of the World*, 9th edition. Copyright ©2011 National Geographic Society. Reprinted by arrangement. All rights reserved.

Area	
Population	502,000
Government	Constitutional Democracy
Capital	Paramaribo 252,000
Life Expectancy	69 years
Religion	Hindu, Protestant (mostly Moravian), Roman Catholic, Muslim, indigenous beliefs
Language	Dutch, English, Sranang Tongo, Caribbean Hindustani
Currency	Surinamese dollar (SRD)
GDP per Cap	$9,000
Labor Force	8% Agriculture, 14% Industry, 78% Services

From *National Geographic Atlas of the World*, 9th edition. Copyright ©2011 National Geographic Society. Reprinted by arrangement. All rights reserved.

TRAVEL**TIPS**

Entry: A passport and a visa are required.

Peak Tourist Season: July and August

National Holiday: November 25 (Independence Day).

Internet TLD: .sr

CULTURAL CAPSULE The population of Suriname is one of the most varied in the world. The major ethnic groups are Hindustani, Creole, Javanese, Maroon (Bush Black), Amerindians, and Chinese. Social relations tend to stay within ethnic groups. The population clusters along the narrow, northern coastal plain.

Tourism Characteristics

Suriname has a small but unique tourist industry within the Guyanas. By 2010 it was receiving around 200,000 visitors a year. Its tourism characteristics are dominated by the linkage between Suriname and The Netherlands. This can be illustrated by the fact that The Netherlands accounts for nearly 50 percent of the total visitors to Suriname, and the major purpose of visits is friends and family. The peak tourist season in July and August with a secondary peak from September through December is characteristic of visitors from Europe and the United States. Paramaribo, the capital, is a modern city with a diversity of cultures expressed in the variety of Catholic cathedrals, Moslem mosques, and Hindu temples. The People's Palace (the old Governor's Mansion), a number of eighteenth- and nineteenth-century Dutch-style buildings, and the restored Fort Zeelandia add flavor to the city. The country has a number of nature reserves providing a rain forest experience with a number of species such as sea turtles and a host of birds.

French Guiana

Introduction

Located in northern South America, French Guiana is densely forested, and most Guianans live along the Atlantic coast. Trade winds help make the hot temperatures comfortable. The Guiana Space Center near Kourou is the major launch facility for the European Space Agency.

Area	86,504 sq km (33,400 sq mi)
Population	226,000
Capital	Cayenne 63,000
Religion	Roman Catholic, Protestant, Hindu, Muslim
Language	French, Guianese Creole

TRAVEL **TIPS** 🧳

Entry: A visa is not required. A passport is required.

Tourist Season: August to October

National Holiday: July 14 (Bastille Day).

Internet TLD: .gf

Tourism Characteristics

French Guiana has one of the most underdeveloped tourist industries in South America. It is the only region in South America that has not yet gained independence. Most of its visitors are from France. Cayenne, the capital, is on the island of Cayenne and is the jumping-off place for visits to the jungle and the notorious penal colony Devil's Island. The second city, Kourou, is the home of the French National Space Agency's Guiana Space Center, from which the European Space Agency's rockets are launched (Figure 20.6).

In Javouhey and Cacao at opposite ends of French Guyana, two Hmong villages contain some 1,200 tribespeople, resettled in areas resembling their former villages in Laos. Tourists can view a wide array of colorful tapestries woven by the Hmong women and purchase traditional Southeast Asian vegetables.

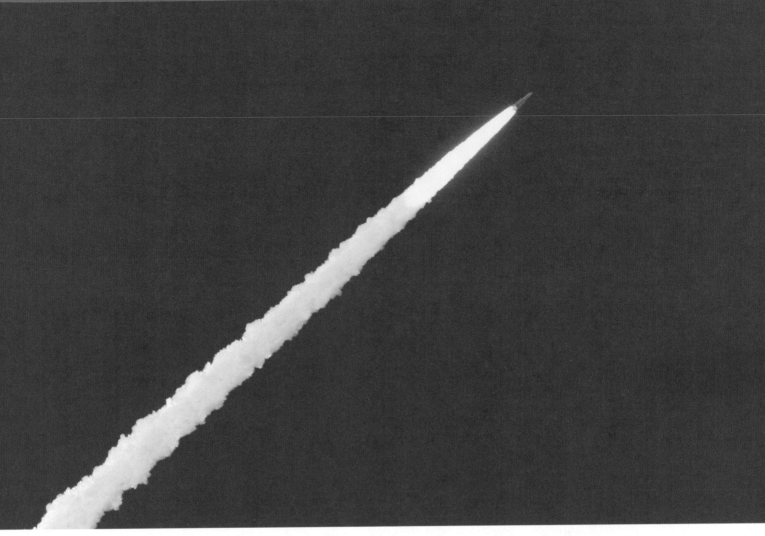

Figure 20.6 Ariane 5 take-off in Kourou, home of the French National Space Agency's Guiana Space Center. © Stephanie Rousseau/www.Shutterstock.com.

REVIEW QUESTIONS

1. What are Brazil's major opportunities and obstacles to develop its tourism industry into the future?

2. What is the outlook for domestic tourism in Brazil?

3. Name Rio de Janeiro's major sites and events.

4. A major export item for Suriname is bauxite. What is it used for?

5. Why is French Guiana an important site for the European Aerospace program?

© Michae.

© 2015 Cengage Learning®

MAJOR GEOGRAPHIC CHARACTERISTICS

- Western Europe has a highly urbanized, skilled, and well-educated population.
- Western Europe's climate is moderate for its northern location.
- Western Europe is the home of the Industrial Revolution.
- Western Europe is one of the wealthiest regions of the world.
- Western Europe has an outstanding network of transportation and communications.
- Western Europe is the most densely populated region of the world.
- Most of the countries of Western Europe were colonial powers and still have important connections with countries that were former colonies.
- Western Europe is one of the major trading centers of the world.
- Western Europe's economy is based on service industries, technology, and manufacturing.
- Western Europe is characterized by cultural fragmentation.
- Northern Europe has a high-latitude location and rugged physical geography.
- Population centers are concentrated along Northern Europe's southern margins.
- Northern Europe is relatively isolated.
- The Lutheran religion predominates in Northern Europe.
- Northern Europe has a homogeneous population with few minorities.
- Individual countries in Northern Europe have high standards of living.
- The lingua franca for Northern Europe is English.
- The population of Northern Europe is highly urbanized, highly skilled, and highly educated.
- Nearly all of Southern Europe has a Mediterranean climate.

(continued)

- Mountains have formed a barrier between Western Europe and Southern Europe.
- Southern Europe occupies three major peninsulas.
- The Mediterranean Sea is an important resource for the culture and economies of Southern Europe.
- The nations of Southern Europe share a common cultural heritage created from the Greek and Roman empires.
- Southern Europe lacks major deposits of important minerals.
- Populations in Southern Europe are located on coastal or riverine plains.
- Agriculture in Southern Europe is concentrated in coastal and river plain locations.
- Agricultural productivity in Southern Europe is lower than in Western and Northern Europe.
- Central Europe and the Balkan States are fragmented culturally and politically.
- Central Europe is located between more powerful countries, which hindered its political development, resulting in repeated conflicts.
- Central Europe historically had a central monarchy and a nobility whose palaces and other relics are important tourist attractions.
- There is a wide range of economic and tourism development, standard of living, and political stability in Central Europe.
- Central Europe is characterized by physical and cultural diversity.

- Most visitors to Northern Europe stay only for short periods of time.
- Southern Europe's major tourism emphasis for Europeans is sun-sea-sand.
- North American and Asian visitors seek out cities and cultural treasures in Southern Europe.
- Tourism costs are lower in Southern Europe than in Western and Northern Europe.
- Religious pilgrimages are important to Southern Europe.
- Cruises and excursions are popular in Southern Europe.
- Tourism to Southern Europe is mostly destination oriented.
- Tourism is highly localized to specific regions within each country in Southern Europe.
- The archaeological and cultural heritage of Western civilization is an important attraction in Southern Europe.
- There is a diversity in entry requirements, but all countries in Central Europe are encouraging international tourism.
- The countries of Central Europe have increased their interest in tourism development.
- There is a wide variety of tourist attractions and landscapes in Central Europe.
- Tourism from the West to Central Europe expanded dramatically after the revolutions of the early 1990s that overthrew the Communist governments in the region.
- Many attractions and accommodations in Central Europe were destroyed during the early 1990s as a result of the conflicts in Slovenia, Croatia, Bosnia, and Serbia, but many sites have been restored and tourists have returned to the region.

MAJOR TOURIST CHARACTERISTICS

- Western Europe generates more tourists than any region of the world.
- Western Europe receives more tourists than any region of the world.
- Western Europe has a long and well-established history of travel.
- Europe leads the world in reducing frontier barriers between countries.
- Western Europe has a highly efficient tourism industry.
- All countries in the region (with the exception of the United Kingdom and Switzerland) use the Euro currency.
- The major attractions in Northern Europe are scenic and outdoor sports related.
- The character of the travel industry varies greatly from country to country in Northern Europe.
- Tourism is less important to the economies of the countries in Northern Europe than to the rest of Europe.
- Fewer tourists visit Northern Europe than other regions of Europe.

MAJOR TOURISM DESTINATIONS

- European Capitals
- London, Stonehenge, Stratford-upon-Avon, and York in England
- Dublin and surrounding area
- Cork and Kerry, Ireland
- Amsterdam and Polder cities northwest of Amsterdam in the Netherlands
- Brussels, Bruges, and Ghent in Belgium
- Paris and the Chateau Region of the Loire Valley
- Cathedral of Notre Dame (Paris, France)
- French Riviera
- French Alps
- Rhine River between Köln and Wiesbaden
- Bavaria
- Berlin
- Swiss Alps and Lakes
- Tyrol area around Innsbruck

- Salzburg region
- Vienna (Danube Basin)
- Capitals of Northern Europe
- Fjords of Norway (Bergen to Trondheim)
- Bergen to Oslo, Norway
- Jutland, Denmark
- Turku to Helsinki, Finland
- King's Road
- Lake Country (Finland)
- Lapland
- Odense, Denmark
- Oresund Bridge
- Malmo, Sweden
- Göteborg to Stockholm, Sweden
- Capitals
- Venice, Italy
- Florence, Italy
- Rome and the Vatican City
- Area around Naples
- Balearic Islands and the Coasts of Spain (Brava, Blanca, and Sol)
- Central Region around Madrid
- Andalusia
- Barcelona
- Lisbon and Its Environs
- Algarve
- Athens and Its Environs
- Island of Peloponnisos
- The Greek Islands
- Capitals of Central Europe and the Balkan States
- Black Sea Resorts
- Karlovy Vary, Czech Republic
- Adriatic Sea Coast
- Transylvania
- Carpathian Mountains
- Tatra Mountains
- Krakow
- Lake Balaton
- Julian Alps
- Dubrovnik
- Valley of Roses
- Dinaric Alps
- Romanian Riviera
- Dalmatian Coast

KEY TERMS AND WORDS

Acropolis	Jutland
Adriatic	Karst
Alhambra	Lapland
Alluvial	Lingua Franca
Ancient Cities	Lochs
Andalusia	Lutheran
Archipelago	Maritime Influence
Austro-Hungarian Empire	Massif Central
Basques	Masurian Lake District
Casbah	Medieval
Castle	Medieval
Cathedral Cities	Medieval
Celtic	Mediterranean
Chateau	Mezzogiorno
Christianity	Midnight Sun
Cirque	Moors
Continental Europe	Mosque
Danube	Mountains (Carpathian, Tatra, Dinaric Alps)
Dayton Accord	
Druids	National Trusts
Eastern Orthodox	North Atlantic Drift
Eastern Orthodox	Old Quarter
English Channel	Ottoman
Euro Zone	Peninsula
European Cities	Peninsular
European Plain	Pilgrimage
European Plain	Po Valley
European Union	Polder
Fens	Punic
Fjord	Queues
Gaelic	Riviera
Glacial drift	Romance Languages
Glaciation	Sagas
Glacier-burst	Sami
Glockenspiel	Scandinavia
Gothic	Skåne
Greek Islands	The Conflict in the Balkans
Hanging Valley	Turkic Ottoman Empire
Hanseatic League	Tyrol
Hidden Economy	Visigoth
Holy Week	Vulcanism
Industry	Welfare State
Insularity	Western Culture
Iron Gate	"White Gold"
Islands	World War II

Introduction

No other continent offers more cultural, physical, and climate diversity than does Europe. Sixty percent of all international travel takes place within the borders of this continent. Seven of the continent's countries rank within the top ten of destinations for world travelers. Attractions include historic monuments, exciting urban centers, world-class beaches, famous ski resorts, and renowned hotels and restaurants. The continents is crisscrossed with an extensive and efficient road, rail, and air transportation network. Over forty countries make up this important travel region. Many are small and each has a distinct history and culture. Many countries in the region have a distinct language and particular way of life. Europe is covered in the next five chapters. Chapter 21 will cover the countries of Western Europe: Ireland, The United Kingdom, France, Monaco, Belgium, the Netherlands, Luxembourg, Germany, Austria, Switzerland, and Liechtenstein. Northern Europe, a region also referred to as Scandinavia, is highlighted in Chapter 22. Countries here include Denmark, Finland, Sweden, Norway, and Iceland. Southern Europe, Chapter 23, includes Greece, Cyprus, Italy, Spain, Gibraltar, Andorra, Portugal, and Malta. Central Europe (until recently referred to as Eastern Europe) is featured in Chapter 24 and includes Poland, the Czech Republic, Slovakia, Hungary, Romania, Bulgaria, and the Balkan states of Serbia, Slovenia, Croatia, Bosnia, and Albania.

INTERNATIONAL TOURISM TO WESTERN EUROPE (IN MILLIONS), 2010.

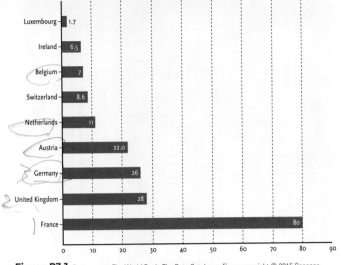

Figure P7.1 Data source: *The World Bank: The Data Catalogue.* Figure copyright © 2015 Cengage Learning®. All rights reserved.

INTERNATIONAL TOURISM TO NORTHERN EUROPE (IN MILLIONS), 2010.

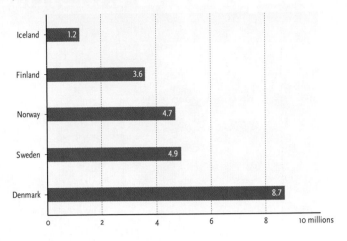

INTERNATIONAL TOURISM TO CENTRAL EUROPE (IN MILLIONS), 2010.

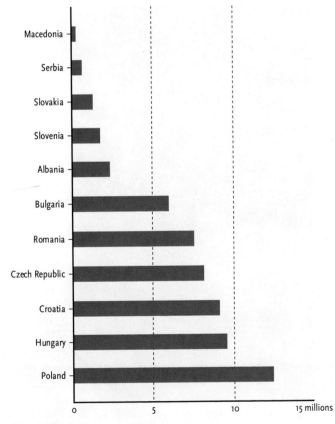

Figure P7.2 Data source: *The World Bank: The Data Catalogue.* Figure copyright © 2015 Cengage Learning®. All rights reserved.

Introduction

The countries of Western Europe combine with the nations of Southern and Northern Europe to form the most important tourist region in the world. Three of the world's top destination countries are from this region (France, United Kingdom, and Germany). In addition, five other countries of this region (Austria, Switzerland, The Netherlands, Ireland, and Belgium) are in the top thirty. Together, these countries account for nearly 25 percent of total world tourist arrivals. They are also major contributors to world expenditures in tourism. These countries, without Ireland, account for over 36 percent of the total world expenditures in tourism. Western Europe is extremely accessible, with major transportation routes both within the region and outside the region.

The region has excellent connections to Anglo-America. The nature of tourism to Western Europe from North America varies considerably from country to country. Germany, Belgium, the Netherlands, and Switzerland are "short stay" countries that tourists visit in connection with a multicountry visit or tour. Austria, France, Ireland, and the United Kingdom are more likely to have a stronger one-country emphasis or be the main destination. All have a high per capita visitor expenditure, but average visitor expense differs markedly from country to country, primarily reflecting differences in length of stay.

Increasing cooperation associated with the European Union combines with deregulation of the airlines to make European travel easier and less expensive. The deregulation of the airlines in Europe has been much slower than in the United States. The latest step in open skies allows airlines to fly between any two cities in the European Union, even on domestic flights inside another country. As in the United States this is creating a new challenge for the national flag carriers as low-cost airlines develop in Europe. Airfares are being driven down on formerly monopolized routes, and discounts are given on heavily traveled routes. The European Union has also removed border requirements between member nations. The European Union has increased investment in tourism development in the countries of Southern Europe and Ireland.

Tourism in Western Europe is quite seasonal. Because European countries have a strong summer holiday tradition a summer peak is typical of Europe. A combination of factors such as climate, school closings, factory vacations, and economic characteristics are important in European seasonality. The degree of seasonality varies slightly depending on location. For example, the United Kingdom and Ireland may have a slightly higher percentage in the winter and a bit lower in July and August because of the more moderate climate. However, the strong peaks in July and August are the same throughout Western Europe. France has an even less-intensive seasonality because of access to the Mediterranean Sea, which attracts more visitors in the winter than Germany and Austria, although they have a strong ski industry.

Ireland

Introduction

An island in the North Atlantic, Ireland features coastal mountains in the west and interior agricultural lowlands, with numerous hills, lakes, and bogs. Ireland occupies about 83 percent of the island of Ireland—Northern Ireland, with 1.8 million people, is part of the United Kingdom.

Irish, or Irish Gaelic (a Celtic language), is the country's first official language and is taught in schools, but few native speakers remain. Éire (AIR-uh) is the Irish name for the republic of Ireland. English is the second official language and is more common.

In 1922, Ireland's Roman Catholic counties won independence, while mostly Protestant Northern Ireland remained under British control. After Ireland joined the EU in 1973, its economy was slowly transformed. From the early 1990s to 2007, Ireland experienced robust growth in construction, manufacturing, and tourism.

Recently, Ireland shifted its economic focus toward biotechnology, financial services, and innovative communications technologies.

From *National Geographic Atlas of the World*, 9th edition. Copyright ©2011 National Geographic Society. Reprinted by arrangement. All rights reserved.

It's long been a staple of Irish rural life: the earthy warmth of burning peat. For centuries families relied on turf bricks cut from raised bogs (left) and dried for fuel. Now a move by the European Union to enforce a 1997 directive to protect these disappearing ancient habitats—rich in decomposing plants and rare species— has turf cutters bristling.

The EU designation of dozens of large bogs for conservation, part of a push to protect environmental diversity, went largely unenforced due to rural Irish sensitivities. But evidence of extensive cutting led the EU to threaten heavy fines last year. Industrial interests continued to cut, citing jobs. A tentative peace was reached this past summer,

with contractors agreeing to halt activity for the rest of the year. But the ground remains unsteady; Irish legislator and turf cutter Luke Flanagan promises a fresh fight next year.

—Erin Friar McDermott, *National Geographic Magazine*, November 2011

Area	70,273 sq km (27,133 sq mi)
Population	4,528,000
Government	republic, parliamentary democracy
Capital	Dublin 1,059,000
Life Expectancy	79 years
Religion	Roman Catholic
Language	Irish (Gaelic), English
Currency	euro (EUR)
GDP per Cap	$42,200
Labor Force	6% Agriculture, 27% Industry, 67% Services

From *National Geographic Atlas of the World*, 9th edition. Copyright ©2011 National Geographic Society. Reprinted by arrangement. All rights reserved.

TRAVEL**TIPS** 💼

Entry: Visas are not required. Passports are required.

Peak Tourist Season: July and August

National Holiday: March 17 (St. Patrick's Day).

Shopping: Common items are Irish tweeds, jackets, suits, skirts, ties, knee rugs, tartans, Irish linen, laces, poplins, knitted goods, fishermen's sweaters, pottery, silver work, Connemara marble souvenirs, and world-famous Waterford glass.

Internet TLD: .ie

 CULTURAL CAPSULE The Irish people are of Celtic origin. There is a significant minority descended from the Anglo-Normans. English is the common language, but Irish (Gaelic) is also an official language and is taught in the schools. The Irish are very friendly and cheerful. The people are about 94 percent Catholic.

Cultural hints: The Irish take great pride in their cultural differences from the United Kingdom so do not make the mistake to assume that the country is part of Great Britain. Lines (queues) are common and respected. Service charges are generally included in the bill. If not, a tip is customary. Typical food includes fresh vegetables, dairy products, breads, seafood (especially smoked salmon), potatoes, chicken, pork, beef, and mutton.

Tourism Characteristics

The Republic of Ireland has not had the volume of tourists received by other Western European countries.

Tourism arrivals have fluctuated greatly during the last ten years from an all time high of 8 million in 2008 to a 12-year low in 2011 when 7 million tourists visited the country. Tourism now accounts for 6 percent of the country's GNP and 7 percent of its total employment. Shortly after joining the European Union (EU) Ireland has had one of the fastest-growing economies in Europe, but the country has experienced a severe recession that started in 2008.

The greatest number and percentage of visitors to Ireland are from the United Kingdom. Excluding Northern Ireland, Great Britain accounts for over half of total tourists to Ireland. Including Northern Ireland, it would be 62 percent. Visitors from the United States rank a distant second, but they have much longer length of stays. Germany and France are the two leading originating countries from the continent. North American visitors account for 10 percent. The domination of Ireland's tourism by visitors from the United Kingdom and the United States is a reflection of historical and cultural ties. During the period between 1840 and 1860, Ireland's population declined from 5 million to just over 2 million, as a blight struck the staple crop of potatoes. Millions migrated to the United Kingdom and the United States, creating strong cultural and family ties that still exist.

Travel linkages with the United Kingdom have been improved with some deregulation of the airline industry and greater competition on the London–Dublin route. The results have been a dramatic drop in airfares and an increase in traffic. These linkages are also expressed in the length of visitor stay of 10.8 days, which is the longest of Western Europe. This destination character of tourism to Ireland reflects the family and cultural linkages as well as Ireland's physical separation from Western Europe. Further, Ireland's membership in the European Union increased European visitors. Today 28 percent of visitors come from Continental Europe. Most indicate holiday as the primary purpose of their visits. The past political troubles in Northern Ireland have hampered the growth of tourism to the Republic of Ireland from North America, as many potential visitors wrongly perceive the problem to be occurring on all of the island. Recognizing the importance of tourism to Ireland, the

Figure 21.1 Fields in County Wicklow, Ireland. © walshphotos/www.Shutterstock.com

government established a National Tourist Board, which is responsible for promotion, development, and marketing of tourism to Ireland. Eight regional tourist organizations promote local areas and provide information services and accommodation reservation facilities.

Tourist Destinations and Attractions

The most important attraction of Ireland is the combination of a scenic cultural landscape in a lush, green setting. The beautiful pastoral scenery that results is a unique characteristic of the countryside (Figure 21.1). The Irish people are some of the most friendly and helpful in all of Europe. Descriptions of the major travel regions follow.

Dublin and Surrounding Area

Dublin is the capital and cultural center of Ireland. It contains a number of important historic buildings such as the Abbey Theater; St. Patrick's Cathedral, built in

1191; Tailor's Guild Hall, built in 1706; Christ Church on the edge of the liberties section of Dublin, which has a history of eight hundred years; the National Museum; the Custom House, dating from 1791; and the O'Connell Bridge, built in 1880. The city hosts numerous festivals including Bloomsday and the St. Patrick's Festival. The single most important attraction in Ireland is Trinity College (Figure 21.2), which was founded by Queen Elizabeth in 1591. It has in its library the remarkable eighth-century *Book of Kells*. To the north of Dublin in the Boyne River valley there are a number of ancient burial places and ruins of both pagan and Christian Ireland. At Newgrange, there is a prehistoric burial mound as impressive as Stonehenge. Archaeologists and tourists alike have marveled at the "Light Box," where at daybreak on a midwinter day (Winter Solstice) the sun's rays penetrate into the recessed area of the chamber. The light box is the slit above the entrance through which the sun's rays shine. The ancient kings of Ireland are buried in the burial mounds along the Boyne at Newgrange and Knowth. The great palace at the Hill of

Tara was the seat of government from the Bronze Age to the Middle Ages.

The Upper West Coast

This region was the home of poet Yeats and is central to his writing. It is a rugged region, where the sea pounds the shores and picturesque castles are located. It is an area much acclaimed for its coastal scenery of cliffs and sandy beaches. Bloody Foreland is named for the intense blood-red beauty of its sunsets. The road to Bloody Foreland twists and climbs around the spectacular coastline, which includes the tallest marine cliffs in Europe. These cliffs tower up to a mile above the sea. Behind the coastal plain rise mountains interspersed with deep glens and innumerable crystal lakes. This is the heart of Yeats country, which inspired his poetry. An important site, Lough Derg, is one of Ireland's most noted places of pilgrimage. In Glencolumbkille, there is a specially created folk village showing how three centuries of Irish have lived in thatched cottages.

Galway and Galway Bay

This is a region of the Irish landscape that inspired legends in song and deed. It has attractive fishing villages and shepherds' whitewashed, thatched-roof cottages. Castles, cathedrals, and Spanish architectural remnants are readily viewed in the landscape. Columbus is reputed to have stopped in Galway as his last port of call in Europe.

Galway City is the gateway to three distinctive regions: the horse-raising and fox-hunting country to the east; the two large lakes, Lough Corrib and Lough Mask to the north, which provide salmon and trout fishing; and Connemara to the west, the harsh land stripped to its rock bone by glaciation, suffused with liquid light and smoky colors, which have been the subject of many Irish painters. The area includes the fjord-like Killary Harbor and Leenane and the beautiful Clew Bay near Westport. Rising from its shores and dominating the surrounding countryside is Ireland's holy mountain, Croagh Patrick.

Figure 21.2 Trinity College, Dublin, Ireland. © Patricia Hofmeester/www.Shutterstock.com

Figure 21.3 The Cliffs of Moher. © Gigi Peis/www.Shutterstock.com

Limerick

Limerick was protected by King John's castle, whose drum tower and ramparts still stand. St. Mary's cathedral tower and fragments of the old city walls add to the historic character of the region. Just to the north of Limerick, the Bunratty castle has been fully restored and furnished in its original style. Its Folk Park, a historical village, depicts the housing styles and history of Ireland. To the west on the Atlantic Coast in County Clare, there are a variety of mighty cliffs, caverns, and sandy bays culminating in the fortress-like Cliffs of Moher (Figure 21.3). They rise seven hundred feet straight above the sea. Burren County provides a lunar landscape and the Poulnabrone Dolmen, another of the Stone Age structures found throughout the country.

Cork and Its Environment

Cork, the second largest city in Ireland, is a port city on the Lee River. It is a major gateway for visitors from the continent arriving by ferry from France. Its history dates back to the sixth century and reflects the influences of the Vikings, Normans, and Oliver Cromwell.

The legendary Blarney Castle and its famous stone are near Cork. Thousands of visitors climb to the top of the Castle to lie down and slide out over a well-like structure to kiss the stone, which is reported to bring them eloquent speech. Nearby is Bunratty Castle popular with visitors for its daily medieval banquets. The drive northwest from Cork to Waterford passes through small market towns, seaside resorts, cliffbound coasts, and mountains. Waterford City is world famous for its handblown lead crystal.

The Dingle Peninsula and Killarney

With its three "magic" lakes, Killarney is reported to be one of the most beautiful spots in the world and is the major resort area in Ireland, with its nearby Macgillycuddy's Reeks Mountains. West, across Macgillycuddy's Reeks, the Dingle Peninsula and the Ring of Kerry have some of the most magnificent coastal scenery and mountain background in Ireland. The region is characterized by lakes, lost valleys, soaring passes, little harbors, and sandy coves. Slea Head is the most westerly point in Europe. The scenic landscape is dotted with peat bogs that are being mined.

The United Kingdom

Introduction

Located in northwest Europe, the United Kingdom (informally called Britain) includes England, Scotland, and Wales on the island of Great Britain, the Channel Islands, and Northern Ireland on the island of Ireland. England takes up over half the land and holds 84 percent of the people. England is mostly flat with rolling hills and some mountains. Scotland consists of southern uplands, central lowlands, and the rugged Highlands. Wales features green hills and valleys in the south, rising to the Cambrian Mountains in the north. Northern Ireland contains the largest lake in the United Kingdom, Lough Neagh. The temperate climate is generally mild, wet, and variable. England's population is more than 51 million, Scotland's 5.1 million, Wales's 2.9 million, and Northern Ireland's 1.8 million. A legacy of empire means that Britain is home to a growing multicultural population; with more than 2.5 million Asians (mostly Indians and Pakistanis) and 1.1 million blacks (from former or current British dependencies in Africa and the Caribbean). Whites make up 92 percent of the total U.K. population, and the largest European foreign-born populations are from Ireland, Poland, and Germany. England and Wales were united in 1536. The addition of Scotland in 1707 created Great Britain, renamed the United Kingdom in 1801 when Ireland was added. The Republic of Ireland fought itself free of British rule in 1922, leaving Northern Ireland as a province of the United Kingdom. The Scottish nation can be traced to the Scoti, a Gaelic-speaking Celtic tribe. Wales also boasts a Celtic culture—the country is called Cymru (pronounced CUM-ree) in the Welsh language. Since 1997 the government has been pursuing a policy of devolution, leading in 1999 to an elected Scottish parliament and Welsh assembly. Economically, London drives Britain and commands the global economy as an international business and financial center.

From *National Geographic Atlas of the World*, 9th edition. Copyright ©2011 National Geographic Society. Reprinted by arrangement. All rights reserved.

Area	242,910 sq km (93,788 sq mi)
Population	61,823,000
Government	constitutional monarchy and Commonwealth realm
Capital	London 8,567,000
Life Expectancy	79 years
Religion	Anglican, Roman Catholic, Presbyterian, Methodist
Language	English, Welsh, Scottish, Gaelic, Irish, Cornish
Currency	British pound (GBP)
GDP per Cap	$35,200
Labor Force	1.4% Agriculture, 18.2% Industry, 80.4% Services

From *National Geographic Atlas of the World*, 9th edition. Copyright ©2011 National Geographic Society. Reprinted by arrangement. All rights reserved.

UNITED KINGDOM

TRAVEL **TIPS**

Entry: Visas are not required. Passports are required.

Peak Tourist Seasons: July and August

National Holiday: The United Kingdom does not celebrate one particular National Holiday.

Shopping: Common items are woolens such as men's clothing, tweeds, raincoats, overcoats; high-quality porcelain, china, and glass; pewter, silverware, cutlery; art works and antiques; fabrics such as cashmere, tartans, yard goods, mohair, and sheepskins; and Scottish handicrafts such as baskets, pottery, jewelry, printed textiles, and stone carvings.

Internet TLD: .gb

CULTURAL CAPSULE The United Kingdom is a mixture of ethnic groups—Celtic, Roman, Anglo-Saxon, and Norse. The many invasions from Scandinavia, Rome, and Normandy are blended in the Britons of today. More recent migrations have created sizable minorities of Indian, Pakistani, African, and Asian ancestry. There is a strong degree of regionalism in Wales, Scotland, and Northern Ireland. The Welsh are descendants of the Britons, who settled the island before the Romans. They have maintained a strong cultural identity through their literature and language.

Cultural hints: Excessive hand gestures are not used. The "queue" (line) is very important. Crowding in is not done. Common English foods include tea, eggs, stewed tomatoes, bacon, sausage, fish and chips, beef, mutton, potatoes, and vegetables. There are many ethnic restaurants throughout Britain as well, especially Asian.

Tourism Characteristics

The United Kingdom consists of England, Scotland, Wales, Northern Ireland, the Channel Isles, and the Isle of Man. Most international statistics on tourism refer to this definition of the United Kingdom. Great Britain consists of England, Scotland, and Wales. Britain is a term that is used interchangeably with Great Britain. Great Britain is the area referred to by British statistics on domestic tourism. England is the most populous and largest area of the three political units in Great Britain. It also dominates both international and domestic tourism markets to the United Kingdom. Eighty-three percent of all domestic holidays and nearly 90 percent of all overseas trips to the United Kingdom include England. However, when adjusting for population base on a per capita basis, tourism to Wales is more important economically than to England or Scotland. The ratio of tourist to resident in Wales is 4 to 5 compared with 2 to 4 for Scotland and 2 to 3 for England.

Residents of the United Kingdom have a high propensity for holidays and travel. One of the strongest characteristics of British international travel has been the growth of package tours. Companies such as Thomas Cook, Thompson, and Cosmos Holidays have specialized in packaging tours for the mass market. These package tours are generally for week-long trips to such places as Greece, Spain, the Caribbean, and other "major destination" areas and are priced and sold inclusive of accommodations, meals, and airfare for less than the typical airfare on regularly scheduled airlines. British companies lease and operate their own airline charter services and hotels in the destination area. Thus, little of the tour package sold to countries and regions outside of Britain actually ends up in the local economy. Hotels in the destination areas even hire British citizens who are willing to work cheaply for the opportunity to live in an "exotic" location for a few months to a year.

The combination of low-priced packaging and poor weather at coastal resorts in Britain has led to a decline in long domestic holidays. Long domestic holidays were historically for the purpose of visiting British seaside resorts. Large English and Welsh resorts such as Torquay, Brighton, Bournemouth, Blackpool, Rhyl, Colwyn Bay, Llandudno, and Aberystwyth have lost up to a third of their visitors. The "short break" market is the fastest-growing market in the United Kingdom and companies are developing strategies to capitalize on this trend.

Domestic tourism has always been highly seasonal. The peak season, which occurs in July and August, accounts for 30 percent of total domestic trips. Adding June and September to July and August, 53 percent of all trips were taken during the summer. The shortness of the British summer season, the school year ending in July, Bank Holiday in August, and the traditional closing of factories the first week of August are the major factors in the sharp seasonality of domestic tourism in Great Britain.

In 2011, 28 million tourists visited the United Kingdom. International tourism to the United Kingdom is dominated by visitors from the United States and Europe. In 2011, nearly 3 million Americans visited the United Kingdom. France, Germany, and Ireland are the three major markets in Europe. The 55 percent of visitors from Europe to the United Kingdom represents the smallest percentage of within-region travel for all the countries of Western Europe. This is due in part to the strong linkages between the United Kingdom and North America and the former colonial empire of Britain. As a result, the United Kingdom receives more visitors from other countries outside of Europe than does any other country in Europe. The average length of stay in the United Kingdom of 11.6 days is the longest of all the nations of Western Europe, indicating the destination character of the nation. Visitors from the United States are comfortable with the language and have a strong cultural link with the country. The location that receives the most international visitors is London (almost 70 percent of all international visitors), with southeast England a distant second at almost 14 percent. Although most visitors enter through airports around London, visitors still concentrate in the city, in many cases taking short day trips to surrounding towns and tourist sites or departing for travel to the Continent. The Olympics caused an upswing in travel to London during the summer of 2012.

The opening of the Channel Tunnel in 1995 increased travel between Britain and France, making day trips between the two nations more practical and increasing the already-established trend. The two nations took advantage of the linkage by creating a joint rail pass.

The combination of domestic and international tourism employs 6 percent of the labor force. This is more employment than is generated by banking, finance, and insurance combined. The importance of tourism in the United Kingdom is evidenced by operations of four independent national tourist boards. They are the British Tourist Authority (BTA), which is primarily responsible for overseas marketing; the English Tourist Board (ETB), which is responsible for marketing and development of tourism in England; and the Wales Tourist Board and the Scottish Tourist Board, which are responsible for marketing and development of tourism in Wales and Scotland, respectively. The growing importance of tourism to employment caused the United Kingdom to create a government department (National Heritage) with Cabinet rank bringing together tourism, arts, museums, sports, and broadcasting.

The United Kingdom is a crossroads for international travel and is highly accessible from the Continent by air, bus, and rail. A large ferry system carries people back and forth into several European ports and countries. Transportation within the United Kingdom is excellent by rail, bus, or automobile.

Tourist Destinations and Attractions

It is impossible to identify all the tourist attractions in the United Kingdom in a few pages. In almost every

Figure 21.4 London, England. © Samot/www.Shutterstock.com

shire, village, or countryside, there are some interesting attractions. Many of the castles, mansions, and some villages have been preserved by National Trusts (British or Scottish) to preserve and maintain history. The National Trust protects or owns about 200 historical buildings, over 400 miles of unspoiled coastline, and more than a half million acres of land. It has thirty complete villages and hamlets, castles, and abbeys, as well as lakes and hills. It owns lengths of inland waterways, bird sanctuaries, natural reserves, wind and water mills, working farms, coastal waterways, conservation camps, gardens, gift shops, and restaurants. The United Kingdom is famous for its many thousands of stately homes. Many are open to the public either by private individuals or the National Trust. One such site receiving much attention is recent years is Highclere Castle in Hampshire. It was used for exterior shots of Downton Abbey and most of the interior filming for the popular TV series.

Descriptions of a few of the major tourist destination centers follow.

London and Surrounding Region

London (Figure 21.4) is one of the world's greatest cities. It has been the center of government since Roman times. Although there were a number of settlements in the region before the Romans, it was under the Romans that London became an important city. It provided good access for shipping of Roman soldiers and supplies. England's role

Figure 21.5 Picturesque Cotswold village of Castle Combe, England. © JeniFoto/www.Shutterstock.com

later as a colonial and industrial power caused London to expand to include surrounding communities, creating Greater London. Because London has mostly avoided skyscrapers, the resulting combination of parks and low buildings gives a feeling of being in an urban village. Greater London is the focal point of all tourism, domestic and international. While the city has several spectacular tall buildings, including The Shard, which opened in 2012, *tradition* is the word that best characterizes much of the attractiveness of London. This tradition is expressed in pageantry: the daily changing of the guards (footguards at Buckingham Palace; horseguards at St. James's Place), the Ceremony of the Keys at the Tower (locking the Tower, a tradition that has existed for seven hundred years), the yearly special occasions, such as the Queen's birthday, the opening of Parliament, and new terms at the Law Courts. The institutions of Britain are expressed in Parliament, Big Ben, The Tower of London (which houses the crown jewels), and churches, such as St. Paul's Cathedral and Westminster Abbey. The large parks retained when Kensington, Chelsea, and Hyde were created combine with few urban highrises to provide a much more human-scale city than is experienced in other world cities.

London has numerous markets, such as Petticoat Lane and Portobello Road; great museums, such as the British, Victoria and Albert, Transport, and Underground War Rooms; art galleries; famous homes, such as those of writers Dickens, Keats, and Ben Johnson; impressive monuments; and theaters that fill with visitors every night. Museums include the British Museum, the Tate Gallery, the National Gallery, and the Victoria and Albert Museum. Two famous department stores are Harrods and Selfridges.

West of London, Greenwich keeps the world's time and is home to the clipper ship the *Cutty Sark* and the National Maritime Museum. Near London, there are important castles, such as Hampton Court, home of Cardinal Wolsey, and Windsor, home of Henry the Eighth. Hampton Court has a large garden and a famous maze. Windsor Castle, 20 miles west of London, is still used by the British Monarchs. Overlooking the River Thames and Eton College, it is the largest functioning castle (with 1,000 rooms) in use today and can be visited when the Queen is not in residence. Windsor Castle also has its pageantry with the changing of the guard and the procession of Knights of the Garter to St. George's Chapel. Near Windsor is Runnymede, where King John signed the Magna Carta in 1215. Just southeast of London in Canterbury are the twelfth-century cathedral and the shrine of Thomas Beckett.

Shakespeare Country and the Cotswolds

The center of one of the most interesting and scenic regions of small towns and villages in all of England is Shakespeare's birthplace, Stratford-upon-Avon. In this region known as the Cotswolds, the limestone-and-thatched-roof cottages provide a picturesque setting (Figure 21.5). Moreton-in-Marsh, Bibury, Broadway,

Figure 21.6 Stonehenge. © David Maska/www.Shutterstock.com

Bourton-on-the-Water, Cirencester, Chipping Campden, Tetbury, and the Slaughters are a few of these Cotswold towns built with the local honey-colored limestone that are still maintained today. Some outstanding castles, especially Warwick and Kenilworth, are fascinating to explore. Lygon Arms and Buckland Manor are some of the great old hotels in the area.

Coventry was firebombed by the Germans in World War II, and the rebuilt modern cathedral is a monument to peace. A statue of Lady Godiva, who, according to local folklore, some nine hundred years ago saved the town from additional taxes by riding through the streets upon her horse with only her long hair covering her body, is Coventry's other unique attraction. To the west in Shropshire, the Stokesay Castle is an excellent example of a moated and fortified manor house, and the world's first iron bridge is at Ironbridge. The bridge symbolizes the Industrial Revolution, when mass production of cast iron (and steel) made bridges longer, higher, and easier to construct.

The cities of Oxford and Cambridge, with their famous universities and their traditions, medieval spires, domes, towers, and ancient walled gardens, are also near this area.

The South and Salisbury Plain

From Brighton, one of the oldest historical resort centers in England, to Dorset County, there are a variety of scenic villages and medieval country towns. Brighton is a reflection of eighteenth-century England when the Royal Pavilion was built as a palace. To the west are Southampton and Portsmouth and the popular summer destinations with sandy beaches on the Isle of Wright. The most visited attraction on the island is the Osborne House, which was the home of Queen Victoria and Prince Albert. Further to the east is Hastings, near where William the Conqueror defeated the last Anglo-Saxon King, Harold, in 1066 A.D. The two great cathedral towns of Salisbury and Winchester provide a rich historical view of Saxon and early history. Stonehenge (Figure 21.6), one of the modern wonders of the world, is the focal point of this region. The standing rocks in formation remain only dimly understood by modern observers. It is impressive to consider that these very large stones, up to twenty tons each, were moved to the area and set in a pattern before the invention of the wheel. Early folklore associated the development with the

Druids. This has been discounted, although the Druids perform special ceremonies at Stonehenge on the twenty-first of June, when the rays of the rising sun fall in harmony with the pattern of the stones. Near Stonehenge at Avebury, there is another large prehistoric site with more than one hundred huge stones in a large circle.

The Southwest Country

The climate of this area is mild, and parts of the area serve as the "English Riviera" with scenic harbors and dramatic landscapes. Land's End, in Cornwall, is the southwestern most point in Great Britain. Tiny coastal villages, such as Penzance, St. Ives, and Polpero, were noted for their smuggling activities. The region has numerous hidden sandy bays, cobbled harbors, and the ruins of King Arthur's legendary castle of Tintagel on a Cornish cliff. Inland in the area, there are the moors, an area of two national parks, Dartmoor in Devonshire and Exmoor in Somerset. Dartmoor is an area of streams and wooded valleys with small villages and market towns on the edge. Plymouth is noted as the place from which the Pilgrims set sail and from which Sir Francis Drake went to battle with the Spanish Armada. On the edge of the area, Bath, with its Roman ruins and unique eighteenth-century Georgian architecture, and Bristol, a large port city, attract an important tourist trade.

North England

On the west side of North England, the Lake District in Cumbria has some of England's most beautiful scenery, with green hills, lakes, and moors. It is the region of the author Wordsworth, with the wooded shores of Grasmere, and the rushing streams and jagged peaks of England's highest mountains. The largest lake is Windermere, a long and beautiful sheet of water with a wooded backdrop. The Lake District is a popular destination region for domestic tourism for hiking, fishing, waterskiing, or pony trekking. Two of the most popular towns are Grasmere and Keswick, which are part of the Lake District National Park. On the central and east sides are the cathedral cities of Lincoln, York, and Durham. York, the most famous of the three, has Roman walls, timbered houses, and narrow twisting lanes.

South of York are the dales and moors that served as the inspiration for the novel *Wuthering Heights*. North of York and the Lake District along the Scottish border, Hadrian's Wall (Figure 21.7) was the northernmost bastion of the Roman Empire. The wall, over seventy-three miles in length, was built by the Emperor Hadrian starting in 122 A.D. The Romans built a fort every five Roman miles. At every Roman mile, a mile castle, a small fort with barracks for a garrison of eight to thirty-two men, was constructed.

Figure 21.7 Hadrian's Wall, Northumberland, England.
© Collpicto/www.Shutterstock.com

The purpose of the wall was to protect the English part of the Roman Empire from the Picts and Scots of Scotland.

Wales

Wales has a rugged, scenic landscape of mountains and coastal areas (Figure 21.8). It is a region of castles, coastlines, and wild landscapes. It too is a popular region for hiking and other outdoor activities, with national parks, mountains, and scenic villages with names such as Betws-y-Coed, Llanberis Pass, Capel Curig, Nant Gwynant, and Snowdon. Snowdon National Park is a mountainous area dissected by cascading rivers and waterfalls (Figure 21.9), interspersed with lakes, forests, and small country towns. Cardiff, the capital and largest city of Wales, has important attractions, such as the impressive Llandaff Cathedral, the historical village, and a mining village illustrating the history of the mining industry of Wales. Cardiff also has its restored castle with a considerable amount of the original foundations.

Figure 21.8 South Stack Lighthouse in Anglesey, Wales. © JuliusKielaitis/www.Shutterstock.com

Figure 21.9 Swallow Falls, Betws-y-Coed, North Wales. © JuliusKielaitis/www.Shutterstock.com.

Figure 21.10 Loch Lomond, Scotland. © Tamara Kulikova/www.Shutterstock.com.

Scotland

The major focal destination in Scotland is Edinburgh with its Royal Mile, a succession of picturesque streets that wind through the Old Town. The Royal Mile connects Edinburgh Castle, high atop Castle Rock, to Holyrood Palace, at one time the home of Mary Queen of Scots. Museums such as the National Gallery of Scotland, the Royal Scottish Museum, the Scottish National Gallery of Modern Art, and the Scottish National Portrait Gallery are major repositories of the history, culture, and art of Scotland. The Edinburgh festival is one of the most famous in the world. It begins in mid-August with the spectacular and colorful Military Tattoo on the floodlit Castle Esplanada and continues for three weeks with music, opera, drama, and art.

Glasgow, Scotland's second-largest city is a large industrial city and considered one of the finest art cities in Europe. Not far from Glasgow and Edinburgh are the fabled scenic landscapes of the lochs. The term *loch* refers to landform features created when glaciers deepened stream valleys, which have since been flooded. Loch Lomond (Figure 21.10) is one of the most beautiful lakes in Europe. Small villages, such as Inverary,

and beautiful fjords adorn the west coast near Glasgow. The Highlands are scenic with tiny villages bordered by lovely bays on the coast and by loch-dotted moorland and steep mountains inland. It is in the Central Highlands that the famous Loch Ness is located. The islands off the coast of Scotland, Orkney to the north and Western Islands to the west, provide both scenic and cultural attractions enjoyed mostly by British visitors. The Orkney Islands were settled more than a thousand years ago by the Vikings, while the Western Islands were a center of Gaelic culture and Scottish Christianity. There are many golf courses throughout Scotland. The most famous is in the medieval university town of St. Andrews. A unique way to experience the beauty of Scotland is on board the legendary train The Royal Scotsman with regular departures from Edinburgh.

The United States and Canada are the source of 40 percent of Scotland's total visitors. Although not as important, Australia and New Zealand also have a higher percentage of visitors to Scotland than the total to Great Britain. All four countries have strong ethnic linkages with Scotland, as many Scots emigrated to those nations.

Northern Ireland

North of the Republic of Ireland, Northern Ireland's major attractions are in the outdoors. Northern Ireland has many lakes, which combine with its coastline to offer many beaches, coves, caves, and cliffs. The region's most famous attraction is the Giant's Causeway (Figure 21.11), a series of honeycomb-shaped columns that are volcanic in origin. The cultural attractions are associated with its Celtic and prehistoric background, which are found in museums, such as the Ulster Museum in Belfast, and in the countryside where castles and other structures dot the landscape. One of the better marine drives is the Antrim Coast Road. It has delightful bays and pleasant villages and towns along the coastline.

Figure 21.11 Giant's Causeway, County Antrim, Northern Ireland. © Paul Krugman/www.Shutterstock.com

France

Introduction

Fertile plains cover two-thirds of France, which is the largest country in Western Europe. With more than half the land under cultivation, it leads the European Union in food exports. The mountain ranges are mostly in the south, including the Alps, Pyrenees, and Massif Central. Forests cover 30 percent of France and are a source of environmental and scenic wealth. The north is humid and cool, while the south is dry and warm. Favorable conditions for grape growing in the south make French wines world renowned.

France is the second most populous country (after Germany) in the European Union. Most French live in urban areas, with more than 77 percent living in cities and towns—nearly one in five live within the urbanized area of Paris. The French population continues to age despite a recent rise in the birthrate, and France would be losing population without immigration. Most immigrants began coming from former French African and Asian colonies starting in the 1960s, and many became French citizens. The French census does not record information on ethnicity or religion, but sources estimate more than 4 million Arabs (mostly Muslim), more than 3 million blacks or Africans, and some 1.5 million Asians.

The national government plays a large role in directing economic activity, and it guarantees full-time workers five weeks of paid vacation each year. France enjoys one of the world's densest and most efficient highway and railway networks. High-speed trains (TGV) run at average speeds of 280 kilometers (174 miles) an hour. A TGV train set a world record reaching 574.8 kilometers (357 miles) an hour. Superior infrastructure benefits the tourism industry, helping to make France the world's most visited country, with 80 million foreign tourists in annually. Nuclear power plants supply more than 75 percent of France's electricity.

From *National Geographic Atlas of the World*, 9th edition. Copyright ©2011 National Geographic Society. Reprinted by arrangement. All rights reserved.

Area	643,427 sq km (248,429 sq mi)
Population	62,621,000
Government	republic
Capital	Paris 9,904,000
Life Expectancy	81 years
Religion	Roman Catholic, Muslim
Language	French
Currency	euro (EUR)
GDP per Cap	$32,800
Labor Force	3.8% Agriculture, 24.3% Industry, 71.8% Services

From *National Geographic Atlas of the World*, 9th edition. Copyright ©2011 National Geographic Society. Reprinted by arrangement. All rights reserved.

TRAVEL**TIPS** 💼

Entry: Visas are not required. Passports are required.

Peak Tourist Season: July and August

National Holiday: July 14 (Fete de la Federation or Bastille Day).

Shopping: Common items vary from high fashion to the Flea Market in Paris. Perfumes, antiques, paintings, and other art objects are found both in galleries and on the street.

Internet TLD: .fr

CULTURAL CAPSULE France has been at the crossroads of trade, travel, and invasion for many centuries. As such, the three basic European groups—Celtic, Latin, and Teutonic (Frankish)—have mixed over the centuries to create the present population. Historically, France has had a high level of immigration. Most immigrants are southern Europeans (Portuguese) and North Africans (Algerian, Tunisian, Moroccans). There are a number of other ethnic groups such as a sizable group of Southeast Asians, especially Vietnamese. About 90 percent of the population is Roman Catholic. Migrants and their children comprise the nearly 4 million Muslims living and working in France. French is one of the official languages of the United Nations and other international organizations.

Cultural hints: Do not rest feet on tables or chairs. Fruit is peeled with a knife and eaten with a fork. Do not speak with food in your mouth. Typical foods include sauces, soups, bread, croissants, crepes, cheese, desserts, wine, beef, and chicken. Crepes with filling such as ham, cheese, jams, and honey are good street foods.

Tourism Characteristics

France has a long history of tourism and a well-established reputation of being the playground of Europe. It was involved in the Grand Tour for the noble and wealthy of Western Europe in the eighteenth century and has been a political and art center of Europe for at least five hundred years. France receives more tourists than any other European country, approximately 80 million. They have a large number of short-term border crossings; but in the summer months of June, July, and August, traffic and hotel occupancies are high.

Some of the elements that make France such an important tourism destination are its location,

centrality, the importance and size of Paris with transportation systems that focus on the city from throughout Europe, large land area, the variety of landscapes, and the multitude of attractions. French landscapes are among the most diverse found in Europe, from the Vosges on the east, which reminds tourists of the Black Forest of Germany; to the varied Atlantic coasts of Le Touquet, La Baukle, and Biarritz; the vitality and variety of Paris; the castles of the Loire; the highest mountain in Europe, Mont Blanc; to the sun and sea of the Cote D'Azur (Riviera), with world-renowned coastal resorts centered on Nice and Cannes. This diversity is even greater with large international theme parks, such as Disneyland Paris, the Hagondange (The New World of the Smurfs), and the Zygopolis Waterpark at Nice.

France has a strong centralized tourist industry, with the Commisariate General au Tourisme directly responsible to the prime minister of the country. It promotes tourism, creates and improves the infrastructure through loans, subsidies, and fiscal incentives, and coordinates the various segments of the tourism industry.

Like the residents of the United Kingdom, a high percentage of French people (58 percent) take a holiday of four days or more annually. However, unlike other European countries, 82 percent of the French stay in their own country. The French use the car for vacation travel more than any other Europeans (81 percent of vacations), and the French are second only to the Dutch in camping activities or owning travel trailers. Domestic travel is highly seasonal, with July and August as the peak. Travel on major highways leaving Paris can resemble a parking lot during some weeks in July and August when many government offices and businesses effectively close for the month.

European countries account for over 88 percent of foreign visitors to France, with neighbors United Kingdom, Germany, and Belgium accounting for 45 percent of arrivals. The United States market contributes a respectable 8 percent of total visitors. All indications are that the future for tourism to France is extremely bright. The Channel Tunnel, connecting France to the United Kingdom by rail, funnels large number of tourists into France.

Tourist Destinations and Attractions

France, one of Europe's largest countries, has multiple attractions and a varied tourist industry. The size and number of these attractions are impossible to detail, but they may be briefly described by dividing France into tourist regions.

Paris and Surrounding Environs

Paris (Figure 21.12) is one of the most striking capitals of the world, rich in history and monuments. Paris was first developed on an island in the center of the Seine River called Ile de la Cité. By the Middle Ages it had grown

Figure 21.12 View of Paris from Notre Dame Cathedral. © lotsostock/www.Shutterstock.com

and extended to both banks of the river. Walls were built around the city in approximately 1200 by King Philip Augustus. Later, additional walls were built to encompass an expanding village. Paris temporarily became the capital in the tenth century, then permanently by the twelfth century. In the mid-1800s, a system of boulevards and traffic circles were planned and built, which combined with the many parks and monuments creates the attractiveness of Paris.

The most famous monument is the Tour d'Eiffel (Eiffel Tower). Built in 1889 as part of the World's Fair held in Paris, it now dominates the visual landscape both day and night. The Arc de Triomphe was erected by Napoleon at one end of the elegant and beautiful shopping street, the Champs Elysees. The Grand Arc, part of Europe's largest shopping center, provides an excellent view of the city and is a gathering place in a long, open-air, central court area. At the other end of this street, in the middle of Paris, is the Place de la Concorde where Louis XIV and Marie Antoinette were guillotined. Some of the world's largest and finest museums are in Paris. The Louvre, with its modern pyramid at the entrance, and the d'Orsay are two of the most famous. They contain important and noted works of art, such as the *Mona Lisa*, *Winged Victory*, *Whistler's Mother*, and the *Venus de Milo*, as well as famous works of Cezanne, Monet, Renoir, Van Gogh, and Lautrec. The Centre Georges Pompidou houses modern art. Other museums include the de Cluny, d'Orsay, and Picasso Museums.

Paris has important cathedrals, parks, and gardens, such as Notre Dame (one of the finest Gothic cathedrals in the world), Sacre-Coeur Basilica, Sainte Chapelle (with a beautiful stained-glass window), Jardin du Luxembourg, Bois de Vincennes, and Jardin des Tuileries, as well as world-famous night life and cuisine. Boat trips occur on the Seine day and night. Several famous palaces are located near Paris. The most famous is the palace of Versailles, built by Louis XIV and considered one of the most magnificent and elaborate royal residences and grounds in the world. Others are Fontainbleau, Chateaux of Vaux-le-Vicomte, Thierry, and St. Germain-en-Laye. Euro-Disney, some twenty miles east, is attempting to rival the historic attractions.

South of Paris, the cathedral in the medieval town of Chartres rivals Paris's Notre Dame, with marvelous Gothic architecture and exquisite stained-glass windows. The Loire Valley contains a number of well-kept chateaus of all sizes and degrees of charm. Within this area alone, there are over a hundred castles that can be visited. Light and sound shows, which were started in the Loire Valley in 1952, bring to life the rich past of kings, queens, and nobility of France as the castles, fortresses, and abbeys of the Loire Valley are brought to life in the brightness of a thousand lights. A few are Blois, with the death chamber of Catherine De Medici; Amboise, where 1,500 Huguenots were massacred in 1560 and Charles VII died; or Chambord, a royal palace of King Francois I, set in a large park as large as Paris. The Loire Valley is also an area of important wine production for France, adding to the picturesque character of the area.

Brittany

West of Paris, along the coast of the English Channel, is a picturesque and distinctive coastal area of cliffs, beaches, and charming fishing and farming villages. The countryside is dotted with giant granite boulders and wild meadows on the moors and thickets and forests in a gently rolling landscape. Sea resorts, ancient cathedrals, religious festivals and pilgrimages, and castles add to the picturesque coastline of Brittany. The high point of a visit to Brittany is St. Malo, with its massive medieval ramparts overlooking the seafront, and the great chateau and fortress.

Normandy

North of Brittany is the traditional home of the Normans, who invaded England in 1066. They left their mark upon the landscape with their unique architectural style in the cities of Rouen, Caen, and Bayeux. The link between Britain and Normandy's history is expressed in the cathedrals of Rouen, Bayeux, Coutances, Sees, and Hambye. Rouen was where Joan of Arc was burned at the stake. The site is now a church, and a monument has been dedicated to this female patron saint. Bayeux is famous for the Bayeux Tapestry, depicting the Norman Conquest of England.

Normandy has three hundred fifty miles of contrasting coastline, with cliffs, pebbly coves, and long stretches of fine golden sand. Resorts along the Cherbourg Peninsula are warmed by the North Atlantic Drift. Inland are forests, tranquil streams, lush pastures, and fruit orchards. Two of the most impressive features of the region are the beaches where the Allied forces landed on D-Day in World War II and spectacular Mont-St.-Michel. Mont-St.-Michel is one of the world's great wonders. The first view of the granite offshore mount, surmounted by a gothic abbey with a tall spire, is breathtaking. It is a popular pilgrimage center where visitors walk through twisted passageways faced by old houses, shops, and restaurants up to the top of the rock to the abbey church, with its spire rising more than five hundred feet.

The major attraction for many North Americans and Britons are the D-Day beaches along the coast. The American Cemetery with its rows of white marble crosses and stars of David overlooking Omaha Beach is a sobering, yet impressive, sight. On the seafront at Arromanches is an excellent museum commemorating the war.

Northern France

This vast, flat land is famous as the path of armies. Towns along the coast, such as Dunkirk, Dieppe, Le Havre, and Calais, are important points of departure to, and entry from, England. They also bring thousands of day trippers from Britain to enjoy the coastal beaches.

The French Alps and Massif Central

The center for this region is the cities of two past Winter Olympics, Grenoble and Albertville. Grenoble serves as a base for visitors to the many ski resorts in the surrounding mountains. High mountains and beautiful lakes characterize this region. It is a region with a reputation for mineral waters for the treatment of specific illnesses and for mountain resorts for the alleviation of respiratory complaints. Famous centers such as Chamonix, Val d'Isere, Vichy, La Bourdoule, Chatel-Guyon, Mont Dore, Royat, and St. Nectaire were built to cater to visitors seeking health treatment. Second homes, holiday villages, and individual chalets are popular in this region. Mont Blanc, just outside Chamonix, is Europe's highest mountain at 15,781 feet.

Cote d'Azur and Principality of Monaco

The international playground of Cote d'Azur, or Riviera, with its picturesque little harbors, marinas, and beach resorts along the Mediterranean and casino in Monaco, equals Paris as a tourist destination in terms of visitors. The region is high on the list of dream places to visit. The climate and warm deep blue sea have fostered fashionable resorts such as St. Tropez, St. Raphael, Cannes, Antibes, Nice, and Menton, along with Monte Carlo. The two most popular cities for American tourists are Nice (Figure 21.13) and Cannes. Both have wide avenues, palm trees, and palatial hotels. The Cannes Film Festival in the spring brings visitors and movie stars from all over the world to the world's largest and most famous film festival. Aix-en-Provence is a picturesque Provencal town. Arles has a famous amphitheater.

Languedoc-Roussillon

The tourist area near the Spanish border, Languedoc-Roussillon, is designed to take advantage of the sandy Mediterranean beaches and take some of the pressure off the Riviera. Montpellier (one of the most attractive towns in southern France) and Narbonne are the major centers for this developing region. It is a culturally unique area with small towns, small buildings with red-tiled roofs, and ancient fortresses on the hills. One of the most impressive medieval fortress towns is inland at Carcassonne. It is impressive both by day and by night with its circle of towers and battlements built by Visigoths and Romans. To the north, in Albi (near Toulouse) is the Toulouse Lautrec Museum.

Figure 21.13 The beach at Nice, France. © LiliGraphie/www.Shutterstock.com

Pyrenees

Along the border with Spain is a scenic mountain area inhabited by a distinctive cultural group, the Basques. Also close to the area is the famous religious shrine of Lourdes. Lourdes is a small town in a beautiful mountain setting on the edge of the Pau Gorge, which attracts thousands of pilgrims to the site where the Virgin Mary reputedly appeared to a young girl near the Massabiel Rock in February 1858. Just north of the Pyrenees, there is an excellent wine-producing area with wineries to visit outside Bordeaux, near Perigod, Medoc, and the Dordogne River valley. Biarritz is a beach resort near the Spanish border.

Corsica

This Mediterranean island, with its rocky coastline, is the birthplace of Napoleon. Corsica lies 100 miles south of the French Riviera, 50 miles from the Italian peninsula, and 8 miles from Sardinia. Half of Corsica's 220,000 inhabitants are concentrated in the two main towns of Ajaccio and Bastia. It is sometimes called the Isle of Beauty. The island is covered with jagged, forested mountains, with small villages perched on the sides of the valleys. The sprawling coastal beaches fringed with palm trees, ancient buildings, and open-air cafés are popular for visitors.

Monaco

Introduction

Monaco occupies a mostly rocky strip of land on France's Mediterranean coast. An unparalleled luxury resort since the mid-nineteenth century, Monaco has a reputation that belies its size. Millions come to Monaco each year for the beachfront resorts, the yacht harbor, the Opera House, and the famous Monte Carlo Casino. The House of Grimaldi has ruled since 1297, except between 1793 and 1814, and Prince Albert II is the current monarch. Tourism and gambling drive the economy, and Monaco is a tax haven for the super wealthy.

From *National Geographic Atlas of the World*, 9th edition. Copyright ©2011 National Geographic Society. Reprinted by arrangement. All rights reserved.

PRINCIPALITY OF MONACO

Location	Western Europe
Area	2.0 sq km (0.8 sq mi)
Population	35,000
Government	constitutional monarchy
Capital	Monaco 35,000
Religion	Roman Catholic

Language	French, English, Italian, Monegasque
Currency	euro (EUR)
GDP per Cap	$30,000
Industry	tourism, construction, small-scale industrial and consumer products

From *National Geographic Atlas of the World*, 9th edition. Copyright ©2011 National Geographic Society. Reprinted by arrangement. All rights reserved.

Tourism Characteristics

The Principality of Monaco is the second smallest independent state in the world, after Vatican City. It is located on the Mediterranean coast some eleven miles from Nice, France, and is surrounded on three sides by France. The people are French (47 percent), Monegasque (16 percent), Italian (16 percent), and other (21 percent).

Monaco is divided into three sections—Monaco-Ville, the old city; La Condamine, the section along the port; and Monte Carlo, the new city, the principal residential and resort area. International air service is available to North America and other countries of the world through the international airport at Nice.

Monte Carlo has become famous as an exclusive resort for the rich and famous and royalty. Monte Carlo's famous Grand Casino (Figure 21.14) is a major source of income for the Principality of Monaco. The mild winter climate with its sunny days makes the Riviera a year-round attraction. Monaco attracted 800,000 visitors in 2011.

Figure 21.14 Grand Casino in Monte Carlo, Monaco. © LiliGraphie/www.Shutterstock.com

Belgium

Introduction

Unity and division define Belgium, a Western European country that is mostly flat, except for the hilly Ardennes region in the south. Belgium's unity comes from Brussels being the headquarters for the European Union and North Atlantic Treaty Organization (NATO). However, division reigns within Belgium between the northern Dutch-speaking region of Flanders and the southern French-speaking Wallonia region. In 1993, the country adopted a federal form of government to give Flanders, Wallonia, and the small German-speaking community greater political autonomy.

From *National Geographic Atlas of the World*, 9th edition. Copyright ©2011 National Geographic Society. Reprinted by arrangement. All rights reserved.

Area	30,528 sq km (11,787 sq mi)
Population	10,792,000
Government	federal parliamentary democracy under a constitutional monarchy
Capital	Brussels 1,743,000
Life Expectancy	80 years
Religion	Roman Catholic, Protestant
Language	Dutch (Flemish), French (Walloon), German
Currency	euro (EUR)
GDP per Cap	$36,600
Labor Force	2% Agriculture, 25% Industry, 73% Services

From *National Geographic Atlas of the World*, 9th edition. Copyright ©2011 National Geographic Society. Reprinted by arrangement. All rights reserved.

TRAVEL**TIPS** 🧳

Entry: Visas are not required. Passports are required.

Peak Tourist Season: June to August

National Holiday: July 21

Shopping: Belgium lace and chocolates are the most famous items. Also tapestries, diamonds, leatherwork, linen, glass, and antiques are common purchases.

Internet LTD: .be

The people of Belgium comprise elements of Celtic, Roman, German, French, Dutch, Spanish, and Austrian origins. Today, the Walloons (French speakers) occupy the southern half of the country, and the Flemish (Dutch speakers) the northern half, referred to as Flanders. French and Dutch are the official languages, but are spoken in their respective regions. English is understood in both areas. There are minorities of Italians, Spaniards, North Africans, and Germans. The majority of the population is Roman Catholic.

Cultural hints: Generally, bills are paid at the table. The tip is generally included in the bill; extra is appropriate. Typical foods include pork, game birds, fish, cheeses, fruits, vegetables, breads, soups, wine, beer (over 1,000 varieties), and mineral water.

Belgium is famous for its chocolates and waffles. French fries are served with a variety of dressings based on mayonnaise rather than ketchup.

Tourism Characteristics

Belgium's tourism is characterized by short stays. Visitors stay only a fraction over two days. The majority of tourists to Belgium come from other Western European countries, with the Netherlands, France, and the United Kingdom accounting for approximately 50 percent of its nearly 7 million visitors. The United States is the largest market outside of Europe, accounting for slightly less than 5 percent of total visitors. Many residents from the United Kingdom come for short stay visits made possible with easy ferry and train (nonstop London–Brussels) connections. Most of the tourists are from the Netherlands, the largest single source of visitors. Belgium's location on major international and European transport routes is conducive to a large number of tourists visiting Belgium as part of a longer visit to Europe in general. As is the case in many European countries, tourism is highly seasonal with the summer months as the high season.

Tourist Destinations and Attractions

The historical cities of Belgium-Bruges, Brussels, Ghent, Liege, and Antwerp are picturesque, combining medieval with modern atmosphere. The town center of the capital, Brussels, is one of the most picturesque of all Europe. The Grand-Place (the town square) consists of the Town Hall, Maison du Roi, and the Guild Houses (Figure 21.15). Excellent parks such as Parc de Bruxelles and the Parc du Cinquantenaire also attract visitors to Brussels. Antwerp, the major port and a diamond center, is the home of the Cathedral of Our Lady, Rubens House, the Gallery of Fine Arts, a weekly flea market, and a popular zoo. Bruges

Figure 21.15 Guild Houses on the Grand-Place, Brussels, Belgium. © EUROPHOTOS/www.Shutterstock.com

Figure 21.16 Canal in Bruges, Belgium. © silver tiger/www.Shutterstock.com

(Brugge) (Figure 21.16), Europe's best preserved medieval city, and Ghent, the "Venice of the North," are popular tourist cities each with its own personality. Museums, churches, monasteries, and palaces maintain the character of the Flemish culture, especially their famous artists.

In the southern part of Belgium, the Ardennes Mountains are where the famous World War II Battle of the Bulge took place. This area is popular with both Belgians and international tourists who are attracted to its spas, parks, quaint villages, beautiful streams, woods, and nature reserves.

The European Union (EU) and the North Atlantic Treaty Organization, housed in Brussels, foster business travel to Belgium. Belgium's coast has some of the better beaches in Western Europe, with promenades, casinos, and aquariums. Beach cities such as Knokke-Heist and Oostende receive large numbers of tourists on ferry excursions from Britain.

The Netherlands

Introduction

The Netherlands faces the North Sea in western Europe. The Dutch have a saying: "God made the Earth, but the Dutch made Holland." The first defenses against the sea went up some 800 years ago. Today more than 17,000 kilometers (10,560 miles) of dikes shield the low, flat land—almost half of which lies below sea level—from invasion by the North Sea. Without the existing dikes, 65 percent of the country would be flooded daily, which explains how the Netherlands (meaning "lowlands") got its name. The country has one of the world's highest population densities, which requires intensive land use. The Randstad (a conurbation combining Amsterdam, The Hague, Rotterdam, and Utrecht) is one of Europe's most economically powerful urban areas. About 60 percent of the country is farmed, with super-efficiency, by just 2 percent of the workforce. Located at the mouth of the Rhine River, the Netherlands is a gateway to northwestern Europe, with Rotterdam being Europe's largest seaport. The Netherlands has a strong market economy that depends on trade. The country's highest value exports are machinery and transport equipment, but its most famous exports are billions of flower bulbs, mostly tulips. Tourism is important to the country, and many come to see Dutch art, architecture—and the flowers. Most of the Netherlands trade is with other EU countries, but it maintains economic relationships with elements of its former empire: Indonesia, Suriname, Aruba, and the Netherlands Antilles.

From *National Geographic Atlas of the World*, 9th edition. Copyright ©2011 National Geographic Society. Reprinted by arrangement. All rights reserved.

Area	41,543 sq km (16,040 sq mi)
Population	16,527,000
Government	constitutional monarchy
Capital	Amsterdam 1,031,000 (seat of government is The Hague)
Life Expectancy	80 years
Religion	Roman Catholic, Dutch Reformed, Calvinist, Muslim
Language	Dutch, Frisian
Currency	euro (EUR)
GDP per Cap	$39,200
Labor Force	2% Agriculture, 18% Industry, 80% Services

From *National Geographic Atlas of the World*, 9th edition. Copyright ©2011 National Geographic Society. Reprinted by arrangement. All rights reserved.

TRAVEL**TIPS** 🧳

Entry: Visas are not required. Passports are required.

Peak Tourist Season: April to September

National Holiday: April 27 (King's Day)

Shopping: Important local items include diamonds, Delft-ware, porcelain, traditional dolls, cheese, paintings, and antiques.

Internet TLD: .nl

CULTURAL CAPSULE The Dutch are primarily from the Germanic culture, with some minorities from Indonesia and Surinam, former colonies of the Netherlands. The two major religious groups are Roman Catholics (40 percent) and Dutch Reformed (27 percent). The Royal Family belongs to the Dutch Reformed Church. The official language is Dutch; however, English, German, and French are generally understood. All three languages are taught (required) in High School.

Cultural hints: Close friends exchange three kisses on the cheek as a greeting and at departure. Do not chew gum while speaking. Touching and close contact are not common. Do not eat before the hostess does. Sample all items of a meal. Leaving the table during a meal is considered rude. Typical food includes bread, cheese, meats, sausage, potatoes, vegetables, fish (herring, smoked eel), and pastries. There are a number of Chinese (Indonesian) restaurants in almost every town. French fries are served with a variety of dressings based on mayonnaise, rather than ketchup.

Tourism Characteristics

Tourism to the Netherlands is characterized by short stays. Europe accounts for 80 percent of all visitors, with Germany and the United Kingdom contributing half of all European visitors. The United States is the largest market outside of Europe and ranks third overall. In 2011, the Netherlands hosted nearly 11 million visitors. Tourism is significant for the economy of the Netherlands, as it has one of the highest daily per capita expenditures in Western Europe. It accounts for 300,000 jobs for the country.

Holland's venerable souvenir is still made the old-fashioned way.

Since the sixteenth century, when Holland's burghers developed an eye for the finer things, the Netherlands has been importing, exporting, and producing some of the world's most exquisite collectibles. While a Dutch master painting may be too pricey to bring home, Delftware, Holland's handmade blue-and-white porcelain, is affordable. At least when you go to the source. The would be De Porceleyne Fles, aka the Royal Delft factory (Rotterdamseweg 196; www.royaldelft.com) in Delft itself, just 44 miles southwest of Amsterdam. The last of the thirty-two earthenware factories established in Delft in the seventeenth century, De Porceleyne Fles was founded in 1653.

The factory's daily guided tours (Apr–Oct) tell the history of the art form and its popularity. Traders with the Dutch East India Company shipped loads of Chinese porcelain into Holland's ports. The blue-on-white elegance of the Asian ceramic appealed to the burgeoning middle class. Delft's factories, only loosely imitating the original and using local lowlands clay, started introducing quintessentially Dutch motifs. "Flowers and windmills are the most common designs," says Simon Van Oosten, a De Porceleyne master painter who still hand-paints each vase. His favorite motifs personalized orders; you can get your own portrait painted on porcelain.

Delftware is available all over the country, ranging in price from 40 euros for a tile to 12,000 for a vase. How do you tell the real thing from imitation Delft? Look for the trademark for Royal Delftware—a bulbous jar sitting above the initials JT and the place-name Delft—on the bottom.

—Raphael Kadushin, *National Geographic Traveler*, April 2010

Tourist Destinations and Attractions

The major attractions of the Netherlands include its famous flower auctions, particularly at Aalsmeer; flower bulb fields such as at Keukenhof Gardens at Lisse, which draws many tourists in the spring; its culture and small villages such as Volendam, Etten-Leur, Gouda, and Zaanse Schans with their old houses, gardens, and residents attired in folk costumes in stores and other places where tourists frequent; its countryside of reclaimed polder lands; and rich farm land with windmills and canals. The major city of Amsterdam, with its famous canals (Figure 21.17), includes other important sites and museums, such as the Rijksmuseum, the Van Gogh Museum, the Rembrandt House, and Anne Frank's house where

Figure 21.17 Amsterdam. ©JeniFoto/www.Shutterstock.com

her family took refuge from the Nazis during World War II. The Rijksmuseum is the national museum of the Netherlands, built around 1885. The most famous work of art in the Rijksmuseum is Rembrandt's *The Night Watch*. The Van Gogh Museum contains about eighty of his works arranged in chronological order to show Van Gogh's stylistic development. The city's newest attraction is the Canal House Museum; an interactive interpretation of seventeenth-century life along Amsterdam's canals. The most popular tour of Amsterdam is the glass-topped boats through the canals.

The Hague (Den Haag), where the government is actually located, has the International World Court of Justice (the Peace Palace) and historic Ridderzaal (Knights' Hall). Near The Hague, the miniature village Madurodam offers a view of almost all of the notable landscapes and buildings of the country on a 1:25 scale. Rotterdam is one of the most dynamic and efficient seaports in the world, with a large free-port center. Other major cities include Utrecht, which has one of the oldest and best-preserved Gothic cathedrals in Europe; Leiden, a university town where the Pilgrims lived before setting out for America; and Delft, with step-gabled houses and a famous porcelain factory where hand-painted Delft's Blue pottery and tiles are produced. Eindhoven is home to the electronics firm Philips.

Luxembourg

Introduction

Luxembourg, a landlocked western European country, has heavily forested hills in the north and open, rolling countryside in the south. It was a founding member of the Benelux, a customs union in 1948 that evolved into today's European Union. Although small in size, Luxembourg's central location, political stability, multilingual population, and tax incentives have made it a major financial center. Foreign investment in high-tech industries and services has offset the decline in steel, once a major industry for the country.

Area	2,586 sq km (998 sq mi)
Population	498,000
Government	constitutional monarchy
Capital	Luxembourg 84,000
Life Expectancy	80 years
Religion	Roman Catholic
Language	Luxembourgish, German, French
Currency	euro (EUR)
GDP per Cap	$78,000
Labor Force	2.2% Agriculture, 17.2% Industry, 80.6% Services

TRAVEL**TIPS** 💼

Entry: Visas not required. Passports are required.

Peak Tourist Season: May to September

National Holiday: June 23 (Grand Duke's Birthday)

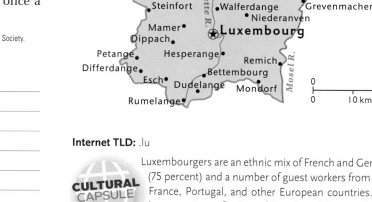

Internet TLD: .lu

CULTURAL CAPSULE Luxembourgers are an ethnic mix of French and German (75 percent) and a number of guest workers from Italy, France, Portugal, and other European countries. The language is a reflection of French and German blend. It is Luxembourgish, a Franco-Moselle dialect mixed with many German and French words. English is widely understood. Over 90 percent of the population is Roman Catholic. The remaining population belongs to various Protestant denominations or is Jewish. In 1815, after four hundred years of domination by various European nations, Luxembourg was made a grand duchy by the Congress of Vienna. It was granted political autonomy in 1838 under King William I of the Netherlands, who was also the Grand Duke of Luxembourg. This explains why Luxembourg and the Netherlands are the only two countries in the world to have the same national flag.

Cultural hints: A light handshake is a common form of greeting. The waiter is usually paid at the table. A service fee is usually included in the bill. Typical food includes ham, freshwater fish (trout and pike), black-pudding sausages, black pudding, potatoes, sauerkraut, and calves liver dumplings.

Figure 21.18 Luxembourg City. © gevision/www.Shutterstock.com

Tourism Characteristics

Luxembourg's central location has been a major factor for its tourist industry. For years, it has been a primary access to Europe by low-cost, scheduled airlines, such as Icelandair. It is on several major transportation routes. Of its 900,000+ visitors in 2010, 90 percent were from other European countries, mostly its neighbors, Germany, Belgium, and France. Tourism is seasonal, primarily in the summer.

Tourist Destinations and Attractions

Luxembourg City, the capital (Figure 21.18), is Luxembourg's major attraction. It has medieval bridges, spires, and ramparts, which are illuminated at night; a gothic cathedral; and museums. The Ademes and Moselle Valleys are green, scenic valleys with old fortresses dotting the landscape.

Germany

Introduction

Germany's geography embraces fertile northern plains stretching south from the North and Baltic Seas, merging into central highlands, and finally rising to the rugged Schwarzwald (Black Forest) in the southwest and to the Alps in the far south. The climate is temperate, and westerly winds bring frequent changes in weather. Germans are highly urbanized; about 88 percent live in cities and towns. With one of the world's lowest birthrates, Germany is a magnet for foreign workers; some 7.3 million foreigners live here, including 1.7 million Turks and 530,000 Italians. About 1.4 million foreigners living in Germany were actually born in

the country, but German law does not grant automatic citizenship to people born in Germany. Most people in Germany are Christians, but there are an estimated 3.3 million Muslims. Germany is Europe's most populous country (outside Russia) as well as its strongest economic and industrial power. Some German industrial names are well known, such as Mercedes, Bayer, BMW, Daimler, Siemens, and Volkswagen; some, like Enercon (wind turbines) and Solon (solar modules), represent newer industries and green technologies.

"Wir sind ein Volk—We are one people," sang crowds on November 9, 1989, as East Germans breached the Berlin Wall. A year later, just after midnight on October 3, 1990, Germany was reunited. One people, divided since the end of World War II, had one country again. Rejoining two populations after 45 years of separation has been difficult. Noxious air and water pollution in East Germany prior to reunification left a legacy of people needing medical care for airway diseases. The economy in eastern Germany remains weaker, and the population is declining as many move west for jobs. But prosperity continues in Berlin, Germany's capital and largest city. Visitors marvel at the innovative architecture, including the Reichstag building, with its new glass dome, and the ultramodern Hauptbahnhof (central train station).

From *National Geographic Atlas of the World*, 9th edition. Copyright ©2011 National Geographic Society. Reprinted by arrangement. All rights reserved.

Area	357,022 sq km (137,847 sq mi)
Population	81,980,000
Government	federal republic
Capital	Berlin 3,406,000
Life Expectancy	80 years
Religion	Protestant, Roman Catholic, Muslim
Language	German
Currency	euro (EUR)
GDP per Cap	$34,100
Labor Force	2.4% Agriculture, 29.7% Industry, 67.8% Services

From *National Geographic Atlas of the World*, 9th edition. Copyright ©2011 National Geographic Society. Reprinted by arrangement. All rights reserved.

TRAVEL **TIPS** 🧳

Peak Tourist Season: June, July, August

Entry: Visas are not required. Passports are required.

National Holiday: October 3 (Unity Day)

Shopping: Items include musical instruments; fine porcelain; crystal; silverware; cuckoo clocks; wood carvings; stainless steel cutlery; Bavarian leather shorts; Tyrolean hats; Mercedes Benz, BMW, Volkswagen, and Audi automobiles; and wine.

Internet TLD: .de

CULTURAL CAPSULE The population of Germany is primarily German; however, there are large numbers of foreign guest workers from Turkey, Italy, and the Baltic States. Changes in East Germany since 1990 have prompted former Yugoslavians and others to migrate to Germany.

An ethnic Danish minority lives in the north, and a small Slavic minority known as the Serbs lives in eastern Germany. In the western region there are refugees from the Middle East, India, Africa, and Asia. The reunification of Germany occurred on October 3, 1990. It has been difficult (and expensive) to try to bring the standard of living of Germans in former East Germany up to the levels of West Germany. German is the language of the country, and English is widely understood and taught in the schools. The two major religions are Roman Catholic (in the south and west) and Lutheran (in the north and east).

Cultural hints: Men rise when a woman enters the room. Coughing or restlessness at a concert is rude. It is common to be seated with other parties if seats are not available at a private table. Do not cut potatoes, pancakes, or dumplings with a knife. Typical foods include potatoes, noodles, dumplings, sauces, vegetables, cakes, pastries, sausages, pork, chicken, and ethnic foods. German sausage, in dozens of different types, is world famous. Regional dishes, such as smoked eels in Hamburg, smoked ham and bacon in the Black Forest, and liver dumpling soup and roast pork in Bavaria, are but a few of the many regional specialties.

Tourism Characteristics

While Germans represent one of the great international and domestic travel markets of the world, the German visitor industry consists primarily of excursionists or travelers in transit. In 2011, 26 million travelers visited Germany. Germany's location on the borders of the Netherlands, France, Switzerland, Austria, Belgium, Luxembourg, Czech Republic, Poland, and Denmark brings many one-day visitors from these countries as well as travelers passing through to visit neighboring countries. Like other countries of Europe, many of Germany's visitors are from Europe itself, as 72 percent of their visitors are European. The Netherlands is the largest single market for nights spent in hotels in Germany, accounting for over 10 percent of visitors. The United States and United Kingdom rank second and third. Americans often stay only a few days, indicating that Germany is part of a larger tour of Europe.

The major purpose for visiting Germany is listed by visitors as a "holiday." Two other reasons given are visiting friends and relatives and business. In addition, a significant number of visitors from Northern Europe (Denmark, Sweden, Norway, and Finland) indicated "in transit" as a major reason for visiting. Business as a tourist attraction is reflected in the increasing convention exhibitors and international fairs in Germany.

The summer months of June, July, and August are the most dominant season for both domestic and international tourism. Most visitors (85 percent) arrive by road from neighboring countries.

Tourist Destinations and Attractions

Descriptions of the major tourist regions of Germany follow.

The Rhineland-Palatinate

One of the most romantic areas of Europe is the Rhine River region. Castles dot the islands of the river and

Figure 21.19 Cologne, Germany. © prasit chansareekorn/www.Shutterstock.com

adjacent hills. Vineyards and picturesque towns are found along the river's length. Although it is one of the world's busiest rivers, the Rhine is also rich in history and legend with its castles and islands. One of the most popular tourist attractions is the Rhine Valley between Bingen and Koblenz. The Rhine cuts deeply into the Rhenish Slate Mountains and is lined with vineyards, castles, and beautiful villages, such as Bingen with its Mouse Tower, Kaub with its Pfalz (toll station) in the middle of the Rhine, St. Goar, St. Goarshausen, Boppard, and Koblenz. The mighty Prussian fortress of Ehrenbreitstein towers over Koblenz. The Rhine and Moselle rivers join near Koblenz.

East of the Rhine, Westerwald and Taunus have nature reserves, the historic old state spa of Bad Ems, and the famous potteries in the Kanenbackerland. West of the Rhine, Eifel and Hunsruck offer crater lakes and wildlife parks; the Benedictine Abbey of Maria Laach, the best-preserved Romanesque edifice in Germany and a historic jewel; and the Ahr Valley, the largest red wine producer in Germany. Between the Eifel and Hunsruck, the Moselle winds its way from Trier to the Rhine, past many renowned wine-producing villages, art treasures, and religious symbols. Trier, Germany's oldest city, prides itself in having the most splendid Roman architecture north of the Alps. The cities in the Rhine region from Cologne (Köln) on the north (Figure 21.19), through Bonn, Frankfurt/Main, and Heidelberg on the Neckar, contain important cathedrals, museums, and picturesque town halls. Cologne, an old Roman city,

boasts a cathedral that dominates the landscape amid a city replete with Romanesque churches, a medieval city wall, and famous museums. To the south of Cologne are Frankfurt and Wiesbaden.

Wurzburg to Fussen

The "romantic road" from Wurzburg to Fussen connects a series of medieval walled cities. Rothenburg is one of the most famous well-preserved medieval towns overlooking the Tauber River. It offers an extensive network of footpaths, wall walks, thirty gates and towers, and magnificent houses and museums. Other communities, such as Dinkesbürhl and Nördlingen, are equally well preserved. Augsburg, an important trade and banking center even in Roman times, is an excellent example of Renaissance architecture. At the end of the romantic road is Fussen in Bavaria.

The Black Forest (Baden-Württenberg)

The Black Forest is an area of scenic beauty, with vineyards, hills, meadows, woods, and splendid vistas of the Rhine plateau. Heidelberg is home to Germany's oldest university town with its world-famous student castle. The Black Forest is famous for its many health resorts, mineral springs, and wooden clocks. The most well-known health resort is Baden-Baden. Other centuries-old spas are at Wildbad, Bad Liebenzell, Baiersbronn, Bad Mergentheim, Bad Durrheim, and Triberg. The gateway

Figure 21.20 The Neuschwanstein castle (Bavaria, Germany). © Tiberiu Stan/www.Shutterstock.com

to the southern Black Forest is the medieval town of Freiburg, which is referred to as the "Gothic city of woods and wines." With its orchards and vineyards, the area around Lake Constance adds to the tropical flora of Mainau Island in the lake to provide a diversity of beauty.

Bavaria

The center of German culture in Bavaria (southern Germany) is Munich, with its large cellar-like beer halls, Oktoberfest Fair, and Fasching, the carnival time preceding Lent. It is home to Marienplatz, the center of Munich; and the Hofbrauhaus, the world's largest beer hall and the center of activities during Oktoberfest. The Alte Pinakothek is the city's foremost art museum. The Deutsches Museum features accomplishments in science and technology. The museums, city halls, and palaces of Bavarian kings abound in the area. Munich was the site of the 1972 Olympic games, and the grounds are today a major attraction with their unique design. South of Munich in the German Alps are high mountains with cogwheel railroads and cable cars, lakes, and some of the best-preserved castles in all of Europe. The Romantic Road is a 200-mile scenic drive connecting castles and villages between Wuerzburg and the Austrian border. Lederhosen and yodeling with the Alps as a backdrop are the most familiar tourist images of Germany. Northeast Bavaria is a storybook land.

King Ludwig II built several castles (Linderhof, Herrenchiemsee, and Neuschwanstein) that represent the apex of castle building in the region (Figure 21.20). They are in excellent condition and set in very picturesque areas. Other important attractions are the passion play at Oberammergau, which occurs every ten years in memory of the town being saved from the Black Plague that swept Europe in the fourteenth century; Garmish-Partenkirchen, from which a train ride can be taken to Zugspitze high in the Alps; and Berchtesgarden near the border of Austria.

Two cities, Nuremberg and Regensburg, serve as examples of the area. Nuremberg has a well-preserved ancient Imperial castle. Regensburg is dominated by many churches and patrician homes. The cathedral of the Old Free City is one of the Gothic masterpieces in Bavaria. The Danube cuts through the region and is navigable from Regensburg to the Black Sea.

Berlin and Former East Germany

Berlin's importance as a travel region has been growing rapidly since the reunification of Germany. Since 1992, Berlin is the official capital of Germany, increasing its importance for business and government travel. The principal attraction in Berlin is the old capital of Germany and its growing importance as a cultural center. The performance of opera, ballet, drama, orchestra, and chamber music is taken seriously. For a more contemporary experience visitors flock to the "Mitte" where over 500 art places are concentrated in the heart of the city. Berlin's attractions include many historic buildings that have been reconstructed or are being rebuilt after suffering damage or destruction in World War II. These include the Schloss

Charlottenburg, summer palace of the Hohenzollern's rulers; the Egyptian Museum and a number of galleries and fine museums; the Brandenburg Gate; the Reichstag building; Humboldt University; Neue Wache; the National Gallery; and Marienkirche, Berlin's oldest church.

Major cities for tourists in eastern Germany are Dresden, Potsdam, Leipzig, and, in general, the southern part of former East Germany. Although Dresden was destroyed completely by fire bombing in World War II, it has been rebuilt. The open plazas with fountains and gardens contrast with the old structures that are being rebuilt. The major attraction is the Zwinger Art Museum, which has an exceptional collection of paintings by Rembrandt and Michelangelo. Just downstream of the Elbe is Meissen, the "Porcelain City." Since 1720, Europe's most famous porcelain "white gold" has been continuously produced in this classic small city that lies on the steep banks of the Elbe. Potsdam, about an hour from Berlin, has been a significant town since the 1600s. The palace Sans-Souci has important works of art. Cecilienhof, a twentieth-century palace near Potsdam, is where the Potsdam Agreement was signed.

Leipzig was the site of a famous battle of Napoleon. During the twelfth century, Leipzig was a famous trade center. Some of the buildings from that period are still standing, reflecting Leipzig's early glory. Along the border region near the Czech Republic is a beautiful wooded mountain landscape with a number of attractive towns such as Freiberg, with its ancient fortifications and tiny miners' houses in narrow streets.

Northern Germany

In northern Germany, a distinctive landscape of woodland, fields and meadows, moors, sky and water, and ports attracts travelers. The fresh, salty, North Sea breezes travel across the blue waters of the countless lakes, bays, fords, inlets, fertile fens (low farmlands), and fishing villages. The coasts of the North Sea, the Baltic, the Frisian Islands, and Heiigoland offer fine sandy beaches and modern spas. Two cities important in the region are Hamburg and Bremen. Hamburg, a Free Hanseatic City in medieval times, has a large harbor and the Old City, which provides a good place to explore. Bremen is one of Germany's oldest cities. The city's historic buildings date from the eighth century. The oldest are grouped around the Market Square, where the Town Hall with its superb façade and one of Europe's finest banqueting halls, the Grosse Halle, may be found.

Austria

Introduction

The Alps cover two-thirds of this central European country. The lowlands of the Danube River Valley hold most of Austria's population and economic activity. The metropolis of the Danube is Vienna, Austria's capital and largest city. Imperial palaces highlight old Vienna, but new Vienna features modern skyscrapers and UN offices, and green Vienna features gardens, parks, and the Riesenrad (Giant Ferris Wheel). Vienna—city of music—plays pop, rock, and jazz as well as Beethoven and Haydn. Besides Vienna, tourists flock to Mozart's Salzburg and to the many Alpine ski resorts.

From *National Geographic Atlas of the World*, 9th edition. Copyright ©2011 National Geographic Society. Reprinted by arrangement. All rights reserved.

Area	83,858 sq km (32,378 sq mi)
Population	8,374,000
Government	federal republic
Capital	Vienna 2,315,000
Life Expectancy	80 years
Religion	Roman Catholic, Protestant, Muslim
Language	German
Currency	euro (EUR)
GDP per Cap	$39,400
Labor Force	5.5% Agriculture, 27.5% Industry, 67% Services

From *National Geographic Atlas of the World*, 9th edition. Copyright ©2011 National Geographic Society. Reprinted by arrangement. All rights reserved.

TRAVEL **TIPS**

Entry: Visas are not required. Passports are required.

Peak Tourist Seasons: July and August

National Holiday: October 26 (National Day)

Shopping: Common items include dirndls (dress), wood carvings, music boxes, felt hiking hats with pins from each place visited, Tyrolean leather goods, porcelain figurines, crystal, ski equipment and mountaineering clothing, and antiques.

Internet TLD: .at

CULTURAL CAPSULE Austria is inhabited by a very homogeneous population (99 percent German speaking). In the last few years, there have been a number of immigrants from Central Europe and Turkey, many of whom work in the service jobs of the tourist industry. There are two significant minority groups, Slovenes in south-central Austria and

Figure 21.21 The Alps mountains in Mayrhofen, Austria. © Alexander Tolstykh/www.Shutterstock.com

Croatians on the Hungarian border. Nearly 85 percent of the population is Roman Catholic. The official language is High German. English is understood by many and is required in high schools. The Austro-Hungarian Empire played a decisive role in Central European history, partly because of its strategic position astride the southwestern approaches to Western Europe and the north-south routes between Germany and Italy. Although present-day Austria is only a tiny remnant of the old empire, it still occupies this strategic position for tourism.

Cultural hints: Hands in pockets when conversing should be avoided. Do not be loud. Wait for all to be served to eat. Place knife and fork next to your plate when finished. Typical food includes potato dumplings, goulash, Wienerschnitzel, bread, beer, wine, cheese, boiled beef, and chicken.

Tourism Characteristics

Tourism is very important to the economy of Austria. Austria ranks the highest in Europe for tourism contribution to GDP. It draws over 22 million visitors annually.

Austria's tourism is extremely dependent upon the European market. Over 88 percent of its visitors are from other European countries. Even the European market is dominated by one major source, Germany, which contributes half of all bed nights. The common language, history, culture, and common border are major factors in this domination by Germany. While the length of stay is much longer than for most of the other Western European nations, it does receive a number of visitors who are in transit from the Northern European countries to the Mediterranean countries of Italy, the Baltic States,

and Greece. There has been an increased flow from the former Communist Central European countries because of Vienna's location. It has become a hub for travelers from both the west and the east to visit the other regions of Europe.

There are two seasonal peaks, the largest being the summer, which coincides with the school holidays and is a popular period for outdoor activities, such as swimming, fishing, and waterskiing. The second peak is in the Alpine areas in the winter for skiing (Figure 21.21). The summer season accounts for over 50 percent of the bed nights and the winter, 30 percent. Austria's cities experience a less seasonal pattern of tourist arrivals. Austria receives an overwhelming number of its tourists by road, with 93 percent coming by car. Most of these are from neighboring countries and are excursionists on short trips or on their way to another destination. Packaged tour groups from the United States and the United Kingdom represent the bulk of air arrivals.

Tourist Destinations and Attractions

Austria is famous for its nature tourism (skiing, hiking), culture, music, and pastry. Three cities in Austria—Vienna, Innsbruck, and Salzburg—are the centers for the three major regions. Vienna, the capital, has famous churches, such as St. Stephen's Cathedral and St. Charles Church (Karlskirche); some of the finest palaces of Europe, including the Hofburg (Hapsburg Palace), the

Schoenbrunn (which rivals Versailles), and the Belvedere Palace (Figure 21.22); museums associated with the history of the Hapsburg Empire; some of the finest musical productions in the world (including the famous New Year Day's performance); the performing Spanish Riding School (the Lippizaner White Stallions); the Vienna Boys' Choir; and the picturesque Vienna Woods. Vienna is the center of Austrian culture. The Kunsthistorisches Museum (Museum of Fine Arts) is one of the major art museums in the world. The Danube is another attraction near Vienna. Farther from Vienna, the countryside offers towers perched on the Alpine foothills, medieval cloisters, and monasteries. Dürnstein is a red-roofed, riverside village where King Richard the Lionhearted was imprisoned during the Crusades.

With its medieval city and fortress, Salzburg is the birthplace of Mozart and provided the location for the popular film *The Sound of Music*. Like Vienna, Salzburg is a center for music and theater and is surrounded by beautiful mountains and lakes. The Salzburg Festival is one of Europe's most important music festivals. The mountain and lake scenery attracts winter sports enthusiasts and summer sightseers alike. Mozart's birthplace is now a museum displaying early editions of his works,

models of sets for some of his famous operas, and other memorabilia. In addition, the medieval Salzburg Castle, Mirabell Palace, and St. Peter's monastery, set on a hill in the center of the town, are major attractions. One of the most unusual palaces in all of Europe, the Hellbrunn, is a short trip from Salzburg. It was built by a prankster, the archbishop Markus Sittikus. Hidden water nozzles in the benches, walls, sculpture, floors, and ceilings spray visitors today as they did in his time. In an area just east of Salzburg, Austria's lake country, the Salzkammergut has scenic lakeshore towns and picturesque countryside.

Innsbruck, which hosted the Winter Olympics in 1964, is the center for summer sightseeing travel to alpine peaks and glaciers, and in the winter is a skier's mecca. Gothic architecture adds to the atmosphere of the city. The city is full of beautiful buildings. The two most-noted sights are the Golden Roof on an ornate stone balcony of an ancient mansion and the Roman-style Triumphal Arch. Innsbruck, Lech, and Kitzbuhel are the main destinations in Tyrol. Throughout Tyrol, there are mountain lakes, green meadows, high mountain peaks, rambling streams, and picturesque resort villages.

Figure 21.22 Belvedere Palace, Vienna, Austria. © clearlens /www.Shutterstock.com

Switzerland

Introduction

Located in west-central Europe, Switzerland is mountainous and landlocked. The Alps rise in the south, and the Jura Mountains dominate the northwest; between the mountains is a central plateau, with rolling hills and lakes, the largest being Lake Geneva. The climate is temperate but varies with altitude. More than 75 percent of the population lives on the central plateau, many in large cities like Zurich. Switzerland has four national languages, representing the ethnic populations of the country: 63.7 percent speak German; 20.4 percent French; 6.5 percent Italian; and 0.5 percent Romansh (an ancient Latin-based language). About 21 percent of the country's population is foreign born, and the foreign languages spoken most often are Serbian, Croatian, and English. Founded in 1291 as a union of three cantons chafing against Habsburg rule, Switzerland has been independent since 1815; its borders now encompass 26 cantons. Switzerland competes in global markets with exports that make up almost half of the nation's economy; however, it voted against joining the EU in 2001. Elaborate civil defense measures and a strong militia back up the Swiss policy of permanent neutrality. Switzerland is firmly committed to world peace, and in 2002 it became a member of the UN. A history of political stability and expertise in technology and commerce make Switzerland a post-industrial economy, reporting one of the highest per capita incomes in the world.

From *National Geographic Atlas of the World*, 9th edition. Copyright ©2011 National Geographic Society. Reprinted by arrangement. All rights reserved.

Area	41,284 sq km (15,940 sq mi)
Population	7,754,000
Government	confederation
Capital	Bern 337,000
Life Expectancy	82 years
Religion	Roman Catholic, Protestant, Muslim
Language	German, French, Italian, Romansh
Currency	Swiss franc (CHF)
GDP per Cap	$41,700
Labor Force	3.8% Agriculture, 23.9% Industry, 72.3% Services

From *National Geographic Atlas of the World*, 9th edition. Copyright ©2011 National Geographic Society. Reprinted by arrangement. All rights reserved.

TRAVEL **TIPS**

Entry: Visas are not required. Passports are required.

Peak Tourist Season: July and August

National Holiday: August 1 (Founders Day)

Shopping: Common items include watches, wood carvings, chocolate, embroidered items, cheese, handicrafts such as music boxes, cuckoo clocks, wood carvings, and antiques.

Internet TLD: .ch

CULTURAL CAPSULE

Switzerland has a number of ethnic groups, German (72 percent, living mostly in the east and central regions), French (18 percent, living mostly in the west), and Italians (10 percent, living mostly in the south). There are a number of foreign residents and guest workers from the Baltic states, Spain, Greece, Italy, and the Middle East. Switzerland has four national languages—German, French, Italian, and Romansch (based on Latin and spoken by a tiny minority)—but only three are official. English is widely known and understood. The canton (province) chooses which language will be official in that province, and all signs are generally in that language. Nearly half of the people are Roman Catholic, and the other half belong to various other Christian churches. There is a small Jewish minority.

Cultural hints: Various customs identify the language groups; however, a handshake is appropriate for greetings and when parting. Maintain good posture. If a restaurant is full, you may be seated with strangers. Typical foods include breads, cheese, meat, sausages, leek soup, fish, wines, and pork. The most famous dish is fondue, which is hot, melted cheese or meat in a chafing dish utilizing long forks to dip bread or meat. A regional dish at the eastern end of Lake Geneva is a potato fondue in which small potatoes are covered with hot, melted cheese. Do not litter.

Tourism Characteristics

The Swiss have a high regard for nature and beauty, and it is reflected in their tourism. With its winter sports and summer sightseeing activities, Switzerland has a strong year-round tourist season; but the busiest months are July and August. Switzerland has a long tradition in the tourism industry. The federal character of Switzerland is reflected in its tourism offices. The Swiss National Tourist Office is primarily concerned with the promotion of Switzerland abroad. Switzerland's location in the center of Europe is an important factor in its tourism industry. Its reputation as an expensive country is not deserved as it provides accommodations and service in a range of prices. The country's decision not to join the EuroZone has made the Swiss Franc the envy of many Europeans as the currency has maintained its strength in international monetary markets throughout the monetary crisis in the early 2010s.

Figure 21.23 Mount Jungfrau in the Swiss Alps . © Fedor Selivanov/www.Shutterstock.com

In 2011, Switzerland hosted 8.6 million international visitors. Switzerland's major market is other European countries. Eighty-four percent of its visitors are European, with Germans, British, and French dominating. Visitors from the United States average about 7.8 percent of all visitors to Switzerland. The average length of stay, 3.8 days, indicates that many tourists come to Switzerland either in transit or as part of a larger trip or a short excursion. This is the case with a majority of the United States visitors, who make a multiple-country tour.

Tourist Destinations and Attractions

The main destinations in Switzerland are in the high, rugged Alps (Figure 21.23), with such ski resorts as St. Moritz, Davos, Arosa, Flims, Zermatt (near the Matterhorn), Gstaad (in the Saane Valley), Murren (which sits on cliffs above the Lauterbrunnen Valley), and Klosters. Mountain climbing is popular. The Matterhorn (Figure 21.24) is one of the most recognizable mountains in the world. The Alpine lakes interspersed between the high mountain peaks offer abundant scenery. Lake Geneva, Lake Leman (the largest lake in Europe), Lake Thun, Lake Brienz, Lake Lucerne, Lake Maggiore (partially in Italy),

Lake Lugano (partially in Italy), and Lake Constance (partially in Germany) are only a few of the summer attractions for tourists. Some of the major tourist towns are Lucerne, Bern, Interlaken, Davos, Geneva, Montreux, Lugano, St. Gallen, Zurich, and Zermatt.

Lucerne is the center of American tourism to Switzerland. It is situated on the shores of Lake Lucerne with mountains nearby for excursions. The city is enhanced by the wooden Chapel Bridge, the Lion Monument, the turreted city walls, and the baroque interior of the Jesuit Church. Lausanne, which is an educational center, hosts many festivals of music, ballet, and opera. Other major tourist destinations are Interlaken with its view and gateway to the Bernese Oberland and the highest railroad line in the world (to the top of the Jungfrau, a ride of 11,333 feet); and Bern, the capital, which offers museums, Swiss handicrafts, and culture to the interested traveler.

Montreux, on the sunny side of Lake Geneva, is famous for its international music festivals. The vistas from the mountains near Montreux are impressive and easy to reach. Major financial and international cities include Zurich, the largest city, and Geneva (Figure 21.25), which claims the title of the world's

Figure 21.24 The Matterhorn. © Jool-yan/www.Shutterstock.com

Figure 21.25 Geneva, Switzerland. © Voronin76/www.Shutterstock.com

premier international city. (Over two hundred international organizations, including the United Nations, have offices in Geneva.) Geneva was the site of the League of Nations, the forerunner of the United Nations.

Basel, representing the Swiss emphasis on practicality, is an industrial town, an old university town, and the beginning of navigation downstream on the Rhine.

Basel is also a city of arts and culture; its art gallery holds important collections. There are over twenty museums in Basel. In eastern Switzerland, St. Gallen has a magnificent baroque cathedral surrounded by an old town. A short distance from St. Gallen are Lake Constance and the famous Pestalozzi Children's Village of Trogen, which was established for the care of orphans.

Liechtenstein

Liechtenstein is a tiny independent state wedged between Switzerland and Austria. In 1719 the princely House of Liechtenstein, which still rules this constitutional monarchy, purchased a strip of floodplain and adjacent mountains located on the east bank of the Rhine River. Because of liberal tax policies and banking laws, Liechtenstein hosts 3,500 businesses, and it is highly industrialized. Liechtensteiners savor one of the world's highest standards of living.

From *National Geographic Atlas of the World*, 9th edition. Copyright ©2011 National Geographic Society. Reprinted by arrangement. All rights reserved.

Area	160 sq km (62 sq mi)
Population	36,000
Government	constitutional monarchy
Capital	Vaduz 5,000
Life Expectancy	80 years
Religion	Roman Catholic, Protestant
Language	German, Alemannic dialect
Currency	Swiss franc (CHF)
GDP per Cap	$122,100
Labor Force	2% Agriculture, 43% Industry, 55% Services

From *National Geographic Atlas of the World*, 9th edition. Copyright ©2011 National Geographic Society. Reprinted by arrangement. All rights reserved.

Figure 21.26 Vaduz Castle, Liechtenstein. © Telegin Sergey/www.Shutterstock.com

CULTURAL CAPSULE Located in the mountains between Austria and Switzerland, the small nation of Liechtenstein (27,825 people) draws tourists who want to buy stamps and mail letters from this tiny country. The population is homogeneous, stemming almost entirely from a Germanic tribe, the Alemanni. The official language is German, but most speak Alemannic, a German dialect similar to that used in eastern Switzerland. The rugged snow-capped mountain peaks, beautiful valleys, old cottages, medieval castles (Figure 21.26), and friendly people set an atmosphere helpful to hikers, skiers, and other tourists. While many tourists visit, the length of stay is the shortest in the world, as few stay overnight. The attractions offered to tourists are at least as varied as the topographical features of the country. The Rhine Valley, where Liechtenstein is situated, is characterized by a wide valley base and the steep western slope of the Dreischwestern mountain range. The mountainous eastern part of the country is made up of three high-altitude valleys, the best known of them being the Malbun Valley. The Castle of Gutenberg dominates the village of Baizers. It is situated upon a 150-foot-high rock formation that rises above the plain.

REVIEW QUESTIONS

1. Why do countries like Holland and Germany have large deficits in their tourism trade balance?

2. Why is the climate of Western Europe more moderate than in the same latitude locations in the United States?

3. Which countries of Europe have a tourism visitor profile that is more transitory in nature? Why?

4. What are the major tourist regions of the United Kingdom?

5. Where do the visitors to Ireland come from? Why?

6. Which countries of Western Europe have large numbers of winter tourists? Why?

7. How do you explain the fact that Germany, one of the largest countries in Europe, has such a short length of stay by visitors?

8. What factors explain the short length of stay by visitors to the Netherlands and Belgium?

9. France has the highest percentage of its residents who remain in their home country. What might explain this pattern?

10. What role do natural features (like the Alps or the Rhine River) play in tourism to Western Europe?

chapter 22: GEOGRAPHY AND TOURISM IN NORTHERN EUROPE

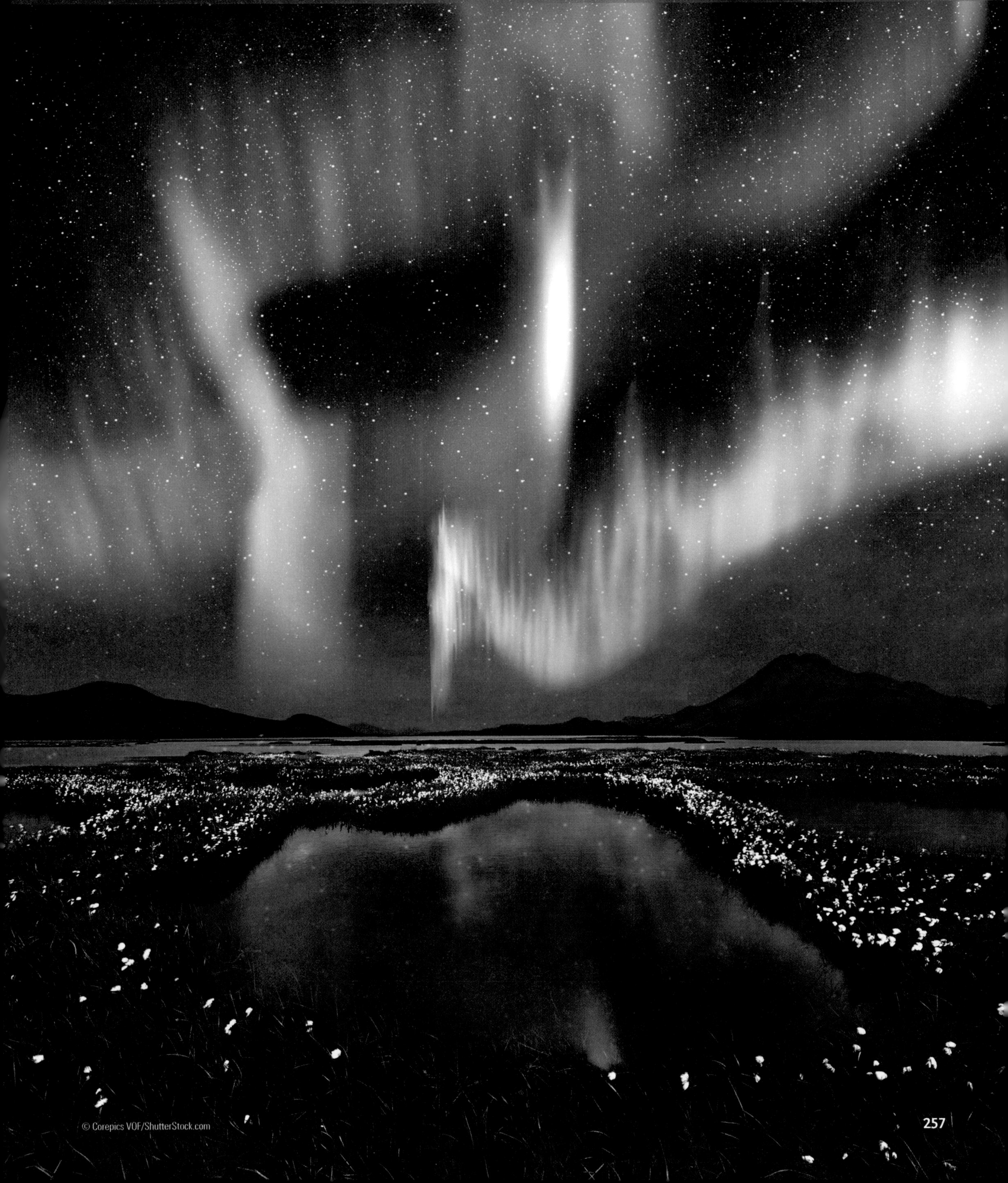

Introduction

Northern Europe occupies a position in Europe comparable to that of Alaska in North America. Its southern point, the border of Germany and Denmark, is situated in the same latitude as the southern tip of the Alaskan Panhandle (55 degrees North). The northernmost point of continental Europe at the North Cape in Norway is at the same latitude as Point Barrow, Alaska (71 degrees North). The distance from the eastern extremity of Finland to the western extremity of Iceland is as great as from the Alaskan Panhandle to the outermost islands of the Aleutian Chain. Northern Europe is nearly 90 percent as large as Alaska.

Northern Europe is one of the wealthiest regions of the world, which is remarkable given the marginal environment that has limited the agricultural base of the individual countries. The region is also referred to as **Scandinavia**. Anciently it was the name of the country of the Norsemen (Vikings). Today the region encompasses Denmark, Norway, and Sweden and is sometimes expanded to include Finland and Iceland. All five countries jointly market tourism under the Scandinavian Tourist Board.

The Northern European nations are on the periphery of Europe both geographically and in terms of tourism. The region receives the fewest tourists of the four major regions of Europe. There are a number of common cultural and physical geographical elements in these northern countries (Figure 22.1). Most have more of their own residents travel as tourists than they have nonresident tourist visitors. The three largest countries—Norway, Sweden, and Finland—have their major population centers in the south.

Climate Characteristics

Because of **maritime influence** on the islands and peninsula of Northern Europe, the marine west coast climate prevails in Denmark and along the coastal margins of Sweden, Iceland, Norway, and islands as far north as the Arctic Circle. The weather is not as cold as the location would suggest, with even the islands north of the Arctic Circle affected by the relatively milder water temperature, reflecting the influence of the North Atlantic Drift. The northern location does dictate cool summers. Temperatures average near or above freezing during most winters and into the mid-60s during the summer. Precipitation, the bulk of which falls as rain, totals between 20 and 30 inches per year.

In northern Scandinavia there is tundra climate across the north of Norway. The mountainous core of

Figure 22.1 Norwegian coastline: Town of Reine, Lofoten Islands, Norway. © Harvepino/www.Shutterstock.com.

Figure 22.2 Field of icebergs. © Sami Sarkis/Getty Images.

the Scandinavian Peninsula and northern Finland have subarctic climates (Figure 22.2), while the inland plain areas of Finland, Sweden, and Norway have a humid continental, cool summer climate. The humid continental climate has winter temperatures below zero and summer temperatures similar to the marine west coast. The greater part of eastern Norway, Sweden, and Finland receive between 20 and 30 inches of precipitation a year, with maximum rainfall in the summer. Southern Sweden and southern Finland have a humid continental, warm summer climate. They have a hot, humid summer with maximum temperatures reaching the eighties during the daytime, and winters with subzero temperatures and permanent snow cover.

Because of insularity, both the Faeroes and Iceland have maritime climates. In the Faeroes, winter temperatures rarely dip to the freezing point, and summer temperatures seldom rise above 50 degrees Fahrenheit. About 60 inches of precipitation are received each year, the maximum in winter and almost all in the form of rain. Because of the North Atlantic Drift, the south and west coasts of Iceland have a milder and wetter climate than the northern and eastern coasts. Winter temperatures in the southwest seldom average below freezing, but in the north and east they normally drop into the low twenties. Snow is more common and longer lasting in the north and east regions. Precipitation averages between 30 and 60 inches a year in the south and west. Over most of the northern half of Iceland, it usually amounts to less than 20 inches.

The high-latitude location of the region causes an additional physical geographic phenomenon that affects both the region's inhabitants and tourism, the twenty-four hours of daylight in the summer. North of the Arctic Circle, the sun does not set for twenty-four hours at a time because of the tilt of the earth (Figure 22.3). This phenomenon is called the "Midnight Sun" and is an important tourist attraction. In the winter, of course, there are an equal number of days without the sun rising. Even south of the Arctic Circle in northern Europe, the summer night is only a few hours long.

Tourism Characteristics

The similarities of economic, geographic, cultural, and historic development among countries in this region are also found in their tourism. The four major countries (Denmark, Norway, Sweden, and Finland) have a similar tourism profile: outdoor activity; high season in

Figure 22.3 Godafoss waterfall in Iceland, after the midnight sunset. © Filip Fuxa/www.Shutterstock.com.

summer due to cold, dark winters and cool summers; a relatively small number of tourists compared with other European countries; the heavy use of the automobile by international tourists; a relatively short stay; the lack of overall importance of tourism to their economies; and more individual tourists and tourist itineraries. Cruises have become popular in this region and one of the major factors in the growth in the number of visitors. While the countries share some common tourism elements, there is also considerable variety in attractions from country to country. Peak numbers of tourists occur in the summer months in all the Scandinavian countries.

Denmark

Introduction

Located in northern Europe, most of Denmark is formed by the Jutland peninsula, which juts north from the continent of Europe and separates the North Sea from the Baltic. The rest of the nation consists of 406 islands, 78 of which are inhabited. Fertile farmland covers 62 percent of the country, which is among the flattest in the world. The flat land contributes to high average winds, which helped make Denmark become a major producer and consumer of wind power and the largest exporter of wind turbines in the world.

Denmark's industrialized market economy depends on trade and services, including tourism; it is a major exporter of food and energy. More and more Danes are using alternative energy sources—wind power, solar, and biomass—for environmental and economic reasons. With its palaces and gardens, Copenhagen hosts more visitors than any other Nordic city. Tivoli, founded in 1843, is a world-famous amusement park in downtown Copenhagen. The Kingdom of Denmark is a constitutional monarchy that includes the self-governing territories of the Faroe Islands, in the Norwegian Sea, and Greenland, the world's largest island.

Area	16,639 sq mi (about twice the size of Massachusetts)
Population	5,529,000
Government	constitutional monarchy
Capital	Copenhagen 1,085,000
Life Expectancy	79 years
Literacy	99%
Religion	Evangelical Lutheran
Language	Danish, Faroese, Greenlandic, German, English
Currency	Danish krone (DKK)
GDP per Cap	$36,000
Labor Force	2.5% Agriculture, 20.2% Industry, 77.3% Services

TRAVEL**TIPS**

Entry: Visas are not required for stays of less than ninety days. Passports are required.

Peak Visitor Season: July and August

National Holiday: June 5 (Constitution Day)

Shopping: Common items include Danish jewelry, furniture, wooden carving boards, salad bowls, and utensils. Also gold, silver, stainless steel flatware, ceramics, glassware, toys, and Danish cheese are popular items.

Internet TLD: .dk

 The Danes are a Gothic-Germanic people who have inhabited Denmark since prehistoric times. Danish is the official language with a small German-speaking minority along the border with Germany. English is widely spoken and understood. Ninety-two percent of the people are Evangelical Lutheran; however, most are cultural Lutherans, limiting church participation to baptism, confirmation of family or friends, and major holidays, such as Easter and Christmas. The Danes are a friendly and informal people.

Cultural hints: A handshake is the most common greeting. Politeness is important. Danes do not use hand gestures in conversation. Typical food includes cheese, pork roast, fish, beans, Brussels sprouts, potatoes, fresh vegetables, and soup. A common breakfast in hotels is a smorgasbord of cheese, fruits, and pastries.

Tourism Characteristics

Tourism to Denmark has been constant for some years at around 8 million visitors annually. The country has the largest tourism industry of the northern European countries. Tourism to Denmark is highly regional in origin, with Sweden, Norway, and Germany responsible for 55 percent of the bed nights. The United States accounts for 6 percent of Denmark's visitors. Tourists from Anglo-America are quite comfortable in Denmark as most of the population can speak the English language. There are a significant number of Americans who have Danish ancestors, in part accounting for the American tourists to the country. A large celebration, the Ribild Fourth of July celebration, takes place each year in recognition of America's independence. A site on Ribild Hills on the northern tip of the Jutland moor was dedicated in 1912 as a national park. In the park stands the Lincoln Memorial Cabin, built of logs from the original thirteen states, and the Immigrant Museum, devoted to mementos of Danish immigration to the United States. The tourist season is quite seasonal. The summer months are the most popular, accounting for more than half of all visitors.

Tourist Destinations and Attractions

Tourist attractions in Denmark are overwhelmingly cultural and historical, reflecting the lack of any individual outstanding physical feature. Most of Denmark's islands are small with very few inhabitants. The country can be divided into three regions in terms of tourism.

Copenhagen

Copenhagen, the capital, is one of Europe's most attractive cities. Located on the island of Zealand, the largest Danish island and connected to the Swedish coast by the Oresund Bridge, Copenhagen was founded in the twelfth century and today is home for a quarter of Denmark's five and a half million inhabitants. Tivoli Gardens, the inspiration for most theme parks, is in the center of town. One block from the train station of Copenhagen, Tivoli is one of the oldest (founded in 1843) and most beautiful theme parks in the world. Surrounding a lake are fountains, amusement rides and games, food establishments of all types and sizes, and theaters where concerts, plays, pantomime, skits, and acrobatic shows occur throughout the day. Copenhagen is a lovely city for dining, shopping, nightclubbing, and sightseeing. The major shopping street is alive with strollers, impromptu entertainment, and Danish ambiance.

The middle of Old Copenhagen is composed of a maze of pedestrian shopping streets offering shops of every conceivable type for every taste. One of the most charming and picturesque areas is the Nyhavn (New Harbor) district (Figure 22.4). It was built along a canal with tall row houses that now express the Danish style

Figure 22.4 Nyhavn ("New Harbor") district, Copenhagen, Denmark. © Yarygin/www.Shutterstock.com.

of architectural design, handsomely painted in rich tones of blues and yellows. Nyhavn was originally sailors' quarters, but today consists of a jungle of bars, cafés, restaurants, and the home where Hans Christian Andersen wrote his first fairy tales. Boat tours leave the area to visit the harbor and attractions along the canals of Copenhagen.

There are a number of museums, such as the Carlsberg Glyptotek Art Museum, the Danish Museum of Art and Design, the National Museum (history), Christiansborg Palace with its collection of rare documents in the Royal Library (including pre-Columbian Viking logs of transatlantic voyages), the Royal Theater (1500), the Royal Museum of Fine Art, and the Citadel. "Langelinie Promenade" along the harbor is where the most photographed mermaid in the world, the Little Mermaid, sits. It is such an important figure that her head was once severed and held for ransom. The ransom was not paid, and the head was recast and reattached to the statue.

Copenhagen's architectural beauty is expressed in the four identical mansions in Amalienborg Palace Square. The Royal House of Glucksborg has always resided here, and the Royal Guard with their striking tall bearskin caps are impressive. The changing of the guard brings tourists and residents to the square. Rosenborg Castle is a beautiful Renaissance palace that is now a museum housing

fine tapestries and royal possessions, including the Danish crown jewels. Surrounding the castle, the Kongens Have (the King's gardens) features beautiful flowers, majestic trees, and walks lined with sculptures.

Many of the morning activities center on the square opposite the Stock Exchange where many vendors have their colorful booths. The Fish Market is the place to watch the daily catch being sold by fishermen's wives. Across the canal, from which many canal and harbor tours depart, is Thorvaldsen's Museum, which contains a large collection of his work.

Outside of Copenhagen and Zealand

North of Copenhagen is a Deer Park near which is the royal hunting lodge of Eremithagen with a fine view over the Sound to Sweden. A large number of old Danish farms, windmills, and historical houses from all over the country have been assembled at Sorgenfri.

Some twenty-five miles north of Copenhagen in the heart of the Grib Forest lies Hillerød. The Frederiksborg Castle, a fairy-tale castle dating back to 1560, is the main attraction of Hillerød. Near Hillerød is the Ebleholt Abbey from the Middle Ages. Northeast of Hillerød is the Fredensborg Palace, the summer residence of the Danish Royal Family, which was built in Italian style in

Figure 22.5 Egeskov Castle, Denmark. © Sukhoverkhova Viktoriia/www.Shutterstock.com.

the early eighteenth century. Further north is Helsingør, a busy port and a major crossing point to Sweden. Kronborg Castle in Helsingør was built in the late sixteenth century and is famous as the setting of Shakespeare's *Hamlet.* Helsingør is one of the best preserved towns in Denmark, and its old section illustrates the old buildings and narrow streets of bygone years. Near the North Zealand fishing ports of Hornbaek, Gilleleje, and Tisvildeleje, there are extensive beaches and pinewoods, which have excellent bathing facilities for the visitor.

West of Copenhagen is Roskilde, one of Denmark's ancient leading cities. The twelfth-century cathedral is compared to Westminster Abbey and is the burial place for more than thirty-eight Danish kings and queens. The Viking Ship Museum has on display five Viking ships, found in Roskilde Fjord.

South of Copenhagen on the island of Amager is the old fishing port of Dragør, which has an old-world charm. From Dragør, tourists visit the bird sanctuaries on the island of Saltholm. Odense, the birthplace of Hans Christian Andersen, is on the nearby island of Funen. A museum with Andersen's books, letters, drawings, and personal belongings is located at Odense. The island of Funen has the greatest concentration of manor houses and castles in Denmark. Egeskov Castle

(Figure 22.5) is one of Europe's best-preserved Renaissance castles, built on oak piles that have been driven down into the lake.

Jutland

The Peninsula of Jutland has miles of broad white sandy beaches that attract many campers from Germany, Sweden, and Norway. Extending out from Aarhus, Denmark's second largest city and seaport, is a series of beaches, lakes, and picturesque small villages and towns. Old Town in Aarhus has narrow cobblestone streets and an open-air museum illustrating life in the sixteenth century. Along the eastern coast of the Jutland Peninsula are jagged fjords, tree-studded slopes, and rolling meadows, with heather moors and fertile fields. The medieval town of Ribe, where storks nest on the roofs of attractive old houses, is located in the moors. Also popular is Legoland, near Vejle, with famous landmarks from around the world created with Lego blocks. Founded in A.D. 948, Ribe is Denmark's oldest town. The peninsula has numerous small museums in most of the small towns. These museums house Viking relics and depict Viking life. The islands of Faeroe, Fano, Aero, Samso, and Bornholm offer glimpses of Danish village and rural life.

Finland

Introduction

Finland, in northern Europe, is low-lying in the south and center with mountains in the north. Forests blanket 75 percent of Finland, while 180,000 lakes cover 10 percent of the country. One-quarter of Finland lies north of the Arctic Circle, and the country experiences long, harsh winters. Most of the population is concentrated in the triangle formed by the cities of Helsinki (the capital), Tampere, and Turku.

After six centuries of union with Sweden, Finland came under Russian rule in 1809; but the Finns gained independence in 1917, during the Russian Revolution. After World War II, Finland developed close economic links with the Soviet Union. Finland strengthened its ties with Western Europe after the Soviet Union collapsed in 1991, and it joined the EU in 1995.

Despite a short growing season Finland is self-sufficient in meat, grains, and dairy products. For years, the wood and paper industry dominated Finland's exports; but the 1990s saw growth in telecommunication equipment, spearheaded by companies such as the Nokia corporation.

From *National Geographic Atlas of the World*, 9th edition. Copyright ©2011 National Geographic Society. Reprinted by arrangement. All rights reserved.

Area	130,558 sq mi (slightly smaller than Montana)
Population	5,387,000
Government	republic
Capital	Helsinki 1,115,000
Life Expectancy	80 years
Literacy	100%
Religion	Lutheran Church of Finland
Language	Finnish, Swedish
Currency	euro (EUR)
GDP per Cap	$36,700
Labor Force	18.2% Agriculture & Forestry, 15.9% Industry, 65.9% Services

From *National Geographic Atlas of the World*, 9th edition. Copyright ©2011 National Geographic Society. Reprinted by arrangement. All rights reserved.

TRAVEL TIPS

Entry: Visas are not required for stays up to ninety days. Passports are required.

Peak Tourist Season: June, July, and August

National Holiday: December 6 (Independence Day)

Shopping: Items include furniture, jewelry, leather goods, furs, toys, glassware, ceramics, textiles, foods such as crispbread, herring, cheese, and liquor.

Internet TLD: .fi

CULTURAL CAPSULE

The majority of the population is Finnish. It is thought their original home was in what is now west-central Siberia. As the Finns moved into the area, they pushed the Lapps into the more remote northern regions. Finland has a small minority of Lapps and some Gypsies. The Finnish language, which over 93 percent speak, is a Finno-Ugric member of the Uralic language family and not Indo-European. Lappish is spoken by a minority of Lapps. Swedish and English are widely understood. Over 90 percent of the population belongs to the Evangelical Lutheran Church, but weekly church attendance is very low. The small minority of Eastern Orthodox results from Finland's past ties to the Russian Empire.

Cultural hints: A handshake is a common greeting even with children. Do not talk with your hands in your pockets. Typical foods include fish, seafood, salmon, wild game, vegetables, potatoes, cheese, wild berries, milk, and rye bread.

Tourism Characteristics

Finland's tourist arrivals have been increasing over the past few years with numbers reaching 4.2 million by 2011. In the past, Finland received few tourists because of its relative remoteness from the prime European markets, higher airfare from America, and its short summer. Finland is second only to Iceland in lowest length of stay in Northern Europe. However, with the breakup of the former Soviet Union, Finland now benefits from its location as an origin point for tours (particularly cruises) to Russia, Estonia, Latvia, and Lithuania. Tourism numbers to Finland has doubled since the late 1990s.

Here in the Ita-Suomi region of Finland where the country bulges eastward into Russia like a swollen lip, land often seems to get swallowed by the endless lakes. The lakeside cottage, or mokki, is as simple as it is inviting, politely deferring to nature's leading role. On long summer evenings, the sun hovers impossibly on the horizon as if someone hit the pause button, keeping the forest soaked in vermillion light until the wee hours, until eyes, defeated, finally close for the night. The cool waters of Lake Haapavesi beckon for a post-sauna dip. (Don't see a sauna? There's probably one just beyond the next curve—there are 2 million of them in this land of 5 million people.) A swarm of opera fans descends on the nearby five-hotel town of Savonlinna every July for the world-class festival held in one of Scandinavia's best-preserved medieval castles, so a quiet mokki may be the best place to stay. Pick up some kalakukko (fish pie), traditional juniper beer, and a can of bug spray, or wait until January and bring cross-country skis. Savonlinna is reached by train—just half a day from Helsinki—but the region is best explored by car and canoe.

— Doug Lansky, *National Geographic Traveler*, July 2010

Finland does benefit from a special relationship with Russia. A former possession of the Russian Empire, Helsinki has long been a business center for East–West trade and is home to a number of international organizations. This location and relationship is seen in the origin of Finland's visitors. The three major markets for Finland are Russia, Sweden, and Estonia. Together, they account for 65 percent of tourists to Finland. The other two major markets are Germany with a little over 6 percent of visitors and the United States with 2 percent. Close economic ties between Russia and Finland diminished somewhat after the USSR was dissolved in 1991. Since then Finland has strengthened links with Western Europe and has joined the EU. Helsinki remains a preeminent center for international diplomacy.

Summer seasonality of visits is the norm, in part reflecting the large number of Germans and Swedes.

Tourism Destinations and Attractions

Finland's major attractions can be divided into four regions.

Helsinki

Helsinki, the capital, was founded in 1550 by King Gustaf Vasa when Finland was still united with Sweden. The city was completely rebuilt after the Great Fire in 1808. It has a very Scandinavian architectural style with many parks. More than 30 percent of its area has been retained as open space. Helsinki is one of the smaller capitals of the world but has been the site of the Olympic games. The places of interest begin with the old center around the Senate Square (Figure 22.6), much of which is in a neoclassic style, forming a homogeneous and attractive whole. It serves as an example of planned, single-style harmony on a large scale. Other places to visit within Helsinki include the Art Museum of the Ateneum, with its comprehensive collection of Finnish paintings; Kansallisteatteri, the Finnish National Theater; the Morning Market Square at Kauppatori, with its colorful array of flower and fruit stalls and handicrafts booths; the Mannerheim Museum; the Observatory Hill Park, which provides an excellent view of the harbor and waterfront; the Parliament Building; and the

Figure 22.6 Senate Square in Helsinki, Finland. © Neil Beer/Getty Images.

Finnish National Museum, which has a section devoted to the Finno-Ugric culture. Helsinki also has a unique church, Temppeliaukio, that is built into a rock and has an impressive interior. Carved from a rock outcrop, the pantheon-like interior is enhanced by the rugged granite walls and the copper-plated cupola. Seurasaari Island is an open-air museum illustrating the original farm and manor buildings from early history, with folk dancing and folk music performances in the summer. Nearby is Tapiola, the forerunner of planned communities.

Turku

Turku is Finland's oldest city, dating from the fourteenth century. It is the southwestern gateway to the country. Formerly the administrative and cultural capital of the country, old Turku has a well-preserved medieval cathedral and castle. There are a number of museums of interest, including the Handicraft Museum, which is a block of houses that survived the 1827 fire, and Sibelius Museum, which has a collection of musical instruments. Turku contains over twenty old shops from the medieval period.

Lake Country

Tampere, second in size only to Helsinki, is on the headland between Näsijärvi and Pyhäjärvi lakes. It is a good location for excursions into the countryside by motorboat for hiking and camping. From Tampere and Aulanko north and east, the country is dominated by lakes and magnificent scenery. The area is popular for chalet and camping holidays combined with watersports on Finland's many lakes and rivers. In the eastern part of the lake district, Savonlinna is one of Finland's most popular tourist destinations for all tourists (domestic and international). The Olavinlinna Castle, established in 1475 on a small island near the center of Savonlinna, is the stage for the Savonlinna Opera Festival each July. It is the biggest cultural event in Finland, attracting over 100,000 visitors. About 15 miles from Savonlinna is what the Finns claim is the world's largest wooden church.

Lapland

Visits to the North Pole center around the towns of Rovaniemi on the Arctic Circle and Kemijarvi, north of the Arctic Circle. Both have winter sports centers and facilities. The emphasis at Rovaniemi are the Lapps, winter sports, and the lumber industry. Near Rovaniemi is the reported home of Father Claus, the original inspiration for the American Santa Claus.

Sweden

Introduction

Sweden lies between Norway and the Baltic Sea on the Scandinavian Peninsula in northern Europe. Sweden's north, called Norrland, takes up more than half of the country and features a pristine landscape of forested mountains and large river valleys. Sweden became the first European country to protect its wilderness with national parks in 1910. Despite its northerly location, Sweden enjoys a favorable climate, with mostly mild summers and winters.

For many years, Sweden was ethnically very homogeneous, except for about 15,000 Sami people in the far north. Sweden has one of the world's longest life expectancies and lowest birth rates. About 1.6 million foreigners reside in Sweden; some came seeking asylum and some for work. Finns are the largest group at 256,000, but there are also 142,000 Iraqis, 78,000 Poles, 75,000 Iranians, 59,000 Germans, and more than 48,000 Africans.

Sweden remained neutral in both world wars and helped those seeking asylum from Nazi Germany during World War II. The country has continued to be a beacon for refugees and asylum seekers, most recently taking in people from Somalia, Iraq, and Afghanistan.

Sweden's political and economic success has been credited to a blending of socialism and capitalism. High taxes finance advanced social programs, from education and health care to child care and paid paternity leave. Sweden joined the EU in 1995, providing more markets to Swedish companies; many are household names, such as Volvo, Ericsson, and Electrolux.

Area	173,732 sq mi (about the size of California)
Population	9,288,000
Government	constitutional monarchy
Capital	Stockholm 1,264,000
Life Expectancy	81 years
Literacy	99%
Religion	Lutheran
Language	Swedish, Sami, Finnish
Currency	Swedish krona (SEK)
GDP per Cap	$36,800
Labor Force	1.1% Agriculture, 28.2% Industry, 70.7% Services

TRAVEL **TIPS** 🧳

Entry: Visas are not required for stays up to three months. Passports are required.

Peak Tourist Seasons: July and August

National Holiday: June 6 (National Flag Day)

Shopping: Common items include Swedish glass and ceramics, hand-woven textiles, wood carvings, antiques, reindeer-skin products, and tableware.

Internet TLD: .se

CULTURAL CAPSULE Sweden has one of the world's highest life expectancies and one of the lowest birthrates. Over 85 percent of the people are ethnic Swedes. The country's ethnic and linguistic minorities include 17,000 Lapps (Sami) and 50,000 indigenous Finnish speakers in the north as well as over 700,000 immigrants, mostly from the Nordic countries, Yugoslavia, Turkey, and Iran. Non-Swedes account for about 12 percent of the population. The Sami live in the north and traditionally herd reindeer for a living.

Swedish is a Germanic language related to Danish, Norwegian, and Icelandic. The Sami speak their own language, and the large Finnish minority speaks Finnish. English is understood by many throughout the country. Most Swedes belong to the Evangelical Lutheran Church, but most rarely attend church services. There has been a growth in Muslims and Jews due to recent immigration.

Cultural hints: A firm handshake is common at greetings and departures. Hands should be kept above the table while eating. Typical foods include meat, fish, cheese, vegetables, fruits, yogurt, and potatoes.

Tourism Characteristics

Sweden has a large deficit in tourism trade balances, with its citizens spending much more money out of the country on tourism than is brought in by visitors.

Sweden had a good growth rate in tourism during the first decade of the twenty-first century with arrivals reaching 5 million in 2010.

Tourism to Sweden is highly regional. Norway and Germany account for 30 percent of the total bed nights in Sweden. The United States accounts for 5 percent of the total bed nights.

Tourist Destinations and Attractions

There are three general tourist regions: Stockholm and the Central Region; the South, centered on Malmö; and the North.

Stockholm and the Central Region

Stockholm (Figure 22.7), the capital of the old kingdom of Sweden, is built on a group of islands in Lake Mälaren and Saltsjön, part of the Baltic Sea. Founded in the early thirteenth century, it has grown into a modern metropolis incorporating the islands and spreading out over the mainland. The most-visited tourist area is the Gamla Stan (Old Town), which has quaint, narrow cobblestone streets and old houses. The Royal Palace is on the same island. Across from Gamla Sta'n are Skansen, an open-air museum of Swedish life and culture; a number of other museums and art galleries; park lands; and the seventeenth-century warship *Vasa*, a symbol of Sweden's former sea might. Boat excursions take visitors to the magnificent eighteenth-century palace of Drottningholm or through the Swedish Archipelago.

To the north is the medieval city of Uppsala, with its old university, cathedral, and burial mounds of Viking kings. Uppsala is the seat of the archbishop and the leading university town of Sweden. Near Stockholm on the northern shore of Lake Mälaren is Sigtuna, the oldest town in Sweden. It was founded by Sweden's first Christian king, Olof Skotkonung, and for one hundred fifty years it was the country's capital. There are ancient towns, quiet villages, farms, large lakes, forests, and many castles and manors throughout the area.

The South, including Skåne and the Lake Country

Skåne is the chateau country of Sweden. There are many castles and manor houses, some of which are open to the public. Glimmingehus and Torup are among the oldest castles. They are thick-walled medieval fortresses. This area is the most fertile area in Sweden. Beautiful farms with half-timbered homes and ancient towns can be seen throughout the countryside. North of Skåne in Smaland, the land is not as fertile or productive. It has rocky soil and dense forests. On the coast of Smaland, the medieval castle at Kalmar is one of Scandinavia's most impressive. The area is filled with meadows, windmills, ancient forts, and Viking burial sites.

Figure 22.7 Stockholm, Sweden. © Neil Beer/Getty Images.

is an attractive area with castles and scenic countryside of narrow valleys, forests, lakes, and waterfalls. On the coast is Göteborg, Sweden's second-largest city and hub of the west coast. Three of the most popular attractions at Göteborg are Liseberg (Scandinavia's largest and most famous amusement park, particularly noted for its floral displays), an excellent maritime museum, and an aquarium. Malmo experienced growth since the opening of the Oresund Bridge in 2000. It connects Sweden with Copenhagen, Denmark. The bridge carries over 20,000 vehicles daily and provides a strategic link between continental Europe and the Scandinavian countries for both commercial and tourism related traffic.

The North

The area northwest of Stockholm to the Norwegian border is characterized by the wooded hills and valleys of Varmland and Dalarna. Jämtland and Lapland contain one of Europe's few remaining wilderness areas (Figure 22.8), a sportsman's paradise providing varied outdoor activities.

To the west, the lake country centers on Lake Vanern and the Göta Canal, which connects the Baltic in the east to Lake Vanern in the west, making it possible to travel by boat from Göteborg to Stockholm. It

Figure 22.8 Reindeer on the road in northern Sweden in winter. © Mikhail Markovskiy/www.Shutterstock.com.

Norway

Introduction

In northern Europe, the thinly populated Kingdom of Norway borders the North Atlantic and Arctic Oceans. The extensive coastline is indented with fjords and edged with islands. The mostly mountainous country is covered with coniferous forests, and the only major lowlands are found along the southern coast. Despite its northerly location, Norway enjoys a temperate climate due to the warming effect of ocean currents.

Norway's population is largely homogeneous and most speak Norwegian, a North Germanic language; also spoken is the Sami language of Norway's indigenous people. There are about 40,000 Sami in northern Norway. Norwegians have a high standard of living based on oil and natural gas exports. Norway's oil needs are modest because virtually all of its electricity comes from hydroelectric power plants.

From *National Geographic Atlas of the World*, 9th edition. Copyright ©2011 National Geographic Society. Reprinted by arrangement. All rights reserved.

Area	125,021 sq mi (near the size of New Mexico)
Population	4,827,000
Government	constitutional monarchy
Capital	Oslo 835,000
Life Expectancy	81 years
Literacy	100%
Religion	Church of Norway (Lutheran)
Language	Bokmal Norwegian, Nynorsk Norwegian, Sami, Finnish
Currency	Norwegian krone (NOK)
GDP per Cap	$58,600
Labor Force	2.9% Agriculture, 21.1% Industry, 76.0% Services

From *National Geographic Atlas of the World*, 9th edition. Copyright ©2011 National Geographic Society. Reprinted by arrangement. All rights reserved.

TRAVEL **TIPS** 🧳

Entry: Visas are not required for visits up to three months. Passports are required.

Peak Tourist Seasons: June, July, and August

National Holiday: May 17 (Constitution Day)

Shopping: Common items include arts and handicrafts such as silverware, handblown glass, carved wood, pewter, ceramics, knitwear, and furniture.

Internet TLD: .no

 CULTURAL CAPSULE Norwegians are predominantly Germanic. There is a minority of Lapps (Sami), who live mostly in the north. Norwegian is the official language. There are two forms, Bokmal, or "book language," which is used in most writing and spoken by the majority of people, and Nynorsk, a rural dialect. The Lapps speak Sami and

learn Norwegian as a second language. English is widely understood and spoken. Norway is in the top rank of nations in number of books printed per capita, even though Norwegian is one of the world's smallest language groups. The Evangelical Lutheran Church is a state church, and over 85 percent of the population are members.

Cultural hints: There is little personal touching except among relatives. Do not speak in a loud voice. Courtesy and good behavior are important. Typical food includes seafood (salmon and cod), meat, potatoes, cheese, yogurt, vegetables, and soup. Some specialties are fish balls, smoked salmon, cod, cabbage and mutton, and sheep's head.

Tourism Characteristics

Norway has the second largest tourist industry of the Northern European countries. The discovery of oil in the North Sea allowed the government to develop its tourism infrastructure in a steady manner. Norway is the world's third largest oil exporter. International arrivals reached 5 million in 2011. The largest tourism markets are Sweden, Germany, and Denmark. The United States accounts for only a small percent of visitors. A large number of Norwegians migrated to the United States in the late 1800s and early 1900s. This cultural tie between the United States and Norway combines with the environmental attractions in Norway to attract travel from the United States to Norway. Ecotourism is important to Norwegians, and over one-third of the families own or share a cabin in the mountains or by the sea.

Tourist Destinations and Attractions

Norway is known as fjord country. No country in the world evokes the mental image of deep valleys and spectacular coastal and lake views as does Norway. The three major tourist regions are Oslo, Bergen and the Fjords, and Trondheim and the Land of the Midnight Sun.

Oslo and Southern Norway

Oslo, the capital, is over nine hundred years old. Oslo's climate is tempered by the waters of the fjord and surrounding lakes. Winter sports are evident even in Oslo itself, with the Holmenkollen ski jump overlooking the city and a ski museum as a part of the city's winter complex. The Edvard Munch Museum holds many of the world's foremost expressionist painter's work, including a version of *The Scream*. Across the harbor on the Bygdøy Peninsula are a number of attractions. The Folk Museum has over one hundred fifty buildings and houses from various parts of Norway and from various eras. The Folk Museum hosts folk-dancing and craft demonstrations in the summer. It also contains a collection of author Henrik Ibsen's works. Also on the peninsula are museums housing Viking ships and *Kon-Tiki*, the raft on which Thor Heyerdahl floated from Latin America to the Polynesian Islands in the 1950s to prove that the people in the two areas were related. The Arctic polar exploration ship, the *Fram*, sailed by Nansen and Amundsen seeking the North Pole, is also found here.

Much activity centers on the harbor area for short excursions to the local fjord and downtown sites of the fourteenth-century Akershus Fortress, the Town Hall with its famous murals, Frogner Park with an outstanding collection of granite statues by Gustdav Vigeland (Figure 22.9), and other art museums. There has been extensive development around the harbor, where a large shopping complex is a major focal point.

The surrounding area has old towns, scenic countryside with red barns, old fortresses and churches, lakes, and relics of Norway's past. North of Oslo, Lillehammer staged the 1994 Winter Olympic games.

Bergen and the Fjord Country

Bergen (Figure 22.10), the former Hanseatic League city of the Middle Ages, is the second-largest city in Norway in the heart of the fjord country. The Hanseatic League, of German origin, was a mercantile association of towns that was founded during the medieval time period by wealthy merchants to control maritime commerce and trade originating in the Baltic and North Seas. The oldest part of Bergen, called Bryggen, dates back to the city's founding in the eleventh century. It has been beautifully restored and is a UNESCO World Heritage Site. The country opened the world's longest road tunnel in 2000 on the main Oslo-Bergen highway. At over fifteen miles the tunnel is a mile longer than the St. Gotthard tunnel in Switzerland and boosted tourism to the spectacular Fjords. Many excursions can be undertaken from Bergen to the fjords, both north and south. Along the waterfront are the old buildings, museums, old homes, and shops of the Hanseatic port. Near Bergen is the home of the composer Edvard Grieg.

Throughout the fjord country, spectacular natural scenery and panoramas combine with fishing villages to create stunning vistas (Figure 22.11). Hardangerfjord south of Bergen is the most striking. Sognefjord, north of Bergen, is the world's longest and deepest fjord, home to the famous Kvikne's Hotel in Balestrand. The Hardangervidda plateau, Europe's largest mountain plateau, is the home of the largest herd of wild reindeer in Europe.

Figure 22.9 Vigeland Park in Frogner Park, Oslo, Norway.
© MARTAFR/www.Shutterstock.com.

A most interesting combination of train, bus, and ferry rides, the Voss-Stalheim-Flam Myrdal route that branches off from the Bergen-to-Oslo route ranks high in scenic panoramas. The train, in fact, stops so passengers can see and photograph the best possible views of magnificent scenery and roaring waterfalls. Legendary Notre Dame football coach Knute Rockne was born at Voss.

South of Bergen, Stavanger is an attractive fishing city that emphasizes its historical role as a fishing village. Today, Stavanger is a major oil center. Steamers connect the two cities and provide excellent views of the coastal fjords.

Trondheim and the Land of the Midnight Sun

Trondheim is the gateway to the north country and summer trips to the Arctic Circle and North Cape, where the sun never sets between May 14 and the end of July. Trondheim's sights include the famous Nidaros Cathedral (English Gothic style), the royal residence Stiftsgarden, and the Bishop's Palace, a relic of Trondheim's medieval glory. The countryside is beautiful, offering an excellent location for those interested in winter sports.

Figure 22.10 Bergen, Norway. © David Buffington/Getty Images.

Figure 22.11 Trolltunga in Norway. © Galyna Andrushko/www.Shutterstock.com.

Norway's Gateway to the Arctic

Flying into Bodø, the plane descends over a seascape covering thousands of isles, while the final approach offers a close-up view of the majestic glaciers and peaks guarding this small capital of Norway's Nordland Province. Arriving by sea (often and deservedly called "the world's most beautiful sea voyage"), the famous Hurtigruten coastal ships give passengers a glimpse to the northwest of the imposing 62-mile chain of spiky mountains that forms the mythic-seeming Lofoten archipelago.

Bodø is less than one degree north of the Arctic Circle. Without the warming effect of the Gulf Stream, the landscape would be a frozen, inhospitable waste at this latitude. In fact, Bodø offers cycling, skiing, hiking, caving, climbing, and fishing. Many visitors come here for the unique Arctic light, whether the soft pastels of winter that crescendo in a display of aurora borealis or the orange glow of summer's midnight sun (the best viewpoint for both is from the Landegode lighthouse). Don't leave without seeing the Saltstraumen sound, where deep, swirling eddies form every six hours with the change in tides as the equivalent of 160,000 Olympic-size pools of water surge through a narrow passage. Above all, northern Norway has this to offer: the absence of distractions and the chance of an intimate encounter with awe-inspiring nature.

— Arild Molstad, *National Geographic Traveler*, December 2012/January 2013

Iceland

Introduction

A volcanic island, Iceland is Europe's westernmost country and home to the world's northernmost capital city, Reykjavík. Although glaciers cover more than a tenth of the island, the Gulf Stream and warm southwesterly winds moderate the climate. Under the Danish crown for more than 500 years, the country became a republic in 1944. Almost all of Iceland's electricity and heating come from hydroelectric power and geothermal water reserves. Explosive geysers, relaxing geothermal spas, and glacier-fed waterfalls attract tourists. Aluminum and marine products are the main exports, and most trade is with European Union countries. In 2009, Iceland applied for membership in the EU.

Area	39,769 sq mi (about the size of Virginia)
Population	321,000
Government	constitutional republic
Capital	Reykjavík 192,000
Life Expectancy	81 years
Literacy	99%
Religion	Lutheran Church of Iceland
Language	Icelandic, English, Nordic languages, German
Currency	Icelandic krona (ISK)
GDP per Cap	$39,600
Labor Force	4.8% Agriculture, 22.2% Industry, 73% Services

TRAVEL **TIPS** 🧳

Entry: Visas are not required for stays up to three months. Passports are required.

Peak Tourist Season: July and August

National Holiday: June 17 (Independence Day)

Internet TLD: .is

CULTURAL CAPSULE

Icelanders are descendants of Norwegian settlers and Celts from the British Isles. The official language, Icelandic, is close to the old Norse language and has remained relatively unchanged since the twelfth century, making it more similar to ancient Norwegian than modern Norwegian. The state church is the Evangelical Lutheran Church or other Lutheran churches. There are a few other Protestant and Roman Catholic congregations.

Cultural hints: Names in a phone book are alphabetized by the first given name. It is necessary also to know the last name. Icelanders use very few hand gestures when talking. Typical foods include fish (cod, haddock, halibut, plaice, herring, salmon, and trout), lamb, and dairy products. Specialties are smoked mutton, yogurt, and potatoes.

Figure 22.12 Reykjavik, Iceland. © Gail Johnson/www.Shutterstock.com.

Tourism Characteristics

Iceland has the least number of visitors in Northern Europe. Its insular location is a major factor in its small number of visitors. Iceland attracts 1.2 million visitors annually. Iceland's income resulting from tourism is low, as the per capita expenditure on tourism is the lowest in the Northern European countries.

The tourist industry is highly dependent upon North America and Europe. The two regions account for over 90 percent of the visitors to Iceland.

Tourism Destinations and Attractions

Reykjavik, the capital (Figure 22.12), was founded over 1,100 years ago. It has an international airport and receives the most visitors. It also is home of almost half of all the population. Attractions in Reykjavik include the Pearl (a unique entertainment venue with shops and restaurants built on top of hot water storage tanks), the

Old Town near the harbor, the University, the National Museum and Art Gallery, Nordic House, a center for Nordic Studies, the Einar Jonsson Museum, the Asgrim Jonsson Museum, the home of Asmundur Sveinsson, and the Folk Museum at Arbaer.

Iceland's proudest cultural achievement is its literary contributions. In the twelfth and thirteenth centuries, Icelandic writers recorded Eddic and Akaldic poetry portraying many of the legends, religious beliefs, and ideas of the pre-Christian Nordic-Germanic people, thereby preserving much of the heritage. These Sagas, almost all of which were written between 1180 and 1300, remain Iceland's best-known literary accomplishments. The Sagas present views of Nordic life and times up to 1100, and they have no counterpart anywhere in the Nordic world. The twentieth-century artist and modern sculptor Asmundur Sveinsson (1893–1982) drew his inspiration from Icelandic folklore and the Sagas.

A short distance from Reykjavik is the national park Thingvellir, where the world's first parliament convened. Also, the region has a unique open plain between tall lava walls and Iceland's largest lake. There are also many fishing villages and towns along the coast. The landscape consists of glaciers, swift rivers, mountain peaks, flower-strewn grasslands, and birchwoods. A unique way to experience the country is to travel the "Ring Road." It is a 850-mile loop along the country's entire coastline.

All through the island, hot springs and volcanoes provide spectacular sights. Three of the most famous are Gullfoss, known as the "Golden Waterfall," and Geysir, a spouting hot spring. Gullfoss is a waterfall that plummets two hundred feet into a deep gorge, creating rainbows. Geysir and other geysers erupt frequently. The 2010 eruption of the Eyjafjallajokull volcano caused enormous disruption in air travel across northern and western Europe.

REVIEW QUESTIONS

1. Describe the climates of Northern Europe. How do they affect tourism?

2. What geographic features do the countries of Northern Europe have in common?

3. Why do you think Sweden has such a large deficit in its tourism trade payments?

4. Compare Scandinavia with Alaska and explain why the climate is different.

5. Where are the major population centers of Northern Europe? Why are they there?

6. Describe the general characteristics of tourism to Northern Europe.

7. Why does Finland receive so many fewer visitors than the other Scandinavian countries?

8. What are the major tourist regions of Norway?

9. What are the major tourist regions of Denmark?

10. Where are the major tourism markets for the Northern European countries? Why?

chapter 23: GEOGRAPHY AND TOURISM IN SOUTHERN EUROPE

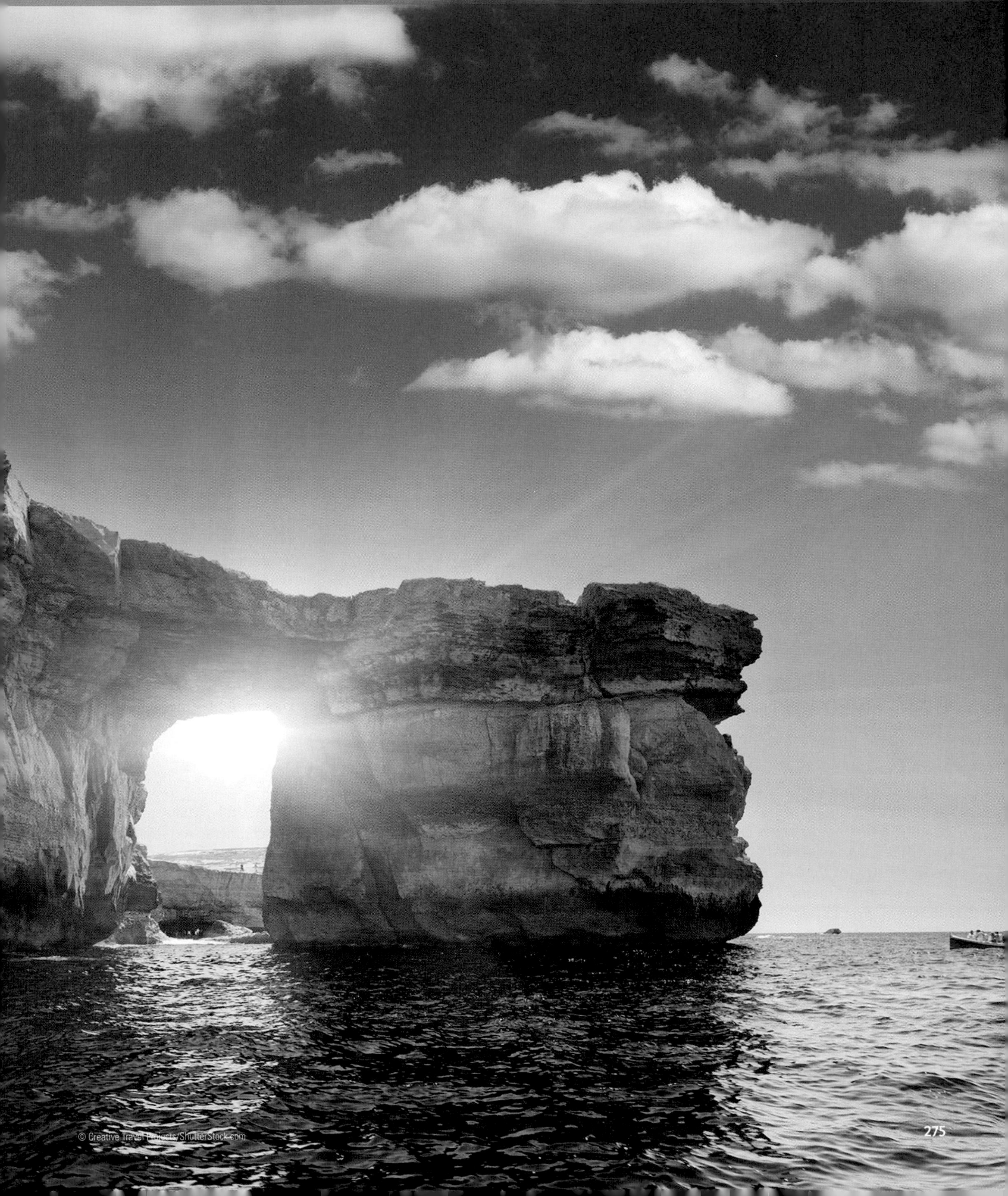

Figure 23.1 Praia da Rocha in Portugal. © StevanZZ/www.Shutterstock.com.

Introduction

Southern Europe has become the major tourism destination of Europe. While there are various places throughout Europe (such as the Riviera) that claim to be Europe's playground, as an entire region, Southern Europe best epitomizes the concept of a continental playground. While there are major cultural and historical attractions in the region, the massive number of European tourists to the region return regularly because of the favorable climate, warm sea, and excellent beaches. By contrast, Americans visit mostly for the antiquities and cultural experiences.

The four major countries of Southern Europe—Portugal, Spain, Italy, and Greece—form a group that is distinct from Western, Northern, or Central Europe and the Balkans. Climatically, there is less variability from country to country. Economically, these nations have been slower to industrialize. However, since joining the European Union (EU), Spain and Portugal has experienced initial rapid economic growth. The average per capita income is still lower than those found in Western or Northern Europe but above those in Central Europe and the Balkan states. Italy has the highest per capita

income in the south, but it is only half that of its neighbor, Switzerland. In the early 2010s, many countries in the region experienced a series of financial austerity measures imposed by Euro Zone partners following bail-out payments made to cover debt situations.

Climate Patterns

For the most part, Portugal, Spain, Italy, Malta, and Greece have Mediterranean climates characterized by summer drought and winter rainfall. Nearly 80 percent of precipitation falls between December and March. The temperatures of the region are warmer than the rest of Europe because of a more southerly location and a lower incidence of cloudiness. The summers are hot, except along the Atlantic shore in Portugal and Spain, with July temperatures averaging between 70 and 85 degrees Fahrenheit. The relative humidity in the summers is very low and fairly rapid nighttime cooling is common, making coastal areas very comfortable and very attractive to tourists (Figure 23.1). The winters are mild. Extended periods of frost are unknown, except in the mountains. Groves of citrus fruit trees dot the landscape of the lowlands of the Mediterranean.

Figure 23.2 The Acropolis, Athens, Greece. © marcokenya/www.Shutterstock.com.

It was in the Mediterranean climate that the **Western culture** was born. This was the home of the Minoan, Mycenaean, classical Greek, Etruscan, Roman, and Byzantine cultures, upon which much of Western civilization is based. Many of the ruins of early cultures are based on abandonment of cities due to extended drought, earthquakes, volcanoes, or conflict.

The Po Valley in Italy is a small zone with humid subtropical climate. Temperatures are similar to those of the Mediterranean region, but it does not have the intense summer drought. In the Iberian Peninsula, there are areas of steppe climate found where the mountain ranges block rain-bearing winds from the ocean. Two of these are the southeast coastal area of Spain and the Ebro Valley northeast of Madrid.

The growth of major cities such as Rome, Milan, Madrid, Barcelona, and Athens has so clogged the road arteries of the cities that air pollution is extremely high. Air pollution is so high that the Acropolis in Athens and other important ruins are in jeopardy. Some cities have completely banned auto traffic from downtown historic districts and have closed antiquities such as the Parthenon on Athens's Acropolis (Figure 23.2) and the Altamire caves at Santander, Spain.

Cultural Characteristics

Southern Europe shares important cultural characteristics. The Catholic Church has been the dominant religious force in the area. The languages, with the notable exception of Greek and a few minor tongues, are based on Latin. Since Latin diffused from Rome, these and other languages based on Latin are known as **Romance languages**. Greece retained its linguistic integrity when it was part of the Roman Empire; unlike the rest of the region, it is dominated by the Eastern (Greek) Orthodox Church.

Tourism Characteristics

Tourism in Southern Europe in the twentieth century rivaled manufacturing as a source of national income. Florence and other cities of the Mediterranean, however, were the focal point of visitors as far back as the Renaissance. As Europe experienced the Industrial Revolution, residents of the more industrialized and

Figure 23.3 St. Peter's Basilica, St. Peter's Square, Vatican City. © Sergii Figurnyi/www.Shutterstock.com.

wealthy nations of Western Europe started turning south to the warm climates of Southern Europe bordering the beautiful Mediterranean. Italy was the earliest destination because of its history and transport connections to Northern and Western Europe. After World War II, tourism increased to Spain and Greece. The Swedes, Germans, and British have historically escaped temporarily from the cloudy, damp, cool lands of the north to the sunny lands of the Mediterranean. Generally, they have grouped in various coastal cities and resorts. Along the Costa Del Sol in Spain, specific communities and resorts are dominated by French, German, British, or Swedish visitors. These communities provide familiar language and food for each nationality group.

Pilgrimages are an important element of tourism to Southern Europe. The Catholic Church has a long tradition of pilgrimages in the region. Pilgrimage sites vary in importance, ranging from small shrines that attract only those faithful who live in the immediate surroundings to world-renowned sites that are visited by Catholic people from all over the world. Fatima, north of Lisbon in Portugal, Santiago de Campostela in Spain, and the Vatican in Rome (Figure 23.3) draw millions of visitors each year. The landscape is dotted with monasteries and impressive churches both large and small. Many early monastic orders were established as agricultural settlements engaged in land reclamation and colonization. Most were secularized over time, but the monasteries remained on the landscape.

Southern Europe can be characterized as a tourism destination region, with a greater number of travelers visiting the area than leaving it. The percentage of Southern Europeans taking a vacation in which they travel to another country, while lower than among Western or Northern Europeans, is rising. Italy is the leader, but the Spanish are also rapidly becoming world travelers. The low percentages of citizens leaving the region are the result of two factors: the lower standard of living of the nations of Southern Europe and the greater distances of the population centers from other European countries.

The three major attractions common to the four countries can be classified as sun-sea-sand, religion, and historic sites. The tourism industry in Southern Europe is both highly seasonal and geographically concentrated in coastal areas and capitals.

Spain and Italy have the greatest number of visitors and have a travel industry as large as any in Europe. Together they account for nearly 14 percent of the world's arrivals. Both Portugal and Greece have a significantly smaller number of visitors. Greece has more visitors than Portugal, reflecting its cultural importance, its location between Europe and the Middle East, a more favorable climate, and its numerous attractive islands. Tourism to Southern Europe grew more than 40 percent in the past decade, slightly more than the rest of Western and Northern Europe.

Greece

Introduction

Greece, part of the Balkan Peninsula in southeastern Europe, is mostly dry and mountainous, with a large mainland and 9,835 islands and islets (220 are inhabited). The climate is generally temperate, with wet, mild winters and dry, hot summers, but the northern mountains in the Greek regions of Macedonia and Thrace are cold in winter.

Since the 1960s, Greeks have been migrating from rural to urban areas, with most rural areas and islands losing population. Athens has been the major destination for migrants; today more than a third of Greece's population lives in the Athens area—on only 5 percent of the land. Since the 1990s, foreigners have been migrating to Greece from poorer neighboring countries; Albanians, by far, make up the largest number of foreigners in Greece at an estimated 460,000. The nation where democracy was conceived in the fifth century B.C. has periodically suffered the loss of freedom and then celebrated its return. After almost 400 years under Turkish rule, Greece won independence in 1830. The nation endured Nazi occupation during World War II and military dictatorship from 1967 to 1974. The military junta fell after a failed Athens-backed coup in Cyprus. An elected government and new constitution followed. Even though Greece and Turkey are both members of NATO, relations have been tense over Cyprus and Aegean issues.

From *National Geographic Atlas of the World*, 9th edition. Copyright ©2011 National Geographic Society. Reprinted by arrangement. All rights reserved.

Area	131,957 sq km (50,949 sq mi)
Population	11,277,000
Government	parliamentary republic
Capital	Athens 3,242,000
Life Expectancy	80 years
Religion	Greek Orthodox
Language	Greek
Currency	euro (EUR)
GDP per Cap	$32,100
Labor Force	12.4% Agriculture, 22.4% Industry, 65.1% Services

From *National Geographic Atlas of the World*, 9th edition. Copyright ©2011 National Geographic Society. Reprinted by arrangement. All rights reserved.

TRAVEL **TIPS**

Entry: Visas are not required for stays up to three months. Passports are required.

Peak Tourist Season: May to September

National Holiday: March 25 (Independence Day)

Shopping: Common items include local handicrafts, woven fabrics, linen, wool carpets, sheepskin jackets, embroidered blouses, fabric bags, silver jewelry, and ceramics.

Internet TLD: .gr

CULTURAL CAPSULE Some 98 percent of the population is ethnic Greek, with small groups of Turks, Albanians, Pomachs, and Slavs. The same percentage (98) belongs to the Eastern (Greek) Orthodox Church, which is supported by the state through taxes. During the centuries of Ottoman Turkish domination, the church preserved the Greek language, values, and national identity and was the central point in the struggle for independence. The Greek language dates back at least 3,500 years. English and French are widely understood. There is a Muslim minority.

Cultural hints: A slight upward nod of the head means yes. To tilt the head to either side means no. Greeks smile both when happy and upset. To beckon, extend the arm, palm down, and make a scratching motion with fingers. The appetizers before and after lunch are finger food. When finished eating, place utensils in an X shape and the napkin next to your plate. Typical food includes lamb, seafood, olives, cheese, potatoes, rice, beans, breads, chicken, fruit, and vegetables. For cooking, oil, garlic, onions, and spices are commonly used.

Tourism Characteristics

Greece is still a relatively inexpensive location for the visitor compared with the rest of Europe. The country attracted 15 million visitors in 2010 but the number of visitors has decreased dramatically since then, following the announcement of financial austerity measures and resulting high unemployment and domestic unrest. It has a shorter length of stay than other southern European countries, due in part to the fact that it is a gateway to the Middle East for both cruises and air travel.

Europe is the overwhelming market area for Greece. Over 93 percent of the visitors to Greece are from Europe, with the United Kingdom and Germany accounting for 25 percent of European travelers. The dominance of these two countries results from the development

Figure 23.4 Athens, Greece. © Anastasios71/www.Shutterstock.com.

of Greece as a major charter destination area by large travel companies in the United Kingdom and Germany. The majority of the European market desires a relaxing holiday in which sun, sea, and sand are the most important elements, things that Greece can provide. In the islands, as well as at Delphi, Olympia, Knossos, and Athens, there are large hotel developments.

Greece is a mecca for youthful travelers, who favor cheap accommodations in campsites, hostels, or rental rooms. Although the climate of Greece is pleasant year-round, the peak tourist season is from May to September. Seasonality is largely a result of institutional holidays, such as school vacations, in the major market countries of Europe.

Tourist Destinations and Attractions

The major attractions of Greece are its classical historical and architectural remains, its scenic islands, picturesque ports, and sheltered coves. The Greek culture is expressed in the villages, flea markets, food, festivals, and friendly people. All are important factors in the future of Greece's tourism. Tourism destination regions can be divided into four broad groups.

Athens and Surrounding Environs

The major destination is Athens (Figure 23.4). Athens is the largest city in the Balkan peninsula with a population in the greater Athens area of over 3 million residents. The city itself is surrounded by an amphitheater of mountains. The focal attraction of Athens is the Acropolis, which dominates the city. The major site on the Acropolis is the Parthenon, a temple of Athena built between 448 and 438 B.C., and Erechtheion, with its Porch of Maidens. Other Acropolis attractions include the Temple of Olympia, Zeus, and the Theseum. Around the base of the Acropolis are other classical ruins, such as the Temple of the Wingless Victory. Other sites in Athens are the Arch of Hadrian, the Monument of Lysirkates, the Olympic Stadium, the Theater of Dionysos, the Odeion of Herodes Atticus, and the Theseion, a focal point of ancient Athenian community life. The history of Christians and Muslims in Greece is on display at the Byzantine Museum and the Benaki Museum.

The Plaka is the oldest and most picturesque quarter in Athens, spreading around the Acropolis with winding, narrow alleys, single-story houses, and elegant mansions. There are small taverns, nightclubs, and shops. The market offers all types of handcrafted goods

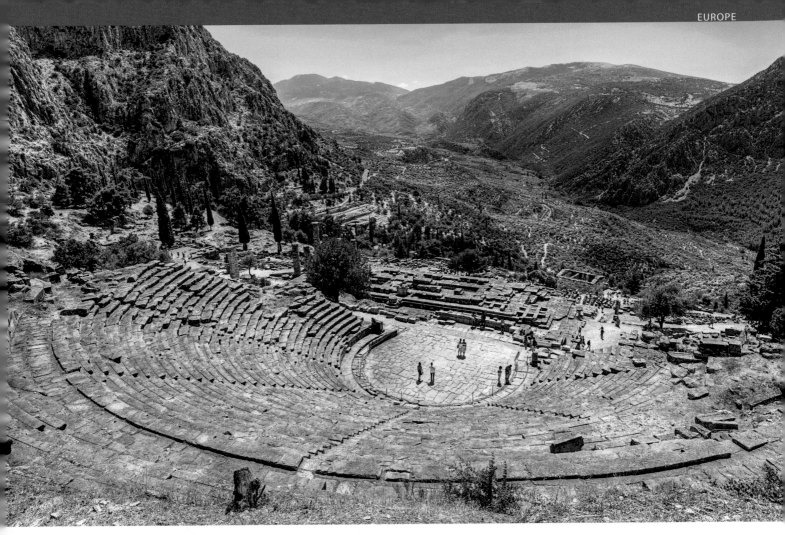

Figure 23.5 Ancient theater in Delphi, Greece. © Anastasios71/www.Shutterstock.com.

such as woven fabrics, linen, wool carpets, sheepskin jackets, embroidered blouses and fabric bags, handmade silver jewelry, ceramics, and gold icons and ornaments. The Parliament is guarded by colorfully dressed soldiers called Evzones. The periodic changing of the Parliament guard is an attraction in its own right. It is a carry-over from the old changing of the guard at the Palace before Greece became a republic. The Greek House of Parliament is a neoclassical building overlooking the Tomb of the Unknown Soldier. Formerly used as a residential palace of Greece's first king, Otto (1832–1862), it has been the Greek Parliament since 1933.

Near Athens, there are a number of easy and interesting one-day excursions. To the south is the Temple of Poseidon overlooking the sea. To the west is Delphi, with its extensive outstanding ruins (Figure 23.5), including the Temple of Apollo, the Treasuries along the Sacred Way, the Theater, the Stadium, the Temples of Athena, and the sacred Castalian spring from which pilgrims drank on their way to the Delphic Oracle. It is considered by many as the most spectacularly beautiful ancient site in Greece, evoking the classical past. Set on the slopes of Mount Parnassos, it offers a view of the plain below and the surrounding countryside.

Between Delphi and Athens is Osios Loukás monastery (the Monastery of St. Luke Stíris). It sits on the brow of a hill with commanding views of Helikon and the surrounding country. The monastery is dedicated to a local beatified hermit, the Blessed Luke (Osios Loukás) of Stíri. His family fled from Aegina during its invasion by the Saracens, and Luke was born in the region. It has beautiful mosaics, which combine with the physical setting to provide a pleasant attraction.

Also near Athens is Marathon, where the ancient Athenians stopped the invading Persians. The 26.2-mile marathon race was derived from the military runner who carried the news of the victory to Athens. South of Athens is Piraeus, which is the major port for Athens and the home of many cruise ships visiting the Greek islands and the eastern Mediterranean.

The Island of Peloponnisos

At the Isthmus of Corinth, the Corinth Canal is a major geographical feature. The canal is 4 miles long, 27 yards wide, and 26 feet deep. It was built to save vessels from going all the way around Peloponnisos. The ancient city of Corinth is spread out at the foot of the huge rock

A bolt of Greece lightning

Thessaloniki's sparkling harbor is almost empty—a good thing. It remains one of the last urban seafronts in southern Europe not hemmed in by a giant marina. Instead, wooden caïques still ply the quiet bay while footpaths trace the meandering waterfront of Greece's second largest city, some 320 miles north—and a world away—from chaotic Athens.

Although the euro crisis has caused ripples of discontentment here, it's the century-old street markets filled with ripe fruits and barrels of fresh feta that symbolize this city. Tucked between relics of Byzantine and Ottoman antiquity are art galleries, bohemian nightclubs, and culinary hot spots, all part of a grassroots vision turned reality by Thessaloniki's large (about 50 percent of the population) do-it-yourself youth culture. "We are driven by our optimism and positive energy for a new way of living that embraces our heritage," says Vicky Papadimitiou, a university graduate who helped Thessaloniki garner official status as the 2014 European Youth Capital.

The best way to get the feel of this mission-driven city is on foot, walking from the ruins of Ano Poli to Aristotelous Square on the waterfront. Then cozy up to a café to nibble grilled calamari washed down with dry Macedonian wine.

— Costas Christ, *National Geographic Traveler*, December 2012/January 2013

---

of Acrocorinth. Its ruins are largely Roman. Corinth includes a Temple of Apollo, one of the oldest in Greece; a marketplace; a theater; and the Odeon. Mycenae on Peloponnisos is a city of pre-Hellenic Greece. It has impressive stone ramparts and tombs. Mycenae was the most powerful, brilliant, and sovereign influence in Greece until 1100 B.C., when it was destroyed by fire. While most of the treasures have been moved to the National Archaeological Museum in Athens, it still offers a glimpse of Greek civilization. The Lion Gate entrance is the oldest example of monumental sculpture in Europe. Excavations have uncovered the palace complex of houses, sanctuaries, royal tombs, and other important buildings.

Nauplion, which was the first capital of modern Greece, has **medieval** fortresses. Epidaurus was the center of the worship of Asklepios, the god of healing. The area is near vineyards and age-old olive groves with mountains in the distance. On a hillside, within the sanctuary, lies the theater of Epidaurus (third century B.C.). It is the most famous and best preserved of all the ancient theaters in Greece. It is built of limestone and can seat twelve thousand spectators. Each summer it offers ancient drama. The acoustics are so good that the merest whisper can be heard in the last row.

Olympia was the site of the first Games, which started in 776 B.C. and continued every four years for a thousand years. The Olympic Games were revived in 1896 by the French historian and educator Pier de Coubertin. Since then, every four years a torch bearer, like the ancient heralds, starts out from Olympia bearing the sacred flame to the place where the Games are held. Near the ancient site the modern village of Olympia has a Museum of the Olympic Games.

Thessaloniki (Salonika) and the North

Thessaloniki is the second largest city in Greece and historically the crossroads of international trade. The old Byzantine city walls still dominate part of the town. Thessaloniki has a number of outstanding Byzantine churches, some with important mosaics. The area also reflects other conquerors, such as the Romans and the Ottomans. The region of northern Greece (Macedonia) has numerous beaches, beautiful villages (some with beaches), and a rugged terrain. Athos, southeast of Thessaloniki, is one of the most beautiful places in Greece. It is the home of many monasteries interspersed among the rocky paths, scrubs, and trees of Mt. Athos. Northeast of Thessaloniki is the beautiful beach town of Kavalla.

The Greek Islands

The Greek Islands have become the playground of the rich and famous. Names such as Corfu, Rhodes, Crete, Mykonos, Naxos, Santorini, and Ithaka have become highly recognized and associated with outstanding Mediterranean islands. These are part of four major island groups: the Sporades, Cyclades, Dodecanese, and Ionian islands. Crete is the largest and most visited of all the islands. It is distinguished by its ruins of the Minoan civilization. It is the fourth-largest island in size in the Mediterranean, following Sicily, Sardinia, and Cyprus. Because of its size, it offers a variety of settings, from mountains capped with snow to palm-lined beaches, caves, and coves. The Minoan ruins are most impressive at the Palace of Knossos.

Located off the west coast of Greece, the Ionian Islands include Corfu, which is probably the most popular of this group. Corfu has lush vegetation, hotels, and beautiful beaches. Other islands in this group are Paxos, Ithaka (an impressive mountainous island with ports, coves, and caves), Sami, and Zakynthos (Figure 23.6) ("the Venice" of the Ionian Sea). Southeast in the Cyclades are Mykonos, with its dazzling white buildings; Santorini (Figure 23.7), with its volcanic remnant landscape; Rhodes, with its walled medieval city built by the Knights of Saint John; Syros, a center of Catholicism in Greece; and Paros, with its whitewashed houses and bougainvillaea draped from balconies and staircases.

Figure 23.6 Blue caves on Zakynthos Island, Greece. © Andrei Pop/www.Shutterstock.com.

Figure 23.7 Santorini Island, Greece. © leoks/www.Shutterstock.com.

In the Sporades Islands, Samos features the three wonders of the ancient world—the harbor mole, the kilometer-long tunnel of Eupalinos cut through Astypalala for a water supply when under siege, and the Temple of Hera. Other islands in this group are Chios, which is reported to contain the hometown of Homer, and Lesvos.

The Dodecanese, like part of the Sporades, closely follow the Turkish coastline. One of the most famous islands for tourism in this group is Patmos, which is a holy island for Christians as it is reputed to be the island where St. John wrote the Book of Revelations and received his vision of the Apocalypse. Other attractive islands are Le'ros, Kalymnos, Kos, and Rhodes. Rhodes was the home for a time of the Knights of St. John, who created a walled, medieval town around the harbor.

Cyprus

Introduction

The third largest island in the Mediterranean, Cyprus is culturally European but with Asian and African influences. The two major Cypriot communities consist of Greek Cypriots, with an estimated 78 percent of the population, and Turkish Cypriots, with 18 percent.

Cyprus won its independence from Britain in 1960, but it has been divided since 1974, when Turkish troops invaded to protect Turkish Cypriots and stop Greek military plans for enosis—a union of Cyprus with Greece. Turkish troops occupied the northern third of the island; Greek Cypriots fled south, while Turkish Cypriots moved north into the occupied area. The UN-monitored cease-fire line, known as the "Green Line," separates the government-controlled area from Northern Cyprus. The capital, Nicosia, is the only divided capital in Europe. Cyprus joined the European Union in 2004, but EU laws apply only to the government-controlled area, pending reunification.

From *National Geographic Atlas of the World*, 9th edition. Copyright ©2011 National Geographic Society. Reprinted by arrangement. All rights reserved.

Area	9,251 sq km (3,572 sq mi)
Population	1,072,000
Government	republic
Capital	Nicosia 233,000
Life Expectancy	78 years
Religion	Greek Orthodox, Muslim
Language	Greek, Turkish, English
Currency	euro (EUR)
GDP per Cap	$21,200
Labor Force	8.5% Agriculture, 20.5% Industry, 71% Services

From *National Geographic Atlas of the World*, 9th edition. Copyright ©2011 National Geographic Society. Reprinted by arrangement. All rights reserved.

TRAVEL**TIPS**

Entry: A visa is issued upon arrival for stays up to three months. Passports are required.

Peak Tourist Season: May through September

National Holiday: October 1 (Independence Day)

Shopping: Common items include silver work, leather goods, and handmade lace.

Internet TLD: .cy

CULTURAL CAPSULE The majority of the people (called Cypriots) are divided between Greek (78 percent) and Turkish (18 percent). The language and religion of Cyprus follows this division: Greek and Turkish for language; and Greek Orthodox and Muslim the dominant religions in the same percentages as ethnic divisions. In 1974 hostilities divided the island into two de facto autonomous areas—a Greek area controlled by the Cypriot government (60 percent of the island's land area) and a Turkish-Cypriot area (35 percent of the island's land area). The two are separated by a narrow buffer zone controlled by the United Nations.

Tourist Characteristics

The conflict between the two major ethnic groups, Greeks and Turks, combined with the problems in the Middle East seriously affect tourism to Cyprus. Most visitors are from Europe (91 percent) and the Middle East (5 percent). The political division still exists, and tourism has experienced little growth over the years, with 2 million visitors in 2010. Travel is complicated by the fact that visitors who arrive in areas controlled by the Turkish Cypriots are not permitted to visit the Republic of Cyprus (Greek Cypriot control).

Figure 23.8 Bellapais Abbey Monastery in Kyrenia. © Grauvision/www.Shutterstock.com.

Tourist Destinations and Attractions

The major tourist destinations and attractions are historical and archaeological, with sites from the Neolithic, Hellenic, Macedonian, Roman, Crusader, and Ottoman periods. This illustrates the crossroads nature of the island in the eastern Mediterranean. It is a major cruise stop at the ports of Limassol and Larnaca. The major sites are Nicosia, with its Venetian walls ringing the old town; Kyrenia (Figure 23,8), with its Crusader Castle; Famagusta, with its walled Turkish quarter; and the Monastery of Stavrovouni at Larnaca. The island is popular for both water and snow skiing.

Italy

Introduction

Italy is famous for its mountainous, bootlike peninsula that extends into the Mediterranean Sea; the country also includes the islands of Sicily, Sardinia, and about 70 other smaller islands. The Alps form Italy's northern border with France, Switzerland, Austria, and Slovenia. Most of Italy has warm, dry summers and mild winters, with northern Italy experiencing colder, wetter winters. There are some notable active volcanoes, such as Vesuvius (near Naples) and Etna (on Sicily). Italy is overwhelmingly Italian. However, there are ethnic Germans in the Trentino–Alto Adige region and ethnic French in the Valle d'Aosta region. Immigration is a major national concern, and more than 4 million immigrants

are in Italy. Most immigrants come from eastern Europe (Romania, Albania) and Africa (Morocco). Italy is a prime arrival point for illegal immigrants from Africa, most coming by boat via Libya. Although decades of struggle unified Italy in 1871, two Italys exist today: the prosperous industrialized north and the less developed agricultural south, known as the Mezzogiorno ("Land of the Midday Sun"). The north is dominated by large commercial cities. Milan reigns as Italy's first city of commerce, and the Po River plain is both Italy's agricultural heartland and southern Europe's most advanced industrial region. Turin, the capital of heavy industry, is home to Fiat—one of the world's largest carmakers.

Italy imports almost all its raw materials and energy, and the country's economic strength is in the processing and manufacturing of goods, primarily in small and medium-size family-owned firms.

Area	301,340 sq km (116,348 sq mi)
Population	60,274,000
GOVERNMENT	republic
Capital	Rome 3,339,000
Life Expectancy	82 years
Religion	Roman Catholic
Language	Italian, German, French, Slovene
Currency	euro (EUR)
GDP per Cap	$30,300
Labor Force	4.2% Agriculture, 30.7% Industry, 65.1% Service

TRAVEL**TIPS**

Entry: Visas are not required for visits up to three months. Passports are required.

Peak Tourist Seasons: June, July, August, and September. Compounded by nearly 40 percent of Italians taking their vacations in July and August

National Holiday: April 25 (Liberation Day)

Shopping: Common items include cameos, glass objects, Pinocchio dolls, embroidered tablecloths, mosaic jewelry, alabaster statues, fruit, leather, shoes, knitwear, and antiques.

Internet TLD: .it

 While Italy is generally ethnic Italian, there is great cultural, culinary, economic, and political diversity in the country. Some minority groups are French, German, Slovenes, and Albanians, all of which are expressed in the languages in the various regions of these minorities. Nearly all Italians are nominally Roman Catholic.

Cultural hints: Italians often touch one another when conversing: physical contact is common. Dress modestly when visiting churches. Women cover their heads and do not wear shorts or sleeveless blouses.

Do not start to eat before host. Meals are a time to visit. Keep hands above the table, not in lap. Do not leave the table until all have finished. Service charge is often in the bill, but a small tip is still appropriate. Restaurants in which clients stand are less expensive than those in which they are seated. Typical foods include pasta, cheese, fish, meat (particularly veal), and vegetables. Salad dressing is oil and vinegar, without spices. Pizza. Pasta is served by itself and meat follows later.

Tourism Characteristics

Tourism is extremely important to Italy's economy. Tourism is a ministry-level responsibility in Italy under the Ministry of Tourism, with each of the twenty-one tourist regions having a tourist board. Each province within a region has a provincial tourist office. The Entre Nazionale Turismo Italiano (ENTI) under the Ministry of Tourism is responsible for promoting tourism abroad. The Ministry of Tourism has the overall political responsibility for tourism through promotion and development strategy. The ministry is responsible for licensing, training, and investment subsidies. The ministry is concerned with negative factors, such as terrorist incidents, public order, and disruptions in the transportation sectors. Italy is concerned with competition from Spain, Portugal, France, and Croatia for the mass budget-minded, sun-sea-sand markets of Northern Europe, especially since Italy has become more expensive. Italy has a long history of tourism, from the Renaissance to the eighteenth century when it was the major destination of the "Grand Tour" taken by the wealthy and nobility of Europe, to the mass tourism of the present.

With its diversity of attractions, Italy is one of the world's leading tourist destinations, ranking fourth in total visitors (43 million). Passage through Italy to ferry ports in southern Italy are very popular for Europeans and other international visitors to Europe. Italy's market is becoming more diverse because more visitor arrive each year from counties outside Europe. This is illustrated by the fact that Japan and China are now major markets for visitors to Italy. Germany, France, and Austria are the three largest markets. The large German market is illustrative of the transit nature of tourism in that many used to be on their way to Croatia and Slovenia, which received a larger number of visitors from Germany than did Italy.

Forty-five percent of all international visitors to Italy were attracted by artistic/historical attractions (Figure 23.9), the climate (43 percent), natural environment (26 percent), or visiting friends and relatives (9 percent). Thirty-two percent indicated a combination of events. The Vatican is a major attraction. Many visitors, whether Catholic or not, combine visiting the historical attractions and the Vatican. Visits to friends and relatives by tourists from the United States are declining as the population of the United States ages and there is less direct connectivity to Italy by United States citizens.

Tourism is highly seasonal, with a summer peak. July and August account for nearly 34 percent of all visitors,

Figure 23.9 The Coliseum, Rome, Italy. © JPF/www.Shutterstock.com.

while May and June account for an additional 22 percent of visitors. The distribution of tourists is concentrated in the northern region of Italy. Mountain resorts account for 19 percent of all tourist arrivals. Tourism in Italy is highly regional, with approximately 60 percent of all international visitors visiting northern locations where most of the cultural attractions and some of the best beaches are located. Fine beaches can also be found in the south and on the islands of Sicily, Sardinia, Calabria, Puglia, and Salento. A major concern of the Italian government is the development of southern Italy (called the **Mezzogiorno**). Because of its poor economy and the potential of tourism to help solve the economic problems of the South, the Mezzogiorno is the focus of tourism development attempts. In 2010, the travel regions south

of Naples received only 9 percent of the total visitors, and one region—Puglia, in which the tourists catch ferries to Greece—accounted for 25 percent of these. Because of its distance from the main European markets, the South must depend upon air-inclusive tour traffic, which puts it in competition with Spain, Greece, and North Africa.

The impact of tourism has reached such a level that there is concern over the quality of life for the residents as well as the ecosystem. UNESCO has funded a study of a number of art cities of Europe, trying to assess the impact of visitors and establish measures to negate the negative consequences. Venice plans to be the first city to limit the number of visitors to the number of bed spaces plus a set number of day visitors. Some days Venice has in excess of fifty thousand day visitors in the city.

Tourist Destinations and Attractions

The Southern Alps and Lake Country

As in Switzerland and Austria, the glaciated lakes, such as Maggiore, Como, Garda, and the high mountain Alps, provide scenic winter and summer resorts. The site of the 1956 Winter Olympics held at Cortina d'Ampezzo is the centerpiece of winter sports in the Dolomites, providing gentle beginning slopes to spectacular runs and late-season skiing, some years into late June or early July. The lake district is full of beautiful lakes with blue waters at the foot of high scenic mountains. The district centers on Maggiore, the most famous lake, with its luxuriant vegetation, much of which is tropical, and sometimes rugged shores. Italy shares Lake Maggiore with Switzerland. The Lake District has a mild climate resulting from its location on the southern side of the Alps, which block the cold winds from the north.

In the northwest corner of Italy the Aosta Valley is a land of great natural beauty with medieval villages and views of some of Europe's highest mountains, Mont Blanc (Monte Bianco) and Monte Rosa. Like the rest of northern Italy, the region has some excellent winter sports resorts with fine skiing. Remains of the Roman Age can be seen along the road from Ivrea to the Piccolo San Bernardo and in Aosta itself. Gothic influence is visible in buildings in Aosta and in the romantic castles of Fènis, Issogne, and Verrès.

Some important tourist cities are Turin, a major industrial center, noted for its cars (Fiat) and computers, featuring several museums and the cathedral in the Piazza San Giovanni, which houses a relic of the Holy Shroud. The city's highest tower is the Mole Antonelliana, which houses a film museum. Turin hosted the winter Olympics in 2006. Milan, another major industrial city and a fine art city centered on the Piazza del Duomo with its great Gothic cathedral, is the second largest church building in Italy, the home of one of the most famous opera houses in the world, La Scala, and many important artworks such as da Vinci's *Last Supper* and Michelangelo's *Pieta*. Bolzano, the capital of Alto Adige, was once the South Tyrol of Austria and is German in character still today.

Italy's Coastal Environment (including the Riviera)

Having five thousand miles of coastline, Italy offers not only excellent beaches, but hilltop villages, white rock stairways, fishermen's villages, reefs, island-rocks, high cliffs over transparent water, and a host of cultural and archaeological sites both along and within easy distance of the coastal areas.

Stretching from the French border to Tuscany is the Italian Riviera. The mild climate has given it a lengthy beach season, which, in turn, extends the tourist season. The area has numerous pocket beaches of sand and rock, woods, prehistoric grottoes, romantic villages and hamlets, plus larger towns and cities with olive-, palm-, and magnolia-lined boulevards. The most famous resort is San Remo, with its casino and funicular railway to the top of Mount Bignone. The capital of the Italian Riviera is Genoa, a busy seaport and birthplace of Christopher Columbus, with an interesting section of medieval churches and houses. Another very important attraction along the Italian Riviera is "Cinque Terre" (Figure 23.10),

Figure 23.10 Village of Manarola on the Cinque Terre coast of Italy. © JeniFoto/www.Shutterstock.com.

Figure 23.11 Grand Canal and Basilica Santa Maria della Salute, Venice, Italy. © Iakov Kalinin/www.Shutterstock.com.

a series of towns situated high on cliffs overlooking the Mediterranean Sea. All along the coast from the Riviera to Sicily are expanses of coast beaches and scenic beauty. A variety of resorts on the Adriatic coast take advantage of the long, sandy beaches and clear water of the sea. On the Adriatic coast the major attraction is the Riviera Romagnola known for its theme parks, water parks, and other forms of family entertainment.

The Cities in Central Italy from Venice to Ancona and Tuscany

Venice (Figure 23.11) is built on over 115 islands separated by 177 canals but connected by 400 bridges, gondolas, and a style of living unlike any city in the world. The Rialto Bridge, Piazza San Marco, the Basilica of San Marco, the Bridge of Sighs, and Doges palaces are household names that remind visitors of Venice. A number of islands are easily reached from Venice. They include the Lido, with its fashionable seaside resorts; Murano, famed for glassblowing and shaping; and Burano, where lace is made.

Florence, the capital of Tuscany, is the center of the art world and was the focal city of the Renaissance. Florence was at one time called the City of the Medici and is the city of Michelangelo, whose famous statue of David is in the Academia of Florence. Much of the art can be seen in the Uffizi Palace, the Piazza della Signoria, the Bargello Museum, the Palazzo Pitti, and the Academia. The center of Florence is the Piazza del Duomo, with its thirteenth-century Baptistery of San Giovanni and Ghiberti's famous bronze doors. The Cathedral of Santa Maria del Fiore in Florence is one of the largest churches in the world. The thirteenth-century Church of Santa Croce is the burial place of both Michelangelo and Machiavelli. High on a hill above the Pitti Palace is the Piazzale Michelangelo, with a much-photographed view of Florence. Florence is noted for its leather goods and market, some of which is on Ponte Vecchio over the Arno River.

A vibrant historical mosaic in Italy

At first glance, there hardly seems to be any comparison between Ravenna and Rome: Ravenna is smaller, sleepier, and without Rome's domed skyline or ruins. But back in the fifth century, it was Ravenna that served as capital of the Western Roman Empire. In this burgeoning city, Roman rulers built monuments celebrating both Christianity and their own power—monuments famous, then and now, for their sweeping mosaics.

Seven of Ravenna's eight buildings from the fifth and sixth centuries are spectacularly decorated with examples of this ancient art. "In the past, many people couldn't read or write," says tour guide and Ravenna native Silvia Giogoli. "Mosaics were a way to explain the religion, and the political situation, to the people."

At the Basilica of San Vitale, a bejeweled Empress Theodora stares across the apse at her husband, Justinian. At Sant'Apollinare Nuovo, two rows of larger-than-life saints march toward the apse. But in Ravenna, mosaics aren't just historical remnants. Visitors admire pieces by contemporary mosaicists including Chagall, Mathieu, and Vedova at the MAR (Museo d'Arte Ravenna) or poke into cluttered bottegas (workshops) where modern artists use the same methods as their Byzantine forebears. At the Parco della Pace, locals relax beside mosaic sculptures; even the city's street signs glitter with glass fragments. At the 2013 Ravenna Mosaico, mosaic mania takes hold. Visitors can gawk at new pieces, listen to musicians, and learn to make their own masterpieces.

— **Amanda Ruggeri,** *National Geographic Traveler,* December 2012/January 2013

In addition to these two gems, there are a host of villages and towns that fascinate visitors (Figure 23.12). Verona, with its rose-red brick architecture, was Romeo and Juliet's city; Ravenna is famous for its fine mosaics; Vicenza for its palladian architecture; Siena is a walled town; and Pisa with its leaning tower, are only a few.

Rome and the Vatican

The Vatican, a separate political entity, is the center of the Roman Catholic Church. St. Peter's Basilica and St. Peter's Square are the heart of pilgrimages to the Holy City. The Vatican City occupies an area of 109 acres situated entirely within the city of Rome. In addition to St. Peter's Basilica and the Vatican Apostolic Palace, its museums, archives, and library, the Vatican City consists of a number of administrative and ecclesiastical buildings, a village of apartments, and the Vatican Gardens. Its population is about one thousand. The cathedral dome and the youthful "pieta" were designed and sculptured by Michelangelo. The canopy of the main altar and St. Peter's Square were designed by Bernini. In addition to housing one of the great museums of the world, the Vatican is the location of the Sistine Chapel. Its fresco ceiling was done by Michelangelo. Apart from the Vatican, a visitor can keep busy in Rome. Ancient Rome is evident in the Colosseum, the Forum, the Pantheon, the Palatine Hill, the Via Appia Antica, the Roman baths, and the Castel Sant' Angelo, which dominates the Tiber River. Relics of early Christianity can be seen in the Catacombs, an underground burial place for early Christians. Other popular attractions include the Spanish Steps, the Villa Borghese, the Trevi Fountain, and the Palazzo Venezia, which was the official home of Mussolini. Other important and interesting churches are the Santa Maria Maggiore, St. John Lateran, St. Paul Outside the Walls, and St. Peter in Chains.

Near Rome, Tivoli is a small town on the Aniene River that is well known for its wine, villas with their cascades and beautiful gardens, and Lido di Roma, a fashionable resort.

Figure 23.12 San Quirico d´Orcia, Tuscany, Italy. © Luboslav Tiles/www.Shutterstock.com.

Naples and Surrounding Area

Naples and many of the ancient cities in the region, such as Pompeii and Herculaneum, were resort towns for ancient Rome, built in the shadow of Mount Vesuvius. The eruption of Vesuvius in 76 A.D. buried both Pompeii and Herculaneum, and the excavated cities are excellent historical sites detailing life during the Roman era. Naples is a city built around a lovely bay that is bounded by Vesuvius, the Sorrento Peninsula, and islands just beyond the harbor. The Mediterranean is best enjoyed from Capri and Ischia, little islands off the coast of Naples. Capri's most famous natural wonder is the Blue Grotto. The crowded streets of Naples are alive with vendors, festivals, refreshment kiosks, and friendly people.

The Sorrento Peninsula, with its colorful villas, scenic villages, shops, and views of the sea, is best observed along the Amalfi Drive. North of Naples in Caserta, the remarkable palace of Charles III rivals Versailles in size and splendor. Further south of Pompeii are the remains of an extremely well-preserved Greek Temple of Poseidon and a beautiful example of Doric architecture at Paestum.

Sicily

Sicily has a tremendous potential for tourism. The island has beautiful beaches with clear and transparent water. Palermo, the largest city, has a fine Greek temple, and there are a number of Greek ruins, such as an amphitheater at the Greek City of Syracuse. Taormina has a rugged picturesque setting, including a fine view of Mount Etna and access by bus to fine beaches. In addition to the Greek temples throughout Sicily, there is architectural evidence of Roman, Norman, Moorish, and Arabian influence.

Sardinia

Sardinia, the second-largest island in the Mediterranean, is the popular luxury resort of the Aga Khan, who built Costa Smerelda. Sardinia is rugged, with mountain ranges extending to six thousand feet in elevation. It has beautiful scenery, excellent beaches, and many historic attractions from the Phoenicians and Romans.

San Marino

San Marino, the world's smallest republic, is in the Apennine Mountains. It is about one-third the size of Washington, D.C. Located in the north-central area of Italy near the east coast, it has few visitors as its tourism facilities are limited. About 2 million tourists visit San Marino each year, attracted by its medieval fortresses and panoramic views. It is only accessible by highway. Most visitors are day visitors. Its language is Italian, and its currency is the Euro.

Spain

Introduction

Spain occupies most of the Iberian Peninsula in Mediterranean, the Canary Islands in the Atlantic, and two enclaves on the North Africa coast, Ceuta and Melilla, which border Morocco. Much of the mainland is high plateau, with mountain ranges, including the Pyrenees, in the north. The plateau experiences hot summers and cold winters—it is cooler and wetter to the north.

The national language is Castilian (usually known as Spanish), but it is not the only language in Spain. Catalan, used by 17 percent of Spaniards, functions as an official language in Catalonia, Valencia, and the Balearic Islands. Gallego (Galician) is an official language in Galicia, and Euskera (Basque) is official in the Basque provinces. Millions of immigrants from Latin America and Eastern Europe add to the country's language diversity. Spain has been a crossroads between continents for centuries. Moors invaded in A.D. 711 and were finally ousted by Christian armies in 1492. Enriched by its New World empire, Spain dominated Europe during the sixteenth century but was in decline by the eighteenth century. General Francisco Franco wielded power from 1936 until his death in 1975, when Juan Carlos became king. Three years later a new constitution confirmed Spain as a parliamentary monarchy, and it joined the EU in 1986. Pro-business policies in the 1990s were blamed for widening the gap between rich and poor and for the bankruptcy of noncompetitive industries—all contributing to high unemployment. Separatist agitation born of historical regional differences, most pronounced in the Basque provinces and in Catalonia, still challenges national unity.

Area	505,988 sq km (195,363 sq mi)
Population	46,916,000
Government	parliamentary monarchy
Capital	Madrid 5,567,000
Life Expectancy	81 years
Religion	Roman Catholic
Language	Castilian Spanish, Catalan, Galician, Basque
Currency	euro (EUR)
GDP per Cap	$33,700
Labor Force	4.2% Agriculture, 24% Industry, 71.7% Services

From *National Geographic Atlas of the World*, 9th edition. Copyright ©2011 National Geographic Society. Reprinted by arrangement. All rights reserved.

TRAVEL **TIPS** 💼

Entry: Visas are not required for stays up to three months. Passports are required.

Peak Tourist Seasons: July, August, and September

National Holiday: October 12 (Columbus Day)

Shopping: Common items include leather, ceramics, glassware, lace, embroideries, inlaid gold metalwork, pearls, wrought iron, and guitars.

Internet TLD: .es

CULTURAL CAPSULE Spanish people are a mixture of Mediterranean and Nordic ancestry and are considered a homogeneous ethnic group, although the Basques disagree. There are four official languages in Spain. Castilian is the main language of business and government. The other three are Catalan (17 percent), Galician (7 percent), and Basque (2 percent). English is common in the tourist centers. While there is no official religion, more than 90 percent of the people belong to the Roman Catholic Church.

Cultural hints: Business cards are commonly exchanged. Eye contact is important, but women should be careful in doing so. Do not put your hands in your pockets when talking. When finished eating, place the knife and fork parallel across the plate. Do not eat while walking in the streets. The service charge is generally in the bill. Tip a small amount also. Typical food includes meat, eggs, chicken, fish, fresh vegetables, potatoes, onions, pork sausages, lamb stew, roasted meats, cold vegetable soup (gazpachos), and rice. Churros, a batter made of flour and butter, deep-fried and sprinkled with sugar, are sold throughout the cities. Paella is the country's national dish.

Tourism Characteristics

Spain has become one of the largest destination countries for international tourists in Southern Europe. Along with France and the United States it is one of the world's leaders in visitors, ranking fourth in total tourism receipts. Most of its importance as a destination for tourists has developed since the end of World War II. Tourism is the most important single element in the Spanish economy, accounting for the highest percentage of export trade in any European country. The character of tourism emphasizes low-priced package tourism oriented towards the coastal areas and the Balearic Islands. In addition, Spain

has a large number of visitors that stay less than 24 hours. These short-stay visitors come mostly from France and Portugal and are not included in the 52 million total foreign tourists Spain receives annually.

Europe is the most important market region, accounting for 90 percent of Spain's total visitors. The United Kingdom and Germany lead in total visitors in hotels. French and Portuguese travelers also generate large total numbers of visitors, but they are short term. France and Portugal account for some 40 percent of the total visitors, but only 10 percent of the bed nights. This indicates the imbalance in the number of visitors and the number of bed nights spent in Spain. Tourism from the United States and Canada accounts for just over 3 percent of all visitors, again indicating the dominance of Europe as the major market.

Tourism to Spain is both highly seasonal and geographically concentrated. The peak season is the summer from June to September, with August being the largest tourism month. Summer tourism is compounded by Spanish holidays in August, when the Spanish move from the hot interior of Madrid and other major cities to the coasts. This high level of seasonality creates serious problems in labor and hotel usage. On the Balearic Islands, the industry has tried to adjust to this problem by closing some hotels and emphasizing a few large hotels in each complex during the off-season. They have developed a program of unemployment compensation that provides for payments to workers during the off-season.

There is a heavy regional concentration, with the Balearic Islands and the Costa Brava (north of Barcelona) having the largest number of visitors. The Costa Blanca, centered on Alicante, and Costa del Sol, between Algeciras and Malaga, are the second ranking destinations. Saturation of the coastal areas creates a distinctive cycle of bustling summer seasons versus the high vacancy rates in the winter months.

Although it is handicapped by its interior location, the area around Madrid is the major interior location for international tourists.

Tourist Destinations and Attractions

Destination regions in Spain can be divided as follows.

Balearic Islands

The Balearic Islands—Majorca, Minorca, Ibiza, and Formentera—are best known for their sun-sea-sand and mass tourism. There are some outstanding cathedrals and fortresses, which provide a diversion from the beaches. Throughout the islands, there are traces of prehistoric, Greek, Roman, Punic, and Arab civilizations.

The Costa Brava and Barcelona

North of Barcelona along a coastline of cliffs and pines are secluded coves, wide sandy beaches, and picturesque seaside villages. South of Barcelona are a number

Figure 23.13 Park Guell, Barcelona, Spain. © Luciano Mortula/www.Shutterstock.com.

of seaside resorts, such as Stiges and the ancient town of Tarragona, with its Roman, Visigoth, Moorish, and medieval ruins.

Near Barcelona, Montserrat and the Benedictine Monastery sit high in the mountains in a spectacular setting. Barcelona itself (Figure 23.13) is a sophisticated city with many cultural and architectural treasures. It is the largest and busiest port in Spain. It was the home of the 1992 Summer Olympics and from where Columbus set sail for America. Located near the Ramblas (the principal pedestrian street), the Gothic Quarter features a series of beautiful restored medieval structures and a cathedral dating from the twelfth century. Throughout the city, there are interesting churches. The unfinished but original Church of the Sagrada Familia by Antonio Gaudi and the oldest church (the Church of San Pablo del Campo) are quite interesting. Museums include the Catalan National Art Museum and the Picasso Museum. Pueblo Espanol, a Spanish village built for the Exposition of 1929, depicts architectural styles and workmanship from the various regions of Spain at that time.

Costa Blanca and Valencia

The Costa Blanca, which extends north and south of Alicante, was at one time a series of coastal fishing villages. They were "discovered" by tourists from Northern and Western Europe and have become large tourist developments, focusing on wide sandy beaches and the warm waters of the Mediterranean. Valencia is a port city that provides ferry access to the Balearic Islands. Valencia is set in a rich agricultural area with gardens of lemon, almond, olive, pomegranate, palm, and orange trees. The city has many fine ancient mansions and gardens and a number of museums.

Andalusia

Andalusia (the south of Spain where Moorish influence is still visible) and the Costa del Sol are often pictured on travel posters and brochures of Spain. The combination of whitewashed houses with red-tiled roofs and the Moorish architecture reflecting the Islamic culture makes this area unique. In the coastal area from Malaga to Algeciras, near the Rock

Figure 23.14 Bath in Alcazar, Seville, Spain. © javarman/www.Shutterstock.com.

of Gibraltar, the small coastal villages have been over-whelmed with tourist developments. The region offers splendid beaches, mild climates, and a host of cities and towns in Andalusia to visit. In Malaga, there is a Renaissance cathedral and a Moorish Alcazaba. Throughout Andalusia, there are fine examples of Moorish culture. The city of Granada is replete with Moorish architecture, the most famous of which is the Alhambra Palace with its stunning towers, halls, fountains, courtyards, gardens, mazes, and gold mosaics. Below the hill on which the Alhambra is located are gypsy caves and a cathedral where King Ferdinand and Queen Isabella are buried.

Northwest of Granada, Cordoba has more ruins from the Moorish period. The **Mosque** at Cordoba (La Mezquita) is considered by many to be the greatest surviving example of Moorish architecture. The third major city in Andalusia affected by the **Moors** is Seville, the unofficial capital of Andalusia. The Moors were a combination of tribes (Arabs, Berbers, Syrians, etc.) from North Africa united by Islam and the Arabic language. Seville was under Roman, Visigoth, and Moorish rule, all of which left their mark. The Cathedral of Seville is one of the most beautiful Gothic cathedrals in Spain. The Moorish Christian Alcazar (Figure 23.14) also adds to the beauty of the city. The Giralda Tower is one of three original Moorish towers that is still erect. The Santa Cruz quarter with its twisting byways, dignified old houses, and flagstoned patios and the Tower of Gold are but two of the many attractions this fine city offers. One of the most celebrated **Holy Week** festivals takes place in Seville. The mountains in Andalusia provide some outstanding attractions. Two of the most famous are Jerez de la Frontera (sherry country) and Ronda, one of the oldest towns and bullrings in Spain. It has an outstanding Roman bridge spanning a deep, rocky cleft. The movie *Lawrence of Arabia* was filmed in Almeria, in southeast Spain.

Madrid and Central Spain

Madrid (Figure 23.15), the capital and cultural center of Spain, has one of the world's great museums, the Prado. The works of El Greco, Velasquez, Goya, and other Spanish masters are found here. The Royal Palace (Figure 23.15) is one of the most beautiful palaces of Europe with Flemish tapestries, porcelain furniture, fifteenth- to eighteenth-century armor, Goya portraits, and an outstanding and attractive garden. Madrid's cathedral was built in the seventeenth century and is a blend of Gothic and Renaissance styles. Madrid is the home of the United Nations World Tourism Organization.

Figure 23.15 Royal Palace Fountain, Madrid. © Josie Elias/Getty Images.

A number of interesting and important towns, cities, and countrysides lie within a day's travel from Madrid. Probably the most famous is Toledo, the religious center of Spain. Toledo has outstanding churches, such as its thirteenth-century Spanish Gothic cathedral, the Church of Cristo de la Luz, which was a tiny mosque in the tenth century, and two former synagogues of the city, Santa Maria and El Tránsito. Toledo was the home of El Greco. His most famous paintings and his restored house can be seen here. The most visual feature of the landscape is the fortress that was rebuilt following the civil war of the 1930s. The scenic landscape with windmills on hilltops that was made famous in the book about Don Quixote is near Toledo.

North of Madrid, the Romanesque city of Segovia has impressive ruins and one of the most beautiful castles in Spain, and Avila, a medieval walled city. Close to Madrid are El Escorial, a huge monastery-palace and burial place for the kings of Spain; the Palace of Aranjuez, inspired by Versailles and the Trianons; and the Valley of the Fallen, a burial place and monument to the former Spanish dictator Franco and the civil war heroes of Spain.

Northern Spain

Santiago de Compostela, one of the major pilgrimage cities of Europe, and the famous government hotel, Hostal de las Reyes Catolicos, one of the most magnificent hotels in Spain and a showcase in itself, are in the Northwest. On the Asturian coast, visitors can tour the city of Santander and see the world-famous 13,000-year-old Altamire cave paintings. (A replica of the caves is located at the national museum in Madrid.) Northern Spain has one of Spain's busiest coasts because of its close proximity to France, the resort town of San Sebastian, and the port city of Bilbao with the spectacular Guggenheim Museum Bilbao. An hour south of San Sebastian is Pamplona, which is famous for its once-a-year festival of the running of the bulls July 6 through 15. Ernest Hemingway was enamored with Spain and its culture. He spent considerable time in Spain and wrote part of his *For Whom the Bell Tolls* at the Casa Botin, an old restaurant in Madrid, first opened in 1725. Both Hemingway and Orson Welles watched a few bullfights in Ronda. Welles's ashes were scattered in Ronda after his death.

Canary Islands

Off the coast of Morocco and about 650 miles south of Spain are the volcanic Canary Islands. Las Palmas on Grand Canary Island and Santa Cruz de Tenerife are the two most frequented locales. The Canaries have been "discovered" by the large tour operators of Germany and Great Britain and have become a highly commercialized sun-sea-sand vacation destination.

Gibraltar

Introduction

The peninsula that is Gibraltar is in southwest Europe on the southern coast of Spain. British control dates to 1704, though Spain still claims the territory. Tourism is growing, with some 8 million visitors a year.

Area	6.5 sq km (2.5 sq mi)
Population	30,000
Capital	Gibraltar 30,000
Religion	Roman Catholic, Church of England, Muslim
Language	English, Spanish, Italian, Portuguese
Internet TLD	.gi

Tourism Characteristics

Gibraltar, famous as "the Rock," has been under control of the British for many years and is a political issue for the Spanish. For many years, the border between Gibraltar and Spain was closed. In order to visit from Spain,

Figure 23.16 The Rock of Gibraltar, as seen from the beach of La Linea, Spain. © Philip Lange/www.Shutterstock.com.

tourists had to travel to Morocco and then return to Gibraltar or vice versa. The border with Spain is now open. Gibraltar received 11 million visitors in 2011, mostly day trippers from neighboring Spain. The major attraction is "the rock" (Figure 23.16), which can be ascended by cable car to see the Barbary apes. It has good beaches, water sports, duty-free shopping, a Moorish castle, and St. Michael's Cave, prominent for military defense, overlooking the Strait of Gibraltar.

Andorra

Introduction

The Pyrenees mountains provide Andorra with ski resorts, tourism, and the highest capital city in Europe—Andorra la Vella. According to legend, Charlemagne founded Andorra in the year 805, because the people of these mountain valleys fought against the Saracens. The country continues a feudal tradition, with the Bishop of La Seu d'Urgell (a nearby town in Spain) and the President of France being co-princes, but today Andorra is governed by a constitution, ratified in 1993, and elected officials.

Area	468 sq km (181 sq mi)
Population	86,000
Government	parliamentary democracy
Capital	Andorra la Vella 24,000
Life Expectancy	83 years
Religion	Roman Catholic
Language	Catalan, French, Castilian, Portuguese
Currency	euro (EUR)

GDP per Cap	$44,900
Labor Force	0.5% Agriculture, 18.5% Industry, 81% Services
Internet TLD	.ad

Cultural Characteristics

The population is concentrated in the seven urbanized valleys that form Andorra's political district. Andorran citizens are a minority, outnumbered three to one by Spanish residents. The national language is Catalan and is spoken by more than 6 million people in the region comprising French and Spanish Catalonia. Andorra has the longest life expectancy of any country in the world.

Tourism Characteristics

Andorra is high in the Pyrenees on the Spanish and French border. Andorra's major attraction is its location and the lowest-cost, duty-free shopping in Europe, which attracts visitors from adjacent Spain and France. Attractions and duty-free shopping in Andorra result in nearly 3 million overnight visitors and more than 6 million day visitors a year. Andorra's setting in the mountains is outstanding, and attractions such as lakes, hiking, camping, and skiing are available. It has resorts such as Pas de la Cosa and Envalira, which are good winter sports areas.

Portugal

Introduction

Portugal, with its long Atlantic coast, lies on the western edge of the Iberian Peninsula in southwestern Europe—the most westerly country on the European mainland. The land consists of highland forests in the north and rolling lowland in the south. It tends to be wetter and cooler in the north. The south can be hot and parched, and it is dotted with reservoirs to conserve water. The Azores and the Madeira Islands are part of Portugal. Most Portuguese live along the coast, with a third of the population living in the urban areas of Lisbon and Porto. There are some small minority groups, mostly coming from countries that were once part of the Portuguese empire, such as Brazilians, Cape Verdeans, and Angolans. Established in the twelfth century, Portugal came to preside over a vast empire that had its roots in the seafaring expeditions of the 1400s. Breakup of the last European overseas empire came in the 1970s, when Portugal relinquished Angola, Mozambique, and other colonies. A coup in 1974 ended forty-two years of dictatorship, and the country became a democracy. Portugal gained membership in the European Union in 1986. To reverse the depopulation and desertification of its southeast region, the government built the Alqueva hydroelectric dam on the Guadiana River, creating Europe's largest freshwater reservoir in 2006. Portugal's service sector, including tourism, is the country's largest employer.

From *National Geographic Atlas of the World*, 9th edition. Copyright ©2011 National Geographic Society. Reprinted by arrangement. All rights reserved.

Area	92,345 sq km (35,655 sq mi)
Population	10,639,000
Government	republic
Capital	Lisbon 2,812,000
Life Expectancy	78 years
Religion	Roman Catholic
Language	Portuguese, Mirandese
Currency	euro (EUR)
GDP per Cap	$21,800
Labor Force	10% Agriculture, 30% Industry, 60% Services

From *National Geographic Atlas of the World*, 9th edition. Copyright ©2011 National Geographic Society. Reprinted by arrangement. All rights reserved.

PORTUGAL

TRAVEL **TIPS** 🧳

Entry: Visas are not required for visits up to sixty days. Passports are required.

Peak Tourist Seasons: July and August

National Holiday: June 10 (Portugal Day)

Shopping: Common items include wine, glazed tiles (Figure 23.17), porcelain, textiles, embroideries, tapestries, leather gloves, filigree jewelry, and decorative pieces in gold and silver.

Internet TLD .pt

The Portuguese are a mixture of an Ibero-Celtic tribe and Germanic, Roman, Arabic, and African peoples. There is a small minority of Africans who migrated to Portugal after decolonization of Portugal's African territories. Portugal is one of the oldest states in Europe. It traces its modern history to A.D. 1140 when, following a nine-year rebellion against the king of Leon-Castile, Afonso Henriques, the Count of Portugal, became the country's first king. After a series of expansions, the present-day boundaries were secured in 1249. The official language is Portuguese. English, French, and German are taught

Figure 23.17 Set of 48 ceramic tile patterns from Portugal.
© homydesign/www.Shutterstock.com.

in the schools and understood by many. Over 95 percent of the people are Roman Catholic.

Cultural hints: The thumbs up with both hands means everything is well. Dinner is a social event taking time. When finished eating, place the knife and fork vertically on the plate. Eat fruit with a knife and fork. A special knife and fork are used for eating fish. Do not use bread to wipe up gravy or juices. Typical food includes fish (cod is popular), chicken, rice, pork, partridge, quail, rabbit, potatoes, vegetables, fruits, and pastry. Olive oil is the favorite cooking oil, and garlic is a popular seasoning substance.

Tourism Characteristics

Portugal has experienced significant growth in tourist arrivals in the last decade. It received 7 million visitors in 2010. Its relative location and attractions have been factors in the past that hindered its tourist trade, but it has overcome them. Portugal's better beaches are similar to those in other Southern European nations; but they are located in the south of Portugal, far from markets, and they are not on the Mediterranean.

Portugal's single largest market is Spain, accounting for some 20 percent of its arrivals. However, they represent less than 10 percent of its bed nights. The United Kingdom, the source for 15 percent of Portugal's arrivals, accounts for 30 percent of all bed nights. In the 1970s and 1980s, Portugal cultivated the sophisticated traveler and the luxury market from North America. In the 1990s, however, they began to market to countries and companies with a strong reputation for mass tourism. This change is expressed in the high volume of visitors from the United Kingdom, Germany and France. Further development will, of necessity, need to emphasize air travel. The crowded Spanish beaches are making Portugal an attractive alternative.

The tourist boom in the Algarve has attracted a host of real estate speculators from all over Europe.

Tourism Destinations and Attractions

The main attractions are found in three areas: Lisbon and its environs, the Algarve, and the Madeira Islands. Coimbra is a smaller destination.

Lisbon and Its Environs

Lisbon, the capital, and the Tagus estuary coast are the major centers for tourism to Portugal. Lisbon is one of the oldest capitals in Europe. The city of Lisbon is spread over seven hills. It was founded by Phoenicians in 1200 B.C. It is a city of contrast between the old and the new, with wide, shady avenues contrasting with the narrow streets and alleys of picturesque old districts. Lisbon is the chief center of administration, business, and diplomatic activity. The influence of the Moors can be seen in the buildings and castles. A number of museums, such as the Museum of Popular Art, the Calouste Gulbenkian, the Maritime Museum, the National Coach Museum, and the National Museum of Ancient Art, are excellent. The Tower of Belem, built in 1515, is a part of a fortress marking the spot of Vasco da Gama's first sailing for India. Jeronimos Monastery is a Manueline Renaissance structure where da Gama is buried. Both of these sites are found in the city. On the hilltop dominating Lisbon is the Castle of Sao Jorge, an old Moorish fort with a medieval village around its base.

The old quarter of Lisbon is called the Alfama, a Moorish and Visigoth district of winding, narrow casbah (bazaar) streets and houses. Near Lisbon, the towns of Estoril and Cascais are resort centers with beaches and casinos. Queluz (National Palace) is described as a miniature Versailles, with outstanding gardens. Three important buildings at Sintra are the Royal Palace, Pena Palace (Figure 23.18), and Moorish Castle. All along the coast north from Lisbon are scenic fishing villages and towns, such as Nazaré, a fishing village that is rich in folklore and has a fine beach. A little over one hundred miles north of Lisbon, Fátima is the location where the Virgin Mary is reputed to have appeared to three shepherd children. Fátima is now an important pilgrimage site in Portugal.

Algarve

The Algarve is Portugal's answer to the Costa del Sol and other coastal beach resorts in Spain. The Algarve

Figure 23.18 Pena National Palace in Sintra, Portugal (Palacio Nacional da Pena). © EUROPHOTOS/www.Shutterstock.com.

is in the southern part of the country and offers the best beaches and water in the country. It stretches from Sagres in the west to the Spanish frontier in the east. It is a sheltered, south-facing coastal strip with a string of small towns and fishing villages that has become Portugal's vacation zone. Its fishing villages are very picturesque, with white houses topped by gracefully carved chimneys. Orchards of oranges, figs, carob, and almond trees dot the landscape.

Madeira and the Azores

Madeira is the main tourist island of the volcanic Madeira Islands, about four hundred miles off the coast of Africa, west of Morocco. Its mild climate, moderate rainfall, and mountainous countryside with deep ravines, vineyards, banana groves, pines, and eucalyptus trees provide a number of resorts and favorable attractions. Madeira is referred to as a garden of thousands of flowers. Funchal, the capital of the island, and the center of tourism, is surrounded by parks and gardens overlooking the ocean. The city itself is worth exploring with its narrow streets and passages in the old part of the city. Santa Catarina's chapel dominates the city from its position on one of the plains along the coast. The builders used violet lava, gray volcanic stone, and black

or white stones in its construction. Its appearance is brightened by white and yellow climbing plants. Relics of the fifteenth and sixteenth centuries are seen in Fort Sao Lourenco, the Santa Clara Convent, the old Customs House, and the Sao Tiago Fort. All can be discovered by walking through streets and squares paved with black and white stones, patterned in such a way that they are often a reminder of the waves on the sea.

The Azores are a group of nine islands about eight hundred miles west of Portugal. The Azores have some seaside resorts and excellent spas. Ecotourism is becoming important in the Azores. The sea is rich in tuna, blue and white marlin, swordfish, and albacore.

Coimbra

The city of Coimbra was founded by the Romans and was the capital of Portugal in the early days of the kingdom. The university here was one of the first in Europe. Coimbra is rich in art, monuments, and historical buildings. Near Coimbra are Conimbriga (ruins of a Roman town), Lorvao (monastery), Pombol (Castle), and Cantanhede (the churches of Sao Pedro and Varziela). West of Coimbra at the mouth of the River Mondego, Figueira da Fox is a resort area and fishing port that offers gambling and an excellent climate to the visitor.

Malta

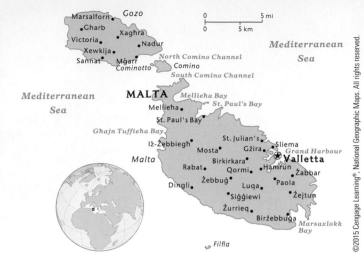

Introduction

The island nation lies just south of Sicily in the middle of the Mediterranean Sea and consists of three small islands: Malta, Gozo, and Comino. The climate is hot and dry in the summer and mild in the winter. Malta's position midway between Europe and Africa has made it a strategic prize. Here, in the sixteenth century, the Knights of St. John repelled thirty thousand soldiers of the Ottoman Empire. It withstood Axis bombs during World War II. In 1964, after almost 150 years as a British colony, the Maltese islands won independence. Tourism is the cornerstone of Malta's economy, and it joined the EU in 2004.

From *National Geographic Atlas of the World*, 9th edition. Copyright ©2011 National Geographic Society. Reprinted by arrangement. All rights reserved.

Area	316 sq km (122 sq mi)
Population	414,000
Government	republic
Capital	Valletta 199,000
Life Expectancy	80 years
Religion	Roman Catholic
Language	Maltese, English
Currency	euro (EUR)
GDP per Cap	$23,800
Labor Force	1.6% Agriculture, 22.8% Industry, 75.6% Services
Internet TLD:	.mt

From *National Geographic Atlas of the World*, 9th edition. Copyright ©2011 National Geographic Society. Reprinted by arrangement. All rights reserved.

Cultural Characteristics

Malta was first colonized by the Phoenicians, followed by the Arabs, the Italians, and the British. Most of the foreign population consists of retired British people. Roman Catholicism is established by law. The two official languages are Maltese (a Semitic language) and English. Malta is one of the most densely populated countries in the world. Flights to Malta are available from Europe and Northern Africa. There is car ferry service from Naples and Sicily.

Tourism Characteristics

Malta gained its independence from Britain in 1964. The island was historically an island fortress because of its strategic location in the Mediterranean. Although the islands' topography consists of low, barren hills, the climate is warm and clear, particularly in the winter. Over 40 percent of Malta's visitors are from the United Kingdom. Malta's previous ties combine with its warm winters to make it very attractive to the British, especially as a retirement destination. Germany and France are the other two markets of significance. Malta has a very long average length of stay, illustrating the destination character of visitors.

Cultural attractions of Malta are associated with the Phoenicians, Romans, Arabs, Normans, Knights of St. John, French, and British. Monuments and remains from temples and idols of prehistoric civilizations are also found.

REVIEW QUESTIONS

1. What are some of the impacts of tourism activity on the physical environment of Southern Europe?

2. Which Southern European country has the most diverse tourism industry? Justify your response.

3. Which country has the shortest length of stay? Why?

4. What are the challenges of tourism development on Cyprus?

5. Compare and contrast tourism to Spain and Portugal.

6. What are five reasons for visiting Greece?

7. Why is tourism so important to the economies of most of the Southern European countries?

8. What are some of the major problems that Spain has with delivering on its tourism potential? How can Spain overcome the problems?

9. Name the main pilgrimage destinations in Southern Europe.

10. What are some general concerns visitors have about going to Southern Europe?

Introduction

The countries of Central Europe and the Balkan States are distinct geographically and as a tourism destination region in three readily identifiable ways. First, the region emerged from Communist domination in 1989. Communist governments made visiting difficult to varying degrees depending upon each individual country's policies. Second, the region spans a wide range of climatic, scenic, and cultural settings, providing a great variety of tourism experiences. Third, portions of this region are a living relic of medieval Europe, something that is unusual because of the extensive conflicts that have affected the continent in the last two centuries.

The Political Geography of Central Europe

The political geography of Central Europe is a function of its location and physical geography. The location is peripheral to the core of Europe centered in France, Germany, and the British Isles. The location is also important because certain countries lie along the trade routes between Asia and Europe, Russia and Europe, and the Middle East and Europe. In consequence they have been invaded and re-invaded, creating an ever-changing mosaic of boundaries and countries. The physical geography of Central Europe that contributed to the fragmentation of the region still affects the area. The contrast in physical geography between the European Plain of Poland (Figure 24.1) and the mountainous peninsula occupied by Serbia, Croatia, Bosnia, and Albania (Figure 24.2) helps explain the present cultural fragmentation, which is partially reflected in the political boundaries of the region. Taken together, the location and physical geography of Eastern Europe continue to be expressed in the extraordinary changes presently occurring within the region.

The nations of Central Europe today share a long history of political and cultural evolution. At varying times, they have been invaded from Russia and the former Soviet Union, Germany, Austria, Turkey, and Rome. The resulting pattern of peoples, languages, and cultural characteristics makes this one of the most complex areas in the world. The most recent factors affecting the political geography of Central Europe and the Balkan States were the impact of **World War II** and the emergence of the Communist Party as the sole political party in each of these countries and the revolution of 1989 that overthrew the Communists, leading to democracy, change, and sometimes conflict.

Figure 24.1 Black Lake in the Suwalki region, Osinkach. Poland.
© Przemyslaw Wasilewski/www.Shutterstock.com.

The Modern States of Central Europe and the Balkan States

The countries of the region range in size from Poland (largest in population and area) to Macedonia (smallest in population and area).

The development of **industry** came late to this region. Industrial development primarily reflects developments

Figure 24.2 Theth village, Prokletije mountains, Albania.
© salajean/www.Shutterstock.com.

since World War II. Even in the Czech Republic the bulk of indu strial development historically occurred in the region adjoining Germany. The initial industrial development in western Czech Republic spread to southern Poland. Since World War II, the industrialization of Central Europe has proceeded more rapidly. The general pattern of industrial development is from north to south, with the Czech Republic and Poland still having the highest level of industrialization. This reflects both their earlier beginnings in industrial development and the amount of assistance that they received from the former Soviet Union.

The relative standard of living across the region reflects the level of economic development. As measured by per capita gross national product (GNP), Slovenia is the highest. It is misleading to assume, however, that the per capita GNP effectively measures the standard of living. The growing importance of private ownership of farms, small shops, and industries and service activities create a **hidden economy** that is not measured by the official GNP.

Climate of Central Europe and the Balkan States

The climate of Central Europe and the Balkan States is transitional between the maritime climates of Western Europe, the Mediterranean climate of Southern Europe,

and the continental climate of Russia. In the north in Poland, the Czech Republic, and Slovakia, the climate is primarily humid continental, with cool summers similar to Wisconsin and Minnesota summers. The summer temperatures tend to be in the 70s or low 80s for the daytime maximums. These three countries are generally humid, but the relatively moderate daytime highs make summers comfortable. The areas south of the Sudetes in the Czech Republic, such as Prague in the west, are less humid because the mountains create a rainshadow effect. Slovakia and Poland are wetter in the summertime.

Poland, the Czech Republic, and Slovakia have winter temperatures that rarely drop below 20 degrees Fahrenheit. This region has a winter climate analogous to that found in areas of the United States such as St. Louis. The humid continental warm summer climates of Central Europe have a summer maximum of precipitation, with most countries receiving between 20 and 30 inches. Across the entire region, the only areas that have more than 30 inches of precipitation are associated with the mountains and highlands. The result is a climatic pattern of moderate to warm summers with seasonal extremes of winter cold in the north, but delightful and extensive autumn periods. North of the Dinaric Alps of Croatia and Bosnia-Herzegovina, snow covers much of the East European region for a prolonged period (Figure 24.3). The average duration of

Figure 24.3 Banska Stiavnica, Slovakia. © Maran Garai/www.Shutterstock.com.

Figure 24.4 Zlatni Rat beach on the island of Brač, Croatia. © Simone Simone/www.Shutterstock.com.

snow cover ranges from forty days in northern Poland to ten to thirty days over most of the highlands of Bosnia-Herzegovina, Hungary, Romania, and Bulgaria. The snow cover lasts longer in the mountains of the Carpathians and Dinaric Alps, making them an important winter resort region.

The highest temperatures found in the region are recorded in the coastal areas of Croatia, Albania, and southern Bulgaria, while the coldest temperatures are found in northeastern Poland, where the continental and latitudinal influences are greatest. The Black Sea Coast regions of Bulgaria and Romania have summer temperatures similar to those found in the Carolinas and Virginia of North America, which makes them attractive to tourists.

A Mediterranean climatic type is found along the Adriatic sea coast of Croatia, Bosnia and Herzegovina, and Albania. The Mediterranean climates of the Adriatic are characterized by long, hot, dry summers and moderate humid winters. Across the Mediterranean region, the precipitation is between 20 and 30 inches, most of which falls in the winter season. The hot dry summers combine with the beaches of Croatia (Figure 24.4), Bosnia and Hercegovina, and Macedonia to make it a most attractive destination for foreign tourists in Central Europe when it is not handicapped by armed conflict. The winter season in the coastal Mediterranean climate has temperatures that range between 30 and 55 degrees Fahrenheit range. The climatic variety found in Central Europe provides a mirror image to that found in Western Europe. The range from the cool continental climates of northern Poland to the Mediterranean climate of Croatia is very similar to the range found from northern Germany to Spain or Italy with their Mediterranean climates.

Tourism in Central Europe and the Balkan States

Tourism in Central Europe and the Balkan States reflects the physical and cultural geography of the region. European cities and towns are central to tourism in Central Europe. The pattern of urban development reflects both the recent changes in industrialization and economic development and the historic population distribution based on the physical geography of the region. Major industrial cities remain the primary economic centers of the individual countries. From Warsaw in Poland to Prague in the Czech Republic to Budapest in Hungary to Belgrade in Serbia, the old cities remain dominant. In part, this reflects their political role, but it also reflects their development over long periods of time as economic and trade centers.

The emergence of medieval states in the Middle Ages was associated with the development of a capital city in each. These capital cities became the focus of the castle and the cathedral in that state. The close association of government and church is manifested in the role the church played in selecting the kings, crowning them, and providing them with skilled administrative staff. These old cities developed on a hill or defensible site such as the Wawel at Krakow, the Hills of Buda in Budapest, or the Hradcany Castle of Prague. Within the fortification was located the castle of the king and the cathedral of the bishop or archbishop. The Wawel at Krakow best retains its appearance of a medieval capital and is a major tourist attraction. The Hradcany of Prague preserves its Gothic Cathedral of St. Vitus, but most of the present buildings on the hill date from the eighteenth century. The other capitals such as Budapest, Zagreb, and Warsaw have been destroyed by wars and later rebuilt.

Other cities developed in the region primarily for trade purposes. The majority of these cities have a castle or monastery as the nucleus around which they developed. The cities were generally planned with at least a number of straight streets intersecting at right angles to create rectangular blocks. One of these central blocks became the marketplace, which is typical of the older merchant cities of Central Europe. The towns contain parish churches, but the churches are rarely as ostentatious or pretentious as the town hall or guildhall. Because of the role of the merchants in most of the cities of Central Europe, the guildhall emerges as the dominant architectural attraction where it has not been destroyed.

The coastal town, whether along the Baltic or the Mediterranean coast, is related to merchant trade of the late Middle Ages. The few towns along the Baltic Coast reflect the trading of the Hanseatic League. Houses are tall and richly decorated, with warehouses built along the waterfront as at Gdansk, Poland. They reflect the tradition of Hamburg and the German traders who came to the Baltic Coast. Mediterranean coastal settlements generally derive from Italy. Rijeka, Croatia (formerly the Italian community of Fiume), was originally a Roman settlement. Split, Croatia, grew around the palace built by the Roman Emperor Diocletian for his retirement.

Some of the older towns have surviving relics from the Roman Period, or churches dating from the second and third centuries. Dubrovnik, Croatia, was originally a small island settlement of Italian merchants. By filling in the narrow channel that separated it from the coast, it was able to expand onto the mainland. Dubrovnik was heavily damaged by Serbian shelling when Croatia declared its independence in 1991 but the city has since been restored. Most of the medieval towns in Central Europe date from medieval times and medieval trade rather than from the Romans or the early Italian state. Initially established for trade, the old core is generally recognizable even today. The medieval settlement was surrounded by a wall or fortification for defense, and the line of these walls is visible in the parks or boulevards that still are found in some cities, such as Budapest or Prague. In a few instances, the medieval walls survive, as at Zagreb in Croatia or in Warsaw, Poland. The newer areas of these towns (1800s forward) are recognizable because of larger or stylistically distinct buildings with wider streets.

An important characteristic of a medieval town was its division into sectors, in each of which there was some specialization by occupation or trade. Prior to World War II, this segregation into districts was most evident in the persistence of Jewish ghettos. The calculated destruction of these overcrowded ghettos during World War II destroyed much of the uniqueness of the ghettos of Central Europe, but the old Jewish cemeteries and tabernacles still exist in some communities, adding to the character of the communities.

The **Turkic Ottoman Empire** had an influence on Bulgaria, parts of Romania, the south of Yugoslavia, Bosnia-Herzegovina, and Albania for many centuries. In these areas occupied by the Turks, the cities' sections were divided on the basis of religious belief or ethnic group rather than occupation. Cities in these regions have characteristic architecture, including mosques dating from the Islamic religion of Turkic invaders and cathedrals of the **Eastern Orthodox** Church, which share many of the architectural characteristics of the mosque. The onion-shaped domes, arches, and uses of tile are typical of the Islamic influence in the Byzantine architecture of this area of Eastern Europe, greatly enhancing its attraction to tourists. Grafted onto the old towns of Central Europe are the structures of the post–World War II Communist period. These are more homogeneous and better planned than the early towns in terms of ease of movement, but they are less interesting. The characteristics of these areas include large apartment blocks, state-run shops, children's playgrounds, and a generally monotonous and egalitarian community. The Communist presence of monumental architecture

(Palace of Culture, the Party Headquarters), fountains, and boulevards with gardens are designed to make the quality of life less crowded and more efficient. They succeed in this, but because they were repeated over and over throughout the region, they are less interesting to tourists than the towns from the previous era. Until 1989, tourism reflected the impact of the Communist governments. Most international tourism in the past was characterized by planned movements of groups between the eastern European countries themselves. The overthrow of Communism has transformed the character of tourism to the region. Western tourism has increased dramatically since the breakup of the Communist bloc. Easing of entry requirements, the emergence of private travel agencies and tour companies offering low-cost travel compared with Western Europe, visits to ancestral homelands, and curiosity about the formerly reclusive region motivated Western tourists to the area. Other factors affecting the number of visitors to individual countries reflect the level of development of the tourism infrastructure. Poland, Hungary, the Czech Republic, and Croatia are the primary destinations.

As would be expected, the level of tourism facilities in Central Europe still reflects the legacy of the Communist system. With few exceptions, hotels and other accommodations are clean and adequate, but many are not luxurious. Since 2005, numerous luxury hotels have been constructed in major cities. There still exist a few major hotels that predate the Communist Revolution in Central Europe, with all of the elegance expected by the wealthy travelers of the pre–World War II era. As with most of the public facilities in the countries of Central Europe and the former Soviet Union, however, these luxury hotels are but a shadow of their former elegance. The service level is also lower than is normally experienced in Western Europe and other countries where the staff has an incentive to ensure that the service provided is outstanding. New hotels have been completed in the three leading tourism destination countries as Western hotel chains invest in the region.

Poland

Introduction

Poland, a large country in central Europe, is bordered on the north by the Baltic Sea, with the Sudeten and Carpathian mountains defining its southern border. The fertile plains are crossed by large, slow-moving rivers, such as the Vistula and Bug. The generally temperate climate is prone to temperature extremes in the mountains and the east. The Polish language and a common religion, Roman Catholicism, unify Poles as a nation. Unlike many of its neighbors, Poland has only a minuscule minority population. The flat topography has made Poland an invasion route for centuries. In 1939, Germany invaded, starting World War II, and the Nazis built the Auschwitz concentration camp complex, where approximately 1.3 million Jews and others were murdered. After World War II, Joseph Stalin seized territory in eastern Poland for the Soviet Union. Communists took power in 1947 but did not win Poles away from Roman Catholicism. In 1980, soaring prices and tumbling wages spawned Solidarity, the Eastern bloc's first free-trade union. In 1989, Solidarity swept Poland's first free elections in more than forty years and began moving the Soviet Union's most populous satellite toward democracy and free enterprise. It was the first Eastern European country to overthrow communist rule. Poland has developed a market-oriented economy, joining the European Union in 2004. The country is a net food exporter, and reform efforts are reducing the number of state-owned companies. Work is underway on developing an efficient road, rail, and air network.

From *National Geographic Atlas of the World*, 9th edition. Copyright ©2011 National Geographic Society. Reprinted by arrangement. All rights reserved.

Area	312,685 sq km (120,728 sq mi)
Population	38,146,000
Government	republic
Capital	Warsaw 1,707,000
Life Expectancy	76 years
Religion	Roman Catholic
Language	Polish
Currency	zloty (PLN)
GDP per Cap	$17,900
Labor Force	17.4% Agriculture, 29.2% Industry, 53.4% Services

From *National Geographic Atlas of the World*, 9th edition. Copyright ©2011 National Geographic Society. Reprinted by arrangement. All rights reserved.

TRAVEL**TIPS** 💼

Entry: Visas are not required for stays up to ninety days. A passport is required.

Peak Tourist Season: May through September

Shopping: Common items include regional costumes, handwoven rugs, lace, embroidery, ceramics, woodcarving, amber jewelry, coral jewelry, leather work, metalwork, peasant dolls, wooden toys, crystal, and art.

Internet TLD: . pl

CULTURAL CAPSULE Poland has the largest population in Central Europe and has the seventh largest population in Europe. It is ethnically homogeneous with 98 percent Polish. Poland is predominantly active Catholic. The Catholic Church was strong during the Communist regime and has been strongly nationalistic.

Cultural hints: Shake hands to greet, with men waiting for women to extend their hand first. Generally do not embrace or touch while talking. Don't chew gum when talking with Poles. At the table, wait to eat until all are served. Common foods include pierogi (dumplings with cream cheese and potatoes), cabbage dishes of all kinds, and potatoes.

Tourism Characteristics

Communism took power in 1947 but did not win Poles away from Roman Catholicism. In 1980 soaring prices and falling wages spawned Solidarity, the Eastern bloc's first trade union. In 1989 Solidarity swept Poland's first free election in more than forty years and began the country toward democracy and a free enterprise based economy. It was the first Eastern country to overthrow communism. It developed a market-oriented economy and joined the European Union in 2004. Poland has some of the greatest cultural attractions of Central Europe, but it is handicapped by the fact that it lacks the major attractions for tourists—sun, sea, and sand. The Polish government is desperately trying to increase the number of tourists to Poland. Tourism in Poland was estimated at 13 million in 2010, but an even greater number of visitors come as day-trippers from neighboring Germany to take advantage of lower prices on nearly all consumer goods. With the change in government it is anticipated that future visitors to Poland will be more diverse. The currency (Zloty) is stable and readily convertible. Poland is experiencing a boom in private enterprise bringing a growth in street markets, new retail shops, restaurants, private hotels, rental car firms, and travel companies.

Tourist Destinations and Attractions

The major destinations in Poland are the cities of Warsaw, Krakow, and the Baltic Coast, especially the port city of Gdansk. Warsaw was the third capital of Poland and was built in the seventeenth century. Destroyed during World War II by the Germans as they resisted Russian attempts to take the city in 1944, it has since been reconstructed. The old structures were rebuilt using street scene paintings, which can be seen in the national museum. The many museums and reconstructed architecture are major tourist attractions, particularly the monument to the heroes of the Jewish ghetto. The monument remembers the nearly half-million Jewish people of Warsaw who were killed by the Nazis during World War II. Near Warsaw is the birthplace of Chopin (at Zelazowa Wola). The Pulski's museum at Warka, the Wilanow and Lazienki palaces of the kings of Poland, and the restored "old town" are also fascinating.

Krakow (Figure 24.5) was not destroyed or even damaged during the war. The Wawel Mount (or Wawel Hill) is dominated by the royal castle, which dates from the 1500s. Originally the second capital of Poland, the royal castle houses crown jewels, royal tapestries, and historical exhibits. The cathedral on Wawel Mount houses the crypts of the Polish kings and reflects the relationship of the church to the state during much of Poland's history. The old town in Krakow is a treasury of old architecture. The important structures are the Gothic Collegium Maius, now the Museum of the Jagiellonian University, the Main Market Square (the Rynek Glowny) with the Cloth Hall and the Church of St. Mary's. Some of Krakow's architecture and art collections date from the early Middle Ages. Not far from Krakow is Auschwitz. The former Nazi concentration camp is now an interpretive museum.

Poznan, an ancient Polish city, has become an important business travel center. The old Market Square with the town hall has a number of classical and baroque-style buildings. Near Poznan is Kornik, the medieval castle of Zamoyskis, with a library of priceless manuscripts. Poland's famous composer, Frederic Chopin, is remembered in his birthplace Zelazowa Wola where the Chopin Museum hosts piano concerts in the summer.

The Baltic Coast has a length of 365 miles with sandy beaches. Water temperatures tend to be cool, but it still attracts numerous visitors during the short summer season. The coastal resort of Sopot and the reconstructed portions of Gdansk and Szczecin, two Hanseatic cities in the north, are major attractions.

The southern mountains have the winter resort area of Zakopane, near the Czech border. It is visited year-round, offering hiking and alpine climbing in the summer and skiing and other winter sports in the winter. Throughout the Tatra mountains, there is a beautiful scenery with steep, austere ridges and peaks, mysterious caves, beautiful forests, swift-flowing streams and waterfalls, and dozens of lakes of all sizes.

Figure 24.5 Krakow, Poland. © Pecold/www.Shutterstock.com.

The Czech Republic

Introduction

The landlocked Czech Republic in central Europe consists of two major regions: Bohemia, with its rolling plains and plateaus surrounded by low mountains, and the eastern region of Moravia, which is mostly hilly. About a third of the country is forested. The country enjoys a temperate climate, with mild summers and cold, wet winters. About 94 percent of the population is ethnically Czech; Slovaks and Roma form the largest minorities, with smaller numbers of Poles and Germans. Citizens are well educated, thanks to a tradition of compulsory education that reaches back to 1774. Central Europe's oldest university was founded in Prague in 1348.

Czechoslovakia was created in 1918 upon the fall of the Austro-Hungarian Empire. In 1939, the Czech lands were annexed to Germany, while Slovakia became a German puppet state. Communists took charge of a reunited Czechoslovakia in 1948, and crushed an attempt at liberalization in 1968. The communist regime fell in 1989, which led to democracy in 1990. Slovak calls for greater autonomy resulted in the peaceful breakup of Czechoslovakia in 1993 and the creation of the Czech Republic and Slovakia. Today the Czech Republic (known informally as Czechia) is a highly industrialized country; it joined NATO in 1999 and the EU in 2004.

Area	78,867 sq km (30,451 sq mi)
Population	10,511,000
Government	parliamentary democracy
Capital	Prague 1,162,000
Life Expectancy	77 years
Religion	Roman Catholic
Language	Czech
Currency	Czech koruna (CZK)
GDP per Cap	$25,100
Labor Force	3.6% Agriculture, 40.2% Industry, 56.2% Services

TRAVEL**TIPS**

Entry: Visas are not required for stays under thirty days. A passport is required.

Peak Travel Season: June through September.

Shopping: Common items include Bohemian crystal, Carlsbad china, handicrafts, and ceramics.

Internet TLD: .cs

CULTURAL CAPSULE The division of Czechoslovakia into the Czech Republic and Slovakia represented ethnic differences. Other ethnic groups include 60,000 Hungarians in Slovakia. Both have some Ukrainians, Germans, and Poles. There are about 250,000 Gypsies, mainly in Slovakia, who represent the fastest-growing minority. Czechs and Slovaks were united after World War I and remained so under Communist control. In 1993 Czechoslovakia split into the two independent states. The division was largely an urban (Czech) and rural (Slovak) division.

Cultural hints: Shake hands on greeting, with men waiting for women to extend their hand first. Eye contact is important. A good topic of conversations is sports. When finished eating, place your knife and fork to one side of your plate. Food differs somewhat by ethnic group, but pork roast, dumplings, sauerkraut, ham, and sausage are the most popular.

Tourism Characteristics

The Czech Republic has a long tradition of tourism. It was part of early European tourism during the development of resort spas in the 1800s. It has a growing tourist industry. Visitors to the Czech Republic increased from 4.5 million in the 1980s to over 8 million today. The country also receive a large number of day visitors. The major tourism markets for the region are Germany, Austria, and Poland, which are also the major sources of day visitors. The Czech Republic is a much more attractive destination than the more rural Slovakia and it attracts visitors from much greater distances. Famous historical spas offering high-quality service are Carlsbad (Karlovy Vary), Marienbad (Marianske Lazne), and Piest'any. Its central location, wide network of transport, and cultural linkage with the rest of Europe have allowed the Czech Republic to have a strong tourist tradition.

Tourism is a rapidly developing sector and millions come to Prague to visit castles, palaces, and spas. Although political and financial challenges somewhat eroded the country's stability and prosperity, the Czech Republic succeeded in becoming a European Union member in 2004. The Czech Republic and Slovakia appear to have the best future for tourism in Eastern Europe. They have natural beauty and an outstanding wealth of places of historic, cultural, and architectural interest. They are within easy accessibility to Europe's main origin markets and do not have the problems of Bulgaria or Romania or the economic difficulties of the Baltic States.

Tourist Destinations and Attractions

The premier tourist destination in the Czech Republic is Prague (Praha). The medieval city of Prague is built on seven hills on both sides of the river Vltava. The statue-lined old Charles Bridge (Figure 24.6),now closed to vehicular traffic, carries visitors to the ancient city and fortress. The beautiful medieval castle city of Prague with its well-preserved buildings of all social classes from the Middle Ages is one of the most important attractions in Central Europe.

The architecture and atmosphere of Prague make it one of the most delightful cities in Europe. Because Prague's old city was not destroyed by war, it allows visitors to see something of what life was like several hundred years ago. The Estates Theater celebrates the city's cultural and music legacies. Today much tourism to the Czech Republic is related to the health spas, which have attracted visitors for centuries. The most notable of these are Karlovy Vary (Carlsbad) and Marienbad. The principal attractions here and at the more than fifty other spas are the waters, which are impregnated with sulfur. The odor is breathtaking, but they are reputed to be remarkably effective in terms of health. Giant Mountains National Park has excellent ski facilities. Medieval Cesky Kumlov, near the Austrian border, portrays Bohemian village life.

Figure 24.6 Charles Bridge in Prague, Czech Republic. © Daniel Korzeniewski/www.Shutterstock.com.

Slovakia

Introduction

A landlocked country in central Europe, Slovakia is mostly mountainous except for southern lowlands along the Danube—where the capital, Bratislava, is found. The high Tatra Mountains shelter historic castles and villages, while also offering national parks and winter sports. Weather differs depending on location, generally mild in the lowlands but with severe winters in the mountains. The country's split from the more affluent, industrialized Czech Republic in 1993 was prompted by Slovak nationalism and grievances over rapid economic reforms instituted by the Czechoslovak government in Prague—reforms that left many Slovaks without jobs. About 86 percent of the people are Slovaks; ethnic Hungarians (9.7 percent) form the largest minority. Since 1993, Slovakia's industrial economy has transformed from one based on central planning to one that is market oriented. Slovakia joined NATO and the EU in 2004.

From *National Geographic Atlas of the World*, 9th edition. Copyright ©2011 National Geographic Society. Reprinted by arrangement. All rights reserved.

Area	49,035 sq km (18,932 sq mi)
Population	5,417,000
Government	parliamentary democracy
Capital	Bratislava 424,000
Life Expectancy	75 years
Religion	Roman Catholic, Protestant, Greek Catholic
Language	Slovak, Hungarian
Currency	Slovak koruna (SKK)
GDP per Cap	$21,200
Labor Force	4% Agriculture, 39% Industry, 56.9% Services

From *National Geographic Atlas of the World*, 9th edition. Copyright ©2011 National Geographic Society. Reprinted by arrangement. All rights reserved.

TRAVEL**TIPS**

Entry: Visas are not required for stays under thirty days. A passport is required.

Peak Travel Season: June through September

Shopping: Slovak ceramics and embroidered articles.

Internet TLD: .sk

CULTURAL CAPSULE The division of Czechoslovakia into the Czech Republic and Slovakia represented ethnic differences. Other ethnic groups include 60,000 Hungarians in Slovakia. Both have some Ukrainians, Germans, and Poles. There are about 250,000 Gypsies, mainly in Slovakia, who represent the fastest-growing minority. Czechs and Slovaks were united after World War I and remained so under Communist control. In 1993 Czechoslovakia split into the two independent states. The division was largely an urban (Czech) and rural (Slovak) division.

Cultural hints: Shake hands on greeting, with men waiting for women to extend their hand first. A stiff forefinger turned on the temple of the head indicates someone is crazy, and is very rude. Toasting is common. Food differs somewhat by ethnic group, but pork roast, dumplings, sauerkraut, ham, and sausage are the most popular.

Tourism Characteristics

The primary destination in Slovakia is Bratislava, which was once the capital of Hungary. As the capital, it developed an international and cosmopolitan atmosphere. The Bratislava castle is 200 feet up on a hill overlooking the city. The architecture, museums, and other attractions make Bratislava an interesting visit. It also has the longest beer hall in Europe. The Tatra Mountains and Tatras National Park are the second major destination for tourists in Slovakia. The mountains have a number of ski resorts and have a relatively long ski season. Tatranska Lomonica is the most famous summer and winter resort in the region.

Hungary

Introduction

The Danube River flows north to south through the middle of Hungary, splitting this landlocked central European country almost in half. Fertile plains lie east of the Danube, with hills to the west and north. Hungarians (Magyars) migrated here from Asia more than a thousand years ago and are distinct from the Germanic and Slavic peoples that surround them. Hungary's support for Hungarian minorities in neighboring countries is a major foreign policy issue. There are 1.6 million Hungarians in Romania, 570,000 in Slovakia, and 341,000 in Serbia. The Hungarian kingdom was defeated in World War I, and it lost most of its land and many of its people to Czechoslovakia, Romania, and Yugoslavia. Hungary tried to regain its lands during World War II, as an ally of Nazi Germany, but was again on the losing side. Communists took over Hungary after World War II, and Soviet tanks crushed an uprising for democracy in 1956. But Hungary rebounded to become Eastern Europe's first purveyor of "goulash communism," blending personal freedom, prosperity, and a pinch of free enterprise. In 1989 the government abolished censorship; dismantled barriers along the Austrian border; and called for privatization of industry, religious freedom, and free elections. Today Hungary is a parliamentary democracy and modern industrial economy; it joined the European Union in 2004.

Area	93,028 sq km (35,918 sq mi)
Population	10,024,000
Government	parliamentary democracy
Capital	Budapest 1,679,000
Urban	68%
Life Expectancy	73 years
Religion	Roman Catholic, Calvinist, Lutheran
Language	Hungarian
Currency	forint (HUF)
GDP per Cap	$18,600
Labor Force	4.5% Agriculture, 32.1% Industry, 63.4% Services

TRAVEL**TIPS**

Entry: No visa is required for stays less than ninety days. A passport is required.

Peak Tourist Season: July and August

Shopping: Common items include hand-embroidered material, peasant pottery, Herend and Zsolnay china figures, and leather work.

Inter- net TLD: . hu

CULTURAL CAPSULE Magyars (the Hungarian name for both the people and the language) comprise 98 percent of the population. There are small groups of Germans, Slovaks, Gypsies, and Romanians.

Cultural hints: Greet with a handshake, with men waiting for women to extend hand first. Avoid uninvited touching of others. Avoid discussions of politics or religion. Popular food includes goulash (a stew of meat, potatoes, and onions), pork, chicken, noodles, potatoes, and dumplings. Paprika is a popular spice. Strudel and pancakes are popular desserts.

Figure 24.7 Parliament Building, Budapest, Hungary. © Ammit Jack/www.Shutterstock.com.

Tourism Characteristics

By the late 1980s reform-minded Hungary had lost faith in communism, shaken by sagging productivity and the highest per capita foreign debt in Eastern Europe. In 1989 the government abolished censorship, opened the border with Austria, and called for privatization of industry, religious freedom, and free elections. Hungary has had a long history of tourism and has an excellent transportation network. Europe accounts for more than 98 percent of the nearly 10 million visitors in 2010 to Hungary with Germany, Austria, and Italy being major market areas. The Slovakian visitors are often on one-day trips, having less impact than the longer staying visitors from Western Europe. The United States accounts for a small percentage of tourists, many of whom are on side trips from Vienna. Tourism from Anglo-America has grown rapidly as Budapest became one of the most popular destinations of Central Europe.

Hungary has both medieval communities and the grandeur of the relics of the **Austro-Hungarian Empire**. (Budapest is often referred to as the Vienna of Central Europe.) Prices on other consumer goods made in Europe can be low as well. Hungarian-made clothing, musical instruments, handicrafts, and artwork are relatively cheap when purchased with foreign currency.

Tourist Destinations and Attractions

The major tourist attraction in Hungary is Budapest. Budapest is the primary destination because of its beautiful location along the Danube, and the sense of being in one of the most beautiful cities of the world.

The city consists of two parts: Buda, which is the hill side of the river and includes Castle Hill with its numerous Gothic structures, including the former Royal Palace on Castle Hill; and Pest, on the other side of the Danube, the newer, low-lying part of the city. The designation as new is somewhat misleading, as even the newer part dates from the Middle Ages. Post–World War II structures are built in the areas surrounding the city. The major attractions include the Parliament Building (Figure 24.7), Varosliget (the city park, which contains both a zoo and a fun center), and the Corso. The Corso is a broad boulevard running along the Danube River's edge. It is popular with residents and tourists alike. Budapest has nightclubs, gambling casinos, and modern hotels that rival western European countries. The final attraction is the excellent shopping opportunities at relatively low costs. Budapest is the starting place for cruises to the Black Sea. To the north is Esztergom, home to the country's largest Roman Catholic cathedral.

The second tourist area of Hungary is Lake Balaton (Figure 24.8). This is the largest freshwater lake in Central

Figure 24.8 Lake Balaton, Hungary. The largest freshwater lake in Central Europe. © Botond Horvath/www.Shutterstock.com.

Europe, and it is surrounded by campgrounds, which attract Hungarians, Italians, and Germans. Water temperatures are in the high seventies in the summer because of the shallow nature of the lake. Spas have always been popular in Hungary, dating back to the occupation of the region by both the Romans and the Turks.

Romania

Introduction

Romania lies on the Black Sea Coast of southeastern Europe. The Carpathian Mountains and the Transylvanian Alps divide the country into three physical and historical regions: Wallachia in the south, Moldavia in the northeast, and Transylvania in the country's center. Almost two-thirds of the country consists of mountains, hills, or plateaus; and Romania's largest plain is along the Danube River in Wallachia. The majority of the people are Romanian (89 percent of the population), and there is a large ethnic Hungarian minority inhabiting the Transylvanian plateau (7.1 percent). After being part of the Ottoman Empire for centuries, Wallachia and Moldavia united to become the Kingdom of Romania in 1881. The new kingdom looked to the West, especially to France, and Romania sided with France and its allies in World War I. After the war, Romania added

Transylvania to its territory. The Soviet army occupied the country in World War II, and the Communist Party took control of the government in 1947. In 1989, security police of the repressive communist government killed demonstrators in the cities of Timisoara and Bucharest—igniting a revolution. The communist government was overthrown in 1989, and elections were held in 1990. Romania is pursuing a path of economic reform and Western integration, joining NATO in 2004 and the European Union in 2007.

Area	238,391 sq km (92,043 sq mi)
Population	21,474,000
Government	republic
Capital	Bucharest 1,942,000
Urban	54%
Life Expectancy	72 years
Religion	Eastern Orthodox, Protestant, Roman Catholic
Language	Romanian, Hungarian
Currency	new leu (RON)
GDP per Cap	$11,500
Labor Force	29.7% Agriculture, 23.2% Industry, 47.1% Services

TRAVEL**TIPS**

CULTURAL CAPSULE

The people are 89 percent ethnic Romanians, tracing their origins to Latin-speaking Romans and Thracian, Slavonic, and Celtic ancestors. Among the principal minorities are Hungarians and Germans with some Gypsies, Serbs, Croats, Ukrainians, Greeks, Turks, Armenians, and Russians. Most of the minority populations reside in Transylvania or areas to the north and west of Bucharest.

Cultural hints: Firm handshake on meeting and departing. Business cards are freely exchanged. Women need to dress conservatively when visiting a Greek Orthodox Church (covered arms and skirts). Foods include mititei (grilled meatballs), patricieni (grilled sausage), and mamaliga (cornmeal mush), soups, and pastries.

Tourism Characteristics

Romania has a variety of good hotels and restaurants. Tourist arrivals reached 7.5 million in 2010. Most of its tourists are from surrounding Central European countries and Russia. Romania's tourism is centered around its rich cultural tradition, some of which predates the Roman occupation (the country is named because it was a colony of imperial Rome). The traditional folk arts, including dance, wood carving, ceramics, weaving, and embroidery of costumes combine with folk music to provide interest for visitors. The country's many Orthodox monasteries along with the Transylvanian Catholic and Evangelical churches have a rich history and many artistic treasures.

Tourist Destinations and Attractions

Three major areas attract the bulk of tourists to Romania. These are the Black Sea Coast; the capital, Bucharest; and Transylvania. Coastal resorts begin in the north near Constanta and extend over 150 miles south to Mangalia. The main attractions include the sun and sea (Figure 24.9), thermal springs, health spas (including

Figure 24.9 Neptun Beach, Romania. © Aleksandar Todorovic/www.Shutterstock.com.

EUROPE

Figure 24.10 The medieval Castle of Bran, at the border between Transylvania and Wallachia, is known for the myth of Dracula.
© Emi Cristea/www.Shutterstock.com.

the conventional bland apartment buildings, skyscrapers, and a unique circular department store. The presence of the village museum adjacent to Bucharest is also a major tourist attraction. The village museum has nearly 500 peasant houses, churches, barns, and other relics that show how peasants in the Danubian Plains lived during past centuries. These peasant dwellings include underground homes, brush homes, log homes, and adobe dwellings.

The Transylvania area is important because of its association with Dracula in the minds of Western visitors. In actuality, the castle of the fifteenth-century prince Vlad Tepes (from whom Dracula is derived) is located in Wallachia rather than Transylvania (Figure 24.10). Vlad's castle is accessible from the Black Sea Coast. Transylvania has the second largest city in Romania, Brasov. It is a medieval city situated in the foothills of the Carpathian Mountains. The primary attractions are the scenic open mountain countryside and peasant villages. The "Romanian Riviera" of the Black Sea stretches south from Constanta for 150 miles. Throughout this region are the typical beach resorts of high-rise hotels and an abundance of nightclubs, restaurants, discos, and bars. Constanta was founded by the Greeks in the sixth century B.C. and was an important seaport under the Romans and the Turks. Today it is an important cruise port.

medicinal mud), and ruins that are 2,700 years old. Bucharest is a large and sprawling city with a variety of architectural relics dating from the influence of Rome to the Turkic Byzantine Empire to the neoclassic styles of the late Renaissance. Modern construction includes

Serbia

Introduction

Located in southeastern Europe, Serbia features a fertile Danube plain in the north, rising to rugged mountains in the south. Serbia was part of Yugoslavia until 2003 and then part of the union of Serbia and Montenegro until 2006, when Montenegro seceded to become an independent nation. Montenegro's secession made Serbia a landlocked country, but the Danube River provides a vital link to most of Europe and the sea. Serbia's recent history revolves around Kosovo, which was a Serbian province with an ethnic Albanian majority when the nationalist government of Slobodan Milosevic began a campaign of ethnic cleansing in Kosovo in 1998. Thousands of Kosovar Albanians were killed, and 1.5 million were driven from their homes, many into Albania and Macedonia. The war in Kosovo ended in 1999 only after NATO bombed Serbia. The UN made Kosovo an international protectorate, and Kosovo declared independence in February 2008. Serbia's economy is recovering from the conflicts of the 1990s, and the government is selling off state-owned

companies inherited from previous communist regimes. The United Nations Environment Programme helped decontaminate areas polluted by NATO's 1999 bombing of Serbia's factories and refineries.

From *National Geographic Atlas of the World*, 9th edition. Copyright ©2011 National Geographic Society. Reprinted by arrangement. All rights reserved.

All flags ©National Geographic Atlas of the World, 9th edition. Copyright ©2011 National Geographic Society. Reprinted by arrangement. All rights reserved.

©2015 Cengage Learning®. National Geographic Maps. All rights reserved.

CHAPTER 24: GEOGRAPHY AND TOURISM IN CENTRAL EUROPE AND THE BALKAN STATES **315**

One of the world's newest nations, little Montenegro packs an outsize punch with its outstanding array of attraction. The small Balkan country of Montenegro has a population of about 680,000—and we locals say, just as many wonders. Situated immediately south of Croatia and surrounded by Bosnia, Albania, and Serbia—from which it seceded in 2006—my homeland is a place where impossibly is possible. We claim our own fjord, although we are a thousand miles south of Scandinavia. We have 800-year-old olive trees that continue to yield some of the finest olive oils in all of Europe. And fairies still tread our misted hills and lakes-dotted valleys.

Smaller than Connecticut, Montenegro has a wonder for everyone. Wilderness? Discover Durmitor National Park, a World Heritage site of black lakes and blacker forests that center on the massif of Mount Durmitor. I like to hike the park's steep-sided Tara River

Canyon—which has been ranked the longest canyon in Europe—where rock climbers and rafter of all levels can challenge themselves, and whose river water is clean enough to drink. Traditionally considered an enchanted place, this mountainous realm is said to be wandered by Starpanja, the father of all fairies.

Sacred wonders? We have many worthy churches, but nothing tops the magnificent Monastery of Ostrog. A seventeenth-century landmark built right into a mountain cliff and the rest place of Saint Basil, it is a major pilgrimage site that is open to visitors of all faiths.

To the south lies a wonder even some Montenegrins don't know: the vast olive groves—at least 74,000 trees—between the coastal towns of Bar and Ulcinj that date to Roman times and constitute one of the largest concentration of olive trees along the Adriatic Sea. So important was olive oil in times past

that local tradition said a man couldn't marry until he had planted an olive tree.

As for our many seaside wonders, best in sow does to the fjord-like Bay of Kotor, a World Heritage site that is actually submerged river canyon spilling into the Adriatic Sea. Along its shore sits the ancient town Perast, established on the remains of a Neolithic settlement and rich with maritime history: during its rule by the Venetian Republic, 1420 to 1797, it was home to four shipyards and more than 15 baroque palaces and churches.

But the most photographed place in Montenegro has to be the tiny tidal island of Sveti Stefan, with its centuries-old red-roofed village—a Lilliputian wonder that is just one chapter in the long story of Montenegro.

— **Milisav Popovic, National Geographic Traveler,** October 2009

Area	77,474 sq km (29,913 sq mi)
Population	7,322,000
Government	republic
Capital	Belgrade 1,099,000
Life Expectancy	73 years
Religion	Serbian Orthodox, Roman Catholic, Muslim
Language	Serbian, Hungarian, Albanian
Currency	Serbian dinar (RSD)
GDP per Cap	$10,400
Labor Force	23.9% Agriculture, 20.5% Industry, 55.6% Services

From *National Geographic Atlas of the World*, 9th edition. Copyright ©2011 National Geographic Society. Reprinted by arrangement. All rights reserved.

TRAVEL **TIPS** 💼

Entry: No visa is required. A passport is required.

Peak Tourist Season: July and August

Shopping: Common items include peasant handicrafts, embroidered blouses, gold and silver filigree jewelry, carpets, leather goods, carved wooden goods, laces, and pottery.

Internet TLD: .yu

CULTURAL CAPSULE

The people are Serbs and ethnic Montenegrins. All are adherents of the Serbian Orthodox Church. There are a few Muslims and Roman Catholics, but the future for minorities is uncertain.

Cultural hints: Handshake upon greeting. Dress conservatively. To beckon a waiter, raise your hand.

Tourism Characteristics

Serbia (Yugoslavia) stood in marked contrast to the rest of Central Europe prior to 1990. The primary source of

tourists to Serbia was not Central Europe, but West Germany. With the breakup of Yugoslavia and the ethnic tension in Kosovo the number of tourists dropped dramatically in the 1990s, and the source region of visitors changed considerably. Many of the Western European visitors went to the coastal and mountain areas of what is now Slovenia and Croatia. By the end of the 1990s neither Serbia nor Macedonia, which became independent in 1995, had many visitors. At the beginning of the twenty-first century, the major markets appeared to be more regional than before the 1990s and by 2010 numbers had only slowly climbed to just over 1.5 million.

Prior to 1990 the accommodations within the country were somewhat uniform in that they tended to reflect the prevailing philosophy of the centrally planned economies of Central Europe in providing basic accommodations. Although Yugoslavia had four classes of hotels plus accommodations in private homes and campgrounds or youth hostels, there was not a marked difference between the highest- and lowest-class hotels in terms of basic accommodations. The hotels of Yugoslavia tended to be geared directly to mass tourism of the middle class from Europe. Primary differences were in the nature and quality of the entertainment and the amenities offered rather than in the accommodations themselves.

Tourist Destinations and Attractions

The Adriatic coastline in Montenegro attracted a large number of visitors before the division of Yugoslavia. Today, it is isolated and remote from major industrial countries of Europe. There is a ferry to Italy from Bar on the south coast. While there are no major islands off the coast, there are excellent long, sandy beaches. Budva is the largest tourist

Figure 24.11 Kalemegdan Citadel, Belgrade, Serbia. © Jessmine/www.Shutterstock.com. com.

center on the Montenegrin coast, drawing mostly inexpensive package visitors. Budva is a restored old-walled town in the center of a beautiful beach. Further north the Bay of Kotor is the longest and deepest fjord in southern Europe, providing picturesque ferry and bus rides.

The major destination in Serbia is the capital, Belgrade. The dominant attraction in Belgrade is the Kalemegdan Citadel (Figure 24.11), a hilltop fortress at the junction of the Sava and Danube rivers. Orthodox churches, medieval gates, Turkish baths, and Muslim tombs are all part of the citadel. The Monument of Gratitude to France and a large Military Museum are here also. Nearby, Stari Grad, the oldest part of Belgrade, contains the National Museum and the Ethnographical Museum with a collection of Serbian

costumes and art. Belgrade's most important museum is the Palace of Princess Ljubice, an authentic Balkan-style palace built in 1831 and still furnished in that time period. Marshal Tito's grave and former residence is a few miles south of Belgrade.

Southern Yugoslavia has a number of Orthodox monasteries with thirteenth- and fourteenth-century frescoes. Near the village of Despotovac is Manasija Monastery built in 1418 and completely enclosed in defensive walls and towers. The oldest and one of the greatest monasteries of medieval Serbia is south of Kraljevo. There are a number of monasteries in the region and Novi Pazar, which is a Muslim town. There are old Turkish mosques, inns, and bathhouses.

Slovenia

Introduction

Slovenia is an Alpine-mountain state in central Europe. The Alps soar over northern Slovenia, taking up 42 percent of the country, and two-thirds of Slovenia is covered in forests. Southern Slovenia features a karst plateau, and plains lie in the northeast. It has a short coastline on the Adriatic Sea. In 1918 Slovenia joined the Kingdom of Serbs, Croats, and Slovenes—subsequently named Yugoslavia. Slovenia proclaimed its independence in

June 1991, prompting a ten-day conflict that brought defeat to the Serb-dominated Yugoslav Army. It is the most prosperous of the former Yugoslav republics, with the region's highest standard of living. Slovenia possesses a highly skilled labor force, with a diversified economy that is based on services and manufacturing. Its Western outlook and economic stability won Slovenia membership in both NATO and the EU in 2004.

Area	20,273 sq km (7,827 sq mi)
Population	2,043,000
Government	parliamentary republic
Capital	Ljubljana 244,000
Life Expectancy	78 years
Religion	Roman Catholic
Language	Slovene, Croatian, Serbian
Currency	euro (EUR)
GDP per Cap	$27,900
Labor Force	2.2% Agriculture, 35% Industry, 62.8% Services

TRAVEL**TIPS** 🧳

Entry: Visas are not required. A passport is required.

Peak Tourist Season: July and August

Shopping: Common items include peasant handicrafts, embroidered blouses, gold and silver filigree jewelry, carpets, leather goods, carved wooden goods, laces, and pottery.

Internet TLD: .si

 CULTURAL CAPSULE The people are predominantly Slovenes, 89 percent, with some Croats and Serbs. The first Slovenes settled in the region in the sixth century A.D., but by the ninth century it was part of the Holy Roman Empire and became Germanized.

Cultural hints: Foods are Germanic in taste and type. Sausages and sauerkraut, game dishes, Austrian strudel, dumplings, and pastries are all tasty.

Tourism Characteristics

Slovenia has been affected less by the division of Yugoslavia and is consequently better able to handle tourists than the other republics. Slovenia is a transition between Central Europe and the Balkans. Much of the area reminds a visitor of the Austrian Alps or Bavaria with its wooded slopes, fertile valleys, scenic rivers (Figure 24.12), and neat little villages. It is the most prosperous of the former Yugoslav republics, with the region's highest standard of living. Slovenia draws a significant number of visitors from the nearby countries of Italy, Austria, Germany, and Croatia.

Figure 24.12 The Soca river, Triglav National Park, Slovenia. © Pecold/www.Shutterstock.com.

Figure 24.13 Center of the old town Ljubljana, capital of Slovenia. © Boris Stroujko/www.Shutterstock.com.

Tourist Destinations and Attractions

The two major destination regions of Slovenia are the area around the capital, Ljubljana, and the Julian Alps. Ljubljana (Figure 24.13) is a small city on the banks of the Sava River. Castle Hill dominates the landscape. Castles, cathedrals, museums, and markets are spread throughout the town. The most famous destination near Ljubljana and the road to Rijeka are the famous Postojna Caves. Visitors are taken by train and on foot through 3 miles of the nearly 17-mile cave. The Skocjan Caves were placed on UNESCO's World Heritage list in 1986 but are more difficult to visit due to their remoteness.

The Julian Alps, shared with Italy, provide both summer and winter activities. The region is one of the finest hiking areas in Central Europe. The area contains the Triglav National Park, which was founded in 1924. It provides mountain huts scattered throughout the region. Hikers pass outstanding waterfalls, narrow gorges, glacial lakes, and scenic valleys. The most fashionable resort in the Julian Alps is Bled (Figure 24.14), set on a beautiful crystal-clear emerald lake.

Figure 24.14 Church on island in the middle of Bled Lake, Slovenia. © Dudarev Mikhail/www.Shutterstock.com.

Croatia

Introduction

A crescent-shaped country in southeast Europe, Croatia extends from the fertile plains of the Danube to the mountainous coast along the Adriatic Sea. In the Adriatic, Croatia has 1,185 islands—many are major tourist areas. The climate along the coast is mild and sunny, while the interior is moderately rainy. Croatia declared its independence from Yugoslavia in 1991, leading to a war with Croatian Serbs and the Serb-dominated Yugoslav army. The 1991–95 conflict caused massive damage to cities and industries. War halted the tourist trade and drastically cut industrial output, including a lucrative shipbuilding business. Tourism came back after 2000, especially to the beaches and historic cities of the Dalmatian Coast, but the economy is hampered by many old state-owned industries. Since 2000, Croatia has become a stable democracy; it joined NATO in 2009 and became a member of the European Union in 2013.

Area	56,594 sq km (21,851 sq mi)
Population	4,433,000
Government	presidential/parliamentary democracy
Capital	Zagreb 690,000
Urban	57%
Life Expectancy	76 years
Religion	Roman Catholic, Orthodox
Language	Croatian
Currency	kuna (HRK)
GDP per Cap	$17,600
Labor Force	5% Agriculture, 31.3% Industry, 63.6% Services

TRAVEL**TIPS** 🧳

Entry: No visa is required. A passport is required.

Peak Tourist Season: July and August

Shopping: Common items include peasant handicrafts, embroidered blouses, gold and silver filigree jewelry, carpets, leather goods, carved wooden goods, laces, and pottery.

Internet TLD: .hr

CULTURAL CAPSULE

The population is largely Croat with the Serbs the largest minority. There are some Slovenes, Italians, and Slovaks. The Croats are mostly Roman Catholics. German and English are widely used through the country—German because of the number of migrant workers to Germany in the past, and English because of the popularity of English in general.

Cultural hints: Shake hands when meeting. A closed hand with the index and little fingers raised is an insult. Check prices before ordering. Food consists of Italian pizza and pasta, seafood on coast, brodet (mixed fish stewed with rice), mushrooms, manistra od bobica (beans and fresh maize soup), and strukle (cottage cheese rolls). Italian-style espresso coffee is popular.

Tourism Characteristics

The war created serious problems for the tourist industry and Adriatic resorts were affected by the war and considerable destruction occurred. This was particularly true farther south at Osijek and Dubrovnik. Tourists have started to return to the country. The majority of visitors are from the region; Germany, Austria, and Italy.

Tourist Destinations and Attractions

The capital, Zagreb, is a medieval city, on the banks of the Sava River. There are many lovely parks, galleries, museums, and cafés. St. Stephen's Cathedral, built in 1899, has Renaissance pews, marble altars, and a Baroque pulpit. The Baroque Archiepiscopal Palace and sixteenth-century fortifications surround the palace. A number of other churches, such as the St. Catherine's Church (Baroque), Stone Gate, and St. Mark's Church (Gothic, painted-tile roof), have important art works. A number of museums, including the Historical Museum of Croatia, the National History Museum, the City Museum, the Archaeological Museum, and the

Figure 24.15 Bay of Milna, Brač Island, Croatia. © Darios/www.Shutterstock.com.

Ethnographic Museum, recall the history and people of the past and present.

The most important coastal destination is the Dalmatian Coast, which occupies the central 150 miles between the Gulf of Kvarner to the Bay of Kotor and includes the offshore islands. The offshore islands are comparable in beauty to those of Greece. The most important resort is at Dubrovnik. Dubrovnik has beautiful beaches, Renaissance palaces, Venetian-style architecture, old stone streets, and massive city walls of the ancient city. It has been hit hard by the war, and much destruction has occurred. Today, the city's attractions and hotels have been restored. Three other major cities

occupy the Dalmatian Coast and attract tourists. Split is built around a well-preserved fourth-century Roman palace. With its fine Roman ruins and much of the old city wall, Zadar is one of the most beautiful towns on the Adriatic.

Numerous smaller communities and resorts have been built along the Dalmatian Coast, all capitalizing on the beautiful pebble beaches, islands, climate, and clear water (Figure 24.15). Along the coast and inland there are seven national parks that remain in Croatia from what was formerly Yugoslavia. One park that is important to domestic tourism and should gain in international popularity is Plitvice Lakes. It is midway between

Zagreb and Zadar. Accessible either by auto or tour bus, it has sixteen lakes that are connected to each other by waterfalls and are set in a beautiful forest. If the armed conflict can be peacefully resolved, tourism is expected to be the primary source for restoring Croatia's damaged economy.

Bosnia and Herzegovina

Introduction

Ethnic nationalism remains a problem in this southeastern European nation consisting of Bosniaks, or Bosnian Muslims (49 percent of the population), Serbs (34 percent), and Croats (15 percent). These ethnic groups fought a 1992–95 war that subdivided the country into two autonomous regions based on ethnicity: Republika Srpska (Serbian Republic) and the Federation of Bosnia and Herzegovina (where most Bosniaks and Croats live). The Bosnian war was part of the breakup of Yugoslavia, and Serbia provided military aid to the Bosnian Serbs in the Republika Srpska in an effort to create a "greater Serbia." The 1995 Dayton Peace Accords ended the war and stabilized an independent Bosnia and Herzegovina, which includes the entities of Republika Srpska and the Federation of Bosnia and Herzegovina. The country depends on international assistance for its economy and security.

From *National Geographic Atlas of the World*, 9th edition. Copyright ©2011 National Geographic Society. Reprinted by arrangement. All rights reserved.

Area	51,129 sq km (19,741 sq mi)
Population	3,843,000
Government	emerging federal democratic republic
Capital	Sarajevo 376,000
Urban	47%
Life Expectancy	75 years
Religion	Muslim, Orthodox, Roman Catholic
Language	Bosnian, Croatian, Serbian
Currency	konvertibilna marka (BAM)
GDP per Cap	$6,300
Labor Force	20.5% Agriculture, 32.6% Industry, 46.9% Services

From *National Geographic Atlas of the World*, 9th edition. Copyright ©2011 National Geographic Society. Reprinted by arrangement. All rights reserved.

TRAVEL**TIPS** 🧳

Entry: No visa is required. A passport is required.

Peak Tourist Season: July and August

Shopping: Common items include peasant handicrafts, embroidered blouses, gold and silver filigree jewelry, carpets, leather goods, carved wooden goods, laces, and pottery.

Internet: .Ba

Tourism Destinations and Attractions

The three cities, Sarajevo, Mostar, and Jajce, are the principal destinations for tourists. Sarajevo, the capital, by the Miljacka River, had seventy-three mosques. It was ruled by the Turks from the mid-fifteenth century until 1878. Thus, it offered the strongest Turkish flavor of any city in the Balkans. It had picturesque Turkish mosques, markets, and color. However, what will remain after the war is uncertain. Sarajevo was the site of the 1984 Winter Olympic Games. It was shelled by Serbs for nearly two years, with tremendous loss of life and property damage.

The second destination city, Mostar, was founded by the Turks in the fifteenth century on a river crossing. It also offered the visitor a view of Islamic culture with its old quarter, mosques, and Turkish Bridge (destroyed by Serbian shelling in late 1993). Like Sarajevo, it has been badly damaged and is now off-limits to tourists. Jajce is a medieval walled city with cobbled streets and old houses set in a hilly country. It was briefly the capital of liberated Yugoslavia in 1943. Medjugorje was a heavily visited pilgrimage site in the 1980s.

Bulgaria

Introduction

Black Sea beach resorts are the main lures for foreign tourists to this southeastern European country—many never see the snowcapped mountains and forests, teeming with wildlife rarely found in the rest of Europe, such as lynx, brown bears, and golden eagles. Cultural attractions include Roman ruins in Plovdiv and the parks, museums, and nightlife of Sofia, the capital city. Emerging from communist rule in 1991, Bulgaria became a parliamentary democracy, and it joined NATO in 2004 and the EU in 2007. Being one of the poorest countries in the EU, Bulgaria works to modernize its economy and infrastructure.

From *National Geographic Atlas of the World*, 9th edition. Copyright ©2011 National Geographic Society. Reprinted by arrangement. All rights reserved.

Area	110,879 sq km (42,811 sq mi)
Population	7,590,000
Government	parliamentary democracy
Capital	Sofia 1,185,000
Life Expectancy	73 years
Religion	Bulgarian Orthodox, Muslim
Language	Bulgarian, Turkish, Roma
Currency	lev (BGN)
GDP per Cap	$12,600
Labor Force	7.5% Agriculture, 36.4% Industry, 56.1% Services

From *National Geographic Atlas of the World*, 9th edition. Copyright ©2011 National Geographic Society. Reprinted by arrangement. All rights reserved.

TRAVEL**TIPS**

Entry: Visas not required for visits of less than sixty days. A passport is required.

Peak Tourist Season: July and August

Shopping: Items include embroidery, woodcarving, pottery, leather and fur clothing, blankets, and carpets.

Internet TLD: .bg

CULTURAL CAPSULE The people are primarily Bulgarian (85 percent). The most important minority is Turkish. The principal religion is the Bulgarian Orthodox Church. Other religions include Islam, Roman Catholicism, Protestantism, and Judaism. Bulgaria's name is derived from a Turkic people, the Bulgars who originated in the steppe north of the Caspian Sea. The Slavic people absorbed the invading Turkic people and were, in general, the precursors of the present-day Bulgarians. The official language, Bulgarian, is a Slavic language using Bulgarian Cyrillic. It is very similar to the Russian alphabet.

Cultural hints: The handshake is the form of greeting. Nodding your head up and down means yes. Nodding your head back and forth means no. Food specialties are lamb, pork, beef, fish, cheese, and Turkish-type desserts with espresso coffee.

Tourism Characteristics

The Bulgarian government views tourism as an important source of foreign exchange to modernize and expand their economy. The industry in Bulgaria is small compared with the developed tourist-receiving countries in Europe, receiving 6 million visitors in 2010. Most of its visitors are from the region. Most of the accommodation facilities are in beach-resort holiday centers along the Black Sea. Romania, Greece, and Germany are the major market for Bulgaria, followed by Turkey and Russia. However, many of the Turks are passing through on their way to Western Europe, mainly Germany. The numbers from the United States are small but are increasing gradually as Bulgaria is a good bargain and has had a peaceful transition from Communism to democracy. New private hotels, restaurants, and shops are eager to please tourists from North America. The major purpose of visits are to transit the country. However, for those visiting, holidays and recreation are the main purposes for visiting the country. There is an abundant supply of hotel rooms and 200 miles of sandy beaches.

Tourist Destinations and Attractions

The tourist destinations in Bulgaria can be classified into three groups: the Black Sea Coast, the capital city Sofia, and the Valley of the Roses. The Black Sea Coast (Figure 24.16) is the dominant international tourist attraction. Balkantourist, the national tourist organization, developed three modern beach resorts on the Black Sea in combination with the traditional centers of Varna and Burgas. Varna, the largest city on the Black Sea, was founded in the sixth century B.C. by the Greeks. It later became a major trading post in the Roman Empire. In addition to swimming and sunbathing, the Black Sea Coast has numerous spas that are reputed to be beneficial for rheumatism, arthritis, and other joint afflictions. One of the more famous is Pomorye, where mudpacks and salt baths are used for the treatment of arthritis and sciatica. The new resorts of Drouzhba, Albena, Zlatni Piassatsi, and Slunchev Bryag (Sunny Beach) provide foreign tourists all of the amenities for a sea-and-sand vacation experience. Rila National Park is Bulgaria's largest.

Sofia is an ancient city in a basin near the Balkan Mountains. Culturally the influence of both Roman and

PRESERVING THE FUTURE | A Short-Sighted Trend in Bulgaria?

Tourism trumps environment as ski resort infringe on parks.

New ski resorts are appearing across Bulgaria as a ban is imposed on their construction in many Alpine countries. This is a slippery slope, say environmentalists. When Bulgaria—the European Union's poorest nation—held a World Cup ski event in 2009 at the Bansko ski resort, protesters in Bulgaria's capital tried to derail it, pointing out that more than half of Bansko's ski runs lie illegally within Pirin National Park, a UNESCO World Heritage site. Major excavation and clear-cutting of century-old trees have resulted in erosion and loss of habitat for wildlife.

> *Major excavation and clear-cutting of century-old trees have resulted in erosion and loss of habitat for wildlife.*

In Rila National Park, a ski lift opened in 2009 without an impact assessment, and some ski runs have been disguised as fire-prevention clearings. Park officials who protested have been fired. The Bansko model is being emulated by illegally built ski resorts in Romania, Ukraine, and Slovakia. Besides ignoring environmental restrictions, many of these resorts are at low elevations and rely on resource-gobbling snow-making technology—a double whammy global warning, and a reason why Swiss banks no longer consider loans to ski resorts below 5,000 feet losing propositions.

— **Charles Kulander,** *National Geographic Traveler,* **March 2010**

Ottoman Turk rule is evident in the architecture. The Alexander Nevsky Memorial Church, built in the nineteenth century as a tribute to Russians who liberated the country from the Turks, is one of the most impressive architectural structures. The Rila Monastery (Figure 24.17) is well known for its exterior frescoes. In addition, the Balkan Hotel contains the remains of the fourth-century church of St. George within its courtyard. Several mosques and the archaeological museum contain important relics from the Turkish past with its Islamic influence.

Figure 24.16 Nessebar beach on the Black Sea in Bulgaria. © Aleksandar Todorovic/www.Shutterstock.com.

Figure 24.17 Rila Monastery, Bulgaria. © auremar/www.Shutterstock.com.

The third area that attracts tourists is Kazanluk and the Valley of the Roses. This is the premier producing region for the roses from which essentially all the world's attar of roses comes for use in perfumes and soap. During May and June, the scent of the harvesting of millions of roses makes this a unique tourist attraction.

Albania

Introduction

Isolation typified Albania during decades of communist rule, which ended in 1991; it remains one of Europe's poorest countries, with nearly 60 percent of all workers employed in agriculture. But market reforms have stimulated the economy, and tourists increasingly visit Albania's Adriatic coast and interior mountains. A new highway connects Kosovo to Albania's port of Durrës, increasing trade and tourism for both countries. Pursuing a policy of European integration, Albania joined NATO and applied for European Union membership.

From *National Geographic Atlas of the World*, 9th edition. Copyright ©2011 National Geographic Society. Reprinted by arrangement. All rights reserved.

Figure 24.18 Temple Of Apollonia in the largest ancient city in Albania. © ollirg/www.Shutterstock.com.

Area	28,748 sq km (11,100 sq mi)
Population	3,196,000
Government	emerging democracy
Capital	Tirana 406,000
Life Expectancy	75 years
Religion	Muslim, Albanian Orthodox, Roman Catholic
Language	Albanian , Greek, Vlach, Romani, Slavic dialects
Currency	lek (ALL)
GDP per Cap	$6,300
Labor Force	58% Agriculture, 15% Industry, 27% Services

From *National Geographic Atlas of the World*, 9th edition. Copyright ©2011 National Geographic Society. Reprinted by arrangement. All rights reserved.

TRAVEL**TIPS**

Entry: No visa is required. A passport is required.

Tourist Season: May through August

Shopping: Common items include black embroidery, linen, native wood carvings, and rugs.

Internet TLD: .al

CULTURAL CAPSULE Ninety-six percent of the people are ethnically Albanian, descendants of the ancient Illyrians who once occupied much of the Balkan Peninsula. Today's Albanians are divided into two groups—the Gegs to the north of the Shkumbin River and the Tosks to the south. Their differences in physical traits, dialects, religions, and social customs are distinguishable but not dramatic. A number of minorities in Albania include Greeks, Vlachs, Bulgars, Serbs, and Gypsies.

Tourism Characteristics

Tourism under Communism was virtually nonexistent, and Albania was withdrawn from the world. In the 1990s tourism grew slowly. Albania has the smallest European tourism market of the region. Europe accounts for some 50 percent of Albania's visitors, with Serbia and Macedonia the two largest European markets. The main tourist centers include Tirane, Durres (an ancient city), Sarande, and Shkodër. The Roman amphitheater at Durrés is one of the largest in Europe. The ancient towns of Apollonia (Figure 24.18) (dating from Roman times) and Berat (known as the "city of a thousand windows"), which is a museum-town with a medieval fortress and mosque, are two of the major historic towns.

REVIEW QUESTIONS

1. Which Central European countries have the most developed tourism industry? Why?

2. What impact does climate have on tourism to Central Europe?

3. Describe tourism to Bulgaria. What are the major attractions?

4. Describe the attractions and major markets for Slovenia and Croatia.

5. How are the countries of Central Europe distinct geographically and as tourism destinations from Western Europe?

6. What role does the Danube play in Central and Eastern Europe?

7. Describe tourism in Hungary.

8. If you had to select one country to visit that would give you the greatest diversity, which Central European or Baltic country would you select? Justify your answer.

part 8 : GEOGRAPHY AND TOURISM IN RUSSIA AND ITS NEIGHBORS

Raymer/National Geographic Creative

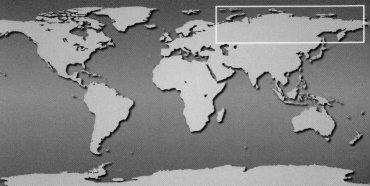

© 2015 Cengage Learning

MAJOR GEOGRAPHIC CHARACTERISTICS

- The weather in this region can be harsh, resulting from its high-latitude location or desert climates.
- Russia has the largest territorial expanse in the world, creating long-distance travel.
- The new countries of the former Soviet Union are in the process of changing from socialist to free-enterprise economies at varying speeds.
- The population is ethnically diverse with Russians found in every country.
- There are limited coastal areas to attract tourists.
- The countries created from the Soviet Union are differentiated by their distinctive physical and cultural geography.

MAJOR TOURISM CHARACTERISTICS

- International visitors generally visit the large cities of Russia, Ukraine, and the Baltic States.
- There is regional concentration of international tourist facilities in a few large cities.
- International tourism is an important revenue source, and most of the countries of this region are building new hotels and entering into agreements with Western businesses to enhance their attractiveness to international tourists.
- There is a limited variety of activities and facilities for all tourists, but in some countries this is quickly changing driven by an increase in domestic tourism.
- Visitors generally have limited knowledge of Russia and other countries created from the former Soviet Union.

MAJOR TOURIST DESTINATIONS

- Moscow and St. Petersburg
- Tallinn and the other capitals and coastal areas of the Baltic States
- Kyiv (or Kiev), the Black Sea Coast, and the Crimean Peninsula in the Ukraine

(continued)

MAJOR TOURIST DESTINATIONS *(continued)*

- Tashkent and the ancient cities of the Silk Road in Uzbekistan
- Eastern coast of the Black Sea in Russia and Georgia
- Lake Baikal and Siberian Russia
- Novgorod and the ancient Russian cities of the Northwest
- Sochi (Host of the 2014 winter Olympic games)

KEY TERMS AND WORDS

Asiatic Russia
Caucasians
Central Planning
Commonwealth of Independent States
Communist Party
Czar
Demokratization
European Russia
Glasnost
Golden Ring
Intourist

Kremlin
Madrassa
Perestroika
Privatization
Republics
Siberia
Slavic
Soviet
Taiga
Trade Unions
Tundra
Turkic

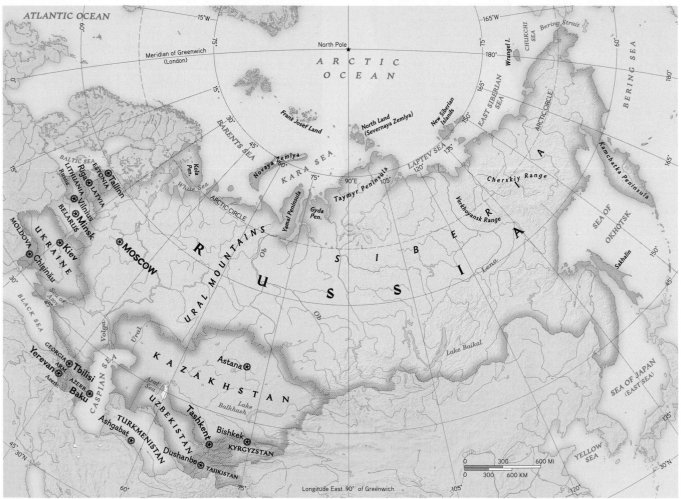

Introduction

The former Union of Soviet Socialist Republics (USSR or simply the Soviet Union) was and, even in its present form of fifteen independent countries, is one of the greatest potential tourist destinations in the world. The Soviet Union disintegrated as a unified country in the fall of 1991. Three of the countries—Estonia, Latvia, and Lithuania (collectively known as the Baltic States)—chose to remain completely independent. The twelve remaining countries have formed a loose political organization called the **Commonwealth of Independent States** (CIS). Within these fifteen countries is one of the largest ranges of ethnic cultures, climates, and vegetation of any comparable group of countries in the world.

The actual powers of the CIS organization are related to coordinating the transition from the unified Soviet state to a system by which the new states are connected by trade, defense, and other agreements. Unfortunately, several individual countries remain unstable, and the future of the region is unpredictable. The political and economic arrangements that the CIS federation and the three independent states ultimately arrive at will greatly affect tourism to this remarkably varied area.

For most people, the countries created from the former Soviet Union remain an enigma. Three important time periods have combined to create the present geography and tourism patterns of these fifteen countries. The first was the emergence of the Russian Empire. Beginning in the fourteenth century, Russian princes expanded their control over the land that stretched from the Baltic Sea in the west to the Pacific Ocean in the east. The centuries of Russian expansion added numerous peoples and cultures to the Russian Empire and resulted in the construction of many beautiful cities, palaces, museums, and churches. These structures remained as major tourist attractions during the other two major time periods that have affected the tourism industry of the region.

The second major time period affecting the countries created from the former Soviet Union began in 1917. The USSR was created from the Russian Empire after the revolution of 1917 that ended with the **Communist Party** dominating the country. Under communist leaders' direction, fifteen **republics** were recognized within the USSR. Russia was the largest of these, comprising nearly three-fourths of the territory of the USSR. The transformation of the historical Russian Empire into the communist-dominated Soviet Union was one of the most significant events affecting the nature and character of tourism in the country at the present. Important results of the 1917 revolution were the establishment of a single-party political system (Communist Party) and an economic system based on the work of Karl Marx as interpreted and expanded by Lenin.

During the seventy years of communist domination, large industrial cities with featureless blocks of housing were constructed as suburbs of old cities or as new cities across the Soviet Union. Many of the old palaces and churches were maintained as tourist attractions, and large new exhibits, museums, and monuments glorifying the communist state were constructed. Many of the most imposing of these were statues of Lenin or museums to his honor. Chief among these is Lenin's tomb (Figure P8.1) in Red Square in Moscow. Until 1987, the USSR relied on a rigidly planned economy controlled by the government. Tourism was a part of this economy, and numerous hotels, camps, and health spas were constructed for citizens of the Soviet Union and the relatively few international tourists who arrived.

Figure P8.1 Lenin's Tomb and the Kremlin, Red Square, Moscow, Russia. © Lloid/www.Shutterstock.com.

The third time period affecting tourism in this region began in the late 1980s. After nearly seventy years of government control, the Soviet Union began to experiment with some modifications to their system to encourage elements of free enterprise. Using the concepts of **glasnost** (free exchange of information and ideas), **perestroika** (restructuring of industry to emphasize quality and profitability rather than simple volume of production whether profitable or not), and **demokratization** (democratic ideals), the leaders tried to change the economy of the Soviet Union. The result was far from what they planned, as the ideas of glasnost and demokratization were adopted into the political arena, resulting in the breakup of the country and the emergence of the fifteen republics as independent countries after 1990.

The democratic movement that has created fifteen new countries is the third period that affected tourism. Each of the newly independent countries has adopted elements of the free enterprise economic system and a democratic government. The official role of the Communist Party has been all but obliterated as even the statues of Lenin and other communist leaders have been removed from most public places. The economic changes created uncertainty as the various governments debated attempts to transfer government-owned farms, factories, banks, stores, and other aspects of the economy into private ownership. Inflation and shortages of many items are causing many residents of the new countries to question whether the dramatic changes were worth the cost. Territorial and other disputes between the various groups in some of the countries create ongoing conflict.

The revolutionary nature of recent events in Russia created a host of issues that are still unresolved, and at this time it is still difficult to predict the end result of the momentous changes set in motion in 1991. The geographic and historical relationships that will ultimately shape these emerging countries and their tourism patterns, however, will be related to the past and present patterns of tourism in the former Soviet Union.

The Geographic Base of the Countries Created from the Former Soviet Union

The geographic characteristics of the countries created from the Soviet Union are distinctive because of their tremendous size and location. With nearly 6.6 million square miles of area, Russia remains the largest country in the world, about twice the size of Canada, China, or the United States. Russia sprawls nearly halfway around the world, extending through 170 degrees of longitude and eleven time zones. Citizens in western cities of Russia, such as St. Petersburg, are just going to bed as those in the far east in Vladivostok are arising for work. If Russia were placed so that its westernmost border coincided with the west coast of Alaska, it would extend across Alaska, Greenland, and the North Atlantic to the west coast of Norway. The other former republics range in size from the tiny Baltic States to Kazakhstan, which is one-third the size of the United States.

The location of the countries is highly varied. The southernmost is Turkmenistan, which extends from 35 degrees to about 42 degrees north latitude. Russia extends from about the latitude of Boston to its islands in the Arctic Ocean at about 78 degrees north. In spite of the northerly location and associated harsh climate (Figure P8.2), Russia and the Baltic countries are among the most densely populated high-latitude lands in the world. Remember that Moscow is north of the southern border of Alaska, and St. Petersburg is located at

Figure P8.2 Siberia, Russia. © Sergey Toronto/www.Shutterstock.com.

Figure P8.3 Caucasus Mountains, Armenia. © Mikhail Pogosov/www.Shutterstock.com.

the same latitude as Stockholm, Sweden. You can understand the challenges created for any political and economic system attempting to develop Russia's vast land.

The People of the CIS

In spite of great ethnic differences, it is possible to divide the population of the fifteen new countries into three broad ethnic groups. The largest group is the Slavic people, consisting of Russians, Ukrainians, and Belarussians. The actual number of each ethnic group does not equal the population of individual countries such as Russia because members of each group are found in many of the new countries. Russians number some 150 million and comprise 51 percent of the fifteen countries' total population. The next largest group is the Ukrainians, with about 50 million people or 17 percent of the population. Between them, these two groups constitute nearly 70 percent of the total population of

the countries created from the former Soviet Union. They represent a substantial minority population even in areas where other nationalities are more numerous. There are 10 million Belarussians, making up about 3.5 percent of the population. Thus, the Slavic population group represents more than 70 percent of the total population of the former Soviet Union.

The second most important population group is comprised of Turkic people: Kirghiz, Tatars, Uzbeks, Kazakhs, and Azerbaijanis. In total, these people constitute approximately 11 percent of the total population of the countries created from the Soviet Union. The Caucasians constitute a third group. They are a diverse people made up of Armenians, Georgians, and a host of smaller ethnic groups. The multiplicity of groups in the Caucasian family results from the isolation of small groups over long periods of time in the Caucasian Mountains (Figure P8.3). A final group, labeled "other," includes people ranging from Estonians who speak a language similar to Finnish to the Aleutian and Yakut tribal groups of Russian Siberia.

Foreign Tourism

Foreign tourism is not yet an important sector of the economy of most of the fifteen countries in the region. The new governments hope tourism will become a primary economic activity, attracting foreign and domestic tourists, however. Tourism was of minor importance in the Russian Empire before the communist revolution of 1917, as it was before the era of mass tourism. Under the communists, domestic tourism was internal since the official policy maintained that the Soviet Union had sufficient variety of natural and cultural features for its residents. Even so, it was not until the 1980s that residents of the Soviet Union could travel relatively freely within the country, and internal passports were required until 1992. Foreign travel for nearly all Soviet citizens was simply not allowed before 1990. Suspicion that outsiders would undermine the socialist society effectively limited the number of foreign tourists entering the Soviet Union until the 1980s.

All tourism in the Soviet era was a state monopoly run by the government agency, **Intourist**. Intourist-controlled hotels, airlines, restaurants, bus systems, spas, and other activities related to tourism. In 1971, foreign visitors totaled 2.1 million, a figure that increased to 3.5 million by 1981. Approximately half of these visitors were from other socialist states, primarily those in Central and Eastern Europe. In the late 1980s and 1990s, the number of foreign tourists continued to increase, reaching 7.8 million in 1989. Since then, tourist numbers have fluctuated wildly, but by 2010 the region had rebounded to more than 52 million visitors, with Russia and the Ukraine accounting for approximately 40 million of these visitors. Most of the visitors to the individual countries of the CIS are from other countries in the region. This is not unlike many parts of the world where a majority of the visitors to a particular country come from within the same region.

Foreign tourists visit the newly independent countries primarily between the first of May and the end of September, reflecting on the climate. The average length of stay is approximately five days, about a day and a half less than the average in Western European countries. The majority of tourists come for business purposes.

There are thousands of independent tourist-related companies in Russia today, but many are small. Fewer than twenty-five agencies handle the great majority of inbound tourists to Russia. VAO Intourist, the relic of the vast Intourist enterprise of the Soviet Union, still handles more than one-quarter of tourist arrivals from countries that were not part of the former Soviet Union, and even more of that from the countries that were. VAO Intourist remains so dominant primarily because of its direct or indirect control of a significant part of the infrastructure of hotels, transportation, restaurants, and entertainment in Russia. In 2011, VAO Intourist established a joint venture with London-based Thomas Cook to further develop and grow the inbound tourism markets.

To provide for the needs of foreign visitors, the umbrella organization that linked the Intourist companies—Intourist-Holding—owns and operates over 75 percent of total beds in the fifteen countries of the former Soviet Union. The largest hotel is the Rossiya near Red Square in Moscow with 3,060 rooms. Built in the early 1970s, it typified the Soviet approach to tourism. Facilities were concentrated in one location, with the hotel having three large restaurants. The Rossiya typified the Soviet Union's approach to foreign tourism, which emphasized **central planning** and control of tourism through use of very large facilities.

The scene is rapidly changing. With Moscow (Figure P8.5) being the most expensive city in the world "for luxury goods," it is not surprising that first-class hotels have appeared on the scene, including the Savoy, the Swiisotel, the Hilton Moscow, and the Ararat Park Hyatt among the finest. Moscow does not lack luxury hotels, rather there is a short supply of good and affordable mid-range properties (even Holiday Inn hotels charge $450 per night). The city today is the center of the country's transportation (four airports), commercial, tourism, government, and education hub.

The CIS countries are changing their approach to tourism, but (except for the large cities where names like Radisson, Marriott, Intercontinental, Best Western, Holiday Inn, Hilton, and Hyatt are present today) it remains far below international standards. In spite of the changes taking place in the old tourist industry of the former Soviet Union, the industry is far different

INTERNATIONAL TOURISM TO RUSSIA AND THE LARGER REPUBLICS OF THE FORMER SOVIET UNION (2005–2010).

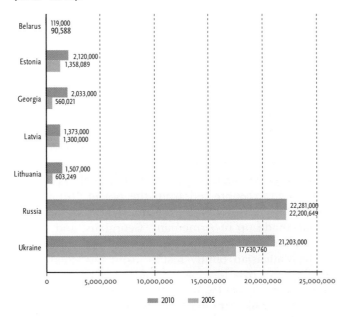

Figure P8.4 Data source: *The World Bank: The Data Catalogue.*

Figure P8.5 Hotel Ukraine and Moscow City business complex in Moscow, Russia. © Pavel L Photo and Video/www.Shutterstock.com.

from that in Western countries. Many workers in the hotel sector still feel that service is demeaning, the bureaucracy remains entrenched, food is at best indifferent in hotels and private restaurants, while increasing in number, are still insufficient. Also, there is little nightlife outside the larger cities and few opportunities for individual tourists to travel without the benefit of organized tours unless they are fluent in Russian.

Future prospects for international tourism to the countries of the former Soviet Union are mixed. Economic and personal ties between Russia and the other CIS countries indicate that most international tourism will continue to be between the new countries themselves. Foreign tourism from beyond the region is handicapped by a variety of factors. First is the strong competition from other East European destinations such as Prague, Budapest, or Warsaw. A second factor, the difficulty of getting a visa to many of the former Soviet Union countries, makes other East European countries even more attractive since visas are not required or easily acquired for most East European countries. The third problem is the continued poor quality of rooms and service at most hotels and other tourist-related establishments. A fourth problem is created by the economic changes that have occurred. Many of the fifteen new countries still use a two-tier pricing structure, charging foreigners substantially more for hotel rooms and

opera, museum, ballet, train, or concert tickets than residents of the former Soviet Union. This is exacerbated by the tendency to charge "Western" prices for hotels and restaurants that clearly do not meet Western standards of quality or service. A fifth problem is the substantially increased crime rate and greater fear for personal safety in the new countries than in other European countries that compete for international tourists. Finally, the slow development of the overall tourism infrastructure lags behind as the government is not yet fully committed to this part of the economy. Together these factors suggest that international tourism from beyond the boundaries of the fifteen countries created from the former Soviet Union will experience only slow growth until these issues are resolved. According to the World Bank, Russia ranked ninth in terms of the total number of inbound tourist arrivals in Europe in 2010. Tourist arrivals to Russia increased to just over 22 million in 2010. The growth in tourist volume could be attributed to factors such as the country's stabilizing economy, rising disposable income levels and government initiatives to promote the country as an attractive tourist destination. Tourist volume in Russia is expected to increase even more by 2014 when the country will host the Winter Olympics. Russia has the potential to become one of the global leading travel and tourism economies over the next decade. Despite the current slow growth trends,

Russia's travel and tourism industry has positive long-term prospects. Over the forecast period, travel and tourism will continue to grow in importance. The outlook for travel and tourism in Russia is positive due to the country's growing economy and increased government initiatives to promote the country as an attractive tourist destination. The Russian government aims to deploy sustainable marketing resources to present the country as a high-quality and safe tourist destination. Short holidays are becoming more popular in Russia as affluent people prefer short breaks due to their busy working lifestyles. The number of small private hotels and recreation centers is increasing in rural areas, especially in areas close to major cities such as Moscow, St. Petersburg, and Sochi.

Internal Tourism in the CIS

Internal tourism dominated the tourism industry of the former Soviet Union. More than 155,000,000 vacation trips are taken inside Russia by its citizens yearly. Russians are granted 15 to 48 days of vacation annually by law. Variations in vacation lengths depended on profession, age, and length of service. Over 50 percent of the working population and more than 75 percent of school children are legally entitled to vacations of 23 days or more. Earlier, the provision of vacation tourism for Russian citizens was under the direction of trade unions. Most workers had their vacations highly subsidized by the place where they worked, resulting in extremely cheap vacation excursions. The various national and local trade union organizations provided a total of about 2 million beds for vacationing citizens of the Soviet Union. The subsidies from the trade unions have largely evaporated, and the emergence of fifteen independent countries has disrupted the old organization for internal tourism within the Soviet Union. Ongoing strife in some of the more popular destinations for citizens of the former Soviet Union (the Black Sea coast, central Asia, and Georgia) have further affected domestic tourism.

The one area in which tourism by citizens of the countries of the former Soviet Union has increased is foreign travel beyond the boundaries of the old Soviet Union. The loss of the former subsidies from trade unions, a relaxation or removal of limits on foreign travel, and the continual problem of the low quality of the tourism experience in the fifteen new countries have prompted many of their residents simply to save until they can visit other countries. European countries have received many of these tourists, but Turkey, China, the United States, Canada, and the Caribbean are destinations for residents of the former Soviet Union. Many of these tourists travel abroad for leisure and business, purchasing goods for resale in their home countries.

Location of Tourist-Related Activities in the CIS

Domestic Tourists

For the internal tourist of the former Soviet Union, the primary vacation destinations are associated with the sea coasts of the Black Sea in Russia and Ukraine, the Baltic Sea Coast in Estonia, Latvia (Figure P8.6), and Lithuania, the Southern Mountains of Central Asia, and to a lesser extent, the Volga River. Vacation facilities along the Black Sea Coast are the basis for a wide variety of communities from Sochi to Batumi and Yalta. Accommodations range from sparse dormitory-style facilities in converted monasteries or large mansions predating the revolution to medical and health spas and to large hotels.

The Baltic Sea Coast is another destination for the CIS and Baltic States tourist. The Volga River is the destination for a popular Russian pastime, a Volga River cruise. The various travel organizations of Russia operate a wide variety of tour boats that provide extended tours on the Volga, including stops at the cities, beaches, and parks along the river.

The mountains in the south of the CIS are a destination for tourists who enjoy hiking in the summer or skiing in the winter. The Caucasus Mountains in Russia and Georgia have the greatest development of these activities. The development of regional recreation centers, such as one on Lake Baikal, capitalizes on unique local features to benefit regional residents. The importance of the Trans-Siberian Railroad as a vacation experience should also be mentioned. Tens of thousands of CIS residents take one-to-two-week vacations simply traveling on the Trans-Siberian. Transportation prices remain relatively inexpensive for residents of the CIS, and entire families vacation by traveling on the railroads.

Foreign Tourists

It is possible to recognize eight broad tourist regions in the countries of the former Soviet Union that foreign tourists visit. The Central Region consists of Moscow, St. Petersburg, and Kyiv. This region receives more tourist visitors than any other in the countries. It is characteristic of the attractions of the former Soviet Union: czarist structures, a unique culture, and a distinctive lifestyle. Moscow is the most important tourist city. Moscow is the business capital of Russia, while St. Petersburg is the cultural capital.

Figure P8.6 Baltic Sea shore, Riga, Latvia. © Aleksey Stemmer/www.Shutterstock.com.

The major attractions in Moscow include the **Kremlin** and Red Square. The Kremlin takes its name from the Russian prefix *kreml*, which refers to a fortification. The Kremlin of Moscow is equally as important because it was the location of the head of government for the Soviet Union historically and now for Russia. The Kremlin consists of a complex of old and new buildings on 64 acres surrounded by fifteenth-century walls. The Kremlin contains the cathedrals of the czars and czarinas and the Armory Museum. Adjacent to the walls of the Kremlin is Red Square. It contains the mausoleum in which Lenin is embalmed, the exquisite St. Basil's Cathedral (Figure P8.7), and the Military Museum. Other important sights in Moscow include several remaining homes of important writers like Pushkin, Tolstoy, and Dostoevski. Famous museums in Moscow contain some of the most important icons, Russian paintings, and European Renaissance artwork in the world.

St. Petersburg remains the second largest city in size and attraction for foreign visitors to Russia. It is a very beautiful city with breathtaking architecture, lively in the summer, and its 300 bridges give it a special charm. The buildings and morphology of St. Petersburg reflect the influence of French and Italian architects and artists employed by Peter the Great. The city has been repainted to reflect the original color scheme, and the canals used to drain the swamplands of the Neva River make it the "Venice of the North." The museums are outstanding, especially the Hermitage. The Hermitage has one of the greatest collections of Western paintings in the world. The summer palace of Katherine the Great is another important attraction. Inside is the Amber Room, considered by some as the eighth wonder of the world.

Kyiv was largely destroyed during World War II and has been rebuilt as a modern city. The wide boulevards and modern buildings are typical of most centrally planned cities in the former Soviet Union. The presence of Russian Orthodox cathedrals (the St. Sophia Cathedral, Trinity Cathedral, and St. Andrew's Church

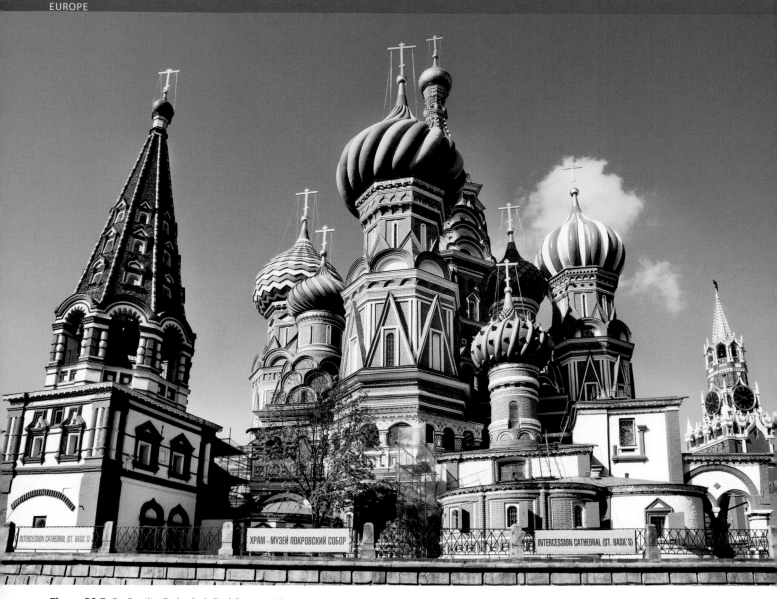

Figure P8.7 St. Basil's Cathedral, Red Square, Moscow. © Nickolay Vinokurov/www.Shutterstock.com.

are among the most significant) and the few remaining architectural gems create an interesting counterpoint to this scene. One of the important attractions is the series of fountains and statuary in honor of those who gave their lives in the Great Patriotic War (World War II).

Smaller towns around these three major cities in the Central Region are interesting for tourists, but the vast majority of foreign tourists visit only these three. Those who do go to smaller towns in the St. Petersburg region opt to visit the wooden villages around Lake Ladoga or Lake Onega. These communities date from the time of the Scandinavian invasion of what is today Estonia and Russia, from the eighth century A.D. onward. They have some of the finest old churches found in Russia. Other trips go out from St. Petersburg to such places as Petrodvorets with its landscaped gardens, fountains, and parks; Peterhof Palace, a fantastic series of old gardens, fountains, and palaces in the town of Peterhof, 20 miles from St. Petersburg; to Pushkin's home outside of Moscow; or to Zagorsk near Moscow where the

historical role of the Russian Orthodox Church can be recognized.

In combination, the remaining seven regions visited by foreign tourists do not attract the number of visitors that come to the Central Region.

The Baltic Region

The Baltic region focuses on the cities of Tallinn, Riga, and Vilnius, capitals of the three Baltic countries. This region is characterized by its European-influenced (particularly Scandinavian) medieval architecture and by sandy beaches on the Baltic. Tallinn has a particularly beautiful old town within its walled fortifications, dating from the Middle Ages.

The Black Sea Region

The Black Sea region includes Odesa in Ukraine, Sochi in Russia (site of the 2014 Winter Olympics), and

Batumi in Georgia. The region attracts tourists because of its coastal location, its excellent resorts, and the Black Sea beaches. The Black Sea region used to be a destination for numerous tourists from the East European satellite countries of the Soviet Union, but tourism is now mostly domestic.

The Southern Coast of the Crimean Peninsula of Ukraine

Major cities of this region include Yalta, Alupka, Evpatoria, and Sudak. The region has been developed for tourism, including prohibition of direct air flights into cities such as Yalta. Incoming tourists land to the north at Simferopol and are taken to Yalta and the surrounding resorts by bus. Automobile traffic is limited within the region, resulting in a very attractive resort setting. The beaches, climate, historical attractions, and spas are among the best in the CIS (Figure P8.8). With their alternating appearance of stark rock and pleasant vegetation, the Crimean Mountains combine with the Black Sea and its beaches to make this one of the most attractive locations in the CIS. The primary users of the Crimean Coast are domestic tourists.

Cities of the Caucasian Region (T'bilsi, Yerevan, and Baku)

The cities of the Caucasus include the birthplace of Stalin, a variety of health resorts that utilize mineral waters of the region, and winter sport facilities. The distinctive culture found in each of these cities makes each of them a unique destination in terms of foods and cultural activities; but as with the Crimea, this region primarily attracts domestic tourism.

The Central Asian Region

The Central Asian region is perhaps the most distinctive region in the former Soviet Union. The major cities (Tashkent, Almaty, Samarkand, and Bukhara) are filled with architectural monuments that reflect the many people who have inhabited this area. The cities are ancient trading centers that now serve as focal points for the cultural groups that are the basis for each of these Central Asian countries. The climate, landscape, language, and old sectors of the communities are distinctively different from anything else found in the CIS. Newer sections of the cities reflect the Soviet penchant for central planning and mass production of buildings and are less interesting than the older section. Because

Figure P8.8 Lastochkino Gnezdo in Yalta, Ukraine. © pil76/www.Shutterstock.com.

of the distance and limited numbers of hotels, this region receives far fewer visitors than does the Central Region.

Siberia

Siberia is a part of Russia. Major cities in Siberia include Novosibirsk, Irkutsk, and Khabarovsk. This region reflects the vastness of the taiga and the harsh Russian climate. Novosibirsk has a winter carnival that attracts some foreign tourists, and Lake Baikal is visited by those coming to Irkutsk, but the total foreign tourist flow to Siberia is extremely low. The Trans-Siberian Railroad attracts a few foreigners who traverse this region and may visit many of the cities along the route, but the lack of an architectural heritage in the new towns of Russian Siberia combines with the distance to minimize foreign tourist visitors to the area. Beyond the regions that dominate tourism in the former USSR, only minor tourist activity occurs in the balance of the large region that was once the Soviet Union.

Tourism: Problems and Potentials

The tourism industry of the region suffers from the same problems that the general economy must face. For the domestic tourist, the industry provided an opportunity to escape from the cities with their seemingly endless blocks of apartment complexes, but the services that were provided were at a basic level. The underlying theoretic guidelines of the Communist Party dictated that the quality of hotels and recreation it provided would be generally uniform throughout the country. Consequently, standards tend to be much lower than those found in typical Western countries. In spite of this, since the domestic tourist has no other choice, tourism is a major economic activity. The present independent governments' emphasis on free enterprise may eliminate some of these problems. If it is effective in the tourism industry, we could expect that individual hotels or resorts would provide their workers an incentive as they generate more profit. If this occurs, it can reasonably be expected that there will be variation in quality of tourism, accommodation, services, and experiences that will change the bland and uniform nature of the domestic tourism experience in the individual CIS countries.

The foreign component of the tourism industry in the former Soviet Union is small, but each of the new countries proposes its expansion. The general low level of service experienced in the industry usually discourages foreign tourists from returning more than once. The exception to this is in the new joint-venture hotels operated by private interests and the emergence of world-class river cruise experiences on the Dnieper and Volga rivers, where the level of service is more typical of what might be found in Western Europe.

In spite of these problems, the CIS countries have attractions that could lead to a major increase in foreign tourism flow if they were exploited. The appeal associated with the unique and the unknown is perhaps the greatest attraction that the new countries have for foreign tourists. The majority of the people of the world know little about Russia or the other countries. Their enigmatic natures continue to attract limited numbers of foreign tourists. Continued improvement in services and goods and development of tourist attractions by each individual country may result in a major change in the number of foreign tourists to the region.

For the individual or organization involved in the tourism industry that interfaces with the countries created from the former Soviet Union, it is important to recognize the strengths and weaknesses of the existing tourist industry. Tourists to the new countries should be made aware that they will not receive the same level of service that they might expect in Western Europe and that facilities will not be at the same standard. If tourists go with a desire to learn more about the cultures of the fifteen countries and their distinctive geography, they will not be disappointed. A visit to these countries can be one of extreme enjoyment if unrealistic expectations are not held. The continuing changes in the region, including efforts to implement incentives in the economy, will lead doubtlessly to an even better experience for foreign tourists in the future.

chapter 25: RUSSIA AND ITS NEIGHBORS

© Asaf Eliason/ShutterStock.com

Armenia

Introduction

Modern Armenia is a small, mountainous, and land-locked country, but ancient Armenia stretched between the Caspian and Mediterranean seas. Its long history includes becoming the first Christian nation in A.D. 301 and being absorbed into countless empires, most recently the Soviet Union in 1920. Armenia's rebirth in 1991 brought war with Azerbaijan over Nagorno-Karabakh, an ethnic Armenian region inside Azerbaijan, which resulted in Armenian control of Nagorno-Karabakh (see Nagorno-Karabakh entry under Azerbaijan). Armenia's developing economy benefits from cash remittances from millions of overseas Armenians.

From *National Geographic Atlas of the World*, 9th edition. Copyright ©2011 National Geographic Society. Reprinted by arrangement. All rights reserved.

Area	29,743 sq km (11,484 sq mi)
Population	3,097,000
Government	republic
Capital	Yerevan 1,102,000
Life Expectancy	72 years
Religion	Armenian Apostolic, other Christian
Language	Armenian
Currency	dram (AMD)
GDP per Cap	$5,900
Labor Force	46.2% Agriculture, 15.6% Industry, 38.2% Services

From *National Geographic Atlas of the World*, 9th edition. Copyright ©2011 National Geographic Society. Reprinted by arrangement. All rights reserved.

TRAVEL **TIPS** 💼

Entry: A passport and visa are required.

Tourist Season: April through October

Shopping: Common items purchased include handicrafts such as folk costumes or other clothing or fabrics, dolls, jewelry, and wooden carvings.

Internet TLD: .am

CULTURAL CAPSULE

Armenia has a long history as a Christian country. An important part of the Roman Empire, Armenia adopted Christianity as the state religion in about 300 A.D. As part of the expanding Byzantine Empire, it was ultimately conquered by Muslim Arabs in 661 A.D. During the late 1000s and 1100s, Armenia was allied with European Crusaders, but was again conquered by the Muslims and became part of the Turkish Ottoman Empire. Nationalistic movements in Armenia in the late nineteenth and early twentieth centuries led to the massacre of as many as 1½ million Armenians and the flight of many to Western countries at the end of World War I. Incorporated into the newly created Union of Soviet Socialist Republics in 1923, Armenia remained a part of the Soviet Union until it declared itself independent on 23 September 1991. The Armenian Orthodox Church has remained dominant throughout the Communist period and today. The Armenians are highly nationalistic and unresolved conflicts with Azerbaijan over

Azerbaijani enclaves within its territory and an Armenian enclave in Azerbaijan lead to war again.

Cultural hints: Armenia is said to be the place where the Middle East meets Europe, so there is great variety in foods and architecture. Shake hands upon meeting, with men waiting for women to extend their hand first. Friends embrace and touch cheeks. Tipping is appreciated, and a gift of money will help you find a seat in a crowded restaurant. Lamb is Armenia's staple meat, and boiled lamb is a specialty. Trout from Lake Sevan are a luxury meal. Brandy is the primary beverage specialty. A variety of Middle Eastern food types are also found here, such as rice pilaf and a wide variety of fruits and vegetables.

Tourism Characteristics

Armenia is a beautiful land with sophisticated people. Armenia's history provides both important tourism opportunities and a great sense of tragedy. Lacking any of the traditional attractions of sun-sea-sand, Armenia has traditionally attracted visitors with ethnic ties to the country or those interested in its long and varied history. Under communist rule the only city open to foreign visitors was Yerevan, the capital. Since independence, the government has lifted many of the restrictions on travel, and tourists are rarely stopped by the authorities. Tourism to Armenia is limited because of ongoing conflicts. Reports of these conflicts frighten potential visitors to the area. Russia, Armenia, and Azerbaijan have signed a declaration to improve the local situation.

Tourism has always been a minor part of the economy of Armenia, although currently it is virtually halted as a result of conflicts. Nevertheless, Armenia has great tourism potential because of its varied and beautiful mountain scenery and the unique Armenian culture and architecture. Someday it may have the stability to capitalize upon its potential.

Tourist Destinations and Attractions

The major destination in Armenia is Yerevan and the surrounding area. Yerevan is a Soviet-built city that is basically drab and featureless, but the vitality of its markets and the emerging cooperative restaurants provide a unique experience. The central plaza in Yerevan has a lovely series of fountains that are enhanced by colored lights at night. The government house on the east side is the seat of the government, and two important hotels are nearby. The Hotel Armenia is being reconstructed and is presently the best hotel in the city. Other places to visit include the Armenian History Museum and the Ancient Manuscripts Library. The library houses over 12,000 Armenian manuscripts dating back to the ninth century. The display of illuminated manuscripts is particularly impressive. The other major site in Yerevan is its memorial to the victims of the 1915 genocide.

Near Yerevan are two important sites. Echmiadzin, the capital of Armenia from 184 to 340 A.D., is a very holy place to Armenians as the site of their most important orthodox cathedral and the residence of the church's leader, the Supreme Catholicos. Sixteen miles east of Yerevan is Garni, where the temple to the Roman god Mithrus was built by the Armenian king in the first century A.D. After Armenia converted to Christianity, Armenian rulers used the temple as a summer residence. Damaged by earthquakes, it was restored in the 1960s and 1970s. There are also ruins of a seventh-century church and a third-century bathhouse with a mosaic floor in the Roman style.

Geghard is an operating monastery 22 miles east of Yerevan. It has marvelous carved churches dating from the early 1200s. There are lovely old Christian sites located in or near all of the major cities of Armenia. The most important medieval Armenian cultural center is at Agartsin. Located 70 miles from Yerevan, it has a classic Armenian church built between the tenth and thirteenth centuries.

Azerbaijan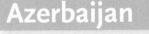

Introduction

Oil-rich Azerbaijan gained independence from the USSR in 1991. It borders the Caspian Sea, where there are sizable oil and gas resources. However, pollution from the petrochemical industry threatens the sea and Caspian caviar. From the populated lowlands bordering the Caspian Sea, the land rises to the rugged, sparsely populated Caucasus Mountains in the north and west. South of Armenia lies Naxçivan, a landlocked exclave of Azerbaijan. The mountainous west harbors Nagorno-Karabakh, where an uneasy cease-fire, following a 1988–94 war with Armenians, drains the country's resources.

Area	86,600 sq km (33,436 sq mi)
Population	8,781,000
Government	republic
Capital	Baku 1,892,000
Life Expectancy	72 years
Religion	Muslim
Language	Azerbaijani (Azeri)
Currency	Azerbaijani manat (AZN)
GDP per Cap	$10,400
Labor Force	38.3% Agriculture, 12.1% Industry, 49.6% Services

TRAVEL TIPS

Entry: A passport and visa are required.

Shopping: Common items include handicrafts such as copper bowls and other ornate metal objects, distinctive folk costumes, and objects related to the Muslim heritage of the country.

Internet TLD: .az

CULTURAL CAPSULE

Azerbaijan was one of the Muslim republics in the former Soviet Union. Culturally it is an extension of the Soviet Central Asia region in terms of its culture and traditions, but its language and ethnic background are tied to Turkish. It shares with the Central Asian republics a tradition of Islam, which has been highly secularized as a result of the seventy years of Soviet rule. Since independence, there has been a resurgence of interest in the Muslim tradition and visitors should be aware of Muslim values in dealing with the people. Most people understand Russian, but a Turkish phrase book will allow you to use basic words that will be understood by the Azeri majority. The written form of Azeri uses the Russian Cyrillic alphabet.

Figure 25.1 Baku, Azerbaijan. © Elnur/www.Shutterstock.com.

Cultural hints: A common greeting is to shake hands, but friends will embrace and may kiss one another upon the cheek. Shake hands with everyone at an office or other gathering. Public displays of affection are usually not acceptable. Before taking photographs, ask permission, especially in mosques or of individuals (who may ask for a small fee). Alcohol should only be consumed in hotels or restaurants catering to foreign visitors or secularized Muslims. Tips will result in better service. Food is served with the traditional black tea, which is drunk in large quantities. Common foods include richly spiced lamb; a pilaf of rice fried with meat, fish, vegetables, or fruit; shish kebabs; minced lamb and vegetables steamed in grape leaves; and soups made from lamb stock. Azerbaijan is famous for its desserts, which are similar to those found in Turkey.

Tourism Characteristics

Azerbaijan is a picturesque and culturally and geographically diverse country. It has received little tourism in the past and receives even less today. During the Soviet period, most visitors were Russians or Georgians and Armenians going to the beaches and spas along the Caspian. Western visitors were extremely few and typically visited only Baku for one or two nights and then the ancient town of Sheki as part of an Intourist tour to the Caucasus and Central Asian republics. Foreign tourism to the southern half of the republic has been basically nonexistent. There was a conflict with Armenia and the resurgence of Islam in the country have reduced tourism to a trickle. Azerbaijan is strengthening its ties with Turkey and Iran and may benefit from tourism from these areas in the future if it is able to develop its Caspian Sea coast. The conflict with Armenia in the 1990s left both countries in poverty. The country is slowly recovering but has ambitious plans for future tourism development, including a ski resort in the Shahdag Mountains.

Tourist Destinations and Attractions

The major destinations in Azerbaijan are Baku, Sheki, and the Caspian coast. Baku (Figure 25.1) is by far the most important tourist attraction. With a quarter of Azerbaijan's population in its limits Baku is the biggest metropolis in all of the Caucasian area and was the fifth largest city in the Soviet Union. It is built on the Apsheron Peninsula, and owes its growth to the discovery of oil in the Caspian Sea and along the coast of Azerbaijan. The city is the site of a school (Madrassa) for Shia Muslims, opened in 1989 as the first in the former Soviet Union. The most interesting tourist attractions in Baku are associated with the old town, a medieval fortress that withstood the Mongol Tartar siege in the thirteenth century. Much of the city heart is pedestrian only. The Dzhuma holds the museum of carpets and applied art. This is the best and most impressive museum in Azerbaijan and includes displays of woven and knotted Azerbaijani carpets, carved wood, metalwork, jewelry, and European and Russian paintings.

Sheki is perhaps the oldest city in Azerbaijan. Located on the southern slopes of the Caucasus Mountains 235 miles from Baku, evidence indicates it was founded over 2,500 years ago. It was the home of a ruler in Azerbaijan in the eighteenth century, and the Summer Palace and Riverside Fortress are still standing. Sheki is

especially important for locally made silk, and its caravanserais (historic inns dating from centuries ago) and bazaars are still famous. The Caspian Sea Coast was an important tourist destination during the Soviet period, with Russians and Armenians joining Azerbaijanis in experiencing the sun-sea-sand. Since the independence of Azerbaijan, this tourism has declined precipitously. The beaches have good potential if they are ever developed properly and the economy and political situation are stabilized.

Belarus

Introduction

Belarus, meaning "White Russia," lies on the edge of eastern Europe and consists of flat lowlands separated by low hills and thousands of lakes. Forests cover a third of this landlocked republic, and the Pinsk Marshes occupy much of the south. The winters are snowy and cold, and the summers are hot and humid. Ethnic Belarusians constitute 81 percent of the population, followed by ethnic Russians at 11.4 percent. Poles (3.9 percent) are concentrated mostly in western Belarus, and the government has been accused of numerous human rights violations against its 400,000-strong Polish minority. Both Belarusian and Russian are official languages, but most people speak Russian on a daily basis. National identity is weak in this former Soviet republic. Until the twentieth century, empires divided Belarus. It became a republic of the Soviet Union in 1922 but suffered intensive Russification under Stalin after World War II, when Russians controlled the government and banned the Belarusian language. Belarus gained independence in 1991, but the autocratic government still depends economically on Russia. The industrial economy hinges on Russian energy and raw materials. Russia provides aid for radiation medicine and safe food production in areas affected by Chernobyl (Chornobyl' in Ukrainian). The 1986 Chernobyl nuclear disaster continues to drain the Belarusian budget with cleanup and health care costs. Even though Chernobyl is in northern Ukraine, more than 70 percent of the radioactive fallout fell on Belarus.

From *National Geographic Atlas of the World*, 9th edition. Copyright ©2011 National Geographic Society. Reprinted by arrangement. All rights reserved.

Area	207,595 sq km (80,153 sq mi)
Population	9,662,000
Government	republic
Capital	Minsk 1,805,000
Life Expectancy	70 years
Religion	Eastern Orthodox, other (includes Roman Catholic, Protestant, Jewish, Muslim)

Language	Belarusian, Russian
Currency	Belarusian ruble (BYB/BYR)
GDP per Cap	$11,600
Labor Force	14% Agriculture, 34.7% Industry, 51.3% Services

From *National Geographic Atlas of the World*, 9th edition. Copyright ©2011 National Geographic Society. Reprinted by arrangement. All rights reserved.

TRAVEL **TIPS** 🧳

Entry: A visa and passport are required.

Tourist Season: May through September

Shopping: Common items include intricately carved wooden boxes (whose geometric designs are made of lacquered straw), wooden trinkets, ceramics, and woven textiles.

Internet TLD: .by

CULTURAL CAPSULE

Belarus is a flat region along the shortest route between Moscow and Poland. Its name means "White Russia," which seems to derive from its ancient inhabitants' clothes. It is a border region that has been fought over for centuries by Russians, Poles, Germans, and others. It suffered grievously during World War II, and was one of three Soviet Republics with a seat in the United Nations before the great independence movements of the 1990s. The people are Slavs who settled the region in the sixth to eighth centuries. The region was dominated by a powerful Lithuanian state in the Middle Ages, and subsequently by Poland. Roman Catholicism became the official religion in 1386. Expansion of Russia caused the peasants who had remained Russian Orthodox to revert to their orthodox religion. During the Soviet period, religion was publicly practiced primarily by the elderly, but since independence there has been a return to the church by many of the young. The language is so similar to Russian that the Russian language is still widely used in spite of independence.

Cultural hints: Shake hands in greeting, but close friends may engage in a hug and a brief kiss to alternate cheeks. As you enter a row of a theater to occupy your seat, if you pass in front of other seated people turn and face them. Public display of affection is avoided. Tips are appreciated.

Figure 25.2 War monument to the brave, Brest fortress, Belarus. © CnOPhoto/www.Shutterstock.com.

During meals toasting with vodka, wine, or beer is common. A typical Belarussian meal includes potatoes, mushrooms, and sausage or other pork. Soups (especially borscht, with its distinctive red color from beets) are common. Potato dumplings are often served with soup. Cucumber-and-tomato salad is common in the summer with lunch and dinner. Sour cream is added to borscht and other soups. Pastries filled with meat are a common main dish. Pies, strudels, and other desserts are a mainstay of major meals.

Tourism Characteristics

Belarus has relatively little to offer in the way of tourism. The major role of Belarus has been as a transit route between Europe and Russia. Consequently, its tourism has been associated with either travel or any disasters that have occurred in the region. As the location of conflict between competing groups, there is a variety of historic sites to visit. In 1996 Belarus entered into a joint economic and political union with Russia. A financial crisis in 2011 caused the economy to falter. Belarus receives few visitors from outside of Europe. Its tourism market is largely regional in character. The majority of visitors are from neighboring Russia.

Tourist Destinations and Attractions

Major destinations in Belarus are Minsk, the hamlet of Khatyn, and Brest on the border. Minsk has an old town, which included the marketplace in the twelfth century. There is a small area of housing on the east bank of the river that has been restored to the seventeenth- and eighteenth-century style to make a quaint attraction.

There are craft shops and functioning churches found in the old center of town. Essentially all of Minsk was destroyed during World War II, and its new buildings reflect the Soviet architectural style. The restored main street of Minsk is the site of major shops and a Belarussian art museum is located only 1½ blocks south. There is a museum of the Great Patriotic War (World War II), which gives a vivid introduction to the destruction and suffering of Minsk during World War II. The art palace exhibits Belarussian arts and crafts, and some reproductions are available for tourists.

Near Minsk are pleasant pine forests and a reservoir (the Minsk Sea) where camping and picnicking are enjoyed by the residents.

The small village of Khatyn is 60 kilometers north of Minsk. Burned to the ground with all of its inhabitants in 1943 as a reprisal by the Germans against local partisans, it is now a memorial to the Great Patriotic War. There is a sculpture and a graveyard commemorating 185 other Belarussian villages destroyed by the Germans. (Do not confuse Khatyn with Katyn, where the Soviets murdered thousands of citizens of the USSR.)

Brest is primarily important for the Brest fortress located here (Figure 25.2). A fort was built in the 1800s and destroyed in the German invasion of 1941. Rebuilt in a monumental style as a memorial after World War II, it features recorded explosions and gunfire to provide atmosphere for visitors. The Defense of Brest Museum is adjacent to the fortress. Also on the outskirts of Brest each Saturday and Sunday is one of the largest markets in the former Soviet Union. Poles and Belarussians sell Western products of all types from guns to computers.

Estonia

Introduction

Estonia, smallest in population of the former Soviet republics, is a low-lying land on the Baltic Sea with bogs, marshes, and 1,200 natural lakes. Forests cover more than half the nation. The average elevation is only 50 meters (160 feet). The country's proximity to the sea means that skies are often cloudy, with frequent rain or snow. Summers tend to be drier and warm. Independence blossomed briefly between 1918 and 1940 after centuries of German, Swedish, and Russian rule. During World War II, Estonia was invaded first by Russian troops, then German, and then Russians again; and it was forced into the Soviet Union in 1944. Since independence in 1991, Estonia deals with the legacy of Russian workers brought in during the Soviet years—25 percent of the population is Russian. As a stable democracy with a market economy, Estonia looks to the West for trade and security, joining both the European Union and NATO in 2004.

From *National Geographic Atlas of the World*, 9th edition. Copyright ©2011 National Geographic Society. Reprinted by arrangement. All rights reserved.

Area	45,228 sq km (17,463 sq mi)
Population	1,340,000
Government	parliamentary republic
Capital	Tallinn 397,000
Life Expectancy	73 years
Religion	Evangelical Lutheran, Orthodox
Language	Estonian, Russian
Currency	Estonian kroon (EEK)
GDP per Cap	$18,700
Labor Force	2.8% Agriculture, 22.7% Industry, 74.5% Services

TRAVEL **TIPS** 🧳

Entry: Visas are not required for tourists from the United States. A passport is required.

Tourist Season: May through September

Shopping: Common items include amber and amber jewelry, woolen textiles, embroidered folk costumes, dolls, and wooden trinkets.

Internet TLD: .ee

CULTURAL CAPSULE Estonia is unique among the former Soviet republics in that it has a language unrelated to any of the Slavic tongues. Estonian is related to Finnish. Estonia has a long tradition of orientation to the West, and several of its cities were dominated by Germans as part of the Hanseatic League. The combination of German, Danish, and Finnish influence has created a Scandinavian feeling in Tallinn and other Hanseatic cities. The major tourist attractions reflect its varied history and are among the most attractive in the former Soviet Union.

Cultural hints: Shake hands to greet. Typical foods include roast pork with onions and mushrooms, soups (including borscht), and a variety of pastries, cakes, and open sandwiches. Fish, chicken, potatoes, cabbage, cheese, pork, and bread are common foods.

Tourism Characteristics

Estonia is unique among the former republics of the Soviet Union in that it maintained a much stronger connection to the West during the entire Soviet period. On a regular basis a long-standing ferry service between Tallinn and Helsinki covered the 50 miles of the Baltic separating them. Of all of the former republics, Estonia had the reputation for the highest-quality consumer goods and the greatest availability of goods and services. Its long connections to Germany and Scandinavia resulted in a culture that is Western oriented and more similar to Scandinavia than to Russia. This can be seen in the visitors to Estonia. More than half are from Finland, while Russia now represents a small percentage. The country is determined to increase its tourism, particularly short-break tourism from Scandinavia and Western Europe. As more facilities are built and older facilities are renovated, it can be expected that tourism to this beautiful country will increase. Its tourism infrastructure is well developed and the level of service is up to Western European standards.

Tourist Destinations and Attractions

The major destinations in Estonia are the cities of Tallinn, Tartu, and Parnu. Tallinn (Figure 25.3) is a lovely Hanseatic League city. In few areas of Europe can you experience the feeling of the fourteenth and fifteenth centuries as you do in Tallinn with its old medieval walls and winding cobbled streets climbing its hills and the needle narrow spires of its churches. It has been judiciously restored to make it extremely attractive. It is divided into the upper town (Toompea) and the lower town. Both are medieval and include a variety of lovely architectural styles in the stores, houses,

Figure 25.3 Towers of old town, Tallinn, Estonia. © Ingrid Maasik/www.Shutterstock.com.

and churches. The upper town occupies the hill overlooking the harbor. The entrance is through a gate tower built in 1380, which separates the upper town on the hill from the lower town. Leading between high walls to the upper town, its cobbled streets are vivid reminders of life during the medieval period. Upper town includes the Toompea Castle, the Russian Orthodox Alexander Nevsky Cathedral, and a variety of beautiful buildings. The castle built by the Danes in 1219 has been largely destroyed, and a baroque replacement dating from the time of Catherine the Great dominates the hill. The castle is now home to the Estonian parliament. Another major attraction in the upper town is the Lutheran dome church (Toomkirik). There are observation platforms in the upper town that provide a dramatic view of the medieval lower town and the Baltic.

The second major attraction is the lower town and its square (Raekoja Plats), which is dominated by the only surviving Gothic town hall in Northern Europe. The square was the center of the first markets held here, from the eleventh to the end of the nineteenth century. In the streets leading off the square are old Lutheran and Catholic churches as well as lovely homes

dating from the fifteenth to the seventeenth century. Roads through the medieval gates of the town are lined with the houses of merchants and gentry built in the fifteenth century or later. Many of the Tallinn guilds (associations of artisans or traders) can also be seen in the medieval lower town.

The second largest attraction in Estonia is the city of Tartu (Dorpat). It is noted for its classical architecture, which results from the comprehensive rebuilding after the town burned down in 1775. Tartu is also home to the most famous university in Estonia. Founded in 1632 when the country was under Swedish control, Tartu University became one of the premier centers of learning in nineteenth century Europe, and its scientific emphasis still persists. Tartu is also home to the Estonian National Museum.

Parnu is a coastal resort 130 kilometers south of Tallinn. This is one of the oldest occupied sites in Europe, with archaeological relics found just inland from the site dating back 9,500 years. It was a Hanseatic port in the fourteenth century, and in the mid-nineteenth century emerged as a sanitorium utilizing its mud baths. Today several sanitoria provide mud baths as well as access to the resort area oriented towards the beach.

Latvia

Introduction

Mostly flat and forested, Latvia lies on the Baltic Sea in northern Europe. Rolling hills and lakes prevail in the east. The climate is mostly temperate, but winters can be severe.

Latvia first gained independence in 1918, but it was occupied by the Soviet Union and Nazi Germany during World War II. Soviet occupation lasted from 1944 to 1991, when Latvia again gained independence. Few former Soviet republics experienced a more profound shift in character during their years of Soviet domination than this Baltic country. From 1939–1989 the proportion of ethnic Latvians in Latvia dropped from 73 percent to 52 percent—due to heavy Russian immigration and Latvian emigration. Since independence in 1991, Latvian ethnicity has started to rebound and now constitutes 59 percent of the population, with Russians at 28 percent. An industrial country with trade ties to the West, Latvia joined NATO and the European Union in 2004.

From *National Geographic Atlas of the World*, 9th edition. Copyright ©2011 National Geographic Society. Reprinted by arrangement. All rights reserved.

Area	64,589 sq km (24,938 sq mi)
Population	2,256,000
Government	parliamentary democracy
Capital	Riga 722,000
Life Expectancy	72 years
Religion	Lutheran, Orthodox
Language	Latvian, Russian
Currency	lats (LVL)
GDP per Cap	$14,500
Labor Force	12.1% Agriculture, 25.8% Industry, 61.8% Services

From *National Geographic Atlas of the World*, 9th edition. Copyright ©2011 National Geographic Society. Reprinted by arrangement. All rights reserved.

TRAVEL **TIPS**

Entry: No visa is required. A passport is required.

Tourist Season: May through September

Shopping: Common items include amber and amber jewelry, woolen textiles, linen fabric, lace, wooden dolls and other trinkets, and embroidery.

Internet TLD: .lv

CULTURAL CAPSULE Latvia has suffered from outside intervention more than any other of the Baltic States. It was not until the late nineteenth century that the idea of a separate country became widespread among the Letts, who are the majority population. The principal city, Rīga, was founded by Germans as a storehouse for traders to the North European Plain. The Germanic Knights occupied the area until the sixteenth century, after which Poles, Russians, Swedes, and Russians controlled it.

Cultural hints: Shake hands to greet, with friends embracing and kissing one another's cheeks. Flowers are often presented by visiting guests. Common foods include borscht, smoked sausage, pork rolls stuffed with carrots, fish, soup, cheese, potatoes, and bread.

Tourist Characteristics, Destinations, and Attractions

Latvia's tourism market is highly regional with few visitors from outside of Europe. Nearly 70 percent of its visitors are from the neighboring countries of Lithuania, Estonia, and Russia. The United States represents half of all its visitors from outside of Europe. The principal destinations in Latvia are Rīga, the Baltic Coast, and the valley of the Gauja River. Rīga is the largest city in the former Baltic Republics of the Soviet Union and is a major commercial and industrial site. It has many old buildings dating from its centuries of occupation, especially by Germans. Old Rīga is the most picturesque of these, containing whole rows of Germanic buildings dating from the seventeenth century. Its crooked streets are mainly pedestrian only, providing the sense of a gigantic outdoor museum. Two towering churches and their squares dominate the old town. The oldest is the brick Dom Cathedral founded by the Germanic Knights in 1211 A.D. Rīga Castle dates in part from the thirteenth century. It contains three museums, the most interesting being the history museum on the fourth floor.

The Baltic coast of Latvia is home to a strip of resorts stretching about twenty miles. The water of the Baltic is cool, and at present so polluted that swimming is prohibited. The main attractions are the sanatoria dating from the nineteenth century, the long sandy beaches, and the pine-covered dunes.

The Gauja River Valley is known for the castles perched above the river valley. Some remnants of the 1207 Germanic Knights' Castle are still standing, and its ruins remind visitors of the host of occupiers and their associated wars that have afflicted the small country of Latvia.

Figure 25.4 Trakai Island Castle, Lake Galvé, Lithuania. © Meoita/www.Shutterstock.com.

Lithuania

Introduction

Lithuania, in northeastern Europe, is the largest of the three Baltic States (the other two are Estonia and Latvia). The landscape consists of gently rolling plains, widespread forests, and 2,800 lakes (Figure 25.4). The French National Geographic Institute (IGN) calculated that a point just north of Vilnius, Lithuania's capital, is the geographic center of Europe. Lithuania's history is reflected in its diverse population, which is 83.5 percent Lithuanian, 6.7 percent Polish, and 6.3 percent Russian. The Lithuanian state was founded in the thirteenth century, formed a union with Poland in the sixteenth century, and then was absorbed into the Russian Empire in 1795. Lithuania was independent again (1918–1940) but then was occupied by the Soviet Union until 1990. Lithuania today is a democracy with a market economy based on information technology and manufacturing; it has seen strong export growth since joining the EU in 2004.

From *National Geographic Atlas of the World*, 9th edition. Copyright ©2011 National Geographic Society. Reprinted by arrangement. All rights reserved.

Area	65,300 sq km (25,212 sq mi)
Population	3,339,000
Government	parliamentary democracy
Capital	Vilnius 543,000
Life Expectancy	71 years
Religion	Roman Catholic, Russian Orthodox

Language	Lithuanian, Russian, Polish
Currency	litas (LTL)
GDP per Cap	$15,400
Labor Force	14.0% Agriculture, 29.1% Industry, 56.9% Services

From *National Geographic Atlas of the World*, 9th edition. Copyright ©2011 National Geographic Society. Reprinted by arrangement. All rights reserved.

TRAVEL **TIPS** 💼

Entry: A visa is not required for residents of the United States. A passport is required.

Tourist Season: May through September

Shopping: Common items include woolen and linen textiles, amber and amber jewelry, embroidered folk costumes, scarves, dolls and other wooden objects, and art objects of tin or other thin metal.

Internet TLD: .lt

CULTURAL CAPSULE

Lithuania has a position on the open European Plain that has made it a focus of repeated invasion. At one time the Polish-Lithuanian empire occupied much of the North European plain. The European influence is obvious in the dominance of the Roman Catholic Church in the culture. Decades of occupation as part of the Soviet Empire did not dull the nationalistic tendencies of the Lithuanians, and Lithuania was one of the first Soviet Republics to demand and obtain independence. The economy is being privatized and is ahead of Estonia and Latvia. Lithuania receives many day tourists from Poland.

Cultural hints: Shake hands upon greeting. Close friends may embrace and kiss cheeks. Flowers are often presented by visitors. Generally do not touch while talking unless it is a close friend. Public display of affection reserved for greeting friends. Pork is a common dish. Other typical foods include caviar, beef, chicken, wild game, eggs, soups, meat pies, potatoes, vegetables, and bread.

Tourism Characteristics, Destinations, and Attractions

The Commonwealth of Independent States accounts for over 55 percent of visitors to Lithuania, with Russia the largest single market. The primary destination in Lithuania is the capital, Vilnius, but tourism to Lithuania has never had very large numbers. In 1994, it ranked fifth of the fifteen countries created from the former Soviet Union. Vilnius, however, is often described as the prettiest and greenest capital of the Baltic countries. Attractions in Vilnius include the red brick tower on the 150-foot-high hill. Part of the old defenses of Vilnius, it provides a good view of the city. The cathedral is now a national shrine, as it was reopened for worship in 1989 and became a symbol of Lithuanian independence. Rebuilt many times since the Gothic structure built in the 1400s, it is now essentially done in the classical style. The old town of Vilnius was built in the fifteenth and sixteenth centuries. Much of this area was a Jewish ghetto during World War II. Lithuanians were involved in the Holocaust, in which essentially all of Lithuania's Jewish population was murdered under German direction. Parts of the old town have been restored to better-than-new condition, while others are dilapidated. The narrow streets and old buildings are among the most interesting attractions in Vilnius. The university in Vilnius was founded in 1579, and today has about 16,000 students. There are numerous other attractions, including lovely Catholic churches, museums, and shops.

At Paneriai about four miles from Vilnius is one of the German death camps, where 100,000 Lithuanian Jews were exterminated. The pits where the thousands of bodies were disposed of are grassed over, but still evoke in visitors a deep sorrow over the inhumanity of the Holocaust.

Kaunas is Lithuania's second largest city. Destroyed repeatedly over the centuries, it contains some lovely restored fifteenth- and sixteenth-century German merchant houses around the old town square. The new town is dominated by a pedestrian street, where the most interesting museums and shops in the town are found. On the outskirts of town is the Ninth Fort, which was turned into a death camp by the Germans. About 80,000 Jews were killed here.

Moldova

Landlocked Moldova lies in eastern Europe between Romania and Ukraine. The country consists of hilly grassland drained by the Prut and Dniester Rivers. Rich black soils make it prime agricultural land. The climate is temperate, with moderate to cold winters and hot summers. Most of Moldova was part of Romania before World War II, and two-thirds of Moldovans speak Romanian (officially known as Moldovan). The region was taken from Romania during World War II and became part of the Soviet Union. Moldovan independence came in 1991. While Moldovans are a majority (78 percent of the population), there are significant minorities: Ukrainians (8.4 percent), Russians (5.8 percent), Gagauz, also known as Christian Turks (4.4 percent). Moldova is one of the poorest countries in Europe, and it depends on foreign aid.

Area	33,851 sq km (13,070 sq mi)
Population	4,133,000
Government	republic
Capital	Chisinau 592,000
Life Expectancy	69 years
Religion	Eastern Orthodox
Language	Moldovan, Russian, Gagauz
Currency	Moldovan leu (MDL)
GDP per Cap	$2,300
Labor Force	40.6% Agriculture, 16.0% Industry, 43.3% Services

From *National Geographic Atlas of the World*, 9th edition. Copyright ©2011 National Geographic Society. Reprinted by arrangement. All rights reserved.

TRAVEL **TIPS** 💼

Entry: A visa is not required. A passport is required.

Tourist Season: No distinct season

Shopping: Common items include embroidered cloth, ceramics, pottery, glassware, and wooden hand-painted icons.

Internet TLD: .md

Tourism Characteristics

Moldova was a minor destination for tourism in the former Soviet Union. Only 1 percent of all tourists to the fifteen new countries created from the Soviet Union went to Moldova in 2010. Since independence from the Soviet Union, Moldova has stated its intention to rejoin Romania. The eastern industrial part of the country, which is predominantly Russian, has declared itself an autonomous republic. Its greatest number of tourists is from Romania at the present, as many come to visit former friends and family separated for fifty years.

Tourist Destinations and Attractions

The major attraction in Moldova is Chisinău (Kishinev). It was largely destroyed during World War II, but has some interesting parks and museums. The old town consists of a few streets of wooden houses near the river. Wine tasting is offered as a form of entertainment.

Other than Chisinău, the road from Romania to Chisinău provides a scenic drive through rolling countryside of vineyards and fields of corn (maize), sunflowers, and sugar beets. There are a number of old monasteries found in the countryside of Moldova. Other cities are less interesting, but provide visitors a view of brandy manufacturing (in Beltsy) or the old forts from the Russian-Turkish conflict over the region (at Bendery and Tiraspol).

Ukraine

Introduction

The Carpathian Mountains rise in the west and the Crimean Mountains in the south, but the heartland of Ukraine is rich, flat earth known as the steppe. Once called the breadbasket of the Soviet Union, Ukraine also has huge deposits of coal and iron that feed heavy industry, particularly in the Donbass (Donets Basin). The climate is subtropical in the Crimean Peninsula and temperate continental in the rest of the country, with greater precipitation in the north and west. Some 130 ethnic groups populate the country. Ukrainians are the largest ethnic group with 77.8 percent of the population; next are ethnic Russians (17.3 percent); followed by Belarusians (0.5 percent) and Crimean Tatars (0.5 percent). Ukrainian is the official language, but Russian is widely spoken in eastern Ukraine. At its greatest extent, the Russian Empire encompassed most of present-day Ukraine; the remainder was part of the Austro-Hungarian Empire. With the fall of the Russian Empire in 1917, Ukrainians tried to become independent, but the country was partitioned between Poland and the Soviet Union. A 1932–33 famine engineered by Stalin brought death to millions

of Ukrainians. Nazi occupation killed millions more during World War II. Ukraine suffered the world's worst recorded nuclear accident in 1986, when a Soviet reactor exploded at the Chernobyl Nuclear Power Plant just north of Kyiv (Kiev), Ukraine's capital. A political meltdown occurred in 1991, when 90 percent of Ukrainians voted for independence from the Soviet Union. Electoral fraud in the 2004 presidential election led to the Orange Revolution, which brought free elections. Ukraine has rich farmlands, industry, and an educated workforce, but government bureaucracy and corruption are holding it

THROUGH VISITOR'S EYES | Crimea

Playground of the tsars

"Russia needs its paradise," Prince Grigory Potemkin, Catherine the Great's general, wrote in 1782 urging the annexation of Crimea, and no wonder.

The Crimean Peninsula, with its voluptuously curved Black Sea coast of sparkling cliffs, is paradise—with Riviera-grade vistas but without Riviera prices. Balmy with 300 days of sun a year ("It is never winter here," said the writer Anton Chekhov, who had a dacha near Yalta), the place served as the playground of tsars and Politburo fat cats. Russians practically wept when, after the breakup of the Soviet Union, Crimea was pulled out of the orbit of Russian rule and became part of an independent Ukraine.

A trace of Soviet hangover endures in the form of unsmiling babushkas and concrete block architecture. Visitors can tour the once secret nuclear-blast-proof Soviet submarine base in Balaklava, a piece of Cold War history, now a museum. Afterward, retreat to one of the briny health resorts of the west and east coasts for a therapeutic mud bath, or go for a run down to Livadia Palace in Yalta, scene of the 1945 conference that reconfigured postwar Europe.

Summer is high season, crowded with Russian and eastern European tourists (North Americans are still rare). In autumn the air turns soft and it's harvest time at vineyards like Massandra, built in the nineteenth century to supply wines for Nicholas II, the last Russian tsar. There you may have the pleasure of tasting a Riesling with the scent of alpine meadows, port the color of rubies, and a nectar called "Seventh Heaven," of which a recent visitor said: "I could kneel in front of this wine."

—Cathy Newman, *National Geographic Traveler*, December 2012/January 2013

---

back. International organizations, like the World Bank, help Ukraine in its transition to a market economy.

Area	603,700 sq km (233,090 sq mi)
Population	46,030,000
Government	republic
Capital	Kyiv 2,709,000
Life Expectancy	68 years
Religion	Ukrainian Orthodox, Ukrainian Greek Catholic
Language	Ukrainian, Russian
Currency	hryvnia (UAH)
GDP per Cap	$6,400
Labor Force	15.8% Agriculture, 18.5% Industry, 65.7% Services

TRAVEL**TIPS** 🧳

Entry: A visa is not required. A passport is required.

Tourist Season: May through September

Shopping: Common items include Pysanky (Ukraine's famous painted eggs), embroidered cloth and clothes, carved wooden boxes and spoons, and ceramics.

Internet TLD: .ua

CULTURAL CAPSULE Ukraine is second only to Russia in population in the countries in the CIS. With nearly 50 million citizens, Ukraine approaches the population of France and the United Kingdom. Ukrainian is a Slavic language that is very closely related to Russian. The word *Ukraine* means "borderland," and this describes the geographic location of Ukraine that has so greatly affected its culture. Affected by repeated invasions and occupations, it developed some major differences from Russia.

One of the major cultural differences is in the Ukrainian Church. Poles occupying what is now Ukraine established the Uniate Church (also known as the Ukrainian Catholic Church) in 1596. This church accepted the Roman Pope as leader, but practiced Russian Orthodox forms of worship involving the old Slavonic language. While many people remained loyal to the Orthodox Church, the combination of distinct church and language ultimately led to independence at various times, culminating with the demands of the Uniate Church for independence from the USSR that began in 1988. Since then the Ukrainian Orthodox Church has separated from the Russian Orthodox Church. The Ukrainian language differs from Russian because of the persistence of old Slavonic pronunciation and the modification caused by centuries of interaction with Poles, Lithuanians, and other countries, which controlled the country at various times.

Cultural hints: Shake hands as a greeting. With friends, Ukrainians embrace and kiss cheeks. Typical foods include chicken (as in chicken Kyiv); cucumber-and-tomato or egg salad with sour cream; borscht with sour cream; small pastries like ravioli filled with meat, potatoes, or almost any combination of meat and vegetables; pancakes with a meat or other filling; potatoes; breads; beef; chicken and pork; and a variety of pastries and cakes.

Tourism Characteristics

Ukraine has some of the best attractions for tourism in the former Soviet Union. Beaches along the Black Sea, while generally covered with small pebbles, provide a sun-sea-sand experience, making them a major destination. Ukraine was second only to Russia in economic importance and power in the former USSR. It has a strong industrial and agricultural base with numerous resources. As it makes the transition to its own currency and creates new markets for its manufactured goods, its economy could become one of the most robust in the CIS. Tourism to the Ukraine is dominated by Russians, but the country has the potential to promote its tourism attractions to other countries outside the CIS.

Tourist Destinations and Attractions

The major destinations in Ukraine are Kyiv, the Crimean Peninsula, and the Black Sea Coast centered on Odessa.

A variety of other cities have important historic sites, but are minor when compared to these three.

Kyiv is one of the most historically important cities of Europe. (It is also spelled Kiev or Kyyiv, but this book has adopted the spelling used on the official travel website of the Ukraine.) The first Russian state, Kyiv Rus, existed here from the ninth to the eleventh centuries, and it was here that the Eastern Orthodox Church was adopted by the rulers. St. Sophia Cathedral (Figure 25.5) dates from the eleventh century, and its interior is an outstanding example of the decorative scheme followed by the Russian Orthodox Church for 900 years. It was opened for Christian services in 1990 following nearly seventy years as a museum under Soviet rule. The second major site in Kyiv is the Caves Monastery, a series of gold-domed churches, underground labyrinths where the mummified remains of generations of monks are placed, and museums with world-class collections of artifacts relating to the earliest occupants of this region. The Kyiv Petchersk Lavra is a district made up of historical buildings and architectural monuments, ranging from bell towers to cathedrals to underground cave systems, and a stone fortification. Other sites in Kyiv include museums, the newly renovated Kyiv Opera House, a variety of churches with outstanding architecture, and the monument to the 100,000 Jews killed at Baby Yar, a ravine outside of Kyiv.

Lviv, in the western part of the country, has a well-preserved medieval city center that is on the UNESCO World Heritage list.

The Crimean Peninsula has been an important tourist destination for Russians since the nineteenth century. It was the number one destination for internal tourists in the former USSR because of its combination of sun-sea-sand and health sanatoria. The major beaches and sanatoria are around Yalta. Yalta is the main attraction with its pedestrian-only area. The beaches have more pebbles than sand and the water is polluted, but there are lovely parks, the famous Russian author Chekhov's house, an aerial tram to the peak behind Yalta for the view, and some lovely old homes to enjoy. The coast near Yalta has some beautiful palaces, parks, and spas that

Figure 25.5 St. Sophia Cathedral, Kyiv, Ukraine. © woe/www.Shutterstock.com.

attract tourists. One was the site of the famed Yalta conference between Roosevelt, Churchill, and Stalin where the division of Europe after World War II was finalized. Ai-Petri is a scenic mountaintop that can be reached via one of Europe's longest cable car rides. On a clear day, visitors can see the coastline of Turkey from atop this site. The beautiful scenery and lovely climate make the coast of the Crimea one of the loveliest spots in the CIS.

Odessa is the biggest Black Sea port and the historic locale for interaction between the Mediterranean to the south and the Ukrainian steppes to the north. It has some good museums that are small enough to be easily enjoyed in a few hours, the famed Potyomkin steps descending from the hill overlooking the harbor, and nearby beaches. Another destination is Sevastopol. The city played an important role in World War II and has deep historic roots.

Russia

Introduction

The world's largest country, Russia spans two continents (Europe and Asia), nine time zones, and all climates except tropical. European Russia, west of the Ural Mountains, features a broad plain with low hills and holds 78 percent of the country's population. Siberia extends east of the Urals to the Pacific, ranging from Arctic tundra, swamps, and forested plateaus in the north to high mountains in the south and far east.

Russia, a multiethnic state, claims more than 130 ethnic groups—but Russians are 80 percent of the population. The Russian Federation designates twenty-one republics for people of non-Russian ethnicity; for example, Tatarstan was created for Tatars, a Turkic and mostly Muslim people. Contrary to world trends, Russia's population has been decreasing since 1991, when it was 148 million. The loss is due to a decrease in the fertility rate and an increase in the mortality rate. The population deficit has brought an estimated 12 million foreign workers into Russia, many from Central Asia. Migrants have flooded into Moscow, giving that city a large Muslim minority. The Muslim population, growing throughout Russia, may surpass 20 million.

Russian expansionism started in the sixteenth century with Ivan IV (Ivan the Terrible), who adopted the ancient title of caesar (tsar in Russian). Russia entered the twentieth century as enormous and imperial. The forced abdication and death of Nicholas II in 1917 ended tsarist rule. Russia became the center of the Union of Soviet Socialist Republics from 1922 to 1991. The Red Army conquered the Caucasus and Central Asia. Soviet planners relocated entire peoples, to reward or punish. Military power held the empire together—until 1991.

Russia became a federal democracy after the disintegration of the Soviet Union. From 1999 to 2008, the economy benefited from strong growth. But oil and gas revenues are crucial, and falling prices adversely affect the Russian economy.

Area	17,075,400 sq km (6,592,849 sq mi)
Population	141,839,000
Government	federation
Capital	Moscow 10,452,000
Life Expectancy	68 years
Religion	Russian Orthodox, Muslim
Language	Russian, minority Languages
Currency	Russian ruble (RUB)
GDP per Cap	$15,100
Labor Force	10.0% Agriculture, 31.9% Industry, 58.1% Services

TRAVEL**TIPS** 💼

Entry: A passport and visa are required.

Tourist Season: May to September, but Moscow and St. Petersburg attract tourists year-round.

Shopping: Common items include Matryoshkas (painted, nested wooden dolls), enameled wooden boxes, bright woolen scarves, brightly painted wooden spoons and other trinkets, and artificial fur hats.

Internet TLD: .ru

CULTURAL CAPSULE Russia has the largest population of the former countries created from the USSR. While Russians are the dominant group, there are important subgroups, such as the Tatars, that create an exciting cultural mosaic. The Russian culture has been shaped by centuries of autocratic government, the Russian Orthodox Church, and a vast, harsh land. From the czars who ruled the Russian Empire

Figure 25.6 Church of the Savior on Spilled Blood, St. Petersburg, Russia. © S.Borisov/www.Shutterstock.com.

to the communist governments of the twentieth century, democracy has been limited and survival the main goal. The Russian people have developed an amazing resilience to withstand hard times, and their culture is characterized by stoicism and tolerance for suffering unknown in the Western world. The church was of paramount importance in people's lives before the revolution, and in spite of seventy years of persecution, it is estimated that there are still some 50 million believers among the Russians. The changes associated with the breakup of the USSR has brought new challenges for the Russian people, but they will no doubt persevere once more. Visitors note that Russians seem to rarely smile while walking the streets, but in the privacy of their homes and among family and friends the Russians seem more happy and friendly than other Europeans. Tourists will find that Russians are a helpful and accommodating host, particularly if visitors take the time to learn even a few Russian words.

Cultural hints: Use a firm handshake and direct eye contact upon greeting someone. Friends typically embrace and kiss cheeks. Flowers are often presented as a gift by visitors. Whistling at public performances is a sign of disapproval. The fork is kept in the left hand, the knife in the right while eating. Individual travelers should tip waiters. Members of groups will find they receive better service at the next meal if they leave a small tip. Typical Russian foods include borscht (or other hearty soups) served with sour cream, caviar served in hard-boiled eggs, cucumber-and-tomato salad, beef stroganoff, meat-stuffed grape or cabbage leaves, chicken, filled pancakes, fish, cabbage and potato dishes of all kinds, small pastries filled with meat and vegetables, breads, and of course the famous Russian ice cream.

Tourism Characteristics

The two leading destinations are Moscow and St. Petersburg (Figure 25.6).

Russia has always suffered from the perception that its facilities and services were below the standards found in other European countries. This was basically true, as under the old system there was little incentive for workers to provide good service, and facilities reflected the planning orientation of the ministry of tourism. With the breakup of the USSR and the emergence of free enterprise, these characteristics are changing. New privately owned restaurants are opening on a regular basis, a variety of tour agencies are available to provide assistance, and new or newly remodeled hotels

City of imperial palaces and cultural aspirations, elegant St. Petersburg has pirouetted back from its gray days as communist Leningrad.

Like all of the structure Russian Tsar Peter the Great built, his new capital city was the triumph of will over nature and reason. On a fever-infested swamp far from the center of Russian Empire or any center of trade rose one of the world's most phantasmagorically beautiful cities, a crucible of political might and cultural prodigality. Today, St. Petersburg—the phenomenon of exuberant Italian architecture in an austere Nordic landscape—remains the best preserved of living cities, despite the destruction wrought by Hitler's armies in World War II. Four hundred miles northwest of Moscow and some 200 miles east of

Helsinki, the city was erected on watery gravel that makes modern high-rise building nigh impossible.

Stroll the length of the city's main thoroughfare, Nevsky Prospekt, and explore the side streets for half a mile on either side (this remains a town for pedestrians). You'll be following in the footsteps of novelist Fyodor Dostoyevsky's protagonists—walking the Raskolnikov, ax under his coat, as he goes to murder the old pawnbroker; perambulating with the Idiot as he frantically roams the city. The buildings, distance, even the stairs, are exactly as Dostoyevsky described them 150 years ago. For more aristocratic contemplation, cruise some of the canals that intersect the main part of the city. Take the smallest

boat on offer, since it can negotiate the narrowest canals that weave past the palazzo of the merchants and noblemen whom Peter the Great forced to migrate here. Like Venice's palaces, St. Petersburg's too are decaying, but in the crepuscular northern cold process seems gentler.

The beauty of St. Petersburg, like the politeness of its elderly inhabitants, is not just the result of cultural pride. Like most striking beauty, it is in part born of suffering stoically endured. This gives the city the dignity of a dowager empress, her power ceded to an uglier, more vulgar rival to the south.

—**Donald Rayfield, *National Geographic Traveler*, October 2009**

provide better accommodations and entertainment. Russia's most important attractions are its rich history, the genuine hospitality of individual Russians, a culture and history that are available nowhere else in the world, and the marvels of the famed buildings and museums of the country.

Tourist Destinations and Attractions

There are almost innumerable tourist attractions in Russia, but the major destinations are Moscow and the surrounding area known as the Golden Ring; St. Petersburg and the surrounding region; the Russian Black Sea Coast centered on Sochi; the Russian Northwest; and Siberia.

The number and variety of attractions in Moscow are so great that only a few can be mentioned. The greatest attraction is the Kremlin and related cathedrals. On Red Square, in front of the Kremlin is the Lenin Mausoleum (Lenin's Tomb) and St. Basil's Cathedral, whose colorful onion domes surmounted by gold crosses symbolize Old Russia. Now open to the public, it is being restored as a house of worship. The Kremlin is the brick fortress built by Ivan the Great. Inside are some of the loveliest examples of Russian Orthodox churches as well as the Armory Museum exhibiting items from the czars. The Moscow Subway is an attraction in its own right, with beautiful mosaic walls and statues. Clean, attractive, and cheap, the Metro (subway) moves millions of Muscovites daily. The Bolshoi Ballet is a prime attraction for visitors to the city. There are a variety of museums (including the Pushkin Museum and Tretyakov Gallery) and churches of interest in Moscow, as well as shops (Old Arbat Street) and stores selling Russian souvenirs and Western amenities, such as Starbucks coffee, McDonald's hamburgers, Pizza Hut pizzas, and

Baskin-Robbins ice cream. Locally made handicrafts and paintings attract foreign shoppers. Moscow is one of the largest (and most expensive) shopping cities in Europe. Gorky Park has become one of the trendiest places in the city. Visitors may observe the city from the observation deck atop Ostankino TV Tower (1200 ft).

There are many cities of interest around Moscow, but some of the more important for tourists are known collectively as the *Golden Ring.* Located northeast of Moscow, they provide a wonderful introduction to Russian history and culture. Suzdal is the best known and was preserved by the Soviet Union as a "museum town." It remains a small town of some 12,000 people with no industry, and its beautiful old Russian Orthodox churches, monasteries, and convents are outstanding. Other cities in the Golden Ring with outstanding old structures are Vladimir, Yaroslavl, and Kostroma.

St. Petersburg remains the second largest city in size and attraction for foreign visitors to Russia. While Moscow hosts more visitors, St. Petersburg has far more attractions for travelers to enjoy. The buildings and morphology of St. Petersburg reflect the influence of French and Italian architects and artists under Peter the Great. The city has been repainted to reflect the original color scheme, and the canals used to drain the swampland of the Neva River make it the "Venice of the North." There are a number of outstanding churches St. Isaac's and the Kazan Cathedral on Nevsky Prospekt (street) being the two most famous. The museums are outstanding, especially the Hermitage. The Hermitage has the greatest collection of Western paintings in the world (over 3 million pieces) and is one of the great art museums of the world. The palace of the emperors and empresses ruling Russia for a century and a half, the Hermitage is one of the greatest treasures of Russia. Other attractions in the city include the Russian Museum, Peter and

Figure 25.7 Olkhon Island at Baikal Lake, Russia. © Mikhail Markovskiy/www.Shutterstock.com.

Paul Fortress, the Ethnographic Museum, Church of the Savior, and Saint Isaac's Cathedral. On Vasilievsky Island visitors may visit the Andreyevski Cathedral, the Erarta Museum and Galleries of Contemporary Art, the Menshikov Palace, and the Zoological Museum. Near St. Petersburg are five palaces, the most impressive being Peter the Great's palace at Petrodovorets on the Baltic. The Catherine Palace at Pushkin is a Baroque extravaganza that shouldn't be missed.

The Black Sea Coast of Russia is centered on the city of Sochi. Nearby is probably the best resort in Russia, Dagomys, which is a completely self-sufficient resort for foreign tourists built by Intourist in the 1980s. The beaches of both Sochi and Dagomys are of pebbles, but Dagomys is less crowded as Russians are concentrated at the beaches of the much larger city of **Sochi**. This city will grow in popularity as it prepares to host the 2016 winter Olympic games. This small stretch of the Black Sea's Coast comprises Russia's sun-sea-sand (ski) attraction.

The Russian northwest is a large area stretching from the Gulf of Finland west of St. Petersburg to the Barents Sea in the north. It provides innumerable opportunities for ecotourism, as well as a number of important towns and cities with architecture reflecting the history of the region. Novgorod is a city dating back to the 800s. It has some of the most diverse and lovely architecture in Russia. Karelia is the name given to the vast area stretching north through forest, lakes, and bogs to the far north of Russia. On Kizhi Island in Lake Onega is found an amazing collection of wooden churches and other buildings. The most impressive of these is the twenty-two–dome Church of the Transfiguration.

Siberia is the vast land stretching east of the Ural Mountains. The most widely known attractions within it are the Trans-Siberian Railroad and Lake Baikal. The railroad skirts the southern margins of Siberia, introducing Russians and hardy foreign tourists to Siberia's vast forests. Lake Baikal (Figure 25.7) is one of the most pristine water bodies in the world and is known as the "Blue Eye of Siberia." Architecturally, Siberia has interesting wooden houses with intricately carved wooden Siberian lace panels. The cities reflect Soviet planning, but have some interesting museums and churches. The far east of Siberia has good potential for Japanese and American tourists interested in experiencing Russia now that travel is possible to this eastern rim of Russia. Vladivostok on the east coast of Russia has seen explosive growth as tourists and business travelers from the United States and Japan now flock to this region. Alaska Airlines and Japan Air offer flights to Vladivostok and other cities of the far east of Siberia, reflecting the growing importance of tourism to this region.

The world's largest freshwater lake is virtually unknown to most travelers, but a major loop trail now under construction could make it a must-see.

Clear as the vodka my hosts are spilling into my glass, Lake Baikal shimmers beneath the evening sky. The Siberians around the fire toast the three miles of trail we've designed, then we hoist our drinks toward the immense lake before us that they call the Sacred Sea.

I'm camped on the narrow beach of a shoreline that extends over a thousand of miles, helping the volunteers of the Great Baikal Trail Association survey a section of the trail they hope to build around the world's oldest, deepest, and clearest lake. Four hundred miles long and containing 20 percent of the planet's fresh water, it is arguably the biggest, too. Lake Baikal forms the epicenter of a vast wilderness ecosystem almost fully encircled by five mountain ranges. Home to sable, nerpa seals, giant sturgeon, and more than 1,500 species—most of which are found nowhere else on the globe—it is environmentally rich beyond measure.

The Great Baikal Trail begins near Irkutsk, where the Trans-Siberian Railway follows the lake's developed southern cusp. The pathway leads backpackers away from all of that into rugged country unbroken except remote villages accessible on foot, aboard a boat, or by crossing the ice of below-zero winters.

North of Mongolia and five times zones east of Moscow, Lake Baikal and its surroundings have tempted exploitation since the days of the Cossack. The eagerness to harvest minerals, forest products, and wildlife has been tempered by those indigenous Buryats still practicing nomadic traditions respectful of nature. Though woefully underfunded, national parks and reserves today buffer much of the lake with a semblance of protection.

In fact, the future of Lake Baikal may rest with idealistic Siberians such as these gathered around the campfire. They reason that the trail they've begun will attract geotourists and increase environmental awareness and activism. They have certainly convinced me. My three-week stay is coming to an end, but I'll be back soon for another four. A place this remarkable and unspoiled deserves my help to keep it that way. And with decades of trail work ahead, there will be plenty of opportunities to lend a hand—and to raise a glass to toast Lake Baikal, the wild heart of Siberia.

—Robert Birkby/*National Geographic Traveler*, **October 2009**

Georgia

Introduction

Georgia, on the Black Sea, is geographically in southwest Asia—the mountains forming its northern border serve as a traditional boundary between Europe and Asia. Rich in farmland and minerals, rugged Georgia is wedged between the Caucasus Mountains and the Lesser Caucasus. The climate is generally mild, ranging from a subtropical coastal region to snowy mountains. Georgia was annexed by Russia in the early nineteenth century. Georgia gained independence with the dissolution of the USSR in 1991. But by 1993 Georgia had lost control of the regions of South Ossetia and Abkhazia due to ethnic strife. Both the Ossetians and Abkhaz enjoyed autonomy during Soviet rule, and both allied with Russia to separate from Georgia. The separatist conflict drained Georgia, but the country stabilized in 1995 as a democratic state. The diverse market economy benefits from the Baku-Tbilisi-Ceyhan (BTC) oil pipeline, which opened in 2006. The 2008 Russian invasion caused extensive damage, but international aid helped restore Georgia. The government seeks to restore Abkhazia and South Ossetia to Georgian control.

Area	69,700 sq km (26,911 sq mi)
Population	4,611,000
Government	republic
Capital	Tbilisi 1,100,000
Life Expectancy	75 years
Religion	Orthodox Christian, Muslim, Armenian-Gregorian
Language	Georgian, Russian, Armenian, Azeri, Abkhaz, Ossetic
Currency	lari (GEL)
GDP per Cap	$4,400
Labor Force	55.6% Agriculture, 8.9% Industry, 35.5% Services

TRAVEL**TIPS** 🧳

Entry: A passport is required. A visa is not required.

Tourist Season: May through October

Shopping: Common items include local handicrafts of wood or embroidered fabric, jewelry, and hand-painted icons.

Internet TLD: .ge

CULTURAL CAPSULE Georgia is one of the most distinctive of the countries created from the former Soviet Union. Even during the Soviet era, Georgians prided themselves on their free-wheeling economic system, which relied unofficially on a strong free enterprise ethic. The Soviet era brought modernization, but Georgia and Georgians experienced a degree of freedom and nonconformity not found elsewhere in the former USSR. Georgia is ethnically heterogeneous, with ancient differences between the individual groups being the basis for conflict with Azerbaijan and with a breakaway northern Black Sea Coastal portion of Georgia known as Abkhazia. Nonetheless, the Georgians are a friendly and hospitable people who welcome guests and treat them like family. Georgia is in many ways reminiscent of a Middle Eastern country with its spicy foods and vocal and friendly people.

Cultural hints: Handshakes are a common form of greeting, but Georgians often embrace upon meeting with a kiss on the cheek. Food is an important part of the culture of Georgia; with meals being a time of hospitality that may extend to people at other tables at restaurants. Toasting with wine or with Georgian brandy or vodka is the norm. Typical foods involve strong spices, herbs, and garlic and include a wide variety of meats, vegetables, and cheeses as well as delicious breads. Typical dishes include green or red beans served with walnuts, beet root, or spinach leaves pounded into a paste with herbs and spices, boiled pigs' feet, spicy meat broth, chicken soup with eggs beaten into it, and tomato and onion used in cooking chicken, mutton, and all kinds of meat.

Tourism Characteristics

Georgia has some of the most scenic tourist attractions among the fifteen former republics of the Soviet Union. If the beaches of the Black Sea were not so pebbly, Georgia would rival much of the Mediterranean in attractiveness. During the Soviet era the coast of Georgia was the ultimate sun-sea-sand tourist destination for Russians. It also has a remarkable vitality among its people that is missing in other areas of the former Soviet Union and ancient cities, such as T'Bilisi, which attracted both domestic and foreign tourists. Georgia is the fourth largest destination for foreign tourists in the former Soviet Union. Individual data from the former Soviet Union countries are not available and noted as CIS. The greatest growth in visitors was from Turkey with a small number from Greece and Israel.

Georgia's tourism has suffered dramatically since the breakup of the Soviet Union. The attraction of the Black Sea Coast has been handicapped by ongoing conflict between the residents of Abkhazi and the central government in T'Bilisi. In 2008 the conflict erupted in a war. As a result, Georgia lost control over Abkhazia and South Ossetia. Foreign tourism has been slow to recover.

Tourist Destinations and Attractions

The major destinations in Georgia are the Black Sea Coast, the city of T'Bilisi, and the Caucasus Mountains. With a population of 1.3 million, T'Bilisi is a large sprawling city set in a bowl between the greater and lesser Caucasus. Its red-tiled roofs, narrow streets, and ancient buildings stand in contrast to the industrialization brought by the Soviet era. The air is highly polluted, but there are still important attractions for visitors. Most important are the museums that detail the unique history of this land, which has been overrun by invaders repeatedly through history. The Georgian state museum and the Georgian state art museum are two of the best. Equally attractive is the old city with its narrow, winding streets that create a maze for visitors and the thirteenth-century Metekhi Church. A second church of importance is the Sioni Cathedral and Caravanserai (inn). This is the center of the Georgian Orthodox Church and contains its holiest relic, a cross supposedly from the fourth century.

The Black Sea Coast of Georgia is a second major attraction, with primary destinations including the cities of Sukhumi and Batumi and the Georgian coast between. The road from T'Bilisi to the Black Sea Coast also takes travelers through Gori, the birthplace of Stalin. Abkhazia, formerly known as Sukhumi, is a city of over 300,000 that combines a resort function with its port and industrial role. For the visitor, the attraction is a warm, sunny climate and the palm and eucalyptus trees that suggest a tropical setting. The beachfront is backed by a pedestrian promenade with vegetation typical of a tropical climate. North of Sukhumi to the border with Russia, there are some resort towns and beaches. From Sukhumi south there is also beachfront, with important resorts at Poti, Kobuleti, and Batumi. All of the towns along the coast have both access for swimming and sun bathing and sanitoria in the hills behind the beach. Batumi is a port resort that includes many of Georgia's Muslims. It has the highest rainfall of any city in the former Soviet Union, typical of a subtropical climate. Citrus and tea production in the surrounding country attracts tourists, but the beach is the main attraction.

The most famous attraction in the Caucasus Mountains is the famed Georgian military road that climbs north from T'bilisi to cross the Caucasus (Figure 25.8). The switchbacks on the road as it climbs the steep southerly slopes of the Caucasus provide some of the most breathtaking views available in any of the fifteen former republics of the former Soviet Union. Along the highway, a route formerly used by the ancient Greeks, are found lovely churches, small towns, and even a small ski resort at Gudauri near the summit of the highway at the Krestovy Pass. At nearly 8,000-feet elevation, it has snow from November to May and a luxury Austrian-built and -run hotel completed in 1990. Hiking to the peaks of the Caucasus are also attractions in this area.

Figure 25.8 Georgian Military Highway, Caucasus mountains. © salajean/www.Shutterstock.com.

REVIEW QUESTIONS

1. How many countries comprise the former USSR? What are their names?

2. What is the difference between European Russia and Asiatic Russia? How does tourism differ in the two areas?

3. Identify and describe five major attractions in Moscow and St. Petersburg.

4. What are the five factors that influence the climate of the region?

5. Describe how climate affects tourism to the region.

6. What are some reasons the number of international tourists to Russia has fluctuated so widely in the past twenty to thirty years?

7. What changes have occurred in tourism in this region since it broke up into independent countries?

8. Describe the major tourist destinations in the countries created from the former Soviet Union.

9. Of the three Baltic States of Lithuania, Latvia, and Estonia, which one has the best potential for increasing the number of its visitors? Why?

10. If you were going to prepare a five-country tour of the CIS, which five countries would you choose? Why?

chapter 26 : THE CENTRAL ASIAN COUNTRIES CREATED FROM THE FORMER SOVIET UNION

© Petrov Andrey/ShutterStock.com

Figure 26.1 Skull caps, Ashkhabad Market, Turkmenistan. © velirina/www.Shutterstock.com.

Introduction

The five countries of the former Soviet Central Asia have never had a large tourist flow. Uzbekistan ranked eighth among the former republics with 1 percent of all tourist arrivals, but Kazakhstan, Kyrgyzstan, Tajikistan, and Turkmenistan in combination received less than 1 percent of tourists. The greatest attraction for tourists to this area, the Islamic and Middle Eastern flavor of the society, is not an important draw for Russians. The architecture dating from the earlier ruling period is magnificent, but the distance and difficulty of traveling to this area is keeping visitors to a low number.

Political instability and ethnic conflict have plagued some of these countries, and the breakup of the old tourist monopoly on travel further disrupted tourist flows. Economic uncertainties combined with increasingly unreliable air transport to further frighten potential visitors. While there are now more visitors from Asia and the Middle East, especially business related, tourism is far below previous levels. The primary destinations in Kazakhstan are Almaty and Astana. Almaty is the cultural capital of Kazakhstan. Astana, the governmental capital, has a very modern look as it was

"planned" by Kisho Kurokawa with many of the building designed by architect Norman Foster. Duman is a large entertainment center in the city.

There are tremendous opportunities for tourism in this region, but it is doubtful whether tourism will see a resurgence in the near future.

TRAVEL **TIPS** 🧳

Entry: All of these countries require a passport and visa. A visa must be obtained before entering the country.

Shopping: Items purchased by tourists are similar across these countries and include local handicrafts such as embroidered rectangular skullcaps worn by Muslim men (Figure 26.1), colorful scarves worn by Muslim women, wool products (including Persian lamb coats, sweaters, etc.), brightly colored cotton and silk fabrics and clothing, and copper or tin utensils or art objects.

CULTURAL CAPSULE

The five countries created in former Soviet Central Asia are distinctive because of the dominance of Islam. The natives were all Muslim at the time of the Communist Revolution, and in the intervening years of official denigration of religion it has become somewhat secularized. Since independence, however, the Muslim people have begun to exercise their former beliefs and practices as they are given control of the mosques that were once museums. The region of countries is highly diverse ethnically, but each is based on a predominant ethnic group. Historically these countries have been the location of kingdoms controlled by either local rulers such as the Uzbeks, or foreign invaders such as the Tatars. The unifying role of Islam combined with these kingdoms to create famous holy and educational cities in the region in the past. The resurgence of Islam means that many of the architectural relics of the bygone era in these countries require that women visitors be clad modestly in either a longish skirt or dress or long pants.

The combination of ethnic diversity and Middle Eastern traditions makes this one of the most culturally vibrant regions in what used to be the Soviet Union. Women dress in colorful dresses covering equally bright trousers. Men in the various republics have distinctive headwear, such as the intricately embroidered square skullcap worn by the Uzbeki men. The veil found in some Islamic countries is rarely seen in this region, but many women cover their hair with scarves.

The people are very friendly and willing to assist tourists, whom they treat with respect. The foods are among the best in the former Soviet Union, relying heavily on the use of mutton, spiced vegetables, and rice. Fruit and vegetables are a regional specialty, as well as delicious flatbread; shish kabob; soups with meat, onion, chilies, and noodles; and a variety of rice dishes such as rice pilaf using meat, vegetables, or fruit. Green tea is the common beverage because of the Islamic prohibitions on alcohol. Remember that this is an Islamic country, and while seventy years of Soviet rule have decreased the intensity of many people's commitment to their beliefs, the use of the right hand in touching or passing food is still essential as you have no way of knowing the degree to which the people with whom you associate are committed Muslims.

Tourist Destinations and Attractions

The two major general destinations for tourists to this region are the capital cities of each country and the famed cities of Samarkand and Bukhara, which were part of the ancient Silk Road and were the capitals of various historic kingdoms in this region. Each of the capitals has lovely architectural relics from the golden age of the empires in this region. Typically associated with mosques or madrassas, they are often characterized by their lovely blue or green glazed tiles. Many of the capital cities also have museums that illustrate the ethnic background of the people and their arts, particularly in weaving and carved wood, or provide access to native crafts. Every city has a bazaar or market.

The main tourist attraction in this region, however, are the cities of Uzbekistan associated with the famed Silk Road and the kingdom of Timur (Tamerlane). Samarkand and Bukhara have some of the most spectacular architecture anywhere in the world. The cities were key stops on the famed Silk Road, and Samarkand was the capital of Timur's empire and contains some of his greatest structures. Bukhara was the capital of a later empire and is a virtual outdoor museum.

Samarkand is the principal attraction in all of Central Asia. Even from the air its beautiful mosques and minarets are visible. The most famous attraction is the Registan (Figure 26.2), which is a group of

Figure 26.2 The Registan, Samarkand, Uzbekistan. © posztos/www.Shutterstock.com.

large madrassas. Covered with brilliant blue mosaics (Figure 26.3), it was once Samarkand's medieval commercial center and market. Other sites are too numerous to mention, but include the gigantic Bibi-Khanym mosque on the northeast of the Registan. Nearby is the Shakh-i-Zinda, a street of tombs, apparently the burial site for the wives, daughters, and other favored family members belonging to Timur and his son and grandson. This has recently been restored to local Islamic control, and a tiny fee is charged, but it provides a good opportunity to see how the wealthy provided for their dead a millennium ago in a Muslim state.

Bukhara is very different from Samarkand. It is a low city built on the edge of the desert, and its brown appearance is deceptive. Much of the center has been preserved to maintain its architecture, and the streets are lined with ancient madrassas and old bazaars. Historically the center of Bukhara was a large marketplace with specialists trading their wares in the traditional Islamic city fashion. The buildings have been largely protected and preserved, and visiting is one of the truly amazing tourist experiences left in the world. Bukhara was the capital of Central Asia's empire before Timur and by the tenth century was its religious and cultural heart, known as the Pillar of Islam. It was a second capital of a sixteenth-century empire and owes much of its appearance

Figure 26.4 Poi Kalon Mosque in Bukhara, Uzbekistan.
© Eduard Kim/www.Shutterstock.com.

to that period. The central bazaar is one of the most fascinating in all the Islam world, and it has a wide variety of minarets, mosques (Figure 26.4), and madrassas to fascinate the visitor. Bukhara is one of a hundred cities recognized by UNESCO as part of a world architectural heritage. Visitors are well repaid for the distance, heat, and poor accommodations found there.

New hotels built by Indian interests were opened in Samarkand and Bukhara, and they make the experience of visiting these famed Silk Road cities even more enjoyable. Because of the summer heat, the best times to visit are April through May, and September to November.

Tashkent is Central Asia's biggest and most European city and was fourth in size after Moscow, St. Petersburg, and Kiev in the former Soviet Union. A transportation hub, it is primarily a city built during the Soviet era. A major earthquake destroyed most of the old town, but there are a few sites including the Kukeldash Madrassa that are of interest. Tashkent has a huge market north of this madrassa where visitors can experience the daily life of the local people.

There are a variety of other attractions in these new countries, but tourism continues to decline because of the problems associated with the changing political and economic picture.

Figure 26.3 Detail of minarets, The Registan, Samarkand, Uzbekistan. © Cardaf/www.Shutterstock.com.

COUNTRY PROFILES

Country	Capital	Language	Population (millions)	Currency	Sq. Mi. and State Comparison Size
Kyrgyzstan	Bishkek	Kyrgyz (Kirghiz)	5.2	Som	76,641 (South Dakota)
Tajikistan	Dushanbe	Tajik	7.2	Somoni	55,251 (Wisconsin)
Turkmenistan	Ashgabat	Turkmen (72%)	5.1	Turkmen Manat	188,456 (California)
Uzbekistan	Tashkent	Uzbek (85%)	25.5	Uzbek Som	172,472 (California)
Kazakhstan	Astana	Qazaq (Kazakh)	16.4	Tenge	1,049,156 (four times Texas)

Tajikistan

Introduction

Mountains cover more than 90 percent of this Central Asian republic (Figure 26.5), whose river valleys are home to a majority of the people. Western Tajikistan is less mountainous and holds the capital, Dushanbe, and most cities. Earthquakes, landslides, and flooding are constant hazards. The lower elevations are hot and dry in summer and cold in winter.

About two-thirds of the people are ethnic Tajiks, and about a quarter are Uzbeks. Shortly after independence in 1991, Tajikistan endured a five-year civil war between the Moscow-backed government and Islamist-led rebels. A peace agreement was signed in 1997, but the political turmoil depressed the economy. Until 2005, Russians guarded Tajikistan's border with Afghanistan against weapons, drugs, and Islamic extremists. Russia still assists Tajik border guards and maintains a military base near Dushanbe. Tajikistan relies on foreign aid, and about half of the country's population lives in poverty.

From *National Geographic Atlas of the World*, 9th edition. Copyright ©2011 National Geographic Society. Reprinted by arrangement. All rights reserved.

Area	143,100 sq km (55,251 sq mi)
Population	7,450,000
Government	republic
Capital	Dushanbe 553,000
Life Expectancy	67 years
Religion	Sunni Muslim, Shiite Muslim
Language	Tajik, Russian
Currency	somoni (TJS)
GDP per Cap	$1,800
Labor Force	49.8% Agriculture, 12.8% Industry, 37.4% Services
Exports	aluminum, electricity, cotton, fruits, vegetable oil, textiles

From *National Geographic Atlas of the World*, 9th edition. Copyright ©2011 National Geographic Society. Reprinted by arrangement. All rights reserved.

Figure 26.5 Valley of the Fann Mountains in Tajikistan.
© Pecold/www.Shutterstock.com.

Turkmenistan

Introduction

The sandy plains of the Garagum desert largely cover the Central Asian country of Turkmenistan. Bordering the vast desert in the northeast is the Amu Darya river valley, and the Caspian Sea lies to the west. The Köpet-dag Mountains rise in the southwest above the capital city, Ashgabat. The mountain region is generally dry and prone to earthquakes.

Turkmenistan has the second lowest population density (after Kazakhstan) in former Soviet Central Asia. The Turkmen people were nomadic herdsmen for centuries, until subdued by Russia in the late nineteenth century. Turkmenistan gained independence in 1991, with the collapse of the Soviet Union. The Garagum Canal, one of the world's longest, is a Soviet-era project that drains water away from the Amu Darya to southern Turkmenistan for cotton production. But the old irrigation canal leaks and creates destructive salt deserts. Turkmenistan's hope lies in the Caspian Sea region, where oil and natural gas fields are concentrated.

From *National Geographic Atlas of the World*, 9th edition. Copyright ©2011 National Geographic Society. Reprinted by arrangement. All rights reserved.

Area	488,100 sq km (188,456 sq mi)
Population	5,110,000

Government	republic
Capital	Ashgabat 744,000
Life Expectancy	65 years
Religion	Muslim, Eastern Orthodox
Language	Turkmen, Russian, Uzbek
Currency	Turkmen manat (TMM)
GDP per Cap	$6,900
Labor Force	48.2% Agriculture, 14% Industry, 37.8% Services

From *National Geographic Atlas of the World*, 9th edition. Copyright ©2011 National Geographic Society. Reprinted by arrangement. All rights reserved.

Uzbekistan

Introduction

Uzbekistan, a landlocked country dominated by the Qizilqum desert, is Central Asia's most populous country. About 80 percent of the country is flat desert, with mountain ranges rising in the far southeast and northeast. The Fergana Valley in the northeast is the country's most fertile region, containing many cities and industries. The Aral Sea, fed by rivers extensively tapped for irrigation, has shrunk to a fraction of its 1960s extent—and could be bone dry by 2018. Uzbeks, who were the third largest ethnic group of the former Soviet Union (after Russians and Ukrainians), descend from Turkic people and are rooted in the Sunni Muslim faith. Uzbeks make up more than three-quarters of the country's population, and the ethnic Russian minority is estimated at 800,000. Also, there are small numbers of ethnic Tajiks and Kazakhs living in Uzbekistan. Most of the population lives in rural areas, where cotton crops, imposed by Soviet planners, make Uzbekistan one of the world's top five producers.

Economic growth and living standards are among the lowest in the former Soviet Union. The world's largest open-pit gold mine is at Muruntau in the Qizilqum desert—some geologists claim it is Earth's largest gold deposit. However, the economic climate is poor because of smothering state control. The autocratic government is becoming more rigid as Islamist groups threaten it.

From *National Geographic Atlas of the World*, 9th edition. Copyright ©2011 National Geographic Society. Reprinted by arrangement. All rights reserved.

Area	447,400 sq km (172,742 sq mi)
Population	27,562,000
Government	republic
Capital	Tashkent 2,184,000
Life Expectancy	68 years

The ancient cities of Samarkand and Bukhara, Uzbekistan, are fabled for their domed mosques and melding of cultures.

Few cities boast a tourist come-on as effective as the 1913 poem "The Golden Road to Samarkand," by James Elroy Flecker, with its lines, "For lust of knowing what should be known / We take the Golden Road to Samarkand." It was that lure of discovering the forbidden that brought me to this fabled Silk Road city in present-day Uzbekistan.

Samarkand is one of the world's oldest inhabited cities, founded more than 2,750 years ago, its name evoking exotic sights and experiences. Conquered over the centuries by a succession of empire makers, including Alexander the Great and Genghis Khan, Samarkand was declared the capital of the fourteenth-century empire assembled by the native son Tamerlane, who commissioned many of the city's present-day landmarks.

Samarkand's competitor for beauty along the Silk Road was, and is, its sister city, Bukhara. Over the centuries these two crossroad settlement—both now World Heritage site—have been a source wonder; oases in a

Figure 26.6 Ark Citadel In Bukhara, Uzbekistan. © Eduard Kim/www.Shutterstock.com.

vast arid landscape, adorned with elaborate complexes of turquoise-domed mosques, mosaic-filled mausoleums, and celebrated madrassas. Bukhara is "the most complete example of a medieval city in Central Asia," according to UNESCO. The Ark of Bukhara (Figure 26.6), the city's massive ancient fortress, looms like an artificial mountain above the surroundings plain. Nearby stands the 155-foot-high Kalyan Minaret, said to have been one of the tallest building in Central Asia when it was erected in the twelfth century.

Then there is the Mago-i-Attari mosque, dating to the eleventh century. Archaeologists

discovered that the site has, at different times, hosted a Zoroastrian fire temple and a Buddhist shirne; today it features a carpet museum. The present-day mosque is so evocative of *The Arabian Nights* that I half-expected a magic carpet to scoop me up and fly me around the domes.

The best time to savor these cities? At twilight, when the stars rise above the domes, and the very air seem to shimmer. Magical indeed.

—**Ian Williams,** *National Geographic Traveler,* **October 2009**

Religion	Muslim (mostly Sunni), Eastern Orthodox
Language	Uzbek, Russian, Tajik, Kazakh
Currency	soum (UZS)

GDP per Cap	$2,800
Labor Force	44% Agriculture, 20% Industry, 36% Services

From *National Geographic Atlas of the World,* 9th edition. Copyright ©2011 National Geographic Society. Reprinted by arrangement. All rights reserved[Q11].

Kyrgyzstan

Introduction

A rugged nation in Central Asia, Kyrgyzstan shares the snowcapped Tian Shan mountains with China. A large salt lake, Ysyk-Köl (Lake Ysyk) (Figure 26.7), occupies a highland basin in the northeast. Some 75 percent of the land is mountainous, and high mountains separate the north—and the capital, Bishkek—from the rest of the country.

In their mountain fastness, the nomadic Kyrgyz, a Turkic-speaking people with loose ties to Islam, have bred horses, cattle, and yaks for centuries. The Kyrgyz came under tsarist Russian rule during the nineteenth century, and thousands of Russian farmers migrated into the region. Kyrgyzstan achieved independence in 1991. The Kyrgyz make up 69 percent of the population, and there are large Uzbek (14 percent) and

Russian (9.1 percent) minorities. Raising livestock remains the principal agricultural activity today, and Kyrgyzstan remains one of the poorest countries of the former Soviet Union. The country is a democracy, but a north–south divide creates political instability.

From *National Geographic Atlas of the World,* 9th edition. Copyright ©2011 National Geographic Society. Reprinted by arrangement. All rights reserved.

Area	199,900 sq km (77,182 sq mi)
Population	5,304,000
Government	republic
Capital	Bishkek 837,000
Life Expectancy	68 years
Religion	Muslim, Russian Orthodox
Language	Kyrgyz, Uzbek, Russian
Currency	som (KGS)
GDP per Cap	$2,100
Labor Force	48.0% Agriculture, 12.5% Industry, 39.5% Services

From *National Geographic Atlas of the World*, 9th edition. Copyright ©2011 National Geographic Society. Reprinted by arrangement. All rights reserved.

Figure 26.7 Ysyk-Köl, Kyrgyztan. © Novoselov/www.Shutterstock.com.

Kazakhstan

Introduction

Stretching across Central Asia, landlocked Kazakhstan is mostly desert and dry steppes. The land is flat in the west, and there are large lowlands along the Caspian Sea. High mountains rise along Kazakhstan's borders in the southeast and east. The climate is continental with hot summers, severely cold winters, and high winds sweeping across the plains.

With independence in 1991, Kazakhs made up about 44 percent of the population, with Russians at 36 percent and Germans at 4 percent. In 2006, the government reported a significant change in ethnic composition due to some 1.5 million Russians and 500,000 Germans emigrating from Kazakhstan. Today the ethnic populations are: 60 percent Kazakh, 24 percent Russian, 2.9 percent Uzbek, 2.7 percent Ukrainian, and 1.4 percent German.

In the fifteenth century the Kazakhs emerged as nomadic stock herders of the steppes, speaking a Turkic language and practicing Islam. Imperial Russia colonized the region in the nineteenth century. An estimated 1 million Kazakhs died during Soviet campaigns in the 1930s to forcibly settle the nomads. The nation confronts a legacy of environmental abuse left behind by the Soviets, such as the desertification of the Aral Sea and radioactivity from nuclear explosions at the Semipalatinsk test site. Economically, Kazakhstan is enjoying strong growth because of its large oil, gas, and mineral reserves.

From *National Geographic Atlas of the World*, 9th edition. Copyright ©2011 National Geographic Society. Reprinted by arrangement. All rights reserved.

Area	2,724,900 sq km (1,052,090 sq mi)
Population	15,880,000
Government	republic
Capital	Astana 585,000
Life Expectancy	67 years
Religion	Muslim, Russian Orthodox
Language	Kazakh (Qazaq), Russian
Currency	tenge (KZT)
GDP per Cap	$11,800
Labor Force	31.5% Agriculture, 18.4% Industry, 50.0% Services

From *National Geographic Atlas of the World*, 9th edition. Copyright ©2011 National Geographic Society. Reprinted by arrangement. All rights reserved.

REVIEW QUESTIONS

1. What is the name of the most modern city in the region?

2. What was the purpose of the ancient Silk Road?

3. What is the region's most populous country?

4. What religion dominates the region?

5. In what country do we find the UNESCO World Heritage Site Samarkand?

part 9 : GEOGRAPHY AND TOURISM IN THE MIDDLE EAST

MAJOR GEOGRAPHIC CHARACTERISTICS

- The Islamic religion dominates the entire region.
- The region is the hearth of early civilization and three major religions: Christianity, Islam, and Judaism.
- Population concentrations reflect water availability.
- The region is one of the driest areas of the world, but is strategically important, especially for oil.
- Political and social conflict in the region affects the region and the world.

MAJOR TOURISM CHARACTERISTICS

- In 2011 protests took place across the Middle East calling for reform and regime change (Arab Spring) with violence erupting in several countries and disrupting tourism to the region.
- Pilgrimages associated with Christianity, Judaism, and Islam are important to tourism.
- International tourism is concentrated in a few countries of the region.
- With their distinctive landscapes, the cities of the region attract regional and international tourists.
- Travel within the region is often difficult.
- Historical and archaeological sites of ancient cultures are major tourist attractions.

MAJOR TOURIST DESTINATIONS

Islamic capitals

Dubai, Abu Dhabi, and Qatar

Petra and Jerash (Jordan)

Jerusalem

Holy Land sites

Cairo, the Great Pyramids, and the Sphinx (Egypt)

Istanbul (Turkey)

Ismir

Central Anatolia

(continued)

© 2015 Cengage Learning

MAJOR TOURIST DESTINATIONS (continued)

Antalya

Damascus

Tunis and Coastal resorts (Tunisia)

KEY TERMS AND WORDS

Arab Spring	Desert Pavement	Jewish	Oasis
Arabian Plateau	Druze	Kasbah	Pilgrimages
Ashkenazim	Friday Mosque	Koran	River Basins
Baksheesh	Greco-Roman	Lake Kinnereth	Sephardim
Bazaar	Islam	Lifestyle	Shiite
Bedouin	Islamic	Medina	Souk (Suq)
Christian	Islamic Cities	Mediterranean	Steppe
Coptic	Islamic Fundamentalist	Middle East	Sunni
Cultural Hearth	Islamic Law	Mosque	
Desert	Islamic World	Muslim	

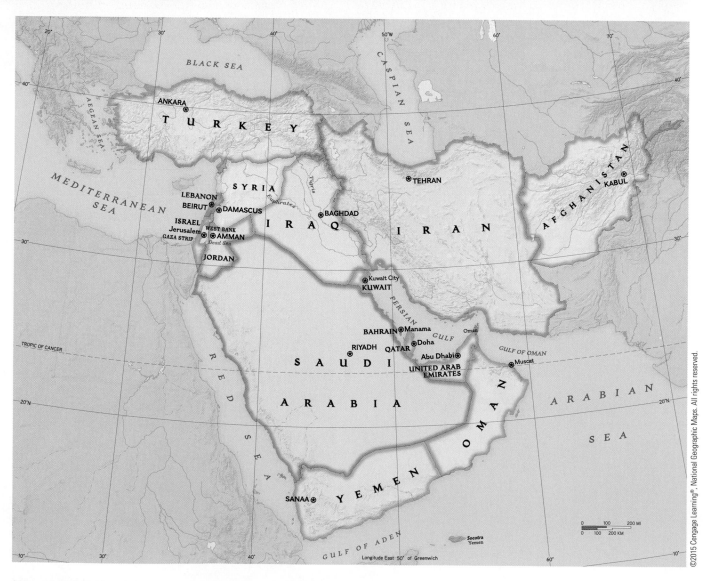

Introduction

The Middle East was the only region in the world experiencing a decline in international arrivals in 2010 (UNWTO). In 2010, visitors to the Middle East represented only 3.2 percent of global international arrivals, down from 5.7 percent in 2000. Tourism is very important to specific areas and countries of the Middle East, but the ranking of specific destinations has changed in the last few decades as a result of political problems in the Middle East and North Africa. Tourism continues to be impacted by geopolitical realities and events. These include efforts to help bring about a change in Iraq; a series of regime changes in several Arab countries as the result of a movement that became known as the Arab Spring; and a further isolation of Iran due to concerns over its nuclear ambitions. These all impact on the region as a tourist destination.

Figure P9.1 Dubai marina. © Anastasios71/www.Shutterstock.com.

The region is dominated by the Islamic religion. (Islam refers to the religion; a Muslim is a believer in Islam). Most countries (other than Israel, Iran, and Turkey) are part of the Arab realm. Most of the Arab countries in the region have joined an Arab Tourism Organization (ATO) to promote and develop local tourism. The chief emphasis has been on developing a Pan-Arab–integrated tourism market, with hopes for increasing the flow of tourism traffic between the Arab nations. The organization's mission calls for it to provide support and services to member countries and to contribute to the growth of the Arab tourism industry. To date they have met with little success in developing a Pan-Arab–integrated tourism market. In some of these countries, European and American tourists are not encouraged and are often faced with restrictions that curtail movement and curiosity. There has been a wave of anti-Western sentiment accompanied by a movement to revive Islamic traditions in many countries. There have also been popular uprisings against authoritarian regimes starting in December 2010 in Tunisia and spreading to Egypt, Libya, and Syria causing rapid change but also concern among potential tourists to the region until these countries regain stability. Some of the wealthier countries that export petroleum, such as Saudi Arabia and Bahrain are not interested in Western tourists because they do not need the income from tourism. Dubai, on the other hand, has a large duty-free airport and seeks to establish itself as a major destination and hub for travel through the region. Dubai's explosive growth has manifested itself in spectacular architectural achievements and a futuristic cityscape (Figure P9.1). Other Arab states are concerned that tourism will affect their population's attitudes toward modernization and lead to adoption of Western dress, behavior, and values, which they feel are distracting from traditional values.

The importance of Islam to this region makes it possible to identify specific tourist types in the Islamic world. The first characteristic is attraction to cities. Muslims enjoy visiting the cities of their region and the world for both pilgrimages and business purposes. The traditional Islamic cities offer attractions, such as the mosques where daily prayers are to be offered, the baths, and the bazaars. The business capitals of the Islamic world such as Damascus, Syria; Beirut, Lebanon; and Cairo, Egypt, are the centers of trade and commerce carried out under Islamic law. Muslims also visit cities for burial pilgrimages. It is the desire of many Muslims to be buried in a sacred place. Holy pilgrimages to Mecca in Saudi Arabia or the Dome of the Rock in Jerusalem involve several million Muslim visitors a year. Residents of the region are attracted to water because of its coolness and the rest it offers to desert-tired eyes. Muslims are not attracted to the sandy beach as are Western tourists, but visit for the water itself. Tourists in this area also make summer visits to the mountains in search of relief from the heat of the cities. A final form of tourism within the region is family-related tourism. Family members visit relatives abroad or return home from foreign residences. In Dubai, for example, nine out of ten workers are expatriates.

Geographic Characteristics

The Middle East is a widely misunderstood region. In much of the Western world the term *the Middle East* evokes images of oil-rich sheiks, conflicts between Arab and Arab or Arab and Israeli, terrorist groups, and nomadic Bedouins crossing the desert in camel caravans. Popular stereotypes of the region are misleading, and even efforts to define the region have problems of

Poets praise their treasures. Profiteers deplete them. Activists now seek to preserve them.

The old fisherman sat on a scrap of carpet in a thatched shelter by the sea.

His face was like a walnut shell, and his eyes squinted with a lifetime of gazing into the white-hot glare of Arabia. The *shamal* was blowing off the sea in scorching gusts, making even the date palms droop. "It is the western wind," the man said in a raspy voice. "I feel its warmth."

Behind him, the village of Film, notched into the mountains of Oman's Musandam Peninsula, shimmered like a brazier. Goats panted in the shade cast by upturned boats and the walls of a mosque. Just breathing made me feel as if my nostrils might burst into flame. Sami Alhaj, my Yemeni dive partner, said: "Underwater, with the corals, we get a little piece of heaven. Above water, with this wind, we get a little piece of hell."

We soon fled the inferno and descended into paradise once more. Color marked our passage between worlds as vividly as temperature did. Where the colors of land were those of the spice suq—pepper, cinnamon, mustard, mace—the undersea world was drenched in the sumptuous hues of a sultan's palace. Long, waving indigo arms of soft corals mingled with pomegranate fronds of feather stars. Speckled-gray moray eels, whose gaping mouths reveal a startling burst of yellow, leered out of crevices, while butterflyfish flitted past in tangerine flashes.

Had the legendary Scheherazade known the richness of these seas, she would have had stories for another thousand and one Arabian nights. She might have piqued the king's curiosity with the riddle of the reefs of Dhofar, in southern Oman; they flourish as coral gardens in winter and seaweed forests in summer. The trigger for this ecological shift—found nowhere else—is the onset of the *khareef*, the southwesterly monsoon, which bathes the coast in an upwelling of cold, nutrient-rich water. Seaweed, dormant in the warm months, responds to the cooler conditions with a burst of luxuriant growth, carpeting the reefs with green, red, and golden fronds.

Or she might have told the story of the tribe of mudskippers that have their sheikh-dom on the shores of Kuwait Bay. Their name in Persian means "lazy ones," because they appear too lethargic to follow the falling tide. Instead, each goggle-eyed fish builds and patrols its own mud-rimmed swimming pool. Shining in slippery coats of mud, they wriggle through the slurry of their ponds, waddle along the walls on their broad pectoral fins, then fling themselves into the air, exuberant as porpoises.

Might she have mentioned the ghost crabs of Masira Island? They build perfect miniature Mount Fujis of sand every night, only to have them leveled by the winds the next day. Scheherazade would have had no shortage of material.

"I am the sea. In my depths all treasures dwell. Have they asked the divers about my pearls?" the Egyptian poet Muhammad Hafiz Ibrahim wrote a century ago. Few survive today of those champions of the sea, the pearl divers of generations past who sought the greatest treasure of all. Forty, fifty, a hundred times a day they dropped to the seafloor, as deep as 65 feet, without goggles and often wearing only a thin woven garment to protect against jellyfish stings. With other risks, they took their chances. Men died from stingray jabs, from poisonous stonefish spines, from shark bites. Clownfish—cruel joke—attacked their eyes. Their eardrums burst, and some went blind from constant exposure to the salty water.

Pearls were the diamonds of the ancient world. In Hafiz's time they were the Persian Gulf's most valuable resource, and 70,000 men were engaged in collecting them. But the divers saw little of the wealth they brought up. The oysters were thrown into a common pile, to be opened the next day, when dead. Even if a diver brought up a pearl of Steinbeckian magnificence, he would never know it. Debt drove them to dive. Debt inherited from their fathers and their father's fathers.

Yet pearling was equally a matter of deep cultural pride, part of a maritime tradition that is as Arabian as deserts and dates. Through the waters of the Persian Gulf, East met West, the wealth of Africa and India flowing to the empires of Europe. Until the 1930s, great Kuwaiti dhows, or booms, with names like *The Triumph of Righteousness* and *The Light of the Earth and Sea*, set their lateen sails to the billowing north-easterly wind that blew them to Zanzibar and Mangalore. Months later the khareef brought them home again. The seasonal fluctuations of the winds were the fuel of Arabian commerce. The winds were Allah's, and the winds were free.

Then came oil, and a seafaring way of life that had endured for millennia melted away at the breath of a new monetary lord. Oil was the genie that granted the wishes of modernization and affluence. Arabia was transformed—from camels to Cadillacs, mud houses to megamalls—as its citizens rode the magic carpet of petro-wealth.

Today human hands are reaching deep into Arabia's seas and taking more treasure than the seas can possibly replenish. Overfishing, pollution, seabed dredging, and massive coastal modification are crippling marine ecosystems by degrading water quality and exacerbating toxic algal blooms. In 2010 a group of marine scientists described the region's most strategic waterway, the Persian Gulf (Figure P9-2), as "a sea in decline," bedeviled by a storm of malign influences. "If current trends continue," they wrote, we will "lose a unique marine environment."

Had the legendary Scheherazade known the richness of these seas, she would have had stories for another thousand and one Arabian nights.

One of the groups at greatest risk are sharks. Of all the insults to Arabia's marine life, none is more grotesque than the mountains of shark carcasses that arrive every evening in the Deira Fish Market in Dubai, trucked from landing sites around Oman and the United Arab Emirates, from there to make their way east—a stinking tide of fins and flesh.

Rima Jabado, conspicuous in her yellow rubber boots and pink top, moves through the market counting and measuring hammer-heads, threshers, bulls, silkies, and makos: the thoroughbreds of Arabia's seas, carted here to be hocked like horsemeat. Totemic animals that divers dream of encountering underwater are hauled out of the backs of trucks with meat hooks and lined up on the pavement, grimy and bloodied, row upon row of scowling mouths.

An auctioneer works his way along the line, followed by a retinue of buyers calculating profit margins on their smart phones. In their wake a man expertly severs the fins and lays them out on plastic tarps for separate sale. A pickup truck pulls up, and the driver unloads a dozen sacks of dried fins. He plunges his hands into a sack and lifts out handfuls of small gray triangles, stiff as plywood. There must be several thousand fins in this one shipment.

"When I started working here, I thought, That's a lot of sharks," Jabado, a doctoral student at United Arab Emirates University, tells me. "But when you see it every day, you ask, How is this possible? How can this last?"

A muezzin gives the evening call to prayer from a mosque whose minarets make artful silhouettes against a golden sky. Across the parking lot, the fish market is crowded with Emirati housewives gliding down aisles of laden stalls, passing their purchases to Pakistani boys who wheel them in garden barrows to a rank of SUVs.

The old name for this part of Arabia was the Pirate Coast. Trading ships carried companies

continues

Figure P9.2 Persian Gulf. © alanf/www.Shutterstock.com.

of archers to repel thieves. But how to solve the plunder of the sea itself? Jabado travels the length of the U.A.E. coast, from Abu Dhabi to Ras al Khaimah, tallying sharks and interviewing fishermen. Everywhere it is the same story: Catches are down, and fishing intensity is up.

One of the questions Jabado asks the fishermen is whether they think sharks should be protected. Some say, No, why should we protect them? Sharks are a gift from God. He will replenish them. Others say that sharks should be protected but that it needs to happen across the region. If we protect them here, do you think the Iranians are going to stop taking them? they tell her. Why should I stop fishing for sharks and miss out on revenue if some other person keeps taking them?

Eight countries border the gulf. "They have the same kind of culture and heritage, mostly speak the same language, face the same problems, and share the same resources," Jabado says. "Why aren't they working together?"

Her concerns run deeper than fisheries management. The impact of an environmental disaster in so shallow and enclosed a waterway is appalling to contemplate. There are many hundreds of oil and gas platforms in the gulf, and tens of thousands of tanker movements annually through a narrow stretch of the Strait of Hormuz between the Musandam Peninsula and Iran. "What if there was a *Deepwater Horizon* event here?" she asks. "The average depth of the gulf is about 30 meters. One big spill could wipe out whole marine ecosystems."

There are inklings that the unified approach Jabado seeks may be starting to take

shape. Several countries are considering following the lead of the United Arab Emirates in giving legal protection to a single species of shark: the whale shark (Figure P10-3), the biggest fish in the sea. The giant filter feeders have been turning up in unexpected places. In 2009 David Robinson, a Dubai-based whale shark researcher, was startled when a Google image search turned up a photograph of whale sharks swimming among the platforms of Al Shaheen, a major oil and gas field off the coast of Qatar.

"The photograph was on the Facebook page of a worker on a gas rig," Robinson said. "I sent him a message, he added me as a friend, and now we're getting a stream of pictures from him and others. In one photograph I counted 150 animals. I'd like to say we discovered the sharks through tirelessly scouring the oceans, but that would be a lie. It was through scouring the oceans of cyberspace! Science by Facebook—a bit embarrassing, really."

The discovery of whale sharks at Al Shaheen has led to other finds. Seasonal mass spawning of lobsters has been observed, with the lobsters rising to the surface at night and turning the sea into a vast crustacean soup. With fishing banned and boat traffic restricted in many oil and gas fields, these areas likely serve as de facto marine reserves. The platforms certainly act as giant fish-aggregating devices. At Al Shaheen, with a flare stack belching flame overhead, I watched a shoal of jacks circle the legs of the platform and spinner dolphins launch their lissome bodies into the air. A hammerhead cruised at the edge of visibility, finding sanctuary within the ring of fire.

A sense of marine guardianship seems to be growing across the region. In Kuwait hundreds of keen amateur divers have formed the ecological equivalent of SWAT teams, dedicated to repairing the environmental damage of war and waste. They lift sunken vessels from the seabed and remove tons of snared fishing nets from Kuwait's coral reefs.

Off the island of Qaruh, I helped cut away a net that was twined around the brittle stubs of staghorn coral—a nightmare of knotted nylon mesh that yielded reluctantly to our collection of chef's knives and garden shears. Our odd assortment of reef repairmen included a computer engineer, a television producer, and a former leader of Kuwait's Grand Mosque. On the return journey, crossing a smooth, tawny sea with a dust storm billowing on the horizon, two of the team found space among the scuba gear on deck to pray. Oblivious to the symphonic thunder of twin 200-horsepower outboards, they prostrated their bodies and uttered the ancient words of invocation and praise, giving voice to the hope that good might come to the world.

At the other end of the Persian Gulf, in Dubai, public-spirited beachgoers collect stranded turtles and take them to a rehabilitation facility in the luxury Burj al Arab hotel. In 2011, 350 juvenile turtles were brought in, many victims of "cold stunning"—inertia caused by the winter drop in sea temperature. "If they survive the first 24 hours, there's a 99 percent chance they'll recover," Warren Baverstock, the aquarium operations manager, said as we walked along a line of bubbling tanks. He reached in to scratch

continues

the backs of splashing turtles, which twisted their necks and flippers in pleasure at the attention. "They always know where the sea is," he said. "They swim up and down the wall nearest the sea, lifting their heads up, looking for it."

Mass releases of the rehabilitated turtles are staged at a nearby beach to publicize the work and reinforce the message that Arabia's marine life is valuable, vulnerable, and in need of protection. Each turtle is implanted with a microchip for identification. In the seven years the project has been operating, no turtle has washed ashore twice.

The hotel's most famous patient was an adult green turtle called Dibba, which had arrived with a fractured skull. Baverstock and his team needed 18 months to rehabilitate the turtle, but Dibba, released with a satellite transmitter glued to its carapace, repaid its caregivers with a 259-day, 5,000-mile migratory journey, looping down the Arabian Sea, passing the Maldives, skirting Sri Lanka, and reaching as far as the Andaman Islands before the transmitter battery failed.

Dibba traced an ancient route imprinted not just on turtles but also on the cultural memory of Arabia's peoples. This way came the dhows laden with Basra dates and pearls. This way they returned, carrying camphor, silks, sandalwood, and cloves. Every Arabian family had its sea captains and sailors, its pearl divers and boat carpenters—a saltwater legacy written in its genes.

Modernity has dimmed that memory. "We have lost the thirst for the sea that can only be quenched by going to the sea," one Omani businessman told me with sadness in his eyes. Yet for others the thirst is returning. Increasing numbers of Arabs are going to the sea not to exploit it but to experience it as it is. They are renewing their bond with ancient shores and rediscovering the poet's truth: "In my depths all treasures dwell."

— **Kennedy Warne, National Geographic, March 2012**

Figure P9.3 Whale shark in the Red Sea.
© Kim Briers/www.Shutterstock.com.

agreement. Most of the area is dry, with precipitation totals under twenty inches per year and in many places less than ten inches per year. Culturally, North Africa and the Middle East are considered a single region by geographers and many others because of the influence of the Islamic religion. The Middle East is the hearth of the Islamic religion. At least 80 percent of the people of the region, including North Africa, are Muslim. Areas suitable for human occupancy are widely scattered, and most of the lands of North Africa and the Middle East have high population densities only in more favorable sites associated with water. Thus for most of the region, the population density of individual countries is low.

Population is concentrated in river or oasis locations, and the vast majority of the people have little to do with nomadism, camels, or the Sahara Desert. The view of the region as the home of wealthy Arab sheiks engaging in conspicuous consumption from their oil wealth is equally erroneous. Not only is the oil wealth concentrated in only a few countries, but within them a significant portion of that wealth is being channeled into development efforts to benefit a broader segment of the population. Even the aridity of the area is modified by elevation and increased precipitation in the highlands. The idea that the region is entirely sand is another error, since most of it is covered by a rocky gravel surface known as desert pavement rather than sand.

The importance of the region to the world centers on its vast reserves of oil and oil-related wealth; its role as cultural hearth for the world's major religions of Judaism, Christianity, and Islam; the importance of the area historically as a cradle of civilization; and its present strategic location and repeated conflicts that threaten to draw other regions of the world into global war.

Climate Characteristics

The Middle East is not as arid as commonly assumed, but in general, the region does have a dry climate. The predominant climatic type is desert or steppe, with precipitation totals of ten inches or less per year. The driest portions are the Sahara and the great deserts of the Arabian Peninsula.

Important areas of Turkey, Syria, Israel, and Jordan have Mediterranean climates. Precipitation totals of fifteen to thirty-five inches make farming more profitable in these areas, particularly fall-planted crops such as barley and wheat, which utilize the winter rainfall.

The temperatures of the Middle East are almost uniformly high during the summer months.

Organization of Life

Of interest to tourism is the organization of life in the region. There are three distinctive lifestyles: city, village, and nomadic. For tourists and residents, the cityscape is dominated by narrow streets, the mosque, and the bazaar. The mosque is the focal point of the city and its neighborhoods, for Muhammad revealed that the faithful Muslim must bow in prayer five times daily while facing Mecca. Fridays are the Sabbath, and the great mosques are referred to as Friday Mosques. Each section of the bazaar specializes in one category of goods, making shopping easier than the maze of winding narrow passageways might suggest to the uninitiated visitor. Closest to the mosque are the merchants selling articles necessary for worship, then those skilled artisans working with silver or gold. Farthest from the mosque are textiles and goods associated with food preparation, which are least compatible with the worship service of the mosque.

Streets remained narrow because the Koran (the words of Allah to the prophet Muhammad) did not provide for public space greater than that needed for a laden camel to pass. The construction of buildings in the Islamic city provides the individual with security and privacy. Islamic architecture is interior-oriented rather than exterior-oriented, with a central court bounded by the rooms of the home and no windows in the exterior walls. Each quarter of the city was set apart for different groups, separated by walls and strong gates for protection.

Early Islamic cities became great learning centers where scholars were responsible for many scientific advancements. Today, these large cities, such as Baghdad, Amman, and Cairo, are the homes of both the very wealthy and the very poor. Contrasts between the rich and poor abound in city life. Problems of sanitation, water supply, unsafe housing, and access to adequate food contribute to a low standard of living among the urban poor. In spite of the dichotomy between rich and poor, the Islamic city is a magnet to tourists and a haven to its residents. The myriad architectural attractions, fascinating street scenes, and tantalizing glimpses into the Islamic lifestyle make the great Islamic cities a unique tourist attraction.

The second lifestyle (which tourists generally only glimpse) is found in the villages. The villagers focus on agriculture—wheat, dates, barley, and other small grains and vegetables for local and national consumption. The location of villages depends upon water. The villages are composed of houses of various sizes and amenities depending upon social and economic level, the mosque, the market or bazaar, and the fields surrounding the village. The village lifestyle is more traditional than the lifestyle in the cities. The pace of life reflects centuries of evolution of a social and political milieu that provided for the needs of each village member. The contrast with the city is apparent to even a casual visitor. For the tourist who has braved the traffic-congested streets of a city, the villages in the region offer an opportunity to pause and reflect on the relative progress brought by the Industrial Revolution. Nearly one-half of the people of this region live in villages, and even city residents return frequently to family homes in the village.

The third major lifestyle is found among the nomads. The nomads account for only 5 to 10 percent of the population of the region, and national boundaries and politics are pressuring them to become sedentary. The nomads use a part of the environment not used by villagers, herding their animals throughout the region. They provide meat, cheese, leather products, and animals for the village and city dwellers. It has become increasingly popular with tourists to visit a Bedouin tent. They observe and learn of the lifestyle of the nomad and feel the trip to the region is more complete having had such fleeting contact with the local peoples.

INTERNATIONAL TOURISM TO THE PERSIAN GULF, 2005–2010.

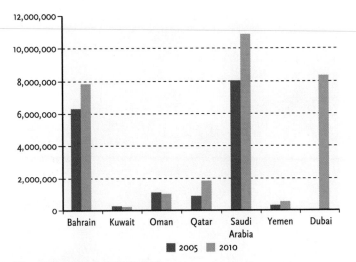

Data source: *The World Bank: The Data Catalogue.*
Figure copyright ©2015 Cengage Learning®. All rights reserved.

INTERNATIONAL TOURISM TO THE MEDITERRANEAN, 2005–2010.

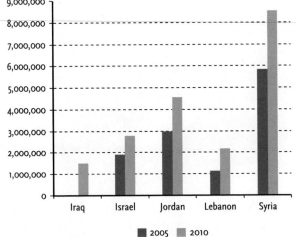

Data source: *The World Bank: The Data Catalogue.*
Figure copyright ©2015 Cengage Learning®. All rights reserved.

World attention is focused upon this region both because of the political situation and its potential. The political situation changed the tourist map of the region. In 2011 protests erupted across the Middle East in the wake of calls for reform and regime change with violence erupting in some counties. The Arab Spring caused the tourism industry in countries such as Tunisia, Egypt, Libya, and Syria to suffer greatly. Other destinations in the region, such as Dubai, Abu Dhabi, and Qatar saw their tourist arrivals increase. The aftermath of two Gulf Wars in the region, the continuing internal stress in Iraq, the distrust between the Western world and Iran, the Israeli–Palestinian dispute, the "Arab Spring," the rise of Islamic fundamentalism, and difficulties between the moderate and radical Arab states combined to inhibit tourism in many parts of the region. Government decrees against Western lifestyles (as in Iran) and minimizing Western tourists in Saudi Arabia and Yemen further reduces tourist activity

The major tourist countries of the Middle East today are Egypt, Israel, Turkey, and Dubai. Historically, other countries of the region such as Iraq and Lebanon have been major international tourist centers. Jordan and Israel signed an accord opening their borders. The impact was almost immediate as tourism arrivals nearly doubled and continued to grow. If and when the political situation stabilizes, tourism should return, but it would be difficult to predict the length of time needed to return to the earlier number of visitors. Despite the turmoil, the region continues to intrigue visitors and is a key market for tourism development. These countries have proven to be resilient to crisis and their historical importance as a cradle of Western civilization, their oil wealth, and demographic growth provide foundations for a tourism rebound.

Israel

Introduction

Israel lies on the Mediterranean coast of Southwest Asia, with most people living along the coastal plain. The eastern interior is dry and includes the Dead Sea—the lowest point on the Earth's surface. North are the rugged hills of Galilee, and south lies the Negev, a desert plateau. Israel's population is about 75 percent Jewish, with Israeli Arabs making up about 20 percent (not including the West Bank and Gaza Strip). The Israeli non-Jewish population is 83 percent Muslim, 8.3 percent Christian, and 8.2 percent Druze. The Arab Christian population is concentrated in Galilee. Nazareth is the largest Arab Christian town. Born in battle after the British left Palestine in 1948, Israel has endured eight major conflicts with Arab countries. In the 1967 Six Day War, Israel captured the Gaza Strip from Egypt, West Bank from Jordan, and Golan Heights from Syria. To secure peace, Israel in 1982 returned the Sinai, which it had taken from Egypt in 1967. But at a time of peace with Egypt, tensions flared with Palestinians and Syrians in Lebanon, and Israel invaded Lebanon in 1982. Palestinian intifadas (armed uprisings), 1987–1992, 2000–2005, and 2012 in the West Bank and Gaza Strip cost thousands of lives. In 2006, Hezbollah forces attacked from Lebanon, and Israel invaded again. Stumbling blocks to peace—and the creation of a Palestinian state—include Jewish settlements in the West Bank, the status of Jerusalem, and the return of Palestinian refugees from neighboring Arab countries.

From *National Geographic Atlas of the World*, 9th edition. Copyright ©2011 National Geographic Society. Reprinted by arrangement. All rights reserved.

Area	22,072 sq km (8,522 sq mi)
Population	7,634,000

Government	parliamentary democracy
Capital	Jerusalem 736,000
Life Expectancy	81 years
Religion	Jewish, Muslim
Language	Hebrew, Arabic, English
Currency	new Israeli shekel (ILS)
GDP per Cap	$28,400
Labor Force	2% Agriculture, 16% Industry, 82% Services

From *National Geographic Atlas of the World*, 9th edition. Copyright ©2011 National Geographic Society. Reprinted by arrangement. All rights reserved.

TRAVEL **TIPS** 💼

Entry: Visas are issued on arrival for stays of less than three months. Passports are required.

Shopping: Common items include locally made sportswear, jewelry, beachwear, copper and glass, ceramics, leather, suede, carved olive wood, religious ornaments, and handicrafts.

Internet TLD: .il

CULTURAL CAPSULE There are three broad Jewish groupings: the Ashkenazim, or Jews who came to Israel from Europe, North and South America, South Africa, and Australia; the Sephardim, who trace their origin to Spain and Portugal; and the Eastern or Oriental Jews, who descend from ancient communities in Islamic countries. The Ashkenazim have generally dominated religion and politics in Israel. The 4.47 million population includes about 200,000 Israeli settlers in the West Bank of Jordan occupied by Israel, the Gaza Strip, the Golan Heights, and East Jerusalem. Seventeen percent of Israel's citizens are Israeli Arabs and members of the Druze and Circassian ethnic groups. The remainder (83 percent) is Jewish. In the occupied West Bank and Gaza Strip are nearly 2 million Palestinian Arabs, a region with a combined area about half the size of New York's Long Island.

Hebrew is the official language of Israel. Arabic is taught in the public schools and is also an official language. English is understood widely and is used in commerce. In the West Bank and Gaza Strip the Palestinian Arabs speak Arabic. A large percentage also speak English or French. Of the Palestinian Arabs, about 92 percent are Muslims (mostly Sunni), while the rest are Christian (Greek Orthodox or Roman Catholic). Stores and shops in Israel, the West Bank, and Gaza Strip are closed on Friday, Saturday, or Sunday, depending upon the owner's religion.

Cultural hints: "Shalom" (peace) is a usual greeting in Israel. "Salaam alaikum" (peace be upon you) is a usual greeting by Palestinians. Men need to wear a skullcap (kipah) when visiting Jewish religious sites. In Palestinian areas it is impolite to pass objects or shake hands with the left hand. There is a variety of food in the region because of the great cultural diversity. Some typical foods are falafel (pocket bread filled with beans, lamb, or chicken); stuffed grape leaves; spiced rice; kebab (meat and vegetables on a skewer); gefilte fish; vegetable salad, mixed with olive oil, lemon juice, and spices; and fruit and eggs. Israelis do not mix dairy products and meat during meals because of their religion; therefore, breakfasts will be meatless with lots of fruit, vegetables, and dairy products.

Tourism Characteristics

Israel, the Holy Land of three religions—Islam, Christianity, and Judaism—is an important world tourist center. Despite a constant threat from geopolitical events in the region, tourism is Israel's largest export income earner and international arrivals reached 3 million in 2010 (up from 2 million in 2000). The United States is the largest source area for international tourists to Israel, accounting for over 605,000 visitors in 2010, a number that has not changed much over a ten-year period.

The government recognizes the importance of tourism. It works actively to promote tourism and has assisted in the development of hotels and other segments of the tourist infrastructure. It has also developed a central reservation system for hotels and encouraged the development of more hotel rooms. It works actively to promote tourism and has organized a vigorous campaign to regain previous visitor levels from the United States and Europe. In 1992 Israel joined with Egypt, Greece, and Cyprus to promote travel from the United States to these four countries. Although Israel receives fewer total tourists than Egypt, Israel receives more from countries outside of the region. Its average length of stay of some twenty-one days is one of the highest in the world. This is due to the nature of the tourists. The United States is the leading source of tourists to Israel, accounting for one-fifth of total arrivals, 75 percent of whom are American Jews. Many have family ties and have a tendency to stay longer in the region. The European countries account for over 60 percent of total tourists to Israel, with Germany and France the leading contributors. The importance of religion other than Judaism cannot be overlooked. Both Christian and Islamic faiths have important religious sites in Israel.

Tourist Destinations and Attractions

The principal attraction of Israel is religion, centering around the old city of Jerusalem (Figure 27.1) and Bethlehem, with holy sites located throughout the country. Jerusalem offers much of the religious significance for all three major religions. The Dome of the Rock is second only to Mecca as a sacred site for Muslims. It is the spot where the Prophet Muhammad is reported to have ascended into Heaven. It is also the site of Solomon's temple. Near the Western Wall is the Wailing Wall, which is important to Jews. Jews call the wall the *Kotel Ha'naaravu* (the Western Wall). The name "Wailing Wall" was applied to it as Jews came here to pray and bewail the destruction of the Temple, the Exile, and the hard fate of the Jewish people. Men and women pray at different sections of the Wall in accordance with Orthodox Jewish customs. Sites associated with Christ, such as Golgotha where Christ was crucified, the Garden of Gethsemane, the Via Dolorosa (the last path Christ walked), the room of the Last Supper, the Church of the Holy Sepulchre, and so on, attract Christians. Some areas of Jerusalem are closed to traffic on the Jewish Sabbath. Also, modern Jerusalem has a beautiful Israel Museum containing the Dead Sea Scrolls, the famous Chagall windows, and the Museum of the Holocaust. Old Jerusalem, surrounded by a wall, has Arab, Christian, and Jewish quarters and markets. It is only a short trip to Bethlehem to visit the site of Christ's birth and Rachel's tomb.

Figure 27.1 Jerusalem old city, Israel. © silver-john/www.Shutterstock.com.

North of Jerusalem is the Sea of Galilee, which is called Lake Kinnereth by Israelis. Surrounding the sea are a number of holy sites, such as the Mount of Beatitudes and Capernaum. It is difficult to travel anywhere in Israel without coming in contact with sites of significant meaning for some segment of the three great religions. For example, the Dead Sea and Negev area, two other major centers of attraction, are associated with locations from biblical times: Masada, the Dead Sea Scrolls, Beersheba, and Sodom. Masada is famous because of a long siege by the Romans that ended in the deaths of all the Jewish defenders. Now Air Force pilots fly over from time to time to emphasize Masada's symbolic importance to Israel today.

The Dead Sea, on the border with Jordan, provides a unique experience of swimming and floating (Figure 27.2). Negev is also a resort and garden center for the region. Israel shares the Gulf of Aquaba with Jordan. Eilat on the Gulf is a well-developed beach resort that provides some excellent water recreation in the clear water of the Gulf of Aquaba (Figure 27.3). Many Europeans are attracted to the modern cities of Haifa and Tel Aviv and the nearby coastal resorts of Netanya and Herzliya. The Museum of the Diaspora is in Tel Aviv. Near Tel Aviv is the ancient city of Jaffa. Old Akko, the home of medieval Crusaders, lies north of Haifa. The Israeli government and other private organizations are conducting excavation projects throughout the country. These areas are becoming important attractions for visitors.

Figure 27.2 Floating in the Dead Sea. © ProfStocker/www.Shutterstock.com.

Figure 27.3 Hawksbill turtle, Eilat, Israel. © Rich Carey/www.Shutterstock.com.

The self-governing, occupied territories of the West Bank, Gaza Strip, and Golan Heights are predominantly Palestinian-Arab and contain many of the region's religious sites. Continued unrest in the West Bank has created some problems for the traveler desiring to visit those sites. The impact of unresolved boundary issues on tourism in the future remains to be seen.

Jordan

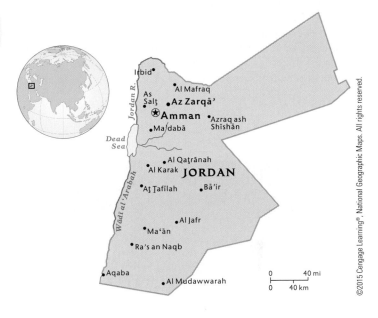

Introduction

Located on desert plateaus in West Asia, Jordan is almost landlocked but for a short coast on the Gulf of Aqaba. Irrigated farmland in the Jordan River valley provides much of the food, and most people live in the northwestern part of the country.

In 1923, after the fall of the Ottoman Empire, Transjordan was designated a British mandate. Independence came in 1946, and the army of Transjordan (the Arab Legion) went to war against the new state of Israel in 1948. Following the 1948–49 Arab–Israeli conflict, the country's name was changed to Jordan. The part of Palestine taken by Jordan in the 1948–49 war became known as the West Bank; it was ruled by Jordan until being conquered by Israel in 1967. The Arab–Israeli wars have flooded Jordan with 1.7 million Palestinian refugees. Jordan is governed by a constitutional monarchy; its economy is based on textiles, potash, and tourism. Most visitors come to see Petra, a city carved from stone, but there are also Roman ruins and biblical sites.

From *National Geographic Atlas of the World*, 9th edition. Copyright ©2011 National Geographic Society. Reprinted by arrangement. All rights reserved.

Area	89,342 sq km (34,495 sq mi)
Population	5,915,000
Government	constitutional monarchy
Capital	Amman 1,060,000
Life Expectancy	73 years
Religion	Sunni Muslim, Christian
Language	Arabic, English
Currency	Jordanian dinar (JOD)
GDP per Cap	$5,300
Labor Force	3% Agriculture, 20% Industry, 77% Services

From *National Geographic Atlas of the World*, 9th edition. Copyright ©2011 National Geographic Society. Reprinted by arrangement. All rights reserved.

TRAVEL**TIPS**

Entry: Visa is required and can be obtained on entry. Passports are required.

Peak Tourist Season: June through August

Shopping: Common items include gold and silver jewelry and local crafts such as wood carvings, leather goods, Nubian basketwork, and camel saddles.

Internet TLD: .jo

Jordanians are Arabic. There are a few communities of Circassians, Armenians, and Kurds. The largest minority today is some 1.5 million Palestinian Arabs, which includes some 850,000 registered refugees. Most Palestinians living in Jordan are citizens.

About one-fourth of the Arabs are of Bedouin descent; however, less than 5 percent are currently nomadic. Many of the Bedouins still live in tents. Arab is the official language of Jordan, but English is widely spoken among the educated. Approximately 90 percent of the population is Sunni Muslim. The Jordanians are good-natured, friendly, and hospitable. While appointments are important, Jordanians may be late as time is not as important in Jordan. Some Palestinians, although having Jordanian citizenship, consider themselves Palestinians first and support the establishment of a Palestinian homeland.

Cultural hints: "Salaam alaikum" (peace be with you) is common. Avoid touching members of the opposite sex in mosques and on the street. Avoid excessive admiration of any object owned by hosts. It is an honor to be invited into a home. It is polite to leave small portions of food on your plate. Eat with the right hand, never the left. Refuse offers of additional food for at least two times, then accept on the third offer if you wish more. Coffee is important. If not wanted, tip the cup back and forth.

A warm desert breeze whispers softly through Jarash's hundreds of Roman columns, the bruised and fallen, the proud and unbending alike. It swishes about the Oval Forum, witness to this city's ancient glory. Just 30 miles north of Jordan's capital, Amman, Jarash was a part of the Decapolis, a set of semiautonomous cities that stretched across the Levant. With the visit of Emperor Hadrian in A.D. 129, it became the temporary seat of an empire.

A new city has arisen, but Jarash remains home to some of the best preserved Roman ruins in the world.

"The city was covered by sand for so many years. Today, you can still feel how these people lived," says tour guide Ayman Khattab. You can see the scars of chariots on the original stones along the Cardo Maximus. At the Hippodrome, you can almost hear the clash of gladiator battles.

And at the South Theater, contemporary sounds emerge. Its annual summertime showcase of national and international music and poetry is Jordan's preeminent cultural event. A modern concert surrounded by these ancient stones deserves a standing ovation.

— **Benjamin Orbach,** *National Geographic Traveler,* December 2012/January 2013

Figure 27.4 The ancient city of Petra, Jordan.
© Aivolie/www.Shutterstock.com.

Tourism Characteristics

Jordan has benefitted from the relative calm along its border with Israel over the past few years, but like Israel and Egypt it has been hurt by the political conflicts and border changes in the area. During 1991 the Gulf War reduced its tourism to almost zero. However, in 1993 tourists began to return to Jordan. The border agreement between Jordan and Israel helped Jordan increase its tourism with arrivals reaching 4.6 million in 2010. Saudi Arabia is the largest market for tourism to Jordan with Syria providing the second largest number of visitors. The United States also contributes a significant amount of tourists to Jordan. Jordan benefits from tourists crossing the border into Israel. Jordan serves as a transit country for visitors to Israel due to some favorable airfares. Along with Israel and Egypt, Jordan is also part of a regional destination area. Jordan is bordered by Syria on the north, Iraq and Saudi Arabia on the east, Saudi Arabia on the south, and the West Bank on the west. The transit nature of Jordan serves two markets: tourists going to Israel and Islamic pilgrims from countries such as Turkey who visit the holy places in Saudi Arabia by land. The major rail line between Turkey and Saudi Arabia traverses Jordan, making such linkages possible. Eighty-five percent of visitors to Jordan are Arabic, and have far less economic impact on the country than the Western visitors to Israel do there. Low expenditures reflect the fact that relatively few of Jordan's visitors are true leisure travelers.

Tourist Destinations and Attractions

The major attractions of Jordan are archaeological relics, such as the city of Petra (The Rose City, Figure 27.4); desert castles; Kavak, a citadel built by the crusaders;

Jerash, a preserved Roman colonial city; Amman, the capital; Roman ruins; and the country's many museums. In Petra, Al-Khazneh is a Nabataean capital, a façade carved into solid rock. It is considered one of the wonders of the world. It is believed to have been carved as a tomb for a king in the century before Christ. It can only be reached by walking (Figure 27.5) or by riding donkeys or horses down a canyon, which is the more popular method. It even has a hotel at the bottom of the canyon. Jerash includes well-preserved examples of Greco-Roman architecture, including a Triumphal Arch, the Temple of Artemis, the Street of Columns, and an amphitheater. Madaba, which dates back to the Middle Bronze Age (2000–1500 B.C.), is mentioned in the Bible as a Moabite town.

Amman (Figure 27.6) has an archaeological museum that emphasizes the life of Nabataean Muslims and other artifacts of the region. Also, there is a fine Roman amphitheater cut out of a hillside in Amman. Jordan has a beach resort with excellent beaches at 'Aqaba at the head of the Gulf of 'Aqaba.

Figure 27.5 Slot canyon entrance to the ancient city of Petra, Jordan.
© robert paul van beets/www.Shutterstock.com.

Figure 27.6 Temple of Hercules on the citadel, Amman, Jordan. © takepicsforfun/www.Shutterstock.com.

Lebanon

Introduction

Lebanon is a small, mountainous country on the eastern shore of the Mediterranean Sea. East of the coastal strip, where most of the population lives, rise two parallel ranges, the Lebanon and Anti-Lebanon mountains. The Bekaa Valley, a high plateau, separates the mountain ranges. After independence from France in 1943, Lebanon prospered as a banking and resort center. It is estimated that two-thirds of the mostly Arab population are Muslim and the rest Christian. No census has been taken since 1932 due to political sensitivity over religious affiliation. There are also 400,000 Palestinian refugees in Lebanon. Fighting between Christian and Muslim militias escalated into civil war from 1975 to 1991. Democracy was restored in 1992 by allocating government positions based on religion. During the civil war both Israel and Syria sent troops into Lebanon, and Syria continues to have a strong influence. In 2006, the militia of the Lebanese Shiite party, Hezbollah, attacked Israel, prompting an Israeli invasion. The conflict caused extensive infrastructure damage and displaced up to a million Lebanese people.

From *National Geographic Atlas of the World*, 9th edition. Copyright ©2011 National Geographic Society. Reprinted by arrangement. All rights reserved.

Area	10,400 sq km (4,015 sq mi)
Population	3,876,000
Government	republic
Capital	Beirut 1,846,000
Life Expectancy	72 years
Religion	Muslim, Christian
Language	Arabic, French, English, Armenian
Currency	Lebanese pound (LBP)
GDP per Cap	$13,100

From *National Geographic Atlas of the World*, 9th edition. Copyright ©2011 National Geographic Society. Reprinted by arrangement. All rights reserved.

TRAVEL**TIPS** 💼

Entry: A passport and visa are required.

Tourist Season: Year-round

Shopping: Common items include gold and silver jewelry, leather goods, and wood carvings.

Internet TLD: .lb

CULTURAL CAPSULE Nearly 93 percent of the population is Arabic, and about 7 percent are Armenians, who live mostly in Beirut. The major religious groups are Muslim and Christians. Shiite Muslims make up the single largest religious group. Many Christian sects are represented in Lebanon, including Maronite, Greek Orthodox, Greek Catholic, Armenian Apostolic, Roman Catholic, and Protestant. The Druze, a group derived from Shiite Islam, constitute another significant minority. Arabic is the official language. French and English are widely understood. The Armenian minority also speak Armenian, and some speak Turkish.

Tourism Characteristics

Lebanon was greatly affected by internal conflicts in the 1980s. Prior to that, it was a major destination and a financial center with outstanding connectivity, sometimes called the "Switzerland of the Middle East." It had very good accommodations and other tourist facilities. It is trying to rebuild its economy, but it is recommended for travelers from the West to use caution. Arrivals reached 2.17 million in 2010.

Tourist Destinations and Attractions

Beirut, the capital, has good beaches and caves to explore from the sea. A day's trip from Beirut are the biblical Cedars of Lebanon (Figure 27.7), from which the cedar for King Solomon's Temple came. South along the coast are the biblical cities of Sidon and Tyre, which remain centers of conflict and unrest. Tripoli is an ancient Phoenician city. It has a crusader castle overlooking the city. As in other Middle Eastern countries, mosques are common throughout Lebanon.

Figure 27.7 A cedar in Lebanon. © Walid Nohra/www.Shutterstock.com.

Syria

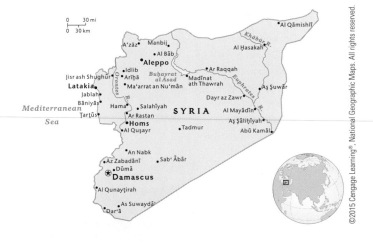

Introduction

Syria lies in West Asia and in the heart of the Middle East. The Mediterranean coastal plain is backed by a low range of hills, followed by a vast interior desert plateau. Most people live near the coast or along the Euphrates River, which brings life to the arid plateau. Damascus, the capital, was built on an oasis and is said to be the world's oldest continuously inhabited settlement. Syrians are mostly Arab, although about 9 percent are ethnic Kurds, who live mostly in the northeast corner of the country. Syria's population is about 90 percent Muslim, mostly Sunni; but the Alawite minority (12 percent of Syrians) is politically dominant. The Alawite-controlled Baath (Renaissance) Party has ruled Syria since 1963. Part of the Ottoman Empire for four centuries, Syria became a French mandate in 1920 and gained independence in 1946. Dreams of a "Greater Syria" were dashed when Britain and France created the smaller states of Lebanon, Palestine, and Jordan in the 1920s. Syrian military intervention in Lebanon from 1976 to 2005 appeared as an occupation to many, and Syrian influence in Lebanon remains strong. Syria has fought four wars with Israel—losing control of the Golan Heights to Israel in 1967. Recovering the Golan has been a matter of fierce national pride for Syrians.

From *National Geographic Atlas of the World*, 9th edition. Copyright ©2011 National Geographic Society. Reprinted by arrangement. All rights reserved.

Area	185,180 sq km (71,498 sq mi)
Population	21,906,000
Government	republic
Capital	Damascus 2,466,000
Life Expectancy	74 years
Religion	Sunni Muslim, other Muslim (includes Alawite, Druze), Christian
Language	Arabic, Kurdish, Armenian, Aramaic, Circassian
Currency	Syrian pound (SYP)
GDP per Cap	$4,600
Labor Force	17% Agriculture, 16% Industry, 67% Services

From *National Geographic Atlas of the World*, 9th edition. Copyright ©2011 National Geographic Society. Reprinted by arrangement. All rights reserved.

TRAVEL**TIPS**

Entry: Visas and passports are required.

Peak Tourist Season: July

Shopping: Common items include silk brocades, carved wood objects, glassware, brass ware, copper work, pottery, gold, silver, and handwoven rugs.

Internet TLD: .sy

 CULTURAL CAPSULE Syrians are of Semitic stock and about 90 percent of the population is Arab. Muslim (Sunnis) constitute the majority (74 percent). The Alawites represent about 16 percent, and Christians represent approximately 10 percent of the population. Arabic is the official language, and English and French are spoken by some of the educated.

Cultural hints: A friendly handshake is a common greeting. Do not point at other people. Do not point the sole of the foot at another person. Syrians generally refuse an invitation for more food twice and accept the third offer. Alcohol and pork are taboo. Typical foods include chickpeas, eggplant, meats, breads, and beans.

Tourism Characteristics

Although Syria officially encourages tourism and has a national tourist office to promote the development of an infrastructure, the current political problems and uncertainties have decreased the volume of tourism from Western nations. Its close ties to Iran provide Syria with oil, but result in few tourists from the West. The Islamic countries of Jordan, Lebanon, Saudi Arabia, and Iran provide the majority of visitors to Syria (8.5 million in 2010). Of the Arab states that promote tourism, Syria has the shortest length of stay, indicating a somewhat transit character to their tourist trade. Syria has little trade from the United States. However, if the political situation were to change, it would offer a number of attractions of interest to North Americans and Europeans.

Tourist Destinations and Attractions

Syria has a number of interesting places to visit, such as the Arab citadel of Aleppo with its mosque and museum; the ruins of ancient Tadmor at Palmyra (Figure 27.8); desert palaces, such as the Krak des Chevaliers, one of the best-preserved Crusader castles in the Middle East; and the Convent of Saint Takla, the oldest convent in the world, where Aramaic is still spoken. The capital, Damascus, is an Arab city with a rich history. The Omayyad Mosque is a major site. The House of Ananias, the Tomb of Saladin, St. Paul's Church, and the Street Straight in Damascus are all referred to in the Bible. Souks (marketplaces) full of copper inlays, brass, wood, and spices provide important handicraft items for the visitor. Roman ruins and a typical Arab bazaar are additional attractions.

Figure 27.8 Tadmor, Palmyra, Syria. Credit to come

Turkey

Introduction

Turkey sits astride Europe and Asia. While the portion of European Turkey may be small (5 percent of its land), the country's largest urban area, Istanbul, is there. With 10.1 million people, Istanbul is the second most populous European city, after Moscow. The dry plateau of Anatolia dominates the Asian part of Turkey, and high mountains flank the plateau in the north, east, and south. The coastal areas of Anatolia consist of fertile lowlands with major cities. The country, especially in the north, suffers from severe earthquakes. About 99 percent of Turks are Muslim, with an estimated 80 percent being Sunni Muslims and 20 percent Alevi (a Shiite sect). The Kurds are Turkey's largest ethnic minority at some 14 million; the majority are Sunnis living in the southeast. Around 500,000 ethnic Arabs live along the Syrian border. Most of Turkey's 70,000 ethnic Armenians reside in Istanbul; prior to World War I, some 1.5 million Armenians inhabited eastern Anatolia. Only about 5,000 ethnic Greeks remain in Turkey, a tiny remnant of a people that once populated much of Turkey's Aegean coast. The Ottoman Empire, defeated in World War I, collapsed in 1922. Mustafa Kemal, known as Atatürk (Father of the Turks), founded the Republic of Turkey in 1923 and sought to transform a conservative Islamic society into a secular Westernized state. Turkey joined the UN in 1945 and NATO in 1952. Although Turkey and Greece both belong to NATO, disputes such as Cyprus strain relations. Turkey invaded Cyprus in 1974 and still maintains troops in northern Cyprus. Another problem arose in southeast Turkey, where Kurdish rebels fought a guerrilla war from 1984 to 1999. Turkey strives toward membership in the European Union. Some 3 million Turks work and live in EU countries. Most of Turkey's trade is with Europe, and millions of European vacationers come to Turkey each year.

From *National Geographic Atlas of the World*, 9th edition. Copyright ©2011 National Geographic Society. Reprinted by arrangement. All rights reserved.

Area	779,452 sq km (300,948 sq mi)
Population	74,816,000
Government	republican parliamentary democracy
Capital	Ankara 3,716,000
Life Expectancy	72 years
Religion	Muslim (mostly Sunni)
Language	Turkish, Kurdish, Dimli, Azeri, Kabardian, Gagauz
Currency	Turkish lira (TRY)
GDP per Cap	$11,200
Labor Force	29.5% Agriculture, 24.7% Industry, 45.8% Services

From *National Geographic Atlas of the World*, 9th edition. Copyright ©2011 National Geographic Society. Reprinted by arrangement. All rights reserved.

TRAVEL **TIPS** 🧳

Entry: Visa is not required for stays up to three months. Passports are required.

Peak Tourist Season: July through September

Shopping: Common items include jewelry, ornaments, copper, brass, silver, meerschaum pipes, daggers, ceramics and pottery, animal skins, rugs, and carpets.

Internet TLD: .tr

CULTURAL CAPSULE Nearly 80 percent of the population are Turks, with a sizeable minority of Kurds. Although 98 percent of the population is Muslim (Sunni), Turkey is officially secular. Turkish is the official language of the country. It is related to the Uralic-Altaic languages spoken in Asia. The Kurdish minority speaks Kurdish. English is somewhat popular, and in major cities many understand it.

Cultural hints: Many Turks remove their shoes when entering a home. Do not eat or smoke on the street. Remove shoes when entering a Turkish mosque. Before taking pictures ask for permission. Some restaurants include a service charge. If so, tip 5 percent. If not, tip 15 percent. Typical food includes seafood, Turkish coffee, tea, cheese, bread, soup, shish kebabs (chunks of lamb on a skewer), vegetables prepared in olive oil, rice, baklava (syrup-dipped pastry), and milk pudding.

Tourism Characteristics

Turkey's location makes it a Mediterranean, Middle Eastern, and Balkan country. Its long (for the region) history of relative political stability encourages the growth of tourism. Tourism has been an important element of Turkey's development plans and these efforts are paying off. Tourism to the country has doubled since 2000 and in 2010 arrivals reached 27 million. Turkey now ranks seventh in international visitor arrivals worldwide. Germany, Russia (mostly from the Muslim southern republics), and the United Kingdom are the leading generators of tourists to Turkey. The United States accounts for only a small percentage of the visitors. Cruises are an important element in the tourist industry, with approximately 25 percent of all arrivals coming by ship. Still, the average of 9.5 days per visitor is impressive, indicating Turkey is a destination country. Americans constitute the largest single source of visitors from cruise ships on day trips from Greek islands close to the Turkish coast. The country undertook many reforms to strengthen its democracy and economy. Turkey is an associate member of the European Union, aspiring full membership.

Tourist Destinations and Attractions

Turkey's tourist regions can be divided into four areas. They are Istanbul and the Northwest, Izmir and the West, Central Anatolia, and the Black Sea and the East.

Millennia-old archaeological treasures dot Turkey's sun kissed Azure Coast, a strikingly scenic crossroads of civilizations.

One of the world's exceptional geographies unspooled along Turkey's storied Azure Coast, which runs from Bodrum in the north to Antalya in the south and has been prized for millennia by all who have happened upon it. This is the land of gods and goddesses, legendary birthplace of the Son of Light, Apollo. Every square inch of its scalloping shoreline bordering the turquoise Aegean Sea has been touched by succession of civilizations. The landscape teems with sophisticated settlements built by the ancient Lycians, a civilization that allied with Troy and crafted perhaps the first federation of cities founded on democratic principles. (American founding fathers Alexander Hamilton and James Madison referred to the Lycian model in their papers.)

I chose to live along this coast because I feel that I have belonged here forever; in my soul, I have always been Lycian. I have walked the Lycian Way, which starts in the colorful seaside town of Fethiye and travels to the many historical sites—ancient rock tombs, Roman amphitheaters and churches—that punctuate this striking land. I seek out the village tucked into the rocky bluffs, where Turkish tea is served at small cafes shaded by mulberry and olive trees. I wander weathered hills that offer a bird's-eye view of mu picturesque hometown of Kas and the infinite horizons of the Mediterranean Sea beyond. I travel to the fishing port of Simean with its medieval hilltop fortress and sunken Lycian city, easily visible in the clear aquamarine waters. I visit the millennia-old town of Myra for its beautifully preserved Roman amphitheater and Lycian tombs boldly sculpted

from soaring cliff faces. I tour the Church of St. Nicholas, named for its gift-giving fourth-century bishop, who would find reincarnation as Santa Claus.

As an artist I marvel at the special light along this coast. At sundown, each rock, each surface shades from yellow to a deep red, an illumination that inspired moniker "Lycian Land of Light." Here, I am in the midst of both the past and the future. Each corner reveals a surprise, each stone whispers the story of a different time. I feel a new excitement on every excursion I take. I hear new sounds, smell new fragrances, glimpse new colors. And always I see myself reflected in the deep history that surrounded me here, and discover myself anew.

— **Aydin Curkurova, *National Geographic Traveler*, October 2009**

Istanbul and the Northwest

Istanbul's location on the Bosphorus has long been a geographical and cultural crossroads, and the cultural landscape expresses that interaction. Constantine's St. Sophia, the "Blue" mosque of Sultan Ahmet, the Hagia Sophia mosque, and the city walls from the Byzantine era are but a fraction of the many mosques and minarets. The Topkapi Palace (the home of the Ottoman sultans) is well worth a visit. In addition, museums, palaces, and narrow streets crowded with shops and people bring to life the old history of Istanbul.

Throughout northwest Turkey, there are resorts on the Black Sea and other evidence of the history of the region with mosques, famous battle sites such as Gallipoli, the Ottoman capital Bursa, and Greco-Roman ruins.

Izmir and the West

This area has one of the most-unspoiled and least-developed coastlines in the Mediterranean, with sandy bays, islands, and fishing ports (Figure 27.9). St. Paul preached in the area, and many sites he visited have become attractions. Greek and Roman ruins (including the birthplace of Herodotus); one of the original seven wonders of the ancient world, the great tomb of King Mausolus; rock fortresses; caravan routes; spectacular waterfalls; and assorted ruins dot the landscape in this region. At Ephesus, some 50 miles from Izmir, is the site of an ancient city that dates back to 4000 B.C. and contains the Temple of Diana, another of the ancient seven wonders of the world, and the statue of the Mother Goddess of Earth. Later, it would become the center of the Roman presence in Asia. Nearby is the Basilica of St. John, which is believed to contain the tomb of St. John. The region also contains an early Turkish citadel, the beautiful Mosque of Isa Bey, and the ruins of the Greek cities of Troy and Aphrodisia. Seaside cities include Bodrum, Marmaris, and the resort region of Antalya.

Figure 27.9 Olympos coast, Turkey. © Nastya22/www.Shutterstock.com.

Central Anatolia

This is a region of spectacular snow-capped mountains forming a backdrop for the coastal plain with its great castles and scenic towns and cities. The region centers on Ankara, a modern city. Old Ankara features the Citadel. However, the most important structure is the Mausoleum of Ataturk, founder of the Turkish Republic, which is built on the highest hill and is visible from throughout the city. The Ethnographical Museum houses exhibits of Turkish history, folklore, and art. Around Ankara, there are a number of other ruins with remains of the Hittites and the Phrygian capital of Gordion, where Alexander the Great cut the famous Gordion Knot that gave him the key to Asia. The Valley of Goreme is a unique area where human activity has blended unobtrusively into the landscape. Konya is the center of the Islamic Sufism sect known around the world for its cultural whirling dance ritual know as the Turn. Cappadocia, further to the east, is a region with a spectacular rock formations and early cave dwellings.

The Black Sea and the East

To date, this is the least-developed region of Turkey. The region offers miles upon miles of deserted sandy beaches, charming fishing villages, cities with bazaars, and remains of former civilizations—Greek, Hittite, Roman, and Seljuk.

Iran

Introduction

Iran is a West Asian country of mountains and deserts. Eastern Iran is dominated by a high plateau, with large salt flats and vast sand deserts. The plateau is surrounded by even higher mountains, including the Zagros to the west and the Elburz to the north. Farming and settlement are largely concentrated in the narrow plains or valleys in the west or north, where there is more rainfall. Iran's huge oil reserves lie in the southwest, along the Persian Gulf. Iran is a pluralistic society consisting of many ethnic and religious minorities. A majority of Iranians are ethnically Persian (51 percent). Azeris, numbering some 18 million, are the largest minority; most live in northwest Iran near Azerbaijan. Smaller minorities include about 4 million Kurds in the northwest, 3 million Arabs in the southwest, and 1.4 million Baluchis in the southeast. Approximately 89 percent of Iranians are Shiite Muslims; the other 11 percent include some 6 million Sunni Muslims, 300,000 Baha'is, and 200,000 Christians. Shah Mohammad Reza Pahlavi came to power in 1941; with Western support he kept the Soviet Union out of Iran after World War II. The shah initiated social and economic reforms financed by petroleum exports, but he became increasingly autocratic. The shah's rule alienated more and more people, including the Shiite clergy, and revolution broke out in 1978. The shah fled, and Ayatollah Khomeini imposed a fundamentalist theocracy in 1979. The official state religion became the Shiite branch of Islam. War with Iraq from 1980 to 1988 claimed at least 300,000 Iranian lives and devastated the economy of western Iran. Oil provides 80 percent of Iran's export earnings, and the economy benefits from rising oil prices; but the country faces international isolation over its nuclear program and poor human rights record.

From *National Geographic Atlas of the World*, 9th edition. Copyright ©2011 National Geographic Society. Reprinted by arrangement. All rights reserved.

Area	1,648,195 sq km (636,372 sq mi)
Population	73,244,000
Government	theocratic republic
Capital	Tehran 7,873,000
Life Expectancy	71 years
Religion	Shiite Muslim, Sunni Muslim
Language	Persian (Farsi), Azerbaijani (Azeri), Turkmen, Kurdish, Arabic
Currency	Iranian rial (IRR)
GDP per Cap	$12,900
Labor Force	24% Agriculture, 31% Industry, 45% Services

From *National Geographic Atlas of the World*, 9th edition. Copyright ©2011 National Geographic Society. Reprinted by arrangement. All rights reserved.

Figure 27.10 Imam Square (Naqsh-e Jahan Square), Isfahan, Iran. © Ko.Yo/www.Shutterstock.com.

TRAVEL **TIPS** 🧳

Entry: Travel to Iran is not advised. Visas and passports are required. Travel is risky because of the political situation.

Tourist Season: April to mid-June and mid-September to mid-November

Internet TLD: .ir

CULTURAL CAPSULE

Just over 50 percent of the population are ethnic Persians. Other groups include Azerbaijanis (25 percent), Kurds (9 percent), Gilakis and Mazandaranis (8 percent), Lurs (2 percent), and a number of other groups. The official language is Persian (Farsi), but there are many languages and dialects representing the various ethnic groups. Turkic, Kurdish, Luri, and Arabic are the major other languages. The state religion is Shiite Islam. It is an Islamic Republic, in which women are expected to be covered from wrist to ankle, veils and hair covering are mandatory, and makeup is frowned upon. Enforcement of these and other strict Islamic prohibitions on alcohol, Western movies, and pork is by young men or women who stop offenders on the streets. They may lecture, warn, or arrest those breaking these rules.

Tourism Characteristics

Iran has little contact with the West. Eighty percent of its tourists come from the neighboring Islamic countries of Azerbaijan, Turkey, Afghanistan, and Pakistan.

Tourist Destinations and Attractions

Pilgrimages to Iran's holy cities of Isfahan and Qom and the sites and museums of the once-great Persian empire, such as Shiraz, Persepolis, and Tehran, are Iran's most important and unique attractions. Tehran provides a contrast between the modern styles and the ancient Muslim buildings. The Shahyad Monument, which was built in 1971 to commemorate the 2,500th anniversary of the Persian Empire, is an impressive structure. The old and historical character can be observed at the Golestan Palace, the Decorative Arts Museum, the National Arts Museum, and the Sepahsalar Mosque. Near Tehran is Rey, considered to have been one of the great ancient cities.

Isfahan (Figure 27.10) was once the capital city of Persia. It has many decorated mosques, regal palaces and gardens, old bridges, and a busy bazaar. Shiraz, which was also once the capital of Persia, includes the New Mosque, one of Iran's largest; the tombs of the lyric poets, located in typical Persian gardens; the Mashidi-I Jumeh Attiq; and the Eram and the Khalili Gardens.

Darius the Great founded Persepolis in 521 B.C. It contains the tombs of Xerxes, Darius, Cyrus, and Artaxerxes. The ruins of Pawargadae, the capital of Cyrus the Great, and the ruins of Naqshe Rustam are nearby.

Iraq

Introduction

Iraq occupies the ancient region of Mesopotamia, a fertile lowland created by the Tigris and Euphrates rivers. Today these rivers sustain large areas of irrigated farmland and one of the highest populations in the Middle East. Beneath the land, Iraq ranks fourth in oil reserves, behind Saudi Arabia, Canada, and Iran. Temperatures can get as hot as 50°C (122°F) in the summer. Millions of Iraqis have become refugees since 2003, and Iraq has not done a complete census since 1987, so statistics on demographics are estimates. Iraq's population is some 75 percent Arab and 15 percent Kurd, with the rest being Turkomans, Assyrians, and others. Iraq is 97 percent Muslim; Shiites form about two-thirds of the population and Sunnis one-third. Shiites populate the Baghdad region and areas south, while Sunnis reside in Baghdad and areas north of the city. More than 4.5 million Kurds (non-Arab and mostly Sunni Muslim) live in mountainous northeastern Iraq. Iraq gained independence from Britain in 1932; it was a monarchy until a 1958 coup brought a series of military dictatorships. In 1979, Saddam Hussein took control of Iraq; he invaded Iran in 1980 and Kuwait in 1990. U.S.-led coalition forces drove the Iraqi occupation army from Kuwait in 1991 and patrolled no-fly zones over Iraq from 1992 to 2003—protecting Kurds and Shiites from Iraqi warplanes. The Kurdish region, defying the Iraqi army, established self-government in the early 1990s. Another U.S.-led coalition invaded Iraq on March 20, 2003. Iraqis voted on a new constitution in 2005 that made it a federal democracy. The economy depends on oil exports and international aid.

From *National Geographic Atlas of the World, 9th edition. Copyright* ©2011 National Geographic Society. Reprinted by arrangement. All rights reserved.

Area	438,317 sq km (169,235 sq mi)
Population	30,047,000
Government	parliamentary democracy
Capital	Baghdad 5,054,000
Life Expectancy	67 years
Religion	Shiite Muslim, Sunni Muslim
Language	Arabic, Kurdish, Turkoman, Assyrian, Armenian
Currency	New Iraqi dinar (NID)
GDP per Cap	$3,600
Labor Force	21.5% Agriculture, 18.7% Industry, 59.8% Services

From *National Geographic Atlas of the World*, 9th edition. Copyright ©2011 National Geographic Society. Reprinted by arrangement. All rights reserved.

TRAVEL **TIPS** 🧳

Entry: Visas and passports are required. Travel is risky because of continued instability.

Tourist Season: September to January and April to June

Internet TLD: .iq

Iraq's two largest ethnic groups are Arabs and Kurds. Other groups are Assyrians, Turkomans, Iranians, Lurs, and Armenians. Most Iraqi Muslims are members of the Shiite sect, but there is a large Sunni population as well. Small communities of Christians, Jews, Baha'is, Mandaeans, and Yezidis exist. Most Kurds are Sunni Muslims, but differ in language, dress, and customs from Iraqis. Iraq, known as Mesopotamia, was the site of flourishing ancient civilizations, including the Sumerian, Babylonian, and Parthian. Muslims conquered Iraq in the seventh century A.D. In the eighth century, the Abassaid caliphate established its capital at Baghdad, which became a famous center of learning and the arts. By 1838, Baghdad had become a frontier outpost of the Ottoman Empire. Iraq became a British mandated territory at the end of World War I. In 1932, it was declared independent.

Tourism Characteristics

As a result of political instability in the area in the wake of a turbulent decade of occupation and insurgence, there are few European and American visitors. Tourists from Europe and the United States accounted for only 10 percent of the total visitors to Iraq before the first Gulf War of 1990–1991. Another U.S.-led coalition would invade the country in 2003. After the removal of President Hussein from office, the country's authority was assigned to the Iraqi Interim Government and two years later a permanent constitution was ratified. The last of the coalition troops left Iraq in 2011. Until the region stabilizes, the tourism industry in Iraq will not contribute to its economy.

Tourist Destinations and Attractions

Iraq has a number of monuments and remnants of such early civilizations as the Assyrians, Babylonians, Sumerians, and Akkadians. Many of the artifacts from these civilizations are in the National Museum in

Figure 27.11 Detail of a lion on a Babylonian city wall. © kerenby/www.Shutterstock.com.

Baghdad. Baghdad also has Tell Harmal, a walled city dating back to Hammurabi, palaces, mosques, minarets, and bazaars. Baghdad is home to one of the world's oldest universities, the Mustansiriyah, founded in 1234 A.D. Some early important landmarks are the Abbasid Palace, the Minaret in Suq al-Ghazil, the Arms Museum, Bab al-Wastani, the Sheik Abdul Qadir al-Gailani Mosque, and Zubaida's Tomb. One of the holy pilgrimage places for Shiite Muslims is the Mosque of Kadhimain near Baghdad. Also in the region is a large palace built by Sassanian Persians in the fourth century A.D., Ctesiphon, with its still-standing arch that is the longest single-span nonreinforced brick arch in the world.

A number of ancient city ruins are added attractions in Iraq. Hatra with the Temple of the Sun; Babylon, Khorsabad, a capital built by Sargon II who ruled Assyria from 721 to 705 B.C., with a palace and the Temple of Sebiti; the site of Jarmo, one of the most ancient cities in the world; Nimrud, with extremely thick walls and massive gateways; Nineveh, ruled by three ancient kings; and Samarra with the great Friday Mosque and the ruins of Beit al-Kalifa, a maze of terraces, artificial lakes, gardens, and pavilions. One of the better cities to visit of the many ancient cities is Mosul. It has over 100 mosques and numerous Christian churches.

Iraq has a number of holy shrines such as Karbala, which is one of the holiest cities in the world for Shiite Muslims, and Najaf, where Ali (the early leader of Shiite Muslims) is entombed. Ur, the home of Abraham, is important for Christians and is one of the earliest cities of the world.

The ruins of Babylon (Figure 27.11) (including the Hanging Gardens, one of the seven wonders of the ancient world) are near Baghdad. They have been rebuilt by the Iraqi government. In addition to the Hanging Gardens, Procession Street, Ishtar Gate, the South Palace, and the Tower of Babel (now being restored) were all in Babylon.

Afghanistan

Introduction

The Hindu Kush dominates much of Afghanistan, soaring to some 7,000 meters (23,000 feet), and is a vast barrier separating the nation's northern plains from the southern desert plateau (Figure 27.12). Almost half the country sits at or above 2,000 meters (6,500 feet), and Afghanistan's northeast is prone to severe earthquakes. Kabul, Afghanistan's capital, sits in a mountain valley at 1,800 meters (5,900 feet). A harsh climate brings hot, dry summers and cold winters with heavy snow, especially in the Hindu Kush. A diverse ethnic geography matches the varied landscape: the Pashtun (about 40 percent of the population) are concentrated south of the Hindu Kush, while Tajiks (25 percent), Hazara (10 percent), Uzbeks (9 percent), and Turkmen (3 percent) live mostly in the north. Islam could be a unifying force, and most Afghans are Sunni Muslims, except for the Shiite Hazara. However, more than two decades of war has bred enmity among the ethnic groups, and the return of 5 million Afghan refugees strains government services. Education is a bright spot, with more than 6 million students and teachers returning to school since 2002.

Current problems began when the Soviet Union occupied Afghanistan from 1979 to 1989. But the mujahideen (Islamic fighters) defeated communist forces. A 1992–96 civil war pitted the Pashtun-dominated Taliban against non-Pashtun militias. The Taliban ruled most of the country from 1996 to 2001, but their brutal regime alienated Pashtuns and non-Pashtuns. Forced from power in 2001, the Taliban resurged in 2006, especially in the south and

Figure 27.12 Hindu Kush mountains, Afghanistan. © Dana Ward/www.Shutterstock.com.

along the Pakistan border. Afghan government forces, with U.S. and NATO allies, fight the insurgency.

Area	652,090 sq km (251,773 sq mi)
Population	28,396,000
Government	Islamic republic
Capital	Kabul 3,277,000
Life Expectancy	44 years
Religion	Sunni Muslim, Shiite Muslim
Language	Afghan Persian (Dari), Pashto, Turkic languages (mostly Uzbek and Turkmen)
Currency	afghani (AFA)
GDP per Cap	$800
Labor Force	78.6% Agriculture, 5.7% Industry, 15.7% Services

TRAVEL**TIPS** 🧳

Entry: Travel to Afghanistan is not advised. Visas and passports are required. Travel is risky because of the political situation.

Tourist Season: Spring and Fall

Internet TLD: .af

CULTURAL CAPSULE

Afghanistan is ethnically and linguistically mixed. The Pukhtun (40 percent), Tajik, Uzbek, Turkoman, Hazar, and Aimaq ethnic groups make up the bulk of the Afghan population. Dari (Afghan Persian) is spoken by a third of the population, and Pushtu is spoken by about half. Turkoman and Uzbeki are spoken widely in the north. There are more than seventy other languages and dialects throughout the country. Afghanistan is a Muslim country. Eight percent of the population are Sunni, and the remainder are Shiite. Islamic practice pervades all aspects of life, and Islamic religious tradition and law provide the principal means for controlling conduct and settling legal disputes.

Tourism Characteristics

Afghanistan has only a token tourism industry due to civil war, presence of NATO troops, and a poor infrastructure with only a few hotels of poor quality. After decades of war, the country is trying to rebuild its economy. In 2004 the country voted its first democratically elected president into office. The government faces many challenges including internal security, the Taliban, and lack of basic services.

Tourist Destinations and Attractions

Two cities, Kabul and Maza{r-e-Shari{f (an ancient city of the kingdom of Bactria), and the hidden valley of Bamiyan (with relics from prehistoric times). One of the largest Buddha statues in the world was located here but it was destroyed by the Taliban. Herat is the home of a mosque that is considered by some to be one of the greatest in the world. It was built in the twelfth century and has been restored several times. Afghanistan is the gateway to the Khyber Pass with its magnificent scenery.

REVIEW QUESTIONS

1. Describe three major cultural aspects of Middle East societies.

2. What are the major tourist destination countries of the Middle East? Why?

3. Why is Jerusalem important to Arab travelers?

4. If the Middle East became politically stable and had open borders, which country would have the largest number of tourists? Why?

5. Explain the popularity of Turkey as an important tourist destination in the world.

While neighboring oil-rich countries on the Arabian Peninsula are building skyscrapers and convention centers, Oman is erecting an opera house and planting desert gardens amid capital city Muscat's white stone buildings. Sultan Qaboos sparked the country's modern renaissance with his rise to power in 1970—adding scores of new schools and hospitals and increasing the miles of paved road from six to over 3,700.

Many of Oman's delights cater to the elite luxury traveler. The ritziest hotel in Muscat offers a helicopter landing pad out back. Pleasure yachts anchor off the coast; it can be easy to forget the sea is Arabian, not Mediterranean.

The more adventurous explore the Daymaniyat Islands Nature Preserve, home to the peninsula's best diving, just offshore from Muscat. This cluster of moonlike rocks juts above Tiffany Blue waters in which sea turtles and parrotfish frolic. But even a backpacker can hop in a rental car and take off along one of the sultan's well-maintained roads (women are allowed to drive here, unlike in Saudi Arabia) into an ancient landscape barren except for the occasional abandoned fort perched on a mountain ledge or a tucked-away wadi oasis revealing a pool of restorative water. The smell of frankincense envelops the country, as it likely has for centuries. (Oman

has been a source for much of the world's frankincense and myrrh since biblical times.) In the suqs, the smoke hangs heavy in the air like perfumed smog. Near the front door of almost every home, a clay vessel burns the ubiquitous resin, a fragrant welcome to all visitors.

Many of Oman's delights cater to the elite luxury traveler.

— Meghan Miner, *National Geographic Traveler, November–December 2011*

The countries of the Arabian Peninsula limit tourism to business travel and Islamic religious pilgrims. Two of the most important Islamic sites are Mecca and Medina in Saudi Arabia. The countries of Saudi Arabia, Dubai, Kuwait, Bahrain, Qatar, United Arab Emirates, Oman, and Yemen comprise the area. Dubai deserves special mention here due to its pro-travel stance and explosive development.

Saudi Arabia

Saudi Arabia occupies most of the Arabian Peninsula and is the largest country in area in the Middle East—but 95 percent of the land is desert. Mountains running parallel to the Red Sea slope down to plains along the Persian Gulf (called Arabian Gulf by Arab states). Below the arid landscape, oil has made this desert kingdom very wealthy.

The oil-enriched economy has drawn some 6.3 million immigrants, mostly from other Arab states or South Asia. The mismatch between the job skills of Saudi graduates and the needs of the job market, as well as constraints on employment for Saudi women, are reasons for the large number of foreign workers. Saudis and immigrants live and work in a highly conservative Muslim society, where Islamic law (sharia) is followed. The workweek is from Saturday to Wednesday; Thursday and Friday being the "weekend," when most services are closed.

King Abdulaziz Al Saud merged warring Bedouin tribes to form Saudi Arabia in 1932. Succession has fallen in turn to his sons, governing through consultation with members of the royal family, religious leaders, and advisers. Saudi Arabia holds Islam's most sacred cities: Mecca, where the Prophet Muhammad received the word of Allah, and Medina, where Muhammad died in A.D. 632. Some 2.5 million pilgrims, most foreign, participate in the hajj (pilgrimage to Mecca) each year.

From *National Geographic Atlas of the World*, 9th edition. Copyright ©2011 National Geographic Society. Reprinted by arrangement. All rights reserved.

Area	1,960,582 sq km (756,985 sq mi)
Population	28,687,000
Government	monarchy
Capital	Riyadh 4,465,000
Religion	Muslim
Language	Arabic
Currency	Saudi riyal (SAR)
Labor Force	6.7% Agriculture, 21.4% Industry, 71.9% Services

From *National Geographic Atlas of the World*, 9th edition. Copyright ©2011 National Geographic Society. Reprinted by arrangement. All rights reserved.

United Arab Emirates

The United Arab Emirates lies on the Persian Gulf coast of the Arabian Peninsula. The land is flat desert that is hot in the summer and mild in the winter. The country of Dubai has created huge artificial island complexes off its coast; two are in the shape of palm trees and

one resembles a world map. Seven sheikhdoms on the Arabian Peninsula combined to form a federation after Britain pulled out of this barren coastal region in 1971. The United Arab Emirates include Abu Dhabi, seat of the federal government and the oil capital, and Dubai, the main port and commercial-industrial hub. The smaller emirates are Ajman, Umm al Qaiwain, Ras al Khaimah, Fujairah, and Sharjah. Oil, discovered in 1958, is the major income earner. Oil wealth brought foreign workers, who now make up about three-quarters of the population.

Area	77,700 sq km (30,000 sq mi)
Population	5,066,000
Government	federation
Capital	Abu Dhabi 603,000
Life Expectancy	77 years
Religion	Muslim
Language	Arabic, Persian, English, Hindi, Urdu
Currency	Emirati dirham (AED)
GDP per Cap	$42,000
Labor Force	7% Agriculture, 15% Industry, 78% Services

Dubai

Dubai has transformed itself, in just twenty-five years, into a major world city, transportation hub, and tourist destinations. In 2011, over 8 million travelers visited Dubai, earning it a ranking among the top ten most visited cities in the world. The region is attracting world attention due to its innovative construction projects, including the world's tallest building (Burj Khalifa), the world's tallest hotel (Burj Al Arab), and the world's largest shopping mall (Dubai Mall). Other attractions in the city include the Gold Souk Shopping Market, the Dubai Fountain (the world's largest dancing fountain), Palm

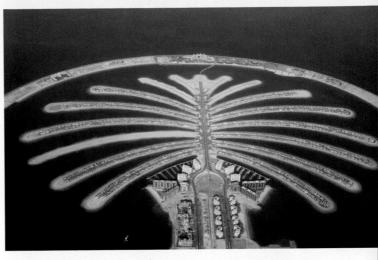

Figure 28.1 Palm Islands, Dubai. © Konstantin Stepanenko/www.Shutterstock.com.

Islands (Figure 28.1) (each island is shaped to resemble a palm leaf and features expensive beachfront housing), the Dubai Ski Dome, and the Wild Wadi Water Park. Each year, from November until late February, Dubai hosts a Global Village event where countries from around the world have a pavilion with a unique representation of their culture, landmarks, and souvenirs.

Capital:	Dubai City
Government:	Constitutional Monarchy. Emirate with special powers delegate to the UAE federal government
Size:	1,600 sq miles
Language:	Arabic, English
Religion:	Varies depending on ethnicity
Tourist Season:	Year-round
Currency:	Dirham
Population:	2.8 million
Internet TLD:	.ae

REVIEW QUESTIONS

1. Explain why Saudi Arabia, despite little efforts to promote tourism, hosts the largest number of visitors in the Middle East.

2. Name some of Dubai's world-class attractions.

3. Name the bodies of water on either side of the Arabian Peninsula. Why is each strategically important?

4. Name the six countries bordering Saudi Arabia.

5. Describe Saudi Arabia's role as the "birthplace" of Islam.

part 10 : GEOGRAPHY AND TOURISM IN AFRICA

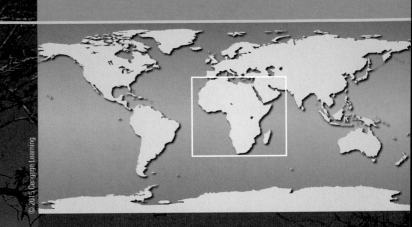

MAJOR GEOGRAPHIC CHARACTERISTICS

- Africa has the most rapid population growth rate in the world.
- Large parts of Africa's physical environment can be labeled "harsh."
- The population distribution is highly rural.
- The physical geography makes access within Africa difficult and limited.
- Africa is rich in important resources needed in industrial nations.
- Conflict and boundary disputes are common, reflecting tribalism and nationalism.
- High incidences of disease and poverty plague many countries.
- Unstable or ineffective governments in some countries handicap tourism growth.

MAJOR TOURISM CHARACTERISTICS

- Wildlife parks dominate.
- There is a lack of tourism infrastructure.
- Africa has the smallest tourism industry of any major region.
- Tourism is mostly to coastal countries.
- A combination of political, economic, and environmental factors handicap tourism development in many countries.

MAJOR TOURIST DESTINATIONS

Luxor, Egypt

Abu Simbel (Egypt)

Algiers

Casablanca, Tangier, and Marrakesh (Morocco)

The Great National Game Parks: Kenya, Tanzania, South Africa, Senegal, Zimbabwe, Zambia, and Namibia

Zimbabwe

Tanzania

(continued)

South Africa

Senegal

Ivory Coast

Seychelles

Swaziland

Botswana

Coastal beaches and waters of Ivory Coast, Kenya, Mauritius, Seychelles, and South Africa

KEY TERMS AND WORDS

African Riviera	Nile
Afrikaaners	Plateau
Boers	Rift Valley
Cataracts	Safari Lodges
Game Reserves	Sahara Desert
Game Viewing	Sahel
Great Trek	Sanctuaries
HIV	Savanna
Horn of Africa	Serengeti
Mt. Kenya	Swahili
Mt. Kilimanjaro	Tropical

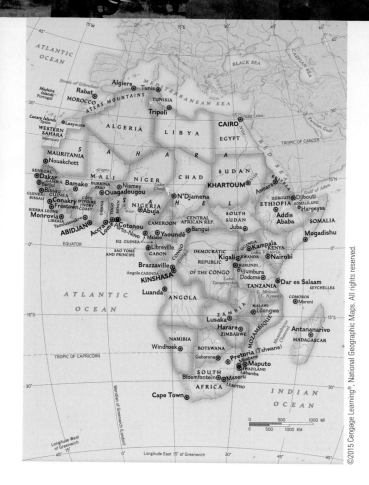

Introduction

Africa is one of the largest continents and is also one of the most sparsely populated and least visited. The entire continent of Africa totals 11,685,000 square miles, second only to Asia. The part of Africa south of the Sahara is itself a large area, totaling approximately 9 million square miles, roughly three times the size of the United States. The sheer size of this landmass has played a major role in its relationship with the rest of the world. Its size handicaps development of transportation and communication linkages, which remain concentrated along coastal areas or navigable waters. In addition to its large size and isolation, Africa generally has a climate that is either too wet or too dry for most agriculture.

Tourism in sub-Saharan Africa is limited. Only three regions attract significant world tourism, East Africa (principally Kenya, Tanzania, Uganda and Mauritius), West Africa (Senegal, Nigeria, Ghana, and Ivory Coast), and Southern Africa (South Africa, Botswana, Zimbabwe, Zambia, and Swaziland).

Africa is a land of poverty, with the lowest per capita incomes in the world. In many countries, $300 a year or less is the norm. Low literacy rates, high birth and death rates, high infant mortality rates, and the predominance of rural village residence indicate the lack of industrial development of the continent. These factors also handicap the development of tourism to Africa. There are signs of hope. The continent holds nine of the world's fastest-growing economies within its borders. According to the World Bank, almost half of Africa's countries have attained middle class status. Major factors underpinning this continued growth include the strong performance of oil exporting countries, continued spending on infrastructure projects, and economic ties with Asian countries. However, Africa remains plagued with numerous challenges, including armed conflict in various parts of the region, rising inequalities, fluctuating commodity prices, and youth unemployment. Despite these uncertainties the world will be looking to Africa to see whether it can shifts from a continent of doom to one of boom during the twenty-first century.

Climate Patterns

The climates of Africa are characterized by too much, too little, or poorly timed precipitation. The location of almost all of the continent within 30 degrees of the equator means that the entire area is warm or hot. The only exceptions are the mountains and highlands of the rift zone of East Africa. Because of its location centered on the equator, the Congo Basin is the center of the tropical rain forest. Extending approximately five to eight degrees north and south of the equator, it is an area with year-round high

Figure P10.1 Wildebeest and zebras on the African savannah.
© moizhusein/www.Shutterstock.com

Figure P10.2 Dried up lake at the northern end of the Sahel zone in eastern Chad © Mike VON BERGEN/www.Shutterstock.com.

temperatures and precipitation. Daytime temperatures average between 70 to 80 degrees Fahrenheit throughout the year, and daily ranges rarely exceed 15 degrees. Precipitation generally exceeds 45 inches per year, and in much of the region exceeds 60 inches.

The savanna climates of Africa extend from between 10 to 15 degrees and 20 to 25 degrees north and south of the equator. These climates are hot and rainy half of the year, and hot and dry the other half of the year. The savanna climate produces vegetation ranging from the tall grasslands of Nigeria, the Sudan, the Ivory Coast, and Kenya to a forest different from the tropical rain forest only in density and number of species of trees. Some savannas, such as those in areas of West Africa, probably resulted from the repeated and persistent burning by both the present and former occupants of the area. The savanna lands are also the home of the last great herds of wild animals and their predators (Figure P10.1). These have become a major tourist attraction.

North and south of the tropical savanna lands is a transition zone of steppe climate. The transitional region immediately south of the **Sahara Desert** is known as the **Sahel** (Figure P10.2), where the world's attention has been focused because of recurring drought and related human suffering. Precipitation totals from 7.5 to 20 inches yearly, and temperature maximums are constantly in the range of 80 to 100 degrees Fahrenheit. The daily temperature range is great, with nighttime lows falling to between 50 and 60 degrees Fahrenheit. This steppe region extends nearly the full width of the African continent, but it is relatively narrow in north-south extent.

South of the southern zone of savanna in Africa is another belt of steppe land. It is composed of Botswana, Zimbabwe, and Zambia, but portions extend into Angola, Namibia, and South Africa. This region is similar to the Sahel and has suffered from similar environmental problems such as drought. North and south of the steppe lands are the great deserts of Africa. To the north is the Sahara (Figure P10.3) (approximately the same size as the United States), the world's greatest desert, and in the south is the Kalahari. These deserts are characterized by temperature extremes, limited precipitation, and isolated settlements. The desert regions of Africa have recorded the world's highest official temperatures of 136 degrees Fahrenheit. Precipitation ranges from two to six inches per year, making settlement difficult. Population is restricted to oases or the valleys of rivers, such as the Nile, which bring the much-needed water from the tropical savanna and tropical rain forest areas. Other rivers penetrate the margins of the Sahara and are the basis for settlements such as Tombouctou (Timbuktu) on the Niger and Kaedi on the Senegal River on the border between Mauritania and Senega.

In southeastern and southwestern Africa, increased elevation or influence from prevailing winds creates areas of subtropical climate similar to the southeastern United

Figure P10.3 Sand dunes and rocks, Sahara Desert, Algeria © Pichugin Dmitry/www.Shutterstock.com.

States. The southwest tip of Africa around Cape Town has a Mediterranean or dry-summer, subtropical climate. The southeast coast has a humid subtropical climate caused by modification of the steppe lands by the higher elevations of the Drakensberg Mountains (Figure P10.4]

Sub-Saharan Africa is the least developed and least visited region of tourism in the world. A number of factors account for the overall general lack of a strong tourist industry in Africa. First is the region's long distance from the major tourist-generating countries of the world and the limited connectivity between North America, Europe, and Africa. There is direct connectivity from North America into some countries, such as Kenya, Nigeria, and South Africa; for other countries direct service is often provided through Europe via the capital cities of their former colonial powers, such as Brussels, Paris, or London. For the region as a whole, transportation is poor and infrequent. In some cases, limited air travel connections exist to world tourist markets. Second, modern transportation systems within Africa are extremely poor or nonexistent. Travel both to and between countries can be circuitous at best. Third, in many countries, there is little or no infrastructure for tourists. Most of the countries are

Figure P10.4 Valley in the Drakensberg Mountains, South Africa © Andre Klopper/www.Shutterstock.com.

INTERNATIONAL TOURISM TO NORTH AFRICA

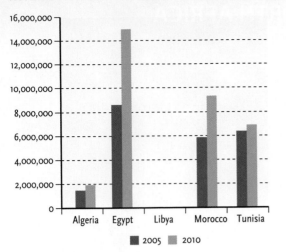

INTERNATIONAL TOURISM TO SOUTHERN AFRICA, 2010

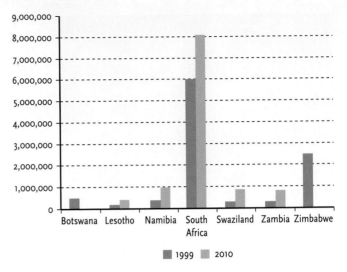

INTERNATIONAL TOURISM ARRIVALS TO WEST AFRICA, 2010

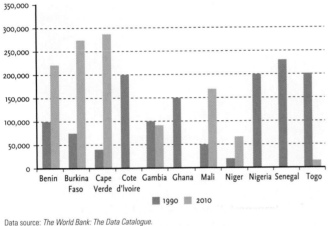

INTERNATIONAL TOURISM ARRIVALS TO CENTRAL AND INTERIOR AFRICA. 2010.

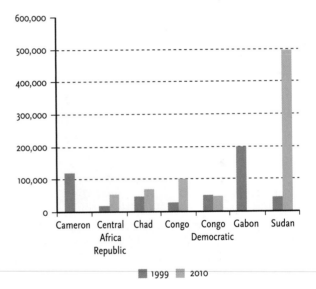

INTERNATIONAL TOURIST ARRIVALS TO EAST AFRICA, 2010

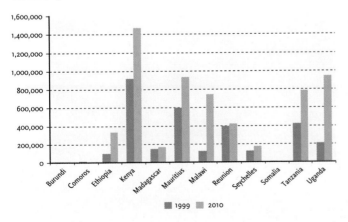

poor and have a difficult time financing their development, and funds have not been available from either international or local sources for tourism development. Fourth, the political unrest in many regions handicaps the tourist market. Fifth, the fear of HIV (human immunodeficiency virus) and reports of its high incidence in Africa is causing a decline in the limited number of tourists coming to Africa south of the Sahara. As yet, except for a few areas, such as those in East Africa, West Africa, and Southern Africa, there is little tourism of consequence in Africa. This region does have a higher percentage of travel for the purpose of business, which has led to the development of some world-class hotels in capital cities. Data are also sporadic, but some idea of the character of tourism to Africa can be illustrated for the various regions.

© Waj/ShutterStock.com

North African countries have gone through the process of being discovered by Europeans seeking the warm coastal beaches of the Mediterranean. The three most visited countries are Egypt, Morocco, and Tunisia. The physical attraction of the beaches in a Mediterranean climate combined with the lure of a culture much different from Europe's intrigues many Europeans. In addition, French is used widely as a lingua franca. The tourist is much more comfortable, therefore, than would be the case with a completely foreign tongue. Egypt, Tunisia, Morocco, and Algeria cater to Europeans and have developed resort centers, allowing the tourists to escape the puritanical milieu of Islam while still being able to enjoy the cultural landscape. Libya, however, does nothing to attract Western tourists. Strict enforcement of Islam's dietary and social restrictions makes most visitors from the Western industrial world uncomfortable in Libya. Tourism's outlook for the region is uncertain in the aftermath of the "Arab Spring" and its unpredictable impact on political and cultural traditions.

The Sahara Desert and its oases, common to all countries of North Africa, are also becoming major tourist attractions. The Sahara provides contact with what Europeans and other Westerners might consider to be exotic cultural experiences. A number of ancient and modern ruins left by the Phoenicians, Romans, Arabs, Spanish, and French serve to augment the modern attractions.

Egypt

Located in northeast Africa, Egypt includes the Sinai peninsula—the only land bridge between Africa and Asia. Egypt controls the Suez Canal, the shortest sea link between the Indian Ocean and the Mediterranean Sea. The country is defined by desert and the Nile, the world's longest river. The Nile runs north out of the East African and the Ethiopian Highlands, cascading over cataracts (waterfalls) through Upper (southern) Egypt and Lower (northern) Egypt to the Mediterranean Sea. The Nile flows through a mountainous desert to the east and a rolling drier desert to the west into a densely populated delta north of Cairo. Egypt is the most populous country in the Arab world and the second most populous in Africa (after Nigeria). About 97 percent of Egyptians live on just 5.5 percent of the land. The Nile Valley is one of the world's most densely populated areas, holding more than 1,000 persons per square kilometer (400 per square mile). Most Egyptians are Muslim Arabs, but there is a sizable Coptic Christian population estimated at more than 7 million—the largest Christian population in the Arab world. Ancient civilizations arose along the narrow floodplain of the Nile, protected by the deserts that were natural barriers to invaders. Some 4,500 years ago, Egypt possessed enough peace and wealth to cultivate a culture devoted to the afterlife, and Egyptians built the Great Pyramid at Giza. At 147 meters (481 feet) high it was the world's tallest building for thousands of years—until the nineteenth century. Today, Egypt has an economy based on remittances from workers abroad, Suez Canal fees, tourism, cotton, and oil. The Aswan High Dam, completed in 1971, provides hydroelectricity, as well as a controlled water supply for year-round irrigation and desert reclamation. A revolutionary uprising, part of the Arab Spring movement, ousted President Mubarak in 2011.

From *National Geographic Atlas of the World*, 9th edition. Copyright ©2011 National Geographic Society. Reprinted by arrangement. All rights reserved.

Area	1,001,450 sq km (386,662 sq mi)
Population	78,629,000
Government	Republic
Capital	Cairo 11,893,000
Life Expectancy	72 years
Religion	Muslim (mostly Sunni), Coptic Christian
Language	Arabic, English, French
Currency	Egyptian pound (EGP)
GDP per Cap	$6,000
Labor Force	32% Agriculture, 17% Industry, 51% Services

From *National Geographic Atlas of the World*, 9th edition. Copyright ©2011 National Geographic Society. Reprinted by arrangement. All rights reserved.

TRAVEL **TIPS** 💼

Entry: Visas and passport are required.

Peak Tourist Season: No significant tourist peak

Shopping: Common items include cotton and linen, gold and silver jewelry, local crafts such as copperware, wood carvings, leather goods, Nubian basketwork, and camel saddles. A cartouche with the visitor's name is also a popular souvenir.

Internet TLD: .eg

CULTURAL CAPSULE Egypt is the most populous country in the Arab world and the second most populous on the African continent. The Egyptians are homogeneous (90 percent), with Mediterranean (Egyptians) and Arab influences in the North. There are some Nubians of northern Sudan in the South and minorities of Bedouin, Greeks, Italians, and Syro-Lebanese. Arabic is the official language in Egypt with English and French used in business and education. Over 90 percent of all Egyptians belong to the Sunni sect of Islam. There is a fairly large number of Coptic Christians (over 5 million).

Cultural hints: Men only shake hands with a woman if she extends her hand. Personal space between men is very close. Tipping (*Baksheesh*) is important for personal services. Carry a lot of small change. Eat finger food only with the right hand. It is considered impolite to eat everything on your plate. Typical foods include rice, bread, fish, lamb, chicken, turkey, tomatoes, yogurt, cucumbers, and stuffed vegetables.

Tourism Characteristics

In recent years, there has been a decline in tourism to Egypt caused by volatility resulting from the political uncertainty after the Arab Spring events in 2011. When the political situation stabilizes tourists will begin to return quickly and numbers should be back at 2010 levels (15 million annually). The country's tourism is somewhat constrained because of the high cost of travel from the main tourist-generating countries of the United States and Western Europe.

Arrivals from western Europe (led by the United Kingdom, Italy, and Germany) accounted for one-third of arrivals. A fast-growing market for Egypt has been Russia with over 2 million visitors to the country in 2010. There were about 321,000 visitors from the United States in 2010. This shift from a regional to a worldwide emphasis has reduced the length of stay. In the 1950s, the length of stay was for almost one month. Today it is approximately six days. A visit to the pyramids and either a cruise up the Nile River or a quick trip to Luxor or the Aswan Dam can be completed easily in a week or less. Arab visitors still stay longer than do those from industrialized countries, however. Most of the visitors from the industrialized countries include Egypt in a two- or three-country visit as part of a regional visit. Egypt is working with Jordan to create a two-center visit that is attractive to Arab visitors.

Tourism demand is year-round, with Arab visitors preferring the summer, the Europeans and North Americans preferring the winter, and the central Europeans and Russians preferring the spring and autumn.

Tourist Destinations and Attractions

Four regions and the Nile cruises comprise Egypt's major attractions. Nile cruises between Luxor and the Aswan Dam, or Cairo to Luxor and then on the Aswan reservoir (Lake Nassar) are the most popular, especially for North American and West European visitors.

Three regions are more important than the fourth. They are Cairo and the surrounding area, Luxor, and Aswan. Cairo, Egypt's capital, is the political and cultural center of much of the Arab world. In Cairo, the three major attractions are the Egyptian Museum of Antiquities (one of the world's great museums, featuring a collection of ancient artifacts, including mummies, art objects, the King Tut collection, and other historical relics), the Khan El-Khalili Bazaar (an enormous marketplace where visitors can purchase almost anything they desire, particularly a variety of gold and silver works, embroidered clothing, leather, and other handicrafts), and the Museum of Islamic Art. In the old city there are a number of Christian churches and monuments illustrating the influence of the Coptic Christians. The city also offers the Arab culture and a host of mosques set in the landscape of a major Arab city. Tahrir Square was the center of pro-democracy activities in 2011.

Near Cairo, the famous Pyramids of Giza and the Sphinx are a must for travelers. The most famous of the group is the Great Pyramid built by King Cheops (IV Dynasty) around 2650 B.C. It is composed of almost 2.5 million blocks of stone. Near the Pyramid of Cheops are three small pyramids dedicated to either his wives or family members. Pictures do not do justice to their impressive nature.

Also near Cairo are Memphis and Sakara. Memphis is the oldest capital of Egypt, built by King Menes. The statue of Ramses II is the most beautiful representation of him in Egypt. The Step Pyramid of King Zoser at Sakara near Cairo is the oldest stone building in the world, dating from before 2500 B.C. It lies on a desert plateau southwest of Cairo.

The second region is Luxor and the Valleys of the Kings and Queens upstream on the Nile. With the magnificent temples of Luxor and Karnak, Luxor (or Thebes as it was known in ancient time) was the summer palace of the pharaohs. At Luxor is the famed Temple of Luxor. It was built by two pharaohs—Amenhotep III and Ramses II. The second temple at Luxor, Karnak (Figure 29.1), is one of the impressive archaeological sites in the Middle East and North Africa. A visit starts

Figure 29.1 Temples of Karnak (ancient Thebes), Luxor, Egypt. © Martin M303/www.Shutterstock.com.

with a walk through the Avenue of the Rams, representing Amun, a symbol of fertility and growth. It has one of the best sound and light shows in the world. The temple was a major setting for the movie *Death on the Nile*. The Valley of the Dead, across the Nile from Luxor, is the ancient burial place for the historic leaders of Egypt, including King Tut. The tombs are multichamber works of art, and several, including those of Ramses VI, Serti, Armenophis, and King Tutankhamen can be visited.

Farther up the Nile near Aswan were the two funerary temples built by Ramses II for himself and his queen. They have been removed from an area now covered by Lake Nasser and have been restored at Abu Simbel on a plateau overlooking the lake.

The fourth important region is Alexandria and the surrounding area, which receives fewer visitors. Alexandria is a Mediterranean resort and main cruise port that was founded by Alexander the Great and was an important post for the Romans. The Greco-Roman ruins today combine with the superb sand beaches along the coast to attract visitors to Alexandria. Many Mediterranean cruise ships use Alexandria as a port of call.

Egypt has been developing holiday villages along the Mediterranean and Red Sea. The combination of dramatic mountain scenery and the clear blue waters of the Red Sea provide a rich resource for tourism development in this area. With the traditional attractions of the Nile cruise and the archaeological ruins, Egypt feels its beach tourism has the potential to increase the number of visitors by providing a more diversified tourism destination. If political calm can be achieved in the region, Egypt's location and many attractions should assist the country in becoming an important tourist center.

Morocco

Lying in northwest Africa, Morocco is dominated by the Atlas Mountains, which separate the fertile coastal regions from the harsh Sahara. The climate is subtropical, but ocean winds give the coastal cities moderate temperatures. It is hot and dry in the south, and cooler and humid in the mountains. Most Moroccans live in cities, such as Casablanca, Rabat, and Tangier, on the coastal plain. Although rural people are crowding into cities, Morocco remains primarily a nation of farmers. Many Moroccans immigrate to Spain and other European Union countries for better economic opportunities. The high mountains helped protect Morocco from European colonialism until 1912. From 1912 to 1956 the country was divided into French and Spanish zones—two small Spanish enclaves remain, Ceuta and Melilla. Mosques, minarets, and bazaars typify Morocco, 99 percent of whose inhabitants are Muslims. King Mohammed VI, who has ruled since 1999, claims descent from the Prophet Muhammad. Morocco today is one of only three kingdoms left on the continent of Africa—the others, Lesotho and Swaziland, are small, southern African countries. Morocco annexed Western Sahara after Spanish colonial forces left in 1976. Economic development in Morocco is progressing due to improvements in education, tourism infrastructure, and manufacturing.

From *National Geographic Atlas of the World*, 9th edition. Copyright ©2011 National Geographic Society. Reprinted by arrangement. All rights reserved.

Area	446,550 sq km (172,414 sq mi)
Population	31,495,000
Government	Constitutional Monarchy
Capital	Rabat 1,705,000
Life Expectancy	71 years
Religion	Muslim
Language	Arabic, Berber dialects, French
Currency	Moroccan dirham (MAD)
GDP per Cap	$4,600
Labor Force	44.6% Agriculture, 19.8% Industry, 35.5% Services

From *National Geographic Atlas of the World*, 9th edition. Copyright ©2011 National Geographic Society. Reprinted by arrangement. All rights reserved.

TRAVEL **TIPS**

Entry: Visas are not required for visits up to three months. Passports are required.

Peak Tourist Season: July and August

Shopping: Common items include copper ware, tooled leather, silver, gold, pottery (Figure 29.2), camel saddles, and other handicraft goods.

Internet TLD: .ma

Morocco is the oldest kingdom in the Muslim world, having been independent since the arrival of Moulay Idriss, a grandson of the prophet Mohammed in the eighth century. The two major groups (99 percent) are Arab and Berber or mixed Arab-Berber. The official language is Arabic. French is a second language particularly in government and commerce. In the northern zone Spanish is spoken. In rural areas any of three Berber vernaculars are spoken. The earlier-known settlers of Morocco were the Berbers, believed to have come from southwestern Asia. After a succession of invasions, the Arabs invaded in the seventh century and brought Islam to Morocco. Islam is the country's official religion. Most Moroccans are Sunni Muslims.

Cultural hints: A handshake with foreigners is a common greeting. Close contact, such as kissing cheeks, is common among close friends. Take shoes off to enter a mosque. Finger food is common, but only eat with the right hand. The host will bring water for guests to wash their hands. Typical food includes lamb, beef, or chicken stew; vegetables; milk; and dates. Muslims do not eat pork or drink alcoholic beverages. Couscous is the national dish. It is generally composed of wheat (semolina) steamed over a stew of lamb or chicken accompanied with vegetables and garbanzo beans. It is traditionally eaten with the fingers.

Tourism Characteristics

Morocco (and Tunisia) compare favorably with Israel and Egypt in terms of their tourism industries. Tourism is the second largest foreign exchange earner after phosphates. The importance the government places on tourism is reflected in the creation of a Ministry of Tourism. Morocco has been one of the most politically

Figure 29.2 Traditional spice market in Essaouira, Morocco. © Bizroug/www.Shutterstock.com.

stable countries in North Africa, which should allow the industry to continue to develop. Its relatively large number of visitors reflects five factors:

1. Cruise ships call at the ports of Casablanca and Tangier. Morocco thus benefits from the large Atlantic ports of Europe.

2. Morocco is close to Spain, and encourages tourists in coastal resort areas in southern Spain to participate in one- to three-day trips to Morocco. Its close proximity to Europe and its excellent beaches make it a major attraction for sun-sea-sand participants in Europe. This proximity effect is very important to tourism in Morocco. Also, this is the principal path for visitors from the United States.

3. The opening of the Algerian and Moroccan border and reestablishment of air service to restore communications between the two countries. Algerians have

flocked across the border to visit family and friends and to shop.

4. Morocco has an excellent network of roads and railroads linking the major cities and tourist destination regions with both ports and cities with international airports.

5. The relative inexpensiveness of travel to and through Morocco makes it attractive to tourists. Morocco has benefitted from the devaluation of its currency (the dirham), and the favorable price structure in the country compared to Spain.

The combination of location, attractions, and relatively low price have led to a rather extended length of stay of eleven days, by far the highest of all countries in North Africa. In part, this reflects visits by Moroccans living overseas. Of the more than 9.3 million annual visitors in 2010, many are Moroccan residents working abroad.

The major market area is Europe, with four countries (France, Spain, the United Kingdom, and Italy) accounting for one-third of all international visitors other than Moroccan residents returning home. While seasonality is not a problem, the low season is in the winter months. Part of the winter visitors are the wealthy wintering in Morocco. Europeans prefer visiting in April and in the fall, with the exception of the Spanish, who follow the traditional patterns of June and August.

Tourist Destinations and Attractions

Cultural and political landscapes compete with the sun-sea-sand of coastal resorts in attracting visitors. Morocco's attractions can be divided into seven regions: Tangier and the surrounding area; Agadir with its beach resorts; Marrakesh; Casablanca; the Imperial cities; Ouarzazate (the "Hollywood" of Morocco); and Tarfaya and its beach resorts.

Tangier, and the surrounding beach resorts of Restinga-Smir, M'Diq, Al Hoceima, Nadord, Saidia, and Asilah are an obvious attraction. Tangier once was considered a pearl, but has lost much of its attraction for tourists. It is still a destination for day trips from Spain.

Agadir, the "Miami Beach" of Morocco, has all the trappings of a major coastal resort attraction and a third of all Moroccan bed nights. Agadir is also a base for tours to the Atlas Mountains. At the foot of the High Atlas Mountains, the famous trade center Marrakesh is one of four Imperial cities. It has many musicians, magicians, snake charmers, storytellers, and markets that immerse visitors in the Moroccan culture. The souk (suq) amid covered alleyways displays traditional handicrafts. To escape the heat of the desert, the Agdal Garden was created in the twelfth century. The garden stretches over an area of some 1,000 acres. It has several pools surrounded by fruit trees.

Casablanca, the major cruise port in Morocco, has the best-developed market for tourists. The old native quarter with the Great Mosque is impressive. A number of beautiful public buildings such as the Courthouse, Town Hall, Post Office, and Bank of Morocco, which is designed in neo-Moorish style, surround the United Nations Square. The Hassan II Mosque (Figure 29.3) is the largest religious building in the world and a striking landmark in Casablanca.

The Imperial cities, Rabat (the capital), Marrakesh, Fèz, and Meknes, constitute an important attraction in their own right. Fèz is the oldest and is both a cultural and religious center of the country. Important attractions are the Karaouine Mosque, Mesbahia Medersa (an old school that is remarkable for its traditional architecture), and Souk. Rabat, the political capital, is also an ancient city with a Kasbah, the Tower of Hassan, the Dar es Salaam Summer Palace, and the Royal Palace. Also of interest are the minaret Tour Hassan, the Mohammed V

Figure 29.3 Great Mosque of Hassan II, Casablanca, Morocco
© photobeginner/www.Shutterstock.com.

Mausoleum (an outstanding example of Moroccan architecture), and the Oudaias with its traditional garden, the museum of handicrafts, and antique Moorish café. Marrakesh is the country's most popular destination with many attractions, including Djemaa el Fina Square with a typical Arab market and bazaar. To the west lies the quiet, tourist-friendly coastal town of Essaouira.

Meknes was built in the seventeenth century to rival Paris. It has a most impressive 25-mile girdle of defensive ramparts. Other important sites are Moulay Ismail's magnificent tomb; the monumental gates of Bab Mansour, Bab Berdain, and Bab Djema En Nouar; and the Dar Jamai Palace, now the Museum of Moroccan Arts. Just outside of Meknes are the historically important town of Moulay Idriss and the splendid 2,000-year-old Roman ruins at Volubilis. A tour of all four Imperial cities is one of the most popular tourist activities in Morocco. The least-developed region for tourists is centered on the film capital of Ouarzazate, near the Algerian border. From Ouarzazate, tourists can visit Berber villages, desert oases, and the Dades valley (the "Grand Canyon" of North Africa). The coastal desert region near Tarfaya has many virgin white beaches. This area still requires considerable development, but it does have some luxury hotels.

Tunisia

Tunisia is on the Mediterranean coast of North Africa. The north is mountainous, and the mountain valleys and coastal plains hold most of the farmland and population. The south is semiarid and arid. Overall, Tunisia's summers are hot and dry, and winters are mild and rainy. Gaining its independence in 1956, after 75 years under French control, this North African nation was ruled by President for Life Habib Bourguiba until his ouster in 1987. Political and economic reforms have since pulled Tunisia from the brink of collapse. The fluctuating economy is based on agriculture, particularly market gardening of vegetables, as well as phosphates and petroleum. Tunisia's sunny Mediterranean coast and ancient history—spectacularly preserved at Carthage—make for a robust tourist industry. Tourism and overseas remittances provide important revenue, and in 2008 Tunisia signed a trade agreement with the European Union that removes trade barriers on manufactured goods.

From *National Geographic Atlas of the World*, 9th edition. Copyright ©2011 National Geographic Society. Reprinted by arrangement. All rights reserved.

Area	163,610 sq km (63,170 sq mi)
Population	10,429,000
Government	Republic
Capital	Tunis 745,000
Life Expectancy	74 years
Religion	Muslim
Language	Arabic, French
Currency	Tunisian dinar (TND)
GDP per Cap	$8,000
Labor Force	18.3% Agriculture, 31.9% Industry, 49.8% Services

From *National Geographic Atlas of the World*, 9th edition. Copyright ©2011 National Geographic Society. Reprinted by arrangement. All rights reserved.

TRAVEL TIPS

Entry: Visas are not required for stays up to four months. Passports are required.

Peak Tourist Season: July and August

Shopping: Common items include blankets, rugs, pottery, copper, silver, leather goods, carved wooden items, brass, ceramics, lace, and embroidery.

Internet TLD: .tn

CULTURAL CAPSULE Some 98 percent of the population is Arab. There are small minorities of European descent. Arabic is the official language, and French is widely used. Many Tunisians also speak some English. Ninety-eight percent of the people are Muslim. The majority are Sunni Muslims. Tunisia has been undergoing a transition from a one-man dictatorship to a much more open society. Tunisia considers itself a Westernized country, and Western clothing is common in both urban and rural areas.

Cultural hints: Good friends brush each other's cheeks and kiss the air on greeting. Personal warmth is characteristic of all greetings. A toss or movement of the head backward means no. Family style or a common plate is customary. "Hamdullah" (thanks to God) means it was a good meal. Wash hands before and after meals. Typical foods include fish, lamb, fruits, chicken, tomatoes, potatoes, onions, olives, oil, and peppers. Alcohol and pork are forbidden by Islam. Couscous is Tunisia's national dish. It is made of steamed and spiced semolina and topped with vegetables and meats.

Tourism Characteristics

Tunisia has a growing tourist industry. Tourism development is a major goal of the government's economic development plans. It is the largest earner of foreign exchange. Tunisia was the source of the Arab Spring movement, when in December 2010 a street vendor set himself on fire in protest over local regulations. It sparked the Tunisian revolution and subsequent demonstrations in Egypt, Libya, and Syria. Tunisia is one of the most modern Arab countries and draws visitors mostly from its neighbors and Europe, principally France and Germany. The country attracted nearly 7 million visitors in 2010.

For the Europeans, Tunisia is mainly a sun-sea-sand center. It has 750 miles of coastline on the

Figure 29.4 Sidi Bon Said, Tunisia © JetKat/www.Shutterstock.com.

Mediterranean, with a number of modern hotels from Tunis to Hammamet on down the coast to Sousse, Sfax, and Djerba. The hotels are some of the best in Africa, and the beaches are wide, sandy, and attractive. United States travelers can find similar amenities available much closer to home. The beaches attract the Europeans, who come by package tours from Germany, Netherlands, France, Britain, and Italy. Europeans account for more than 60 percent of the total visitors to Tunisia. The average length of stay is 8.4 days.

Tourist Destinations and Attractions

As indicated, the principal attraction is the beautiful Mediterranean setting with wide, sandy, attractive beaches. The historical cultural landscape reflects a variety of groups: Berbers, Phoenicians, Romans, Vandals, Byzantines, Arabs, Turks, and the French. The culture of the area offers opportunities for excursions into the Sahara that are different enough from the Mediterranean resorts in Spain, France, and Italy to attract those seeking experiences other than sea-sun-sand. The first Club Med vacation village was founded in Tunisia.

Tunis, the capital, is an attractive city with broad boulevards and the ruins of Carthage, which was founded by the Phoenicians and conquered by the Romans. Attractions in the city include the Bardo Museum, the Medina old quarters, and the Great Mosque. Nearby, with its bright homes with iron balconies and sky-blue doors, Sidi Bon Said (Figure 29.4) is popular with artists. Sousse, some 70 miles from Tunis, has extensive Christian catacombs. Near Sousse, Monastir is a picturesque walled city; and Kairouan, one of the most Holy Cities of Islam, has the Grand Mosque of Sidi Okba, which dates back to the eleventh century. The beach resorts are Sidi Bou Said, Hammamet, and the island resort of Djerba.

Algeria

The Tell, Algeria's heartland, is a fertile coastal region of hills, plains, and the Tell Atlas mountain chain (part of the Atlas Mountains). About 91 percent of the country's people live near the coast, on just 12 percent of the land, due to the fact that the Sahara spans 85 percent of Algeria—an area larger than Alaska. The coastal areas enjoy a warm climate, with most rainfall coming during the mild winters, but the rest of the country is hot and arid. Algeria is Africa's second largest country, after Sudan, but the livable area is quite small. Algeria's economy depends on oil and gas revenue, which accounts for 97 percent of export earnings, so the government's budget suffers when oil and gas prices fall. The country faces problems of population growth, rapid urban migration, and high unemployment, especially among youth. Because Algeria was once a French colony, many Algerians continue to immigrate to France for economic opportunities. Some 2 million Algerians and people of Algerian descent live in France, but France recently put limits on Algerian immigration, due to terrorism and absorption fears.

From *National Geographic Atlas of the World*, 9th edition. Copyright ©2011 National Geographic Society. Reprinted by arrangement. All rights reserved.

Area	2,381,741 sq km (919,595 sq mi)
Population	35,370,000
Government	Republic
Capital	Algiers 3,354,000
Life Expectancy	72 years
Religion	Sunni Muslim
Language	Arabic, French, Berber dialects
Currency	Algerian dinar (DZD)
GDP per Cap	$7,000
Labor Force	14% Agriculture, 13% Industry, 73% Services

From *National Geographic Atlas of the World*, 9th edition. Copyright ©2011 National Geographic Society. Reprinted by arrangement. All rights reserved.

TRAVEL TIPS 🧳

Entry: Visas are required. Passports are required.

Peak Tourist Season: March through October

Shopping: The souks have a multitude of things to buy. Common items include Moorish-style jewelry, leather slippers and handbags, baskets, toys, brass trays, chiseled copperware, tapestries, antiques, silver-inlay daggers, and woven rugs.

Internet TLD: .dz

CULTURAL CAPSULE About 83 percent of the population is Arabic and 16 percent are native Berber. There is a very small European minority. Most of the population (91 percent) lives along the Mediterranean. Nearly all are Sunni Muslim. Arabic is the official language. French is commonly used along the coastal areas for business and among the older generation.

Cultural hints: Typical foods include fish, lamb, fruits, chicken, tomatoes, potatoes, onions, olives, oil, and peppers. Alcohol and pork are forbidden by Islam. Couscous is Tunisia's national dish. It is made of steamed and spiced semolina and topped with vegetables and meats. A light handshake and sometimes an embrace are common forms of greeting. Personal space is close. Do not hold hands or express affection in public with a person of the opposite gender. Tilting the head backward means no. Do not touch food with your left hand. Leaving some food on the plate is a compliment to host. Typical food includes lamb, chicken, stews, pasta, vegetables, and fruits. Muslims do not eat pork or drink alcoholic beverages.

Tourism Characteristics

Algeria differs from Morocco and Tunisia in that its tourist sector is entirely state controlled, with the exception of a few small businesses that supply the industry with consumer goods. While Algeria has a host of rich natural attractions for tourism—expansive beaches on the Mediterranean, mountains, and archaeological sites of Roman, Berber, Arab, and French cultures—its tourism industry is small. In the last half of the nineteenth century, Algeria was the major destination for the wealthy from Britain. From then until 1984 the government did little to promote tourism. Although it began implementing plans and programs in 1984, the government has been slow to respond to tourism potential. Visitors stay only a short time, and individual tourist expenditures are the smallest for the North African region. Outside of North Africa itself, France is the major market region, reflecting former colonial ties. Most tourists are from other Arabic countries of North Africa totaling 2 million in 2010.

Tourist Destinations and Attractions

Algeria offers the tourist a variety of scenery. It has broad beaches, rocky coves, scenic mountains, cascading waters, and desert sand dunes. In the mountains, there are picturesque fortified villages, such as Constantine (which sits on a precipitous rock overlooking a deep canyon). In addition, Algeria has Roman ruins, such as at Timgad, with an impressive number of villas, and temples and arches, such as at Djemila. The government has tried to stress the craft industry, and has also utilized the unique Moorish architecture in structures built for the tourist industry. The capital, Algiers, is a beautiful city on the blue Mediterranean. The medina is most interesting, with narrow winding lanes full of craftspeople and shops. The Kasbah on a hill is full of a variety of cultures such as Berbers, Arabs, and Kabyles. Some important buildings are the Franchet-d' Esperey Museum, a fortress, and the Stephane Gsell Museum, containing Roman, Islamic, and Berber archaeology. The Greco-Roman city Cherchell and the Notre Dame d'Afrique are nearby. Constantine has a biblical history, and the Palace of Almond Bey was the home of a harem of three hundred women.

Libya

Narrow sections of fertile lowlands along Libya's Mediterranean coast give way inland to the Sahara, with vast expanses of rocky plains and sand seas. The coastal areas experience a temperate climate, but inland it is hot and arid.

Water-poor, oil-rich Libya has one of the highest per capita incomes in Africa. About 90 percent of Libyans live along the Mediterranean coast on less than 10 percent of the land, many in the cities of Tripoli and Benghazi. The largest water development project ever devised, the Great Manmade River Project, brings water from aquifers under the Sahara to the coastal cities. Since 1969 this former Italian colony, independent since 1951, has been an authoritarian socialist state under Muammar Quaddafi—whose backing of terrorism led to the U.S. bombing of Libya in 1986 and UN sanctions in 1992. In 2003 Libya ended its international isolation and abandoned its weapons programs.

From *National Geographic Atlas of the World*, 9th edition. Copyright ©2011 National Geographic Society. Reprinted by arrangement. All rights reserved.

Area	1,759,540 sq km (679,362 sq mi)
Population	6,283,000
Government	Jamahiriya (a state of the masses)—in theory, governed by the populace; in practice, an authoritarian state
Capital	Tripoli 2,189,000
Life Expectancy	73 years
Religion	Sunni Muslim
Language	Arabic, Italian, English
Currency	Libyan dinar (LYD)

GDP per Cap	$15,200
Labor Force	17% Agriculture, 23% Industry, 59% Services

From *National Geographic Atlas of the World*, 9th edition. Copyright ©2011 National Geographic Society. Reprinted by arrangement. All rights reserved.

TRAVEL TIPS

Entry: A passport is required. A visa is not required providing that visitors hold a letter from an established company in Libya sponsoring their visit.

Tourist Season: Year-round

Internet TLD: .ly

CULTURAL CAPSULE

Libyans are primarily a mixture of Arabs and Berbers. Small tribal groups, Tebou and Touareg, are nomadic or semi-nomadic in southern Libya. There are a number of foreign workers, such as Egyptians, Turks, Pakistanis, Indians, Sudanese, Moroccans, South Koreans, and Europeans. Many foreign workers are employed in the oil fields, but many left in 1993 after atrocities by Islamic fundamentalists. Libya has a small population and a large land area. More than half of the population is concentrated in the two largest cities, Tripoli and Benghazi.

Tourism Characteristics

Libya's tourist industry is at present small and is dominated by other Arab countries, which account for approximately 80 percent of the total visitors to Libya. The average length of stay and income generated as a result of tourism is the smallest in North Africa. In 2011, after months of fighting, a pro-democracy movement (the Transitional National Council) succeeded in overthrowing and killing Muammar Quaddafi, but the current political situation in Libya is still a major deterrent to travel. In 2012 an attack on the United States' embassy killed four Americans, including the U.S. ambassador.

Tourist Destinations and Attractions

There are numerous beaches in the 1,242 miles of Mediterranean coast. The major cities, such as Tripoli and Benghazi, have modern hotels. Libya also has a number of archaeological sites from the Greek, Roman, Byzantine, and Islamic cultures. The traditional Islamic culture is very much in evidence, with women enveloped in veils and the social, legal, and political system based on the Koran. Tripoli, the capital, is an attractive city located on the Mediterranean. The Old City with its narrow, winding streets, the Hammam (bathhouse) of Sidi Dargut, the Mosque of Shaib el Ain, the House of Ali Pasha Karamanli, and the Roman Arch of Marcus Aurelius are major sightseeing areas of the city. Leptis Magna, some 75 miles from Tripoli, was at one time an important Roman city. Along the coast are many picturesque villages, beaches, and coves for swimming and sightseeing.

REVIEW QUESTIONS

1. What two bodies of water are connected by the Suez Canal?
2. Name Cairo's three major attractions.
3. Morocco is home to the world's largest religious building. What is it name? Where is it located?
4. What European country greatly influenced the history and culture of Algeria?
5. What is the name of the most important early Roman city in North Africa? Its extensive ruins are in present-day Libya.

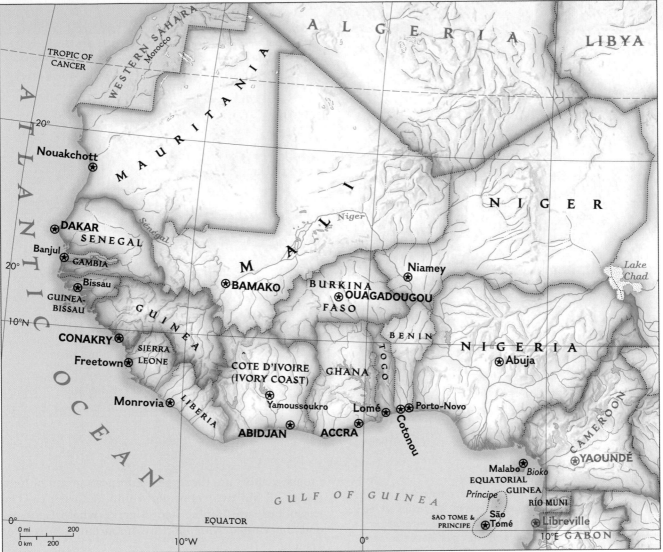

TRAVEL **TIPS** 💼

Entry: A passport is required. Most of the countries with the exception of Senegal require a visa, and some require proof of sufficient funds.

Health: Protection for yellow fever, rabies, malaria, cholera, tetanus, typhus, and typhoid should be taken. Also in most cases tap water is not potable. Meats should be well cooked and fruits and vegetables carefully cleaned and prepared. Visitors should avoid swimming in freshwater streams and lakes. In most countries there is a high incidence of HIV infection among prostitutes.

Shopping: Common items include hand-carved wooden objects, brass, leather goods, masks, jewelry, handwoven fabrics, and handicrafts of the individual country.

West Africa is sub-Saharan Africa's most populous region, and the southern half of the region is home to the majority of people. It was from this region that much of the slave trade came. With the exception of Liberia, all the states of West Africa were created by European colonial powers—France, Germany, Britain, and Portugal—during the late nineteenth century.

CULTURAL CAPSULE West Africa is composed of a number of tribal groups, such as the Malinke, Fulani, Hausa, Mandingoes, and Mossi. The Malinke journeyed from their early center in Mali to the coastal areas of Guinea, Senegal, and Gambia. Malinke also moved into Burkina Faso, Liberia, and Sierra Leone, where they came to be known as Mandingoes. The Fulani have been migrants throughout the region, spreading Islam. The Hausa mostly live in Northern Nigeria and Niger, but are widespread through West Africa; and their language is sometimes suggested as a possible lingua franca for Africa. There has been large regional migration in West Africa from the poor inland states of Burkina Faso, Mali, and Niger to the wealthier states of the Ivory Coast and Ghana. Many Ghanaians, Togolese, Beninois, and Cameroonians have taken up residence in Nigeria.

The two major destination countries, Senegal and Ivory Coast, have a number of ethnic groups, with both countries having a large European (dominated by French) population. The Ivory Coast has more than 5 million non-Ivorian Africans living in the country. Islam is the dominant religion of the two countries, at 90 percent in Senegal and 25 percent in the Ivory Coast. Tribal religions are strong throughout both countries.

COUNTRY PROFILE

Country	Capital	Language	Currency	Population (2001) (millions)	Population (2011) (millions)	Square Miles and State Comparison
Benin	Porto-Novo	French, Fon, Yoruba	CFA franc	6.6	9.3	43,484 (Pennsylvania)
Burkina Faso	Ouagadougou	French, Sudanic	CFA franc	12.3	15.7	105,869 (Colorado)
Gambia	Banjul	English, Mandinka, Wolof	Dalasi	1.4	1.7	4,361 (2 3[CE2] Delaware)
Ghana	Accra	English, Akan, Moshi-pagoma	Cedis	19.9	24.2	92,100 (Oregon)
Ivory Coast	Yamoussoukro	French, Dioula	CFA franc	16.4	20.6	123,847 (New Mexico)
Liberia	Monrovia	English, Nigeran, Congo	Liberian dollar	3.2	3.7	43,000 (Pennsylvania)
Mali	Bamako	French, Bambara	CFA franc	11.0	14.5	478,766 (Texas and California)
Mauritania	Nouakchott	Arabic, Pular, Soniwk-wolof	Ouguiya	2.7	3.1	397,955 (Texas and California)
Niger	Niamey	French, Hausa, Djerma	CFA franc	10.4	15.7	489,191 (3 3 California)
Nigeria	Lagos	English, Hausa, Yoruha, Ibo, Fulani	Naira	126.6	170	356,669 (2 3 California)
Senegal	Dakar	French, Wolof, Pulaan	CFA franc	9.7	12.8	75,955 (South Dakota)
Sierra Leone	Freetown	English, Mende, Temne	Leones	5.4	6.3	27,925 (South Carolina)
Togo	Lome	French, Ewe, Mina	CFA franc	5.2	6.6	21,925 (West Virginia)

© 2015 Cengage Learning®.

The typical food dishes include fish, rice, oil, poultry, onions, ground peanuts, and spices. They have been influenced greatly by French cooking. In Senegal the sexes and different age groups eat separately. Clean hands and eating with the right hand are important.

Taxis are hailed by raising one arm. Men and women keep their distance in public and are expected to be dignified and reserved around the opposite sex. Shaking hands is a common greeting. Punctuality is important in the Ivory Coast.

While the official languages and some African languages are listed in the table of countries, there are a wide variety of languages and dialects spoken in each of the countries, as in all of Africa. The official language is used in the large cities but not necessarily by a majority of the population.

Tourism Characteristics

Senegal and the Ivory Coast, despite a violent aftermath of disputed election results in 2012, are the major beneficiaries of tourism to the region. Senegal acts as a transit area connecting North and South America and Europe with many African countries. Of the areas in West Africa, the Ivory Coast has the best tourist infrastructure, with fine restaurants and good hotels. Nigeria and Ghana experienced a significant increase in the number of tourists. France, a former colonial power in the region, is the dominant market for the region.

French visitors are the largest European group of tourists in all but two countries within West Africa. The exceptions are Gambia and Nigeria, where Germany and the United Kingdom are important sources for visitors.

Tourist Destinations and Attractions

The focal point of tourism on the Ivory Coast is its beautiful beaches set amid plantations and picturesque fishing villages. Inland towns and villages are "living museums" that demonstrate the culture and way of life of the people in the country. The people of Ivory Coast suffered greatly due to continuing violence because of a civil war. Fighting ended in 2004 but the country remains split. Elections were held in 2010 but resulted in widespread fighting. UN peacekeepers remain vigilant in the country. Abidjan, a port city and administrative capital, is a colonial town providing attractions, such as the public market. Near Abidjan at Buna, there is a wild animal preserve. The Catholic Basilica holds 18,000 people inside and 300,000 people outside in its

Figure 30.1 Coast of Dakar, Senegal © Anton_Ivanov/www.Shutterstock.com.

adjacent square was built in a former president's home village 160 miles north of the capital city of Abidjan. Pope John Paul II visited and consecrated this basilica in September 1990. It contains four times the stained glass of the cathedral in Chartres, France, and the dome is twice the size of the dome of St. Peter's Basilica in Rome.

Senegal is a hub for international flights and also offers beautiful beaches (Figure 30.1). The capital, Dakar, has a number of interesting museums, such as the IFAN Museum of African Art, the House of Slaves on the island of Goree, and a "French town" similar to that in New Orleans or St. Louis. Dakar is an attractive city with shining blue, white, and pink houses and walls covered with bougainvillea. Senegal also has one of the finest game reserves in West Africa with a variety of wildlife and good accommodations. The game park, Niokola-Koba, also is the home of the Bassari people, who offer an interesting cultural experience, demonstrating their unique dress and festivals.

Although they do not have a well-developed tourist trade, the other West African countries have the potential for future tourism, relying upon a variety of African cultures, the wildlife, the colorful scenery, and some excellent beaches. However, they will have to overcome serious political, economic, and environmental problems.

Nigeria suffers from overcrowding, poor sanitation, and high prices in its cities, but those who visit Lagos, will find a fine museum of African art, the Museum of Nigerian Antiquities, the National Museum, and one of the largest markets of Africa at Tafawa Balewa Square. Lagos is built on a series of islands with connecting bridges and overpasses. The city contains beautiful homes built in the Portuguese and Brazilian styles. There are fine beaches near Lagos, such as crowded Bar Beach, Ibeno Beach, and Lekkl Beach. Ibadan, north of Lagos, is the site of an early African medical school. The city is enclosed by thick sun-dried mud walls and has attractions such as markets and colorfully dressed members of the Yoruba tribe. Jos, Nigeria's mining center, has a museum that houses a terra-cotta display that is over 4,000 years old. The ancient mud-walled Islamic city of Kano in northern Nigeria exhibits the Islamic cultural environment to the visitor. Tribal cultures and ancient archaeological sites are important tourism attractions that could be developed in Nigeria. The new capital, Abuja, is located in the heart of the country. Attractions here include the International Conference Center and the National Mosque. Nearby, rock climbers will delight in the challenge provided by the Gawa and Gwagwa Hills.

Togo, near the Ivory Coast, has a tourist trade similar to Nigeria. It has made a serious attempt to improve its tourist business and draws heavily from its neighbors of Ghana and Nigeria. It too has good beaches, picturesque fishing villages, and some unique African tribal cultures. Lome, the capital, is located on an excellent beach. It provides a scenic view of African life with picturesque fishermen's huts and colorfully dressed citizens. North of Togo,

Figure 30.2 The rooftops of Timbuktu, Mali. © James Michael Dorsey/www.Shutterstock.com.

tours into the scenic highlands provide the visitor excellent views of mountain villages set above lush green valleys.

The other countries of West Africa receive only a small number of tourists. Most countries have good beaches and their people illustrate African tribal culture, but lack of facilities and promotion combine with political unrest to prevent significant growth in their tourist trade.

Benin has some national parks and game preserves, but their quality is questionable. There is a restored fortress at Ouidah that dates back to the Portuguese explorers, and it was the site of the last recorded slave ship from Africa, in 1870. For the more daring, the Temple of the Serpents, which houses pythons, is also at Ouidah.

Ghana shares excellent beaches with the Ivory Coast. Accra, the capital, is a modern city in an African setting. Accra serves as a jumping-off place for trips to diamond and gold mines where visitors can observe the mining process. Near Accra along the coast, there are castles and forts that were built by the early Portuguese, Dutch, English, French, and Danish colonial powers.

Liberia is worth mentioning as it received a large portion of its visitors from the United States in the past. Liberia was a nation created for freed slaves who returned to Africa from the United States prior to the American Civil War. The country gained its independence from the United States in 1847. A civil war has devastated the country and, even though democratic elections were held in 2005, it will be some time before the travel industry can recover.

The desert nations, such as Mauritania and Mali, have French settlements and offer camel caravan trips to such places as Timbuktu in Mali (Figure 30.2). Mauritania has some good beaches that can be developed; Chinguetti, the seventh holy city of Islam; and other Islamic buildings worth seeing.

REVIEW QUESTIONS

1. Describe the founding origin of the country of Liberia.

2. What is the most densely populated country in the region? How many people live here?

3. What has kept Ivory Coast from fully developing its tourism potential?

COUNTRY PROFILE

Country	Capital	Language	Currency	Population (2001) (millions)	Population (2011) (millions)	Square Miles and State Comparison
Burundi	Bujumbura	Kirundi, French, Swahili	Franc	6.2	10.2	
Comoros	Moroni	Arabic, French, Comoran	Franc	0.6	.8	838 (1/2 of Delaware)
Ethiopia	Addis Ababa	Amharic, Arabic	Birr	65.4	82.1	472,434 (4/5 of Alaska)
Kenya	Nairobi	English, Swahili	Shilling	29.8	41	224,961 (Texas)
Malawi	Lilongwe	English, Chichewa	Kwacha	10.5	14.9	45,747 (Pennsylvania)
Mauritius	Port Louis	English, Hindi	Rupees	1.2	1.2	790 (Rhode Island)
Rwanda	Kigali	Kinyarwanda, French, Kiswahili	Franc	7.3	11.3	10,169 (Maryland)
Seychelles	Victoria	Creole, French, English	Rupee	0.1	.1	171
Somalia	Mogadishu	Somali, Arabic	Shilling	7.5	9.9	246,200 (Texas)
Tanzania	Dodoma	Swahili, English	Shilling	36.2	43.1	364,900 (2 x California)
Uganda	Kampala	English, Luganda, Swahili	Shilling	24.0	32.3	91,134 (Oregon)

© 2015 Cengage Learning®.

TRAVEL **TIPS** 🧳

Entry: A passport is required. Visas are required by most countries, but in some (Kenya and Seychelles, for example) they can be obtained at the airport. Most require proof of funds, onward or return transportation, and an airport tax.

Health: In most areas tap water is not potable. Water should be boiled or filtered. Many large hotels in Kenya, Tanzania, and the Seychelles filter their water. Fruits and vegetables should be carefully cleaned and prepared. Cholera, yellow fever, and malaria are major concerns for travel to East Africa. Uganda has a serious AIDS and HIV problem, especially among prostitutes.

Shopping: Items include hand-carved wooden objects, brass, leather goods, masks, jewelry, handwoven fabrics, and handicrafts of the individual country.

CULTURAL CAPSULE The East African region is an area of great diversity. The islands are the homes of distinctive civilizations with ties to Asia, yet their interactions with the African mainland require they be placed in this region. The region is one of animals, camels, cattle, goats, and sheep. People have migrated through the region since the existence of humankind; in fact, most of the human fossils of early people have been uncovered in this region.

The languages of the people are tied to either the Bantu or the Nilotic linguistic families. The official languages noted in the table are a result of European colonialism and are spoken by a minority in the major cities.

The area has had considerable Islamic influence through Muslim Arab traders or proximity to the

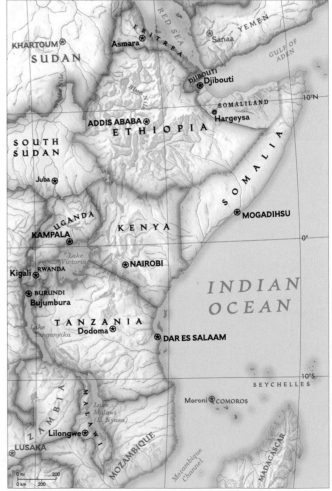

THROUGH VISITOR'S EYES | Malawi: Africa's Liquid Asset

Locals call it the "Lake of Stars," and it's easy to see why. After nightfall, paraffin lamps illuminate Lake Malawi with a constellation of firefly-like flickers; fishermen in dugout canoes work the glassy waters as they have since before the era of the Maravi kingdom.

Deep and clear, the teal lake—Africa's third largest—glimmers in the Great Rift Valley. Bordering Tanzania, Mozambique, and Zambia, Malawi is an increasingly steady presence within a dynamic continent. Last year, a political transition introduced the world to Joyce Banda, a progressive new president

and the second female chief of state in sub-Saharan Africa. More than a domestic shift, this turning point presents an invitation to explore Africa's best kept secret.

"When you make friends with a Malawian, they watch out for you," says Moses Mphatso Kaufulu, a blogger from the historic British capital of Zomba. "The depth of African experience rests on friendship—this is what makes my country second to none in the world."

Where better to befriend a local than by the lake? Swimming boys laugh as a

kaleidoscope of brightly colored fish glitter to the surface. The only high-rise in sight is a jumble of sunbleached boulders. Malawi offers much more than serene lakes. Dusty roads connect towns, and mountains give way to plains of green maize punctuated by baobab trees. But the nation's heart is a watery realm where waves lap the sand, leaving streaks of silt.

— Andrew Evans, *National Geographic Traveler*, December 2012/January 2013

Arabian Peninsula. Mogadishu, the capital of Somalia, began as an Islamic trading post in the tenth century. Islam dominates throughout the Horn of Africa, except in the Ethiopian interior and southern Sudan. In the first half of the nineteenth century the sultan of Oman moved his capital to Zanzibar. The region was a source of a large slave trade to Egypt and the Middle East, the Persian Gulf, and the Indian Ocean islands.

South Asian laborers were brought in by the British to build the East African railroad. Traders and business people settled in Kenya and Tanzania. South Asian laborers were brought in to work on the sugar plantations of Mauritius. East Asians now comprise two-thirds of this island's population. The region of the Horn can be characterized by drought and violence. The people of Kenya, Tanzania, Uganda, Burundi, and Rwanda have shared a similar background of tribal kingdoms and political division along ethnic lines. For example, the Tutsi—a ruling warrior class—and the Hutu—a peasant class—compete in Rwanda and Burundi.

The Comoros, Madagascar, Mauritius, and the Seychelles each has its own unique characteristics while sharing some common traits. All four islands have been influenced by contacts with Asia as well as with mainland Africa and Europe. Madagascar and the Comoros have populations that began in the Middle East, Africa, and Indonesia. The people of Mauritius and the Seychelles are a combination of European, African, and Asian origins.

All four have been influenced by France, with the British taking control of two islands during the 1830s and abolishing slavery. Local French Creole remained the major language on the islands.

The four major tourist destinations are Kenya, Mauritius, Tanzania, and Seychelles. While Kenya's population is largely African, it is divided into as many as forty ethnic groups along linguistic lines. English is the official language and widely used in large cities for business and official use. Swahili is the national language, and each ethnic group speaks its

own language. The major religions are Protestant and Roman Catholic. The Muslims, who comprise about 6 percent of the population, live along the coast and in the Northeast. Tanzania's population is equally diverse. The majority of Tanzanians, including such large tribes as the Sukuma (the only group with more than a million members) and the Nyamwezi, are of Bantu stock. There are three Nilotic ethnic groups, two Khoisan, and two Afro-Asiatic. Zanzibar's population has a strong Arabic influence.

Mauritius was colonized in 1638 by the Dutch. Waves of traders, planters, and their slaves created a strong Asian influence. Mauritius's Creoles trace their origins to the plantation owners and slaves who were brought to work the sugar fields. Indo-Mauritians are descended from Indian immigrants who arrived in the nineteenth century to work as indentured laborers after slavery was abolished in 1835. Most Seychelles people are descendants of early French settlers and African slaves brought to the Seychelles in the nineteenth century by the British who freed them from slave ships on the East African coast. Indians and Chinese account for slightly over 1 percent of the rest of the population. Creole is the native language of 94 percent of the people, with English and French as common languages. English is the language of commerce and government. The handshake is the common greeting in the four major tourist destination countries. They understand most of the European gestures. In many cases using the left hand alone or to pass items is not polite. The verbal "tch-tch" sound is considered an insult in Kenya and Tanzania. Photographing people should not be done without permission. European cuisine (and Indian in major cities) is common in all four major tourist destination countries. The two island nations—Seychelles and Mauritius—have typical Creole, Indian, and Chinese food. Fresh seafood, fruits, and vegetables are common in these islands. Tanzania's foods include grains, fruits, rice, cooked bananas, and vegetables. Kenya's typical dishes are goat, beef, lamb, chicken, fish, red bean stew, and fruits.

Tourism Characteristics

Tourism is significant in East Africa, but a number of countries, especially the countries of the Horn of Africa, have low numbers of visitors due to the environmental and political problems of the region. Kenya receives the largest amount of visitors to the region (just over 1.5 million in 2012), and it is second in Africa only to South Africa in total visitor numbers. Kenya leads Africa in non-African visitors. (South Africa has more visitors, but it has a strong regional flow from other African countries.) Tanzania has opened its borders with Kenya in order to take advantage of Kenya's large tourist industry. Kenya and Tanzania also benefit from tours combining the two countries. The largest number of visitors to Tanzania are by land, while Kenya's visitors come by air.

Along with the governments of other East African countries, Kenya recognized the importance of tourism early and has established governmental agencies to plan, develop, and promote tourism. All of the nations of East Africa have set out to improve their infrastructure for tourism by providing money to build hotels, lodges, airports, and so on. European travelers make up the majority of Kenya's visitors, with Germans dominating. The United States is the most important country outside of Europe for tourists to Kenya. Some concern is expressed by officials that Kenya may be at the saturation point of its tourist-carrying capacity. Most visitors are associated with tours and groups. European visitors to Kenya (German and British) visit longer and combine visits to the game parks with a week on the coast for a sun-sea-sand vacation. North Americans typically visit for just a week and spend their time on safari, then return home.

The islands of Mauritius and Seychelles in the Indian Ocean enjoy a tourism trade that is as large as they can effectively handle and maintain. The Seychelles have targeted their tourism industry at the upscale market. They feel this will provide them with the highest possible income and have less impact upon their islands. The Seychelles market is largely European, with minor markets from South Africa.

Mauritius had significant growth and now has the second largest volume of visitors to East Africa after Kenya. It is dependent upon three major markets: Europe (43 percent), East Africa (20 percent), and Réunion Island (10 percent). In an effort to diversify, Mauritius has tried to attract tourists from Asia and several direct flights are presently operating.

Kenya

The East African country of Kenya rises from a low coastal plain on the Indian Ocean to mountains and plateaus at its center. Most Kenyans live in the highlands, and Nairobi, the capital, is here at an altitude of 1,700 meters (5,500 feet). Even though Nairobi is near the Equator, its high elevation brings cooler air. To the west of Nairobi the land descends to the north-south–running Great Rift Valley—the valley floor is at its lowest near Lake Turkana. Most of northern and eastern Kenya consists of rugged desert or semiarid grasslands.

More than forty ethnic groups, including Kikuyu farmers and Masai cattle herders, crowd the countryside, still home to three-quarters of Kenya's people. About 75 percent of Kenyans work in agriculture, most as subsistence farmers. Intense competition for arable land drives thousands to cities, where unemployment is high. In Nairobi, East Africa's commercial hub, skyscrapers abruptly give way to slums. Both free enterprise and a measure of political debate helped make Kenya one of Africa's most stable nations after it achieved independence from Britain in 1963. Tourism is essential to the economy, and Kenya is one of Africa's major safari destinations. The tourism industry bounced back after the 1998 Nairobi bomb attacks but declined after post-election violence in 2007 and 2008. Remittances, tea, and horticulture (cut flowers, processed fruits and vegetables) are also key contributors to the economy.

Location	Eastern Africa
Area	580,367 sq km (224,081 sq mi)
Population	39,070,000
Government	Republic
Capital	Nairobi 3,010,000
Urban	22%
Life Expectancy	54 years
Religion	Protestant, Roman Catholic, Muslim, indigenous beliefs
Language	English, Kiswahili, many indigenous languages
Currency	Kenyan shilling (KES)
Gdp Per Cap	$1,600
Labor Force	75% Agriculture, 25% Industry & Services

Figure 31.1 African flamingoes, Lake Nakuru National Park, Kenya. © Anna Omelchenko/www.Shutterstock.com.

Tourist Attractions

The principal tourist attractions of Kenya are its forty national parks. The Nairobi National Park is important for observing African wildlife. Tsavo National Park, the largest national park in the world, offers spectacular scenery along with a wide variety of animals and birds. A major attraction in Tsavo is Mzima Springs. Elephants, hippos, and crocodiles are found in its waters, while gazelle, zebra, and giraffe wander along the banks.

The Masai Mara Reserve, where the culture of the Masai people is partially protected, provides an opportunity to observe African wildlife and Masai culture. Masai Mara is one of the most visited game preserves in Africa, and its most prominent feature is the annual migration of the wildebeests from Serengeti in Tanzania. Lake Nakuru National Park has a variety of bird **sanctuaries**. At Lake Nakuru more than a million pink flamingoes can be seen feeding the shore (Figure 31.1). Close to Lake Nakuru, in the Nakuru National Park, is

the first black rhino sanctuary constructed as part of the government plan to save the rhino from extinction. Amboseli National Park is on the border with Tanzania. It has a large elephant population and offers spectacular views of Mt. Kilimanjaro in Tanzania.

Amberdares National Park exhibits the extraordinary mountain scenery of the Rift Valley and some picturesque villages, including an old town with narrow winding streets illustrating native culture. **Mt. Kenya**, Africa's second highest mountain, attracts climbers and hikers. Its slopes have two of the most famous hotels in Africa—Treetops and the Ark, which provide close-up viewing of game as they come out of the forest to salt licks. Nakuru and Thomson's Falls offer scenic views of the Great Rift Valley. Mombasa, on the Indian Ocean, is a Muslim center and has a host of mosques, a Portuguese fort, Fort Jesus, and a number of beaches. It is Kenya's main cruise port.

Nairobi, the capital, has a number of interesting attractions, including the National Assembly Building,

Figure 31.2 Young mountain gorilla with adults on both sides. © Photodynamic/www.Shutterstock.com.

the National Theatre, the University of Nairobi, the National Museum with exhibits of African tribal lore and Kenyan history, and Nairobi National Park where visitors are introduced to the country's wildlife.

Of the other East African countries, Uganda has very little tourism due to the undeveloped nature of the industry as well as its unstable political situation. Uganda has three national parks, with the primary attraction being Murchison Falls, the source of the Nile, surrounded by mountain scenery and an excellent variety of wildlife. Bwindi National Park is home to mountain gorillas (Figure 31.2). Uganda is considered by many to be one of the most beautiful countries in Africa. Lake Victoria is very picturesque. The two major cities are the capital city of Kampala and Entebbe. Both are on Lake Victoria, and travel between the two passes through small villages and farms. Kampala, like Rome, is built on a series of seven hills; it offers the visitor a mosque, the tombs of Kabakas, and the Uganda Museum.

Tanzania

Tanzania, one of the largest countries in East Africa, includes the spice islands of Zanzibar, Pemba, and Mafia and contains Africa's highest point—Kilimanjaro, at 5,895 meters (19,340 feet). Kilimanjaro, a dormant volcano, is snowcapped even though it is near the Equator. Most of the country features a savanna plateau, which is east of the Great Rift Valley containing Lake Tanganyika. The coastal areas are temperate, but the interior is semiarid.

The population of Tanzania consists of more than 120 ethnic groups. About half of the people practice Christianity, more than one-third follow Islam, and there are numerous traditional and immigrant religions. Most Muslims live along the coast and on Zanzibar.

Some 75 percent of Tanzanians farm at subsistence levels. In many areas tsetse fly infestation hampers animal husbandry, as well as tourism.

Tanganyika, a British-controlled UN trust territory, gained independence in 1961; and Zanzibar, a British protectorate with an Arab population, became independent in 1963. Tanganyika and Zanzibar united to form Tanzania in 1964. Until resigning as president in 1985, independence leader Julius K. Nyerere guided the country through decades of socialism—adapted to the *ujamaa* policy of village farming. Tourism contributes to the economy, with popular safaris to Serengeti National Park and Ngorongoro Crater, a huge caldera created by a collapsed volcano. Visitors also come to climb Kilimanjaro, affectionately known as "Kili." Trekkers can walk to the summit, but the climb is strenuous and takes about a week (four days up and two days down).

From *National Geographic Atlas of the World*, 9th edition. Copyright ©2011 National Geographic Society. Reprinted by arrangement. All rights reserved.

Location	Eastern Africa
Area	945,087 sq km (364,900 sq mi)
Population	43,739,000
Government	Republic
Capital	Dar es Salaam (administrative) 2,930,000; Dodoma (legislative) 183,000
Life Expectancy	54 years
Religion	Muslim, indigenous beliefs, Christian
Language	Swahili, Kiunguja (Swahili on Zanzibar), English, Arabic, local languages
Currency	Tanzanian shilling (TZS)
Gdp Per Cap	$1,400
Gdp Growth	4.9%
Labor Force	80% Agriculture, 20% Industry & Services

From *National Geographic Atlas of the World*, 9th edition. Copyright ©2011 National Geographic Society. Reprinted by arrangement. All rights reserved.

Tourist Attractions

Tanzania receives half as many tourists as Kenya and has the same general attractions as Kenya and Uganda. Game parks, mountain scenery, and one of the world's most famous mountains, Mt. Kilimanjaro (Figure 31.3), which attracts climbers and hikers, are part of its tourist destinations. Ngorongoro Crater is one of the largest craters in the world, nearly ten miles

Figure 31.3 Mount Kilimanjaro, Tanzania. © Graeme Shannon/www.Shutterstock.com.

wide. A wide variety of wildlife, including antelopes and elephants, can be seen in the crater. Just outside of the crater is Serengeti, noted for its tree-climbing lions. Serengeti National Park has a large concentration of wildlife and is one of the better viewing parks in the world.

Dar es Salaam, the capital and port city of Tanzania, is an attractive city with attractions, such as the Ministries of the Government, the Arab Asian sectors, Tanzania National Museum, and the harbor area. Just off the coast is Zanzibar Island, which was a Persian and Arab trading center. With its ornate Arabian homes, Stone Town is most interesting in Zanzibar. Both Kenya and Tanzania have some excellent beaches that are attractive to Europeans who enjoy both the national parks and the sun-sea-sand environment.

Seychelles and Mauritius islands offer exotic Indian Ocean sun-sea-sand experiences for visitors. They offer beautiful scenery, placid lagoons, and coral reefs with spectacular snorkeling and skin diving. Madagascar, the fourth largest island in the world, receives few tourists. Ethiopia and Somalia have few tourists because of the conflicts in and between the countries. Both have suffered from extensive droughts, and the world news has emphasized the problems of the two countries and others in the semiarid Sahel.

REVIEW QUESTIONS

1. What is the name of Africa's highest mountain? Where is it located?

2. What country is home to the world's surviving group of mountain gorillas?

3. What is the Lingua Franca of East Africa?

© PhotoSky/ShutterStock.com

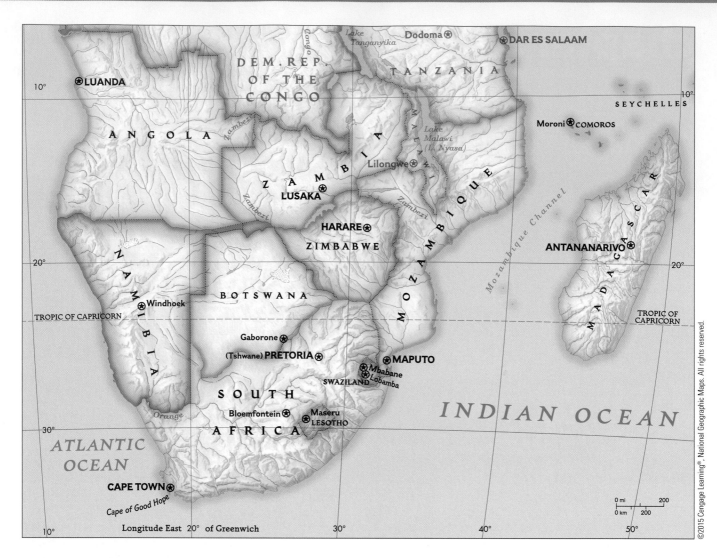

COUNTRY PROFILE

Country	Capital	Language	Currency	Population (2001) (millions)	Population (2011) (millions)	Square Miles and State Comparison
Botswana	Gaborone	English, Setswana	Pula	1.1	2.0	231,804 (slightly less than Texas)
Lesotho	Maseru	English, Sesotho, Zulu, Xhosa	Loti	2.2	2.0	11,716 (Maryland)
Madagascar	Antananarivo	French, Malagasy	ariary	15.9	21.9	228,880 (slightly less than Texas)
Mozambique	Maputo	Portuguese	metical	19.4	22.8	481,353 (2 x California)
Namibia	Windhoek	English, Afrikaans, German	dollar	1.8	2.1	318,261 (1/2 of Alaska)
South Africa	Pretoria	Afrikaans, English	Rand	43.6	50.5	433,680 (4/5 of Alaska)
Swaziland	Mbabane	English, Swati	lilangeni	1.1	1.2	6,704 (Hawaii)
Zambia	Lusaka	English	Kwacha	9.8	12.9	290,585 (Texas)
Zimbabwe	Harare	English	various	11.4	12.5	151,000 (California)

© 2015 Cengage Learning®.

"Who knew?" might be the common refrain by the lucky visitors who discover the surprising beauty and stories past of Mozambique's Quirimbas. Archipelago.

"You can't leave without visiting the Quirimbas Archipelago," everyone told me when I first started working in Mozambique in 2006. That September, I boarded a dhow in the coastal village of Tandanhangue to travel to Ilha do Ibo, the crown jewel in the unspoiled 32-island archipelago. Many tropical islands tend to look alike—white sands, palm tree—but the Quirimbas islands are different. The beaches are backed by dense bush. The islands are surrounding waters pulse with wildlife. You'll likely see humpback whales, hawksbill turtles, bottlenose dolphins, and a diversity of birds, from storks and spotted eagle-owls to crab plovers and kingfishers.

I took long walks at low tide, when it's often possible to stroll from one island to the next. Days revolved around the beach, diving pristine coral reefs, eating the freshest lobster and tuna, and meeting the locals, who are very tall and lean. They are dark skin but possess strong Arabic feature, and some even have green eyes. They strike me as some of the most beautiful people I have ever seen.

I've returned twice since then, visiting other islands, but my favorite island remains Ibo, once an important trading post for silks, cotton, ivory, and, tragically, slave trafficking. In Stone Town, Ibo's main settlement, African, Arab, and European cultures mingled. Stone Town now has a forgotten, ghost-town feel, its once grand avenues strewn with ruins. In one of the old forts, lo-

cal silverwork artisans will ask you for a coin, and several hours later will have transformed it into a filigree necklace or some other piece of exquisite jewelry.

Many tropical islands tend to look alike—white sands, palm tree—but the Quirimbas islands are different.

The Quirimbas Archipelago constantly surprises. Visitors might expect little from this part of Africa—known for civil war and health crises—but they end up finding an unforgettable paradise of many-layered riches.

— Alexandra de Cadaval, *National Geographic Traveler*, October 2009

TRAVEL**TIPS**

Entry: A passport is required. Visas are required for some of the countries. In many cases they require proof of transportation and sufficient funds.

Health: Malaria, yellow fever, and in some cases cholera protection should be taken. Water in major cities of Southern Africa is potable, but care should be taken to use bottled and boiled water elsewhere. Visitors should avoid swimming in fresh water. Hepatitis has been a problem in some of the cities of the region.

Shopping: Common items include animal skins, precious stones, hand-carved wooden objects, brass, leather goods, masks, jewelry, handwoven fabrics, and handicrafts of the individual country.

CULTURAL CAPSULE Southern Africa is a diverse region. The dominant theme in current history has been the evolving struggle of the region's indigenous black African majority for majority rule. The area was settled at least by the eighth century by a variety of black African ethnic groups who spoke languages belonging to the Bantu as well as the Khoisan linguistic classifications. The early groups practiced both agriculture and pastoralism. Some groups had organized into strong states by the fifteenth century as the Kongo of northern Angola and the Shona people of the Zimbabwean plateau. Others like the Nguni speakers lived in smaller communities.

In the sixteenth century small numbers of Portuguese began settling along the coasts of Angola and Mozambique. In 1652, the Dutch established a settlement at Africa's southernmost tip, the Cape of Good Hope. The Dutch expanded steadily into the interior throughout the eighteenth century, seizing land of the local Khoisan communities. The Dutch imported slaves from Asia as well as elsewhere in Africa. The region became racially divided between free white settlers and subordinated people of mixed African and Afro-Asian descent.

The British took over the Cape during the Napoleonic Wars and in 1820 began to send colonists to the region. During this period, the Zulu state emerged under the great warrior Prince Shaka. During the 1830s the British abolished slavery throughout their empire and extended limited civil rights to nonwhites at the Cape. A large number of white Dutch-descended farmers known as Boers migrated (the Great Trek) into the interior to be free of British control. Lesotho and western Botswana kingdoms preserved their independence from the Boers. During the second half of the nineteenth century, white migration spread throughout the rest of Southern Africa, dominated by British migrants. The discovery of diamonds and gold in northeastern South Africa brought further occupation and expansion by the British. Boer farmers moved to the growing towns and cities, and the term "Afrikaaners" was applied to all whites of Dutch ancestry.

In the 1890s, the British South Africa Company occupied modern Zambia and Zimbabwe. British traders, missionaries, and settlers also invaded the area now known as Malawi. The Germans seized Namibia, while the Portuguese began to expand inland from their coastal enclaves. Thus, by 1900 the entire region was under white colonial control.

After World War II, movements advocating black self-determination developed throughout the region. By 1968 Botswana, Lesotho, Malawi, Swaziland, and Zambia had gained their independence. In 1974 Angola and Mozambique, 1980 Zimbabwe, and 1990 Namibia gained independence.

South Africa is now a democratic country, after a 1992 vote by the whites to abolish official racial segregation. Until 1992 South Africa divided the population into four major racial categories: Africans, whites, coloreds,

Earlier this year, the presidents of five southern African nations—Namibia, Botswana, Zambia, Angola, and Zimbabwe—announced a game changer: the creation of **Kavango Zambezi Transfrontier Conservation Area** (KAZA). Although not the first, KAZA could be the largest cross-border protected area in the world. Stretching 169,885 square miles (nearly the size of Sweden), the conservation area brings 36 national parks and reserves together under one umbrella, including celebrated Victoria Falls (Figure 32.1) and the Okavango Delta, creating a wildlife wonderland for animals and ecotourists. The hope is that one day a single tourist visa will allow for easy movement between the five countries.

Until then, tour operators such as African Travel can help you plan a KAZA safari.

"Unlike past top-down conservation efforts in Africa, KAZA will involve local communities from the start," says Chris Weaver, managing director for World Wildlife Fund Namibia, "making sure that they, too, get the benefits and opportunities from increased tourism."

— **Costas Christ,** *National Geographic Traveler,* **November 2012**

Figure 32.1 Rainbow over Victoria Falls on Zambezi River, border of Zambia and Zimbabwe. © Przemyslaw Skibinski/www.Shutterstock.com.

and Asians. The Africans are mainly descendants of the Sotho and Nguni peoples who migrated southward centuries ago. The largest African ethnic groups are the Zulu (6 million) and Xhosa (5.8 million). Whites are primarily descendants of Dutch, French, English, and German settlers, with small mixtures of other Europeans. Coloreds are mostly descendants of indigenous people and the earliest European and Malay settlers. They represent 9 percent of the population and live primarily in Cape Province. Asians are mainly descendants of the Indian workers brought to South Africa in the nineteenth century to work as indentured laborers on sugar estates in Natal. They constitute about 3 percent of the population.

As of 1996, South Africa has officially dropped its apartheid laws, and all individuals are equal before the law. In practice, the white minority still controls the wealth of the country, but the change to a democracy with Africans in the major political positions has occurred without the race war predicted by many.

Tourism Characteristics

Southern Africa suffers because of the great distances to the major industrial nations of the world and the political situation in the region. Of the nations of South Africa, three—Zimbabwe, Botswana, and South Africa—have a significant tourist industry. Namibia, a

newly independent nation, is building a tourist industry. Zimbabwe has an increasing tourist trade, as its political situation stabilized in the 1980s. Tourist numbers now exceed 2.3 million annually.

The social and political problems in South Africa hurt Zimbabwe as well as South Africa since traditionally Zimbabwe was included in tour programs with South Africa. Both tour operators and airlines canceled their South African trips due to South African racism. Tourism is now growing, and more cooperation is occurring in the region.

The tourism market for the region has become a regional market. More than 75 percent of Zimbabwe's tourists are now from the regions of East and South Africa. The United Kingdom and Germany have remained important sources of visitors to the region, but have decreased in relative importance compared with African source regions. The United States has about the same percentage of total visitors as it had in the past, but because total tourism numbers are up, there are actually more Americans visiting today.

Namibia's independence has led to the opening of the country to tourism. Currently a majority of its visitors are South Africans who comprise nearly 40 percent of the visitors. There is an increase in European visitors, with Germany being the main source, accounting for some 20 percent of visitors.

Botswana's visitors are mostly from other African countries (about 60 percent). Most travel independently, taking short camping safari vacations. The government has given priority to promote overseas tourism to the country. Its location and the location of its tourist resources provide opportunity to join its market with

Zimbabwe, which will also help to increase the number of visitors. Chobe National Park is a resource shared by Botswana, Zambia, Namibia, and Zimbabwe. It holds Africa's largest population of elephants. Non-African tourists are mostly European (English). The United States only accounts for 1 percent of the visitors to Botswana.

South Africa

Introduction

South Africa is Africa's southernmost nation and most developed economy. A fertile coastal plain rises to mountains in the south and east, with a high plateau beyond the mountains. South Africa's subtropical location means warm and dry conditions, with unreliable rainfall. Having oceans on three sides allows South Africans to bask in generally mild temperatures, although the northwest has a hot desert climate. The ethnic and linguistic composition of South Africa is complex. Blacks account for 79 percent of South Africans, with the biggest groups being Zulu (24 percent) and Xhosa (18 percent). Whites make up the second largest ethnic group at 9.6 percent, with about 60 percent being of Afrikaans (Dutch) ancestry and the rest of British descent. Coloureds (mixed race) are 8.9 percent, and ethnic Indians and Asians are 2.5 percent of the population. The government recognizes eleven official languages (including English). From 1948 to 1991 South Africa's political system was dominated by apartheid, a policy of segregation. In 1989 a reform-minded government, spurred by international economic sanctions as well as domestic protests, began the process of dismantling apartheid. A year later Nelson Mandela, the long-jailed leader of black nationalism, was released. By the middle of 1991 all remaining apartheid legislation was revoked. The first multiracial parliament was elected in 1994, and Nelson Mandela became South Africa's first black president. In the twenty-first century, South Africa is a democratic country representing all its diverse people—often called the rainbow nation. South Africa produces high-tech equipment and is a world leader in the output of gold and diamonds. South Africa seeks to help develop other southern African countries by improving trade and transport and reducing hunger and disease.

Location	Southern Africa
Area	1,219,090 sq km (470,693 sq mi)
Population	50,674,000
Government	Republic

Capital	Pretoria (Tshwane) (administrative) 1,338,000; Cape Town (legislative) 3,215,000; Bloemfontein (judicial) 417,000
Demonym	South African(s)
Life Expectancy	52 years
Religion	Zion Christian, Pentecostal, Roman Catholic, Methodist, Dutch Reformed, other Christian
Language	IsiZulu, IsiXhosa, Afrikaans, Sepedi, English, Setswana, Sesotho, Xitsonga, siSwati, IsiNdebele, Tshivenda
Currency	rand (ZAR)
Gdp Per Cap	$10,100
Labor Force	9% Agriculture, 26% Industry, 65% Services

Tourism Characteristics

Tourism to South Africa itself has grown rapidly since the 1990s with the change in government. Nearly 80 percent of its visitors are from other countries in the region. Outside of Africa, the greatest number of visitors to South Africa are from the United Kingdom, because of former colonial and commonwealth links. About 3 percent of South Africa's tourists are from the United States. In 2010, when South Africa hosted the Soccer FIFA World Cup, tourism arrivals surged past 10 million.

Tourist Destinations and Attractions

The major attractions of neighboring Zimbabwe and Zambia are the spectacular Victoria Falls and the upgraded game viewing areas. The falls are over a mile wide between Zimbabwe and Zambia and can be viewed from both countries. The Zimbabwe Ruins near Fort Victoria are impressive, with ruins of stone buildings dating from 700 B.C. The Wankie Game Reserve and the Hwange National Park are excellent for observing African wildlife. Matobo National Park has a fantastic granite rock–sculptured landscape.

South Africa has game reserves, such as the Kruger National Park (Figure 32.2), the Kalahari Gemsbok National Park, and the Umfolozi Game reserve. The major cities of Cape Town, Pretoria, Durban, Port Elizabeth, Pietermaritzburg, and Johannesburg have

Figure 32.2 Giraffes in Kruger Park, South Africa. © jaroslava V/www.Shutterstock.com.

museums and strong historical ties to the Afrikaaner culture. Reached by a cable car ride, Table Mountain provides a fantastic view of Cape Town and the coast. Cape Town has evidences of the Dutch and British colonial period. The most historic castle in South Africa is in Cape Town.

Pretoria, the administrative capital, has government buildings and the Voortrekker Monument in honor of the Boer trek to settle the Transvaal.

Durban is the seaside resort center of South Africa. It also has Hindu temples and mosques and Indian markets that add to the area of best beaches in South Africa. It has a number of Bantu markets and is only a short drive from Zululand. Kimberley is the diamond mining center (DeBeers), where visitors can watch the mining process.

The smaller countries of southern Africa receive few visitors from outside of Africa. A major development for Swaziland, Lesotho, and Botswana has been the development of gambling casinos and large resort complexes.

These places are very attractive to South Africans and other residents of the region, providing an important tourist industry to these countries. Most famous is Sun City with the spectacular Palace of the Lost City hotel.

Zambia, a landlocked country, shares Victoria Falls with Zimbabwe and also has a number of game reserves with abundant wildlife. In addition to Victoria Falls, Zambia has nineteen game and wildlife parks. A specialty of the South Luangwa Park is walking safaris. Kafue National Park is one of the largest game sanctuaries in Africa, occupying an area as large as Wales. It offers both a rich variety of African wildlife as well as a spectacular array of bird life. Botswana boasts of the most pristine and best-managed park and game reserves in Africa. Chobe National Park has a large concentration of elephants along with rhino, sable, and roan antelope. The Okavango Delta has a wide variety of birds.

Namibia is one of the few countries of the world where the black rhino still exists. In addition to the Etosha National Park it has nineteen park and game reserves.

Cape Town Calling: From Penguins to Politics in This Worldly South African City

Yes, vineyards may surround it, and oenophiles may sip glass after glass at its waterside cafés, but there's more to Cape Town (Figure 32.3) than wine. This sunny coastal city, long divided between the wealthy metropolis and outlying townships, was revitalized by the 2010 World Cup, with improvements to public transportation and the grimy downtown area known as City Bowl. Main draws include hiking, kite-surfing, miles of sandy beaches, and a world-class shopping and dining scene, all less than an hour and a half's drive to the storied Cape of Good Hope. Nevertheless, ongoing racial tensions—though not a threat to visitors' safety in central areas of town—are a haunting legacy of apartheid.

What to Do

After a multimillion-dollar renovation, the Robben Island Museum, where former President Nelson Mandela spent 18 of his 27 years in prison during apartheid, reopened to the public in 1997. Visitors arrive at the World Heritage site by ferries departing from a waterfront terminal and are taken to what used to be the island's maximum-security prison, where they see Mandela's cell. The island also serves as a nature conservation area, home to the African penguin (Figure 32.4) and herds of springbok, South Africa's beloved national mascot.

The frequently foggy flat top of Table Mountain, in expansive Table Mountain National Park, dominates this city's every vista. Most tourists opt to take an aerial cableway, which reaches the top in five minutes, though there's a steep path all the way to the summit for hardy hikers. Once there, replenish at the Table Mountain Café. Visitors meander along level hiking trails or simply admire the view from a bench near the mountain's edge.

On the other side of the park is the Silvermine Nature Reserve. Once a site of Dutch silver prospecting, it's now a popular spot for a leisurely stroll and features a wheelchair-accessible boardwalk. "Being here feels as if you're in the countryside," says Kathryn Pettit, business and project manager at Cape Town's African Impact, a leading volunteer-tourism organization. "The lake is always warm and a deep red in color."

At the foot of Table Mountain and covering more than 1,235 acres, the Kirstenbosch National Botanic Garden was the first garden devoted to flora native to South Africa. A sculpture garden displays contemporary African stone artwork. Easy-to-follow trails wind through fynbos (shrubland) and mountain

Figure 32.3 Cape Town. © michaeljung/www.Shutterstock.com.

Figure 32.4 Penguins crossing the sandy beach at Boulders in South Africa.
© Four Oaks/www.Shutterstock.com.

forest. The strenuous Smuts Track (named after former Prime Minister Jan Smuts) traverses Skeleton Gorge. In summer, a Sunday-evening concert series brings out residents and tourists.

In a sprawling art deco building, the South African National Gallery's permanent collection includes African and European art, beadwork, masks, and sculpture, and its temporary exhibits showcase local talent, such as Peter Clarke, whose multimedia works have made him one of Cape Town's most acclaimed artists.

Nearby stand the Houses of Parliament, with their porticos, red walls, and towering white columns. Dating back to 1885, the complex includes the Library of Parliament and is the site of the annual State of the Nation address. Buy tickets for the public gallery and check out the live parliamentary sessions (only allowed the first six months of the year), or take a guided tour of the facilities. Afterward, walk next door to the Tuynhuys, South Africa's official presidential

residence. From its famous steps in 1992, former President F. W. de Klerk announced that his country had "closed the door" on apartheid.

Where to Shop

Situated on a tree-shaded, cobbled square in the business district, the open-air Green Market has aisles packed with jewelry, textiles, paintings, and curiosities from every corner of South Africa—but be prepared to haggle. Musicians and other characters populate the square, built in 1696 as a trading post; find a good bench to sit and people-watch.

The Victoria and Alfred Waterfront is Cape Town's epicenter for shopping and dining. More than 450 retail outlets have set up shop here, flanked by a breezy seaside boardwalk. Check out the Victorian Gothic-style clock tower and then hop a ride on the 131-foot-high observation wheel.

continues

Surrounding an outdoor courtyard, the shops at Cape Quarter Lifestyle Village—a development in the chic Green Point neighborhood—sell contemporary African crafts, locally designed fashions, and home decor. The Quarter is designed in the Cape Malay architectural style influenced by the area's Dutch settlers, with dark beams and multicolored façades.

The Red Shed Craft Workshop, on the V&A Waterfront, provides an alternative to megamall glitz. Bargain hunters troll stalls for recycled-glass vases, antique silver jewelry from Ethiopia, and hand-painted cushions in safari animal shapes.

Where to Eat

Long Street—a traditional backpackers' hub—is lined with one-of-a-kind craft shops and eateries in every price range, open until early morning, when Cape Town's liveliest avenue finally closes down. The menu at Long Street Café, located in a former bookstore, runs the quirky gamut from Thai wraps to waffles and ice cream. Join the cosmopolitan crowd for Wednesday night karaoke. Down the street, Lola's lists its fare on a chalkboard: sweet corn fritters, anchovies on toast, and steamed west coast mussels. At Fork, the seasonal small-plates menu ranges from deep-fried goat cheese with port-and-onion marmalade to mini kudu (antelope) fillets with chili potato puree.

In Camps Bay, an affluent area sandwiched between white-sand beaches and the far side of Table Mountain, Camps Bay Retreat hotel holds a traditional South African *braai* (barbecue) on Wednesdays and Saturdays amid impeccable lawns, herb gardens, and restored fynbos ($39 per person).

Roundhouse, in a 1786 former guard station, features contemporary South African cuisine and a long wine list. Its more casual, outdoor sister, Rumbullion, serves picnic-style breakfasts and lunch pizzas with expansive views of Camps Bay and the Twelve Apostles mountain range.

Though its decor and formal ambience now come off as a bit dated, La Perla in beachy Sea Point has become a local legend since opening in 1959 (Marlene Dietrich once ate here). Stick to the fresh seafood, and request a seat on the recently refurbished terrace, a popular spot for "sundowners," the British colonial tradition of outdoor sunset cocktails.

— Karen Leigh, *National Geographic Traveler*, June/July 2012

Other attractions than game include the Fish River Canyon in the southwest, one of the biggest outside of the Grand Canyon, hot springs resorts, and the Cape Cross seal reserve on the northern coastline. Namibia's colonial history provides plenty of evidence of architectural gems in Luderitz and Swakopmund of the German colonial days.

Tourist data are not available for Angola and Mozambique. They have severe political problems, which hinder the development of tourism. Mozambique does have some natural attractions upon which to develop a tourism industry when the political problems are overcome. It has a rich variety of wildlife in its national parks, reserves, and the countryside.

Madagascar, the fourth largest island in the world, is increasingly gaining recognition as a world renowned ecotourism destination. It offers secluded tropical beaches, coral reefs, ancient palaces, beautiful scenery, and considerable French influence. However, it is far from Europe and North America, and there are many sun-sea-sand exotic locations closer and more developed than Madagascar. Madagascar is recognized for its unique flora and fauna, including more than sixty varieties of ring-tailed lemur monkeys (Figure 32.5). It is becoming an important ecotourism destination as

Figure 32.5 Lemur, Madagascar. © sunsinger/www.Shutterstock.com.

90 percent of its wildlife is unique to the island and not found anywhere else on earth. Populations expansion, ecosystem destruction, and species loss are major challenges on Madagascar.

REVIEW QUESTIONS

1. Name two European countries that had an early colonial presence in South Africa.

2. What is the name of the large diamond mine in South Africa?

3. Name the large island off the east coast of Africa. What would you see if you went there for a visit? (Why is it unique?)

4. Name the two countries that were former colonies of Portugal.

5. Where is Victoria Falls located?

chapter 33: GEOGRAPHY AND TOURISM IN CENTRAL AND INTERIOR AFRICA

COUNTRY PROFILE

Country	Capital	Language	Currency	Population (2001) (millions)	Population (2011) (millions)	Square Miles and State Comparison
Cameroon	Yaounde	English, French	Franc	15.8	19.1	183,568 (California)
Central African Republic	Bangui	French, Swahili, Sanglo, Arabic	Franc	3.6	4.4	242,000 (Texas)
Chad	N'Djamena	French, Arabic, Sara, Sango	Franc	8.7	10.3	596,000 (Texas and California)
Congo Democratic, Republic of the	Kinshasa	French, Lingala, Swahili	Congolese franc	53.6	71.7	905,063 (almost 1/4 of U.S.)
Congo, Republic of the	Brazzaville	French, Lingala, Kilongo	Franc	3.1	3.6	132,000 (Montana)
Gabon	Libreville	French, Fang, Myene	Franc	1.2	1.4	102,317 (Colorado)
Sudan	Khartoum	Arabic, Nubian, Ya Bedawie	Pound	31.8	30.8	967,500 (1/4 of U.S.)
South Sudan	Juba	English, Sudanese indigenous languages	South Sudanese pound	NA	8.2	239.285 (Texas)

© 2015 Cengage Learning®.

TRAVEL **TIPS**

Entry: A passport is required. Most of these countries require visas, sufficient funds, and proof of return or onward transportation.

Health: Cholera, yellow fever, and malaria are major concerns. Also, typhoid, polio, and hepatitis inoculations are recommended. Raw fruits and vegetables should be carefully prepared. In most cases tap water is not potable. In most cities local transportation is crowded. Taxis are available.

The countries of Central and Interior Africa incorporate a variety of people, cultures, resources, environments, and systems of government. Islam has influenced Chad, Sudan, and the northern part of Cameroon. In most areas Christianity coexists with indigenous tribal systems of belief. All of the states except Chad and Sudan encompass equatorial rain forests. French is the predominant language of the region as French was the principal colonial power in this region. Many of the ethnic groups, such as the Fang in Cameroon, Equatorial Guinea, and Gabon, the Bateke of the Congo, Gabon, and the Congo overlap national boundaries.

Tourism Characteristics and Destinations

Tourism to Central and Interior Africa is very limited. It is the most inaccessible region with the poorest tourist support facilities in the world. Cameroon has the best tourism development in the region, and along with Gabon receives the most visitors. Differing from the other countries in this region, it has a coastal location

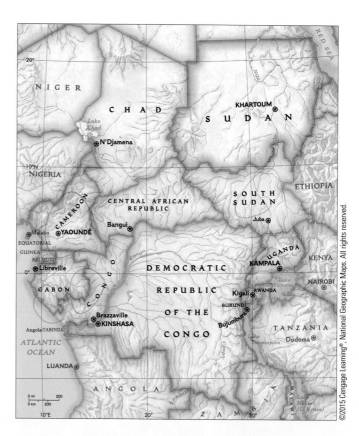

and offers a variety of attractions from coastal to scenic volcanic mountains. It has several fine game reserves with a great variety of wildlife.

Gabon is one of the most prosperous nations of Africa. Beaches, hunting, and photographic safaris are the major attractions of Gabon. Some important attractions are Kango, the M'Bei Waterfalls, and Ogooue' River. Franceville, Ndjole, and Booue are picturesque townships. Dr. Albert Schweitzer worked at Lambarene.

With its large game reserves, rivers, mountains, native villages, and pygmies, the Democratic Republic of the Congo has the potential for tourism, but it is a poorly developed industry. Albert National Park includes not only a variety of animals but a very scenic area that encompasses the Great Rift Valley with its volcanoes, grassy plateaus, alpine scenery, and tropical rain forest. Lake Kivu, the highest lake on the continent, is located in a picturesque setting. Kinshasa, the capital, is an attractive city providing good restaurants and accommodations. St. Anne's Cathedral, the King Albert Monument, the Museum of Native Life, and the markets provide good attractions for the visitor. Kinshasa serves as a good example of the weak tourism market. It is a city of crime, political collapse, poverty, and garbage. Founded by Henry Stanley, Kisangani reveals evidence of its Arab past and also has the pretty Bovoma Falls (formerly Stanley Falls).

The Central African Republic, too, is an undeveloped country with wildlife and national parks and pygmy cultures offering tourism potential. Bangui, the capital, has some interesting attractions in its colorful Central Market, Mamadou M'Baiiki (trading center), Kina, the Fatima Catholic Mission, and an arts and crafts center. Visits can be made from Bangui along the Ubangi River to observe life and visit coffee and rubber plantations and pygmy villages. However, like the Congo, the Central African Republic has not wanted to create a formal, highly visual tourist trade.

Sudan, South Sudan, and Chad in the Sahel receive few visitors. Khartoum and Wadi Halfa are the most promising locations in Sudan. Khartoum, the capital, is the meeting place of the Blue and White Nile Rivers. Wadi Halfa has a number of antiquities in its museum and the Temple of Hatshepsut and Thutmose III at Buhen, which are close to Wadi Halfa. Excursions from Wadi Halfa visit ruins of temples, pyramids, tombs, and fortresses dating back to the Egyptian pharaohs. South Sudan became an independent state in 2011. Chad has the potential to provide good excursions into either desert or tropical environments. N'Djamena, the capital, is a good central location to visit the region for safaris.

REVIEW QUESTIONS

1. Why are there few tourists to the interior of Africa?

2. What European country was the former colonizer of the Congo region?

3. Africa's newest country is in this region. What is its name?

part 11: GEOGRAPHY AND TOURISM IN ASIA

Iurii Yavnik/www.Shutterstock.com

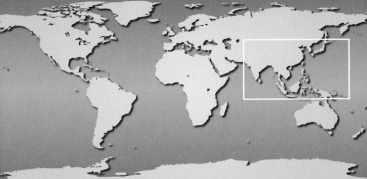

MAJOR GEOGRAPHIC CHARACTERISTICS

- East Asia has a long tradition of civilization and human occupancy, with China being the world's most populous country.
- East Asia's cultures developed essentially in isolation and reflect the influence of China.
- Modern Chinese, Korean, and Japanese cultures are each distinctive.
- South Korea and Japan illustrate that a limited resource base does not doom a country to poverty.
- Individual countries in East Asia (Singapore, South Korea, Taiwan, and China) have rapidly growing economies.
- The population of South and Southeast Asia is concentrated in the river basins.
- Coastal cities in South and Southeast Asia originated along major sea routes and many developed into global centers of trade and commerce.
- The monsoon impacts the economy and life in South Asia.
- Village life dominates throughout South and Southeast Asia.
- There is fragmentation of the political, cultural, and physical geography in South and Southeast Asia.
- Large and rapidly growing populations combine with political and cultural conflict to make South and Southeast Asia important.

MAJOR TOURISM CHARACTERISTICS

- East Asia is part of the Pacific Asia region, which has a high growth rate for tourism arrivals.
- The mystique of the region's culture attracts many first-time tourists, especially to China.
- The opening of China to international tourism in 1978 changed the ranking of tourism destinations in the region.
- Cultural tourism and business travel are major factor for international tourism in East Asia.

(continued)

- China's population makes its potential for domestic tourism the largest in the world.
- The region of South and Southeast Asia is located far from the markets of the Western industrialized countries of the world.
- The exotic is emphasized in attracting tourists to South and Southeast Asia.
- The political problems of Southeast Asia has slowed the growth of tourism development.
- Tourism in South and Southeast Asia is localized in a relatively few countries and places in the region, such as the Himalayan Mountains and the beaches of Thailand.
- Tourists from industrialized countries visit only one country, but tourists from the region visit multiple countries in South and Southeast Asia.
- India, due to its rapid growth and development, is giving rise to a large middle class resulting in increases in domestic tourism and international travel by Indians.

MAJOR TOURIST DESTINATIONS

- Beijing
- Shanghai
- Guangzhou
- Hangzhou
- Lijiang
- Yangtze River
- Pingyao
- Llasa
- Huangshan (Mount)
- Shanxi
- Yunnan
- Xian, Guilin, Kyoto, Osaka, and Tokyo in Japan
- Hong Kong (Special Administrative Region)
- Macau (Special Adninistrative Region)
- Seoul, South Korea
- Buyeo and and Gongju, Gyeongju in South Korea
- Jeju Island, South Korea
- Busan, South Korea
- Taipei, Taiwan
- Kathmandu, Nepal
- Mumbai, Delhi, Agra, and Jaipur, India
- Bangkok, Pattaya, and Phuket, Thailand
- Singapore
- Bali and Jakarta, Indonesia
- Kuala Lumpur and Penang, Malaysia
- Manila and Luzon Island, Philippines

KEY TERMS AND WORDS

Archipelago	Overseas Chinese
Buddha	Pagoda
Circular Tours	Pinyin
Daibutsu	Population
Deccan Plateau	River Valleys
Demilitarized Zone	Shinto
Edo	South Asia
Forbidden City	Southeast Asia
Geomancy	Special Administrative
Ginza	Region
Golden Triangle	Stupa
Great Wall	Subtropical
Han	Taj Mahal
Himalayas	Temple
Hindu	Tiananmen Square
Japan Alps	Tsunami
Kimono	Village
Ming Tombs	Wafuku
Monsoon	Wat
Mosque	Yurt
Mt. Fuji	

Introduction

East Asia

East Asia consists of North and South Korea, the People's Republic of China (and the Special Administrative Regions of Hong Kong and Macau), Taiwan (an Area of Special Status), and Japan. By the end of 2010, the region had the greatest growth in international arrivals of tourists. The opening of China to mass tourism in 1978 and its tourism development was the primary reason for this rapid growth. The interest in China led to increased numbers of visitors for all the countries of the area. Japan and Hong Kong serve as gateways into China and visitors from industrialized nations normally combine a visit to China with visits to several other countries in the region. Hong Kong became a Special Administrative Region of China in 1997 by agreement with the United Kingdom. The agreement provided for a continuation of Hong Kong's unique social, economic, and legal systems.

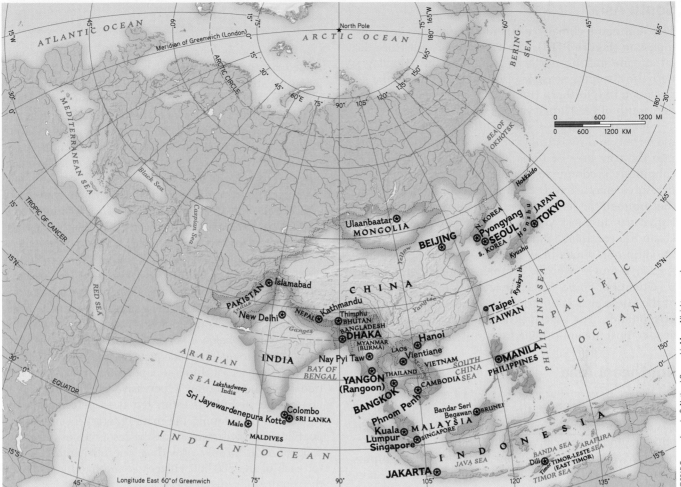

Relationship between China and Taiwan are evolving quickly and the island is now viewed as an Area of Special Status.

East Asia is a very diverse region economically and geographically. It contains one of the most successful industrialized countries of the world in Japan, and a number of growing newly industrialized countries (China, Hong Kong, Taiwan, and South Korea). Japan, China, South Korea, Taiwan, and Hong Kong, now share in the greater wealth and higher standard of living of industrialized countries, and they are an exception to most of the countries of Asia. China's economy is increasing the most rapidly resulting in dramatic economic and social changes in the country.

South and Southeast Asia

With the exception of a few countries, tourism to South and Southeast Asia has been slow to develop. The region's isolated location from the major tourism generating countries of the world, poverty and inequality, natural disasters (earthquakes, tsunamis, and floods), the political problems of the region, rapid urbanization, and the developing economic character of the area are important factors in the lack of development of the tourist industry in South and Southeast Asia. Nearly all of the region's climate is either tropical rain forest or tropical savanna, which also hinders tourism development because of high temperatures and humidity during at least part of the year.

Climate Characteristics

East Asia

East Asia's mainland has the warmest regions in winter in the south. In summer the coolest spots are far to the north. Much of China's climate is characterized by dry seasons and wet monsoons. In winter, winds coming from the north are cold and dry while in the summer winds turn to come from the south (from the sea) and are moist and warm. In the northern regions, summer tends to be short but with plenty of sunshine. Winters are cold. Japan's climate is tropical in the south and cool in the north.

South Asia

The dominant climatic element in South Asia is the **monsoon (Figure P11.1)**. The monsoons result from the jet stream shifting north and south of the Himalayas with the changing seasons of the year. In winter, the jet stream in the Northern Hemisphere is divided, with one part south of the Himalayas.

This arm of the jet stream effectively prevents air movement and moisture from the oceans from moving into the core area of India along the Ganges, and dry conditions predominate. During this dry season, temperatures may exceed 95 degrees Fahrenheit. During the summer, the jet stream moves entirely north of the Himalayas in most years; allowing moist air to penetrate the continent. During the summer season, when the monsoon winds blow from the ocean, the air mass rises as it moves over the continent, causing orographic precipitation. Some years, the jet stream remains south of the Himalayas late into the summer season, limiting precipitation. For tourists, the monsoon season of the year is most uncomfortable for travel.

Southeast Asia

Southeast Asia is characterized by a homogeneous climate. No other area of the world of comparable size has such a uniform climate. The climate throughout the entire region is tropical, with temperatures exceeding 60 degrees Fahrenheit throughout the year. Although portions of the region have a dry period from a monsoon or a more savanna-type climate, there is no truly arid region in Southeast Asia. Prevailing winds in the islands and along the coasts of the continent cause rain shadows in some locales, but the region generally receives high precipitation. Abundant rain falls every month, but it comes in the form of convectional precipitation with brief, heavy showers each day.

Population Issues

One of the impressions gained by tourists to this region is related to its people. East Asia has the world's highest population density. Nearly twenty-five percent of the world's population live in this region. China alone is home to 1.3 billion people, but with a fertility rate of 1.7 percent (less than two children born per woman) the country's population is not expected to increase dramatically in the near future. Japan's population is expected to shrink even faster, as it had a negative fertility rate in 2012. South and Southeast Asia have large population numbers and a high growth rate. As of 2011, the absolute increase in numbers each year in India is second only to China, totaling nearly 20 million people per year—more than live in all but a few of the most populous states of the United States. India's population problem is typical of that of less industrialized countries. The perpetually increasing numbers of Indians help to keep India one of the poorest countries of the world. It is estimated that more than 400 million people in India (35 percent of the population) live below the country's national poverty and below a level to maintain adequate health.

The impact of India's population on attempts to transform the economy is pervasive and insidious. The literacy rate of India is estimated at 45 percent, and the logistics of overcoming the mass illiteracy, even without population growth, would tax the resources of the entire subcontinent. Simply providing one elementary school for each of the 580,000 **villages** is an ongoing challenge the country is trying to meet.

Pakistan's mushrooming population exceeds the country's food production. Pakistan is a nation of farmers, with a limited resource base that helps keep it in the less developed realm of the world. Bangladesh has similar problems. It has one of the highest rural population densities in the world. Food production is inadequate for the country whose population reached 160 million in 2011.

Figure P11.1 Heavy monsoon rain causes a flash flood in Varanasi, India. © Daniel J. Rao/www.Shutterstock.com

INTERNATIONAL TOURISM TO EAST ASIA (1999–2010).

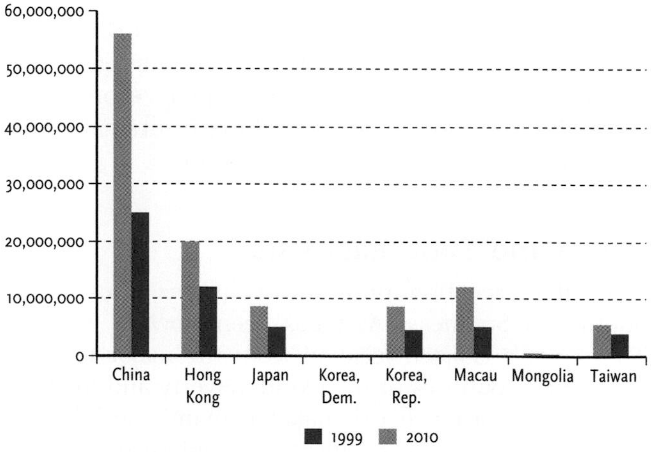

Figure P11.2 Tourism to East Asia. Data source: *The World Bank: The Data Catalogue.*
Figure copyright © 2015 Cengage Learning®. All rights reserved.

Population is also a major challenge in much of Southeast Asia. The island of Java is one of the most densely populated locations in the world. As with the rest of Southeast Asia, however, the bulk of the country of Indonesia has low population densities. Indonesia has reduced its population growth rate, but as with other Southeast Asian countries, it still faces the difficult challenge of channeling its growing populations into less densely settled locales, improving literacy and health standards, and providing jobs for its burgeoning populations.

Tourism in Asia

East Asia

The most significant feature of tourism to East Asia has been the opening and development of tourism to the People's Republic of China. Although the region has one of the highest rates of visitor increases, it is somewhat difficult to interpret. Various data sources indicate different numbers of visitors. The numbers used in this text are the World Bank's estimates of visitor numbers, East Asia accounts for the highest percentage of all tourists to the larger Pacific Asia region.

South and Southeast Asia

South and Southeast Asia are sensual destination regions of the world. For most of the industrialized Western nations, both the environment and the culture are much different than those in which they live or with which they have considerable contact. Tourism is also localized in South and Southeast Asia, with a few countries receiving most of the tourists. Within the countries receiving the tourists, tourism is localized to a few specific regions. Tourism development and growth have been limited

INTERNATIONAL TOURISM TO SOUTH ASIA, 1999–2010

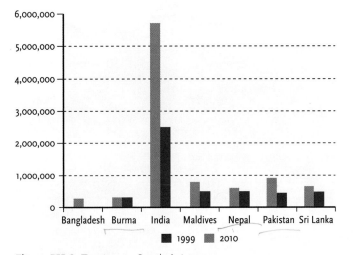

Figure P11.3 Tourism to South Asia. Data source: *The World Bank: The Data Catalogue.* Figure copyright © 2015 Cengage Learning®. All rights reserved.

INTERNATIONAL TOURISM TO SOUTHEAST ASIA, 2010

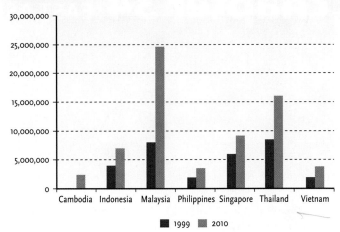

Figure P11.4 Tourism to Southest Asia. Data source: *The World Bank: The Data Catalogue.* Figure copyright © 2015 Cengage Learning®. All rights reserved.

because of the political problems, development challenges, and the emergence of nationalistic movements. Many countries of the region lack accommodations for middle-income tourists. This situation is somewhat offset by the lower food and labor costs that keep tour packages reasonable. A major tourist organization is the Pacific Asia Travel Association (PATA). Membership consists of over 80 governments, state, and city tourism bodies who work together to promote tourism through research, development, education, and marketing.

A significant percentage of international tourism in the region is regional in character. With its huge population, India provides the largest segment of international visitors to the other countries of South Asia. India also receives the most income from tourists, but in contrast to the other South Asian countries, visitors from within the region are far less important. India's international visitors come from many countries, but a significant percentage of those traveling from Europe are from the United Kingdom, reflecting ties from the colonial period. Many residents from South Asia, particularly India and Pakistan, migrated to Britain. Until recently, residents of former colonies of the United Kingdom that were members of the Commonwealth of Nations could migrate freely to the United Kingdom. With family ties in South Asia, visitors from England have trips of long duration, averaging nearly 30 days for India and 27 for Pakistan.

Tourism to India reflects the great regional variation in visits to the region. Climatic factors (the hot, humid monsoon), sociopolitical problems, and tourist attractions and development combine to determine the level of tourism activity in each individual country. An important recent development in the region has been the rapid growth of budget airlines. Nonexistent just ten years ago, companies like IndiGo (India), Air Asia (Malaysia), and Wings Air (Indonesia) now make up 25 percent of all regional air travel.

chapter 34: EAST ASIA

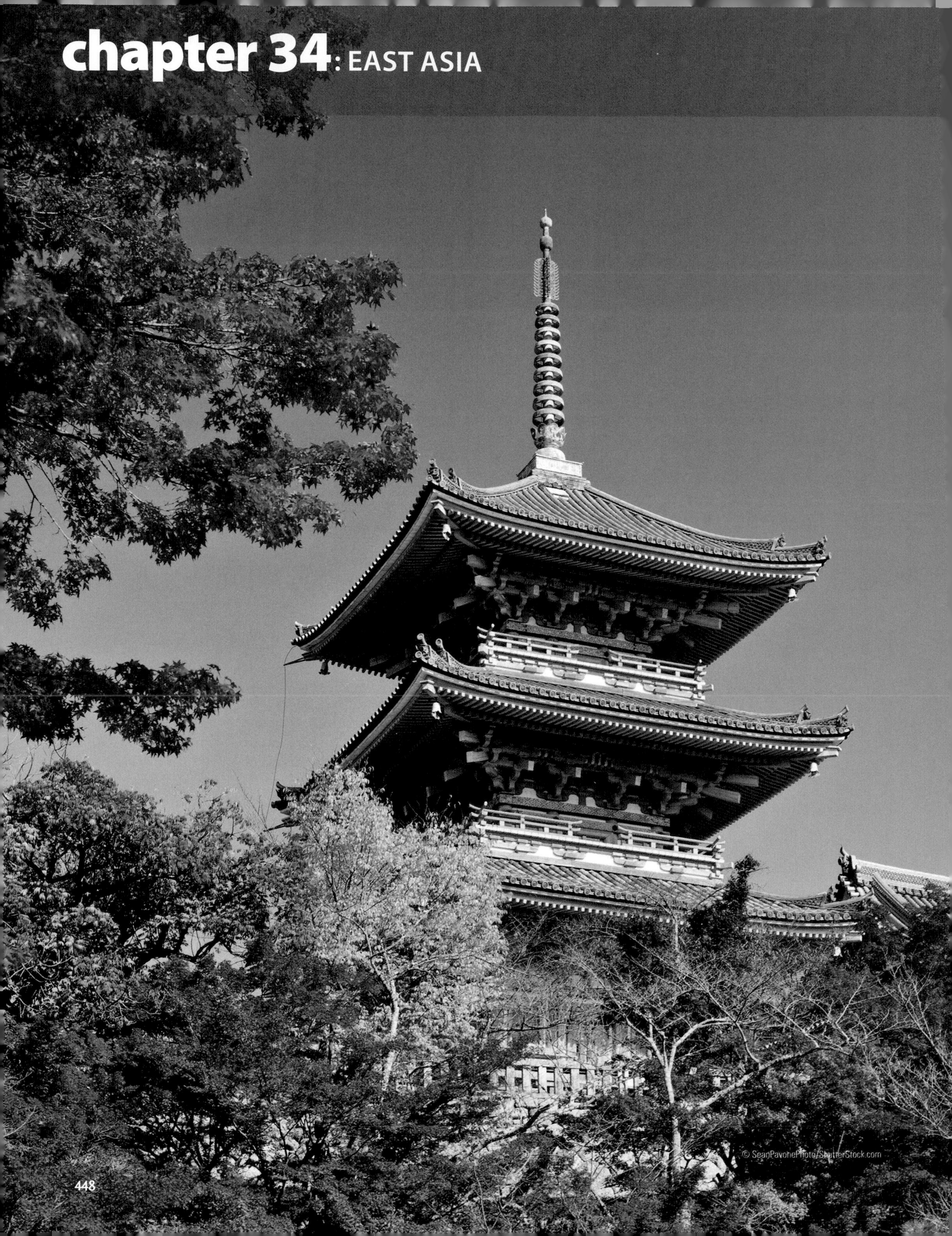

Japan

Japan, a country of mountainous islands, extends along the Pacific coast of Asia. The largest island is Honshu; the other major islands are Shikoku and Kyushu to the south and Hokkaido to the north. More than 4,000 smaller islands surround the four largest. East of Hokkaido lie the islands known as the Northern Territories, consisting of the Habomai Islands, Shikotan, Kunishiri, and Etorofu (called "Iturup" by Russia). Taken by Soviet forces at the end of World War II, Japan still claims these Russian-held islands. Japan has some 80 active volcanoes and experiences earthquakes and typhoons. The islands enjoy a mostly temperate climate, except for cold, snowy winters in northwest Honshu and Hokkaido. Some southern islands, including Okinawa, are subtropical.

About 73 percent of Japan is mountainous, and all its major cities, except the ancient capital of Kyoto, cling to narrow coastal plains. Only an estimated 18 percent of Japan's territory is suitable for settlement—so Japan's cities are large and densely populated. Tokyo, the capital, is the planet's largest urbanized area at 35.6 million people. Medical technology and a healthy diet provide Japanese with the world's highest life expectancy. But Japan's population is aging faster than that of any other country, and 30 percent of Japanese will be 65 or older by 2020.

Aggressive expansion across the Pacific led to war with the United States in 1941, and the U.S. occupation imposed a democratic constitution after World War II. Despite a lack of raw materials, the economy was revived with the help of U.S. grants, high rates of labor productivity, personal savings, and capital investment.

Currently, Japan's innovative market economy is one of the world's largest. High-speed trains (known as *shinkansen*, or bullet trains) efficiently connect its major cities. Japanese automakers pioneer fuel-efficient and green cars, and Japan leads the way in commercial robotics, with more robots than any other country.

From *National Geographic Atlas of the World,* 9th edition. Copyright ©2011 National Geographic Society. Reprinted by arrangement. All rights reserved.

Area	377,915 sq km (145,914 sq mi)
Population	127,568,000
Government	Parliamentary Government with Constitutional Monarchy
Capital	Tokyo 35,676,000
Life Expectancy	83 years
Religion	Shinto, Buddhist
Language	Japanese
Currency	yen (JPY)
GDP per Cap	$32,600
Labor Force	4% Agriculture, 28% Industry, 68% Services

From *National Geographic Atlas of the World,* 9th edition. Copyright ©2011 National Geographic Society. Reprinted by arrangement. All rights reserved.

TRAVEL **TIPS** 🧳

Entry: A passport is required. Visas are not required for stays less than 90 days with proof of return or onward transportation.

National Holiday: December 23 (Birthday of Emperor Akihito)

Peak Tourist Season: October

Shopping: Common items include Japanese handicrafts and art objects, jewelry, silks, furs, pottery pieces, paper lanterns, dolls, and hand-painted dishes and bowls. The manufactured items known the world over can be purchased, but they are expensive and can be purchased for less in other cities such as Hong Kong.

Internet TLD: .jp

CULTURAL CAPSULE

Japan is one of the most densely populated nations in the world with a population of 127 million (nearly one-third that of the United States), living on less than 5 percent of the total territory of the United States. The three major metropolitan areas of Tokyo, Osaka, and Nagoya contain nearly 45 percent of the population of Japan. The Japanese, about 99 percent of the population, are a Mongoloid people, closely related to the major groups of East Asia. There are small numbers of Koreans (675,000) and Chinese. Buddhism and Shinto are the major religions. Most Japanese still consider themselves members of one of the major Buddhist sects. Shintoism is an indigenous religion founded on myths, legends, and ritual practices of the early Japanese. Neither Buddhism nor Shintoism is an exclusive religion, and most Japanese observe both Buddhist and Shinto rituals, the former for funerals and the latter for births, marriages, and other occasions. Confucianism also influences Japanese thought. About 1.5 million people are Christians. Approximately 50 percent are Protestant and 40 percent Roman Catholic.

Devotion, conformity, loyalty, and hard work can best describe the Japanese people. The society is group oriented, and loyalty to one's superiors takes precedence over personal feelings. Conformity in dress is the general rule. Businessmen wear suits and ties in public. The traditional kimono or wafuku, which is a long robe with sleeves, wrapped with a special sash, is worn on special occasions and at leisure.

Cultural hints: A bow is the traditional greeting. Japanese will shake hands with Westerners, but avoid an overly firm handshake. Formal titles are important. Do not show signs of affectionate physical contact in public. Lines are respected. An open mouth is considered rude;

cover your mouth when yawning. When counting, the thumb represents the number five. Snack foods sold on the streets are generally eaten at the stand. Present gifts and business cards with both hands. Also, bow slightly. Toasting is common in Japan. At public restaurants or private homes, remove your shoes before entering.

Traditional meals are eaten with chopsticks from bowls that are held at chest level. Western foods are eaten with Western utensils. Typical foods are rice, fresh vegetables, seafood, fruit, and small portions of meat. Some typical dishes are miso (bean paste) soup, noodles, curried rice, sashimi (uncooked fish), tofu, pork, and sushi (combination of fish, cooked or uncooked, and rice with vinegar).

Tourism Characteristics

Japan has not historically looked to tourism as a major foreign income earner as it had such a huge trade surplus in the 1980s. Since the 1990s it has taken a more active role in promoting inbound tourism. Japan has a well-organized tourist industry. The government is involved with both domestic and international tourism, with offices in many cities of the world outside of Japan to promote and provide information about tourism to Japan. The government has also established a number of programs and offices to develop a broad variety of tourist attractions in Japan while maintaining the quality of its natural environmental settings.

Three factors appear to limit Japan's growth from the main generating markets of North America and Europe: (1) its prime attractions are culture, history, customs, and traditions that appeal to a relatively narrow segment of the long-haul tourist market; (2) there is a language and cultural barrier that deters some people from visiting; (3) high travel and land costs limit market demand. The image that Japan is expensive limits the number of visitors to the country.

According to data compiled and released by the Japan Tourism Marketing Company, tourists arrive in Japan from throughout the world. The largest origin countries are South Korea (1.6 million), China (1.3 million), and Taiwan (994,000), which combined for about half of total visitors in 2010. The United States is fourth, generating 565,000 arrivals. Europe, led by Great Britain, accounts for 14 percent of visitors. Most of the European visitors are business travelers. Europeans have the highest incidence of business travel of any region's visitors to Japan. Tourism arrivals from all counties were down sharply in 2011 following the impact and aftermath of an earthquake and tsunami that hit northern Japan in March 2011. The event caused 20,000 casualties and resulted in massive property damage and a slowdown of the Japanese economy.

The most popular time for visitors is October, followed by July and August. The winter months are the slowest, and the government desires to encourage and promote more winter events and conventions to level out the seasons. Domestic tourism has risen dramatically in Japan over the past decades. The decreasing work days and increasing prosperity of the country are beginning to overcome the traditional cultural restraints against taking vacations. However, many Japanese still work on their days off and refuse to take vacations. This is changing slowly, which has an important effect on tourism. Tokyo's financial firms are no longer open on Saturdays. The government is encouraging the establishment of a five-day work week.

One of the remarkable achievements in the Japanese travel industry has been the increase in international travel by the Japanese during the last 30 years. One factor encouraging the Japanese to travel is that goods can be purchased abroad more cheaply than at home. One of the characteristics of Japanese travel overseas is that it too is seasonal, with August as the peak and April the low point. When Japanese travel overseas popular destinations are China (3.8 million), the United States (3.2 million), South Korea (3.1 million), Taiwan (1.2 million), and Thailand (1.1 million). (Source: Japan Tourism Marketing Co. 2012)

Tourist Destinations and Attractions

The attractions most frequently visited by the Japanese themselves are temples and historical and cultural places, especially in the older cities of Osaka, Kyoto, and Nara. Each of these was at one time the capital of Japan, and they have great historical value and ancient treasures. In Nara, for example, the Horyuji Temple, which was built over 1,350 years ago and is the oldest of all wood buildings now existing in Japan, attracts Japanese. National parks are the second most important vacation attractions. There are 28 national parks, 55 nationalized parks, and 299 state parks. National parks are maintained by the Natural Environment Preserve Committee. Another major attraction is hot springs, which have been popular for generations. Japan has an outstanding internal transportation system, by rail and by air, for both domestic and international visitors.

There are eight travel regions in Japan that serve as the major destinations for foreign visitors. First is Hokkaido, the northernmost island in the Japanese archipelago. Sapporo, the capital city, was the site of the 1972 Winter Olympics. Its annual winter carnival (Snow Festival) is a major attraction. It has hundreds of gigantic snow sculptures created by talented artists. Other attractions in the city are the Hokkaido University, Botanical Gardens, Historical Museum (illustrating Hokkaido treasures of Ainu and Giliak costumes, canoes, harpoons, and other objects), and Odori Promenade. The promenade is decorated year-round with flowers. Below it, there is an underground shopping arcade with some 150 restaurants, souvenir shops, and coffee houses. The characteristics of Hokkaido as a vacationland are its natural beauty and unique fauna and flora. The volcanoes, lakes, and spas form a rich variety of outdoor activities for the tourist. Hokkaido has five important national parks with a variety of

Figure 34.1 Tokyo skyline and Tokyo Skytree at dusk. © skyearth/www.Shutterstock.com

volcanoes, caldera lakes, hot spring resorts, forests and wild flowers, and spas.

A second travel region is Tohoku, which is located in the northeastern section of the main island of Honshu. It has scenic areas that include three national parks and many hot springs. The parks offer mountaineering and skiing. The Tohoku region also boasts handicrafts, historical and traditional festivals, and folk dancing. The major tourist center in this region is Sendai, the capital of Miyagi Prefecture and the cultural, economic, and political center. Formerly a castle town, the city is very popular and serves as a center for trips to scenic spots in the district.

The third tourism region in Japan is Tokyo and the surrounding area. It has many shrines and temples along with the attractions of a great modern city. Historically Tokyo first became the seat of the Shogunate government in 1603. Under the Shogun's great influence, the city (then called Edo) enjoyed all the privileges of a virtual national capital for the next three centuries even though Kyoto remained the legal capital until 1868. Today Tokyo is the center of national politics, education, and finance. Narita International Airport is the gateway into the country for most international travelers. Although it is a highly westernized metropolis, it still retains much of its Oriental charm. Tokyo is particularly attractive to visitors because of its unique capacity to blend the East and the West, the old and the new. Side by side with the bustling activity of its business sections, there remain traditional ways and habits of old Japan interspersed with many colorful festivities.

An important attraction is the Imperial Palace surrounded by a high stone wall and moat. While visitors cannot enter the palace, the surrounding area is pleasant and interesting. The Meiji Shrine, which is located in a thickly wooded parkland and flower garden, is a popular attraction for Japanese and foreign tourists. The Roppongi District is the cultural heart of Tokyo. Museum here include the Mori Art Museum, the Suntory Museum of Art, and the National Art Center. One of the most popular attractions in Tokyo is the Ginza, the famous shopping district of Japan. It has many prestigious department stores, large and small specialty shops, restaurants and coffee shops, and upscale nightlife. The Ginza district is also home to the largest fish market in Asia, the Tsukiji Fish Market. Tokyo Tower offers a great view of the city. Tokyo Skytree (Figure 34.1), the second tallest free standing structure in the world, opened in

As darkness falls, **Tokyo** crackles to life in bursts of neon energy. Scrolling signs slide along the sides of skyscrapers. Multistory TV screens flaunt hot young bodies flashing hotter new gadgets. On the streets, designer girls in ice-pick heels download horoscopes onto their iPhones, chattering to each other like a flock of sparrows. Tuxedoed Svengalis urge potential customers into darkened bars.

But there is another side of Tokyo; you catch glimpses of it in Asakusa, a village deep in the heart of old Tokyo—a village that became a city yet remained a village. People here still leave their doors unlocked at night. Old-fashioned cottage industries fill the summer air with the scent of fresh-cut *tatami* straw or the sour tang of fermenting soybeans. And if you look carefully, you'll even find the occasional stiff-backed woman in a three-layered kimono surreptitiously enjoying a burger in a corner fast-food restaurant.

Dig deeper, and you will find Tokyo's feudal heritage in moments as ephemeral as the first cherry blossoms in spring. Tokyo is one of few places in the world where a flower can bring an entire city to a state of heightened excitement. Cherry blossoms last for less than two weeks and in Japanese culture symbolize the impermanence of life, the sadness that underlies all exquisite beauty. Cherry blossoms fall in their prime, as samurai warriors were meant to do.

Over the past century, Tokyo has been virtually annihilated twice: first in 1923, during the Great Kanto earthquake and subsequent firestorm, and again in World War II, during devastating bombings by Allied forces. Each time it has risen like a phoenix from the ashes, reborn in an ever more modern reflection of itself, yet with the past woven into its present. It is precisely this balance that gives Tokyo both the resilience and the flexibility to survive everything from catastrophic fires to Hello Kitty as it moves confidently into the 21st century.

—**Karin Muller,** *National Geographic Traveler,* **October 2009**

2012. The Asakusa Kannou Temple, founded in 645 A.D., is surrounded by a multitude of souvenir shops, theaters, and amusement spots, indicating the importance of the temple as a tourist attraction. Tokyo Disneyworld and Tokyo DisneySea are family favorites. The surrounding area has lovely mountain scenery, hot springs, and many historic spots.

The most famous symbol of Japan is snow-capped Mt. Fuji (Figure 34.2). Five lakes on the fringes of Mt. Fuji and the mountain itself provide a variety of outdoor recreational and spiritual activities. Hakone is a mountain resort and spa town with Mt. Fuji as a backdrop. Lake Ashi, boiling hot springs, and a splendid reflection of Mt. Fuji are among the attractions in Hakone. Kamakura, a small quiet town, was once a feudal government headquarters. It has a number of old temples and shrines. Some highlights are the Great Image of Buddha, the colorful Tsurugaoka Hachimangu Shrine, and the picturesque Enoshima Island. The gorgeous Toshogu Shrine, Lake Chuzenji, and the beautiful Kegon Falls, which fall 330 feet, are in and around Nikko.

Kamakura, 30 miles southwest of Tokyo, was also a seat of a feudal government. Today it is a lovely seaside resort. Kamakura is the site of Daibutsu or Great Buddha, a huge 700-year-old bronze image of Buddha, and the Tsurugaoka Hachimangu Shrine.

The fourth region, Chubu, is the center of the main island of Honshu, in which there are seven national parks and the "Japan Alps." The area has splendid mountain scenery, beautiful plateaus, swift rivers, hot springs, mirror-like lakes, and excellent ski resorts. The largest city of central Honshu is Nagoya, with a history that dates back to the seventeenth century when Ieyasu Tokugawa (1542–1616), the generalissimo who established his government in Edo (now Tokyo), built an imposing castle, which is now the city's symbol. Ise is considered the most sacred city in Japan. The Ise Grand Shrines, sacred to mythological creators of the country, are located there. The Grand Shrines have numerous pilgrims year-round.

Figure 34.2 Mt. Fuji. © prasit chansareekorn/www.Shutterstock.com

Figure 34.3 Kinkaku-Ji Temple, Kyoto. © DmitrySerbin/www.Shutterstock.com

One of the most scenic mountain areas in Japan is often compared to the European Alps, causing them to be called the Japan Alps. The center for travel into and through the Alps of Japan is Matsumoto. Matsumoto is a castle town, with a distinctive local culture and an unexploited countryside. Japan's oldest medieval castle is in Matsumoto and provides a panorama of the superb countryside. In the valley, from Shiojiri in the south to Otari in the north, there are charming old post towns and villages surrounded by lush agricultural land and flowing rivers. There are summer and winter resorts in the Japan Alps; the region hosted the 1998 Winter Olympic games in Nagano.

The fifth region is Kansai, with the metropolitan cities of Kyoto and Osaka on the southern half of the island of Honshu. This is a major destination for international visitors. The area has superb scenic beauty, like Ise-Shima National Park with its seascapes. In addition, the ancient capitals of Japan are in this area. Kyoto, the capital of Japan from 794 to 1868, has some 400 Shinto shrines and 1,650 Buddhist temples, as well as villas with elaborately designed gardens. One of the most impressive sites is the Kinkaku-Ji Temple (Temple of the Golden Pavilion) (Figure 34.3). In the early 1300s the pavilion was constructed as a villa for the aristocrat Saionji Kintsune. It was purchased in 1397 by the third shogun of the Ashikaga,

Yoshimitsu. Yoshimitsu used the pavilion as a place to store his art and literature collection. After his death the palace became a Zen temple and remains the most recognized site in Kyoto. The gold-leafed temple consists of three different types of architecture: the first floor is traditional fujiwara court style; the second is Kamakura period samurai house style; and the third floor is Chinese Zen temple style. Kyoto is a city of festivals as well, with many centuries-old events to remind the visitor of life in the ancient world. It is Japan's top center for folk arts, silk fabrics, brocades, lacquerware, earthenware, porcelain fans, dolls, and bronze, all of superb workmanship.

The city of Nara, just south of Kyoto, is a popular day trip from Kyoto. Nara has an even older history than Kyoto and was the cradle of Japan's arts. It contains ancient tombs, ruins, and other historical relics. The most widely known symbol of Nara is the Kofukuji Temple, built in 710 A.D. Moved from Asuka to its present site, its five-story pagoda is a distinctive landmark. An attraction not to be missed in Nara is the Deer Park, a 1200-acre park with hundreds of very visitor-friendly deer.

Osaka serves as an excellent base for trips to Kyoto and Nara. Osaka has a long history as a commercial and transportation center of Japan. Contact between Japan and the countries of Korea and China took place in Osaka, and several emperors established their courts here. Kobe, near Osaka, is also an important port city. Its business and shopping centers vie with its architecture reflecting foreign influence, preserved from the Meiji Period, to attract visitors.

The sixth region is Chugoku, the western end of the island of Honshu. It has beautiful beaches, coastal plateaus, and the Inland Sea National Park. It includes Hiroshima, site of the first atomic bomb used in warfare, and one of the three most beautiful Japanese landscape gardens, Korakuen Garden. The central city in the district is Okayama, an old castle town. The attractions in Okayama include the Korakuen Garden and Washuzan Hill, which provides one of the best views of the Inland Sea. Hiroshima has been restored and has adopted the name "the City of Peace." The attractions in Hiroshima include Shukukeien Garden, Hiroshima Castle, Peace Memorial Park and Hall, Atomic Bomb Dome, Memorial Cenotaph for the A-bomb victims, and Memorial Cathedral for World Peace.

The seventh region is the island of Kyushu, which has a subtropical climate and six national parks and offers spectacular scenery, hot springs, and numerous historical sites. One major city in this region is Fukuoka, which is divided into the modern commercial district and the old trading port. Fukuoka has been undergoing development to stimulate more tourism. It is known for its Hakata-ori silk textiles and gala festivals of Hakata Dontaku. Nagasaki also contains a number of attractions, including some memorials to the suffering caused by the atomic bomb dropped on the city.

The eighth region is the Okinawa Islands, which have many historical ties to Japan. Okinawa has a wealth of natural beauty, including coral reefs and emerald water, sunny skies, and subtropical plants. Tourist attractions include Naminoue Shrine, dedicated to a god of land management, and Sogenji Temple, the mausoleum for successive Ryiukyuan kings and others.

South Korea

The Republic of Korea, or South Korea, consists of the southern half of the Korean Peninsula in East Asia, as well as many islands lying off the western and southern coasts. The largest island, Jeju, has the highest mountain in South Korea at 6,398 feet. The South Korean terrain is mountainous, though less rugged than in North Korea.

South Koreans are culturally homogeneous and highly urbanized. Korean is the official language, but English is taught as a second language in most schools—and more than 2.1 million ethnic Koreans reside in the United States. The population is 81 percent urban, with the Seoul urban agglomeration holding half of South Korea's people. To reduce pollution and traffic congestion, South Korea launched high-speed rail service between Seoul and Busan in 2004. The high-speed train line serves 71 percent of the population and carries some 38 million people a year.

The end of World War II freed Korea from Japanese rule; unfortunately, U.S. and Soviet occupation zones then divided Koreans along the 38th parallel. South Korea gained independence in 1948 but was invaded by North Korea in 1950. After the Korean War, South Korean society shifted from being 75 percent rural to being an overwhelmingly urbanized and industrialized society. Since 1987 it has grown as a multiparty democracy, and the government has pursued peace initiatives and trade with the unpredictable North Korean regime. South Korea is one of the world's top trading nations and a major exporter of cars, consumer electronics, and computer components—due in part to huge export-oriented conglomerates, such as Hyundai, LG, and Samsung. The country has experienced high economic growth over the last three decades.

SOUTH KOREA

To enhance its competitiveness, South Korea pursues free trade agreements (FTA) with large economies.

From *National Geographic Atlas of the World*, 9th edition. Copyright ©2011 National Geographic Society. Reprinted by arrangement. All rights reserved.

Area	99,720 sq km (38,502 sq mi)
Population	48,747,000
Government	Republic
Capital	Seoul 9,796,000
Life Expectancy	80 years
Religion	Christian, Buddhist
Language	Korean, English
Currency	South Korean won (KRW)
GDP per Cap	$28,000
Labor Force	7.2% Agriculture, 25.1% Industry, 67.7% Services

From *National Geographic Atlas of the World*, 9th edition. Copyright ©2011 National Geographic Society. Reprinted by arrangement. All rights reserved.

TRAVEL**TIPS** 🧳

Internet TLD: .kr

CULTURAL CAPSULE Korea is one of the most homogeneous countries in the world (ethnic Korean). Korea was first populated by a Tungusic branch of the Ural-Altaic family, which migrated to the peninsula from the northwestern regions of Asia. It has a small Chinese minority (50,000).

Korean is a Uralic language remotely related to Japanese, Hungarian, Finnish, and Mongolian. The language uses numerous Chinese words. Many older people retain some knowledge of Japanese from the colonial period (1910–1945), and most educated Koreans can read English. Shamanism and Buddhism are the traditional religions of Korea. Shamanism, a folk religion, involves geomancy, the process of divination, avoiding bad luck or omens, warding off evil spirits, and honoring the dead. Nearly 30 percent of the population is Christian. The Confucian ethic of hard work and filial piety is important to the society. There are many rituals of courtesy, formality in behavior, and customs regulating social relations.

Cultural hints: A slight bow and handshake is a common greeting between men. Women shake hands less often than men, usually just acknowledging with a nod. Avoid touching, patting on arm, shoulder, or back unless good friends. Use both hands to pass and receive objects. Shoes are removed before entering a home. Periods of silence are common during meals. Pass food and other objects with right hand. A service charge is usually included in the bill. Tipping is not expected. At a restaurant, one person usually pays for all. When dining, the elderly are served first and the children last. Typical food is spicy. Common foods are rice, spicy pickled cabbage, red beans, chicken, marinated and barbecued beef, barley tea, and fruit for dessert.

Tourism Characteristics

Tourism to South Korea is recognized as a national industry, and the government works to improve the industry and promote increased tourism to Korea. The South Korean tourism industry has increased dramatically for both outgoing and incoming tourists. The combination of Asian Games followed in 1988 by the Summer Olympics and FIFA Worldcup in 2002 greatly benefited tourism to the country. Tourism in South Korea developed much later than in Japan. The Korean War, from 1950 to 1953, devastated the country and its economy. In 1962, there were only 15,000 foreign visitors to Korea. In 1999, there were 4.6 million. In 2010 the country hosted 8 million visitors. Japan dominates the market, accounting for 34 percent of total visitors. Japan's proximity and the similarity of culture and language attract Japanese travelers, as do low prices for travel and consumer items. The United States accounts for less than 10 percent of the total foreign visitors to Korea. Presently few Europeans visit Korea.

The Olympics in Seoul (held in September 1988) helped the country develop accommodations and other tourist infrastructure, as well as showcased the country in Europe and North America as the pageantry of the summer games received broad coverage in those regions. Pyeongchang will host the 2018 Winter Olympic Games. The 600th anniversary of Seoul as the nation's capital took place in 1994, and as such it was designated as the "Visit Korea Year." The government has undertaken an extensive campaign, especially in the United States, to stimulate travel to Korea. Spring and autumn have been the peak seasons, but seasonality does not represent a problem as it has not overloaded the accommodations to date.

Tourist Destinations and Attractions

There are three main attractions for tourists to South Korea. Seoul, the capital (Figure 34.4), has palaces and folklore museums with Korean architecture. Now an Olympic city, Seoul is the gateway to the Republic of Korea. Seoul's historic heritage is evidenced in the palaces, shrines, and monuments still standing through the city. A number of palaces are important attractions. Toksu Palace blends both Western and Korean architecture. The Kyongbok Palace was built in 1395

Figure 34.4 Skyline of downtown Seoul, South Korean, from Bongeunsa Temple. © SeanPavonePhoto/www.Shutterstock.com

by King Taejo of the Choson Dynasty and was rebuilt in 1868. Many of the nation's historic stone pagodas and monuments, including a ten-story pagoda, are on its grounds. The Secret Garden within the Changdok-kung Palace contains forty-four pavilions scattered amid small streams with bridges and other idyllic spots. Changgyonggung Palace has been restored and depicts the life and arts of the ancient royal family.

There are many other attractions in Seoul. One of the attractions is a museum to commemorate Seoul's 600th anniversary. The Great South Gate of Seoul (Nandaemum) has been designated as the foremost National Treasure. Chogyesa Temple (a large Buddhist temple) and the Temple of Heaven are two highly visible Buddhist temples in the city. In the vicinity there are the royal tombs, with the Tonggurung or East Nine Tombs as the best known and most accessible. The royal remains are entombed in huge mounds of earth, each surmounted by an altar stone on which sacrifices used to be offered on ritual days.

West of Seoul, at Inchon, is Chayu Park and the MacArthur Monument, commemorating the American Army's landing at Inchon in the Korean conflict, and the Memorial Hall for the Inchon Landing Operation. South of Seoul, the fortress city of Suwon boasts a restored fortress that was originally built in the late eighteenth century by King Chongjo to honor his father. The Korean Folk Village (Figure 34.5) just outside of Suwon provides a view of Korea's past. Here in reconstructed farmhouses, residences of the nobility, and other buildings of several centuries ago, a functioning community of potters, millers, weavers, blacksmiths, pipemakers, and other craftsmen work as their ancestors did. At the Everland Resort, the Global Town exhibits various traditional cultural scenes from 21 different countries around the world. North of Seoul is the Demilitarized Zone (DMZ). P'anmunjom, in the middle of the DMZ, is the site of the armistice negotiations. East of Seoul, there are a number of lakes, providing a water vacationland for the visitor.

The second major area is the southwest area centering on Buyeo and Gongju, former Baekje Kingdom capitals, known for their temples, museums, monasteries, sacred mountains, and royal tombs. Buyeo, the last capital of the kingdom, has many ruins dating back to 600 A.D. A fortified castle sits on a steep hill in Buyeo's's city center. The Buyeo National Museum is a fine example of Korea's modern architecture. Also, the government built an exhibition hall in Buyeo highlighting the Baekje culture, which flourished from 57 B.C. to 668 A.D. At Gongju, the Gongju National Museum houses the valuables of King Muryeong tomb. Near these ancient capitals at the town of Nonsan is the massive Unjin Miruk Buddha, Korea's largest stone Buddha, dating from the tenth century.

Figure 34.5 Kimchi pots in front of a traditional Korean house at Suwon Folk Village, South Korea. © Gina Smith/www.Shutterstock.com

A third major area is the southeast area centered around Gyeongju. Gyeongju was the capital of the Shilla Kingdom and at one time was one of the great cities of the world. UNESCO selected Gyeongju as one of the ten ancient historic cities in the world. The Chumsungdae Observatory, a bottle-shaped stone tower, may have been used for observing the stars. The layout of a series of stones around the base creates an attraction comparable to Stonehenge in England. Gyerim Forest, the remains of Panwolsong Castle, Anapchi Pond (a pleasure resort), and Tumuli Park (site of large royal tombs) are all impressive reminders of the Shilla period. Some of the tombs have been excavated and are open for viewing. At the Punhwangsa Temple, one of only five brick pagodas in Korea still stands. The Gyeongju National Museum houses a treasure of objects from Shilla tombs, including the famous gold crowns, gold girdles, jewelry ceramics, sword hilts, and other artifacts. The countryside is dotted with temples, tombs, and fortresses, each of which is impressive in its own right.

Busan is the second largest city in South Korea. Haeundae Beach with fine sand and beautiful scenery is one of the best beaches around the South Korean coastline. Near Haeundae Beach, camellia and pine trees in Dongbaek Park on Dongbaek Island create a magnificent scene. It attracts over 600,000 tourists every year. At Busan, the United Nations Memorial Cemetery serves as a reminder of the Korean conflict. Today Busan is Korea's principal port, and its warmer southern location extends the season for ocean beach resorts and hot springs in the vicinity.

Throughout the country, there are many natural and cultural attractions that provide a rich potential for travelers. There are spectacular mountain scenery, clean sandy beaches, many natural harbors and waterfalls, distinctive cuisine, and many historical and archaeological sites. Health spas are in abundance and along with winter sports are important to a developing domestic market. One area the government feels has a tremendous potential is Jeju Island, which is an exotic semitropical island known for its female deepsea divers, and Mt. Hallasan, the tallest mountain in South Korea. Its striking scenery, lack of pollution, and warm climate make the island an important potential tourist attraction for Korea.

North Korea (Democratic People's Republic of Korea)

NORTH KOREA

The Democratic People's Republic of Korea, or North Korea, occupies the northern part of the Korean peninsula in East Asia, with mountains covering more than 80 percent of the land. Coastal plains are wide along the west coast but narrow and discontinuous along the east coast. One of the most extensive plains surrounds the capital city, Pyongyang (*pyong* means "flat" and *yang* means "land"). The continental climate brings cold, dry winters and warm, wet summers. Since the early 1990s, an estimated 500,000 to 2 million North Koreans have starved to death. Food shortages and human rights abuses in North Korea have forced thousands of North Koreans to escape to China. It is estimated that 30,000 to 300,000 North Koreans are in hiding in China, blending in with an estimated 1 million Chinese of Korean descent near the border. Refugees are subject to exploitation because, if discovered, they are returned to North Korea. One of the few remaining communist states, reclusive North Korea is one of the world's most secretive societies. The country lost subsidized trade relationships with the fall of the Soviet Union in 1991, causing economic decline. North Korea lags far behind South Korea in economic development, devoting large amounts of money to the military, while its people suffer persistent and chronic food shortages. North Korea maintains one of the world's largest armies, missiles that threaten South Korea and Japan, and a nuclear weapons program.

Area	120,538 sq km (46,540 sq mi)
Population	22,665,000
Government	Communist State, one-man dictatorship
Capital	Pyongyang 3,300,000
Life Expectancy	63 years
Literacy	99%
Religion	Buddhist, Confucianist, some Christian and syncretic Chondogyo
Language	Korean
Currency	North Korean won (KPW)
GDP per Cap	$1,900
Labor Force	37% Agriculture, 63% Industry & Services

Figure 34.6 Pyongyang, North Korea. © Maxim Tupikov/www.Shutterstock.com

 CULTURAL CAPSULE The country's President Kim Jong Il died in 2011 and leadership was placed in the hands of his son Kim Jong Un. It is too early to tell what this change in leadership means for the country's economic development and its future relationship with the rest of the world. Korea was first populated by a Tungusic branch of the Ural-Altaic family, which migrated to the peninsula from the northwestern regions of Asia. The Koreans and Manchurians are physically similar. Koreans are racially and linguistically homogeneous. Korean is a Uralic language remotely related to Japanese, Mongolian, Hungarian, and Finnish. North Korea differs from South Korea in that it does not use a mixed script of Chinese and Korean. Russian, Chinese, and English are taught in the schools. Although religious groups (Buddhism, Shamanism, and Chondogyo) nominally exist in North Korea, the government severely restricts their activity. Chondogyo is an indigenous religion founded in 1860 as an eclectic combination of Buddhist, Confucian, and Christian beliefs. The government allows Christians to meet in small groups under the direction of state-appointed ministers.

Tourism Characteristics

Data are not available concerning North Korea's tourism. Entry is extremely limited and by invitation only. It is estimated that North Korea averages about 150,000 visitors a year. Few visitors are South Koreans or Americans. The major market is Koreans living in Japan. A few Korean-Americans have been allowed to visit their families in North Korea. Few people visit beyond Pyongyang, the capital (Figure 34.6). The major attractions in the city are reconstructed Buddhist temples, which are no longer used as places of worship, and the Grand Theater. North Korea wants to increase its tourist industry and is offering group tours for rock climbing, bird-watching, sunbathing, and lessons in the martial arts. In recent years, special visits from South Korea have been allowed to allow for family reunions.

Taiwan

This mountainous and subtropical island lies off China's southeast coast. Nationalists started ruling Taiwan after losing China to Communist forces in 1949. Taiwan transformed into a high-technology economy and became a multiparty democracy in 1989. However, the People's Republic of China claims Taiwan as a province, and most countries and the UN recognize China's claim.

Area	35,980 sq km (13,892 sq mi)
Population	23,079,000
Capital	Taipei 2,603,000
Religion	Buddhist, Taoist, Christian
Language	Mandarin Chinese, Taiwanese (Min), Hakka dialects

TRAVEL **TIPS** 🧳

Entry: No visa is required for stays up to 90 days. A passport is required.

Tourist Season: Year-round

National Holiday: October 10 (Republic Day)

Health: Drinking water in major hotels is safe, but care should be taken elsewhere to drink bottled or boiled water.

Caution: Do not take photographs inside Buddhist temples without permission.

Shopping: Items include rosewood furniture, textiles, rattan, rare books, classical Chinese musical instruments, and traditional Chinese art and handicrafts.

Internet TLD: .tw

CULTURAL CAPSULE The native Taiwanese (20.5 million) are descendants of Chinese who migrated from the crowded, coastal mainland areas of Fujian and Guangdong provinces in the eighteenth and nineteenth centuries. There are also more than 2 million mainland Chinese who migrated after World War II. About 425,000 aborigines, inhabiting the mountainous central and eastern parts of the island, are believed to be of Malayo-Polynesian origin. The official language is Mandarin Chinese. Most native Taiwanese speak a variant of the Amoy (Hokkien) dialect of southern Fujian. Hakka, another Chinese dialect, is also spoken. Many Taiwanese over age 50 also speak Japanese. English is taught in urban areas as a second or third language.

The predominant religion is a combination of Buddhism and Taoism brought to Taiwan by the original Chinese settlers. The Confucian ethical code is considered by some to be the official religion of Taiwan. There are more than 600,000 Christians, mostly Protestant, in Taiwan.

Cultural hints: A nod and a smile are considered appropriate for first meeting. Remove your shoes before entering a home. Do not put your arm around the shoulder of another. Shaking one hand from side to side with palm forward means no. Present and receive gifts with both hands. Toasting is common before and during dinner. Chopsticks are the normal eating instruments. Hold bowls of food directly under your lower lip and use the chopsticks to push the food into your mouth. Place long, slippery noodles in your mouth and slurp or suck. Don't use your chopsticks for communal dishes of food. Host will place food on your plate, or a separate pair of serving chopsticks will be near the serving dish. Typical foods are rice, soup, seafood, pork, chicken, vegetables, and fruit. Sauces are important, and most foods are stir-fried.

The People's Republic of China claims Taiwan as its 23rd province. Taiwan's government (Republic of China) maintains there are two political entities. The islands of Matsu, Penghu (Pescadores), Dongsha (Pratas), and Kinmen (Quemoy) are administered by Taiwan.

TAIWAN (China)

Tourism Characteristics

The government of Taiwan encourages and promotes tourism as an excellent source of income and a means of displaying Chinese culture. Originally called Formosa (meaning "beautiful") by Portuguese explorers, its first people were Polynesian. However, through time the population became dominated by Chinese influences, creating a distinctive Taiwanese population. Mainland Chinese fleeing the Communist Revolution in 1949 seized the island's government and ruled until 1987, when a Taiwanese native was elected president. Distinctive population groups today include the Taiwanese (84 percent of the population), Chinese (14 percent), aborigines, and sizeable communities from Korea, Vietnam, and Japan.

Taiwan's tourism industry has grown from 2 million visitors per year in the 1990s to 4.3 million in 2010. Relations between the People's Republic of China and Taiwan have improved and direct air service between the two countries was established in 2008 as part of the "Three Links" agreement (postal, transportation, and trade). The dominant political issue, going into the future, will be the nature of the relationship between China and Taiwan, especially Taiwan's eventual status. Today, most countries in the world and the United Nations view Taiwan as an Area of Special Status (as claimed by the PR of China).

Figure 34.7 Taroko Gorge, Taiwan. © Marc Venema/www.Shutterstock.com

A unique feature of Taiwan's tourism trade is the large number of "overseas Chinese" who account for about 17 percent of tourists. These overseas Chinese represent mainlanders who have migrated throughout Asia to major urban centers. The vast majority of the overseas Chinese arrive in Taiwan from Hong Kong. It is difficult to assess the linkages other than ethnic in that many of the overseas Chinese do not state the purpose of their trip. For those that do state the purpose, 33 percent are for business. Taiwan has one of the highest average visitor expenditures in the world. The peak number of visitors occurs in the spring and autumn. This is largely caused by the climate, which is subtropical. There is a rainy season in May and June, and the highest temperatures occur between May and September. The December-to-March period is the coolest time of the year, but the Chinese New Year in February attracts some visitors.

Taiwan has a sizable domestic market. The increasing standard of living has been helpful in the growth of the domestic market. The government has created a network of national parks and resort development areas to facilitate travel. The leading attraction for domestic visitors is the China Lake (just outside Kaohsiung), which is visited by nearly 2.5 million people per year, followed by Yangmingshan (outside Taipei), with 2 million visitors annually, and Shihmen Dam, with 1.7 million visitors.

Tourist Destinations and Attractions

Taiwan has three main tourist areas. North Taiwan, an urban/rural region, contains the capital, Taipei, and has mountain resorts, a wildlife park, and numerous beaches. The main attraction in Taipei is the National Palace Museum, which contains a magnificent collection of Chinese art. Other important attractions in Taipei are Taipei 101 (a landmark skyscraper), the Presidential Mansion, and the Taiwan Jinja Shrine. Lungshan Szu (Dragon Mountain Temple) is the oldest and most famous Buddhist temple in Taipei. The Martyr's Shrine is modeled after Beijing's Forbidden City. The aristocrats' compound in Panchio; the Taoist Chihnan Temple, 1,000 steps up Monkey Hill; and the ten monasteries atop Lions Head Mountain are near Taipei.

Central Taiwan is the second region and is an area of great natural beauty. Taroko Gorge (Figure 34.7), a twelve-mile-long, marble-sided natural feature, is the centerpiece of the region. Skiing and forest recreation are popular in this region. The city Tai-chung, in the center of the Sun Moon lake district, is one of the most scenic areas in the world.

The third region is in South Taiwan. This area around Kaohsiung is the intellectual center, the industrial center, and the main port of the nation. South Taiwan has Kenting National Scenic Area and some good beaches. The aboriginal villages of Taoyuan and Orchid Island are also in the south.

China (The People's Republic of China) and the special administrative regions of Hong Kong and Macau

The People's Republic of China claims Taiwan as its 23rd province. Taiwan's government (Republic of China) maintains there are two political entities.

In both size and population, China dwarfs its neighbors and most other countries. The world's most populous nation and the fourth largest in area (after Russia, Canada, and the United States), China is a large and complex country, but geographers often divide it into three physical regions. Southwestern China encompasses the massive Plateau of Tibet, which covers a quarter of the country; known as the "roof of the world," the plateau towers over the rest of China—averaging 4,260 meters (14,000 feet) in elevation—and its melting snows feed many of Asia's major rivers. Northern China, a mostly arid region, stretches from the desert basins of northwestern China to the end of the Gobi desert in China's northeast. Eastern China, the third region, largely contains low-lying, fertile coastal plains and river valleys.

China's geography contributes to uneven population distribution and economic development. Some 90 percent of China's people, mainly ethnic Han, live on the plains of eastern China, many in megacities. A growing economic disparity exists between urban China and the rural hinterlands, causing millions to migrate to teeming cities from poor farming villages. Economic inequality extends to the large Tibetan and Uygur minorities in western China and contributes to civil unrest. The Communist Party has controlled China since its forces defeated the Nationalists in 1949. The party's decision to allow multinational corporations to use China as an export platform, taking advantage of an almost endless supply of low-cost and hardworking labor, has propelled the nation into a manufacturing giant—with wealth concentrated in the coastal provinces. Coal has fueled the rapid industrialization that began in the 1980s, resulting in major pollution problems. China has one of the world's largest economies, and its economic growth outpaces domestic energy reserves, making it one of the world's top oil importers.

From *National Geographic Atlas of the World*, 9th edition. Copyright ©2011 National Geographic Society. Reprinted by arrangement. All rights reserved.

Area	9,596,961 sq km (3,705,407 sq mi)
Population	1,331,398,000
Government	Communist State

Capital	Beijing 11,106,000
Life Expectancy	73 years
Religion	Taoist, Buddhist, Christian
Language	Standard Chinese or Mandarin, Yue, Wu, Minbei, Minnan, Xiang, Gan, Hakka dialects
Currency	renminbi (RMB); also referred to as the unit yuan (CNY)
GDP per Cap	$6,600
Labor Force	39.5% Agriculture, 27.2% Industry, 33.2% Services

From *National Geographic Atlas of the World*, 9th edition. Copyright ©2011 National Geographic Society. Reprinted by arrangement. All rights reserved.

TRAVEL **TIPS**

Entry: Visas and passports are required.

Peak Tourist Season: June to September

National Holiday: October 1 (Founders Day)

Health: Concern should be taken for malaria and cholera. Outside of the large hotels water is not potable.

Shopping: Common items include Chinese handicrafts, art, historical artifacts, handwoven bags, hats, clothing, carved chess sets, leather coats and bags, and a host of souvenirs at major attractions.

Internet TLD: .cn

 CULTURAL CAPSULE
The largest ethnic group is the Han Chinese, who comprise about 94 percent of the total population. Fifty-five minorities make up 8 percent of the population, of which 15 have a population of more than a million people. They include Zhuangs, Hui, Uygurs, Yi, Mio, Manchus, Tibetans, Mongols, and Koreans. The national language is Putonghua (based on Mandarin). Other principal dialect groups include Cantonese, Shanghainese, Fujianese, and Hakka. Chinese does not have a phonetic alphabet. It uses characters to express words, thoughts, or ideas. A romanized alphabet (pinyin) is used to teach Chinese in school and for international communication.

Cultural hints: A nod or a slight bow is also used as a greeting. Use a person's title and last name when addressing him or her. Business cards are exchanged. They should be printed in both English and Chinese. Spitting and blowing the nose in public is common. Pushing and shoving in stores or boarding public transportation is common. Chopsticks are used. Bones and seeds are placed on the table or in a dish. Refusing food may be impolite. Just poke it and move it to the side of your plate. Toothpicks are common, but cover your mouth when using them. Chinese will hold bowls directly under their lips and push food into their mouths with chopsticks. While dining, guests sit at the left of the host. Typical foods are rice, potatoes, corn meal, tofu, pork, beef, chicken, and fish. Specialties vary from region to region, including duck in Beijing or spicy dishes in Sichuan. Fruits and vegetables are eaten in season. Sauces are mixed with vegetables and meats and eaten with rice.

Tourism Characteristics

One of the most significant features of world tourism has been the opening and development of tourism to China from the West. The first important year for Chinese tourism was 1978. In 1978, the Eleventh Party Central Committee of the Chinese Communist Party decided that tourism was a means to earn much-needed foreign currency. By 2010, China was receiving over $235 billion annually from tourism (4% of total export earnings), compared to just 1 billion on 1985. This growth is remarkable not only in numbers but also because starting in 1978 there was little tourist infrastructure.

When China first began a major tourism program in 1978, it was designed for special interest groups such as doctors, nurses, and teachers. In October of 1982, China simplified admission procedures to allow individuals to visit and increased the number of cities that could be visited. In 1982, there were only 29 cities allowing visitors, although there were 120 cities open to foreign visitors. This was in part due to the lack of trained personnel and adequate facilities (both accommodations and air service) to provide proper service to visitors. Further liberalization occurred in 1986 when the State Council approved a law allowing foreigners to travel to all 274 open cities' areas without a travel permit. Today most of the country is open for visitors with inbound travel services facilitated by the CITS (China International Travel Services).

A tremendous growth has occurred in accommodations, particularly at the major centers of Beijing, Xi'an, Guilin, Shanghai, Hangzhou, and Guangzhou. More areas have been opened and facilities built with the assistance of foreign investment and management skills established to support a more diversified travel industry. Hosting the 2008 Olympic Games was an important catalyst for major improvements to the country's tourism infrastructure. Today there are hundreds of new hotels serving major destination. In addition, the country has opened over 40 new airports. China has updated its fleet of aircraft and opened numerous tourism programs in universities and colleges.

Domestic tourism is relatively new for the Chinese, developing only since the 1980s. By 2010 it was estimated that there were about 2.1 billion domestic tourists visiting such places as the gardens of Suzhou, the Great Wall, Beijing, the West Lake in Hangzhou, Shanghai, and the seaside resorts of Qingdao, Yantai, and Qinhuangdao.

Some 100 million non-mainland visitors to China were from Hong Kong and Macau. The most significant growth in the past five years has been the increased Taiwan market. Since Taiwanese visitors have been included in the compatriot count, data are somewhat limited. In 2010, it was estimated that 4 million visitors were from Taiwan. Direct air service was inaugurated in 2008.

Of those classified as foreign visitors by China, Japan, South Korea, and the United States are the largest markets for China.

The average length of stay is 8.1 days, and for the foreign visitors, seasonal, with April through June and September through November the peak periods.

The most popular regions for foreign groups appear to include Beijing, Xi'an, Shanghai, Guilin, Guangzhou, Lijiang, Chengdu, Pingyao, Mount Huangshan, Suzhou, Wuxi or Hangzhou, and Nanjing.

Tourism Destinations and Attractions

The dominant attraction is the Chinese culture itself, as modified by subsequent experiments with socialism. China is a large country but many of the attractions are clustered, especially in the vicinity of Beijing and Shanghai. The ten major cities in order for tourism are Beijing, Guangzhou, Shanghai, Shenzhen, Guilin, Xi'an, Hangzhou, Nanjing, Suzhou, and Wuxi. Xiamen, a new city situated across the bay from Taiwan, is growing in popularity due to its cosmopolitan beauty and coastal proximity to Taiwan. Visitors who return repeatedly to China note the changes that can take place even over a short period. Beijing, the capital with the Imperial Palace (the Forbidden City) (Figure 34.8) at its center, serves as the anchor for tourism to China. The Imperial Palace covers 250 acres and consists of over 1,000 buildings some with golden roofs, marble balustrades, and the Palace Museum. Tiananmen Square is just south of the Forbidden City and is the center of Beijing. Its name comes from the huge gate (Gate of Heavenly Peace) on its north side that was built in 1412. It is a parade ground and has monuments, such as the tomb of Mao, and museums. On the west side of Tiananmen Square is the Great Hall of the People with the National People's Congress used for conventions and receptions of foreign dignitaries.

Figure 34.8 The Forbidden City, Beijing, China. © ChameleonsEye/www.Shutterstock.com

In front of the Mausoleum of Mao Zedong are the Museum of Chinese History and the Museum of the Chinese Revolution. Northwest of the Forbidden City is Beihai Park, a beautifully landscaped park of artificial hills, pavilions, temples, halls, bridges, and covered walkways. The Beijing Zoo is one of the world's great zoos. The giant pandas are the star attraction at the zoo. The Temple of Heaven (Tian Tan) is a cluster of ceremonial buildings of the fifteenth century. The most impressive is the "Hall of Prayer for Good Harvest" (Zi Nian Dian). It is constructed entirely of wood without nails. Near Beijing is the Summer Palace of pagodas, pavilions, temples, courtyards, and nearby hills, lakes, and terraced gardens. The Summer Palace was the rest-and-recreation area of the royal families. It dates back to 1000 A.D. The grounds include Longevity Hall and Kunming Lake with the famous Marble Boat and the Seventeen Arched Bridge. The Long Corridor here with its Painted Gallery is most impressive.

Also near Beijing is one of the world's great cultural artifacts, the Great Wall, and the extremely interesting Ming Tombs. The Great Wall (Figure 34.9) is 4,000 miles long and parts are 2,600 years old. The thirteen Ming Tombs are equally as impressive, with the famous Sacred Way of Stone Animals guarding the entrance to the area. The tombs lie in a natural amphitheater, and the approach is lined with statues of men and animals. The tomb of the thirteenth emperor, Wan (1773–1620), has been completely excavated and can be visited. It is equal to the tombs of the pharaohs in Egypt.

Shanghai, the largest city and most European in design, also has an old Chinese town, with Yu Yuan Yu (the Mandarin's Garden), the Temple to the Town Gods, and the Garden of the Purple Clouds of Autumn. The Mandarin's Garden was built by the Pan family

Figure 34.9 The Great Wall, Hebei Province, China. © axz700/www.Shutterstock.com

in the sixteenth century. It is noted for its many halls and pavilions, bridges, and towers. The Temple of the Town Gods next to the Mandarin's Garden is one of the few surviving such temples in China. The Garden of the Purple Clouds of Autumn behind the Temple of the Town Gods is known for its ornamental lake and pavilions. The Children's Palace, once the home of a wealthy merchant, is now one of the most famous attractions in China. It is a school for children learning dancing, singing, music, painting, and handicraft. The Shanghai Museum, the Shanghai Art Museum, the Temple of the Jade Buddha, the Carpet Factory, and the Jade Carving Factory are other important attractions in Shanghai. The Bund is the name of Shanghai's waterfront boulevard with its rich architectural history. The Pudang area, across the river, affords great views of Shanghai. Parts of Shanghai are very modern and the new Shanghai Tower is a sign of "things to come" for the rest of the country. The city hosted the World Expo in 2010.

A hundred miles south, a short train ride from Shanghai, is West Lake near Hangzhou (Figure 34.10), China's "Paradise on Earth" and one of the most beautiful places in the country. The lake is extremely beautiful and is controlled by dikes, some of which were built around 820 A.D. Many pavilions and temples have been built around the lake. The Pagoda of Six Harmonies and the Lingyin Monastery are earlier reminders of the region. Buddhist rock carvings can be seen at the Lingyin Temple. The sunsets, sunrises, and misty days are exceptionally beautiful and are used often on pictures of China. A cable car between the temple and north peak provides a view of the lake.

At Suzhou (Heaven on Earth) is Huqiu Hill (Tiger Hill), the burial place of the father of King Wu. The pagoda on the top was built in 961 A.D. Suzhou has more than a dozen Chinese gardens dating from the eleventh century. Each was designed to represent an idealization of the natural world (rocks = mountains, ponds = oceans, shrubs = forests). Some are very small, while others are large multi-acre parks. The West Garden dates back to the Ming Dynasty and contains some 500 arhats that guard the temple.

Nanjing, an ancient capital, has the tomb of China's first president, Dr. Sun Yat-sen, and the tomb of a Ming emperor, which also has a Sacred Way like Beijing. Nanjing is China's university city and it has many tourist sites, attractions, and activities. Around Nanjing, tourists also visit the Yangtze River Bridge and the People's Commune of National Minorities. Wuxi, some 80 miles west of Shanghai, is considered the Venice of China. Lake Taihu and the Grand Canal connect seventy-two islands with beautiful scenes, pavilions, and towers. Suzhou is noted for its silk factories, gardens, and canals. The region is a top tourist destination in China.

Figure 34.10 West Lake, Hangzhou, China. © chungking/www.Shutterstock.com

Some 500 miles southwest of Shanghai, Lushan is a famous summer resort. The best-known attraction is the Fairy Cave or "Cave of the Immortals." The cave is located on a sheer cliff. Near Lushan, Hanpo Pass is the beginning of Poyang Lake, one of China's largest lakes. It is a scenic area, particularly at sunrise. Flower Path Park is one of the most fascinating parks in China. There are miniature trees set in water in porous rock, rock formations, bridges, and so on.

Another region popular with tourists centers around Xi'an. The ancient city of Xi'an is the site of the excavation of Emperor Qin Shi Huang's gigantic buried army of 6,000 life-size terra-cotta soldiers and horses discovered in 1974 (Figure 34.11 a and b). Bronze horses and soldiers were excavated in its vicinity after they were discovered in 1974. The Provincial Museum contains more than 2,000 ancient artifacts, including the oldest collection of stone tables (steles) in China and historical relics and the Gallery of the Stone Sculpture. Also in Xi'an are the Dayan Pagoda, known as the Big Wild Goose Pagoda; the Emperor Qin Shi Huang Mausoleum; the Ban Po Museum, a neolithic village of the Ban Po people who settled the area some 6,000 years ago; and the Bell Tower, which is 119 feet high and constructed of wood and brick.

Another important attraction in the broad region around Xi'an is Luoyang. Luoyang has the impressive Longmen Grottoes dating to 494 A.D. There are some 1,300 grottoes and 40 pagodas containing at least 100,000 Buddhas, the largest of which is 56 feet tall. In the Working People's Park, there are two Han tombs dating back to 206 B.C. Lushan is a famous summer resort for the Chinese.

Two of the most scenic cities are Guilin and Kunming. Guilin is a popular attraction for international visitors who enjoy hiking and backpacking. With its unique karst topography and river cruises on the Li River, Guilin is a delight to the visitor. The karst mountains are best viewed from Yangshuo. There are sensational views of mist-covered hills and valleys, rock formations, rapids, and bamboo groves. Ludiyan (Reed Flute Cave) has a number of beautiful formations and colors and has a large grotto (Crystal Cave) that can hold 1,000 people. Kunming's most unique attraction is the Stone Forest, which was formed when limestone rose from the receding seawater. In Xishan Park, there are a number of ancient temples set on the shore of Kunming Lake. The atmosphere includes an interesting market, ruined pagodas, the Yuantong Temple, stores selling tribal handicrafts, and traditional Chinese teahouses. Nearby is the Stone Forest of Lunan, which consists of incredible, uniquely shaped rock formations created by erosion. Chengdu is a lovely city and a transportation gateway to Tibet. A Breeding Research Center for the giant pandas has been established in Chengdu.

Figure 34.11a Terra-cotta soldiers and horses, Xi'an, China.
© AJancso /www.Shutterstock.com

Figure 34.11b Close-up of terra-cotta soldiers.
© Jarno Gonzalez Zarraonandia/www.Shutterstock.com

Far to the west on the Silk Road is Urumqi, the capital of the Xinjiang Uygur Autonomous Region, which provides visitors with an excellent view of western China. It has an outstanding museum of ancient artifacts dating to the Stone Age. The Lake of Heaven and the Carpet Factory are other important attractions in this remote city. Visits to Xizang (Tibet), under Chinese control, center in Lhasa. The Potala Palace (Figure 34.12), now a Chinese Museum, on the slopes of the Red Hill in the Old City originally served as the Winter Palace of the individual Dalai Lama who was ruling the country at a specific time. Norbu Lingka, the Dalai Lama's Summer Palace, is located 62 miles west of the Potala Palace. The Jokhang Temple, with its golden tiles on the roof, was built in the seventh century A.D. Other attractions are the Drepung Monastery, constructed in 1416, and the Ganden Temple, which is one of the three major temples of the Ghelu Section of Tibetan Buddhism in Lhasa.

Many visitors entering China arrive from Hong Kong at Guangzhou (formerly Canton), considered the southern gateway to China. The city is a commercial center and its annual Trade Fair attracts thousands from all over the world. Attractions in Guangzhou include the Memorial Garden to the Martyrs (sometimes called the Red Flower Garden), which has a pure white stone tomb; the mausoleum of the seventy-two martyrs; the Zhenhai tower, which was built about 1480 and contains both a museum and an observation tower of the famous Pearl River; and the Dr. Sun Yat-Sen Memorial Hall. The Ancestral Temple of Foshan, an ancient Taoist temple, is near Guangzhou. The old European section has colonial architecture

from the nineteenth century. The Qingping Free Market is an experience. Among the stalls visitors will find snakes being skinned alive, freshly slaughtered cuts of meat, and all kinds of live animals such as monkeys, cats, large wild birds, and so on. The city of Shenzhen, designated as a Special Economic Zone, is situated adjacent to Hong Kong. It grew from 20,000 inhabitants in 1970 to over 8 million in 2010. Datong on the Mongolian border and Hohot in Mongolia are the major attractions in the Mongolian region. Datong contains the world-famous ancient Yungang grottoes. These cave temples, some of which reach heights of 60 feet, were carved in the period from 386 to 534 A.D. The Nine Dragon Screen, which is 147 feet long and 6 feet high, is colorful and impressive. Hohot provides a good view of the famous Mongolian grasslands and offers the experience of staying in a typical Mongolian Yurt (felt hut).

The Three Gorges on the Yangtze River can be viewed by visitors from cruise ships, but the Chinese have built a dam on the river that submerged many spectacular attractions. In the western Sichuan tourist district around Chengdu is the world's largest Buddhist statue. It is carved on Mount Leshan and surrounded by a region of unusual scenic beauty. In the tourist district of central Shandong Province is Confucius' hometown in Qufu, Mount Tai and Jinan City. The large palace-like Confucian temple, estate, and tomb are in Qufu. Near Qufu, Mount Tai is an imposing mountain with ancient architecture and cultural relics.

China's attractions are as many and diverse as the size of the country itself. From the deserts and

Figure 34.12 Potala Palace, Lhasa, Tibet. © huafeng207/www.Shutterstock.com

grasslands of the north and the high mountain region of Xizang (Tibet) to the hot, humid south, scenic beauty, ancient wonders, and modern ways are inviting to tourists. With the further development of the industry, greater access to more places, and prices becoming competitive with other tourist destinations, China is earning a reputation as one of the great tourist destinations in the world.

Hong Kong

After more than 150 years of British rule, Hong Kong became a special administrative region of China in 1997. It is governed under the principle of "one country, two systems," and maintains a high degree of autonomy economically, with its own currency and customs status.

Area	1,104 sq km (426 sq mi)
Government	Hong Kong Special Administrative Region
Population	7,037,000
Capital	NA
Religion	local religions, Christian
Language	Chinese Cantonese, other Chinese dialects, English

TRAVEL**TIPS** 🧳

Entry: Visas and passports are required.

Peak Tourist Season: Year-round

National Holiday: October 1 and July 1

Shopping: Hong Kong is a shopper's paradise. Items include rosewood furniture, textiles, rattan, rare books, classical Chinese musical instruments, and traditional Chinese art and handicrafts.

Internet TLD: .hk

CULTURAL CAPSULE

Hong Kong is ethnically homogeneous with nearly 98 percent being ethnic Chinese and 2 percent mostly European. Cantonese is the official Chinese dialect, and English is widely understood and also official. The religious characteristic is one of diversity. Strong elements of Taoism and Confucianism with folk religion practices are widespread. Ancestorial worship is important. Many homes contain brightly decorated boxes with pictures of deceased relatives, smoking incense sticks, or symbolic offerings of fruit to venerate ancestors. About 10 percent of the population is Christian.

Cultural hints: The Chinese are reserved and modest when dealing with others. Aggressive behavior is offensive. To beckon someone, hold the palm down and wave your fingers. Never use the index finger to beckon. Toasting is common. Chopsticks and knives and forks are used. Service is generally included in the bill, but it's still customary to leave a tip. Do not eat on the street. Typical foods are rice, fish, pork, chicken, and vegetables.

Tourism Characteristics

Hong Kong is a unique state, a special administrative region of China occupying the northeast side of the broad estuary of the Xi (Hsun) River. On July 1, 1997, the United Kingdom relinquished its claim to the territory, handing it back to China. China has pledged to keep Hong Kong's situation practically the same as under British rule, including tourism.

Hong Kong is one of the most densely populated areas in the world. The majority of the population is concentrated on the island of Hong Kong itself, which is only 32 square miles in area. Geographically it is part of China, and even the population is 98 percent Chinese. Economically, it lacks natural resources and relies on China for food and water.

Hong Kong provided China access to the West during the life of Mao, when the government nominally refused relations with the industrial world. Contacts with Western firms were handled through the firms of Hong Kong Chinese, enabling China to gain needed technology. Since the change in view of the Chinese government after Mao's death, China does not rely on Hong Kong as much, but the colony still provides an important arena for trading with the West. Hong Kong's own industrial productivity provides important technology for China and makes it one of the rapidly industrializing countries of the world. The continued importance of Hong Kong to mainland China as a supplier of manufactured goods and technology, as well as the potential for China to show Taiwan that former territories can rejoin China and still have local autonomy, suggests that China will fulfill its promises concerning the status of Hong Kong.

The government's Hong Kong Tourist Association is charged with the task of promoting, monitoring, and stimulating tourism. It has had a long history as a tourist center because of its nature and relationship with mainland China. Tourism is the third largest earner of foreign exchange for Hong Kong after garments and electronics. Arrivals jumped from 11.3 million in 1999 to 17 million in 2010. Hong Kong has benefited from the increasing tourism to China as many of its visitors also went to China. The future of the tourism industry in Hong Kong depends upon its future as determined by China. However, as more direct connections are established between the industrialized countries of the world and China, Hong Kong's importance as a gateway into China may decline.

In terms of origin of visitors, China, Taiwan, and Japan are the largest sources. Taiwan can be accounted for by increased travel to China by the Taiwanese and a liberalization of travel restrictions by the Taiwan government. The United States and major European Markets account for over 15 percent of visitors. The main purpose given for visiting Hong Kong is pleasure, but the role of the city as a financial center can be seen in the fact that in 2010 about 40 percent of visitors came for business reasons. The average length of stay is short, suggesting that it is a transit area combined with a large tour package or visit. The Hong Kong Visitors Bureau has adopted a major slogan, "Stay an extra day," in an attempt to convince tour operators to increase the stay in Hong Kong.

Tourist Destinations and Attractions

Hong Kong's attractions are shopping and the scenery, including the skyline from the top of the Peak reached by a tram ride (the Peak Tram). Hong Kong is synonymous with shopping. Merchants in Kowloon (across the bay from Hong Kong) and in Hong Kong present a variety of goods from the latest electronics and cameras to fine watches and jewelry. Ocean Park, an oceanarium and fun park; Sung Dynasty Village, a model Chinese cultural village; and Hong Kong Disneyland add to its shopping attraction. Tiger Balm Gardens are a complex of statuary and tableaux, depicting tales from Chinese mythology. The harbor (Figure 34.13) offers fishing, restaurants, and an outstanding view of the skyline. Stanley, at the southern tip of Hong Kong Island (reached by the famous Star Ferry), has a popular outdoor market. Cultural attractions in the city include the Hong Kong Museum of Art, the Art Museum of the Chinese University of Hong Kong, and the Hong Kong Science Museum.

Figure 34.13 Traditional wooden sailboat in Victoria Harbor, Hong Kong. © chungking/www.Shutterstock.com

Macau

Introduction

Portuguese fishermen settled in Macau in the sixteenth century, and it was ruled by Portugal, until 1999 when it became part of China. The Macau Special Administrative Region's economy is based on tourism and gambling.

Area	28 sq km (11 sq mi)
Population	555,000
Capital	NA
Religion	Buddhist, Roman Catholic
Language	Chinese (Cantonese, other dialects), Portuguese English

 TRAVEL**TIPS**

Internet LTD: .mo

Tourism Characteristics

Macau was a Portuguese territory until its return to China in December of 1999. U.S. passport holders (and those from most of the other major Western tourist markets) no longer need visas to stay up to twenty days.

Macau is located on the southern coast of China at the mouth of the Pearl River. Macau consists of the municipality of Macau, situated on a narrow peninsula, and Taipa and Coloane, two islands to the south. About 99 percent of Macau's population is Chinese, primarily Cantonese and some Hakka. The official language is Portuguese, although Chinese (Cantonese) is spoken extensively.

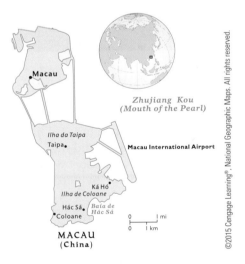

Figure 34.14 Casino Lisboa, Macau. © SeanPavonePhoto/www.Shutterstock.com

Macau, the oldest European settlement in the Far East used to be quiet and somewhat laid back. Today, it has a reputation for gambling and nightlife (Figure 34.14). Most visitors stay a very short while (1.5 days) and are usually on excursion by ferry from Hong Kong. Tourism and gambling account for 25 percent of its Gross Domestic National Product (GDNP). Since Macau was a Portuguese colony, many shows feature Portuguese folk dancing and Fado singing in addition to the Chinese shows.

Mongolia

Located in East Asia, Mongolia is a large landlocked country between two larger countries—Russia and China (Figure 34.15). Founded on mountains and plateaus, it is one of the world's highest nations, with an average elevation of 1,580 meters (5,180 feet). Mongolia undergoes temperature extremes, and the sands of the Gobi desert extend over southern Mongolia.

Figure 34.15 Horses grazing at Plateau Ukok, the junction of Russian, Mongolian and Chinese borders.

Genghis Khan's Mongol horsemen conquered much of Asia and Europe during the thirteenth century. Mongolia became a communist country in 1924, but in 1990 multiparty elections were held. In 1991, Mongolia started its transition from a communist-controlled to market-oriented economy. The proportion of the economy in private hands has risen from 4 percent to more than 70 percent. The economy is based on agriculture, and more than a third of the people are nomadic herders. Poverty is high, and international development assistance contributes to progress. Mining (primarily gold and copper) and tourism help grow Mongolia's economy.

Area	1,564,116 sq km (603,909 sq mi)
Population	2,708,000
Government	Parliamentary
Capital	Ulaanbaatar 885,000
Life Expectancy	65 years
Religion	Buddhist Lamaist, Shamanist, Christian, Muslim
Language	Khalkha Mongol, Kazakh, Russian
Currency	togrog/tugrik (MNT)
GDP per Cap	$3,200
Labor Force	34% Agriculture, 5% Industry, 61% Services

TRAVEL**TIPS** 💼

Entry: A visa and passport are required.

Tourist Season: June through August

National Holiday: July 11 (Independence Day)

Internet TLD: .mn

CULTURAL CAPSULE Over 90 percent of the people are comprised of subgroups of the Mongol nationality. The largest is the Khalkha (79 percent). Other Mongols are Buryads, Dorwods, Oolds, Bayads, Dzakhchin, Uriyankhais, Uzemchins, and Bargas. The largest non-Mongol ethnic group is the Kazakhs, about 6 percent of the population. The Mongols are pastoral nomads. Mongols have practiced a combination of Tibetan Buddhism and Shamanism. The Dalai Lama of Tibet is the religion's spiritual leader. The people practice ritualistic magic, nature worship, exorcism, meditation, and natural healing as part of their shamanistic heritage. While many monasteries were closed under communist rule, many have reopened; and Muslims are allowed to practice Islam.

Cultural hints: People are called by their given names. Use the right hand for making gestures. Passing items with the left hand is impolite. Tea and milk are common. Guests give the hosts a small gift. Typical foods are dairy products, meat (mutton or beef), barley, and wheat. Rice is common in urban areas.

Tourist Characteristics and Tourism Destinations

The tourism industry is small, and there is little data available pertaining to Mongolia. The major destinations and attractions are the dinosaur graveyard in the Great Gobi Reserve, the ancient city of Karakorum, the medieval Erdene-Dzuu monastery, and the summer palaces of the last living Buddha. Russia and China are currently the major sources for visitors to Mongolia, although there are increasing numbers of Westerners and non-Chinese visitors (especially Japanese and Koreans).

REVIEW QUESTIONS

1. Outbound travel from Japan declined after 2008. Why?

2. What factors explain the rapid growth in tourism to China?

3. What are Hong Kong's primary attractions?

4. What are the three major classifications of tourists to China?

5. Compare and contrast two of the major tourist regions of Japan.

6. Discuss the economic characteristics of the various nations of East Asia.

7. What are the major attractions of Taiwan?

8. What are the major markets for Taiwan's tourism industry?

9. As China increases its standard of living and starts generating more international visitors to the rest of the world, what countries do you think would be major destinations for Chinese tourists? How should they prepare?

10. Why has Hong Kong's importance as a gateway to China declined?

chapter 35: SOUTH ASIA

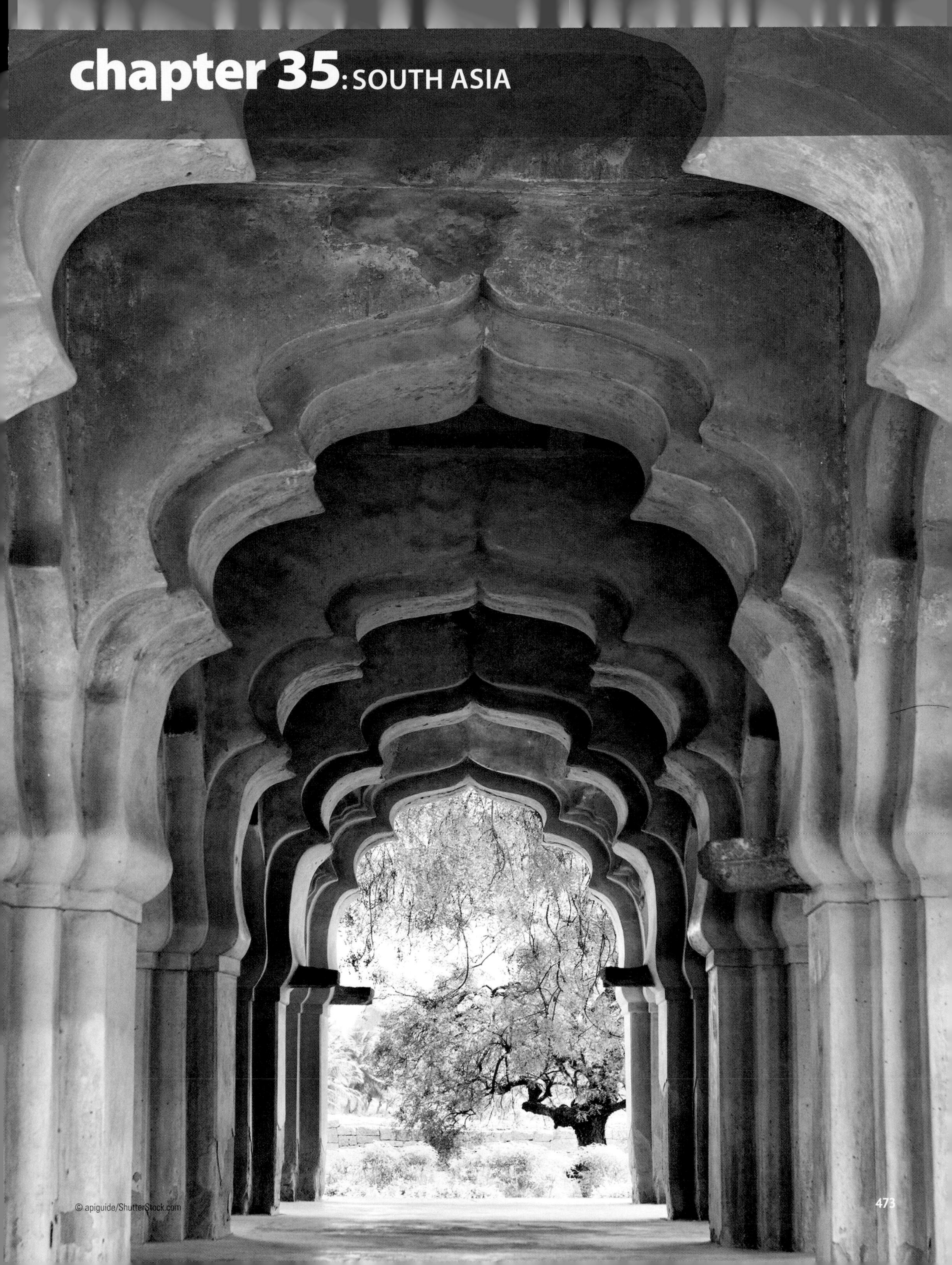

Bangladesh

River deltas form most of Bangladesh, the largest delta system in the world. Some 700 rivers flow through the country, including the Ganges. This great deltaic plain is quite fertile, supporting high-density farming. However, 80 percent of the country consists of flood plains, and floods frequently destroy homes and crops. The tropical climate is governed by the monsoon winds, which from June to September bring heavy rainfall of up to 5 meters (200 inches). While monsoon floods are destructive, the water also enriches the soil and builds new land. Despite a difficult environment, Bangladesh has moved forward since its independence from Pakistan in 1971. Farming employs millions of Bangladeshis, with rice as a primary crop, but expansion of irrigation and flood control networks has increased food production and caused crop diversification. New jobs, mostly for women, have been created in the garment industry, with clothing now being a major export. Bangladesh also has benefited from foreign aid donors, such as the World Bank, and remittances from workers overseas. Economic progress has helped the poverty rate fall from 57 percent of the population in 1990 to less than 37 percent in 2010.

From *National Geographic Atlas of the World,* 9th edition. Copyright ©2011 National Geographic Society. Reprinted by arrangement. All rights reserved.

Area	143,998 sq km (55,598 sq mi)
Population	162,221,000
Government	Parliamentary Democracy
Capital	Dhaka 13,485,000
Life Expectancy	65 years
Literacy	48%
Religion	Muslim, Hindu
Language	Bangla (Bengali), English
Currency	taka (BDT)
GDP per Cap	$1,600
Labor Force	45% Agriculture, 30% Industry, 25% Services

From *National Geographic Atlas of the World,* 9th edition. Copyright ©2011 National Geographic Society. Reprinted by arrangement. All rights reserved.

TRAVEL TIPS 🧳

Entry: A visa and passport are required.

Peak Tourist Season: December through February

National Holiday: March 26 (Independence Day)

Health: Malaria, cholera, typhoid, hepatitis, and yellow fever are concerns for protection. Do not drink water other than bottled or boiled. Do not eat food from street vendors. If you cannot peel it or it is not cooked, do not eat it.

Shopping: Items include pottery, products of papier-mâché, textiles, carpets, leather goods, brass, wood carvings, and gold and silver filigree jewelry.

Internet TLD: .bd

CULTURAL CAPSULE Bangladesh is the most densely populated agricultural country in the world. The population of Bangladesh is about 98 percent ethnic Bengali and speak Bangla. They are of an Indo-European heritage, with some Arab, Persian, and Turkish influence. There are some Urdu-speaking non-Bengali Muslims of Indian origin (Assamese). They are often referred to as "Biharis" or stranded Pakistanis. There are also various tribal groups, mostly in the Chittagong Hill Tract. Most Bangladeshis (85 percent) are Muslims, and Hindus are the largest minority (14 percent). There are a small number of Buddhists, Christians, and Animists. English is understood and spoken in the urban areas and among the educated. Small groups along the southeast border speak their own language.

Cultural hints: Women do not wear pants and men do not wear shorts. Remove shoes before entering a mosque. Do not take pictures without asking permission. Never use the left hand to eat. Men and women often dine separately. Do not transfer food from one person to another. It is acceptable to eat with your fingers. Do not pass objects with your left hand. Bones and food wastes are placed on bone plates. Typical food is rice, fish, carrots, cucumbers, and tomatoes. Food is spicy (cumin, ginger, coriander, tumeric, and pepper) and often marinated.

Tourism Characteristics

Bangladesh receives most of its visitors from Asia and the Pacific. Of the 500,000 visitors to the country in 2011, more than 30 percent came from India, with the rest of the Asian and Pacific countries accounting for an additional 30 percent of the visitors. Of countries outside of the Asian and Pacific realm, the United Kingdom contributes the most visitors, due to the colonial ties and linkages, which took a number of citizens of Bangladesh to the United Kingdom.

Bangladesh is presently not an important world destination country. With only two major cities, it lacks both an infrastructure (roads, airports, sewage systems) and suprastructure (hotels, restaurants, entertainment). Most international visitors from the industrialized nations of the world are there for business or, as suggested, if from the United Kingdom, to visit friends and family.

Tourist Destinations and Attractions

Dhaka, the capital, and Chittagong, the major port city, have mosques, markets (Figure 35.1), and crowded, active street scenes. In Dhaka, a huge fort (the Lal Bagh Fort) and the tomb of Pari Bibi (a daughter of one of the moguls) are attractions. Near Chittagong, there is an excellent seaside resort (Cox's Bazaar), with beaches stretching 70 miles on the Bay of Bengal. On the Karnaphuli River around Rangamati, the local tribes build their bamboo houses in the jungle high on stilts. Bangladesh has a few archaeological sites and the Dhaka Museum of Antiquities, which displays relics of the early civilizations of the region.

Figure 35.1 Market, Dhaka, Bangladesh.
© Jorg Hackemann/www.Shutterstock.com.

Bhutan

A thunder dragon symbolizes Bhutan on its flag; and in the native language, Dzongkha, *bhutan* means "thunder"—a roar of dragons. Often thunder comes from the violent monsoon storms and gale-force winds in the eastern Himalaya. In 2008, this South Asian Buddhist kingdom underwent a peaceful transition from absolute monarchy to constitutional monarchy. The economy depends on agriculture, although tourism and exports of hydroelectric power to India are growing in importance. Tourists come for the pristine mountain valleys, ancient *dzongs* (fortresses), and monasteries.

Area	46,500 sq km (17,954 sq mi)
Population	683,000
Government	Constitutional Monarchy
Capital	Thimphu 83,000
Life Expectancy	68 years

Literacy	47%
Religion	Lamaistic Buddhist, Indian- and Nepali-influenced Hindu
Language	Dzongkha, Tibetan dialects, Nepalese dialects
Currency	ngultrum (BTN); Indian rupee (INR)
GDP per Cap	$5,400
Labor Force	63% Agriculture, 6% Industry, 31% Services

Figure 35.2 Taktshang Monastery (Tiger's Nest), Bhutan. © Hung Chung Chih/www.Shutterstock.com.

TRAVEL **TIPS**

Entry: Tourists are admitted only in groups prearranged with Bhutan's **Ministry of Tourism.** A visa and passport are required.

Peak Tourist Season: December through March

National Holiday: December 17 (National Day)

Health: Cholera, yellow fever, tetanus, typhoid, poliomyelitis, and hepatitis immunizations are recommended. Special food-handling methods and water purification are essential.

Internet TLD: .bt

CULTURAL CAPSULE The people of Bhutan are divided into three ethnic groups—Sharchops, Ngalops, and Nepali. Sharchops, the earliest major group, live in eastern Bhutan and appear to be closely related to the inhabitants of northeast India. The Ngalops are considered to be of Tibetan origin, arriving in Bhutan in the eighth century A.D. and bringing with them the culture and Buddhist religion that are dominant in the northern two-thirds of Bhutan. The Nepalis, most of whom are Hindus, arrived in the late nineteenth and early twentieth centuries. They farm Bhutan's southern foothill region. The official language of Bhutan, Dzongkha, is related to classical Tibetan and is written partly in a classical Tibetan script. Nepali predominates in southern Bhutan. English is the official working language and is taught in schools. It is widely used. More than 90 percent of the people are employed in subsistence farming and animal husbandry. Terrace agriculture is extensive, with rice paddies as high as 8,000 feet.

Tourism Characteristics and Tourist Destinations

Bhutan has little tourism. Until recently, the few visitors allowed were official or business visitors. While it now encourages tourism, tourists continue to be very limited with only 60,000 visitors in 2012. Yet this number represents a doubling in just three years since 2009. Bhutan has a very small private tourism sector, as tourism is organized directly by the government. It has little access and remains largely a mystery to the rest of the world.

Bhutan's main tourism attractions are the breathtaking Himalayan scenery and the country's culture. The Bhutan countryside has numerous monasteries (Figure 35.2), and the monks are a distinctive part of the culture. Punakha, the former capital, is the religious center of the country and beautiful **temples** and interesting fortresses are located in Paro, a city set in a scenic valley dominated by Mount Chomolhari. The Skimtokha Dzong in Thimbu is located on a high mountain perch. The Manas game sanctuary, with the rare golden langur monkeys, could become an important attraction if more visitors were allowed.

Burma (formerly Myanmar)

Myanmar is once again known as Burma. In 1989 the largest nation of mainland Southeast Asia changed its name from Burma to Myanmar and that of its capital from Rangoon to Yangon—the name changes were made by an unelected military regime, and many continue to use the old names. Geographically, the country's Irrawaddy basin is surrounded on three sides by densely forested mountains and plateaus. Most people live in the fertile valley and delta of the Irrawaddy River.

The majority of Burma's people are ethnic Burmans (69 percent); other ethnic groups include Shan (8.5 percent), Karen (6.2 percent), Rakhine (4.5 percent), Mon (2.4 percent), Chin (2.2 percent), and Kachin (1.4 percent). Ethnic minorities are dominant in border and mountainous areas: Shan in the north and east (bordering India and Thailand), Karen in the southeast (frontier with Thailand), and Kachin in the far north (bordering China). The military regime has brutally suppressed ethnic minorities, sending thousands of refugees to neighboring countries. Many ethnic insurgencies operate against the military.

Independence from Britain in 1948 was followed by isolationism and socialism. Military governments have ruled Burma since 1962 and have been accused of corruption and human rights violations—including forcible relocation of civilians and use of forced labor. In 1990 national elections were held for parliament, but the military refused to recognize the results. Today, democracy is slowly gaining a foothold in the country and freedom of the press is increasingly "tolerated."

From *National Geographic Atlas of the World*, 9th edition. Copyright ©2011 National Geographic Society. Reprinted by arrangement. All rights reserved.

Location	Southeastern Asia
Area	676,578 sq km (261,228 sq mi)
Population	50,020,000
Government	Military Junta
Capital	Nay Pyi Taw (administrative) 930,000; Yangon (Rangoon) (legislative) 4,088,000
Life Expectancy	61 years
Religion	Buddhist, Christian, Muslim
Language	Burmese, ethnic languages
Currency	kyat (MMK)
GDP per Cap	$1,100
Labor Force	70% Agriculture, 7% Industry, 23% Services

From *National Geographic Atlas of the World*, 9th edition. Copyright ©2011 National Geographic Society. Reprinted by arrangement. All rights reserved.

TRAVEL TIPS

Entry: A visa and passport are required.

Peak Tourist Season: November through January

National Holiday: January 4 (Independence Day)

Health: Inoculation for yellow fever, cholera, tuberculosis, typhoid, and malaria are needed. The plague and leprosy are endemic to the country. Boil all drinking water and eat only well-cooked meat and vegetables.

Shopping: Common items include local jade and other gemstones and native handicrafts.

Internet TLD: .mm

CULTURAL CAPSULE The dominant ethnic group of the country is Burmans (25 million). More than 2 million Karens live throughout southern and eastern Burma. The Shans, ethnically related to the Thai, number some 2 million and live mainly in the eastern plateau region. Other major indigenous groups are the Rakhins in the west, Chins in the northwest, and Kachins in the north. There are large groups of ethnic Chinese, Indians, and Bangladeshi living in the country. Theravada Buddhism, an older form of Buddhism, is the major religion (85 percent). Other religions include Islam, Christianity, and traditional practices.

Burma's ethnic groups speak numerous languages and subsidiary dialects. Burmese is related to Tibetan and spoken by most of the people. English is a second language and spoken among the educated and official people.

Tourism Characteristics and Tourist Destinations

In most geographies, Burma is considered a nation of South Asia. However, the World Travel Organization lists it as part of Southeast Asia. A new constitution was adopted in 2011 with election held in 2012. Aung San Suu Kyi, who had been placed under house

The once isolated nation at the culturally rich crossroads of India and China is a land that imbues even the most jaded traveler with a sense of wonder.

In Myanmar, government reforms since 2010 and the election of democracy activist (and Nobel Peace Prize recipient) Aung San Suu Kyi to parliament have propelled a profoundly gracious land, formerly known as Burma, onto the world stage. It's about time.

Decades of reclusion have preserved a vibrant culture deeply steeped in Buddhism; especially outside the major urban centers of Yangon and Mandalay, daily life has remained largely untouched by Western trends. Rudyard Kipling's words in *Letters From the East* still ring true: "This is Burma and it will be quite unlike any land you know about."

The best Burmese travel experiences require a bit of planning, but the rewards are great—especially in Bagan, the arid, pagoda-studded plain along the Ayeyarwady River in Upper Burma where the first Burmese Buddhist kings, their courtiers, and other merit-seeking patrons built thousands of religious monuments from the eleventh to thirteenth centuries (Figure 35.3). According to Burma scholar Donald Stadtner, these 16 square miles —despite the misguided restoration of some temples in the 1990s—rank among Southeast Asia's most significant sacred ancient sites.

Secure an early morning bird's-eye view of the monuments by booking a Balloons Over Bagan hot-air-balloon-and-sparkling-wine trip; profits fund community service projects on the ground. Spend the afternoon exploring dusty trails by bicycle. At sunset, find a perch and gaze over the panorama of castle-like structures shimmering in the golden light.

— **Ceil Miller Bouchet,** *National Geographic Traveler*, December 2012/January 2013

Figure 35.3 Ancient temples and pagodas in Bagan, Burma. © Chantal de Bruijne/www.Shutterstock.com.

arrest just a few years earlier, was elected president of the country. Conditions suggest that the country is still a long way from having an open democratic system. It has little tourism and for a number of years was closed to most of the world's tourist market countries. Tourism is still very limited and will remain small compared with other countries in the region. The dry season from November to February is the best time to visit. Few cities outside of Yangon have accommodations for travelers. Yangon, the capital, has been influenced by the British and has old colonial public buildings and wide streets. It has parks, gardens, lakes, and colorful **pagodas**, of which the magnificent Shwedagon Pagoda is the focal point. The Shwedagon Pagoda historically served as the center of the religious and cultural life.

A number of smaller shrines and temples, each with images of **Buddha**, surround the pagoda. Passageways and bazaars selling Burmese handicrafts, flowers, and incense are located around the pagoda.

Mandalay, in the northern part of the country, was the former capital and remains the cultural center of Burma. Like other Asian towns, its marketplace, bazaars, monasteries, and golden pagodas are the major attractions. Near Mandalay, Maymyo, which was the summer capital under the British, is now a popular resort for the Burmese people. Pagan, the ancient capital, has extensive ruins of more than 5,000 pagodas. The government is in the process of restoring some thirty of the most impressive temples. Moulmein, across the Gulf of Martaban, has been called the most beautiful town in Burma.

India

The South Asian country of India is a land of great contrasts in geography. The barren, snowcapped Himalaya, the world's tallest mountain system, rises along its northern border. South of the Himalaya, the low, fertile Ganges Plain is India's most populous region. Farther south, the dry Deccan Plateau stretches to the southern tip of the peninsula. The Thar Desert (also known as the Great Indian Desert) (Figure 35.4) consumes the western frontier with Pakistan, but eastern India receives some of the highest rainfall in the world during the monsoon season (June to October).

India is second only to China in population—but India is growing faster (some 18 million a year) and may surpass China by 2030. Indian society is highly diverse. Hindi and English serve as official languages, but the government recognizes twenty other languages that are used in various parts of the country. Although 81 percent of Indians are Hindu, India also has 161 million Muslims—one of the world's largest Muslim populations. Christians number some 25 million. Hindu culture evolved out of the mingling of indigenous Dravidian peoples and Aryan-speaking nomads who arrived from Central Asia in 1500 B.C. Islam spread across the subcontinent starting in the eighth century A.D. From the seventeenth century to the mid-twentieth century, India was part of the British Empire. Guided by Mahatma Gandhi, Indians won nationhood in 1947. From British rule India inherited parliamentary government, the English language, and a dense rail system, which helped knit the multiethnic country into a secular democracy—often called "the world's largest democracy."

Decades of sustained economic growth have reduced poverty, created a burgeoning middle class, and produced a diversified economy with industries like pharmaceuticals, information technology, and entertainment. Mumbai (Bombay) is India's largest city and is

home to "Bollywood"—India's film industry. Bangalore is India's Silicon Valley.

From *National Geographic Atlas of the World*, 9th edition. Copyright ©2011 National Geographic Society. Reprinted by arrangement. All rights reserved.

Area	3,287,263 sq km (1,269,219 sq mi)
Population	1,171,029,000
Government	Federal Republic
Capital	New Delhi 15,926,000
Life Expectancy	64 years
Literacy	61%
Religion	Hindu, Muslim, Christian, Sikh
Language	Hindi, English, 20 other official languages, Hindustani (popular Hindi/Urdu variant in the north)
Currency	Indian rupee (INR)
GDP per Cap	$3,100
Labor Force	52% Agriculture, 14% Industry, 34% Services

From *National Geographic Atlas of the World*, 9th edition. Copyright ©2011 National Geographic Society. Reprinted by arrangement. All rights reserved.

Figure 35.4 Women going for water in the Thar Desert near Jaisamler, India. © Rafal Cichawa/www.Shutterstock.com.

TRAVEL **TIPS**

Entry: Visas and passports are required.

Peak Tourist Season: November and December

National Holiday: January 26 (Republic Day)

Health: Typhoid, tetanus, hepatitis, diphtheria, cholera, and malaria shots are recommended. Water is unsafe. Drink bottled or carbonated water.

Shopping: Common items include handicraft goods, exquisite jewelry in gold and silver, Kashmir carpets, wood and ivory carvings, silks, fur, leather hides, saris, marble tabletops, and intricately inlaid items.

Internet TLD: .in

CULTURAL CAPSULE

India is a nation of villages. About 80 percent of the population live in the more than 550,000 villages throughout the country. Northern India has been invaded from the Iranian plateau, Central Asia, Arabia, and Afghanistan throughout its ancient and pre-modern history. The blood and culture of these invaders have mixed freely with those of the indigenous people to create the current character. Today Indo-Aryans make up 72 percent and the Dravidians account for 25 percent of the population. The remaining 3 percent is made up of a number of other groups, including Mongoloids. Religion, caste, and language are major determinants of social and political organization. More than 1,600 languages are spoken in India, with twenty-four having more than a million users each. Sixteen are officially recognized languages, and English is an unofficial lingua franca. Hindi is the most widely used, with 30 percent of the people speaking it. English is particularly common in business and government. Although 83 percent of the people are Hindu, India also has approximately 125 million Muslims, giving it one of the world's largest Muslim populations. India also includes Christians, Jews, Sikhs, Jains, Buddhists, and Parsis. The Sikhs are recognizable because of their distinctive dress (including turbans for men). Extremely nationalistic, they are trying to create a Sikh state in Punjab. The caste system, comprising the traditional social categories of Indian society, has been historically based on occupation-related categories ranked in a theoretically defined hierarchy. Four castes were identified plus a category of outcasts (untouchables). However, there are thousands of subcastes. Despite laws against discrimination against lower castes and lower-end untouchables, the system remains an important factor in India.

Cultural hints: Traditional greeting is palms pressed together, fingers up below the chin and a slight bow. The term "namaste" is a common greeting and goodbye. Ask permission to take pictures. Women should cover their heads when entering a sacred building. To grasp one's earlobes is to express remorse or honesty. To point, use

Figure 35.5 Indian sacred cow in front of a house, Madhya Pradesh, India. © Aleksandar Todorovic/www.Shutterstock.com.

the chin, full hand, or thumb but not a single finger. Remove shoes before entering a temple or mosque. Beckoning a waiter is done by a snap of fingers and hiss. Transfer food from the communal dish to your plate with a spoon. Indian food is quite spicy. Typical food varies by region. In general it includes rice, wheat bread, and curry (eggs, fish, meat, or vegetables in a spicy sauce). Vegetarianism is common for religious reasons (Figure 35.5). Muslims eat no pork and drink no alcohol. Betel leaves and nuts are commonly chewed or eaten after meals.

Tourism Characteristics

India, the second most populous country of the world, received 5 million visitors in 2010, which ranks it fourth in the region (after Malaysia, Thailand, and Singapore). Tourism grew slowly in the 1980s and early 1990s as a result of civil problems in the country, but many within India felt that the government stifled tourism growth because of a bureaucratic administration and lack of tax and investment incentive. A National Action Plan for Tourism was introduced. The purpose was to encourage private investment, both domestic and foreign. The objective was to increase India's share of world tourist arrivals by upgrading the tourist infrastructure and the identification and development of selected areas. Seventeen tourist circuits and destinations were identified

for development. Special targets were wildlife tourism, trekking, river rafting, mountaineering, rock climbing, water skiing, river running, paragliding, and helicopter skiing.

India has the most dispersed tourism markets of all the South Asian countries. Europe, led by the United Kingdom with its historical colonial ties, is the major source area. Seasonality is strong, with the monsoon months having the lowest number of visitors and the peak months being in December, January, February, and March during the dry season. India has one of the longest lengths of stay for foreign visitors in the world. The average stay of tourists is approximately 30 days. The combination of Indians returning home and the long distance and huge size of the country contribute to the long visit.

Tourist Destinations and Attractions

While tourist attractions are dispersed throughout India, the industry is concentrated in the north. The major tourism regions follow.

The Golden Triangle—Agra, Jaipur, and Udaipur

If there is a modern "Seven Wonders of the World," one would be the Taj Mahal (Figure 35.6) in Agra. Along with the Great Wall and the Pyramids, the Taj Mahal is one of the best-known structures in the world. Pictures do not do justice to the beauty of the structure. The intricate artwork, using semiprecious stones, such as sardonyx, coral, amethyst, chalcedony, agate, lapis lazuli, and turquoise, and outstanding workmanship manifested in the marble screens and minarets make a visit to the Taj Mahal an overwhelming experience. The Taj Majal was built some 500 years ago by Shah Jahan as a tomb for his second wife and queen, Arjummand Bano Begam.

The Red Fort is also in Agra and nearby is the abandoned city of Fatehpur Sikri, a pilgrimage center for Indian women desiring larger families. Fatehpur Sikri was developed as a new capital city several hundred years ago at great cost. It was abandoned due to lack of water, but all of the buildings remain. It is a fascinating attraction for international tourists, and the abandoned temple is a fertility symbol because a Hindu priest's prayers successfully enabled the maharajah's wife to bear him an heir when the city was occupied.

The Red Fort at Agra was built three-quarters of a century before Delhi's famed Red Fort. Within the area of the Red Fort, there are a number of buildings of interest. The Red Palace was believed to have been built by Akbar for his son, Jahangir. The Khas Mahal, or Private Palace, contains the Golden Pavilions, with beautiful curved golden roofs. The Sheesh Mahal, or Palace of Mirrors, and Musamman Burj, or Saman Burj (the Prisoner's Tower), are nearby. There is an excellent view of the Taj Mahal from the tower. Around Agra, there are a number of impressive structures, such as the Itmad-ud-Daula (a forerunner of the Taj) and Akbar's Tomb.

Figure 35.6 Taj Mahal, Agra, India. © James Gritz/Getty Images.

of the surrounding countryside. One unique aspect of Amber is the use of elephants to carry many tourists (Figure 35.7).

The last of the **Golden Triangle** cities is Udaipur. A walled city in a desert state, Udaipur is in a fertile valley with lakes that add to the beauty of its white buildings, palaces, temples, and unique architecture. Elegant marble palaces appear to be floating on blue lakes, giving it a fairyland appeal. Gulab Bagh, a series of beautiful gardens, surrounds the lake.

Delhi

Delhi, the capital, is two cities: Old Delhi and New Delhi, which was built by the British to be the capital of India. New Delhi contains the government buildings, which are dominated by the India Gate, built by the British in the style of the Arc de Triomphe in Paris. Several sites such as Connaught Place, Parliament Street, Rajpath, and Janpath are part of the well-planned New Delhi and provide an impressive visit. Connaught Place consists of three concentric circles radiating out from the center, with Janpath and Parliament Streets forming spokes of the wheel. The most impressive government buildings are the Parliament House and the President's House, a cream-and-red sandstone palace, that covers 330 acres. Old Delhi is a crowded, colorful bazaar of small shops and stalls (Figure 35.8). With its high walls and a complex of elegant palaces, the Red Fort is the focus of visitors to Old Delhi. Across the street from the Red Fort is the Jama Masjid, the largest **mosque** in India. Made of red sandstone inlaid with white marble, it is very impressive. Also not far from Red Fort, the Mahatma Gandhi Memorial Raj Ghat marks the spot where he was cremated. The Imperial Palace of Shah Jahan, builder of the Taj Majal, is inside the Red Fort. The Muslim influence is evident in the 234-foot-high Qutab Minaret, a minaret built between the thirteenth

Located near the second city in the triangle, Jaipur (known as the Pink City), are the marble quarries from which the marble for the Taj Mahal was obtained. The old city contains both Hindu and Muslim architectural styles. The town was built in the eighteenth century on a grid plan with large plazas and extremely wide avenues, necessary for elephant parades. The focus of the old town was the Hawa Mahal, or the Palace of the Winds. The Hawa Mahal is a beautiful flamingo-colored five-story structure. The Jantar Mantar, an observatory, is a remarkable attraction. Near Jaipur, the old fortified hill city of Amber was deserted after the construction and movement of the capital to Jaipur in the plains. Not only is the palace beautiful, but it offers a panoramic view and fourteenth centuries. It dominates the nearby areas and is visible from far away.

Mumbai

Mumbai, formerly Bombay, on the west coast, is a major international gateway into India and the country's business center. It is a cosmopolitan seaport and was the home of Mahatma Gandhi from 1917 to 1934. His home, Mani Bhavan, has become one of the featured attractions of Mumbai. One of India's best museums, the Prince of Wales Museum, is in (Mumbai) Bombay. Other places of interest are the Jehangir Art Gallery Colaba, a Jain Temple, St. John's Church, and the Taj Mahal Hotel. The Elephant Caves, which contain splendid stone sculptures of religious figures, are nearby on an island. The Kamia Nehru Park includes the Towers of Silence, where the Parsis (a religious sect) place their dead. Vultures pick the flesh from the bones, after which the bones are cremated.

About 150 miles north and east of Mumbai are the Aurangabad, Ellora, and Ajanta caves, which are among

Figure 35.7 Decorated elephant at the annual elephant festival in Jaipur, India. © jo Crebbin/www.Shutterstock.com.

the modern wonders of the world. The rocky hills of the region became the home of rock-cut temples of various religious communities. The temples—twelve Buddhist, seventeen Hindu, and five Jain—were built between the fifth and seventh centuries. Construction of these temples ranks with the task of building the pyramids in Egypt.

Kashmir and the Floating Gardens of Srinagar

Kashmir is a fertile green valley at the foot of the Himalayas with lakes and gardens. Srinagar, the capital, is a city of canals, and the major transportation network is by water. The city has numerous mosques, Hindu temples, and brick and wooden houses that have grass growing on their mud roofs. Houseboats (long, elegant, flat-bottomed types) are common on the water. Specific sites of interest are the Juma Masjid Mosque, built of wood; the Mosque of Madani; the Mosque of Shah Hamada; the Mughal Gardens, which include the large Nishat Bagh or "Gardens of Delights"; Shalimar Gardens; the Shankaracharya Temple on a hill overlooking the city; the Sri Prata Singh Museum; and the Hazrat Bal Mosque, which is supposed to contain a hair of the prophet Mohammad that was preserved as a sacred relic. Near Srinagar, visits can be made into the high scenic areas of Gulmarg, Sonamarg, and Pahalgam.

Between Srinagar and Delhi in Punjab, Chandigarh, designed by the famed architect and city planner Le Corbusier, is the capital of Punjab. The city has broad avenues and gardens and a number of impressive buildings such as the Secretariat, the Assembly, and the High Court.

The Holy City of Varanasi and the Erotic Temple of Khajuraho

Situated on the banks of the Ganges River, Varanasi is the holiest city in India. Hindu pilgrims flock to the city to bathe, perform their rituals, and cremate their dead. Scattered along its narrow, winding streets are over 3,000 temples that are visited by the Hindu faithful. Varanasi is considered to be one of the most ancient cities in the world and has other attractions, including the Durga Temple (Monkey Temple); the Golden Temple, or the Temple of Vishwanath; Benares Hindu University; the Mother India Temple, a national monument; and an interesting bazaar area. Varanasi is also a principal departure point for trips into Nepal. A sacred city to Hindus, it is a pilgrimage site for visitors to its temples, the Ganges River, or those cremating their dead so that their ashes can be scattered on the Ganges.

Located approximately 200 miles west of Varanasi, Khajuraho is the home of the famous erotic temples built by the Chandella Dynasty between 950 and 1050 A.D. The temples may be the greatest examples of medieval Hindu architecture and sculpture in India. Of the eighty-five temples built, only twenty-two have survived, but they comprise an important and unique attraction.

Figure 35.8 Jama Mashid bazaar, Delhi, India. © Jorg Hackemann/www.Shutterstock.com.

Kolkata (Calcutta)

Kolkata is India's largest city. It is also the city to which Western stereotypes of India (population, poverty, disease, etc.) are most commonly applied. Although there are problems in Kolkata, the stereotypes are exaggerated. The British left their mark on Kolkata with stately government buildings, which, combined with the Indian Museum and Zoological Gardens and Indian life, are the focal point of tourism. Some of the British influence and other attractions can be observed in St. John's Church; St. Paul's Cathedral, the Anglican center in Calcutta; the Raj Bhavan, the residence of the Governor of Bengal; famous Chowringee Street, noted for its fine shops and hotels; the Maiden, the city's principal park, with its cricket ground; the business district around Dalhousie Square; the Zoological Gardens; Calcutta University; Victoria Memorial Hall; Howrah Bridge, one of the largest in the world; and the Botanical Garden, which has a 200-year-old banyan tree. A number of temples are worth a visit, namely the Dakshineshwar Kali; Sheetalnathji, a Jain temple; the Kali Temple; the Belur Math Temple; and the Nakhoda Mosque, which is modeled after the tomb of Akbar at Sikandra near Agra. The Marble Palace has a fine collection of art, including works by Rubens, Reynolds, Courbet, and Corot. Near Kolkata is the magnificent Sun Temple of Konarak near the city of Bhubaneshwar. It is designed in the form of a gigantic chariot, with carvings depicting the joys of earthly life.

Kolkata is the gateway for Darjeeling, known for beautiful sunrises on Mt. Everest, the nearby Annapurna, and the countries of Sikkim and Bhutan. Darjeeling provides excellent views of the Himalayan Mountains (Figure 35.9) with excursions to Tiger Hill for the sunrise view of Everest. The Ghoom Monastery and St. Andrew's Church are also worth visiting.

Madras Region

Although it is much less important for international Western visitors, South India centered on Madras is the final major tourist region in India. On the southeast coast of India, Madras is the gateway for southern India.

Figure 35.9 View of Mount Kanchenjunga from Tiger Hill, Darjeeling, India. © David Evison/www.Shutterstock.com.

Madras offers excellent historical, artistic, and religious sites. The National Art Gallery, Government Museum, old Fort St. George, the Cathedral of San Thome, and the Kapaliwarer Temple associated with Shiva are important attractions in Madras that provide a diversity of experiences. The cave and rock temples and open-air reliefs of the Pallava Dynasty are near Madras. These caves have huge boulders carved into monolithic art forms. Madurai, an ancient town, has an unusual Meenakshi Temple that is adorned with gopurams, as well as other lovely carved temples.

Other destinations

Other important tourism sites in the country include the backwaters of Kerala. These are spectacular inland lakes connected by a network of canals. The state of Goa is home to India's finest beaches. Here, the coastline on the Arabian Sea provides the setting for some of the most beautiful beaches in the world. India's unique wildlife is on display in the numerous national parks throughout the country. Kaziranga National Park, a World Heritage Site, is in the state of Assam. The park is famous for the one-horned Indian rhinos and Red pandas.

Maldives

The island nation of Maldives is south of India in the Indian Ocean. The islands are small and none rise more than 1.8 meters (6 feet) above sea level. Like necklaces draped along an undersea plateau, 1,200 coral islands—about 200 inhabited—form the Maldives. In 1968, three years after independence from Britain, the sultanate gave way to an Islamic republic. Tourism and fishing sustain the economy. In 2010 more than 650,000 tourists came to this tiny nation, and ninety of its islands are designated as tourist islands.

From *National Geographic Atlas of the World*, 9th edition. Copyright ©2011 National Geographic Society. Reprinted by arrangement. All rights reserved.

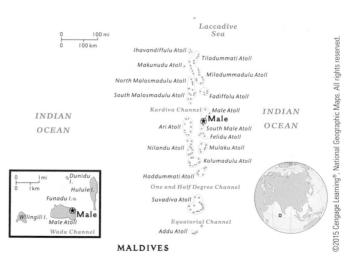

MALDIVES

Figure 35.10 Maldivian island in the shape of a heart. © romrf/www.Shutterstock.com.

Area	298 sq km (115 sq mi)
Population	315,000
Government	Republic
Capital	Male 111,000
Life Expectancy	73 years
Religion	Sunni Muslim
Language	Maldivian Dhivehi, English
Currency	rufiyaa (MVR)
GDP per Cap	$4,200
Labor Force	11% Agriculture, 23% Industry, 65% Services

From *National Geographic Atlas of the World*, 9th edition. Copyright ©2011 National Geographic Society. Reprinted by arrangement. All rights reserved.

TRAVEL **TIPS** 💼

Entry: A passport is required. A visa is issued upon arrival. Proof of sufficient funds and onward or return transportation is required.

National Holiday: July 26 (Independence Day)

Health: Valid immunization against yellow fever may be required. Malaria is a risk in the Maldives.

Internet TLD: .mv

CULTURAL CAPSULE Of the 1,200 islands, 202 are inhabited, with the greatest concentration on the capital island, Male. The earliest settlers were probably from southern India, speaking languages of the Dravidian family. They were followed by Indo-European speakers from Sri Lanka in the fourth and fifth centuries B.C. In the twelfth century, Arab and East African sailors came to the islands. Maldivian ethnic character is a blend of these cultures. Unlike the rest of South Asia, the Maldivians have never been ruled by colonial powers for long periods of time. Originally Buddhists, Maldivians were converted to Sunni Islam in the mid-twelfth century. Islam is the official religion and is adhered to by the entire population. The official language is Dhivehi, an Indo-European language related to Sinhala, the language of Sri Lanka. The writing system, like Arabic, is from right to left, although the alphabets are different. Some social stratification exists on the islands, with the social elite concentrated in Male. The country's long-term sustainability is uncertain because the coral islands are vulnerable to rising ocean levels and the threat of tsunamis; the highest point on the islands is only 9 feet above sea level.

Tourism Characteristics

The travel industry is small, averaging 700,000 tourists a year, who stay for an average of 9.2 days. Direct charters to Europe have made Europe (United Kingdom, Germany, and Italy), the largest markets, accounting for over one-third of the visitors. Russia and China are the next largest market with a 10 percent share.

Tourist Destinations and Attractions

The attractions in the Maldives are mostly sun-sand-sea (Figure 35.10), with diving and other water sports activities. The majority of the 90 or so tourist resorts in the Maldives are located on Kaafu Atoll, with a limited amount of development on Alif Atoll.

Nepal

Nepal lies in the eastern Himalaya mountains between China and India in South Asia. Most Nepalese live in the central, hilly region, which embraces the Kathmandu Valley, and in the southern plain known as the Terai. Rivers that spring from the Himalaya generate electricity for local use and potentially for export. The central region possesses a temperate climate, and the southern plain is subtropical. Nepal possesses the greatest altitude variation on the earth—from the lowlands near sea level to Mount Everest at 8,850 meters (29,035). Mount Everest, named after British surveyor Sir George Everest, is known by the local Sherpas as Chomolungma (meaning "Goddess Mother of the World"). The Nepali name for Everest, Sagarmatha, is often translated as "Forehead of the Sky." Sherpas benefit from the mountaineering boom and tourism in the Everest region. The different regions of Nepal are home to a diversity of peoples. The 2001 census of Nepal recorded 103 caste and ethnic groups in this mostly Hindu nation. There are also ninety-three languages and dialects. This diversity has led to political instability. A Maoist insurgency, started by caste and ethnic groups in western Nepal in 1996, culminated in the Maoists becoming part of the government and ending the 240-year-old monarchy in 2008. Instability has contributed to Nepal's remaining the poorest country in South Asia.

From *National Geographic Atlas of the World*, 9th edition. Copyright ©2011 National Geographic Society. Reprinted by arrangement. All rights reserved.

Area	147,181 sq km (56,827 sq mi)
Population	27,504,000
Government	Federal Democratic Republic
Capital	Kathmandu 895,000
Life Expectancy	64 years
Literacy	49%
Religion	Hindu, Buddhist, Muslim, Kirant
Language	Nepali, Maithali, Bhojpuri, Tharu, Tamang, Newar, Magar
Currency	Nepalese rupee (NPR)
GDP per Cap	$1,200
Labor Force	76% Agriculture, 6% Industry, 18% Services

From *National Geographic Atlas of the World*, 9th edition. Copyright ©2011 National Geographic Society. Reprinted by arrangement. All rights reserved.

TRAVEL **TIPS** 💼

Entry: A passport is required. A visa is required for stays up to thirty days and issued at Kathmandu Airport.

Peak Tourist Season: October through December

National Holiday: May 29 (Republic Day)

Health: Polio, typhus, and meningitis inoculations are suggested, and gamma globulin and malaria suppressants are recommended. Water is not potable; therefore, drink bottled or boiled water.

Shopping: Common items include handicraft jewelry, jewel boxes, wood carvings, brass vessels, prayer wheels, wool blankets, and woven shawls and rugs.

Internet TLD: .np

CULTURAL CAPSULE The Nepalese are descendants of migrants from India, Tibet, and central Asia. Nearly 50 percent are Indo-Aryans. These people reside in the Ganges Basin plain and trace their ancestors to the Brahman and Chetre caste groups from India. People of Indo-Aryan and/or Mongoloid descent live in the hill region. Religion is important, and Nepal is the only official Hindu state in the world (88 percent of the population). Hinduism has been influenced by the large Buddhist minority. The Hindu temples and Buddhist shrines are mutually respected, and Buddhist and Hindu festivals are occasions for common worship and celebration. In addition, Nepal has small Muslim and Christian minorities. Certain animistic practices of old indigenous religions also exist. Nepali is the official language, although a dozen different languages and about thirty major dialects are spoken throughout the country. English is understood in government and business. Hindi is spoken by about 90 percent of the population.

Cultural hints: The palms in prayer position in front of the chin and a slight bow is a traditional greeting. "Namaste" is a greeting and good-bye. Use a person's title in greetings. Do not touch another person's hair or shoulders. Use the right hand to eat. When drinking water from a communal container, the lips do not touch the rim. Typical food includes rice, lentil soup, vegetable curry, goat, chicken, water buffalo, fruits, and vegetables. Many people are vegetarians.

Tourism Characteristics

Nepal, the "rooftop of the world," is most famous as the jumping-off place for climbers in the Himalayas, including Mt. Everest (Figure 35.11). The country has only been open to tourism for about 30 years. Unlike its neighbors, the Hindus and Buddhists of Nepal have lived for nearly 2,000 years in peaceful coexistence. Ashok, Nepal, was the birthplace of Buddha. Ashok is an important religious attraction. Although it is a small country, Nepal contains the greatest range of altitudes in the world, from almost sea-level tropical jungle to the rugged relief of Mt. Everest, over 29,000 feet above sea level.

Nepal is "the" place for trekkers in the world, bringing visitors from a wide variety of places. Pokhara, about 100 miles west of Kathmandu, is the starting point for treks toward the Himalayas. Tourism is the only real earner of foreign exchange, helping Nepal to finance its imports. The

Figure 35.11 Mount Everest. © AntonSokolov/www.Shutterstock.com.

most important country for tourists is India, accounting for 31 percent of visitors. The close proximity and huge population base are important factors in this number. Indian-owned travel companies that deal with tourism to Nepal handle 70 to 80 percent of the tourist business to Nepal.

The European market (30 percent) is diverse, lacking the high percentage of visitors from the United Kingdom that is found in India or Pakistan. The major purpose of visiting is pleasure (almost 75 percent), with 14 percent for trekking and mountaineering. The remaining reasons for travel—business, official, and visiting friends and relatives—account for only slightly over 10 percent of the visitors. The opening of the border between Nepal and China had a positive influence on tourism. Tour operators in Kathmandu have established tours from three to fifteen days to Lhasa, the capital and holy city of Tibet. However, they are either expensive or difficult for budget travelers who must travel by truck to Lhasa over rugged mountain roads.

Tourist Destinations and Attractions

The two major areas of tourism in Nepal are the Kathmandu Valley and Terai, in the southern lowland, where the famous Tiger Tops for viewing wildlife is located. The three important cities in Kathmandu Valley—Kathmandu, Patan, and Bhadgaon (also called Bhaktapur)—are also the areas with the greatest concentration of accommodations. Kathmandu (Figure 35.12), the gateway

to the Himalayas and trekking, focuses on Durbar Square with its many-tiered temples, winding streets, and brick buildings that look somewhat like medieval Europe. The most important temples are Maju Deval with its nine-stage platform that has some erotic carvings, the Shiva-Parvati Temple, the Krishna Temple, and the golden-pagoda-style Taleju Temple. The market area behind Durbar Square has the Kasthmandap, an intricate wooden temple. The Swayambhunath Temple, famous for the monkeys that live there, is on Swayambhu hill. Flights over Mt. Everest and the rest of the Himalayan Range are offered. Mosaics and all of the local crafts are available in Kathmandu. Mount Everest sits east of Kathmandu near the Tibet border.

Patan, the second largest city, is over 2,000 years old and has museums, temples, monuments, courtyards, elaborately carved wooden structures, and prayer wheels. It is also the home of some of the best South Asian handicrafts. Patan's attractions include the famous Krishna Mandir, which was influenced by Indian styles and has a tall pillar on which sits the mythical bird-man Garuda with folded hands; King Yoganarendra Malla's tall column; several Shiva temples with erotic carvings; the Bhimsen Temple; the Hiranya Varma Mahavihara or "Golden Temple"; and the Tibetan refugee center of Jawlakhel.

Bhadgaon, at the east end of the Kathmandu Valley, has numerous shrines and artistic designs expressed in its elaborately carved palace and temples. Bhadgaon (or Bhaktapur) is reported to be the oldest town in the Kathmandu Valley. Attractions include an art gallery

For sixty years climbers have dumped gear and trash en route to the top of Mount Everest, often in the low-oxygen "death zone" above 26,000 feet, where shedding a few pounds can preserve precious energy.

In recent years melting ice has begun to reveal the scope of the high-altitude imprint, exposing oxygen tanks and other long-frozen jetsam. Though tons of refuse are removed annually from base camps, last spring two Nepali groups, Extreme Everest Expedition and Eco Everest Expedition, targeted the peak's upper reaches and hauled down seven tons of waste, including debris from a 1973 helicopter crash.

Nepalis are also concerned about corpses collecting on the mountain they consider holy. Since 1996 some eighty climbers have perished above base camp; most remain near the spot they died. In May two bodies, a Swiss and a Russian, were removed along with a pair of unidentified arms, one wearing a watch. Bringing back corpses was long considered logistically unfeasible, says Linda McMillian of the International Mountaineering and Climbing Federation. But as traffic on Everest has risen, she notes, so too have the desire to clean it.

— Peter Gwin, *National Geographic Magazine*, October 2010

---

containing rare paintings and manuscripts from medieval Nepal; a Golden Gate; a fifty-five–window palace; a bell of barking dogs; an exact replica of the Pashupatinath Temple with erotic carvings; the five-story Nyatapola Temple; and the Bhairabnath Temple.

The holiest temple in Nepal is Pashupati, en route to Bodhnath. The temple is located on the banks of the holy Bagmati River and as at the Ganges, cremations occur frequently. At Bodhnath, one of the biggest Buddhist **stupas** in the world (with four eyes) is an important attraction.

The second major destination center, Tiger Tops, is in the jungles of the Terai Valley, which is an extension of the Ganges River Plain. Tiger Tops, which is closed during the monsoon season, offers the full range of wildlife viewing.

Figure 35.12 Kathmandu, Nepal. © HamsterMan/www.Shutterstock.com.

Pakistan

Pakistan, an arid and densely populated country, lies in the northwest part of South Asia. The Indus River brings life to Pakistan's dry landscape, and most Pakistanis live along the river. West of the Indus, the land becomes increasingly arid and mountainous. To the north the land rises to the great mountains of the Hindu Kush and Karakoram—including K2, the world's second highest mountain after Mount Everest, at 8,611 meters (28,251 feet). The climate in the lowland areas is generally hot and dry, with a high rate of evaporation for summer rains. Generally, Pakistan suffers from a deficiency of rainfall. Language is a marker of ethnic identity in Pakistan, and there are some seventy languages. Although Urdu is the official language, it is spoken as a native tongue by only about a tenth of the people. Urdu is largely used in Pakistan's urban areas, but most Pakistanis are rural and use a regional language. Nearly half of all Pakistanis (48 percent) speak Punjabi; the next most common language is Pashtu (15 percent), followed by Sindhi (14 percent), and Baluchi (3.6 percent). The military has loomed large in Pakistan since 1947, when the country was created for Muslims at the end of British rule, and military coups have marred Pakistani democracy. Relations with India, embittered by conflict over Kashmir, worsened when India helped East Pakistan become Bangladesh in 1971. Tensions with India came to a head in 1998, when both countries tested nuclear weapons. The Indo-Pakistani conflict over Kashmir continues as Pakistan seeks to protect Kashmir's Muslim population. Recently, Pakistan has had to focus on its border with Afghanistan, by supporting Afghan resistance forces during the 1979–1989 Soviet occupation and coordinating Afghan-Pakistani border security since 2001. The economy is based on agriculture, which is concentrated in the irrigated Indus Basin. Poverty and low literacy rates challenge the government, which depends on foreign development aid.

From *National Geographic Atlas of the World*, 9th edition. Copyright ©2011 National Geographic Society. Reprinted by arrangement. All rights reserved.

Location	Southern Asia
Area	796,095 sq km (307,374 sq mi)
Population	180,808,000
Government	Federal Republic
Capital	Islamabad 780,000
Life Expectancy	66 years
Literacy	50%
Religion	Sunni Muslim, Shiite Muslim
Language	Punjabi, Sindhi, Siraiki, Pashtu, Urdu, Baluchi, English

Currency	Pakistani rupee (PKR)
GDP per Cap	$2,600
Labor Force	43.0% Agriculture, 20.3% Industry, 36.6% Services

From *National Geographic Atlas of the World*, 9th edition. Copyright ©2011 National Geographic Society. Reprinted by arrangement. All rights reserved.

TRAVEL TIPS

Entry: A visa and passport is required.

Peak Tourist Season: November through January

National Holiday: March 23 (Republic Day)

Travel Caution: Travel in rural areas, particularly in Sindh Province, is not recommended. Rallies, demonstrations, and processions that are anti-American or anti-Western in nature occur periodically in many cities.

Shopping: Common items include local jade and other gemstones and native handicrafts.

Internet TLD: .pk

CULTURAL CAPSULE

The people of Pakistan are divided into four major ethnic groups: the Punjabi (65 percent), Sindhi (12 percent), Baluchi (9 percent), and Pashtuns (8 percent). A fifth group is the Muhajir, composed of immigrants from India and their descendants. Pakistan is an Islamic republic, and their laws are based on the Koran. Ninety-seven percent of the people are Muslims (77 percent Sunni and 20 percent Shiite). Fatalism is common in the rural areas.

The two official languages are English and Urdu. The government is gradually replacing English with Urdu. Languages reflect ethnic background, with Punjabi spoken by 65 percent of the population. Eleven percent speak Sindhi, and the remaining 24 percent are other languages, such as Saraiki, Baluchi, and Brahui. Urdu, Punjabi, Pushtu, and Baluchi are of the Indo-European language group, while Brahui is believed to have a Dravidian origin.

Cultural hints: Men refrain from touching or shaking hands with a Pakistani woman unless she extends her hand. Use title and last name

Figure 35.13 Karachi, Pakistan. © Pichugin Dmitry/www.Shutterstock.com.

when addressing someone. It is customary to offer coffee, tea, or other refreshments. It is impolite to reject such offers. Women are often kept separated in social situations. Women dress and act modestly in all settings. Ask permission to photograph Pakistani women. Remove shoes before entering a mosque. Public buses are crowded with much touching, shoving, and pushing. When using utensils, use the fork in the left hand to push food into the spoon. Men and women often eat in separate areas. Typical food is an unleavened bread (chapati or roti), buttermilk, yogurt, rice, vegetables, and meat, but not pork. Pakistani food is generally hot and spicy, using curry as a common spice.

Tourism Characteristics

Tourism is not a major earner of foreign exchange for Pakistan. In 2010, just over 800,000 travelers visited the country. Relations with the United States and other western countries are complex as the country is struggling to control domestic insurgents, many of whom are located in the tribal areas adjacent to the border with Afghanistan. Pakistan receives almost half of its visitors from European countries, especially the United Kingdom. Like India, it has strong ties to the United Kingdom, which accounts for over one-third of the international visitors. Historically travel to visit friends and family has been the major purpose of travel, but just over 40 percent of total visits are for this reason. The average length of stay of twenty-seven days, one of the longest in the world, is another factor indicating the importance of family ties for visitors.

Travel to Pakistan has been impacted by unrest at home, the complicated situation along the country's border with Afghanistan, and the perception of many residents of the Western industrialized countries that India offers a better set of tourist attractions than Pakistan. As in the rest of South Asia, the monsoon season affects the tourist season. The most-favored season is from September through March. The three major destinations are Karachi, Lahore, and the capital city of Islamabad.

Tourist Destinations and Attractions

Karachi (Figure 35.13), the former capital and still the largest city, is the center of the country's commerce and industry, largely related to its port characteristics. It is the country's commercial hub and engine of the economy. Although it is not an outstanding or unique city, Karachi does have interesting bazaars, gardens, a zoo, and a national museum. The principal attractions of Karachi are the Mausoleum of Quaid-i-Azam, the founder of the nation; the Defense Housing Society Mosque; Frere Hall in the Jinnah Gardens; and the National Museum. The ancient towns of the Chaukundi Tombs, Thatta, and Moenjo are near Karachi. A number of resorts are found on the tiny island of South Manora and at Hawke's Bay. Tatta, 65 miles southeast of Karachi, was the home of a number of dynasties. The mosque begun by Emperor Shah Jahan, the builder of the Taj Mahal, is the most notable Mogul architecture remaining.

Lahore, the second largest city of Pakistan, is in a picturesque region and is the educational and cultural center of the country. The Shalimar Gardens, built in 1637, are Pakistan's greatest attraction. Called the city of gardens, Lahore has Indo-Muslim architecture and the Badshai Mosque, Emperor Jehangir's Mausoleum, and the Great Mughal with its famous Hall of Mirrors. The Badshai Mosque is one of the world's largest mosques. Shah Jahan, who built the Taj Mahal, also built in Lahore one of the first mausoleums of the East for his father, the Emperor Janagir. The red sandstone tomb sits above the banks of the Ravi River, surrounded by the Dilkusha Garden.

Northwest of Lahore is Taxila, which at one time was the principal center of Buddhist learning and culture. A number of ruins of old cities and the monasteries at Mohra Moradu and Jaulian are the best preserved of their kind in Pakistan. The Zoroastrian Temple is impressive because of its architecture.

Moenjo-Daro (Mound of the Dead) is located some 400 miles north of Karachi and is one of the most impressive ancient sites in the world. This large urban complex included a sophisticated system of waste disposal and drains for fresh water. Other impressive features are the Great Bath, the Great Granary, and a citadel with walls up to 45 feet thick.

To the north are cities less developed for tourism, including Rawalpindi, the capital until Islamabad was completed; Islamabad, the capital of Pakistan; and Peshawar, gateway to excursions into the mountain valleys and the Khyber Pass. Rawalpindi is near a number of mountain resorts. Islamabad, a relatively new city, is an administrative center for Pakistan and is an interesting example of a planned city. Peshawar is the terminal point for trips into the Khyber Pass. The Khyber Pass is 33 miles in length and has a rich history, as Greek, Tartar, and Mongol conquerors passed through it. Peshawar is known for its bazaars, the most famous of which is the Quissi Khawani Bazaar. The Bijori Gate Bazaar was the meeting place for caravans from many places. In the last decades, the Peshawar region has become home to over a million residents of Afghanistan who fled the war in that country.

Sri Lanka

Sri Lanka is a tropical island lying in the Indian Ocean, close to the southern tip of India and near the equator. From the coast, the land rises to a central plateau, where tea plantations are found. A monsoon climate brings ample rainwater to the southwest. A 2004 tsunami inundated coastal areas and caused more than 32,000 deaths. Sinhalese form the country's majority at 74 percent of the population, and Tamils are the largest ethnic minority, at 18 percent. Population density is highest in the island's southwest corner—where Colombo, the capital, is located. The Tamil minority tends to be concentrated geographically along the eastern and northern coastal areas. Most Sinhalese are Buddhist, while most Tamils are Hindu. Under European control for some 450 years, Ceylon won independence from the United Kingdom in 1948. A new constitution in 1972 renamed the country as Sri Lanka, made Sinhala the only official language, and promoted the Buddhist religion. By 1973, Tamils were demanding a separate state, called Tamil Eelam. The Liberation Tigers of Tamil Eelam (LTTE), or Tamil Tigers, was founded in 1976. Conflict between government forces and Tamils escalated into civil war in 1983. After more than twenty-five years of violence, the civil war seemed to end in May 2009, when government forces defeated the Tamil Tigers and took control of the northern Tamil region. The economy, based on the service sector, had been oriented to defense expenses but continues to develop other areas, including telecommunications, banking, and information technology.

SRI LANKA

Area	65,525 sq km (25,299 sq mi)
Population	20,502,000
Government	Republic
Capital	Colombo (administrative) 656,000; Sri Jayewardenepura Kotte (legislative) 120,000
Life Expectancy	71 years
Literacy	91%
Religion	Buddhist, Muslim, Hindu, Christian
Language	Sinhala, Tamil
Currency	Sri Lankan rupee (LKR)
GDP per Cap	$4,500
Labor Force	32.7% Agriculture, 26.3% Industry, 41% Services

TRAVEL TIPS 🧳

Entry: A passport is required. Visas are not required for stays up to six months.

Peak Tourist Season: December through March

National Holiday: February 4 (Independence Day)

Health: Malaria suppressants are advisable. Water is not safe and foods should be peeled or cooked before eating.

Travel Caution: Ongoing civil war is related to violence in Sri Lanka, and visitors should check with the Department of State before departure.

Shopping: Common items include rubies, sapphires, amethysts, opals, hand-dyed batik, tailor-made clothing, and the country's many famous varieties of tea.

Internet TLD: .lk

 CULTURAL CAPSULE The two largest population groups are Sinhalese—comprising 75 percent of the population and concentrated in the densely populated southwest—and Tamils—comprising about 12 percent. A third smaller group is the Indian Tamils, whose ancestors were brought from India during the British colonial era to work on tea plantations. Moors comprise 7 percent of the population, and Malays, Burghers, and Veddahs make up the other 1 percent. The Burghers are descendants of Dutch colonists, and the Veddahs are a remnant of the island's original inhabitants. Sinhala, an Indo-European language, is the native tongue of the Sinhalese. Tamils and most Muslims speak Tamil, part of the South Indian Dravidian linguistic group. Use of English is common but declining. Both Sinhala and Tamil are official languages. Most Sinhalese are Buddhist (Theravada Buddhism), and most Tamils are Hindu. Most of the Muslims are Sunnis. Sizable minorities of both Sinhalese and Tamils are Christians, mostly Roman Catholic.

Cultural hints: Typical food is an unleavened bread (chapati or roti), buttermilk, yogurt, rice, vegetables, and meat, but not pork. Pakistani food is generally hot and spicy, using curry as a common spice. While a handshake is a common form of greeting, differences exist between ethnic groups. Women are forbidden to touch a Buddhist monk. Use titles when addressing people. Typical foods are rice, curries, peas, beans, pulses, and tea. Sri Lankans consume little meat, and the Muslims do not eat pork.

Tourism Characteristics

Sri Lanka (formerly Ceylon) is an island paradise. Lying off the southern tip of India, Sri Lanka is smaller than Ireland or Tasmania. Tourism to Sri Lanka has been hurt by the Tamil guerrilla fighting that continued until 2007 in the northern and eastern provinces.

The peak tourist season is November to April, reflecting both the monsoon season and the high number of tourists from Europe who desire a warm climate during the European winter. Of the 654,000 visitors in 2010, nearly 65 percent came from Europe. The average length of stay is nine days.

Numerous international tourists also arrive from India, primarily because of duty-free shopping in Sri Lanka.

Tourist Destinations and Attractions

The major historical sites are Kandy, Anuradhapura, Polonnaruwa, and Sigiriya. Anuradhapura, 128 miles from Colombo, the capital, is the historical cultural capital of the Sinhalese kings and the religious center. Kandy, the former capital of Kandyan kings, is the home of scholars, writers, artists, and musicians. Temples and a Kandyan palace dot the landscape. Principal attractions in Kandy are the Temple of Tooth, Kandy Lake, the Royal Botanical Gardens, the University of Ceylon, and the Kandy Museum.

Polonnaruwa, 134 miles from Colombo, another capital city (built in A.D. 1100), is the home of the Jewel of Sri Lanka, the Lankatilaka, a colossal standing figure of Buddha. The ruins of King Parakramabahu's Royal Palace, the Royal Audience Hall, the Royal Bath, the circular Vatadage with its Buddhas facing four entrances, the Trivanka Image House and the 55-foot-high Lankatitaka Vihara, and an unusual eleven-foot-high statue of King Parakramabahu I are impressive attractions. Sigiriya has impressive cave paintings that are outstanding in quality near the top of a 400-foot-high rock fortress.

Colombo, the present capital, is a pretty city with a British heritage seen in its Victorian homes and administration buildings. The National Museum contains treasures and artifacts from all over the island. A number of other attractions are the Cinnamon Gardens, an exclusive residential area; the Bandaranaike Memorial International Conference Hall, the beautiful Vihara Maha Devi Park, the elegant Town Hall, and a few Buddhist temples.

The beaches of Sri Lanka are outstanding. The interior includes the national parks of Wilpattu, Ruhunu, and Gal Oya, which have lush vegetation and wild-game preserves. Many visitors to the island also enjoy visiting sights related to the country's celebrated tea-growing industry. Sri Lanka is the world's third largest exporter of tea leaves, and Ceylon tea is world famous.

REVIEW QUESTIONS

1. What are the three major religions of South Asia?
2. What is the most important climatic feature of South Asia? Why?
3. What are the major tourist regions of India?
4. Which country in South Asia has the greatest potential for increasing its visitor numbers over the next twenty years? Why?
5. When India's economy improves enough for India to become an even more important generator of tourists, which Asian country will benefit the most? Why?

chapter 36: SOUTHEAST ASIA

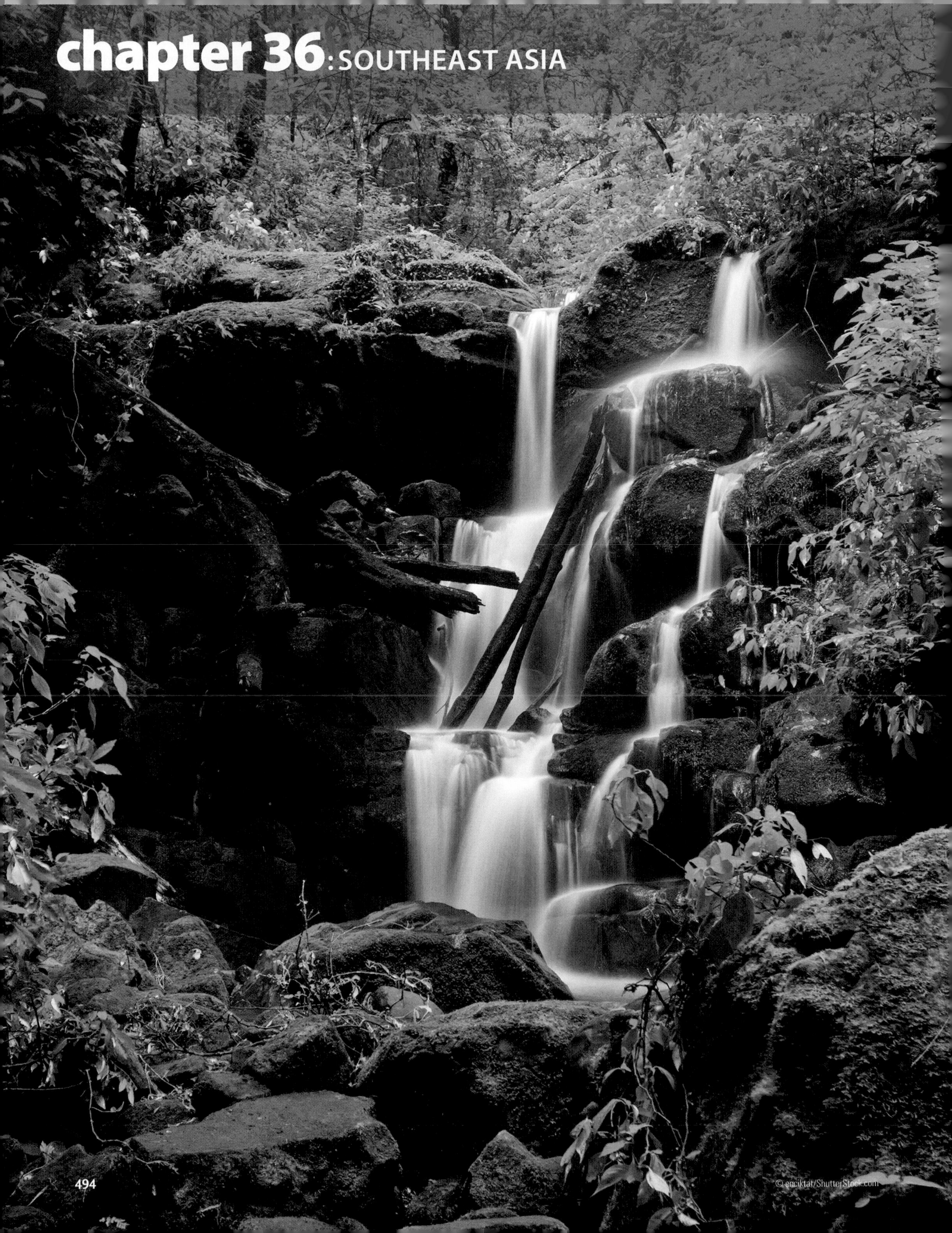

Tourism has not affected all of Southeast Asia evenly, but as a region Southeast Asia has received far more tourists than South Asia. The South Asia region welcomed over 65 million visitors in 2010, a dramatic increase when compared to 5 million in 1990. Leading destination countries are Malaysia (23 million), Thailand (14 million), and Singapore (13 million). And yet, this is but a fraction of total world international tourists, estimated at 1 billion in 2012. If the region can overcome the problem of distance from the major world markets, lack of adequate accommodations, and political tension, there is a considerable, untapped potential for tourism to the region. A major characteristic of the region is the unifying element of the tropical climate. A major tourism characteristic is that much of the travel is intraregional. The largest segment of visitors to Southeast Asia is from other nations of Southeast Asia, with the exception of the Philippines, which draws strongly from East Asia and the United States.

Travel from industrialized countries includes both destination and **circular tours**. Circular tours visit a number of countries as part of a tour of the Pacific region. Both Thailand and Singapore benefit from major international transit traffic. Since visitors are passing through, they will stay and sightsee or purchase goods. This is illustrated in the relatively low length of stay of 3.5 days for Singapore and 5.9 days for Thailand.

Indonesia

Indonesia is a vast equatorial archipelago of 17,508 islands extending 5,150 kilometers (3,200 miles) east to west, between the Indian and Pacific Oceans in Southeast Asia. The largest islands are Sumatra, Java, Kalimantan (Indonesian Borneo), Sulawesi, and Papua (the Indonesian part of New Guinea). Islands are mountainous with dense rain forests, with some 100 active volcanoes. Severe earthquakes are a recurring hazard. Indonesia, the fourth most populous nation on earth, is 85 percent Muslim—and the world's largest Islamic country, though it is a secular state. Some 11 percent of Indonesians are Christian and 2 percent Hindu. Indonesians are separated by seas and clustered on islands. The largest cluster is on Java, with some 130 million people. Sumatra, much larger than Java, has only about a third of Java's people. The country is highly diverse, with over three hundred ethnic groups—45 percent are Javanese (the largest group). There are more than seven hundred languages and dialects, most ethnically based. Indonesian is the official language; English is the top foreign language. After independence from the Netherlands in 1949, the new republic started as a democracy, but secessionist rebellions on many islands brought dictatorship. Authoritarian government persisted from 1959 to 1998. Public unrest, including violent rioting, forced President Suharto—in office since 1967—to resign in 1998. Direct presidential elections started in 2004. The democratic government negotiated a settlement to end secessionist activity in Aceh (northern Sumatra) in 2005. An independence movement on resource-rich Papua remains a concern for the central government. The Indonesian economy hinges on oil and

gas revenue, but it is diversifying into other mining exports (coal and gold) as well as manufacturing. Government priorities include reducing poverty and conserving rain forests and coral reefs.

From *National Geographic Atlas of the World*, 9th edition. Copyright ©2011 National Geographic Society. Reprinted by arrangement. All rights reserved.

Area	1,904,569 sq km (735,358 sq mi)
Population	243,306,000
Government	Republic
Capital	Jakarta 9,125,000
Life Expec	71 years
Literacy	90%
Religion	Muslim, Protestant, Roman Catholic, Hindu
Language	Bahasa Indonesia (modified form of Malay), English, Dutch, local dialects
Currency	Indonesian rupiah (IDR)
GDP per Cap	$4,000
Labor Force	42.1% Agriculture, 18.6% Industry, 39.3% Services

From *National Geographic Atlas of the World*, 9th edition. Copyright © 2011 National Geographic Society. Reprinted by arrangement. All rights reserved.

Raja Ampat has been dubbed the Amazon of the Oceans. Is that hyperbole? Not really. There are single reefs here containing more species than the entire Caribbean (Figure 36.1). A mini-archipelago of rain-forest-clad islands, cays, mangroves, and pearlescent beaches off the coast of West Papua, Indonesia, this marine frontier brims with life. Expect close encounters with recent discoveries such as Raja Ampat's walking shark and pygmy seahorse, along with more familiar creatures—manta rays, leatherback turtles, and bumphead parrotfish. Not to mention three-quarters of all known coral species.

The scenery proves just as spectacular above the surface. On Wayag (Figure 36.2), steep limestone karsts drenched in jungle bisect a cobalt lagoon. Tree canopies filled with rare birds offer lofty theater. It's well worth rising at 3 a.m. to witness the amorous, flamenco-like mating dance of the endemic red bird of paradise.

Remote doesn't mean rough here. Cruise the region aboard an upscale conversion of a traditional phinisi schooner or stay at a hideaway such as Misool Eco Resort, with its swanky overwater bungalows. Diving is the draw, but kayaking and trekking are picking up. This is nature at its most vivid, above and below the water.

— **Johnny Langenheim,** *National Geographic Traveler*, **December 2012/January 2013**

Figure 36.1 Coral reef, Raja Ampat, Indonesia. © FAUP/www.Shutterstock.com.

Figure 36.2 Limestone islands in Wayag, Raja Ampat, Indonesia. © Ethan Daniels/www.Shutterstock.com.

TRAVEL **TIPS** 🧳

Entry: A visa and passport are required.

Peak Tourist Season: August and September

National Holiday: August 17 (Independence Day)

Health: Tuberculosis, malaria, dengue fever, hepatitis, typhoid, and cholera protection is needed. Water and food in the international hotels are safe. Outside of hotels water is not potable and care should be taken to drink boiled or bottled water.

Shopping: Common items include Indonesian crafts of batik, silver work, wood carvings, palm-leaf fans, shadow puppets, dolls, leather goods, bone figurines, and Chinese ceramics, wayang puppets, and antique batiks.

Internet TLD: .id

CULTURAL CAPSULE Indonesia includes numerous related but distinct cultural and linguistic groups, mainly of Malay origin. The Javanese (Malayan) account for 45 percent; the Sundanese, 14 percent; the Madurese, 7.5 percent; and the Coastal Malays, 7.5 percent. The remaining

26 percent belong to various smaller groups. Indonesian, the national language, is a form of Malay that has spread throughout the archipelago and has become the language of all written communication, education, government, and business. English is the most widely spoken foreign language. There are approximately three hundred other languages spoken in the country. About 87 percent of the population is Muslim, 9 percent is Christian (mostly Protestant), and 3 percent is Hindu. A few people still practice animistic religions.

Cultural hints: Remove sunglasses when speaking to someone or entering a home. Use the thumb to point. On buses give up seats to women and elderly. In Bali do not photograph people washing and bathing nude or topless. Eating while walking on the street is inappropriate. In crowded restaurants others will ask to sit with you. Tips are usually included in the bill. Cover the mouth if using a toothpick. Typical foods include rice, vegetables, fish, hot sauces, tea, fruits, beef, buffalo, chilies, and coconut milk. Muslims do not eat pork.

Tourism Characteristics

The island of Bali, probably the most recognizable name relating to tourism in the Pacific, is in Indonesia. Indonesia had 7 million visitors in 2010. The five most important generating countries, all Pacific countries: Singapore, Malaysia, Australia, China, and Japan, account for over 50 percent of all visitors to Indonesia. Tourists also come from various European countries, with the United Kingdom, Germany, and the Netherlands the major market nations.

Most of the recent growth has come from Australia. Most Australian and other visitors are attracted by the island of Bali, which receives more than 27 percent of all visitors to Indonesia and an estimated 60 percent of all leisure arrivals. The United States leveled off in number of visitors to Indonesia, with a current market share of 2.6 percent. Japan sent fewer tourists to Indonesia each year since 2000. China's share of visitor tripled since 2005 to 450,000 in 2012. Since China and South Korea are strong trading partners, this resulted in these countries being markets with tremendous potential for Indonesia. Monthly fluctuations in arrivals to Indonesia are small, suggesting there is no real tourist season as the climate does not change noticeably from one season to another.

There is still considerable potential for increasing tourism to Indonesia. Indonesia has not grown as rapidly as most of the other tourist nations of Southeast Asia. The country suffers from inadequate overseas promotion and the need for improved flight connectivity and frequency. The government has liberalized the process to obtain a license to build a hotel. Bali was opened to foreign airlines, and visa requirements have been dropped for more than twenty countries.

Tourist Destinations and Attractions

The major destinations include the following:

Bali

Bali is considered one of the most exotic, romantic islands in the world. It is frequently referred to as the "island of the gods" and has numerous festivals. Bali is a lush, exotic, and extremely colorful island that has attracted visitors for centuries. Religion and art are the central elements of the rich Balinese culture. With some 20,000 temples, there are almost daily temple festivals celebrated on the islands. Religion and temples are very important in the life of the Balinese. A temple is a place for communicating with the divine spirits through offerings and prayers (Figure 36.3). Temple festivals include purification by the sprinkling of holy water, bringing baskets of food and flowers for offerings. Music, dances, food, flowers, and fruits are all part of the rituals to please the gods and to placate evil spirits.

Women and children wearing their colorful costumes are accompanied by men bearing bountiful offerings on their heads for the temple deities. Bali is also famous for its shops, galleries, and artists who produce stone and wood carvings, highly ornamental gold and silver jewelry, traditional paintings, and woven handlooms. Most visitors fly into Denpasar and stay at one

Figure 36.3 Traditional Balinese god statue in a temple, Bali, Indonesia © Ye Choh Wah/www.Shutterstock.com.

of the many beach resorts. The Bali Museum has an excellent presentation on native Balinese arts and crafts. Ubud, in the mountains, is the spiritual and artistic center of the island. The famous Amandari Resort Hotel is located here.

North Sumatra

An ancient culture dating back to prehistoric periods is the basis for this province's culture and tradition. The tourist sites include Hilisamatano, a village on the island of Nias with ancient traditional houses; Sipisopiso Waterfall; Pematang Purba, a 200-year-old village that is famous for the houses of its tribal chiefs; Lake Toba, one of the largest and highest inland lakes in the world; the island of Samosir in the middle of Lake Toba; Bawomataluo Village, which is 400 meters above sea level and accessible by 480 stone steps; and the great mosque.

West Sumatra

The home of the matrilineal Minangkabau people is a region of spectacular natural beauty. The name Minangkabau means triumphant buffalo. Throughout its highland terrain, there are lakes and deep canyons such as the magnificent Sianok Canyons. Among the high mountains and picturesque valleys are the remnants of the old Minangkabau Kingdom of Pagaruyung with art centers for silver, hand weaving, embroidery, and woodcarving.

Java and Jakarta

The island of Java and its capital city of Jakarta illustrate the nation's historic, cultural, political, and economic character. Jakarta's origin was the small, early sixteenth-century harbor town of Sunda Kelapa, renamed Jayakarta on June 22, 1527. The Dutch East Indies Company captured the town and destroyed it in 1619, changed its name to Batavia, and used it as a base for the expansion of their colonies in the East Indies. Shortly after the outbreak of World War II, Batavia fell to the Japanese, who changed the name to Jakarta as a gesture aimed at winning the sympathy of the Indonesians. The name was retained after Indonesia achieved national independence. Jakarta is a colorful city. In the early 1970s restoration began on the oldest section of Jakarta, known as Old Batavia. The old Portuguese Church and warehouse have been rehabilitated into living museums. The old Supreme Court building is now a museum of fine arts. The old Town Hall has become the Jakarta Museum, displaying rare items, such as Indonesia's old historical documents and Dutch-period furniture. One of the most interesting tourist attractions is the

"Beautiful Indonesia in Miniature Park" called Taman Mini. Built to portray the variety of cultures found within the many islands contained in the Republic of Indonesia, it is an open-air museum exhibiting the many architectural styles, arts, and traditions of all twenty-seven provinces. The Amsterdam Gate, of white-washed brick, Dutch architecture, and other reminders of the Dutch are evident along the remaining canals in the older section of the city.

Near Jakarta are Bogar, which has an outstanding botanical garden, and Puntjab, a resort town. West Java is dotted with rice granaries and with tea, rubber, and quinine plantations. It has several natural reserves; one of them, Ujung Kulon, is the home of the nearly extinct one-horn Java rhino. Pulau Dua, another reserve, is a stopping place for many migrating birds. Bandung, the capital of West Java, provides a panorama of mountains and the active volcano crater of Mt. Tangkubanperahu. Bandunk is an educational center. Unique to the area are the music, which is played on bamboo instruments, and the costumed wooden puppets (Wayang Golek).

Central Java has an interesting landscape with a number of excellent temples. The most famous temple is the Borobudur (Figure 36.4), which was built in the eighth century. It is basically a giant Buddhist stupa containing nearly 400 meditation Buddhas. Its site is a quiet and beautiful hill overlooking lush green rice fields outside Jogjakarta. Jogjakarta, the former capital, also contains ruins of the old Water Palace and the Kraton, the palace city of the sultans. Jogjakarta is the island's center for local art and most famous are the finest Indonesian batik, as well as silverware and leather goods.

East Java has a number of attractions, including sanctuaries and temples of architectural splendors that provide images of past empires. Each village, town, or city has its own unique historical relics and legends. East Java is a tropical jungle with many volcanoes. Surabaya, the provincial capital, and the Singosari Temple are particularly noteworthy. The district also offers visitors mountain resorts that are famous for their magnificent scenery.

Sulawesi

Sulawesi has been a tourism development area. It has some excellent beaches and coral reefs. The Spanish and Portuguese influence is evident. South Sulawesi offers a panorama of nature's wonders. Tana Toraja, the land of the Torajans, is known for the grand and unique burial ceremonies and cliffs with their hanging graves. The most important festival is the "Feast of the Dead," but it is limited to only a very few visitors.

Figure 36.4 Borobudur Temple, Java, Indonesia © Nokuro/www.Shutterstock.com.

Malaysia

The Southeast Asian nation of Malaysia stretches from the Malay Peninsula to northern Borneo. Central mountains divide the peninsula, separating the narrow eastern coast from the fertile western plains. The Malaysian states of Sarawak and Sabah share the island of Borneo with Indonesia and Brunei, where swamps rise to jungle-covered mountains. The entire country experiences a humid tropical climate. Malaysia is a multiracial society. Malays make up 57 percent of the population, and almost all Malays are Muslims. Ethnic Chinese constitute 26 percent of Malaysia's people and Indians some 10 percent—both groups are concentrated on the peninsula's west coast. Sabah and Sarawak have some sixty

indigenous ethnic groups; these states are sparsely populated and hold only about 20 percent of the country's population. In the mid-nineteenth century, Britain began importing Chinese to work the tin mines of Muslim sultanates on the Malay Peninsula; by the turn of the twentieth century, rubber plantations employed imported Indian laborers. In 1957 the Federation of Malaya gained independence from Britain. Six years later the colonies of Sarawak and Sabah, on the island of Borneo, and Singapore joined Malaya to form the Federation of Malaysia; Singapore withdrew in 1965. Malaysia, a federal democracy with a ceremonial king, has a strong high-tech economy based on manufacturing and services.

Area	329,847 sq km (127,355 sq mi)
Population	28,295,000
Government	Constitutional Monarchy
Capital	Kuala Lumpur 1,448,000
Life Expectancy	74 years
Literacy	89%
Religion	Muslim, Buddhist, Christian, Hindu
Language	Bahasa Malaysia (Malay), English, Chinese, Tamil, Telugu, Malayalam, Panjabi, Thai, indigenous languages
Currency	ringgit (MYR)
GDP per Cap	$14,800
Labor Force	13% Agriculture, 36% Industry, 51% Services

TRAVEL TIPS 🧳

Entry: A passport is required. Visas are not required for stays up to three months.

Peak Tourist Season: May to December

National Holiday: August 31 (Independence Day)

Health: Cholera and malaria are the two diseases with which travelers should be concerned. Tap water in major cities is considered safe to drink.

Shopping: Common items include batik sarongs, silver and gold brocade, and silver and locally manufactured pewter.

Internet TLD: .my

CULTURAL CAPSULE Malaysia's population is comprised of many ethnic groups; the Malays are a slight majority. The Malays are indigenous and, by constitutional definition, all Muslim. Nearly one-third of Malaysia's people are Chinese. They are mainly urban residents engaged in trade, business, and finance. The majority are Buddhists, Taoists, or Christians. Malaysians of Indian descent represent about 8 percent of the population. About 85 percent of the Indian population are Tamils. They are divided among Hindus,

Cultural hints: Show respect for elderly people. Among the Malays and Indians avoid touching a person's head. Give and receive gifts with both hands. Remove your shoes before entering mosques. Malayans do not form a line for public buses. Malays and Indians eat with hands and spoons. Chinese eat with chopsticks and spoons. Typical foods

include rice, fish, and spiced foods such as hot peppers, vegetables, and fruits.

Tourism Characteristics

Malaysia has the largest number of visitors of all Southeast Asian countries (23 million in 2010). Its location between Thailand and Singapore results in 60 percent of its visitors coming from these countries, making it one of the strongest regional destinations in Southeast Asia. This regional bias is also expressed in the short length of stay of five days, which is only surpassed by Singapore. Malaysia has some excellent resorts, largely responding to the newly industrialized countries of Southeast Asia with their growing middle-class populations. Singapore is the largest generator of visitors (53 percent) to Malaysia. The European nations contribute 5 percent, with the United Kingdom having the greatest share among European nations.

Tourist Destinations and Attractions

The major destinations are Kuala Lumpur, the capital; Penang, one of the oldest trading centers in the East; and the major resorts (with legal gambling) located on the beaches and in the hills. Kuala Lumpur (Figure 36.5) combines narrow streets and a maze of ancient buildings with modern steel and glass structures (the recently completed twin towers of the national petroleum company are the tallest buildings in the world) to offer a wide variety of attractions. It grew from a wild tin-mining town to a thriving capital city in 100 years. It has not discarded its past colonial British heritage. The National Mosque is near the railway station, distinctive because of its 225-foot-high minaret. The Pusat Islam Center houses an Islamic exhibition hall displaying relics from Muslim civilization, such as pottery, coins, calligraphy, weapons, navigational instruments, and various Islamic manuscripts. The influences of Hinduism are also observable. One of the busiest and most colorful parts of the city is Chinatown in Petaling Street. With open markets selling textiles, herbs, household goods, fruit, flowers, cakes, and vegetables, it is a major attraction. Nearby are the Batu caves, which contain a Hindu shrine, Templar Park, and the National Zoo.

Penang (the Pearl of the Orient), just across the border south of Thailand, is a free port with white sandy beaches. The town of Penang, George Town, has temples, colonial architectural relics, and good tourist accommodations. The Snake Temple is probably the only one of its kind in the world. The snakes coil around objects on the altar and throughout the temple. The island is considered another tropical paradise with its lush foliage of giant palms and luxuriant ferns, flowering trees and shrubs, colorful gardens, fruit orchards, rich rice paddies, and coconut groves. It has one of the

Figure 36.5 Skyline of Kuala Lumpur, Malaysia. © leungchopan/www.Shutterstock.com.

most beautiful shorelines in the country. The clear, blue waters of the Straits of Malacca allow good visibility for diving and underwater viewing.

One hundred miles south of Kuala Lumpur, Malacca is one of the oldest towns in the country. Malacca has a long history as a trading center for ships from India, Arabia, China, and Europe. It was colonized by the Portuguese, Dutch, and British. The old fortress on a small hill; the Portuguese Catholic Church, Christ Church; Stadhuys; and Malacca Museum add to the attractions at Malacca, and many provide good examples of Dutch architecture. Mini-Malaysia reflects a cultural heritage emphasizing the unique traditional architecture of various Malay states. There are thirteen Malay traditional houses of various designs, each containing works of art and crafts unique to each state. The coastal areas have beach resorts and offer an excellent

variety of water sports. The east coast includes beaches, fishing villages, batik, and turtle watching. Kota Bharu, Kuala Trengganu, and Rantau Abang are popular towns along the east coast that have a number of handicraft materials and access to good water activities. At Rantau Abang in September, some 1,500 female giant sea turtles migrate to the coast in order to lay their eggs.

Visitors to East Malaysia ride longboats through the Borneo jungles and visit the Iban people in their longhouses situated on the banks of the river. Some can frolic with the baby orangutans in the tropical forests of the state of Sarawak in East Malaysia. The Sarawak Museum in Kuching, the capital of the state of Sarawak, is one of the finest in Asia. It houses a number of artifacts from the many ethnic groups of Borneo. The Tua Pek Kong Temple, Fort Margherita (now a police museum), and Istana (Palace) are additional sites in and around Kuching.

Philippines

The Philippines, in southeastern Asia, consists of more than 7,100 islands lying between the South China Sea and the Pacific Ocean. The islands of Luzon and Mindanao account for two-thirds of the land area. Most of the largest islands are mountainous and forested, and there are about twenty active volcanoes. Earthquakes are relatively frequent, though most are minor. The islands experience a tropical climate with plenty of rain, and typhoons make landfall annually. The majority of Filipinos are of Malay descent and many have mixed ancestry, with Chinese and Spanish being large influences. About eighty-seven languages and dialects are spoken, but Filipino (based on indigenous Tagalog) and English are official languages. More than 80 percent of the population is Christian due to 400 years of Spanish and American rule. An estimated 5 percent of Filipinos are Muslim, and most live on Mindanao, Palawan, and smaller islands that are close to the Muslim countries of Malaysia and Indonesia.

In 1521 Ferdinand Magellan claimed the Philippines for Spain, which ceded the islands to the United States in 1898 after the Spanish-American War. Independence came in 1946, after Japanese occupation ended. Philippine democracy is based on the American model, with a president, senate, and house of representatives. Traditionally, most politicians have come from the wealthy elite, many being descendants of Spanish settlers. Widespread poverty, political corruption, and voting irregularities have sparked social unrest.

Industrial and service sectors are strong but are limited to major urban areas because of poor rural infrastructure. Almost a quarter of the country's labor force works overseas, and remittances prop up the national economy.

From *National Geographic Atlas of the World*, 9th edition. Copyright © 2011 National Geographic Society. Reprinted by arrangement. All rights reserved.

Area	300,000 sq km (115,831 sq mi)
Population	92,227,000
Government	Republic
Capital	Manila 11,100,000
Life Expectancy	69 years
Literacy	93%
Religion	Roman Catholic, other Christian, Muslim
Language	Filipino, English
Currency	Philippine peso (PHP)
GDP per Cap	$3,300
Labor Force	35% Agriculture, 15% Industry, 50% Services

From *National Geographic Atlas of the World*, 9th edition. Copyright © 2011 National Geographic Society. Reprinted by arrangement. All rights reserved.

PHILIPPINES

TRAVEL TIPS 🧳

Entry: A visa and passport are required.

Peak Tourist Season: December through February

National Holiday: June 12 (Independence Day)

Health: Water is safe in Manila; however, untreated or unboiled water should not be drunk outside the city. Eat only fruits and vegetables that can be peeled or properly cleaned with safe water. Sanitation is not always good, and dysentery is common.

Shopping: Common items include handbags, abacca or rafia rugs, shoes, pearl and coral jewelry, embroidered shirts, wooden handicrafts, brassware, and pineapple fiber textiles.

Internet TLD: .ph

CULTURAL CAPSULE

The majority of Philippine people are of Malay descent who migrated to the islands long before the Christian era. The most significant ethnic minority group is the Chinese, who have played an important role in commerce since the ninth century. As a result of intermarriage, many Filipinos have some Chinese and Spanish ancestry. Americans and Spaniards constitute the next largest minorities in the country. The remainder includes a number of different ethnic groups such as Negritos, who inhabit the uplands of the islands around the Sulu Sea, and the Igorot and Ifugao, who inhabit the mountains of northern Luzon. Over 90 percent of the people are Christian (predominantly Roman Catholic). They were converted during the nearly 400 years of Spanish and American rule. The major non-Hispanic groups are the Muslim population, concentrated in the Sulu Archipelago and western Mindanao, and the mountain groups of northern Luzon. About eighty-seven native languages and dialects are spoken, all belonging to the Malay-Polynesian linguistic family. The three principal indigenous languages are Cebuano, spoken in the Visayas; Tagalog, predominant in the area around Manila; and Ilocano, spoken in northern Luzon. Since 1939, in an effort to develop national unity, the government has promoted the use of the national language, Filipino, which is based on Tagalog. English is the most important nonnative language and is used as a second language by almost half of the population. Spanish is spoken by few Filipinos, and its use is decreasing.

Figure 36.6 Carnation tree coral with diver, Cebu, Philippines. © Sphinx Wang/www.Shutterstock.com.

Cultural hints: Respect is shown for elders. Ask permission to take photographs of people. Filipinos seldom observe lines. A 15 percent tip is customary. Leave a little food on plate when finished. Typical foods include rice, fish, vegetable, pork, garlic, stew of chicken, milk, seafood, and a drink of sweetened beans.

Tourism Characteristics

Travel to the Philippines reached 3.1 million in 2010. Tourism to the Philippines is the most diverse of all Southeast Asian countries. It has the lowest regional numbers of visitors, with less than 10 percent coming from other Southeast Asian countries. The major generators of tourism to the Philippines are South Korea, the United States, and Japan. The major purpose of visiting is listed as "holiday," accounting for over 68 percent of the visitors. A majority of those visiting are repeat visitors, with North America having the highest percentage of repeat visitors (64) compared to an average of 51 percent for all tourists.

Tourist Destinations and Attractions

The major destinations centers are in Manila and Luzon Island. Manila is situated on a large bay on Luzon Island and is the site of the official capital (Quezon City), relics of the Spanish colonial era in Fort Santiago, and the reconstructed Cathedral of San Augustine. The Spanish colonizers moved the capital from Cebu to Manila in 1571, beginning the Walled City as the seat of both church and state. Manila has attractive parks, impressive modern buildings, and a cultural center. The Spanish colonial architecture with iron grillwork and balconies is evident throughout the city. Of special note for Americans are Manila's island fortress, Corregidor, site of General MacArthur's wartime headquarters and a famous World War II battle site, and the American Memorial Cemetery. The Church of St. Augustine is the oldest church in the city.

The Philippines offers good shopping both in modern stores and the bazaar-type markets throughout the country. The Nayong Filipino (Philippine Village) has scaled-down replicas of Bicol's Mayon Volcano, the Banaue Rice Terraces, the Chocolate Hills of Bohol, and Magellan's Cross of Cebu. Also, there are clusters of houses and their architecture reflective of six of the thirteen regions in the country to form a miniature village.

The Pagsanjan River on Luzon has one of Asia's lushest jungles and rapids and waterfalls of great beauty. Just south of the town of Pagsanjan is one of the most beautiful falls in the island. Other attractions on Luzon include Lake Taal, with a unique double volcano, and the eighteenth-century bamboo organ at Las Pinas. The beach resort of Baguio is considered one of the great resorts of the world.

Cebu City in the province of Cebu, the second international gateway to the country after Manila, is referred to as the "Queen City of the South." Cebu Province is composed of 167 islands with a variety of resorts. In addition to good diving (Figure 36.6) and other water sports, its historical attractions include Magellan's Cross, planted by the Portuguese explorer Ferdinand Magellan to mark the spot where the first Filipinos were baptized, and the Basilica Minore del Santo Nino, which houses the oldest religious relic in the Philippines, the statue of the Sto. Nino (Child Jesus).

Mindanao Island is an exotic island where wild carabao are found. Zamboanga, one of Mindanao's cities, has rolling surf, palm-fringed beaches, natural swimming pools, and lovely orchids. Zamboanga is noted for its beautiful hanging gardens and parks along with the minarets and domes of its mosques. People of the Moros tribe perform their ceremonial dances in the Muslim village and mosque at Taluksangay on Mindanao. Unfortunately, the rebellion of the Muslims on the island makes it unsafe for visitors.

Singapore

The country of Singapore, consisting of Singapore island and some 50 smaller islands, is located in Southeast Asia at the tip of the Malay Peninsula. It is connected to the peninsula by a causeway that is 1.2 kilometers (0.75 mile) long. Singapore is low-lying, and nearly 20 percent of its surface area is reclaimed from swamps and the sea. Thousands of multinational companies have offices on this tropical island because of its location at the entrance to the Strait of Malacca—the shortest sea route between the Indian Ocean and the South China Sea. As a trade center of the British Empire, Singapore attracted thousands of Chinese settlers—now 77 percent of the population. Independent since 1965, Singapore is Southeast Asia's financial hub and the world's busiest container port. Singapore approved gambling in 2005, and huge resort casino complexes and theme parks have opened to lure tourists and business travelers.

From *National Geographic Atlas of the World*, 9th edition. Copyright © 2011 National Geographic Society. Reprinted by arrangement. All rights reserved.

Area	660 sq km (255 sq mi)
Population	5,113,000
Government	Parliamentary Republic
Capital	Singapore 4,790,000
Life Expectancy	81 years
Literacy	93%
Religion	Buddhist, Muslim, Christian, Taoist, Hindu
Language	Mandarin, English, Malay, Tamil
Currency	Singapore dollar (SGD)
GDP per Cap	$50,300
Labor Force	0% Agriculture, 23.8% Industry, 76.2% Services

From *National Geographic Atlas of the World*, 9th edition. Copyright © 2011 National Geographic Society. Reprinted by arrangement. All rights reserved.

TRAVEL TIPS

Entry: A passport is required. A visa is not required for stays up to two weeks. Proof of onward or return transportation is required.

Tourist Season: Year-round

National Holiday: August 9 (National Day)

Health: No vaccinations are needed to visit unless entering from a country that has yellow fever. The water is safe to drink.

Caution: Singapore has strict enforcement of littering, jaywalking, and drug possession.

Shopping: Common items include goods from many countries as Singapore is a free port. There are many Chinese goods, handicrafts, and Thai silk. Gold and silver are also popular items.

Internet TLD: .sg

CULTURAL CAPSULE

Singapore is one of the most densely populated countries in the world. It has a varied linguistic, cultural, and religious heritage. More than 76 percent of the population are Chinese. Fifteen percent are Malay, and a little over 6 percent are Indian. Malay, Chinese, English, and Tamil are all official languages. English is widely used in professions, businesses, and schools. The Chinese speak a number of Chinese dialects, such as Hokkein, Chaozhou, and Cantonese. Singapore has religious freedom. Almost all Malays are Muslim; other Singaporeans are Hindus, Sikhs, Taoists, Buddhists, Confucianists, and Christians. The Christians are generally either Chinese or European.

Singapore has created a very strict society. As indicated they have very strong littering, jaywalking, and drug possession laws. They also have strong laws related to quality of goods sold in stores. If a visitor feels a purchase is defective or of poor quality and the store personnel do not correct the problem, they can be prosecuted.

Cultural hints: Shoes are removed before entering a mosque. Visitors are expected to be punctual. Some foods are eaten with a spoon, some with the hands. As service charge is included in bill, tips are not necessary. Typical foods include rice, fish, seafood, peanut sauce, Indian curries, Chinese dishes, and fruits.

Tourism Characteristics

Singapore benefits from its central location in Southeast Asia and its history of being the crossroads of shipping routes between the Indian and Pacific oceans, As an administrative center and military base for the British, it was well on its way to becoming an important international commercial center before World War II. Since World War II, Singapore has emerged as an important industrial producer and commercial center for the entire region. Singapore's important position in Southeast Asia reflects its situational relationship, which offsets its small size. Like Hong Kong, Singapore is a duty-free port; consequently shopping is central to the tourism industry. Visitors have the highest daily per capita expenditure in the region.

Tourists to Singapore reflect a regional market. Asian visitors accounted for over 50 percent of all arrivals in 2010. Growth in tourism has continued with 2010 arrivals reaching nearly 10 million. Outside of the Southeast Asian region, China and Japan contributes the most visitors to Singapore. Outside of Asia, Australia, the United Kingdom, and the United States send the largest number of tourists to Singapore—Australia because of its proximity, the United Kingdom because of historical ties, and the United States, whose travelers use it as a gateway or crossroads to Southeast Asia. A high percentage of visitors visit Singapore as part of a larger tour, as reflected in the low average length of visit, 3.2 days. Singapore is committed to providing a good experience for visitors. It has a very strict "anti-cheaters" law, which literally forces shop owners and merchants to sell quality goods. Should a visitor buy a defective item, he or she can go directly to the store or shop and get a refund or a replacement.

Tourist Destinations and Attractions

Singapore's first and foremost tourist attraction is the duty-free shopping. The city's premier mall is Ngee Ann City. Chinatown offers all the usual Chinese sights, sounds, smells, shops, food, folk medicines, and handicrafts. The architecture of Singapore illustrates its varied population, with Malay Chinese, Indian, and Hindu temples, as well as Islamic mosques and Western churches and architecture. The Raffles Hotel is a famous tourist attraction and well known for its fine restaurants.

Some attractions in addition to the shopping are excellent zoological and botanical gardens; Jung Bird Park, with a variety of tropical Asian birds; Haw Par Villa (Tiger Balm Gardens), which houses a priceless collection of jade; Arab Street; Little India; and Chinatown. A major attraction is the 20-acre Asian Village consisting of three villages representing Southeast Asia, South Asia, and North Asia. It showcases Asian lifestyles, food, entertainment, handicrafts, and architecture. In the Underwater World Singapore, Asia's largest tropical oceanarium with more than 2,300 fish, you can wander along the bottom of the ocean in a 273-foot clear acrylic tube. Esplanade Theater, an architectural signature building for the city, is situated on the river and is home for exhibits and performances related to the fine arts. Nearby is Sentosa Beach.

Thailand

Thailand, in Southeast Asia, is dominated by the Chao Phraya river basin, which contains Bangkok, the capital and largest city, with some 6.7 million people. Bangkok presents a distinctive Buddhist landscape, with gold-layered spires and giant Buddha statues. To the east rises the Khorat Plateau, a sandstone plateau with poor soils supporting grasses and woodlands. The long southern region, which connects with Malaysia, is hilly and forested. The highest mountains are in northern Thailand, where rich soils in remote mountain valleys form part of the opium-producing Golden Triangle region. The population is largely homogeneous, with most people being ethnic Thai and professing Buddhism. Those of Chinese origin form the second largest ethnic group, and they are well integrated into Thai society due to intermarriage. Some 3 million Muslims live in the south near the border with Malaysia. About 160,000 refugees from Myanmar exist in decades-old camps along the border. The UN High Commissioner for Refugees estimates that Thailand shelters 3.5 million stateless people.

In the nineteenth century, kings of Siam introduced Western education and technology but preserved the character of a devout Buddhist society. The only nation in Southeast Asia to escape colonial rule, Siam changed its name in 1939 to Thailand, meaning "land of the free." However, Thailand has not escaped military coups—more than a dozen since 1932.

Area	513,115 sq km (198,115 sq mi)
Population	67,764,000
Government	Constitutional Monarchy
Capital	Bangkok 6,704,000
Life Expectancy	69 years
Literacy	93%
Religion	Buddhist, Muslim
Language	Thai, English, ethnic and regional dialects
Currency	baht (THB)
GDP per Cap	$8,100
Labor Force	42.4% Agriculture, 19.7% Industry, 37.9% Services

TRAVEL **TIPS** 🧳

Entry: A passport is required. A visa is not required for stays up to 30 days.

Peak Tourist Season: December

National Holiday: December 5 (Birthday of King Phumiphon)

Health: For travel in rural areas vaccinations are needed for typhoid, cholera, rabies, and hepatitis. Malaria suppressants are advised. Avoid tap water, raw milk, ice cream, uncooked meats, and unwashed fruits and vegetables.

Caution: Visitors are sometimes victimized by individuals offering to be guides who take tourists to gemstone dealers where the dealer will overcharge for poor-quality stones.

Shopping: Common items include Thai silk and cotton, jewelry, silver, gold lacquerware, bronze ware, Celadon pottery, teak carvings, and rattan and bamboo furniture.

Internet TLD: .th

CULTURAL CAPSULE

Thailand's population is relatively homogeneous. More than 85 percent of the people speak a dialect of Thai and share a common culture. It is divided into Central Thai (36 percent), Thai-Lao (32 percent), Northern Thai (8 percent), and Southern Thai (8 percent). The largest minorities are the Chinese (12 percent) and the Malay-speaking Muslims in the south (3 percent). Other groups include the Khmer, the Mon, and the Vietnamese. Thai is the official language and is used in schools, but each region has its own language, such as Khmer, Mon, Miao, Malay, and others. English is spoken by the educated. Theravada Buddhism is the religion of more than 90 percent of the Thai. Traditionally, all young men were expected to become Buddhist monks for at least three months to study Buddhist

principles. The practice is not strictly enforced today. About 4 percent of the population is Muslim, and there are a small number of Christians. Spirit worship and animism are important in Thai religious life.

Cultural hints: The Wai greeting. Place the palms of the hands together, with fingers extended at chest level, and bow slightly to greet others. This is also used to say thank you, good-bye, or I am sorry. Remove shoes before entering a home. Do not step on the doorsill when entering a dwelling. Thais believe a deity resides in the doorsill. Women must never touch a Buddhist monk or offer to shake hands. Remove your shoes before entering a mosque. Use the fork (left hand) to push food onto the spoon. Tips are not necessary, but some give a small amount (5 percent). Typical foods include rice, spicy dishes of meat, vegetables, fish, eggs, and fruits. Curries and pepper sauces are popular.

Tourism Characteristics

Like Singapore, Thailand is a crossroads for travel between Europe and Asia, and for some Europeans to the South Pacific. The country received 16 million visitors in 2010 and tourism represents 6 percent of the country's economic activity. In 2012 the country embarked on an ambitious five-year National Tourism Development Plan. The country seeks to remain a top destination in Asia by improving the infrastructure, rehabilitate tourism sites, and integrate domestic and international tourism. Visitors to Thailand stay longer than in Singapore, indicating the greater diversity of attractions that Thailand offers compared to Singapore. Like Singapore, however, Thailand receives most of its visitors from Asia. Outside of Southeast Asia, Japan, China, and the United States are the most important individual countries. Japanese tourists include a large percentage of business travelers, often combining business with entertainment unavailable in Japan or coming specifically on package tours for such entertainment. For visitors from the United States and the European countries, Bangkok provides an attractive option on circular tours because of its unique and diverse cultural attractions.

Tourist Destinations and Attractions

Bangkok, the capital, has an impressive and fascinating life along its canals, with shops, teak houses on stilts, temples, and snake farms. Like many nations of the world where a large proportion of the population is engaged in agriculture, Thailand has periodic markets where fresh produce is sold. Thailand's markets are unique because they are floating. The floating markets, such as the Damnoen Saduak (Figure 36.7), reflect the traditional importance of the canals and streams found in the delta of the Menam River of Thailand. Wearing enormous straw hats, men and women bring their products to the market in long, narrow boats piled high with rice, fruits, and vegetables, dried beef and fish, flowers, and other goods and buy and sell from the water.

Figure 36.7 Damnoen Saduak floating market, Ratchaburi, Thailand. © topten22photo /www.Shutterstock.com.

Within Bangkok, the Royal Grand Palace, which was the home for the king of Siam, is one of the wonders of the world. On the grounds of the palace is Wat Phra Kaeo, the chapel of the Emerald Buddha, one of the most impressive attractions in Asia. Patpong is Bangkok's nightlife and shopping district. The Pasteur Institute, operated by the Thai Red Cross, houses the world's largest collection of poisonous snakes. Outside of Bangkok is the "ancient city," a large outdoor museum containing sixty-five of Thailand's most beautiful and impressive temples and reconstructed historical monuments and the Thai Cultural Center (Rose Garden). Throughout the country, there are ornate temples (Figure 36.8) and charming people. A final attraction is the Kwai River, made famous by the film depicting Japanese efforts to make American and British prisoners of war in World War II build a railroad bridge. Nakhon Pathom, some 40 miles west of Bangkok, is the site of the 380-foot Phra Pathom Chedi, the world's tallest Buddhist monument. Ayutthaya, some 40 miles upstream from Bangkok, was the Siamese capital from 1350 to 1767. It has some magnificent ruins of medieval splendor. Nearby is the Bang Pain Palace, the summer residence of early Bangkok monarchs. Phetchaburi, some 80 miles southwest of Bangkok, is the site of Buddha-filled caves, historic temples and palaces, and Kaeng Krachan.

In northern Thailand along the Burma and Laos border, there are forested mountains and fertile river valleys. This area is part of the fabled Golden Triangle and was the cradle of Thai civilization. Major places of interest are Sukhothal, where massive stone Buddhas sit within the old city walls; Si Satchanalai; Lampang, a Thai provincial capital where horse-drawn carriages are still in use; Doi Inthanon National Park, which covers Thailand's highest mountain and includes beautiful waterfalls; and Chiang Rai, the heart of the Golden Triangle.

Pattaya Beach is one of the best-known seaside resort areas in Asia. It offers excellent swimming, snorkeling, and sailing but it is crowded and overdeveloped. Also along the coast are a number of fishing villages with bays and superb beaches. Phuket, on the west coast is a popular beach for European visitors. Koh Phi Phi (near Phuket) and Koh Samui (south of Bangkok) islands are known for their stunning views and idyllic scenery.

Figure 36.8 Wat (Temple) Chong Kham, Mae Hong Son Province, Thailand. © Valery Shanin/www.Shutterstock.com.

REVIEW QUESTIONS

1. What are the four major obstacles to tourism development found in Southeast Asia? Why?

2. Which country in South Asia has the most well-developed tourist industry? Why?

3. Which country in Southeast Asia receives the largest number of visitors? Why?

4. What accounts for the fact that the United States provides so many tourists to the Philippines?

5. If you were planning a trip to Southeast Asia and wanted to experience contrast and diversity, which four countries would you select? Why?

chapter 37: INDOCHINA—VIETNAM, CAMBODIA, AND LAOS

Country	Capital	Language	Currency	Population (2001) (millions)	Square Miles and State Comparison
Cambodia	Phnom Penh	Khmer	Riel	14	69,898 (Arkansas)
Laos	Vientiane	Laotian, French	Liberation kip	6.5	91,429 (Utah)
Vietnam	Hanoi	Vietnamese, French	Dong	86	120,000 (New Mexico)

These three countries of Southeast Asia have experienced extensive conflict and military occupation. Tourism to the three is growing rapidly.

Vietnam

Vietnam, in Southeast Asia, stretches 1,600 kilometers (1,000 miles) north to south but is only about 40 kilometers (25 miles) wide at its narrowest point near the country's center. The Red River delta lowlands in the north are separated from the huge Mekong Delta in the south by long, narrow coastal plains backed by the forested Annam highlands. Hanoi, the capital, is the main city on the Red River and Ho Chi Minh City (formerly Saigon) is the main city on the Mekong. The tropical climate features summer monsoons. Vietnam has fifty-four ethnic groups, but ethnic Vietnamese are by far the largest at 85 percent of the population. The next largest ethnic groups are the Tay (1.9 percent), Thai (1.8 percent), Muong (1.5 percent), and Khmer (1.3 percent). Most of the people occupy the river deltas and work as farmers or fishermen. Independent for almost a thousand years, Vietnam fell prey to French colonialism in the mid-nineteenth century. During Japanese occupation in World War II, communist leader Ho Chi Minh formed the Vietminh, an alliance of communist and noncommunist nationalist groups. Armed struggle won independence from France in 1954 and led to the partition of Vietnam. For two decades noncommunist South Vietnam, aided by the United States, fought North Vietnam (backed by China and the USSR). American troops withdrew in 1973, and the country was reunified under a communist regime in 1976. War continued after reunification, with the Vietnamese army fighting both Cambodia and China in 1979. Vietnam lost decades of economic development due to numerous wars. But the country turned away from communist economic policies in the late 1980s, and is now one of the fastest-growing economies in Asia.

From *National Geographic Atlas of the World*, 9th edition. Copyright ©2011 National Geographic Society. Reprinted by arrangement. All rights reserved.

Location	Southeastern Asia
Area	331,114 sq km (127,844 sq mi)
Population	87,263,000
Government	Communist State
Capital	Hanoi 4,378,000
Life Expectancy	74 years
Literacy	90%
Religion	Buddhist, Roman Catholic
Language	Vietnamese, English, French, Chinese, Khmer
Currency	dong (VND)
GDP per Cap	$2,900
Labor Force	51.8% Agriculture, 15.5% Industry, 32.7% Services

From *National Geographic Atlas of the World*, 9th edition. Copyright ©2011 National Geographic Society. Reprinted by arrangement. All rights reserved.

Figure 37.1 Halong Bay, Vietnam. © Galyna Andrushko/www.Shutterstock.com.

TRAVEL **TIPS** 🧳

Entry: Vietnam—A visa and passport are required. Laos—A visa and passport are required. Proof of sufficient funds for stay and onward or return transportation required. Cambodia—A visa and passport are required.

National Holiday: Vietnam, September 2 (Independence Day); Laos, December 2 (Republic Day); Cambodia, November 9 (Independence Day)

Transportation: International access to all three countries is generally through Bangkok.

Health: Cholera and malaria protection is needed. Tap water is not potable. Care should be taken by eating fruits and vegetables that can be peeled or cooked.

Caution: Many areas of Cambodia are considered unsafe to travel and may be restricted.

CULTURAL CAPSULE Ethnic Vietnamese constitute almost 90 percent of the population. Originating in what is now southern China and northern Vietnam, the Vietnamese people pushed southward beginning in 939 A.D. to occupy the entire eastern seacoast of the Indochinese Peninsula. Various ethnic groups make up the remainder of the population. Chinese is the largest group, found mostly in cities. The second largest minority is the southern Montagnards (mountain people), comprising two main ethnolinguistic groups—Malayo-Polynesian and Khmer. About 30 groups of various cultures and dialects are spread over the highland territory. The third largest minority is the Khmer Krom (Cambodians), numbering about 600,000, who are concentrated in southern provinces near the Cambodian border and at the mouth of the Mekong River. Buddhism is the most common religion (55 percent), followed by Taoist (12 percent), and Roman Catholic (7 percent). Some of the minorities are animists. Vietnamese is the official language. There are a number of accents in the various regions of the country. Most officials understand English.

Tourism Characteristics and Tourist Destinations

Vietnam is welcoming tourists with aggressive marketing campaigns. Visits have increased from 1.5 million in 1996 to more than 5 million foreign tourists arrivals in 2010. China is the most important market for travel to Vietnam. The United States represents the second largest international market for Vietnam. Vietnam veterans and other interested travelers are returning to the country to observe and see the places of interest such as Ho Chi Minh City (Saigon), Cu Chi Tunnels, Mekong, Danang, and Non Nuoc Beach (China Beach). Hue, an ancient royal capital, is about a 3-hour drive from Danang. The Citadel of Hue is being restored with the help of UNESCO. The Citadel comprises the Defensive Wall, the Royal Wall, and the Forbidden Purple City. In Hue also are found the seven Royal Tombs. The Cu Chi Tunnels offer a view of the war. A glass box containing a model of the former war zone, complete with light bulbs to indicate the areas of action, acts as an introduction. Visitors are then led through narrow and dark burrows to obtain a feel of life during the war. Hanoi, the capital, was a picturesque city combining the modern French-built sectors with the Vietnamese character. Two historical monuments, the Single Pillar Pagoda and the Great Buddha Pagoda, are important attractions. Natural attractions in the country include islands dotted Halong Bay (near Hanoi) (Figure 37.1), the Mekong River Delta, and the Tonkinese Alps near the border with Laos and China.

Cambodia

This Southeast Asia country is forested and largely flat, except for the Cardamom Mountains in the southwest and the Dangrek Range in the north—both help form a natural border with Thailand. The Mekong River and Tonle Sap (Great Lake) occupy Cambodia's heartland. The Tonle Sap, Southeast Asia's largest lake, grows larger during the summer rainy season when the Mekong runs high. The capital, Phnom Penh, is located at the confluence of the Mekong and Tonle Sap, and most Cambodians live in this densely populated region. The climate is tropical, with high temperatures throughout the year. Millions of tourists come to see the ruins just north of Tonle Sap. Angkor, the capital of the Khmer empire, fell into ruins some 600 years ago, but its vast urban extent was the size of New York City's five boroughs. Angkor Wat, the world's largest religious monument, represents the greatness of Khmer culture and is pictured on Cambodia's flag.

Cambodia's recent history, which includes the genocidal Khmer Rouge regime and 1979–1989 Vietnamese occupation, devastated the country and made it one of the world's poorest nations. The democratic government is reducing poverty by turning the agrarian economy toward garment production and Angkor-based tourism and events.

Location	Southeastern Asia
Area	181,035 sq km (69,898 sq mi)
Population	14,805,000
Government	Multiparty Democracy under a Constitutional Monarchy
Capital	Phnom Penh 1,466,000
Life Expectancy	61 years
Religion	Buddhist
Language	Khmer, French, English
Currency	riel (KHR)
GDP per Cap	$1,900
Labor Force	67.9% Agriculture

CULTURAL CAPSULE The largest ethnic group is the Khmer (over 70 percent of the population). Next is the Sino-Khmer (mixed Chinese and Khmer), which accounts for about 10 percent of the population. The Chams (5 percent) are descendants of the Champa Kingdom, which was centered in present-day Vietnam and contained people of Malaysian origin. There are a number of Vietnamese and Chinese in Cambodia. The Khmer language comes from an older language called Paali, which developed as a successor to Indian Sanskrit. Thai and Lao share common words with Khmer. French is used to communicate in business and among government officials. Cambodians are Theravada Buddhists. The Cham minority are Islam.

Tourism Characteristics and Tourist Destinations

Cambodia had 2.8 million visitors in 2010 (up from 368,000 in 1999). Vietnam is the reported major source, followed by South Korea, Japan, and China. The remainder are largely inter-regional arrivals. Cambodia is trying to implement a comprehensive plan for the tourism industry. The plan includes renovation and construction of airports, hotels, entertainment facilities, and other segments of the tourism infrastructure. It is designed to preserve Cambodia's cultural and environmental assets while encouraging sustainable tourism growth.

Cambodia's capital, Phnom Penh, is the center of the tourism industry. Much has changed because of the conflict and repeated changes in policy. The Angkor Wat Ruins are the best-known tourist attraction in all of Indochina. Angkor Wat, located in central Cambodia, was the capital city of the old Khmer Empire and a number of architecturally important ruins still remain. Angkor Wat was the masterpiece of the Khmers, built between 1130 and 1160. The five cone-shaped towers rise from the jungle like little volcanoes. Jungle vines are mixed among spectacular ruins (Figure 37.2), adding a sense of greatness.

Hue, the old imperial city, has important attractions, such as the Imperial Palace, the Gold Water Bridge, and the River of Perfumes, much of which was destroyed by war.

Laos

A landlocked nation in Southeast Asia, Laos is mostly a land of forested mountains and plateaus. The climate is tropical with monsoon rains. Agriculture, mostly subsistence farming, dominates the landscape. Ethnically complex, Laos includes some forty-seven major ethnic groups, with the Lao group making up 52 percent of the population. Most people live in the valleys of the Mekong River and its tributaries, where rice can be

grown on fertile floodplains. Soon after independence from France in 1953, the country fell into turmoil; in 1975 the communist Pathet Lao seized power with help from North Vietnam. Many fled the regime, and the United States resettled some 250,000 Lao refugees. One of the few remaining communist states, Laos is hampered by poor roads, no railroad, and limited access to electricity. The country depends on international aid from Japan, China, and Vietnam.

Figure 37.2 Tree covering the stones of Ta Prohm temple in Angkor Wat, Siem Reap, Cambodia. © FCG/www.Shutterstock.com.

Location	Southeastern Asia
Area	236,800 sq km (91,429 sq mi)
Population	6,320,000
Government	Communist State
Capital	Vientiane 745,000
Life Expectancy	65 years
Literacy	69%
Religion	Buddhist
Language	Lao, French, English, various ethnic languages
Currency	kip (LAK)
GDP per Cap	$2,100
Labor Force	80% Agriculture, 20% Industry & Services

From *National Geographic Atlas of the World*, 9th edition. Copyright ©2011 National Geographic Society. Reprinted by arrangement. All rights reserved.

CULTURAL CAPSULE

About half of the people are ethnic Lao, who live in the lowland regions. The Lao descended from the Thai people who migrated southward from China in the thirteenth century. Mountain tribes of Sino-Tibetan (Hmong, Yao, Aka, and Lahu) and Thai ethnolinguistic heritage are found in Northern Laos. In the central and southern mountains, Mon Khmer tribes predominate. Some Vietnamese and Chinese minorities remain in cities. The predominant religion is Theravada Buddhism. Animism is common among the mountain tribes. The official and dominant language is Lao, a tonal language of the Thai linguistic group. French is understood by older people who worked in government and commerce.

Tourism Characteristics and Tourist Destinations

Tourism to Laos was slow to develop but tripled in ten years to 1.2 million between 2001 and 2010. Major attractions in Laos are Luang Prabang, the royal capital with its Royal Palace, and Vientiane, the modern capital, on the Mekong River. Vientiane has many temples, of which the hilltop temple of Wat Phou and the Luang Prabang are the most important as the latter is said to contain Buddha's breastbone.

REVIEW QUESTIONS

1. What is the name of the region's great river?

2. The world's largest religious monument is in Cambodia. What is its name?

3. What is the most developed country in th...

4. What is the least developed country in th...

part 12: GEOGRAPHY AND TOURISM IN AUSTRALIA, NEW ZEALAND, AND THE ISLANDS OF THE SOUTH PACIFIC

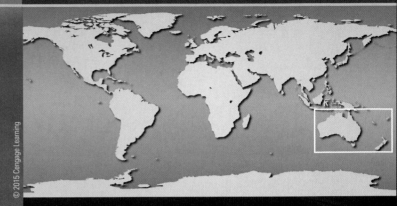

MAJOR GEOGRAPHIC CHARACTERISTICS

- The South Pacific region consists of three island groups: Melanesia, Micronesia, and Polynesia; and Australia and New Zealand.

- The islands of the Pacific can be divided into the high volcanic islands and the low coral islands.

- The Pacific region covers the largest area of any world travel region, yet has a very small land area.

- Australia and New Zealand have strong economic and cultural ties to Europe.

- The economies of Australia and New Zealand rely heavily upon agriculture and natural resources.

MAJOR TOURISM CHARACTERISTICS

- The area is remote from the population and industrial centers of the world, requiring long-haul visitors.

- The Pacific Islands are perceived as both culturally and physically exotic.

- Australia and New Zealand have some of the longest lengths of stay for visitors.

- Tourism to Australia and New Zealand is highly associated with their cultural linkage to Europe and North America.

MAJOR TOURIST DESTINATIONS

Tahiti

Fiji

Guam

Saipan

Auckland, New Zealand

Rotorua, New Zealand

Christchurch, New Zealand

Southern Alps

Queensland and Milford Sound

Southeast coastal area between Sydney and Melbourne

Coastal areas of Queensland (Great Barrier Reef)

Alice Springs, Australia

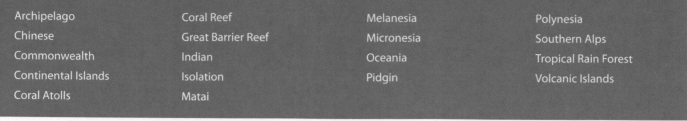

KEY TERMS AND WORDS

Archipelago	Coral Reef	Melanesia	Polynesia
Chinese	Great Barrier Reef	Micronesia	Southern Alps
Commonwealth	Indian	Oceania	Tropical Rain Forest
Continental Islands	Isolation	Pidgin	Volcanic Islands
Coral Atolls	Matai		

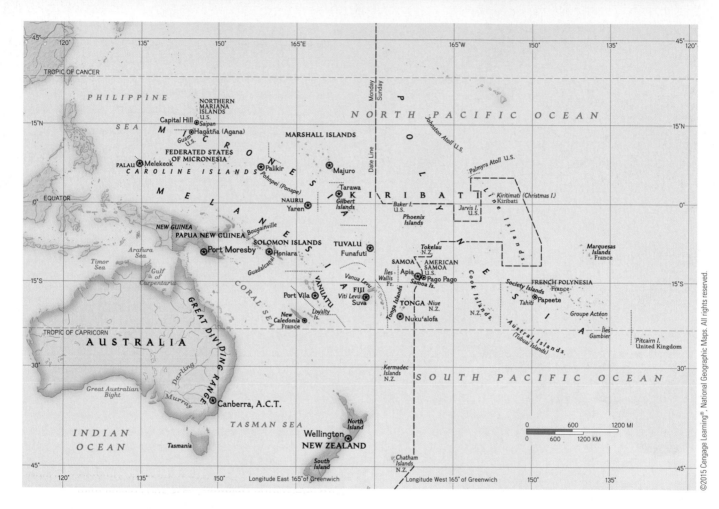

Introduction

The South Pacific is one of the fastest-growing areas for tourist arrivals. However, it must be kept in mind that the numbers are relatively small. The islands of the Pacific (other than Hawaii, which is part of North America because of political ties), Australia, and New Zealand are isolated due to their long distances from the rest of the world. The Pacific Islands are further handicapped because their isolation is compounded by their small size. Their small size hinders development of major manufacturing, resources, and agricultural commodities to justify more transportation links with the rest of the world, which would be helpful in increasing development of tourism.

Australia and New Zealand have benefited from their larger size and close cultural and economic ties to Europe and North America. While isolated from their European cultural hearth, the first European settlers developed towns, governments, and societal values reflecting their European origins. Both Australia's and New Zealand's earliest European inhabitants were English, and they consciously developed societies that replicated the perception of their homeland. Both nations have highly developed economies that have all

Figure P12.1 Coral reef islands, Palau, Micronesia. © tororo reaction/www.Shutterstock.com.

the characteristics of developed nations. They have high literacy levels, high incomes, large amounts of leisure time, and the individualism and materialism found in other regions of the industrialized world.

Australia and New Zealand are different in physical geography, with one large and the other small, one mineral-rich and the other with few mineral resources, one an island nation and the other occupying a continent, and one reliant upon agricultural exports almost exclusively and the other reliant upon both mineral and agricultural exports.

Physical Characteristics

The South Pacific Islands

The islands of the South Pacific region (often referred to as Oceania) can be divided into three island groups: Melanesia, Micronesia, and Polynesia. Melanesia is closest to the Southeast Asian archipelago, and the islands are larger and have a tropical climate similar to that of the Southeast Asian mainland and the Indonesian archipelago. Melanesia extends from the Southeast Asian

mainland to Australia and consists of a number of large islands, the largest being Papua New Guinea. The size of the islands in Melanesia has led some geographers to refer to them as continental islands, to distinguish them from the much smaller islands of Micronesia and Polynesia. The mountains of the large islands of Melanesia are extremely rugged, with plateaus and precipitous interior valleys. The lower and coastal areas are divided by rivers with alternating swampy areas and coastal plains.

Micronesia (Figure P12.1) is a complex of a few high mountainous volcanic islands and many tiny coral atolls. Atolls consist of a coral island or islands with a coral reef surrounding a lagoon. Coral atolls are low, and many rise only a few feet above the high-tide level. Volcanic islands, such as Guam, can reach elevations of over 2,600 feet (800 meters). The low atolls have a shortage of fresh water, which restricts tourism. The higher volcanic islands receive more precipitation, especially on their higher slopes.

Polynesia covers the largest area of the South Pacific, but its total land area is extremely small. Physically, this region includes both low coral atolls and volcanic islands. Many of these high volcanic islands have steep cliffs and mountain ranges divided by deep valleys. As

Figure P12.2 Desert near the old Canning Sock Route in Western Australia. © Edward Haylan/www.Shutterstock.com.

air masses cross these mountains, cooling associated with higher elevations results in condensation, clouds, and precipitation in a process known as orographic precipitation. The heavy precipitation provides a source of fresh water. In some cases the volcanic islands are surrounded by fringing reefs that provide good fishing. While atolls are found throughout the Pacific, most of Micronesia is atolls. The atolls are extremely vulnerable to severe weather disturbances such as typhoons, unusually high seas, or droughts.

With the exception of Easter Island and New Zealand, the climate of the islands of the South Pacific is tropical rain forest with year-round precipitation and warm-to-hot temperatures with seasonal winds to temper the high humidity. Most of the islands in the South Pacific have a uniformly warm year-round temperature, ranging from nighttime lows near 68 degrees Fahrenheit to highs in the mid to high 80s. On the windward side of the high islands and on atolls, the warm temperatures and high humidity are offset by the cooling of the trade winds. On the leeward side and in the interior of the mountainous islands, humidity can make it very uncomfortable. In the highlands of the Melanesian Islands, particularly Papua New Guinea, it can be quite cool, with very rare frost.

While there are no real seasonal changes as in the mid-latitudes, the year can be divided into rainy and dry seasons, especially in the savanna climate. North of the equator, the heaviest rainfall occurs from June to October, and south of the equator, from November to March. In the westernmost Pacific, monsoon winds produce heavy seasonal rains in the western Carolinas, Papua New Guinea, and the Solomon Islands of Melanesia.

The most severe storms in the Pacific are cyclonic storms known as typhoons (hurricanes). They begin in the east and move westward. They can occur at any time of the year, but they are most frequent during the rainy season and cause great destruction and often denude and reshape the configuration of entire atolls.

The coral atolls, volcanic islands, and tropical climate combine to create a setting perceived as exotic by residents of the industrialized nations.

A Unique Landscape: Australia and New Zealand

Australia

Most of Australia has an arid (desert or steppe) climate (Figure P12.2), which limits agricultural activities and

Figure P12.3 Great Barrier Reef, Australia. © gary yim/www.Shutterstock.com.

settlement, but its large landmass includes five general climatic regions.

The eastern coastal area from Brisbane south to Melbourne has abundant precipitation year-round. The climatic types range from humid subtropical in the Brisbane area, which is a major tourist region similar to Miami, to the marine west coast in the south around Melbourne and Canberra, where the tourist season is shorter. The major highland of Australia, the Great Dividing Range, extends along this eastern coast in a belt 100 to 250 miles wide. These rugged but low mountains rarely exceed 3,000 feet in elevation. The highest point, Mount Kosciusko, is at only 7,316 feet, which is also the highest elevation in Australia. It is in this region that the film *Man from Snowy River* was filmed, which increased international tourism interest. It is the eastern and southeastern portions of Australia that are the centers of population for Australia. The two largest cities alone, Sydney and Melbourne, account for 40 percent of the total population of the nation.

The southwestern and southern parts of Australia have a Mediterranean-type climate characterized by hot, dry summers and mild, moist winters, similar to that of Southern California. Since it is in the Southern Hemisphere, the summer dry season is from October to April and the winter wet season is from June to September. This area of Australia is an important producer of grapes and other crops typical of the Mediterranean climates of Southern Europe and Southern California. The combination of summer drought and the region's remoteness from population centers has limited the development of truck farming on a scale similar to that found in Southern California and Southern Europe. The northern coastal regions of Australia have a savanna climate with rainy summers and dry winters. Precipitation exceeds 20 inches throughout most of this northern region, but a dry season and high temperatures handicap agriculture. The northeast region does have the internationally known Great Barrier Reef (Figure P12.3), which has led to the development of one of the better tourist regions of Australia.

Figure P12.4 Mount Cook, New Zealand. © mrmichaelangelo/www.Shutterstock.com.

The majority of Australia is arid and semiarid. The central portion receives less than 10 inches of rainfall per year and is surrounded by a steppe land that receives 10 to 20 inches. This great, dry interior is referred to by Australians as the Outback and covers more than one-half of the total continent.

New Zealand

New Zealand consists of two large and a number of small islands. North Island contains the majority of the 4.3 million residents of New Zealand, while the larger South Island and the small islands have fewer people. The population is centered on the Canterbury Plain of the east central portion of South Island and the coastal plains and the lower slopes of the uplands of North Island. New Zealand's landforms are dominated by high mountain ranges, particularly the Southern Alps of South Island, which reach 12,349 feet at Mt. Cook. The mountainous nature of

Tourism

As indicated, tourism to this region experienced a rapid rate of growth. However, this rate is misleading since it occurred from a relatively small base that makes small numerical increases result in a large percentage increase. The change in Australia/New Zealand from 5.8 million in 1999 to 8 million in 2010 represents a

New Zealand provides for an extensive park system in the Southern Alps and the major tourist attraction of its highest peak, Mt. Cook (Figure P12.4). With active glaciation and many waterfalls, cirques, matterhorns, and fjords along the southwest coast, it is an area of outstanding scenic beauty.

The climate of New Zealand is a marine west-coast climate, and half of the nation is suitable for intensive grazing. The production of wool and mutton for export to Europe has been the major economic activity from the time of the first European settlements. The island character of New Zealand influences the climate. Although New Zealand lies in latitudes similar to those between San Luis Obispo, California, and the mouth of the Columbia River, its climate is cooler and more moderate because of the surrounding water. Precipitation is well distributed seasonally and varies from more than 120 inches annually along the southwest coast to less than 30 inches on the east-coast lowlands.

growth of over 5 percent per year. While the percentages demonstrate a rapid growth *rate*, this rate will probably slow as the numbers of tourists reach the level that tourism development in the South Pacific islands can support.

The area can be characterized by its isolation, great distances from the major tourist-generating countries of the world, poor airline connections to most of the islands, the low level of both economic and tourism

520   PART 12: GEOGRAPHY AND TOURISM IN AUSTRALIA, NEW ZEALAND, AND THE ISLANDS OF THE SOUTH PACIFIC

INTERNATIONAL TOURISM TO THE SOUTH PACIFIC (1999–2010)

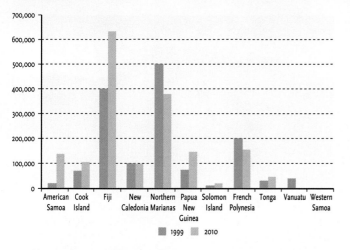

Data source: *The World Bank: The Data Catalogue.*
Figure copyright ©2015 Cengage Learning®. All rights reserved.

INTERNATIONAL TOURISM TO AUSTRALIA, GUAM, AND NEW ZEALAND, 2010

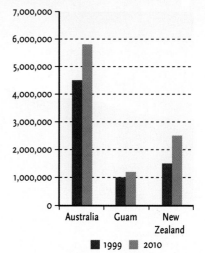

Data source: *The World Bank: The Data Catalogue.*
Figure copyright ©2015 Cengage Learning®. All rights reserved.

development, and the intervening opportunities of tropical environments closer to the major industrialized countries of North America and Western Europe. Tourism to the region reflects the combination of distance and cultural linkages with former colonial ties. Tourists will go to the closest place for a tropical experience unless long distances are overcome by cultural linkages between a specific area and its former colonial country. This is reflected in the region of origin of visitors. Most of the visitors are from the more adjacent Pacific region, which includes Asia and Southeast Asia. The three major origin countries of Oceania are the industrialized countries of Australia, New Zealand, China, and Japan.

South Pacific

The perception of the South Pacific by the residents of the industrialized world is of islands that are of extraordinary and exotic natural beauty with mountains and South Sea vegetation interspersed along the beaches and lagoons. These tropical islands have a pleasant climate, beautiful sunsets, good beaches, and friendly citizens. Europeans also perceive the region as having a variety of South Pacific cultures with many native arts and crafts that are very beautiful and interesting. The perceived characteristics are particularly true for the South Pacific islands. Tourism is viewed by many of the Pacific Island states as an opportunity to reduce their dependency on uncertain aid income. It is estimated that for every thirteen international tourists who visit the islands, one full-time tourist job is generated. This would mean that the 2 million visitors to the islands would generate 150,000 jobs or approximately 12 percent of the region's total employment.

The major origins of tourism to the Pacific Islands are the United States, Japan, China, and Australia and

New Zealand. The Japanese dominate the trade to Guam, Northern Marianas, and New Caledonia; Australia and New Zealand dominate tourism to Fiji, Papua New Guinea, and the Cook Islands. Tahiti receives the largest number of their visitors from the United States, which accounts for one-quarter of the total visitors. The percentage of visitors from the United States has declined, largely because of an increased use of more efficient airplanes allowing nonstop flights to Australia and New Zealand from the United States. The second largest group of visitors to Tahiti is from France, reflecting its status as an overseas territory.

Other than the direct linkages from a few islands, such as Guam, Fiji, and Tahiti, there are poor international connections and even less inter-island transportation. Fewer ships call at most of the islands of the Pacific today than did fifty years ago. Combined with the lack of transportation service is the poor tourist infrastructure. The small size of the islands also provides a less diverse resource base to attract international tourists. The high degree of dependency upon sun-sea-sand created by the tropical environment leaves the region vulnerable to competitive locations that have the same tropical environment but are closer to the major tourist-generating countries of North America and Western Europe.

The average length of stay is relatively long for the islands, with the exception of Guam. The majority of tourists to Guam come from Japan for either a honeymoon or the short traditional vacations taken by the Japanese. The longer length of stay in the rest of the region indicates that most of the islands are major destinations rather than part of a group of islands visited like the Caribbean. A growing trend in the Pacific is the travel in and throughout the region by the Japanese for the purpose of visiting places where either they or relatives were involved in World War II.

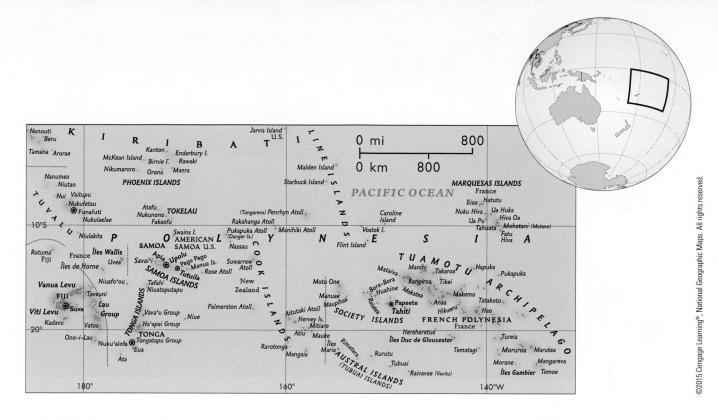

COUNTRY PROFILE

POLYNESIA

Country	Capital	Status	Population 2010 (millions)	Area in Square Miles	Currency
American Samoa	Pago Pago	Unincorporated territory of the United States	0.7	76	U.S. $
Cook Islands	Avarua	Self-governing	0.1	93	N.Z. $
French Polynesia	Papeete	Territory of France	0.27	1,545	C.F.P.
Pitcairn	Adamstown	Dependent of Britain	—	1.7	N.Z. $
Tonga	Nuku'alofa	Constitutional Monarchy	0.1	260	T.P.
Tuvalu	Funafuti	Independent State	0.01	10	AS. $
Wallis and Futuna	Mata Utu	Territory of France	0.0015	48	C.F.P.
Western Samoa	Apia	Independent State	0.2	1,141	W.S.T.

© 2015 Cengage Learning®

French Polynesia (Tahiti)

French Polynesia consists of five South Pacific archipelagos: Austral, Gambier, Marquesas, Society, and Tuamotu. The 118 islands span an area the size of Western Europe. The largest island, Tahiti (one of the Society Islands), is home to world-class resorts and pearl shops.

Location	Oceania, South Pacific
Area	4,167 sq km (1,609 sq mi)
Population	266,000
Capital	Papeete 131,000
Religion	Protestant, Roman Catholic
Language	French, Polynesian

Figure 38.1 Black sand beach in Tahiti. © Thierry Dagnelie/www.Shutterstock.com.

TRAVEL **TIPS** 🧳

Entry: A passport is required. A visa is not required for stays up to thirty days.

National Holiday: July 14 (Bastille Day)

Shopping: Common items include French perfumes, lingerie, and bathing suits. Tahitian items include tiki effigies and fabrics.

CULTURAL CAPSULE While the majority of the population is Polynesian (78 percent), there is considerable mixing with Chinese or European. About 10 percent of the population is French, and another 12 percent is Chinese. French is the official language and is taught in the schools. Tahitian is a regional language for the Society Islands and is the language for the majority of the people as it is the language spoken in the home. The Chinese speak either the Hakka dialect of Chinese or French. English is understood in tourist areas. Each of the island groups in French Polynesia has its own language. Missionaries brought Christianity in the eighteenth century and currently almost 55 percent are Protestant (Evangelical Church), 30 percent are Roman Catholic, and the other 16 percent are divided between a number of religions including Judaism and Buddhism.

The population of French Polynesia is approximately 270,000 people. Half (135,000) live on the island of Tahiti in the Society Islands. The capital, Papeete, is the largest city, with over 80,000 people living in the urbanized area. The balance of the population is scattered over five archipelagos that comprise French Polynesia. The Society Islands, the Tuamotu Islands, and the Marquesas Islands are the largest of these. Tahiti, Papeete, and the Society Islands in general are the major tourism destinations. The visitors enjoy the blend of volcanic peaks and lush tropical forests, with white, sandy beaches surrounding each island.

Cultural hints: Tips are expected on the islands. A handshake is a common greeting. (Shake hands with all in a gathering). Remove shoes before entering a Tahitian home. To stop "le truck" (local transportation), hold out your hand. Wash hands before eating as Tahitians usually eat with their hands. Typical food consists of fish, other seafood, chicken, pork, sweet potatoes, breadfruit, fruits, and vegetables. There is a strong French influence in the tourist facilities.

Tourism Characteristics

French Polynesia has benefitted from its location as a stopover between North America and Australia and New Zealand. However, as indicated, more flights are now going directly between the two regions. While worldwide arrivals have increased, arrivals from North America have declined. Consequently, the Tahiti Tourist Promotion Board has begun a campaign on the West Coast of the United States designed to increase interest in Tahiti.

Tourism Destinations and Attractions

French Polynesia is made up of exotic mountain islands with deep valleys, sandy beaches, and beautiful lagoons. Its capital is on the island of Tahiti in Papeete. The island is highly dependent upon tourism and an annual subsidy from France. Most of the jobs are generated by tourism. Many consider the islands of French Polynesia to be the "Pearl of the Pacific." There are six major islands for tourism in the group: Tahiti, Moorea, Bora Bora, Raiatea, Tahaa, and Huahine. Tahiti and its capital, Papeete, attract the largest number of tourists. Many of the island's sandy beaches consist of broad expanses of black sand (Figure 38.1). The island is ringed by a road passing picturesque clusters of native straw- or tin-roofed huts. The interior is a mountain of sheer cliffs, verdant valleys, and plunging waterfalls.

Moorea, a short 90-minute ferry ride from Papeete, is less developed and less populated than Tahiti. It represents the remains of a volcano and offers a lush landscape of mountains and beautiful beaches with many resorts spread around the island. Bora Bora, about 140 miles from Tahiti, is ringed with atolls, turquoise waters, and palm-studded beaches. The flora and fauna of the ocean are spectacular. Bora Bora is one of the most picturesque islands of the Pacific. James Michener described it as the most beautiful island in the world. Raiatea, a tall volcanic island of some 6,500 inhabitants, and Tahaa are even less developed than Moorea and they are an underwater delight for fishing and photography. The islands' mountains and lagoons are most picturesque and further development will likely continue. Huahine, the most isolated and least developed island, is beginning to attract visitors and development. In addition to the volcanic mountains and lagoons, there are many archaeological relics on the islands.

American and Western Samoa

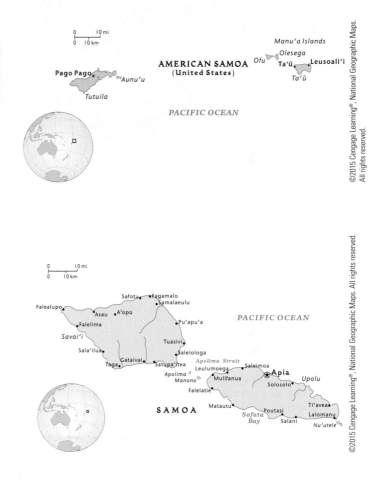

The island groups of American and Western Samoa are volcanic, providing mountain ranges with some small coral atolls in American Samoa. The climate is pleasant because of trade winds, and has frequent rains falling mostly between December and March. Locals elect their own government, and canned tuna is the territory's major export.

From *National Geographic Atlas of the World*, 9th edition. Copyright ©2011 National Geographic Society. Reprinted by arrangement. All rights reserved.

Location	Oceania, South Pacific
Area	199 sq km (77 sq mi)
Population	71,000
Capital	Pago Pago 58,000
Religion	Christian Congregationalist, Roman Catholic, Protestant
Language	Samoan, English, Tongan

From *National Geographic Atlas of the World*, 9th edition. Copyright ©2011 National Geographic Society. Reprinted by arrangement. All rights reserved.

TRAVEL TIPS

Entry: A passport is required. A visa is not required for stays up to thirty days.

National Holiday: June 1 and July 4 (Independence Day)

Shopping: Common items include local handwoven tapa cloth, lavalavas and traditional men's and women's costumes, shells, laufala mats and carvings, baskets, bags, and teak bowls.

CULTURAL CAPSULE Over 2,000 years ago, waves of Polynesians migrated from Southeast Asia to the Samoan Islands. Samoans are the second largest Polynesian group, after the Maoris of New Zealand, and speak a Polynesian dialect. The majority of the people are ethnic Samoan, of Polynesian descent (90 percent). About 7 percent are Euronesians, or people of mixed European and Polynesian descents. Two percent are Caucasian and 2 percent Tongan.

Samoans have tended to retain their traditional ways despite exposure to European influences. Most Samoans live within the traditional social system based on the aiga, or extended family group, headed by a matai, or chief.

Both nations of Samoa speak Samoan, a language related to Hawaiian and other Polynesian languages. In American Samoa, English is the second official language. Nearly all of the people are Christian, with the Congregational Church representing about half of the population. Forty percent are divided between Roman Catholics and Methodists.

Figure 38.2 Apia, Western Samoa. © Chris Jenner/www.Shutterstock.com.

Cultural hints: Greetings are usually formal and effusive. When visiting a home, wait for an invitation to enter from the host and remove shoes. Accepting and giving gifts is common when visiting. Samoan foods are eaten with the fingers. Take a small amount of all food offered. When offered Kava (the national drink) spill a few drops before drinking. Typical foods are bananas, breadfruit, pineapples, papayas, coconuts, copra, yams, taro, pork, chicken, and fish.

Tourism Characteristics

Western Samoa receives nearly four times the number of visitors as American Samoa—139,000 to 34,000. The origin of the visitors is different as Western Samoa's market is more regional, while the visitors from the United States dominate travel to American Samoa. The United States accounts for 69.3 percent of the visitors to American Samoa, while the largest percentage of visitors to Western Samoa is from American Samoa, accounting for 36.5 percent of its visitors. Australia and New Zealand generate over 38 percent of the visitors to each of the countries.

Tourism Destinations and Attractions

American and Western Samoa are both Polynesian and are reported to have some of the world's friendliest people. Periodic markets with colorful Samoan handicraft add to the sun-sea-sand attraction. Like the French Polynesia Islands, the natural sights are spectacular. Tourism is centered around the capitals, Pago Pago on American Samoa and Apia on Western Samoa.

Pago Pago is located on a scenic harbor and is the center for exploring the island of Tutuila. This island has lush, densely wooded mountains and beautiful villages. Apia (Figure 38.2) offers both a beach setting and some architecture indicative of its history. The home and tomb of Robert Louis Stevenson are here. Excursions from Apia take visitors through picturesque Samoan villages, delightful beaches, and scenic waterfalls.

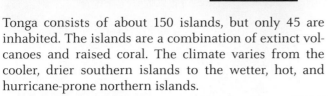

Tonga

Tonga consists of about 150 islands, but only 45 are inhabited. The islands are a combination of extinct volcanoes and raised coral. The climate varies from the cooler, drier southern islands to the wetter, hot, and hurricane-prone northern islands.

TRAVEL **TIPS** 💼

Entry: A passport is required. A visa is not required for stays up to thirty days. Proof of onward or return transportation is required.

National Holiday: June 4 (National Day)

Shopping: Common items include woven mats, shells and bamboo curtains, stuffed-animal toys, shell jewelry, slippers, grass skirts, woven hats, tapa cloth, wooden carvings, and other native goods.

 Nearly two-thirds of the population live on its main island, Tongatapu. Tongans, a Polynesian group with a very small mixture of Melanesian, represent more than 98 percent of the people. The rest are European, mixed European, and other Pacific Islanders. Everyday life is heavily influenced by Polynesian traditions and especially by the Christian faith. For example, all commerce and entertainment activities cease from midnight Saturday until midnight Sunday. The two major religions are the Free Wesleyan (Methodist) Church and the Church of Jesus Christ of Latter-Day Saints (Mormons). Tongan and English are both official languages. Government documents are in both languages, but Tongan is the most common language of daily communication.

Cultural hints: A handshake is a common greeting. Tongans usually call people by their first names. Do not use hand motions to call anyone other than children. It is not customary to leave a tip for service. Eating and drinking while standing is not appropriate. Typical foods include yams, taro leaves, sweet potatoes, cassava, fish, fruits, and pork.

Tourism Characteristics, Destinations, and Attractions

Tonga receives from 40,000 to 45,000 visitors per year. Its visitors' market is relatively dispersed, with 13 percent from the United States, 70 percent from Australia and New Zealand, and 6 percent from Europe. The proximity of Australia and New Zealand is an important factor in the large percentage of visitors

TONGA

from those two countries. There is a significant Tongan population in the United States that helps account for the strong percentage of visitors from the United States.

As in Samoa, the residents are extremely friendly. Unlike Tahiti, the islands are mostly coral atolls with only a few of volcanic origin. Tonga is still ruled by a native form of government of kings and queens. Of the three major groups, Tonga has the smallest tourism trade. The main island of Tongatapu is the tourist center. However, there are a number of attractions, including a Victorian white-framed royal palace and chapel in Nuku'alofa, famous blow holes at Houma (Figure 38.3), and scenic areas, such as Hufangalupe with its huge natural coral bridge under which seawater churns, towering cliffs overlooking the sea, and a beautiful beach at the bottom of a steep downhill trail. The ancient remains of the Ha'amonga'a trilithon stones enabled the early people to identify the seasons. It consists of two 40-ton upright coral stones topped by a horizontal connecting stone. The Port of Refuge in the Vava'u Islands is one of the most picturesque harbors in the Pacific.

Figure 38.3 Blowholes at Houma, Tongatapu Island, Tonga. © Andy Heyward/www.Shutterstock.com.

Cook Islands

The Cook Islands incorporate a variety of geographic settings. The northern atolls are submerged volcanic peaks covered with coral and the steep, raised volcanic peaks of Rarotonga with its narrow, fringing reef. The islands of the northern group, including Manuae and Takutea, are coral atolls, while the remaining six islands of the southern group are mountainous. The climate is warm and humid from December to March. It is milder from April to November.

From *National Geographic Atlas of the World*, 9th edition. Copyright ©2011 National Geographic Society. Reprinted by arrangement. All rights reserved.

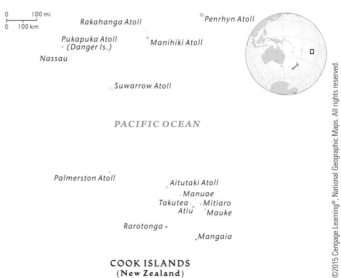

Figure 38.4 Aitutaki Atoll, Cook Islands. © fbxx/www.Shutterstock.com.

TRAVEL **TIPS**🧳

Entry: A passport is required. A visa is not required for stays up to thirty-one days. Proof of sufficient funds and onward transportation is required.

National Holiday: First Monday in August (Constitution Day)

CULTURAL CAPSULE The population is 82 percent Polynesian, 7.7 percent mixed Polynesian and European, and 7.7 percent Polynesian and other. The majority of the people belong to the Christian Church. English is the official language, and Maori is spoken widely.

Tourism Characteristics, Destinations, and Attractions

Only the Cook Islands of the remaining Polynesian islands have any tourist industry of consequence and even then it is small, attracting most of its visitors from Australia and New Zealand (80 percent of visitors). Visitors from the United States and Europe increased in numbers. Accommodations are somewhat limited, but locations are increasing. Like the rest of Polynesia, the Cook Islands are known for their volcanic mountains, beautiful beaches, and crystal-clear lagoons (Figure 38.4). Tourism centers around the capital,

Rarotonga, with a slow-paced, Polynesian, friendly tourist industry. The coral reef and lagoons are centers of interest for snorkeling and scuba diving. The history of the islands can be observed in the historical road of Ara Metua and stone seats near the road. Cook Islands' Christian Church and the Mission House, which is a restored church museum, add to the historical understanding of the Cook Islands.

Other Polynesian Islands

The other Polynesian Islands of Pitcairn, Tuvalu, and Wallis and Futuna have little tourism. They have poor communication and transportation facilities.

REVIEW QUESTIONS

1. Why is tourism to the Pacific relatively small?
2. On which island group in the South Pacific is tourism the least developed? Why?
3. Describe the physical characteristics of the two different types of islands in the South Pacific.
4. Of the Cook Islands, Tonga, and Samoa, which has the best potential to develop a strong tourist industry? Why?
5. If a client has visited Hawaii a number of times, what might motivate him or her to visit the islands of the Pacific?

chapter 39: MELANESIA, MICRONESIA, AND OTHER PACIFIC ISLANDS

© Martin Valigursky/ShutterStock.com

COUNTRY PROFILE

MELANESIA

Country	Capital	Status	Population 2010 (millions)	Area in Square Miles	Currency
Fiji	Suva	Independent State	0.8	7,055	Fiji $
New Caledonia	Noumea	Territory of France	0.2	7,476	C.F.P.
Papua New Guinea	Port Moresby	Independent State	6.6	178,258	K.
Solomon Islands	Honiara	Independent State	0.5	11,496	S.
Vanuatu	Port-Vila	Independent Republic	0.2	4,587	N.F.H.

© 2015 Cengage Learning®

Of the Melanesian Islands, only Fiji, New Caledonia, and the Solomon Islands have a significant number of visitors.

It is a region that has not developed economically and has poor visitor access. Other specific island nations are more exotic in the minds of travelers.

Fiji

The Fiji Islands comprise some 330 islands in the South Pacific, with beaches, coral gardens, and rain forests. Most people live on the largest island, Viti Levu, where the capital, Suva, is located. After 96 years as a British colony, Fiji gained independence in 1970. During British rule, indentured servants from India came to work in the sugarcane fields—Indo-Fijians currently make up more than 37 percent of the population. Indo-Fijians are mostly Hindu, while the majority of native Fijians are mostly Christian. Tensions between the two communities led to military coups in 1987, 2000, and 2006.

From *National Geographic Atlas of the World*, 9th edition. Copyright ©2011 National Geographic Society. Reprinted by arrangement. All rights reserved.

PACIFIC OCEAN
FIJI

Area	18,274 sq km (7,056 sq mi)
Population	844,000
Government	Republic
Capital	Suva 224,000
Life Expectancy	68 years
Religion	Christian, Hindu, Muslim
Language	English, Fijian, Hindustani
Currency	Fijian dollar (FJD)
GDP per Cap	$3,900
Labor Force	70% Agriculture, 30% Industry & Services

From *National Geographic Atlas of the World*, 9th edition. Copyright ©2011 National Geographic Society. Reprinted by arrangement. All rights reserved.

TRAVEL **TIPS** 🧳

Entry: A passport is required. A visa is not required for stays up to four months. Proof of sufficient funds and onward transportation is required.

National Holiday: Second Monday of October (Independence Day)

Shopping: Common items include tortoiseshell jewelry, Indian silk saris, and an array of spices.

CULTURAL CAPSULE

Indigenous Fijians are a mixture of Polynesian and Melanesian, resulting from the original migrations to the South Pacific many centuries ago. The Indian population has grown rapidly since being brought in from India between 1879 and 1916 to work in the sugarcane fields. The rest of the population includes Pacific Islanders, Chinese, Europeans, and other ethnic groups. Fijians are Christian, 78 percent of them Methodist. Roman Catholics account for about 8.5 percent. Indians are either Hindu or Muslim, and the Chinese are either Christian or Buddhist. The Fijians are generous, friendly, and easygoing. They are relaxed and casual. Ethnic tension does exist between Fijians and the Indians. English is the official language. Bauan, a Fijian dialect, is spoken by most indigenous Fijians. Hindustani, a dialect of Hindi, is spoken by many Indians.

Cultural hints: Remove shoes when entering a home. Eye contact is important when talking with someone. To beckon someone, hold palm down and wave the fingers. It is impolite to touch a Fijian's head. Tips are not expected, but will be accepted. Visitors should accept food

Figure 39.1 Matamanoa Island, Fiji. © Ondrej Garaj/www.Shutterstock.com.

that is offered them. Visitors should accept food that is offered them. Typical foods include seafood, coconut milk, chicken, pork, tapioca, and Indian cuisine. Foods are rarely deep fried.

Tourism Characteristics

Fiji vies with Northern Marianas for the largest tourist industry of the South Pacific Islands. Its location close to Australia and New Zealand provides it with an excellent market, with the two countries accounting for over half of Fiji's visitors. In addition, it is somewhat of a crossroads for visits to other islands of the Pacific. It is a major stopover for airlines from North America to Australia and New Zealand.

Periodically, Fiji has had some political conflict between the Indians and the Fijians that has hurt tourism. However, the tourism arrivals began to increase, reaching approximately 630,000 in 2010. The United States

accounts for less than 10 percent of the visitors, and the number has decreased over the last 15 years. The change in aircraft allowing nonstop trips between the United States and Australia and New Zealand is an important factor in this decline. Most of the American market is comprised of travelers to Australia and New Zealand stopping off en route or returning from these two destinations. Its attractions are similar to other Pacific Islands. It offers sandy coral and volcanic islands (Figure 39.1). The high number of Asians provides a unique cuisine that combines Chinese and Indian cooking. Tourism is centered in Suva, the capital and point of origin for trips to other Pacific Islands, and the west coast of Fiji, with its excellent water and beaches. A number of cruises depart from Suva to the surrounding islands. There are a number of resorts and two major cultural centers to entertain visitors. The nightlife is lively and the tropical climate is moderate most of the year.

New Caledonia

New Caledonia is east of Australia in the South Pacific and consists of the main island, the Loyalty Islands, and some smaller islands. An emerald green lagoon surrounds the main island; the economy is based on tourism, nickel mining, and French aid.

Area	18,575 sq km (7,172 sq mi)
Population	251,000
Capital	Nouméa 156,000
Religion	Roman Catholic, Protestant
Language	French, 33 Melanesian-Polynesian dialects

Cultural Characteristics

New Caledonia is an overseas territory of France. The ethnic character is 42.5 percent Melanesian, 37.1 percent European, and 8.5 percent Wallisian, with small groups of Polynesian, Indonesian, Vietnamese, and others. The official language is French. There are approximately twenty-eight Melanesian-Polynesian dialects spoken. Sixty percent are Roman Catholic, and 30 percent are Protestant.

Tourism Characteristics, Destinations, and Attractions

New Caledonia's tourism has suffered from political unrest. Tourism declined to about 60,000 visitors annually in 2000. However, like Fiji's tourism, it increased to 98,000 visitors in 2010. The three major contributors of tourists to New Caledonia are France, Japan, and Australia. The United States accounts for only 1 percent of tourists. Because of political ties with France, New Caledonia has enjoyed good airline connections to the West. The French flavor is abundant in New Caledonia. Noumea, the capital, is considered the "Paris" of the South Pacific, although in spite of containing one-half of the total population of the nation, it is still a small city. Its streets, nightlife, and foods provide a French flavor set in a South Pacific physical and cultural environment of native handicrafts and art. New Caledonia is surrounded by the second largest coral reef in the world, providing clear blue, fish-filled waters for fishing, swimming, snorkeling, and sailing.

Vanuatu

The Vanuatu Islands are rocky and mountainous with only limited plains. The climate can be cool May to September, while in the southern hemisphere summer from December to April, there are frequent heavy storms.

Cultural Characteristics

The population is 94 percent indigenous Melanesian. Christianity is very important, and the majority are Protestant, belonging to the Anglican Church. A local pidgin, Bislama, is the national language. (Pidgin is a language that is simplified and modified through contact with other languages.) English and French are also official languages.

Tourism Characteristics, Destinations, and Attractions

Vanuatu (formerly New Hebrides) and the Solomon Islands have a small regionalized tourist trade. Vanuatu had 97,000 tourists in 2010, and this represented a 47 percent increase over 2000. Most of the tourists are from Australia and New Zealand (90 percent). There is presently little prospect for the islands being "discovered" because of their isolated location and lack of tourist infrastructure. If development occurs, it has some excellent attractions. The mixture of French and British institutions and some water sports and scenic volcanoes could provide the base for a tourism industry. It has been suggested that bungee jumping is based on the age-old ritual practiced by "land divers" of Vanuatu's Pentecost Island. Villagers collect vines and wind them into long cords, climb high wooden towers, tighten the vines around their ankles, and jump. This practice was adapted on the South Island of New Zealand to become "bungee jumping."

Solomon Islands

The major islands of the Solomons are rugged and mountainous. Many of the outer islands of the group are coral atolls and raised coral reefs. The climate is tropical, with the most comfortable time between May and October when southeast trade winds occur.

Cultural Characteristics

The Solomon Islands are a parliamentary democracy within the British Commonwealth. (A commonwealth is a voluntary association of countries.) The population is overwhelmingly Melanesian (93.3 percent), but there are some Polynesians (4 percent) and Micronesians (1.5 percent). In addition, there are small numbers of Europeans and Chinese. Most people reside in widely dispersed settlements along the coasts.

Most Solomon Islanders are Christian, with the Anglican, Roman Catholic, South Seas Evangelical, and Seventh-Day Adventists faiths predominating. Most

Solomon Islanders maintain their traditional social structure, which is rooted in family and village life.

Tourism Characteristics, Destinations, and Attractions

The Solomons receive only a few tourists each year. They average less than 20,000 visitors per year. Most of their visitors are from Australia and New Zealand, with the United States accounting for about 6 percent of the total visitors. The major interests for most are the World War II sites. For example, at Guadalcanal one of the fiercest battles of the war occurred. There are war relics and major battle sites.

Papua New Guinea

Papua New Guinea, an island country in the western Pacific, spans the eastern half of the island of Papua New Guinea and includes many islands, with the largest being New Britain, New Ireland, and Bougainville. On the mainland, almost half the land area is mountainous, and about 20 percent consists of swampy plains that are seasonally flooded. The islands have a tropical monsoon climate.

Papua New Guinea gained independence from Australia in 1975. The indigenous population is highly heterogeneous because the mountainous terrain has separated communities for centuries. Some 860 native languages have been identified, but there are likely many more, some with only a few hundred speakers. The country is a parliamentary democracy but has had some difficulty in governing the far-flung island nation. A ten-year rebellion on Bougainville Island was resolved in 2001 by giving the island more autonomy. Papua New Guinea possesses a modern economy based on oil and mining and a traditional economy where 75 percent of Papua New Guineans rely on subsistence agriculture.

Area	462,840 sq km (178,703 sq mi)
Population	6,610,000
Government	Constitutional Parliamentary Democracy and a Commonwealth Realm
Capital	Port Moresby 299,000
Life Expectancy	59 years
Literacy	57%
Religion	Roman Catholic, Evangelical Lutheran, United Church, Seventh-Day Adventist, Pentecostal, other Protestant
Language	Tok Pisin, English, Hiri Motu, 860 indigenous languages
Currency	kina (PGK)
GDP per Cap	$2,400
Labor Force	85% Agriculture

PAPUA NEW GUINEA

Cultural Characteristics

The indigenous population of Papua New Guinea is extremely heterogeneous. It has several thousand separate communities, most with only a few hundred people. Divided by language, customs, and tradition, some of these communities have engaged in tribal warfare with their neighbors for centuries. Melanesian Pidgin (based on English) and, in Papua, Motu serve as lingua francas. Pidgin has tended to supplant Motu. English is spoken by educated people and in Milne Bay Province. Almost two-thirds of the population is nominally Christian. The two major Christian faiths are Roman Catholic and Lutheran.

The people feel a strong attachment to the land. Most Papua New Guineans still adhere strongly to the traditional social structure, with its roots in family and village life.

Tourism Characteristics, Destinations, and Attractions

Papua New Guinea has a small tourist industry, attracting some 145,000 visitors to the island in 2010. About 55 percent of all visitors are from Australia and New Zealand, with the United States accounting for 5.7 percent of the total visitors.

Figure 39.2 Goroka Tribal Festival, Goroka, Papua New Guinea. © isaxar/www.Shutterstock.com.

Papua New Guinea offers vast contrasts in climate, scenery, and terrain. Festivals have become a major attraction. Some of the most popular are at Goroka (Figure 39.2), Eastern Highlands, and Mountain Hagen. They rotate location from year to year with dancing, feasts, and group singing. World War II cemeteries at Bomana, Lae, and Bita Paka are impressive and serve as reminders of the war. Located along a beach, Port Moresby, the capital, has a colorful market, a town museum, and a nearby stilt village of Hanuobaba. The Rouna Falls and Louki Gorge are nearby. Goroka is the gateway to the highlands for views of scenic tropical forests, sunken gardens, rivers, and native villages with their thatched-roof stilt houses and group singing.

MICRONESIA

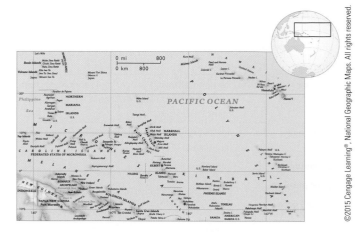

Micronesia, or "little islands," is a group of coral atolls and volcanic islands scattered across the western Pacific. Of the main island groups, the Carolina Islands, the Gilbert Islands, Northern Mariana and Guam, the Marshall Islands, and Nauru, only the Northern Marianas and Guam have a significant tourist industry. Both are commonwealths of the United States, thus enjoying the resources of development from an industrialized country. The bulk of their tourists are from Japan, with Guam receiving 82 percent and Northern Marianas

The heavy iron anchor and chain tumbled noisily into the water. We lowered two red skiffs from our research vessel, loaded our diving gear, and sped off toward the lagoon. After a five-day sail from Fiji to Kanton island, we were anxious to see if reefs here had survived a rare ocean disaster—a lethal spike in the temperature of local seawater. During the El Niño of 2002–03, a body of water more than 1°C (1.8°F) warmer than usual had stalled for six months around the Phoenix Islands, a tiny archipelago in the central Pacific. We'd heard that the hot spot had severely bleached the region's corals. As I descended toward the lagoon floor, I was hoping things weren't as bad as we'd been told.

Settling down beside the reef, I saw dead coral everywhere. What had been flourishing, overlapping, overflowing brown and auburn plates of corals were now ghostly, broken reminders of their former beauty. When I'd first visited the Phoenix Islands a decade ago, these reefs had supported numerous species of hard corals, as well as giant clams, sea anemones, nudibranchs, and great populations of fish, from blacktip reef sharks to parrotfish to bohar snappers. Because the islands have remained undisturbed for so long, they'd largely avoided overfishing, pollution, and other harmful impacts of modern civilization. But they hadn't been able to avoid climate change, which most scientists believe amplifies El Niños.

Not ready to accept this setback, I was heartened to see lots of reef fish and vibrant corals growing up through the rubble—early signs of recovery. Was it possible that the reefs of the Phoenix Islands, like their mythical namesake, were rising from the ashes of a terrible warming?

Ten years ago, I'd flown to Tarawa, capital of the Micronesian country of Kiribati, which includes the Phoenix Islands, to meet with government officials. At the time, the airport terminal was no bigger than a house, open-air with a thatched roof. I was met at the fisheries ministry by David Obura and Sangeeta Mangubhai of CORDIO, an Indian Ocean conservation organization, who had helped me carry out the first systematic underwater surveys of the Phoenix Islands. An ancient air conditioner rattled away in the meeting room as we presented a slide show to the ministers of fisheries and environment, showing them scenes of sharks, flourishing coral, and dense clouds of colorful fish. Accustomed to the degraded reefs closer to their towns and villages, the ministers and their staff were as amazed as we had been at the "like new" reefs of the Phoenix Islands.

"Do you realize, Greg, that you're the first scientists who ever bothered to come tell us what they learned in our waters?" said Tetebo Nakara, then minister of fisheries.

During our subsequent talks with government officials, we found out that a fourth of Kiribati's income ($17 million in 2000) came from selling access to their reef fish, sharks, tunas, and other wild marine resources to nations such as Japan, South Korea, and the United States. In return for a commercial fishing license, a foreign company paid about 5 percent of the wholesale value of anything they took out of Kiribati waters.

I asked Nakara if Kiribati might consider receiving a payment in lieu of the access fees to leave the fish in the water. That way, it would receive badly needed income, but its underwater haven would be preserved. Without living reefs, these islands could rapidly erode. He smiled and said, "This could be good for Kiribati"—as long as his nation could keep receiving income from the "reverse fishing license." Anote Tong, Kiribati's president, enthusiastically backed the project and has since led it to fruition.

Formally declared a reserve at the 2006 Convention on Biological Diversity in Brazil, the Phoenix Islands Protected Area (PIPA) was expanded two years later to become what was then the world's largest marine protected area. At 157,000 square miles, it was nearly as big as California. But many questions remained: How could Kiribati put a fair price on its marine life? Where would the money come from? Who would police such a vast reserve?

To address such questions, I enlisted the help of Conservation International (CI), which in 2001 had created the Global Conservation Fund to protect rain forest and other habitats through a similar strategy. Receptive to the idea, the Kiribati Parliament created the PIPA Conservation Trust with trustees from the New England Aquarium (NEA), CI, and the government of Kiribati, and fund-raising began for a $25-million endowment.

Now I'd returned to Kanton with David Obura and Randi Rotjan, a coral expert from NEA, and other scientists to assess the impact of the El Niño event. The bleaching had killed all the coral on the lagoon floor, but almost half appeared to be growing back—the fastest recovery any of us had ever seen. The reason seemed clear: abundant fish. When coral bleaches, seaweed can grow out of control, stifling reef recovery. But fish eat the algae, keeping it from smothering the coral. Because fish populations had been protected here, the reefs remained surprisingly resilient even after suffering one of the worst bleaching events ever recorded.

As oceans continue to absorb the impacts of human activities and of climate change, we'll need more large protected areas like PIPA to help ecosystems survive. The oceans are our life-support system. There's never been a more important time to take care of them.

— **Gregory Stone, *National Geographic Magazine*, January 2011**

COUNTRY PROFILES

MICRONESIA

Country	Capital	Population Status	2010 (millions)	Area in Square Miles	Currency
Guam	Agana	Unincorporated U.S. Territory	0.2	21	U.S. $
Kiribati	Tarawa	Independent Republic	0.1	378	Aus. $
Kosrae	Kosrae	Federated States of Micronesia	—	42	U.S. $
Mariana Islands	Saipan	In Association with the United States	—	182	U.S. $
Nauru	Yaren	Independent Republic	0.01	8.5	Aus. $
Ponape	Kolonia	Federated States of Micronesia	—	145	U.S. $
Truk	Moen	Federated States of Micronesia	—	45.5	U.S. $

receiving 75 percent of their respective visitors from Japan. Of the Pacific Islands, Guam has the best tourist facilities, with more hotel beds available than any other island, while the Northern Marianas rank fourth in availability of hotel beds in the islands of the Pacific. Both spend more money advertising their islands than any other Pacific islands.

Guam is somewhat special, as it is an important destination for Japanese honeymoons. It has large, well-designed hotels, and its attractions include beautiful beaches that are ideal for water sports such as skindiving and snorkeling on the coral reefs surrounding the island. It has some remarkable rock formations and a spectacular cliff. The Northern Marianas, in addition to their close proximity to Japan, were important during World War II, and there is significant travel for the purpose of visiting war sites and identifying places where relatives died.

Other Pacific Islands

There are a number of Pacific islands not discussed in this book. They have little tourism or facilities to support tourism. Easter Island, however, deserves some mention. Its location and ties to Chile cause some books to list Easter Island as part of South America. It has a small tourist industry, attracted primarily to the giant stone statues carved by early inhabitants of the island.

REVIEW QUESTIONS

1. What is Papua New Guinea's unique appeal?
2. What are the "legends" associated with (1) Easter Island, (2) Pitcairn Island, and (3) Juan Fernandez Island?
3. Describe the physical characteristics of the two different types of islands in the South Pacific (Volcanic and Coral).
4. Which islands would you suggest a client visit on a two-week circle tour of the Pacific Islands? (Assume connectivity is not an issue.) Explain your selection.
5. How important is the cruise industry to the Pacific region? What are opportunities/obstacles for future growth?

chapter 40: NEW ZEALAND AND AUSTRALIA

© Sigurcamp/ShutterStock.com

New Zealand

New Zealand, located in the southwestern Pacific, consists of the North and South Islands and many smaller islands, including the Chatham Islands. National parks and protected offshore islands preserve unique plants and wildlife, such as the kiwi, a flightless bird after which both New Zealanders and the fruit are named. North Island features most of the active volcanoes, while South Island has the Southern Alps running its entire length. The north is subtropical and the south is temperate.

New Zealand's population is diverse and unevenly distributed. Ethnically, about 67 percent of New Zealanders are European, 14.6 percent indigenous Maori, 9.2 percent Asian, and 6.9 percent Pacific peoples (such as Samoans, Cook Islanders, and Tongans). More than 76 percent of the population lives on the North Island. The Maori and Pacific peoples residing in Auckland, New Zealand's biggest city, make it the world's most populous Polynesian city. New Zealanders prosper from the mixed economy, with large agricultural and manufacturing exports.

From *National Geographic Atlas of the World*, 9th edition. Copyright ©2011 National Geographic Society. Reprinted by arrangement. All rights reserved.

Area	267,710 sq km (103,363 sq mi)
Population	4,317,000
Government	Parliamentary Democracy and a Commonwealth Realm
Capital	Wellington 366,000
Life Expectancy	80 years
Literacy	99%
Religion	Anglican, Roman Catholic, Presbyterian, other Christian
Language	English, Maori
Currency	New Zealand dollar (NZD)
GDP per Cap	$27,300
Labor Force	7% Agriculture, 19% Industry, 74% Services

From *National Geographic Atlas of the World*, 9th edition. Copyright ©2011 National Geographic Society. Reprinted by arrangement. All rights reserved.

TRAVEL **TIPS** 🧳

Entry: A passport is required. A visa is not required for stays up to three months (Visa waiver).

Peak Tourist Season: November and December

National Holiday: February 6 (Waitangi Day)

Shopping: Common items include jewelry made from the iridescent paua shell, Maori handicrafts such as wood carving and ornaments made of greenstone, sheepskin rugs, and knitted garments.

NEW ZEALAND

Internet TLD: .nz

CULTURAL CAPSULE
The majority of the people are of British ancestry. The British and other Europeans comprise about 88 percent of the population. Nine percent are Maori (Polynesian). Close to 3 percent are other Polynesians, mostly from Tonga, Samoa, and the Cook Islands. Auckland has the largest urban Polynesian population in the world.

Most of the people live on the North Island. English and Maori are official languages, but almost all Maoris speak English. The population is 81 percent Christian, with the Anglican Church the largest. Other Christian faiths include Presbyterians, Roman Catholics, and Methodists, but about 1 percent of the people are Hindu or Buddhist.

In 1840, the United Kingdom annexed New Zealand and, through the Treaty of Waitangi signed that year with Maori tribes, established British sovereignty. Early European settlers were attracted to New Zealand for lumbering, seal hunting, and whaling.

Cultural hints: After greeting, first names are used frequently. Loud speech and excessively demonstrative behavior are inappropriate. Chewing gum or using a toothpick in public is offensive. Ice is not served with drinks. Water is served only on request. Tipping is not expected. Typical foods are traditionally British, consisting of meat (beef, pork, mutton), potatoes, seafood, vegetables, fruits, sausage, cheese, and ice cream.

Tourism Characteristics

Although New Zealand is remote from the leading world population centers, tourism is one of its fastest-growing industries. In 1992 it surpassed the million mark for annual visitors; today the number of annual visitors exceeds 2.5 million. The government actively promotes tourism, with offices in many of the industrialized

A violent struggle created this world, according to Maori mythology: Indigenous New Zealanders say Sky Father and Earth Mother were ripped from each other's arms to make room for mountains, forests, and oceans. Around Rotorua, a Maori heartland and home of the mineral-rimmed Champagne Pool (Figure 40.1), it's easy to believe the struggle continues, as the eerie landscape bubbles and churns like some primordial stew. Geysers erupt, mud boils, and steam seeps from cliffs and sidewalks, leaving a sulfurous scent in the air.

Start there on the Pathway of Fire to see—and smell—the tumultuous display. Pedal this 46-mile bike trail (classification: easy) past Whakarewarewa, a Maori village hundreds of years old, and Waimangu Volcanic Valley, earth's youngest geothermal system. The pathway is one of eighteen Great Rides of the New Zealand Cycle Trail (Nga Haerenga, in Maori, meaning "the journeys"). The trail's 1,243-plus miles open in 2012.

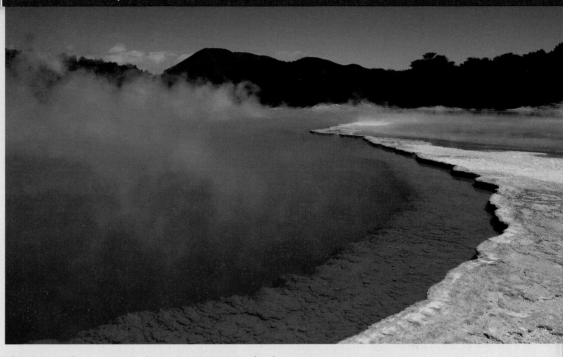

Figure 40.1 Champagne Pool, Rorotunga, New Zealand. © Daryl H/www.Shutterstock.com.

In a land where adrenaline lovers ride rockets suspended on wires and roll downhill inside giant plastic balls, biking seems one of the saner ways to plunge into a landscape that compels exploration: hot springs, glaciers, rain forests, and volcanoes, encircled by nearly 10,000 miles of coastline, packed into a country barely bigger than Colorado. New Zealand is made for journeys, physical and spiritual.

— **Suzanne B. Bopp,** *National Geographic Traveler,* November–December 2011

nations of the world. North Island and South Island, the major populated areas, are the focus of tourism.

New Zealand's strong ties with the United Kingdom since the early 1800s resulted in colonization by British settlers. This strong tie is expressed in the high numbers of visitors from the United Kingdom arriving for the purpose of visiting friends and relatives. Nearly one-fourth (23 percent) of all visitors come to New Zealand for this reason.

Tourism Characteristics

The average length of stay is long, twenty days, reflecting the long distances as well as the high percentage of people visiting friends and relatives. Arrivals are highest in the summer months (October to April), but those traveling to visit friends and relatives prefer December and January during the holiday period.

The major markets are Australia, both because of proximity and cultural linkages; the United States, with about 80 percent from the state of California, where promotional activities are concentrated; the United

Kingdom; China; and Japan. Australia is the most important market for New Zealand, accounting for approximately 44.6 percent of its visitors.

Chinese, Japanese, and United States travelers represent larger potential markets than does Australia. Travelers from the United States stay longer, averaging seventeen days. The primary reason for United States visits to New Zealand is reported to be vacation. Visitors from the United States are more independent than the Chinese and Japanese, using both tours and fly-drive programs, which are increasingly popular. Increased numbers of tourists from the populated, industrial countries of the United States, China, Japan, and the United Kingdom reflect in part an increased promotional campaign and the adoption of larger aircraft that make travel more comfortable.

The future of tourism to New Zealand is bright as long as the general world economy is strong. The government has increased its promotional budget significantly and has overseas offices in London, Frankfurt, Singapore, Beijing, Tokyo, Osaka, Vancouver, San Francisco, Los Angeles, New York, Sydney, Perth, Adelaide,

Figure 40.2 Auckland, New Zealand. © GeebShot/www.Shutterstock.com.

and Brisbane. The efforts of the New Zealand Tourist Publicity Department have diversified and broadened the visitor base to New Zealand and improved its image as a destination, accounting for the growing numbers visiting on vacations.

Tourist Destinations and Attractions

There are a wide variety of attractions on New Zealand's two main islands. New Zealand has encouraged eco-tourism both for preservation and as a major source of attractiveness for visitors. Also, throughout the country the Maori culture is a major tourist attraction and is well presented for the visitor. The major museum, which is in Auckland, emphasizes Maori history and culture; Rotorua, one of the major destination areas, has a fortified Maori village with displays and a small museum. Hotels throughout the country offer Maori music and dancing.

New Zealand has a diverse, scenic physical environment, from subtropical beaches in the north through the North Island's volcanic and thermal belt, to the impressive Southern Alps and fjords of the South Island. Four major tourism regions can be identified in New Zealand.

Auckland is the first region and major gateway city. It is the largest city and has the major international airport for New Zealand. Auckland is built on two hills with two harbors and is surrounded by forests that provide scenic drives through the city and its nearby environs. Auckland (Figure 40.2) has Kelly Tarlton's Underwater World, a waterfront family attraction. Parnell Village is a delightful collection of restored colonial-style shops, the Victoria Street Market, and various craft markets are all popular shopping attractions for visitors. To the north of Auckland are the Bay Islands, a subtropical area that is a center for watersports. The Bay Islands Maritime and Historic Park administers a number of scenic, historic, and recreational reserves. Across the waters of the bay is Russell, the first capital of New Zealand. It is a charming Victorian town with a preserved waterfront where nineteenth-century buildings have been maintained. In the north of New Zealand, Ninety Mile Beach to Cape Reinga is an area of South Pacific beach with incredible coastal scenery and beautiful sandy beaches. South of Auckland is the village of Waitomo, known for its caves, particularly the Glow Worm Grotto, which is one of the most spectacular cave experiences in the world.

Figure 40.3 Traditional Maori carving in national historic park in Rotorua, New Zealand. © George Burba/www.Shutterstock.com.

Rotorua on North Island is the largest tourist attraction in New Zealand, attracting approximately 60 percent of all holiday visitors to the country. It is the center of the Maori culture (Figure 40.3) and has the Maori Arts and Crafts Institute, a model village, museum, and shop selling Maori handicrafts. Programs that emphasize the history and music of the Maori are presented daily. Rotorua is a large thermal area, much like Yellowstone Park in the United States, with geysers, boiling mud, hot springs, and steam geysers. A number of other tourist attractions have been developed in the area, such as the sheep demonstration farm, which provides visitors with examples of the various breeds of sheep and their habitats, sheep dogs at work, and shearing demonstrations. North of Rotorua is Tauranga on the Bay of Plenty. Tauranga's attractions include a number of pleasant gardens, a historic village, mineral pools, a kiwi-fruit winery, a mission house, and an exotic bird garden.

Wellington, the capital, and its harbor serve as the major link to the South Island. Its attractive harbor, wooden houses, and the surrounding forested hillsides add to unusual museum and botanical gardens to

provide an interesting attraction. Within easy driving of Wellington are the mountains and lakes of the North Island. About 130 miles to the north of Wellington, just past Lake Taupo, is Petone, a restored village displaying early settlement in New Zealand. Lake Taupo is the geographical center of the North Island. It is extremely popular for trout fishing, and there is no closed fishing season, allowing fishermen to try their luck year-round. Huka Falls, Aratiatia Rapids, Cherry Island, Honey Center, and Acacia Bay Deer Park and Rabbit Ranch are other popular attractions in the Taupo area.

Christchurch on the South Island is considered the most English city outside of England. It is a garden city and has an international airport. Christchurch's similarity to England includes a Gothic cathedral built in the nineteenth century, a stream through town called the Avon, a beach called New Brighton, and a university named Canterbury. The city sustained serious damage when an earthquake jolted the region in 2010.

Queensland, on the edge of Lake Wakatipu, and the nearby old gold-mining town of Arrowtown are the second-most-visited areas in New Zealand. Queensland's year-round appeal includes summer activities associated with the lake and the rugged Remarkable Mountains surrounding the city and lake for winter skiing. Near Queenstown is the historic and picturesque settlement of Arrowtown, where many of the original gold-rush buildings remain.

The Southern Alps centered on Mt. Cook, the highest mountain in Australia and New Zealand and nearby Tasman Glacier, offer spectacular alpine scenery. Fjordland National Park (Figure 40.4), with its Norwegian-like fjords, forests, and lakes, is easily accessible. Milford

Figure 40.4 Milford Sound and Mitre Peak, Fjordland National Park, New Zealand. © Pi-Lens/www.Shutterstock.com.

Figure 40.5 Moeraki Boulders at sunset, New Zealand. © Khoroshunova Olga/www.Shutterstock.com.

Sound is the favorite destination to enjoy the fjords. The southern lake district, which provides the entrance to Milford Sound, is varied and beautiful. Lake Te Anau is one of the best freshwater fishing areas in the world. From Lake Te Anau to Fjordland, a visitor will pass through the spectacular forest of Eglinton and Hollyford valleys, past Lakes Gunn and Fergus and Mount Christina through a long man-made tunnel (Homer Tunnel) to a road that drops down through the Cleddau Valley, crossing some eighty bridges with outstanding vistas along the route.

Dunedin is called the "Edinburgh of the South," with such Scottish names as Glenfalloch Gardens, Larnach's Castle, Macandrew's Bay, and Princes Street and a statue of Robert Burns. Dunedin is a city of architectural eye-catchers where spires, turrets, towers, and gables adorn the roofs of many of the gracious stone buildings. Not far from and just north of Dunedin, near the fishing village of Moerake, are the intriguing Moeraki boulders (Figure 40.5)—huge, strange spherically shaped rocks that weigh several tons and are up to 6 yards in circumference. Near Queenstown, at the Kawarua Bridge, bungee jumpers started forming the world's first commercial bungee jumping site.

Australia

Continent and country, Australia is the only nation to govern an entire continent and its outlying islands. It is about the same size as the forty-eight contiguous United States, but Australian settlement is concentrated along the temperate, southeastern coastal region, where the largest cities—Sydney, Melbourne, and Brisbane—are found. The interior of the country, the outback, consists mostly of sparsely populated arid and semiarid deserts, with some tropical wetlands in the north. Since 1945, more than 6 million people have migrated to Australia; most speak English, but many speak Chinese, Italian, Vietnamese, Greek, Arabic, and more than 220 other languages. Aborigines, numbering some 460,000, speak 145 different languages—many of which are threatened with extinction. Most Aborigines in urban areas speak English, and the native languages largely survive only in the outback. Agriculture and mining account for most exports, but services dominate the economy, including tourism. Tourists can see native wildlife found nowhere else on earth, such as kangaroos, koalas, and 350 species of unique birds.

From *National Geographic Atlas of the World,* 9th edition. Copyright ©2011 National Geographic Society. Reprinted by arrangement. All rights reserved.

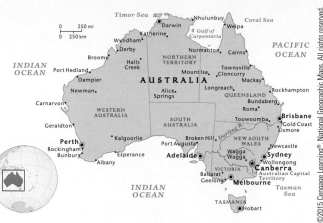

Location	Continent between Indian Ocean and South Pacific
Area	7,692,024 sq km (2,969,907 sq mi)
Population	21,852,000
Government	Federal Parliamentary Democracy and a Commonwealth Realm
Capital	Canberra 378,000
Life Expectancy	81 years
Literacy	99%
Religion	Roman Catholic, Anglican, other Christian
Language	English
Currency	Australian dollar (AUD)
GDP per Cap	$38,800
Labor Force	3.6% Agriculture, 21.1% Industry, 75% Services

From *National Geographic Atlas of the World,* 9th edition. Copyright ©2011 National Geographic Society. Reprinted by arrangement. All rights reserved.

TRAVEL TIPS 🧳

Entry: A passport and visa are required. Proof of onward or round-trip ticket is required.

Peak Tourist Season: December

National Holiday: January 26 (Australia Day)

Shopping: Common items include opals and gems, sheepskin hats and coats, toy koalas, and boomerangs made by Aborigines.

Internet TLD: .au

CULTURAL CAPSULE Captain Cook claimed Australia for the United Kingdom in 1770. At that time the native population numbered some 300,000 in as many as 500 tribes speaking many different languages. Today the aboriginal population numbers about 230,000 representing about 1.4 percent of the population. Today 95 percent of the people are Caucasian. Sixty percent of them are of Anglo-Celtic heritage. The Asian population represents about 4 percent of the population. In addition the cultural mosaic is enriched by people of Vietnamese, Polynesian, Polish, Lithuanian, Latvia, Italian, Greek, German, French, Estonian, Dutch, and Cambodian ancestry.

Today, tribal aboriginals lead a settled but traditional life in remote areas of northern, central, and western Australia. English is the national language. Only about 50 Aboriginal languages have survived.

Approximately 76 percent are Christians, divided among the Anglicans (24 percent), the Catholics (26 percent), and other denominations. Religion does not play a strong role in Australian life.

Cultural hints: A warm, friendly handshake is a common greeting. Respect for queues or lines is important. Common North American gestures are understood. In homes a guest receives a plate with food already served on it. Ask for water if desired. The entree is an appetizer rather than a main dish. Typical foods are fish, mutton, beef, seafood, vegetables, and fruits.

Tourism Characteristics

Like New Zealand, Australia has had rapid growth in both tourism numbers and diversity.

Australia is a large country, nearly as large as the United States. It consists of a federation of six states and two territories with dependencies, including Christmas Island, Cocos (Keeling) Islands, Heard and MacDonald Islands, Lord Howe Islands, Macquarie Island, and Norfolk Island. The federal government has long recognized the importance of tourism and early established the Australian Tourist Commission (ATC). The ATC is responsible for coordinating the planning and development of the travel and tourist industry in both the public and private sectors. It has overseas offices in London, Frankfurt, New York, Los Angeles, Tokyo, Beijing, Singapore, and Wellington.

Figure 40.6 Sydney Opera House, Sydney, Australia. © Selfiy /www.Shutterstock.com.

The average length of stay of visitors is twenty-three days, largely due to its remoteness from major population and industrial centers of the world. Visiting friends and relatives accounts for nearly 24 percent of all visitors, mostly from the United Kingdom, New Zealand, Oceania, and Canada.

The rapid growth of the Chinese market has moved Japan into third place in number of visitors. Because of its proximity and common culture, New Zealand is historically the source for the largest number of tourists. Tourism remains high from New Zealand, totaling nearly 20 percent of visitors to Australia in 2010. An increase also occurred from Asian nations such as China, Japan, South Korea, and Singapore. Europe has a 24 percent share, while the United States accounts for 8 percent of international travelers to Australia.

Tourist Destinations and Attractions

Sydney and Melbourne, the two largest cities, have major international airports and account for 55 percent of all arrivals in the country.

The seasonal shift from the Northern Hemisphere's winter to the Southern Hemisphere's summer is a major attraction. Australia has a variety and diversity of attractions resulting from its size and history. Nature has provided some unique animals, which make the zoos and botanical gardens of Australia most interesting, showing kangaroos, koalas, emus, and platypuses.

The southeast of Australia, represented by Sydney and Melbourne, are the two poles of attraction for tourists. Sydney, Australia's oldest city, is attractive, in some ways resembling London, but on a smaller scale. Its Opera House (Figure 40.6) adorns many calendars

Figure 40.7 Tasmanian Devil. © Flash-ka/www.Shutterstock.com.

and pictures promoting Australia. Many of the historical sites have been renovated and redeveloped into excellent tourist markets, such as the Rocks. The city is famous for its Sydney Harbor Bridge (you can walk across the span), harbor cruises, the Kings Cross entertainment district, and shopping at the Queen Victoria Building.

The Jenolan caves, with ancient aboriginal paintings, and a number of game park reserves are a short distance from Sydney and Melbourne. The Blue Mountains of New South Wales lie west of Sydney. The country's wine region lies to the north of the city.

Australia's second largest city, and the capital of Victoria, is the original capital, Melbourne. It has stately homes and major sights such as the Victoria Cultural Center, the War Memorial Shrine, Botanical Gardens, and a variety of neighborhoods along the rivers cutting through the city. Many think it is Australia's most beautiful city. Short trips from Melbourne take visitors to old gold-rush towns and Phillip Island, home of penguins and seals.

Between Sydney and Melbourne is Canberra, the capital of Australia. It is a modern planned city focusing on Australia's House of Parliament. Canberra is coiled around a man-made lake and has more than twelve million trees and shrubs lining the avenues, circles, and crescents.

An hour's plane ride south of Melbourne is Hobart, the capital of the island state of Tasmania. Hobart has old, narrow, winding, hilly streets. Tasmania itself is a land of plateaus and precipitous mountains set in a green meadow landscape. It is a treasury of outdoor activities. One can fish for trout in beautiful inland lakes and rivers or for huge bluefin tuna offshore; take a bushwalk in wild and wonderful country, some of which is still unexplored; shoot the white-water rapids in a canoe or brave Tasmania's challenging peaks. Cradle Mountain National Park has rugged mountains while coastal Freycinet National Park is home to Tasmania's famous Wineglass Bay. And yes, the Tasmanian Devil is real (Figure 40.7) and lives, in the wild, only on the island of Tasmania.

In Arnhem Land, within Australia's Northern Territory, set aside your maps and let the songs of the Aborigines lead you.

Arnhem Land is my home. It is my birthplace. It is where my family is. It is where my culture is. It is where the stories I sign come from. It is the place where I belong. It is where my ancestors have lived for thousands of years and where everything has a song or story attached to it.

Nothing is unrelated in Arnhem Land: The trees, the rocks, everything has a name and a relationship to the people. You can travel as an Aboriginal person through Arnhem Land by following the songs. They are our maps. Songs tell us where we are, whose country we are in. They show us the connections with people, land, and animals.

I know that Arnhem Land is lush and beautiful, but because I was born blind, I cannot speak to that. Visitors to Arnhem Land should try to close their eyes and listen. There is beauty in what you can hear: the stories, the songs, the ceremony. There are not many places in Australia left where the people still carry on their traditions so strongly, or where so much knowledge is borne by song.

I am a Gumatj man born in northeast Arnhem Land speaking the languages of the Gumatj people and singing the songs of my mother's and father's clans. We eat good food here-turtles, wallabies, oysters, damper, and fish.

When I was little, I remember riding my push bike down the hill at Elcho Island, with everyone calling out directions—"Go left! Go right!" It was a bit scary. But the community looked after me. That was my first impression of Arnhem Land. I also recall the singing of the old people. I could hear the songmen at night. I loved to listen and learn, and I still do.

— **Geoffrey Gurrumul Yunupingu,** *National Geographic Traveler,* October 2009

Figure 40.8 Green turtle and coral, Great Barrier Reef, Australia.
© Regien Paassen/www.Shutterstock.com.

Queensland has Australia's greatest attraction, the Great Barrier Reef, stretching for 1,200 miles along the eastern coast. A series of islands and cities provide excellent access to the spectacular underwater views of the Great Barrier Reef. The Great Barrier Reef is made up of some 2,500 individual coral reefs ranging in size from less than 2 acres to 100 square kilometers. There is a rich and diverse ecosystem along the reef (Figure 40.8), containing more than 300 species of hard corals and 1,500 species of fish. It is also rich in birdlife. The Great Barrier Reef Marine Park protects the future of the area while providing for local and tourist use.

Located on the east coast just south of Brisbane, with easy access to the population centers of Sydney and Brisbane, Queensland has the greatest tourist development in such towns as the Gold Coast and the Sunshine Coast. It is comparable to the coastal resort developments in Spain and could be similar to Waikiki Beach in Hawaii. The Gold Coast, south of Brisbane, is a strip of white sandy beach nineteen miles long and has a number of major attractions such as Dreamworld and Sea World. Surfer's Paradise is a must for those who want to challenge the waves. To the north, Cairns has a tropical environment, and has established an international airport in order to draw more visitors to the region.

South of Alice Springs in the Northern Territory is the memorable Ayers Rock (Figure 40.9), which is part of Uluru National Park. Uluru National Park includes both Ayers Rock and Mount Olga. They are famous peaks of an otherwise buried mountain range and dominate an

Figure 40.9 Ayers Rock (Uluru), Australia. © Stanislav Fosenbauer/www.Shutterstock.com.

open landscape of sandplains, dunes, and Mulga woodland. Both are colorful and impressive formations that, together with the surrounding country, have always held great significance for Aborigines. Ayers Rock is a sacred mountain for the Aborigines. It has been given back to the Aborigines, but is leased to the park service for maintenance. In addition to the area's natural beauty, visitors can see sites, rock formations, and paintings that form an important part of Central Australian Aboriginal mythology. Alice Springs is an oasis in the remote Outback, accounting for the low number of tourists to the Northern Territory.

Darwin, the Northern Territory capital, is the base for either short or extended tours into Kakadu National Park, a vast wilderness east of Darwin that abounds with wildlife and Aboriginal rock paintings unique to Australia.

Adelaide, the capital of South Australia, is the center of the country's wine-making industry due to its Mediterranean climate. Adelaide is near numerous nature reserves and opal mines, which provide nice day trips from the city. Adelaide has wide European-style boulevards, magnificent green parklands, and a number of interesting buildings such as the Parliament House, Constitution Museum, and Government House.

Perth in Western Australia has become well known because of the America's Cup. This is a sailing race held whenever there is a challenge to the reigning cup holder. Its climate is similar to that of Southern California, and it is the center of agriculture, mining, and industry for Western Australia. Perth is a delightful city for strolling and people watching. London Court, a sixteenth-century Tudor-style arcade, is a reminder of England. The Western Australia Museum includes a fine Aboriginal gallery as well as vintage cars, World War II memorabilia, meteorites, and the skeleton of a huge blue whale. While it offers a far better climate, water sports, and a large wildlife reserve within the city limits, its distance from population centers handicap its tourist industry.

Once Australia's roughest port town ruled by those of ill repute, Fremantle or "Freo," 30 minutes southwest of Perth, dramatically changed in the 1950s with a new wave of European immigrants. Then in 1983, after Australia won the America's Cup and Fremantle looked forward to hosting the sailing race in 1987, the locals rejoiced and the town's streets became lined with cafés, boutiques, museums, and buskers. The revelers may have dispersed, but the party stuck around.

SEAFARERS, ARTISTS, AND MISFITS

Check out the America's Cup winning yacht and an old pearling lugger (the boat pearl-shell divers operated) displayed at the modern, steel-and-glass **Western Australian Maritime Museum** on Victoria Quay. Nearby, stroll the 15-acre **Fremantle Prison** and discover a gruesome past as you visit the gallows where hangings took place on Monday mornings right up until 1964. In 2010, the limestone prison was the first building in Western Australia granted UNESCO World Heritage status. Climb down steel ladders to the labyrinth 65 feet below, where prisoners were ordered to hard labor in the tunnels that served as a water catchment. On Wednesday and Friday nights, meet at the prison gatehouse for a guided, torchlit tour. Make your own great escape to the new-Gothic **Fremantle Arts Centre**, built by convicts in 1864 as a criminal lunatic asylum, to view one of the largest collections of local and Australian art in the state, and watch live performances in the intimate courtyard. (*4 hours*)

ISLAND WILDLIFE

Join Capricorn Seakayaking for a guided paddle to the **Shoalwater Islands Marine Park** that encompasses Seal and Penguin

Figure 40.10 Fairy penguin. © Ina Raschke/www.Shutterstock.com.

Islands. Bring your binoculars and view up to 16 unique seabird species seldom seen on the mainland, including whimbrels and the Caspian tern. On Penguin Island, watch fairy penguins (Figure 40.10)—the world's smallest—being fed at the **Penguin Island Discovery Centre**. Snorkel alongside dolphins and explore limestone reefs in the island's underwater wonderland. (*6 hours*)

BEACH IT

The coast is dotted with glorious beaches, but you don't need to travel far to dig your toes into the sand. **Bathers Beach** is located within walking distance of downtown Fremantle, making it an ideal spot for a refreshing dip and for exploring the historic West End bookstores and galleries featuring Aboriginal artwork. If the brilliant white sands and calm waters of the Indian Ocean beckon, then swim or snorkel at **Port Beach**. Or head to **Cottlesloe Beach** along Marine Parade (5 miles north of Fremantle) for its shady Norfolk pines and endless coastal views. (*3 hours*)

GO FISH

Cast a line for snapper and mulluway at the **Fremantle Fishing Boat Harbour**, a historic working port with some 400 fishing boats. If the fish aren't biting, join locals and visitors alike for fresh seafood (including crabs, oysters, and crispy fish and chips) at the 109-year-old, family-owned **Cicerello's**. Afterward, tour the airy **Little Creatures Brewery**, located in a former boat yard, and enjoy a cold ale on its deck with views of Rottnest Island. (*3 hours*)

— Carmen Jenner, *National Geographic Traveler*, June/July 2012

REVIEW QUESTIONS

1. Where are the major market regions of visitors to Australia? Why?

2. What do Australia and New Zealand have in common? How are they different?

3. Where are the major population centers of Australia?

4. Discuss the Aborigines of Australia and the Maoris of New Zealand and their importance to the tourist industry of their respective countries.

5. If tourists only had a week and wanted to visit either New Zealand or Australia (not both), which would you suggest they visit to provide the most diverse experience in the least amount of time? Why?

A

ABC Islands The Netherlands Antilles Islands of Aruba, Bonaire, and Curacao.

Absolute Location The position or place of a point on the surface of the earth expressed in degrees, minutes, and seconds of latitude and longitude.

Accessibility The ease by which interchange or travel can occur between two places or people.

Acropolis The upper fortified part or citadel of the ancient Greek city of Athens.

Adriatic Of or pertaining to the Adriatic Sea or to the people inhabiting its islands and its coast. The Adriatic Sea is an arm of the Mediterranean, 500 miles long and up to 140 miles wide, between Italy and Croatia.

African Pertaining to Africa, its people, or its language; a person born in Africa.

African Riviera The coastal area of the Ivory Coast between Abidjan and Sassandra of beautiful beaches, plantations, casinos, and picturesque fishing villages.

Afrikaaners An Afrikaan-speaking descendant of the early Dutch settlers to South Africa.

Aiga The extended family groups in traditional Samoan cultures.

Alemannic A High-German dialect spoken in Alsace, parts of southern Germany, and Switzerland.

Alhambra Moorish palace in Granada built on the hill overlooking the city. It has imposing towers and halls, rooms decorated with lacy carvings, colored tiles, and gold mosaics, and courtyards with fountains, hidden gardens, and hedges.

Alluvial Deposits of mud, silt, and sand by rivers and streams. Alluvial plains adjoin many larger rivers. Alluvial deltas mark the mouths of rivers, such as the Mississippi. Alluvial fans mark the outlet of canyons of streams.

Alps An alpine chain of high, rugged mountains in central Europe.

Altitudinal Zonation Vertical regions of South and Middle America. Each zone has a different physical, environmental, and population characteristic.

Amazon A river of South America that originates in the Peruvian Andes and flows north then east through northern Brazil to the Atlantic Ocean.

Amazon Basin The lowland, tropical rain forest area of the Amazon River drainage region in South America.

AMTRAK Name used by the National Railroad Passenger Corporation (a semipublic corporation formed by the Rail Passenger Service Act of 1970 and charged with managing and rejuvenating United States intercity passenger railroad service).

Ancient Cities Cities that developed early in the history of humankind.

Andalusia A region of southern Spain comprising the provinces of Almeria, Granada, Jaen, Malaga, Cadiz, Cordoba, Huelva, and Seville. Strongly influenced by the Moors of Northern Africa.

Andes A 4,000-mile-long mountain system stretching the length of western South America from Venezuela to Tierra del Fuego.

Anglican A member of the Church of England or any church related to it.

Arabian Plateau Plateau in the Arabian Peninsula.

Arawaks Indian people living in parts of Guyana, Suriname, and French Guyana; the language spoken by these Indians.

Archaeological The study of material evidences of human life and culture in past ages.

Archipelago A group or chain of islands in close proximity to one another.

Ashkenazim Jews from Western and Central Europe.

Asia The largest of the continents, it occupies the eastern portion of the Eurasian landmass and adjacent islands.

Asiatic Russia The southern regions of Russia bordering on Kazakhstan, Georgia and Azerbaijan that are Islamic and of Asian origin.

Atacama Arid desert of Chile between the Pacific Ocean and the Andes Mountains. One of the driest deserts in the world.

Atolls Coral islands that are low and have an open lagoon surrounded by a reef.

Austro-Hungarian Empire A former dual monarchy of central Europe, formed by the union of Austria, Bohemia, Hungary, and parts of Poland.

B

Baksheesh A tip in Arab countries.

Balance of Payments Statement of international monetary transactions; the amount of money leaving a country for goods and services, as opposed to that spent to purchase goods and services within a country.

Balkan Peninsula A peninsula in southeastern Europe including the countries of Greece, Albania, Yugoslavia, and Bulgaria.

Barrios Low-income neighborhoods in Middle and South America.

Basques A people of obscure racial and linguistic origin who retained autonomy until the nineteenth century. Concentrated in Northwestern Spain and Southern France (around the Pyrenees Mountains).

Bazaar An Arabic market usually consisting of a street or streets lined with shops and stalls.

Bedouin Nomadic group in the Middle East and North Africa.

Biomass The amount of vegetative (organic) matter in an ecosystem in a designated surface area.

Boers Descendants of Dutch colonists in South Africa.

Bord Failte Eireann Irish National Tourist Board.

Border Towns Towns and cities along borders between two countries that receive large numbers of day visitors.

Buddha A representation of Gautama Buddha who was the originator of Buddhism.

Buddhism A religion found today in Southeast Asia, China, Japan, and Korea; an attempt to reform the Hindu belief system. Buddhism maintains that the path of salvation is based on four truths. These truths are: first, recognition that life is full of suffering; second, awareness that desire is the cause of suffering; third, that happiness and satisfaction (the end of suffering) come from overcoming desires; and fourth, that proper conduct, including honesty, forgiveness, compassion, and consideration, is the means of overcoming cravings and desire.

C

Caldera A large crater formed by volcanic explosion or by collapse of a volcanic cone.

Caliph The leader, both religious and secular, of a Moslem state.

Calypso Music of the West Indies centered in Trinidad. Uses improvised lyrics on topical or humorous subjects.

Canadian Shield The low, crystalline rock shield that extends over half of Canada, from Labrador southwest around Hudson Bay and northwest to the Arctic Ocean.

Capital A town or city that is the official seat of government in a state, nation, or other political entity.

Capital Transfers A part of the balance of payments in which money is transferred from one country to another in the form of foreign aid or some kind of cash grant.

Caravanserai Inn for travelers and traders along the Silk Road and other routes of Central Asia.

Carib An original inhabitant of the Lesser Antilles and northern South America.

Caribbean An area of the Atlantic Ocean bordered by North America, Central America, and South America; characterized by its warm climate and beaches; a major tourism area.

Caribbean Tourism Organization A Caribbean organization consisting of eighteen countries that provides statistics and deals with common tourism problems of the region.

Carrying Capacity The number of animals, crops, or people an area can support on a continual basis without degrading the environment. The carrying capacity varies with technology, land-use techniques, and geographic characteristics.

Castellano A regional dialect of Catalonia in northwestern Spain.

Castle A stronghold or a fortified medieval town.

Cataracts A series of large waterfalls.

Cathedral Cities Cities in which a dominant characteristic of the landscape is the cathedral.

Cathedrals Large, impressive churches that contain the official throne of the bishop.

Catholic A member of any Catholic Church, particularly Roman Catholic.

Catholic Inquisition The medieval effort of the Catholic Church to combat heresy.

Caucasians A division of humanity comprising the major ethnic groups of Europe, North Africa, and Southwest Asia.

CEDOK The official tourism organization of the Czech Republic and Slovakia.

Celt An ancient people of western and central Europe, including the Britons and the Gauls.

Celtic A subfamily of the Indo-European family of languages.

Central America Consists of all the countries south of the Mexican border to the northern border of Colombia.

Central Location Places that are located central to their market.

Central Place A community that possesses a certain measure of centrality and forms the urban focus for a particular region.

Central Planning Planning and economic development that are controlled by the central government.

Chateau A French castle or manor house.

Chinese A native of China, a person of Chinese ancestry, or a group of Sino-Tibetan languages and dialects spoken in East Asia.

Christian Those who follow the teachings of Jesus Christ.

Christianity The Christian religion, based on the teachings of Jesus.

Cinder Cone The cone formed in the center of a volcano.

Circular Tours Tours that visit a number of places between the origin and return point in a circular manner.

Cirque A steep hollow occurring at the upper end of mountain valleys. Formed by glaciation.

Civil War A war between two factions or regions of one country.

Climate Generalized statement of the prevailing weather conditions at a given place, based upon statistics of a long period of record and including average values, departures from those averages, and the probabilities associated with those departures.

Colonial Of or relating to being controlled by a European or other foreign power. Individuals in the controlled countries may be called colonials.

Colonial Territories Territories controlled by a foreign power.

Common Market Name given to a group of fifteen European countries (as of 1996) that belong to a supranational association to promote their economic interests. The official name is the European Union (EU).

Commonwealth Formerly the Commonwealth of England, today it refers to independent countries that were once colonies of England and are now part of a political community. Major member countries include the United Kingdom, Australia, New Zealand, India, and Canada.

Commonwealth of Independent States The newly independent republics of the former Soviet Union except Estonia, Latvia, and Lithuania.

Communism The economic system whereby all factors of production are owned by the state in the name of the workers. Private ownership is nonexistent and competition is unacceptable. Individuals perform for the benefit of society rather than the individual.

Complementarity Production of goods or services by two or more places in a mutually beneficial fashion.

Coniferous A cone-bearing evergreen tree with needle leaves, straight trunks, and short branches.

Continent One of the major landmasses of the world; Africa, Antarctica, Asia, Australia, Europe, North America, and South America.

Continental Europe The countries of Europe that are on the continent.

Continental Islands The large islands of the Pacific stretching from the Southeast Asian mainland to Australia.

Continentality A characteristic of climate in large landmasses where the land heats and cools quickly, creating large daily and yearly changes in temperature.

Copper Belt The area of Zambia and Zaire that has a large concentration of copper.

Coptic The Christian Church of Egypt.

Coral Atoll A coral island or islands with a reef surrounding a lagoon.

Coral Reef A marine ridge or mound consisting of compacted coral.

Creole Persons born of European descent in the West Indies or Spanish America. The French patois is spoken by these people.

Crown Colony Colony of Great Britain.

Cruise Ships Luxury passenger ships in which the purpose is vacation and recreation in a given region of the world.

Cultural Centers Cultural attractions that display and maintain important cultural artifacts and ways of life.

Cultural Geography The study of peoples and their works, the site, situation, and specific time.

Cultural Hearth A region of origin for a group of people.

Cultural Links Ties and interactions between two cultures.

Currents The patterns or movements of air and water in a constant direction.

Czar The emperor in the former Russian Empire.

D

Daibutsu Great Buddha. A huge 700-year-old bronze image of Buddha.

Danube The major river of southeastern Europe.

Deccan Plateau A triangular plateau extending over most of peninsular India.

Deciduous A tree that loses its leaves at the beginning of winter or the start of the dry season.

Delta A flat, fertile lowland created by a river as it deposits its load of soil near the mouth when the water slows.

Demilitarized Zone An area wherein military control forces, weapons, and installations may not be established.

Demokratization The movement to democracy in the former Soviet Union.

Desert A region that is barren or partially barren and receives little or no rainfall.

Desert Pavement A relatively smooth area in a desert region with pebbles closely packed together to create a hard surface.

Developing The economic development of a country associated with industrialization and an improved standard of living for its people.

Druids A priestly caste of ancient Gaul and Britain that performs incantations and enchantments.

Druze A member of a religious sect in Syria and Lebanon whose primarily Muslim religion contains some elements of Christianity.

E

Eastern Orthodox Division of Catholicism derived from the church of the Byzantine Empire that acknowledges the primacy of the patriarch of Constantinople.

Economic The production, development, and management of material wealth of a country, household, or business enterprise.

Economic Colonialism The control of a less industrialized economy or businesses by companies in an industrialized country.

Ecotourism Tourism that is based on interest in nature and the environment.

Edo The early name of Tokyo during the Shogunate government in the 1600s.

English Channel A portion of the Atlantic Ocean between England and France, connected with the North Sea by the Strait of Dover.

Environment The total circumstances surrounding an organism or group of organisms, including physical, cultural, and social surroundings.

EU European Union. (*See* Common Market.)

Euronesians Persons of mixed European and Polynesian ancestry.

European Cities The major cities of Europe.

European Plain Low, flat, fertile area of Western Europe.

European Russia The area west of the Ural mountains of Slavic origins. The Russian ethnic group predominates the area and is the area of most of the population of Russia.

Excursionist A temporary visitor staying less than 24 hours in a country.

F

Fall Line The point in rivers on the coastal plain at which waterfalls occur, thus limiting navigation up stream. Cities and industrial centers are often located at the fall line.

Far East An area commonly including the Koreas, Japan, China, and the islands belonging to them. Sometimes used to refer to all of Asia east of Afghanistan.

Fens A low-lying, marshy land.

Fjord Narrow, steep-sided, elongated, and coastal valley deepened by glacier ice that has since melted away, allowing the sea to create an inlet. Found especially along the coasts of Norway, Alaska, and New Zealand where they are important tourist attractions.

Flood Plain The level, low valley floor bordering a river.

Folk Culture The way of life of a traditional society.

FONATUR Mexican State planning office; Fondo Nacional De Fomento al Turismo.

Forbidden City Palace of the former emperors of China in Beijing.

Friday Mosque Islamic mosques in which Friday prayers are held.

G

Gaelic The language of the Gaels. The Celtic language of the Irish and the Scottish Highlanders.

Game Reserve Area set aside by government legislation to protect and manage the habitat of wild animals. While preservation is a major goal, controlled accessibility by visitors for viewing, photographing, and in some cases hunting is also desired.

Game Viewing The national parks of Africa provide an opportunity for visitors to watch animals in a natural setting.

Gaming Official name for gambling entertainment, especially in the United States.

Gauchos An Argentine cowboy in the Pampas region.

Geographic Location Where something is permanently located; an area on a map.

Geography The study of the earth as the home of mankind.

Geomancy The belief that the earth has a spirit and can influence human activities.

Ghetto A section or quarter of a European city to which Jews were restricted. Also used to refer to slum areas of American cities or any poor section of a city whose population is dominated by a distinct ethnic group.

Ginza Major shopping street in Tokyo.

Glacial Drift Glacial deposits on the earth's surface.

Glacial Features Landscape features resulting from glaciation.

Glaciation An area which at one time was covered by glaciers.

Glacier-burst The breaking opening of glaciers.

Glasnost A Russian term meaning "openness." It refers to an open policy in social, economic, and political issues that was introduced in the Soviet Union in the late 1980s.

Global Interdependence The dependency of countries and regions of the world upon each other for production of goods.

Glockenspiel Clock and tower in German-speaking countries.

Golden Ring A group of cities northeast of Moscow that illustrate Russian history and culture consisting of old Russian Orthodox churches, monasteries, and convents. The towns are almost living museums of Russian architecture and life.

Golden Triangle The area of India encompassing Delhi, Agra, and Jaipur; a major tourism region in India.

Gothic The architectural, painting, cultural, and literary style prevalent in Western Europe from the twelfth through the fifteenth centuries.

Grand Tour Itinerary of extended duration or relative luxury. Started in the eighteenth century for the sons of wealthy Western Europeans who traveled for some 3 years. Major destination was Florence, Italy.

Great Barrier Reef The extensive coral reef off the northeast coast of Australia.

Great Trek The Dutch, who settled South Africa, became in conflict with British. The Dutch, as a group, moved to the interior of South Africa.

Great Wall The Great Wall of China was completed about 200 B.C. It was built to protect China's eastern farmers from the pastoral herders of the Asian interior.

Greco-Roman Pertaining to the culture of both Greece and Rome.

Greek Islands The islands of the Aegean Sea and Mediterranean that are culturally and politically Greek.

Gulf Stream A warm ocean current of the North Atlantic issuing from the Gulf of Mexico and flowing east through the Straits of Florida, then northeast along the southeastern coast of the United States, then east to the North Atlantic current.

H

Hacienda A term referring to large estates in Latin America, commonly used in Mexico.

Hajj The pilgrimage to Mecca. The Islamic religion includes the belief that each believer should ideally make the pilgrimage at least once in his or her lifetime.

Hall of Fame Museum that honors outstanding individuals in a particular sport or endeavor.

Han The ethnic group referred to as Chinese.

Hanging Valley The valley of a tributary that enters a main river valley from a considerable height above the bed of the latter, and so forms rapids or waterfalls.

Hanseatic League A mercantile association of towns formed to control trading throughout Europe in the Middle Ages.

Health Resort Complex of facilities and natural features used by tourists interested in health-giving qualities, such as mineral waters, sun, air, exercise, and expert health personnel.

Hemisphere The northern or southern half of the earth as divided by the equator; the eastern or western half as divided by the Prime Meridian.

Hidden Economy The trading, bartering, buying, and selling of goods without a record for government accountability.

Himalayas A high mountain range in south central Asia.

Hinduism The religion of the majority of the population of India.

Historical Houses Houses preserved for historical purposes, frequently important for tourism.

HIV Human immunodeficiency virus. The virus associated with AIDS.

Holiday A day established by law or custom on which ordinary work is suspended; outside the United States, a vacation or time away from work.

Holy Week The week before Easter in Christianity.

Horn of Africa The area of Ethiopia and Somalia that extends out into the Indian Ocean.

Hurricanes Tropical cyclonic winds in excess of 75 miles per hour.

I

IATA (*See* International Air Transportation Association.)

Iberian Peninsula A 230,000-square-mile peninsula in Europe occupied by Spain and Portugal.

Ibero-European European people of the Iberian Peninsula or the influence of this region.

Impact Envisioned or actual consequences (negative or positive) of a decision. The impact may be economic, sociocultural, political, environmental, or other; direct or indirect; intended or not; favorable or unfavorable.

Indian Indigenous populations of North and South America.

Indian Markets Markets in Latin American countries with Indian populations. Usually held once a week, the market allows Indians to exchange, sell, and buy goods and products.

Industrial A highly developed industry.

Industrial Revolution The Industrial Revolution involved the substitution of machine power for muscle power sources, allowing production increases and creating a growth in demand for resources.

Industry A business employing labor, as the tourist industry.

Infrastructure Investments, such as utilities (water, sewer, electricity), transport (roads, harbors, airports), site development, health care, and schools.

Insularity An island or, by extension, being isolated like an island.

Interaction The relationship between places in terms of tourism, trade, etc., that creates joint action.

International Air Transportation Association (IATA) World association of international airlines. It promotes a unified system on international routes by setting fares, rates, safety standards, and the appointment of travel agents to sell international tickets.

International Date Line The line where the date changes by exactly one day as it is crossed. It is approximately 180 degrees West or East.

International Travel Itinerary involving the crossing of the border between countries, usually requiring some degree of formal permission or recognition.

Intervening Opportunities The substitution of a desired destination for a location similar but closer in time and cost.

Intourist The privatized travel agency of Russia and countries that were formerly part of the Soviet Union.

Invisible Exports Tourism, banking or other services that do not result in the export of goods.

Invisible Trade The flow of invisible exports and imports out of and into a country.

Iron Gate Gorges created by rock masses between the Hungarian Plain and the Wallachian Plain of the Danube River.

Islam Religion founded by the prophet Mohammed (Muhammad) in Saudi Arabia around 624 A.D. Islam is the name of the religion and means submission to the will of one God (Allah). Muslim or Moslem refers to a member, one who submits himself or herself to the will of Allah.

Islamic The Moslem religion.

Islamic Cities Cities that have developed according to Islamic beliefs and are in the Islamic cultural region.

Islamic Fundamentalism The movement among some Islamic faithful to return to more conservative Muslim beliefs, practices, and social-political systems.

Islamic Law Some countries of the Islamic World base their political and legal systems on the Koran, the holy book of Islam.

Islamic World The countries of North Africa, the Middle East, and South and Southeast Asia where the great majority of the people are Muslims.

Island A landmass that is smaller than a continent and surrounded by water.

Isolation The condition of being geographically cut off or far removed from mainstreams of thought and action. It also denotes a lack of receptivity to outside influences, caused at least partially by inaccessibility.

J

Jainism A branch of Hinduism that denies the existence of a perfect or supreme being.

Japan Alps The central mountain region of Japan.

Jet Age The era since the development and use of the jet engine.

Jewish Characteristic of the Jews, their religion, or their customs.

Jungle An area of dense vegetation and trees, normally referring to tropical like conditions.

K

Karst Topography A limestone region of hills, gullies, and valleys in which most or all of the drainage is by underground channels, the surface being dry and barren.

Kasbah The old native quarter consisting of housing, the citadel, and the palace, in Arabic cities of North Africa.

Kimono A long, loose, widesleeved Japanese robe, worn with a broad sash.

Koran The book of sacred writings of the Prophet Muhammad.

Kremlin The old walled fortress from which the czars ruled the Russian Empire. Now home to the government of Russia, it is also an important tourist attraction.

L

Lake A large inland body of fresh or salt water.

Lake Kinnereth Name given to the Sea of Galilee by the Israelis.

Landforms The configuration of the land surface into distinctive forms, such as hills, valleys, and plateaus.

Language Any method of communicating ideas by a system of symbolic sounds, or the corresponding written symbols where a written form of the language exists.

Latitude Angular distance north or south of the equator, measured in degrees, minutes, and seconds.

Leeward The side of an island or mountain that is opposite to the side that receives the prevailing winds.

Legal Systems A system of law.

Lifestyle A person's way of life as indicated by the daily or regular activities of the person in clothing, food, drink, leisure, opinions, occupation, work, friendships, and the like. Lifestyle factors are a major influence on a person's tourism behavior and preferences.

Lingua Franca Refers to use of a second language spoken and understood by many peoples to overcome diversity of language in an area.

Location Where something is found.

Loch A lake, fjord, or arm of the sea in Scotland.

Loess Fertile soil created of fine dust deposited by wind.

Longitude Distance east or west of the meridian of Greenwich, measured in degrees, minutes, and seconds.

Lutheran A branch of Protestantism started by Martin Luther, common in Northern Europe and areas settled by migrants from this area.

M

Madrassa Islamic school or seminary training young men.

Maquiladoras Industrial plants established along the Mexican–United States border given special import and export considerations.

Maritime A climate characterized by moderate temperature, medium to high rainfall, and generally high humidity. Usually found along coasts.

Maritime Influence Of or relating to the influence of the ocean on countries with a maritime location.

Massif Central Plateau region of southeastern France.

Masurian Lake District Lake region in Poland.

Matai Chief of Samoan traditional society.

Matrilineal A society in which ancestry is traced through the female line.

Mayan World Circuit The countries of Mexico, Belize, Guatemala, Honduras, and El Salvador have begun joint marketing of the Mayan ruins in Middle America.

Mecca The most sacred city in Islam. Muslims face Mecca for daily prayers and make pilgrimages to the city.

Medieval (Middle Ages) Period of time in history from A.D. 700 to A.D. 1500.

Medina The site of the Prophet Muhammad's tomb in eastern Saudi Arabia.

Mediterranean The Mediterranean Sea, the region surrounding the sea, or the climatic type found in the area characterized by hot, dry summers and mild, warm winters that are excellent for coastal tourism.

Melanesians A cultural group of people who have very dark skins and dark hair.

Memorial An object or event designed to commemorate a person or event.

Meridians Great circles passing around the poles at right angles to the equator.

Mestizo An individual in Latin America whose parentage and lineage are composed of both European and Indian descent.

Mezzogiorno The southern part of Italy. An area economically behind northern Italy.

Micronesians Inhabitants of a small island group in the Pacific north of Melanesia and east of the Philippines.

Middle America The region from the northern Mexican border to the southern Panamanian border.

Middle Class People who occupy a social or economic position between the laboring class and those who are wealthy in terms of land or money.

Middle East The area in Asia and Africa between and including Morocco in the west, Pakistan in the east, Turkey in the north, and the Arabian Peninsula in the south.

Midnight Sun At high latitudes around midsummer the sun does not sink below the horizon and so may be seen at midnight.

Ming Tombs The burial tombs of the rulers during the Ming Dynasty (1364–1644).

Monsoon Technically refers to a seasonal reversal of winds, but it also brings heavy precipitation.

Moonscape A view or picture of the surface of the moon or, by extension, any desolate landscape.

Moors A Muslim people living mainly in northern Africa who invaded Spain in ancient times.

Mosque A Muslim house of worship.

Mt. Fuji The highest peak in Japan (12,388 ft), it is considered a sacred mountain. It is 70 miles west southwest of Tokyo.

Mt. Kenya The highest mountain in Kenya (17,058 feet).

Mt. Kilimanjaro Highest mountain in Africa (19,340 feet).

Mountains A mass of land considerably higher than its surroundings, and of greater altitude than a hill.

Muslim (Moslem) A follower of Islam.

N

Nation Refers to a group of people with a distinct culture that may or may not coincide with political boundaries.

National Museum A museum that contains several artifacts and documents of national interest, or a museum designated as the official repository of such items.

National Park Area designated by the federal government for public education and enjoyment. In some cases, such areas must be limited in access to preserve their unique qualities. Areas so designated are unique by reason of history, geological formations, or ecological resources.

National Trust An organization in Great Britain dedicated to the preservation of historical sites.

Nation-state A country whose population possesses a substantial degree of cultural homogeneity and unity. A political unit wherein the territorial state coincides with the area settled by a certain national group or people.

Nile A river in East and North Africa and the longest on the continent (3,405 miles).

North Atlantic Drift The relatively warm currents of the Atlantic resulting from the Gulf Stream.

Nucleated Settlements A closely packed settlement, village, or hamlet sharply demarcated from adjoining farmlands.

O

Oasis A fertile green spot in a desert created by a spring, well, or other local water source.

Oceania The islands of the South Pacific.

Office Ladies Japanese women who are single and work in offices.

Old Quarter The old part of a town, which characterizes the history of a town.

Orient The countries of the Asian continent, excluding Russia and the former states of the Soviet Union.

Orographic Precipitation Precipitation caused by an air mass being forced to cross a physical barrier, such as a mountain range.

Ottoman Referring to the empire centered on Turkey, 1299 to 1923 A.D.

Ottoman Empire The Turkish Empire from 1299 to 1919 in southwestern Asia, northeastern Africa, and southeastern Europe. The capital was Constantinople. Also known as the Turkish Empire.

Outback The arid interior of Australia.

Overseas Chinese Chinese who live outside of China.

P

Package Tour Any prearranged (usually prepaid) journey to one or more destinations and returning to the point of departure. Includes transportation, accommodations, meals, sightseeing, and other components of travel.

Pagan One who is not a member of an organized religion.

Pagoda A religious building of the Orient, such as an ornate Hindu temple or many-storied Buddhist tower.

Pampas The plains of South America extending for nearly 1,000 miles from the lower Parana River to south central Argentina. It is an important livestock-raising area.

Parallels Parallels of latitude are lines drawn round the earth parallel to the equator and may thus be described as approximate circles with the two poles as centers. The circles become smaller with increasing proximity to the poles.

Party Customer or group of customers to be serviced in the same way; members of the same tour group.

Patagonia Region in South America south of the Limay and Rio Negro rivers to the Strait of Magellan. It is barren tableland between the Andes and the Atlantic Ocean.

Patrilineal A society in which ancestry is traced through the male line.

Peninsula A long, narrow projection of land into water.

Peninsular Having the characteristics of a peninsula, as Europe is peninsular.

Perception The view or understanding of a place or people.

Perestroika Russian term meaning restructuring. One of the key ideas of the late 1980s that helped lead to the breakup of the Soviet Union.

Permafrost Permanently frozen water in the soil and bedrock, as much as 1,000 feet in depth, producing the effect of completely frozen ground. Generally found in high latitudes, it can thaw near the surface during the brief summer season.

Phoenician An inhabitant of ancient Phoenicia.

Pidgin A simplified language used to communicate in areas with numerous distinct languages.

Piedmont Hilly, rolling land, lying at the foot of a mountain range and forming a transition between mountain and plain.

Pilgrimage Travel to and for the purpose of visiting a location regarded as sacred by the traveler.

Pinyin Created by China's communist government to simplify the written form of the Chinese language throughout China.

Place Any specific site that can be recognized, as a town, house, and so forth.

Plateau Upland surface, more or less flat and horizontal, upheld by resistant beds of sedimentary rock or lava flows and bounded by a steep cliff.

PLO Palestine Liberation Organization, founded in 1962 by displaced Arabs from Israel.

Po Valley The agricultural and industrial heartland of Northern Italy.

Polder Land adjacent to shore reclaimed from the sea by constructing dikes and pumping out the water.

Pollution Foreign matter placed into nature by human activity.

Polynesia An area east of Micronesia and Melanesia. It forms a triangle stretching from the Hawaiian Islands to Chile's Easter Island to New Zealand.

Population The total number of inhabitants of a particular race, group, or class in a specified area.

Population Density The number of people in a given area, usually a square mile or kilometer.

Port A place where goods are brought into and out of a country.

Poverty The condition of being poor. The lack of means to provide basic necessities of living.

Preexisting Forms The character of an area (physically and culturally) before changed as a result of tourism.

Prime Meridian Reference to meridian of zero longitude; normally accepted as the Greenwich Meridian.

Privatization The process of changing ownership of property from state ownership to private ownership.

Province A territory governed as an administrative or political unit or a country or empire.

Punic Of or relating to ancient Carthage.

Pyramid An ancient, massive monument with a broad base tapering to a point above. Found especially in Egypt and Mexico.

Q

Qanat A gravity-fed underground irrigation tunnel in the Middle East.

Queues A term used in Britain, New Zealand, and Australia for a line of people waiting to purchase some service or product.

R

Racism The belief that one's own racial group is superior to others.

Rain Forest An area of dense broadleaf vegetation that receives heavy rainfall year-round.

Rainshadow Areas with low rainfall because they are on the leeward side of mountain ranges, which trap the moisture in air masses.

Relative Location Refers to location of a place or region with respect to other places or regions. Used interchangeably with situation.

Republic A political order that is not a monarchy.

Resort Geographic or business area offering a variety of facilities, services, and activities for the accommodation, use, and enjoyment of visitors.

Rift Valley Trench-like valley with steep, parallel sides; association with crustal spreading; East Africa's Rift Valley is the most famous.

Ring of Fire Volcanic mountain region encircling the Pacific Ocean.

River Valleys Valleys that have formed as a result of the rivers.

Riverine Located on or adjacent to a river.

Riverine Basins Basins formed as a result of rivers.

Riverine Population Concentrations The population clusters found in the river basins of the world.

Riviera A narrow coastal strip that is a famous resort area and extends along the Mediterranean Coast from Italy to France and includes the towns of Monte Carlo, Nice, and Cannes.

Roman Era A time period in history associated with the Roman Empire.

Romance Languages Languages that have developed from Vulgar Latin. The principal languages are French, Italian, Portuguese, Rumanian, and Spanish.

Royalty A person of royal lineage.

S

Safari Lodges Lodges built in game parks and reserves from which visitors travel to view game.

Sagas Poetry recounting the legends and beliefs of the pre-Christian Nordic-Germanic people who settled in Iceland.

Sahara The large desert of North Africa.

Sahel Semiarid zone across most of Africa between the southern margins of the arid Sahara and the moister savanna and forest zone to the south.

St. Lawrence Major river between United States and Canada.

Sami Native people of the Arctic regions of Scandinavia. Sometimes referred to as Lapps.

Sanctuaries A reserve area in which animals or birds are protected from hunting or other molestations.

Savanna The tropical regions of the world that have climates with seasonal wet and dry periods, or the grassland with scattered trees and bushes that characterizes this climate.

Scandinavia Geographically, it refers to the northwest European countries of Norway, Sweden, Denmark, and Iceland. Finland is often included, although it is not technically part of Scandinavia.

Sensible Temperature The temperature as "sensed" (felt) by the body. Ninety degrees with high humidity feels hotter than 90 degrees with low humidity.

Sephardim One of the two main divisions of Jews. A Spanish or Portuguese Jew or one of his descendants.

Serengeti A national park in Tanzania known for its abundant wildlife.

Sex Tourism Tourism in which prostitution, pornography, and related activities are important attractions.

Shatterbelt Region located between stronger countries (or cultural-political forces) that is recurrently invaded and/or fragmented by aggressive neighbors.

Shiite An Islamic minority concentrated in Iran and Syria. They believe the leader of Islam should be a direct descendent of Muhammad.

Shinto The aboriginal religion of Japan, marked by the veneration of nature spirits and of ancestors.

Shrine A sacred place.

Siberia A large region in Russia extending from the Ural Mountains to the Pacific Ocean.

Sikh Member of a religion concentrated in the Punjab region of northwest India. Members are characterized by the common surname Singh, and males wear long hair, a full beard, a turban, and a dagger.

Sikhism A religious group that developed on the interface between Islam and Hinduism in India.

Site The internal locational attributes of a place, including its local spatial organization and physical setting.

Situation The external locational attributes of a place; its relative location with reference to other places.

Skåne A region in southern Sweden. A popular tourist destination region.

Slavic A group of languages or peoples living in Eastern Europe.

Social and Cultural The way of life of a group of people.

Socialism A variety of political and economic theories and systems of social organization based on collective or governmental ownership and distribution of goods.

South Asia The countries of Asia south of the Himalayas.

Southeast Asia The countries of Asia east of Myanmar to China and southeast to Papua New Guinea.

Southern Alps Chain of high, scenic mountains in New Zealand.

Soviet Russian term meaning a council.

Spa (*See* Health Resort.)

Spatial Interaction Interaction that occurs between two regions or places, such as trade or tourism.

State The formal name for the political units we commonly call countries.

Steppe Plains landforms with vegetation class consisting of short grasses sparsely distributed in clumps and bunches and some shrubs, widespread in areas of semiarid climate in continental interiors of North America and Eurasia; also called short-grass prairie.

Stupa A dome-shaped Buddhist shrine, often with a cupola on top.

Submergent Coast Coastal areas that have sunk.

Submergent Landforms Land areas that have sunk along coastal areas or river mouths, causing permanent flooding.

Subtropical Warm, humid areas on the eastern coasts of continents.

Sunni (Sunnite) The major religious division of Islam found in North Africa, Pakistan, and Indonesia.

Sun-Sea-Sand Coastal areas that have plentiful sun and sand are major attractors of tourists.

Suq (Souk) Market areas in Arabic towns filled with shops and eating establishments.

Swahili An African Bantu language of eastern and central Africa. It is widely used as a lingua franca.

Symbiotic Mutually beneficial relationships in which both parties in a relationship are better off than they would be if they were operating alone.

T

Taj Mahal The famed tomb in Agra, India, built between 1630 and 1652 by the emperor Shah Jahan for his second wife.

Taxes A contribution or levy for support of a government, or the fee charged members of an organization to support it.

Temple A sacred place of worship.

Territory An area of land; a district or region.

Tiananmen Square The major central square in Beijing, China. Around the square are the Forbidden City, Mao Zedong's mausoleum, and the People's Hall.

Tierra Caliente The hot coastal lowlands and piedmont (usually below 2,500 feet in elevation) in the Andes Mountains of Latin America.

Tierra Fría The cool upland elevations (usually above 6,000 feet) in the Andes Mountains of Latin America.

Tierra Templada The temperate middle elevations (usually between 2,500 and 6,000 feet) in the Andes Mountains of Latin America.

Time Zones The 24 longitudinal divisions of the earth's surface in which a standard time is kept. Each zone is 15 degrees of longitude in width, with local variations.

Tourist Any person traveling outside his or her normal commuting radius for the purpose of pleasure. A tourist is a person who has traveled away from home, is visiting other locations, and does not plan to relocate or stay away from home permanently.

Tourist Patrol Green patrol cars in Mexico that offer assistance to motorists in trouble.

Trade Unions A labor-specific union limited to people of that specific trade.

Transferability The level of ease or difficulty with which one can move from one place to another.

Transit Cities Cities where transit tourism is important. They are cities in which visitors change types of transportation or major directions when traveling.

Transportation The process of carrying passengers, goods, material, or the like.

Tribalism The practice of tribal religion.

Tropical A hot and humid area.

Tropical Rain Forest Vegetation of dense forest areas in the tropics.

Trust Territories A trust territory is a former colonial holding assigned by the United Nations to one of the industrialized nations for development assistance.

Trustee A person holding legal title to a property.

Tundra A zone between the northern limit of trees and the polar region in North America, Europe, and Asia. Tundra areas have only one summer month with an average temperature above freezing; their vegetation is composed of grasses, sedges, lichens, and shrubs.

Turkic A region or subdivision of the Middle Eastern area.

Tyrol A mountain region in Austria east of Salzburg.

U

Urban Pertaining to a city; city life.

V

Village Small town.

Visigoths Members of the western Goths that invaded the Roman Empire in the fourth century A.D. and settled in France and Spain, establishing a monarchy that lasted until the early eighth century A.D.

Volcanic Islands Islands that are volcanic in nature.

Vulcanism Volcanic activity or force. The movement of magma from the interior of the Earth to or near the surface.

W

Wafaku The traditional Japanese clothing of a long robe with sleeves, wrapped with a special sash.

Wat A Buddhist monastery and temple.

Wealth An abundance or large quantity of a valued resource or material possessions.

Welfare Health, happiness, and general well-being; relief work.

Welfare State A country that provides a general social service coverage for their citizens in education, health, and unemployment benefits.

Westerlies The prevailing winds at the middle latitudes flowing from the west to the east.

Western Culture Characteristics typical of the western hemisphere.

White Gold The idea that a white beach or excellent white snow is as valuable as gold for tourists.

Wilderness An unsettled, uncultivated area left in its natural condition.

Windward Area or side of a mountain, island, or other location that receives the prevailing winds directly.

World War II A war fought from 1939 to 1945 in which the United Kingdom, France, the Soviet Union, the United States, and other allies defeated Germany, Italy, and Japan.

X

Xerophytic A plant living in a region where little moisture is available. Its roots are long or enlarged, leaves are small and thick or lacking, as in cactus plants. The plant stores water for extremely long periods of time.

Y

Yurt A circular, domed, portable tent used in Mongolia and by Mongols of Siberia.

Altinay, L., and Paraskevas, A. *Planning Research in Hospitality and Tourism.* Butterworth-Heinemann, 2008.

Anderson, K., ed. *Handbook of Cultural Geography,* Sage Publishing. 2003.

Atkinson, B., Baxter, S., and VerBerkmoes, R. *Lonely Planet's Best in Travel 2013.* Lonely Planet Publications. 2013.

Bain, A., and Deliso, C. *Lonely Planet 1000 Ultimate Experiences.* Lonely Planet Publications. 2009.

Baldwin, R. *Economic Geography and Public Policy.* Princeton University Press. 2003.

Beaver, A. *A Dictionary of Travel and Tourism Terminology.* CABI. 2005.

Bone, R. *The Regional Geography of Canada.* Oxford University Press. 2005.

Bryson, J., ed. *The Economic Geography Reader.* John Wiley. 1999.

Brunn, S., Hays-Mitchell, M., and Zeigler, D. *Cities of The World.* The Rowman and Littlefield Publishing Group. 2010.

Burke, R. *Marketing and Selling the Travel Product.* Cengage/Delmar. 2003.

Bushell, R., and Eagles, P., eds. *Tourism in Protected Areas.* Stylus/Cabi Publishing. 2007.

Chon, K. S., ed. *Journal of Travel and Tourism Marketing.* Routledge Taylor and Francis Group. 2009–2013.

Clark, G., Feldmen, M., and Gertler, M., eds. *The Oxford Handbook of Economic Geography.* 2000.

Collins, V. R., ed. *The Tourism Society's Dictionary for Tourism Industry.* CABI. 2005.

Fouberg, E., Murphy, A., and deBlij, H. *Human Geography.* John Wiley and Sons, 2011.

Garfield, S. On the Map. *A Mind-Expanding Exploration of the Way the World Looks.* Penguin Group. 2013.

Goeldner, C., and Ritchie, J. R. *Tourism: Principles, Practices, and Philosophies.* John Wiley. 2012.

Gorman, R. *Travel Perspectives: A Guide to Becoming a Travel Professional.* Cengage/Delmar. 2007.

Hall, C. M. *The Geography of Tourism and Recreation.* Routledge. 2002.

Hall, C. M., and Page, S. *The Geography of Tourism and Recreation.* Routledge, 2006.

Harris, R., Griffin, T., and Williams, P. *Sustainable Tourism: A Global Perspective.* Butterworth Heinemann. 2002.

Henderson, V., ed. *New Economic Geography.* Edward Elgar Publishing. 2005

Ionnides, D., and Debbage, K. *The Economic Geography of the Tourist Industry: A Supply Side Analysis.* Routledge Chapman & Hall, 1998.

Jordan-Bychkov, T., and Domosh, M. *The Human Mosaic: A Thematic Introduction to Cultural Geography.* W.H. Freeman Press. 2003.

Lew, A., Hall, C., and Dallen, J. *World Geography of Travel and Tourism: A Regional Approach.* Butterworth-Heinemann-Elsevier, 2008.

Mancini, M. *Selling Destinations. Geography for the Travel Professional.* Cengage/Delmar. 2010.

McCann, L., and Gunn, A., eds. *Heartland and Hinterland: A Regional Geography of Canada.* Prentice Hall Canada. 1998.

Mitchell, D. *Cultural Geography: A Critical Introduction.* Blackwell Publishers. 2000.

Newbold, B. *Population Geography: Tools and Issues.* The Rowman and Littlefield Publishing Group. 2010.

Page, S., and Dowling, R. *Ecotourism.* Prentice Hall. 2002.

Page, S., and Connell, J. *Tourism a Modern Synthesis,* Third Edition. Cengage Learning. 2009.

Page, S., and Hall, C. M. *Managing Urban Tourism.* Prentice Hall. 2003.

Park, C. *Sacred Worlds: An Introduction to Geography and Religion.* Routledge. 1994.

Pattullo, P., and Minelli, O. *The Ethical Travel Guide.* Earthscan Publishing. 2009.

Richards, G., ed. *Cultural Tourism.* The Haworth Press. 2007.

Rumney, T. A. *Canadian Geography.* The Rowman and Littlefield Publishing Group. 2010.

Santella, C. *Once in a Lifetime Trips: The World's 50 most Extraordinary and Memorable Travel Experiences.* Potter Style Publishing. 2009.

Schultz, P. *1,000 Places To See Before You Die.* Workman Publishing. 2011.

Schultz, P. *1,000 Places To See in the United States Before You Die.* Workman Publishing. 2011.

Shaw, G., and Williams, A. M. *The Geography of Tourism and Recreation: Environment, Place and Space.* Routledge. 2002.

Spellman, F. *Geography for Nongeographers.* The Rowman and Littlefield Publishing Group. 2010.

Stoddard, R., and Morinis, A., eds. *Sacred Places: The Geography of Pilgrimages.* Louisiana State University Press, 1997.

Stump, R. *Boundaries of Faith: Geographical Perspectives on Religious Fundamentalism.* The Rowman and Littlefield Publishing Group. 2000.

Stump, R. *The Geography of Religion.* The Rowman and Littlefield Publishing Group. 2010.

Van Egmond, T. *Understanding Western Tourists in Developing Countries.* Stylus/Cabi Publishing. 2007.

Williams, Stephen. *Tourism Geography: A New Synthesis.* Taylor & Francis, 2009.

Warkentin, J. *A Regional Geography of Canada: Life, Land, and Space.* Prentice Hall Canada. 2000.

Woodard, C. *American Nation. A History of the Eleven Rival Regional Cultures of North America.* Penguin Group. 2011.

Additional important sources of information:

ASTA Worldwide Destination Guide 2013/2014. ASTA. Alexandria, VA.

The World Factbook. CIA. www.cia.gov/library/publications/the-world-factbook/index.html

International Travel and Health. World Health Organization. 2010.

National Geographic Atlas of the World. Ninth edition.

National Geographic Reader. Travel and Tourism. First edition. Cengage Delmar. 2013.

National Geographic. *Journey's of a Lifetime: 500 of the World's Greatest Trips.* National Geographic. 2007.

National Geographic. *World's Best Travel Experiences: 400 Extraordinary Places.* National Geographic. 2012.

The Travel Book. *A Journey Through Every Country in the World.* A Lonely Planet Book. Lonely Planet Publications. 2011.

Canadian Tourism Commission. Canada's Official Tourism Website: http://us.canada.travel/

United States Travel Association (USTA). http://www.ustravel.org/

USA Office of Travel and Tourism Industries (OTTI). http://tinet.ita.doc.gov/

The European Travel Commission. http://www.etc-corporate.org/

Pacific Area Travel Association. www.pata.org

Caribbean Tourism Association. http://www.onecaribbean.org/

African Travel and Tourism Association. http://www.atta.travel/

World Tourism Organization. *Yearbook of Tourism Statistics.* 2012.

The World Bank. International Tourist Arrivals. Dataset: http://data.worldbank.org/indicator/ST.INT.ARVL

www.fodors.com/world

www.frommer.com/destinations

www.letsgo.com

www.lonely planet.com/destinations

www.ricksteves.com